AMERICAN PASSAGES

VOLUME II: SINCE 1865

BRIEF FOURTH EDITION

Edward L. Ayers
University of Richmond

Lewis L. Gould
University of Texas at Austin, Emeritus

David M. Oshinsky
University of Texas at Austin

Jean R. Soderlund
Lehigh University

WADSWORTH
CENGAGE Learning

Australia • Brazil • Japan • Korea • Mexico • Singapore • Spain • United Kingdom • United States

American Passages, Volume II: Since 1865,
Brief Fourth Edition
Edward L. Ayers, Lewis L. Gould, David M.
Oshinsky, Jean R. Soderlund

Senior Publisher: Suzanne Jeans

Senior Sponsoring Editor: Ann West

Development Editor: Colleen Kyle

Assistant Editor: Megan Chrisman

Editorial Assistant: Patrick Roach

Senior Marketing Manager: Katherine Bates

Marketing Coordinator: Lorreen Pelletier

Marketing Communications Manager:
    Caitlin Green

Senior Content Project Manager: Jane Lee

Senior Art Director: Cate Rickard Barr

Senior Print Buyer: Sandra Milewski

Senior Rights Acquisition Specialist: Katie Huha

Production Service: S4Carlisle Publishing
    Services

Text Designer: Diane Beasley

Senior Photo Manager: Jennifer Meyer Dare

Cover Image: Walter Ellison, American,
    1899–1977, *Train Station*, 1935. Oil on
    cardboard. 20 x 36 cm. Credit:
    Charles M. Kurtz Charitable Trust and
    Barbara Neff Smith and Solomon Byron
    Smith funds; through prior gifts of Florence
    Jane Adams, Mr. and Mrs. Carter H. Harrison,
    and the estate of Celia Schmidt, 1990.134.
    Reproduction, The Art Institute of Chicago.

Compositor: S4Carlisle Publishing Services

For product information and technology assistance, contact us at
Cengage Learning Customer & Sales Support, 1-800-354-9706

For permission to use material from this text or product,
submit all requests online at **www.cengage.com/permissions**
Further permissions questions can be emailed to
permissionrequest@cengage.com

Library of Congress Control Number: 2010929826

Student Edition:
ISBN-13: 978-0-495-91521-8
ISBN-10: 0-495-91521-1

Wadsworth
20 Channel Center Street
Boston, MA 02210
USA

Cengage Learning is a leading provider of customized learning solutions with
office locations around the globe, including Singapore, the United Kingdom,
Australia, Mexico, Brazil, and Japan. Locate your local office at
international.cengage.com/region

Cengage Learning products are represented in Canada by Nelson Education, Ltd.

For your course and learning solutions, visit **www.cengage.com**

Purchase any of our products at your local college store or at our preferred
online store **www.cengagebrain.com.**

Printed in the United States of America
1 2 3 4 5 6 7 14 13 12 11 10

BRIEF CONTENTS

15 Reconstruction: Its Rise and Fall, 1865–1877   338

PASSAGES 1877 to 1914   364

16 An Economy Transformed: The Rise of Big Business, 1877–1887   368
17 Urban Growth and Farm Protest, 1887–1893   392
18 A Troubled Nation Expands Outward, 1893–1901   412
19 Progressivism: Agendas for Change, 1901–1914   434

PASSAGES 1914 to 1933   466

20 Over There and Over Here: The Impact of World War I, 1914–1920   470
21 The Age of Jazz and Mass Culture, 1921–1927   498
22 The Great Depression, 1927–1933   520

PASSAGES 1933 to 1960   538

23 The New Deal, 1933–1939   542
24 The Second World War, 1939–1945   566
25 Postwar America, 1946–1953   592
26 The Eisenhower Years, 1953–1960   612

PASSAGES 1960 to 2010   634

27 The Turbulent Years, 1960–1968   638
28 Crisis of Confidence, 1969–1980   664
29 From Reagan to Clinton, 1981–2000   692
30 A Conservative Nation in a Globalizing World, 2000–2010   720

APPENDIX   A-1
GLOSSARY   G-1
INDEX   I-1

CONTENTS

15 Reconstruction: Its Rise and Fall
1865–1877
338

Reconstruction Under Andrew Johnson, 1865–1867   339
Wartime Reconstruction in the South   340 / Andrew Johnson   341 / Johnson and the Radicals   341 / The Reconstruction Act of 1867   343

From Johnson to Grant, 1867–1868   344
The Election of 1868   344 / The Fifteenth Amendment   345

The First Grant Administration, 1869–1873   345
A Troubled Administration   345 / Grant, Congress, and Republican Discord   346 / The Problem of the Ku Klux Klan   347 / Farmers and Railroads   348 / Indian Policies   348

Women in the 1870s   351
● DOING HISTORY **Women's Rights and Black Suffrage During Reconstruction   352**
The Rise of Voluntary Associations   352 / Women at Work   353

Political and Economic Turmoil   353
The 1872 Election   354 / A Surge of Scandals   354 / The Panic of 1873 and Its Consequences   355

The Failure of Reconstruction, 1875–1877   356
The Stigma of Corruption   356 / The Resurgence of the Democrats   357 / The Centennial Year, 1876   357 / The Race for the White House   358 / Why Reconstruction Failed   360

CHAPTER REVIEW, 1865–1877   361

PASSAGES 1877 to 1914
364

16 An Economy Transformed: The Rise of Big Business
1877–1887
368

Railroads and a "Locomotive People"   369
The Railroad Business and Network   369 / The Railroad as a Social and Political Issue   371 / Regulating the Railroads   371

Big Business Arrives   372
John D. Rockefeller and the Emergence of Trusts   373 / Andrew Carnegie and Steel   374 / The Pace of Invention   374

Americans in the Workplace   375
The New Workforce   375 / The Rise of Unions   376 / Competing Unions   377 / Social Darwinism   378

The Changing West   379
The Mining and Cattle Frontier   380 / Farming on the Great Plains   381

The New South?   382
The Industrial South   383 / Problems of Southern Agriculture   383 / Segregation   384

American Life and Politics During the 1880s   385
Arts and Leisure in the 1880s   385 / Political Life, 1877–1887   386
● DOING HISTORY **Debating the Protective Tariff   387**
CHAPTER REVIEW, 1877–1887   389

17 Urban Growth and Farm Protest
1887–1893
392

The New Urban Society   392
The Structure of the City   394 / The New Immigration   395 / The Urban Political Machine   396

The Diminishing Rights of Minority Groups   397
The Spread of Segregation   398

A Victorian Society   399
The Rules of Life   399 / A Sporting Nation   400

Voices of Protest and Reform   400

Looking Outward: Foreign Policy in the Early 1890s   401
The Roots of Imperialism   402 / New Departures in Foreign Policy   402

Agrarian Unrest   404
The Rise of the Farmers' Alliance   404
● DOING HISTORY **The Causes of Agrarian Discontent   406**
The Presidential Election of 1892   407
CHAPTER REVIEW, 1887–1893   410

18 A Troubled Nation Expands Outward
1893–1901   412

The Panic of 1893   413
Economic Downturn   413 / 1894: A Significant Election   415

The 1890s Depression   415
Reshaping the Economy   416 / The Reform Campaigns   416 / Substantive Due Process and Its Critics   418 / Pragmatism and Realism   418 / African Americans and Segregation   419
● DOING HISTORY **Lynching and the Rights of African Americans, 1898–1900   421**

Foreign Policy Challenges   422
The Cuban Crisis, 1895–1896   422 / The Battle of the Standards: 1896   423 / Bryan and the Cross of Gold   423

The War with Spain and Overseas Expansion, 1898–1900   425
Spain and Cuba   425 / The Sinking of the *Maine*: February 15, 1898   425 / The Spanish-American War, 1898   426 / The 1900 Election and a New Century   430
CHAPTER REVIEW, 1893–1901   432

19 Progressivism: Agendas for Change
1901–1914   434

Theodore Roosevelt and Modern America   435
Social Changes   436 / A Nation of Consumers   436 / Theodore Roosevelt in Power   437 / Controlling Big Business and the Trusts   438 / Labor and Race Relations in the Roosevelt Era   439 / Roosevelt and Foreign Policy   441 / The Election of 1904   442

Progressive Campaigns to Reform the Nation   442
Currents of Reform   442 / The Muckrakers   443 / Women and Progressive Reform   443 / Reform in the Cities and States   444

Roosevelt, Taft, and the Modern Presidency   445
The Expansion of Regulation   445
● DOING HISTORY **Theodore Roosevelt and the Regulation of Business   446**
Roosevelt and World Politics   447 / Roosevelt's Domestic Policies   448 / The 1908 Presidential Election   450 / Taft's Conservative Presidency   450 / The Battle over Conservation   451 / Roosevelt's Return   452

Progressive Victories   452
Woman Suffrage and Prohibition   452 / Restriction of Immigration   453 / Saving Children   453 / Reforming the Workplace   454 / Varieties of Labor Protest   454

Republican Discord and Democratic Opportunity   456
The Struggle Between Roosevelt and Taft   457 / The Democratic Opportunity   457 / Woodrow Wilson and the 1912 Election   457

Reform and Social Change During the Wilson Years   459
Tariff Reform   459 / The Federal Reserve System   460 / Wilson and the Progressive Agenda   460 / Modern Technology and Mass Markets   461 / Artistic and Social Ferment   462 / The New Leisure   463
CHAPTER REVIEW, 1901–1914   464

PASSAGES 1914 to 1933   466

20 Over There and Over Here: The Impact of World War I
1914–1920   470

Staying Neutral in a World Conflict   471
New Freedom Diplomacy   471 / War's Outbreak in Europe   472 / The War and American Public Opinion   474 / The *Lusitania* Crisis   474

Social Change During the Period of Neutrality   475
Enduring Racism   475 / The Rise of the Movies   477 / Shifting Attitudes Toward Sex   477 / The Persistence of Reform   478 / A Hazardous Neutrality   479

The 1916 Presidential Election   480
Mediation and Intervention   480 / The Outbreak of Hostilities   481

A Nation at War   482
Managing the Wartime Economy   483 / Black Americans in the War   484 / Women's Issues in the Great War   485 / Civil Liberties and the Limits of Dissent   485

The Road to Victory   486

Wilson's Peace Program   488 / The Paris Peace
Conference   489 / The Shadow of Bolshevism   489 /
Wilson and the Treaty of Versailles   489

● DOING HISTORY The League of Nations Debate, 1919   490

The Senate and the League of Nations   491

From War to Peace   493

The Waning Spirit of Progressivism   493 / The Struggles
of Labor   493 / Harding and "Normalcy"   495

CHAPTER REVIEW, 1914–1920   496

21 The Age of Jazz and Mass Culture
1921–1927

498

An Urban Nation   499

Immigration Restricted   499 / The Sacco-Vanzetti
Case   500 / White and Black Militance   500 / Dry
America: The First Phase   502 / Harding as President   503

The New Economy   504

The Car Culture   504 / Electrical America   505 / 1920s
Movies and Advertising   505 / Troubled Farmers and
Workers   506 / The Harding Scandals   507 / Keep Cool
with Coolidge   507 / The Discordant Democrats   507

Modern Cultural Currents   508

The Harlem Renaissance   508 / The Sound of Jazz   508 /
An Age of Artistic Achievement   509 / Youth Culture
and Sports   510

Fundamentalism and Traditional Values   511

The Fundamentalist Movement   511

● DOING HISTORY Bryan Versus Darrow: The Scopes Trial   512

The Scopes Trial   512 / Prohibition in Retreat   513

New Roles for Women   514

Women in Politics   514 / The New Woman   514

Coolidge in the White House   515

Coolidge's Foreign Policy   515 / Diplomacy and Finance
in the 1920s   516 / Lucky Lindy and Retiring Cal   516

CHAPTER REVIEW, 1921–1927   518

22 The Great Depression
1927–1933

520

The Stock Market Crash of October 1929   521

Causes of the Crash   522 / Underlying Economic
Weaknesses   523

Brother, Can You Spare a Dime: The Great
Depression   524

The Depression Takes Hold   525 / Hoover's Programs to
Fight the Depression   526 / Everyday Life During the
Depression   527 / Mass Culture During
the Depression   528

A Darkening World   529

A Challenge to the League of Nations   530 / Germany
Moves Toward the Nazis   530

A Political Opportunity for the Democrats   530

A New Deal   532

● DOING HISTORY 1932: The Clash of Philosophies   533

The Economy in Distress   534 / The Bonus March   534 /
The 1932 Election   535 / Hoover Defeated   535

CHAPTER REVIEW, 1927–1933   536

PASSAGES 1933 to 1960

538

23 The New Deal
1933–1939

542

Taking Charge of the Crisis, 1932–1933   543

The Banking Crisis   543 / Extending Relief   544 /
Conservation, Regional Planning, and Public
Power   545 / Agricultural Recovery   545 / Tenants and
Landowners   548 / Centralized Economic Planning   548

New Deal Diplomacy, 1933–1934   549

The Soviet Question   549 / The Good Neighbor   550

Critics Right and Left, 1934–1935   550

The American Liberty League and the 1934 Election   550 /
"Every Man a King"   551 / The Radio Priest
and the Pension Doctor   551

The Second New Deal, 1935–1936   552

Jobs, Jobs, Jobs   552 / Social Security   553 /
"Class Warfare"   553

The Fascist Challenge 555
Hitler and Mussolini 555 / The Neutrality Acts 555
● DOING HISTORY **The Battle over Neutrality** 556

The American People in Transition 557
The 1936 Election 557 / African Americans and the New Deal 558 / Popular Culture in the Depression 559

Losing Ground, 1937–1939 561
Union Struggles 561 / Fascists on the Rise 562 / An End to Reform 563
CHAPTER REVIEW, 1933–1939 564

24 The Second World War
1939–1945 · 566

War in Europe, 1939–1940 566
Blitzkrieg 567 / A Third Term for FDR 567

The End of Neutrality, 1940–1941 568
Lend-Lease 568 / The Road to Pearl Harbor 569 / Early Defeats 570 / War Production 571 / Making Do on the Homefront 572

Opportunity and Discrimination 572
Women and the War Effort 573 / The "Double V" Campaign 574 / Internment of Japanese Americans, 1942–1945 575

The Grand Alliance 577
North Africa, Stalingrad, and the Second Front, 1942–1943 578 / The Normandy Invasion, June 1944 579 / Facing the Holocaust 580

The Pacific War, 1942–1945 581
● DOING HISTORY **Bombing the Death Camps** 582
Turning the Tide, May–June 1942 582 / Closing in on Japan 583

A Change in Leadership, 1944–1945 584
The Yalta Accords 585 / Truman in Charge 585 / The Atomic Bombs, August 1945 587
CHAPTER REVIEW, 1939–1945 589

25 Postwar America
1946–1953 · 592

Affluence and Anxiety 592
Economic Reconversion 593 / Lurching Toward Prosperity 594 / The Postwar American Family 594 / Suburbia 596

The Soviet Threat 597
Containment 597 / The Truman Doctrine and the Marshall Plan 597

Liberalism in Retreat 599
The Cold War at Home 599 / The Domestic Agenda 600 / Breaking the Color Line 600 / Man of the People 601

The Cold War Intensifies, 1949–1953 603
The Fall of China and the Creation of NATO, 1949 603 / War in Korea, 1950–1953 604

McCarthyism and the Election of 1952 606
The Rise of Joe McCarthy 606 / "I Like Ike" 607
● DOING HISTORY **Senator Smith Confronts Senator McCarthy** 608
CHAPTER REVIEW, 1946–1953 610

26 The Eisenhower Years
1953–1960 · 612

A New Direction, 1953 613
Modern Republicanism 613 / A Truce in Korea 614

The Cold War at Home and Abroad, 1953–1954 614
The Hunt for "Subversives" 614 / Brinksmanship and Covert Action 616

The Civil Rights Movement, 1954–1955 617
Brown v. Board of Education 617
● DOING HISTORY **The Long Reach of *Brown*** 618
The Montgomery Bus Boycott 619

American Families at Mid-Century   620
The Golden Age of Television   621 / A New Kind of Music   622 / The Beat Generation   623

Crises and Celebration, 1955–1956   624
Conquering Polio   624 / Interstate Highways   624 / Hungary and Suez   625

A Second Term, 1957–1960   626
Confrontation at Little Rock   626 / *Sputnik* and Its Aftermath   627 / End of an Era   628 / The Election of 1960   629
CHAPTER REVIEW, 1953–1960   631

PASSAGES 1960 to 2010   634

27 The Turbulent Years
1960–1968   638

Early Tests, 1961   639
Idealism and Caution   639 / The Bay of Pigs   640 / The Berlin Wall   640 / The Freedom Riders   641 / The New Economics   641

Social and Political Challenges, 1962–1963   642
The Battle for Ole Miss   642 / The Missiles of October   642 / Trouble in Vietnam   643 / From Birmingham to Washington   644 / Feminist Stirrings   645

Tragedy and Transition   646
Kennedy's Assassination   646 / LBJ's Strong Start   647 / Landslide in 1964   648 / The Great Society, 1964–1965   649 / Health Care and Immigration Reform   649

The Expanding War, 1965–1966   650
Point of No Return   650 / Early Protests   651
● DOING HISTORY Visions of the "Multiversity"   652

The Rights Revolution: Center Stage   653
Voting Rights   653 / The Watts Explosion   653 / Black Power   655 / "Sisterhood Is Powerful"   656 / The Counterculture   656

A Divided Nation, 1968   657
The Tet Offensive   657 / The President Steps Aside   659 / A Violent Spring   659 / The Chicago Convention   660 / Nixon's the One   661
CHAPTER REVIEW, 1960–1968   662

28 Crisis of Confidence
1969–1980   664

America United and Divided   664
The Miracles of 1969   665 / Vietnamization   666 / Confrontation at Home   666 / My Lai and the Pentagon Papers   667

Activism, Rights, and Reform   668
Expanding Women's Rights   668 / Minority Power   669
● DOING HISTORY Women Debate the Equal Rights Amendment   670
Black Capitalism and Civil Rights   672 / The Burger Court   673

New Directions at Home and Abroad   673
Rethinking Welfare   673 / Protecting the Environment   674 / A New World Order   675 / Détente   676

Four More Years?   676
The Landslide of 1972   676 / Exit from Vietnam   677 / Watergate and the Abuse of Power   678 / OPEC and the Oil Embargo   680

Gerald Ford in the White House   681
The Watergate Legacy   681 / The Fall of South Vietnam   681 / Stumbling Toward Defeat   683 / The Election of 1976   683

The Carter Years   684
Civil Rights in a New Era   685 / Human Rights and Global Realities   685 / Economic Blues   686 / The Persian Gulf   687 / Death in the Desert   688
CHAPTER REVIEW, 1969–1980   689

29 From Reagan to Clinton
1981–2000   692

The Reagan Revolution   693
The Election of 1980   693 / Carrying Out the Reagan Agenda   694 / Deregulation   695 / Rivalry with the Soviet Union   696 / Strategic Defense Initiative   697

Social Tensions of the 1980s   697
The Challenge of AIDS   698 / New Technologies   698 / The American Family in the 1980s   698 / The Religious Right   699 / The 1984 Presidential Election   699

Reagan's Second Term   700

Toward Better Relations with the Soviet Union   700 /
Political Controversies   700 / Reagan and Gorbachev:
The Road to Understanding   701 / The 1988 Presidential
Election   701

The Bush Succession   702

Bush's Domestic and Economic Policies   702

● DOING HISTORY **Debating Ronald Reagan's Legacy   703**

The Continuing AIDS Crisis   704 / Foreign Policy Successes,
1989–1990   704 / War in the Persian Gulf   705 /
The Battle over the Clarence Thomas Nomination   706

An Angry Nation   706

The 1992 Election Campaign   707 / Clinton's Domestic
Agenda   708 / Clinton and the World   710 / The

Republican Revolution: 1994   710 / Race, Ethnicity,
and Culture Wars   710

The Republicans in Power   712

Domestic Terrorism in Oklahoma City   712 / Clinton
Resurgent: Bosnia and the Government Shutdowns   713 /
Clinton and the Republican Congress   713

Clinton: Triumphs and Missteps   714

The 1996 Election   714 / An Ambitious Foreign
Policy   715 / An Economic Boom   715 / The Rise of the
Internet   716 / Clinton Impeached and Acquitted   716

CHAPTER REVIEW, 1981–2000   718

30 A Conservative Nation in a Globalizing World
2000–2010

....   720

**The Disputed Presidential Election
of 2000: Bush Versus Gore   720**

The Presidency of George W. Bush   722

September 11, 2001, and After   723 / The Dilemma
of Iraq   724 / The Erosion of the Bush Presidency   726

A Society in Crisis   726

Hurricane Katrina   727 / The Immigration Debate   727

● DOING HISTORY **The Torture Debate   728**

Social Activism, Left and Right   730 / Globalization
and Economic Troubles   731 / The Climate Change
Crisis   731 / The 2006 Midterm Elections   732

A Change of Course: President Obama   733

2008: An Historic Election   733 / The "Great
Recession"   734 / The Obama Presidency   736

CHAPTER REVIEW, 2000–2010   738

APPENDIX   A-1

GLOSSARY   G-1

INDEX   I-1

SPECIAL FEATURES

Doing History

Women's Rights and Black Suffrage During Reconstruction 352

Debating the Protective Tariff 387

The Causes of Agrarian Discontent 406

Lynching and the Rights of African Americans, 1898–1900 421

Theodore Roosevelt and the Regulation of Business 446

The League of Nations Debate, 1919 490

Bryan Versus Darrow: The Scopes Trial 512

1932: The Clash of Philosophies 533

The Battle over Neutrality 556

Bombing the Death Camps 582

Senator Smith Confronts Senator McCarthy 608

The Long Reach of *Brown* 618

Visions of the "Multiversity" 652

Women Debate the Equal Rights Amendment 670

Debating Ronald Reagan's Legacy 703

The Torture Debate 728

MAPS

MAP 15.1 Sharecropping in the South by County, 1880 339

MAP 15.2 Indian Reservations in the West 349

MAP 15.3 Reconstruction in the South 358

MAP 15.4 The Election of 1876 359

MAP 16.1 The Railroad Network, 1850–1900 370

MAP 16.2 Railroad Land Grants 372

MAP 16.3 Settlement of the Trans-Mississippi West, 1870–1890 379

MAP 16.4 The Election of 1884 388

MAP 17.1 Immigration and Urbanization 395

MAP 18.1 The Election of 1896 424

MAP 18.2 The Spanish-American War, 1898 427

MAP 18.3 U.S. Overseas Expansion, 1867–1899 429

MAP 19.1 Theodore Roosevelt: National Parks and Monuments 449

MAP 19.2 The Election of 1912 459

MAP 20.1 Europe on the Eve of World War I 473

MAP 20.2 The Great Migration, 1930 476

MAP 20.3 The March of Woman Suffrage 479

MAP 20.4 The War in Europe, 1914–1918 487

MAP 20.5 Europe After the Peace Conference, 1920 492

MAP 22.1 The Election of 1928 521

MAP 23.1 The Tennessee Valley 546

MAP 23.2 The Dust Bowl, 1936–1940 547

MAP 24.1 Japanese American Relocation, 1942–1945 577

MAP 24.2 The War in Europe 580

MAP 24.3 The War in the Pacific 584

MAP 25.1 The Election of 1948 602

MAP 25.2 Cold War Europe, 1945–1989 605

MAP 25.3 The Korean War 606

MAP 26.1 The National Highway System Proposed in 1957 625

MAP 26.2 The Election of 1960 630

MAP 27.1 Black Voter Registration in the South, 1960–1971 654

MAP 27.2 The Vietnam War 658

MAP 27.3 The Election of 1968 661

MAP 28.1 The Struggle for the Equal Rights Amendment 671

MAP 28.2 The Election of 1976 684

MAP 29.1 The Election of 1980 694

MAP 29.2 The United States in the Caribbean and Central America, 1981–2008 697

MAP 29.3 The Election of 1992 708

MAP 29.4 The Changing Latino Population of the United States, 2000 712

MAP 30.1 The Presidential Election of 2000 722

MAP 30.2 The War in Iraq and Its Effects 725

MAP 30.3 The Election of 2008 734

PREFACE

Like other teachers of history, we have seen our students intrigued by the powerful stories of this nation's past. But textbooks often bear little resemblance to our favorite works of history or to the best kinds of teaching. Textbooks tend to replace the concrete with the abstract, the individual with the aggregate, the story with the summary. They can remove entire regions and ethnic groups from the flow of American history and relegate them to separate chapters, isolated and frozen in time. They can give away the end of the story too easily, squandering drama.

We believed that we could write a book that captured what we love most and what explains the most about history. We decided to write the first U. S. history text in which time stood front and center. Time is what makes history *History* rather than sociology, anthropology, or economics. Time—and the dramatic pace of events—is what most textbooks have sacrificed in the name of convenience and false clarity. In short, we set out to write a more *historical* history text.

Now in its fourth brief edition, *American Passages* is unique in its insistence, in every part of every chapter, that time, with the characteristics of sequence, simultaneity, and contingency, is the *defining nature* of history. Sequence shows how events grow from other events, personalities, and broad changes. Political, social, and cultural history naturally intertwine, and simultaneity shows how apparently disconnected events were situated in larger shared contexts. Contingency shows how history suddenly pivots, how it often changes course in a moment.

The focus on time is easily apparent in the table of contents, in the Passages sections, in the timelines, in the Doing History features, and in the narrative analytical history that is the core of the book. Every chapter covers a specific time period and integrates the themes and events of that period as they cannot be integrated in a more distended account. Our account of the post–Civil War era, for example, deals with integrated periods rather than abstractions such as "urbanization" and "industrialization."

❖ Organization and Pedagogy

American Passages is written to convey the excitement and uncertainty of this nation's past—to see it whole. To balance the chronological approach—to help students see long-term developments and processes—eight "Passages" essays and chronologies help students see long-term developments and processes.

Each chapter in the text contains a wealth of review material to help students keep track of major events, important people, and larger movements. They begin with chapter outlines, chronologies, and "Making Connections" questions that review earlier material in context. "Identification" terms appear in boldface throughout the chapters, are defined on the page where they first appear, and are listed at the end of the chapter for easy review. At the end of every chapter, chapter summaries review key points, and "Making Connections" sections guide students forward to place the current chapter's content in perspective.

❖ Features

The features for the Brief Fourth Edition have been streamlined while maintaining *American Passages'* chronological emphasis.

Doing History

In each chapter, "Doing History" boxes feature two to four brief excerpts from primary sources on related topics, presenting varying perspectives and providing students with manageable opportunities to "do history." Brief commentary by the authors guides students, and assignable "Questions for Reflection" encourage critical thinking or can be used to spark class discussion.

Doing History Online

To give students additional exposure to primary source material, "Doing History Online" notes in the text margins connect students to an array of online resources that permit them to explore history in a deeper and more systematic way. Links to these sources may be found on the student CourseMate website for *American Passages*.

Making Connections

To emphasize recurring themes and trends and spark critical analysis, we have included a section at the beginning of every chapter (except for the first chapter) that highlights key points of the previous chapter and a section at the end of every chapter (except for the last chapter) that previews the content to come. "Making Connections: Looking Back" and "Making Connections:

Looking Ahead" will help remind students of the importance of relating events from one period to another—and will help to keep the narrative a seamless stream in spite of chapter-by-chapter assignments.

❖ Changes to the Brief Fourth Edition

Offering a streamlined narrative and features program, the Brief Fourth Edition has been revised to highlight *American Passages'* strengths while providing a more flexible, briefer text. Unique to the Brief Fourth Edition, the overall chapter count has been reduced from 32 to 30 chapters. Two chapters on the Civil War, 1861–1865, have been combined into one, and two chapters on the Progressive Era have also been combined and streamlined into one. The final two chapters of the text have been restructured: Chapter 29 now covers the presidencies of Ronald Reagan, George H. W. Bush, and Bill Clinton. Chapter 30, "A Conservative Nation in a Globalizing World," covers the period from 2000 to 2010, including updated coverage on the 2008 election, the "Great Recession," and the recent historic passage of health care legislation.

Throughout the text, details have been carefully pruned, enhancing narrative coherence and providing flexibility for instructors who wish to assign additional materials. At the same time, the narrative is still animated by excellent political history coverage, modern scholarship, and vivid quotes and examples. The overall narrative has been reduced by 25 percent.

The pedagogy supporting each chapter has been augmented with detailed chapter outlines and "Looking Back" questions at the beginning of each chapter, glossary definitions, and streamlined end-of-chapter materials that make it easier for students to find what they need. Doing History feature boxes emphasize primary source analysis skills and offer students competing perspectives on key issues.

The colorful new maps in this brief edition include helpful locator and topographical features that make them easier to read and richer as learning tools. Many of the images are new and also larger so that students can better see important details.

In addition to the changes in formatting and appearance, we have carefully reviewed each chapter for clarity and new scholarship and incorporated revisions and updates throughout. We are grateful to the reviewers who provided many helpful suggestions as well. Specific revisions include the following.

Revisions to Chapters 1 through 8 include new Doing History features on the Deerfield Raid of 1704 and the gradual abolition of slavery in the North. Special attention was given to tightening up the end of Chapter 8 ("The New Republic Faces a New Century, 1800–1815")

to allow for a smoother transition into Chapter 9, which covers the period following the War of 1812.

Chapters 14 and 15 have been combined to cover the entirety of the Civil War, and Chapter 16 has been reworked to cover Reconstruction only. In addition, there is a new Doing History feature on Religion and Reform.

In Chapters 17 through 23, the two chapters on Progressivism have been combined into one Chapter 19, titled "Progressivism: Agendas for Change, 1901–1914." New Doing History features include McKinley and the start of the Philippine insurrection in 1899 as well as the torture issue.

In Chapters 24 through 30, most changes relate to popular culture, science, and medicine. There is a longer and more detailed section on the growth and impact of television and sports and a section on how wonder drugs and other discoveries have increased our life span. There is new material relating to the story behind the Iwo Jima flag raising, the impact of Soviet spying, the Cuban Missile Crisis, the importance of Cesar Chavez, and the legacy of Watergate (including the self-identification of Deep Throat). Chapter 30 takes the story up to 2010, with coverage of President Obama's first term, the economic downturn, the debate over the definition of marriage, and deepening debates over climate change.

❖ Learning and Teaching Aids

The *American Passages Brief* program includes a great variety of learning and teaching aids—many linked to specific text features. The instructor supplements are aimed at providing instructors with useful course management and presentation options. The student supplements are designed to expand learning opportunities—and to provide students with a solid source of review material to ensure their success in the course.

Instructor Resources

The *Instructor Website* (**www.cengage.com/login**) contains a wealth of teaching resources for instructors using American Passages, 4e. An **Instructor's Resource Manual** written by James Mills of the University of Texas at Brownsville and Texas Southmost College is available at the website and includes chapter-by-chapter lecture outlines and teaching tips as well as suggestions for class discussion and essay assignments. Also available on the Instructor Website are **PowerPoint® lecture** and **personal response system** slides, access to general teaching resources, and a link to HistoryFinder (see description below), which instructors can use to create their own primary source–based student assignments or lecture presentations.

eInstructor's Resource Manual Prepared by James Mills of the University of Texas at Brownsville and Texas Southmost College, this manual has many features, including instructional objectives, topics for discussion, class starters, writing assignments, chapter outlines, and suggested readings and resources. It is available on the instructor's companion website.

PowerLecture CD-ROM with ExamView® and JoinIn® This dual platform, all-in-one multimedia resource includes the Instructor's Resource Manual; a test bank written by D. Antonio Cantù of Bradley University; Microsoft® PowerPoint® slides of both lecture outlines and images and maps from the text that can be used as offered, or customized by importing personal lecture slides or other material; and *JoinIn®* PowerPoint® slides with clicker content. Also included is ExamView, an easy-to-use assessment and tutorial system that allows instructors to create, deliver, and customize tests in minutes. Instructors can build tests with as many as 250 questions using up to 12 question types, and using ExamView's complete word-processing capabilities, they can enter an unlimited number of new questions or edit existing ones.

HistoryFinder This searchable online database allows instructors to quickly and easily download thousands of assets, including art, photographs, maps, primary sources, and audio/video clips. Each asset downloads directly into a Microsoft® PowerPoint® slide, allowing instructors to easily create exciting PowerPoint® presentations for their classrooms.

WebTutor™ for BlackBoard or WebCT® With WebTutor's text-specific, preformatted content and total flexibility, instructors can easily create and manage their own custom course website. WebTutor's course management tool gives instructors the ability to provide virtual office hours, post syllabi, set up threaded discussions, track student progress with the quizzing material, and much more. For students, WebTutor offers real-time access to a full array of study tools, including animations and videos that bring the book's topics to life, plus chapter outlines, summaries, learning objectives, glossary flash cards (with audio), practice quizzes, and weblinks.

CourseMate *History CourseMate* Cengage Learning's History CourseMate brings course concepts to life with interactive learning, study, and exam preparation tools that support the printed textbook. Watch student comprehension soar as your class works with the printed textbook and the CourseMate content developed for the *American Passages* Brief Fourth Edition. History CourseMate goes beyond the book to deliver what you need! History CourseMate includes an integrated eBook, interactive teaching and learning tools including quizzes developed by Thomas Born of Blinn College, flash cards, videos, and more. It also includes EngagementTracker, a first-of-its-kind tool that monitors student engagement in the course. Go to login.cengage.com to access these resources and look for this icon 🖥 which denotes a resource available within CourseMate.

Student Resources

CourseMate *History CourseMate* For students, CourseMate provides an additional source of interactive learning, study, and exam preparation outside the classroom. Students will find outlines and objectives, focus questions, flash cards, quizzes, primary source links, and video clips. In addition, CourseMate includes an integrated ***American Passages Brief*** eBook. Students taking quizzes will be linked directly to relevant sections in the ebook for additional information. The ebook is fully searchable and students can even take notes and save them for later review. The ebook links to rich media assets such as video and MP3 chapter summaries, primary source documents with critical thinking questions, and interactive (zoomable) maps. Students can use the ebook as their primary text or as a companion multimedia support. Go to login.cengagebrain.com to access these resources, and look for this icon 🖥 to find resources related to your text in CourseMate.

Wadsworth American History Resource Center gives students access to a "virtual reader" with hundreds of primary sources including speeches, letters, legal documents and transcripts, poems, maps, simulations, timelines, and additional images that bring history to life, along with interactive assignable exercises. A map feature including Google Earth™ coordinates and exercises will aid in student comprehension of geography and use of maps. Students can compare the traditional textbook map with an aerial view of the location today. It's an ideal resource for study, review, and research. In addition to this map feature, the resource center also provides blank maps for student review and testing. Ask your sales representative for more information on how to bundle access to the HRC with your text.

cengagebrain.com Save your students time and money. Direct them to www.cengagebrain.com for a choice of formats and savings and a better chance to succeed in class. Students have the freedom to purchase à la carte exactly what they need when they need it. There, students can purchase a downloadable ebook or electronic access to the American History Resource Center, the *American Passages Brief* premium study tools and interactive ebook in CourseMate, or eAudio modules from *The History Handbook* (see below). Students can save 50 percent on the electronic textbook, and can pay as little as $1.99 for an individual eChapter.

Reader Program. Cengage Learning publishes a number of readers, some containing exclusively primary sources, others a combination of primary and secondary sources, and some designed to guide students through the process of historical inquiry. Contact your sales rep or go to Cengage.com to browse through the many options.

Rand McNally Atlas of American History, 2e This comprehensive atlas features more than 80 maps, with new content covering global perspectives, including events in the Middle East from 1945 to 2005, as well as population trends in the United States and around the world. Additional maps document voyages of discovery; the settling of the colonies; major U.S. military engagements, including the American Revolution and World Wars I and II; and sources of immigrations, ethnic populations, and patterns of economic change.

Custom Options

Cengage Learning offers custom solutions for your course—whether it's making a small modification to *American Passages* to match your syllabus or combining multiple sources to create something truly unique. You can pick and choose chapters, include your own material, and add additional map exercises along with the Rand McNally Atlas to create a text that fits the way you teach. Ensure that your students get the most out of their textbook dollar by giving them exactly what they need. Contact your Cengage Learning representative to explore custom solutions for your course.

❖ Acknowledgments

I am grateful to my husband, Rudolf Soderlund, and my family for their support throughout this project. Many colleagues in the colonial and early national periods shared their ideas orally and through their publications. I have appreciated the feedback from instructors and students on earlier editions. As always, I am indebted to my co-authors Edward Ayers, Lewis Gould, and David Oshinsky for their collegiality and commitment to making this a great U.S. history text.

Jean R. Soderlund

I would like to thank Amanda Mushal for her imagination, hard work, and good advice in the revision of this edition. Finally, I am very appreciative of my co-authors, who have been engaged scholars, thoughtful critics, devoted teachers, and good friends throughout the years it took us to write *American Passages*.

Edward L. Ayers

I would like to acknowledge the help of the following former students who contributed in constructive ways to the completion of this textbook: Martin Ansell, the late Christie Bourgeois, Thomas Clarkin, Stacy Cordery, Debbie Cottrell, Scott Harris, Byron Hulsey, Jonathan Lee, John Leffler, and Nancy Beck Young. Karen Gould gave indispensable support and encouragement throughout the writing of the text. At Cengage Learning, I benefited from the guidance, patience, and understanding of Jane Lee, Charlotte Miller, Amy Pastan, Henry Rachlin, Jennifer Sutherland, and Ann West. I am grateful as well to all of the readers of my chapters who made so many useful and timely criticisms.

Lewis L. Gould

I would like to thank my colleagues and students at the University of Texas for allowing me to test out an endless stream of ideas and issues relating to modern American history, and also for their thoughts on how a good college textbook should "read" and what it should contain. As always, the support and love of my family—Matt, Efrem, Ari, and Jane—was unshakable. Above all, I must commend my co-authors and my editors for their remarkable patience and professionalism during this long collaborative process.

David M. Oshinsky

Reviewers

The authors wish to thank the following reviewers, who provided essential advice for the preparation of the fourth edition:

Charles Cox, *Bridgewater State University*
Brian Daugherity, *Virginia Commonwealth University*
David Fitzpatrick, *Washtenaw Community College*
Yolanda Harding, *University of Central Florida*
Scott Holzer, *Jefferson College*
Marc Horger, *Ohio State University*
Timothy Kelly, *West Valley College*
Paul Kelton, *University of Kansas*
Patricia Knol, *Triton College*
Arnold Krammer, *Texas A&M University*
Timothy Lehman, *Rocky Mountain College*
Peter Mathison, *St. John's Prep*
Richard McMillan, *Los Angeles Pierce College*
Michael Namorato, *University of Mississippi*
Phillip Papas, *Union County College*
Gail Parsons, *Gordon College*
Keith Pomakoy, *Adirondack Community College*
David Rayson, *Normandale Community College*
Horacio Salinas, *Laredo Community College*
James Sefton, *California State University, Northridge*
Howard Segal, *University of Maine, Orono*
David Snead, *Liberty University*
Timothy Wood, *Southern Baptist University*
Steven Woodsum, *Brunswick High School*

ABOUT THE AUTHORS

EDWARD L. AYERS is President and Professor of History of the University of Richmond. Named National Professor of the Year in 2003, Ayers has written and edited ten books. *The Promise of the New South: Life After Reconstruction* (1992) was a finalist for both the National Book Award and the Pulitzer Prize. *In the Presence of Mine Enemies, Civil War in the Heart of America* (2003) won the Bancroft Prize for distinguished writing in American history and the Beveridge Prize for the best book in English on the history of the Americas since 1492. Ayers created *The Valley of the Shadow: Two Communities in the American Civil War,* a website that has attracted millions of visitors.

LEWIS L. GOULD is the Eugene C. Barker Centennial Professor in American History *emeritus* at the University of Texas, where he won awards for both undergraduate and graduate teaching. He is currently the editor of the Modern First Ladies series with the University Press of Kansas and the general editor of the Documentary History of the John F. Kennedy Presidency with LexisNexis. His recent books include *The Modern American Presidency* (2003); *Grand Old Party: A History of the Republicans* (2003); *The Most Exclusive Club: A History of the Modern United States Senate* (2005); and *Four Hats in the Ring: The 1912 Election and the Birth of Modern American Politics* (2008).

JEAN R. SODERLUND is Professor of History and Deputy Provost for Faculty Affairs at Lehigh University.

Her book *Quakers and Slavery: A Divided Spirit* won the Alfred E. Driscoll Publication Prize of the New Jersey Historical Commission. Soderlund was an editor of three volumes of the *Papers of William Penn* (1981–1983) and co-authored *Freedom by Degrees: Emancipation in Pennsylvania and Its Aftermath* (1991). She has written articles and chapters in books on the history of women, African Americans, Native Americans, Quakers, and the development of abolition in the British North American colonies and early United States. She is currently working on a book-length study titled, *Violence and Peace on the Delaware: The Evolution of Liberal Society in Colonial New Jersey and Pennsylvania.*

DAVID M. OSHINSKY is the Jack S. Blanton Chair in History at the University of Texas at Austin and a Distinguished Scholar in Residence at New York University. Among his publications are *"A Conspiracy So Immense": The World of Joe McCarthy* (1983), which was voted one of the year's "notable books" by the *New York Times,* and won the Hardeman Prize for the best work about the history of the U.S. Congress; and *Worse Than Slavery* (1996), which won both the Robert F. Kennedy Book Award for the year's most distinguished contribution to human rights, and the American Bar Association's Scribes Award for distinguished legal writing. His most recent publication, *Polio: An American Story* (2005), won both the Pulitzer Prize for History and the Hoover Presidential Book Award.

15

Reconstruction: Its Rise and Fall

1865–1877

MAKING CONNECTIONS

◄‖‖ LOOKING BACK

Chapter 14 described the series of catastrophic events known as the Civil War. At every point, both Northerners and Southerners thought the conflict might end with one more key victory by their side. Instead, each battle seemed to bring another. Before starting Chapter 15, you should be able to answer the following questions:

1. What did the Confederacy need to accomplish in order to claim victory in the Civil War?

2. Did the Civil War have a turning point—a point beyond which it became clear that the United States would defeat the Confederacy? What would you identify as this point?

3. How did emancipation become the Union's central goal for the war?

Reconstruction Under Andrew Johnson, 1865–1867

Wartime Reconstruction in the South
Andrew Johnson
Johnson and the Radicals
The Reconstruction Act of 1867

From Johnson to Grant, 1867–1868

The Election of 1868
The Fifteenth Amendment

The First Grant Administration, 1869–1873

A Troubled Administration
Grant, Congress, and Republican Discord
The Problem of the Ku Klux Klan
Farmers and Railroads
Indian Policies

Women in the 1870s

Doing History: Women's Rights and Black Suffrage During Reconstruction

The Rise of Voluntary Associations
Women at Work

Political and Economic Turmoil

The 1872 Election
A Surge of Scandals
The Panic of 1873 and Its Consequences

The Failure of Reconstruction, 1875–1877

The Stigma of Corruption
The Resurgence of the Democrats
The Centennial Year, 1876
The Race for the White House
Why Reconstruction Failed

Wth the death of Abraham Lincoln in April 1865, a new president sought to reunite the nation at the end of the Civil War. The presence of Andrew Johnson in the White House took the Republican Party and the newly freed slaves in directions that shaped the way the North made policy toward the defeated South. The process became known as Reconstruction, and it has remained one of the most controversial periods in all of American history.

Reconstruction set out to change the South and better the lives of the people, white and black, who lived there. But these important efforts left many aspects of the southern economy in no better, and sometimes worse, shape than before Reconstruction began. A depressed economy and increased debt made sharecropping the lot of many southern farmers of both races by 1880 (see Map 15.1). Still, former slaves played a decisive role in building institutions and carrying on campaigns to expand their political impact in the South. The opportunity to build a multiracial society after the Civil War was a fleeting one, but it represented an important chapter in the lives of those individuals who formerly had been in bondage.

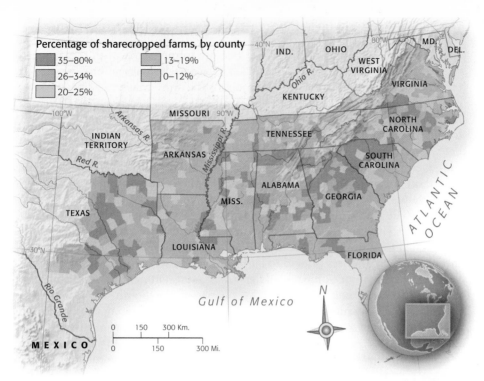

MAP 15.1

Sharecropping in the South by County, 1880
Just fifteen years after the start of Reconstruction, the economic system of sharecropping had taken over agriculture in the South. Hard times, racial discrimination, and an absence of capital forced many farmers into this difficult situation, raising the question of the extent to which Reconstruction really changed the South.

Percentage of sharecropped farms, by county
- 35–80%
- 26–34%
- 20–25%
- 13–19%
- 0–12%

Source: U.S. Census Office, Tenth Census, 1889, *Report of the Production of Agriculture* (Washington, D.C. Government Printing Office, 1883), Table 5.

❖ Reconstruction Under Andrew Johnson, 1865–1867

In the wake of Lincoln's assassination, the nation looked to the new president for leadership. Andrew Johnson was an unknown element to most, but his promise to pursue Lincoln's policies seemed reassuring. As it turned out, Johnson had a firm idea of how he wanted to deal with the South, but his Reconstruction policies proved neither effective nor in tune with majority opinion in the North.

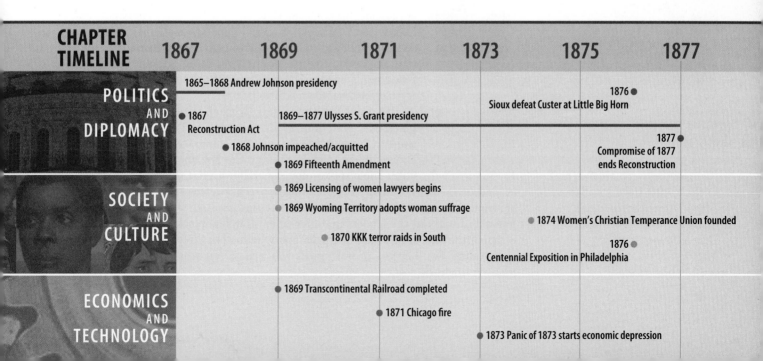

CHAPTER TIMELINE	1867	1869	1871	1873	1875	1877
POLITICS AND DIPLOMACY	1865–1868 Andrew Johnson presidency ● 1867 Reconstruction Act ● 1868 Johnson impeached/acquitted	1869–1877 Ulysses S. Grant presidency ● 1869 Fifteenth Amendment			1876 ● Sioux defeat Custer at Little Big Horn	1877 ● Compromise of 1877 ends Reconstruction
SOCIETY AND CULTURE	● 1869 Licensing of women lawyers begins ● 1869 Wyoming Territory adopts woman suffrage ● 1870 KKK terror raids in South			● 1874 Women's Christian Temperance Union founded 1876 ● Centennial Exposition in Philadelphia		
ECONOMICS AND TECHNOLOGY	● 1869 Transcontinental Railroad completed ● 1871 Chicago fire		● 1873 Panic of 1873 starts economic depression			

Wartime Reconstruction in the South

Toward the end of the Civil War, slaves became former slaves with the passage of the Thirteenth Amendment. Some seized their freedom at the first opportunity, taking their families to Union camps or joining the army. Many freed people set off on journeys in desperate efforts to find family members sold away in earlier years. For others, sheer survival was the highest priority. Freedom came in the late spring, barely in time to get crops in the ground. Some former slaves figured that their best bet was to stay where they were for the time being. They had heard rumors that the government would award them land. Between July and September 1865, however, those dreams died. Union officers had promised land to former slaves in Virginia, Louisiana, Mississippi, and South Carolina, but then Washington revoked the promises. The land would be returned to its former owners.

White southerners also responded in many different ways. Some former slave owners fled to Latin America; others whipped and chained workers to keep them from leaving. Still others offered to let former slaves stay in their cabins and work for wages. The presence of black soldiers triggered resentment and fear among former slave owners; one declared, "The people of the South are in very great danger. . . . I tell you most seriously that the whole south is resting upon a volcano."

Many African Americans had no choice but to compromise with white landowners. At first, in the spring of 1865, planters insisted that the former slaves work as they had worked before emancipation, in "gangs." In return for their work, they would receive a portion of the crop, shared among all the workers. Many black people chafed at this arrangement, preferring to work as individuals or families. In such places, landowners found that they had little choice but to permit black families to take primary responsibility for a portion of land. These former slaves, called "sharecroppers," provided the labor and received part of the crop in return. Planters realized they had few choices: they possessed little cash to pay wage workers and no alternative labor.

The Bureau of Refugees, Freedmen, and Abandoned Lands—the **Freedmen's Bureau**—oversaw the transition from a slave economy to a wage economy. Its agents, approximately nine hundred for the entire South, dispensed medicine, food, and clothing from the vast stores of the federal government to displaced white and black southerners. It created courts to adjudicate conflicts and draw up labor contracts between landholders and laborers. It established schools and coordinated female volunteers who came from the North to teach in them. Although many white southerners resented and resisted the Freedmen's Bureau, it helped smooth the transition from slavery to freedom, from war to peace.

Throughout the South, former slaves and former free blacks gathered in mass meetings, Union Leagues, and conventions to announce their vision of the new order. They wanted, above all else, equality before the law and the opportunity to vote. Their spokesmen generally did not demand confiscation of land or speak extensively of economic concerns. Let us have our basic rights before the courts and at the ballot box, they said, and we will take care of ourselves. But without the leadership of Abraham Lincoln, black southerners rightly worried, the forces of reaction might overwhelm their freedom and economic opportunity. Southerners of both races watched to see what President Andrew Johnson might do.

Freedmen's Bureau Federal agency created in 1865 to supervise newly freed people. It oversaw relations between whites and blacks in the South, issued food rations, and supervised labor contracts.

(Photographic History Collection, National Museum of American History, Smithsonian Institution)

African American Mother and Child. After slavery ended, African Americans pursued education with determination. Here a daughter was photographed as she taught her mother how to read.

Andrew Johnson

Johnson had been chosen for the vice presidency in 1864 because he was a Unionist southerner. As a result, both northerners and southerners distrusted him. The new president's well-known disdain for the wealthy planters of the South appealed to equally disdainful Republicans in Washington, and his public statements suggested a harsh peace for the Confederate leaders: "*Treason* is a crime, and crime must be punished." Unlike some Republicans, however, Johnson held little sympathy for black people or for expansion of the powers of the federal government. Johnson saw himself pursuing Lincoln's highest goal, reuniting the Union. Reunification should start by winning the support of white southerners.

Johnson enjoyed a brief period in which to enact his vision of how to return the South to the Union. Congress was not in session at the time of Lincoln's death and would not be for seven months, so Johnson used the opportunity to implement his plan of reunion. In "Presidential Reconstruction," Johnson offered amnesty to former Confederates who took an oath of loyalty to the Union, restoring their political and civil rights and immunizing them against the seizure of their property and prosecution for treason. By 1866, Johnson had granted more than seven thousand pardons to wealthy southerners and Confederate senior officers who applied individually for pardons.

Johnson's plans for political reunion left out any provision for black voting or participation in politics. Indeed, his plan would give the South even greater national power than it had held before because the entire African American population would now be considered individually when the number of representatives was calculated, not merely as three-fifths of a person as before the war. White southerners could hardly believe their good fortune. The members of the state conventions elected in 1865 flaunted their opinions of the North. Some refused to fly the American flag, some refused to ratify the Thirteenth Amendment, and some even refused to admit that secession had been illegal. Former Confederates filled important posts in state governments. Georgia elected Alexander H. Stevens, the former vice president of the aborted nation, to Congress. Even Johnson recognized that "there seems, in many of the elections something like defiance."

The North erupted in outrage when the new state governments enacted the so-called **black codes**, laws for controlling former slaves. The southern white legislatures granted the barest minimum of rights to black people: the right to marry, to hold property, to sue and be sued. Most of the laws decreed what African Americans could not do: move from one job to another, own or rent land, testify in court, practice certain occupations. When the members of Congress convened in December 1865, they reacted with fury. To northerners, the former Confederates seemed to deny all the war had decided with this blatant attempt to retain racially based laws. Many blamed Johnson for the turn of events.

black codes (colonial) Laws passed by colonial assemblies to define slavery and control the black population.

Johnson and the Radicals

Northern leaders who came to be known as the Radical Republicans were particularly incensed by presidential reconstruction. Senator Thaddeus Stevens called for land to be seized from wealthy planters and given to the former slaves; Senator Charles Sumner wanted immediate and universal suffrage for blacks. But other northerners simply resented the easy pass given to former Confederates. "As for Negro suffrage," wrote a Chicago newspaper editor, "the mass of Union men in the Northwest did not care a great deal. What scares them is the idea that the rebels are all to be let back . . . and made a power in the government again." Moderates tried to devise plans acceptable to both sides.

[handwritten margin note: ← Would things had been different had Johnson not done this? Even today?]

(LC-B8184-10690)/Library of Congress Prints and Photographs Division)

Andrew Johnson.   Andrew Johnson attempted to forge a new alliance between white northerners and white southerners, callously abandoning black southerners in the process.

Ku Klux Klan Founded in 1866 as an organization to terrorize blacks in the South during Reconstruction. It was revived in 1915 as a means of enforcing, often through violence and intimidation, the cultural values of rural, prohibitionist America against minority groups including African Americans, Jews, and Catholics.

Though understaffed and underfunded, the Freedmen's Bureau offered some measure of hope for former slaves by mediating between whites and blacks. Its commissioner, General Oliver Howard, advocated education as the foundation for improving living conditions and prospects for blacks. By 1869, approximately three thousand schools, serving more than 150,000 students, reported to the bureau. The bureau also insisted on the innovation of formal contracts between laborer and landlord. Moderate reformers also pushed for a civil rights bill to define American citizenship for all those born in the United States, including blacks. Citizenship would bring with it equal protection under the law, though the bill said nothing about black voting. The bureau struggled against a public that, in the words of one Mississippi commissioner, failed to "conceive of the Negro having any rights at all."

Republicans supported the Freedmen's Bureau and civil rights bills as the starting point for rebuilding the nation. But Johnson vetoed both bills, claiming that they violated the rights of the states and of white southerners who had been excluded from the decision making. Republicans closed ranks to override Johnson's veto, the first major legislation ever enacted over a presidential veto.

To prevent any future erosion of black rights, the Republicans proposed the Fourteenth Amendment, which, as eventually ratified, guaranteed citizenship to all American-born people and equal protection under the law for those citizens. The amendment decreed that any state that abridged the voting rights of any male inhabitants who were over age twenty-one and citizens would suffer a proportionate reduction in its congressional representation. It was the first constitutional amendment to use the word *male*, angering feminist abolitionists, who challenged the denial of suffrage based on sex. On Johnson's advice, the southern states refused to ratify the amendment.

Throughout the second half of 1866, the North watched, appalled, as much that the Civil War had been fought for seemed to be brushed aside in the South. Not only did the southern men who met in the state conventions refuse to accept the relatively mild Fourteenth Amendment, but they fought back in every way they could against further attempts to remake the South. The spring of that year saw riots in Memphis and New Orleans in which policemen and other whites brutally assaulted and killed black people and burned their homes with little or no provocation. It was in 1866, too, that the **Ku Klux Klan** appeared. Founded by Nathan Bedford Forrest in Tennessee, the Ku Klux Klan dedicated itself to maintaining white supremacy. The Klan became, in effect, a military wing of the Democratic Party, intimidating and killing white and black men who dared to associate with Republicans or support black rights.

Johnson toured the country in the fall of 1866 to denounce Republicans and their policy, to no avail. Republicans won control of Congress as well as the governorship and legislature in every northern state. The Republicans felt they had a mandate to push harder than they had before, but they faced internal disagreements over the vote, land distribution, the courts, and education. Some wanted to put the South under military control for the indefinite future; others sought to return to civilian control as soon as possible. Finally, on March 2, 1867, as time was running out on the session, they passed the Reconstruction Act.

The Reconstruction Act of 1867

The Reconstruction Act placed the South under military rule. All of the southern states except Tennessee, which had been readmitted to the Union after it ratified the Fourteenth Amendment, were divided into five military districts. Once order had been instituted, the states could proceed to elect conventions to draw up new constitutions, but those constitutions had to accept the Fourteenth Amendment and provide universal manhood suffrage. Once a majority of the state's citizens and both houses of the national Congress had approved the new constitution, the state could be readmitted to the Union.

To ensure that Andrew Johnson did not undermine the plan, which soon became known as "Radical Reconstruction," Congress sought to curb the president's power. With no threat of his veto after the 1866 elections, the Republicans called Congress into special session and voted to limit the president's authority as commander-in-chief of the army. They also passed the Tenure of Office Act, which prevented the president from removing officials who had been confirmed by the Senate. Johnson, characteristically, did not accept such restrictions of his power. When he violated the Tenure of Office Act by removing Secretary of War Edwin Stanton in the summer of 1867, many in Congress decided that Johnson warranted **impeachment.** Proceedings dragged on throughout the fall, while the first elections under the Reconstruction Act took place in the South. Finally, on May 16, 1868, Johnson was acquitted in the Senate by one vote, as even his political foes came to realize that using impeachment for anything less than criminal offenses while in office would have been unwise. But the constitutional and political significance of Johnson's impeachment endured.

After word of the Reconstruction Act circulated in the spring and summer, both black and white men claimed leadership roles within the Republican Party. Black northerners came to the South looking for appointive and elective office. Ambitious black southerners, many of whom had been free and relatively prosperous before the Civil War, put themselves forward as the natural leaders of the race. Such men became the backbone of the Republican Party in black-belt districts that had a predominantly African American population.

White southerners sneered at supporters of the Republican cause. They called white northerners who came South to support Radical Reconstruction "carpetbaggers." These men were supposedly so unsuccessful back home that they could throw everything they had into a carpetbag (a cheap suitcase) and head south as soon as they read of the opportunities Radical Reconstruction had created. But the majority of white northerners who became Republican leaders in the South had been well educated in the North before the war, and many held property in the South. Like white southerners, however, the northern-born Republicans found the postwar South a difficult place in which to prosper. Meanwhile, white southern Republicans were labeled "scalawags" by their enemies and considered traitors to their race and region. Few white Republicans emerged in the plantation districts because they endured ostracism, resistance, and violence. In the upcountry districts, however, former Whigs and Unionists asserted themselves against the planters and Confederates. The Republican Party became strong in the mountains of eastern Tennessee, western North Carolina, eastern Kentucky, northern Alabama, and northern Georgia. Blacks, largely propertyless, called for an activist government to raise taxes and provide

impeachment The act of charging a public official with misconduct in office, impeachment is the constitutional procedure for removing presidents who are found guilty of "treason, bribery, or other high crimes and misdemeanors" as interpreted by Congress. Presidents Andrew Johnson, Richard Nixon, and Bill Clinton have been the subject of impeachment proceedings.

(Cheekwood Museum of Art)

African American Man Voting.
African American men voted during Reconstruction in the South but they often put their lives on the line in doing so.

schools, orphanages, and hospitals. Many whites, who owned land, called mainly for lower taxes.

Throughout the South, most whites watched, livid, as local black leaders, ministers, and Republicans mobilized black voters in enormous numbers in fall 1867. Membership in Union Leagues swept the region, with local leagues assisting with labor contracts and school construction as well as political activity. An Alabama league demanded recognition of black citizenship: "We claim exactly the same rights, privileges and immunities as are enjoyed by white men—we seek nothing more and will be content with nothing less." While many white Democrats boycotted the elections, the Republicans swept into the constitutional delegate positions. Although many black men voted, African Americans made up only a relatively small part of the convention delegates. They held the majority in South Carolina and Louisiana, but much smaller proportions elsewhere. About half of the 265 African Americans elected as delegates to the state conventions had been free before the war, and most were ministers, artisans, farmers, and teachers. During the next two years, these delegates would meet to write new, much more democratic constitutions for their states.

Republicans in 1867 believed that they had taken important steps toward a newer and more just society. "We have cut loose from the whole dead past," said Timothy Howe of Wisconsin, "and have cast our anchor out a hundred years." But the struggle over black rights that had begun during the Civil War was far from over. Many white voters in the North thought that the Radicals had gone too far in their concern with black rights and wanted officeholders to devote their energies to problems closer to home. In the South, in the decade that followed the war, blacks pursued their dreams of political equality and economic opportunity, while many whites sought to preserve as many of the features of slavery as they could. Violence, brutality, election fraud, and raw economic intimidation ended the experiment in multiracial politics known as Reconstruction.

In the mid-1870s, a severe economic depression made African American rights seem a less urgent issue. For many in the North, the hum of industry, the spread of railroads, and the rise of cities seemed more in tune with national progress than preserving the rights of former slaves. With a western frontier to open and Native Americans to subdue, the nation retreated from the principles for which the Civil War had been fought. By the disputed presidential election of 1876, white Americans no longer wished to be involved with the fate of blacks in the South.

❖ From Johnson to Grant, 1867–1868

During the months of Johnson's impeachment and trial, Congress completed expansion on the North American continent with the purchase of Alaska from Russia. The Alaska purchase was a major strategic and geographic victory for the United States. Amid the controversy over the impeachment of Johnson and the upcoming presidential election, the acquisition of this northern territory did not attract great attention, however.

The Election of 1868

The issues of the Civil War defined the 1868 presidential race. The Republicans nominated the great hero of the conflict, Ulysses S. Grant, whose popularity transcended partisanship. Republicans believed that they had selected a candidate "so independent of party politics as to be a guarantee of peace and quiet." In his official letter of acceptance, Grant said, "Let us have peace," and that phrase became the theme of the Republican campaign. The Republicans were not campaigning on any promise to expand Reconstruction or to do more for the rights of black Americans.

The Democrats turned to the former governor of New York, Horatio Seymour. Along with his running mate, Frank Blair of Missouri, Seymour relied on racial bigotry and white supremacy as the keynotes of his appeal. To win, the Democrats agreed, they had to arouse "the aversion with which the masses contemplate the equality of the negro." Grant garnered 53 percent of the vote; Seymour totaled 47 percent. Although Grant carried the electoral college by a margin of 214 to 80, the signs were not good for a continuation of Reconstruction. Over time, white voters had become less willing to help African Americans; whatever goals African Americans sought, they would have to achieve them on their own. The high point of post–Civil War racial reform had passed.

The Fifteenth Amendment

After the 1868 election, Republicans pushed for the adoption of the Fifteenth Amendment to the Constitution to finish the political reforms that Reconstruction brought. Under its terms, the federal and state governments could not restrict the right to vote because of race, color, or previous condition of servitude. Congress approved the amendment in February 1869 over Democratic opposition. The purpose of the change was to limit the legal right of the southern states to exclude African Americans from the political process. Democrats assailed it as a step toward black equality and a social revolution. In fact, the new amendment did not ensure African Americans the right to hold office, and it left untouched the restrictions that northern states imposed on the right of males to vote. Nevertheless, state legislatures endorsed the amendment promptly, and it was added to the Constitution in 1870. The adoption of the three Civil War amendments had changed the nature of the government as the administration of President Grant got under way, but American politics responded slowly to the impact of these new additions to the nation's fundamental law.

❖ The First Grant Administration, 1869–1873

Ulysses S. Grant, who came to the White House without political experience, believed that he should administer the government rather than promote new programs. "I shall on all subjects have a policy to recommend," he said in his inaugural address, "but none to enforce against the will of the people." He promised, unlike Andrew Johnson, to carry out the laws that Congress passed. Those who hoped for a period of calm after the storms of Johnson's presidency were soon disappointed, however. Grant's passive view of the presidency and aversion to partisan battles allowed Congress to play a dominant role. Without a clear objective of a war before him in which victory was the goal, the president seemed confused, and he followed a shifting policy in selecting his cabinet and making appointments. His cabinet mixed some strong appointments, such as Secretary of State Hamilton Fish, with other individuals whose qualifications were questionable. As a result, the executive office itself lost some of the authority Lincoln had acquired for it.

A Troubled Administration

Hard choices confronted the new president, particularly in the South. Southern Republicans begged for help from Washington to fight off resurgent Democrats. Yet many party members in the North believed that support for black aspirations seemed an electoral loser. As a result, African Americans in the South had to rely more and more on their own resources and personal courage. They made valiant efforts to involve themselves in regional politics, often at the risk of their lives. For their part, Democrats played down their racism in public statements and argued that former Confederates should now be allowed to participate in public life. The strategy produced mixed results in 1869: Republicans did well in Mississippi and won a close race for governor in Texas, while Democrats triumphed in Virginia and Tennessee. Overall, the results suggested that Republican strength was eroding as the Democrats reentered politics.

Making matters worse were allegations of scandal against the new administration. In the summer of 1869, two speculators, Jay Gould and Jim Fisk, manipulated the gold market to achieve huge profits for themselves. The price of gold rose until financial turmoil erupted on September 24, 1869. Investors who had promised to sell gold at lower prices faced ruin. Then the government sold its own gold supplies, the price of gold broke, and the market returned to its normal level. In the resulting inquiries, the public learned that some members of Grant's family had helped Gould and Fisk carry out their plan. Doubts spread about the ethical standards of Grant's presidency.

To the odor of corruption was soon added White House disarray and incompetence. The administration talked of forcing Spain to give up Cuba and then backed away from the idea. The president wanted to annex the Dominican Republic (Santo Domingo). An agent of the president worked out a treaty of annexation with Santo Domingo's rulers, and the pact was sent to the Senate. Grant pushed hard for its approval, but the Senate, fearful of the influence of speculators and lobbyists, balked. As a result, the treaty was defeated and the president embarrassed.

Grant's administration had more success with American claims for maritime losses against Great Britain. The claims were related to the *Alabama*, one of several Confederate raiders constructed in British shipyards during the Civil War. The *Alabama* had sunk numerous Union vessels. Charles Sumner, chair of the Senate Foreign Relations Committee, wanted to use the claims as leverage in an effort to acquire Canada. In 1871, the State Department worked out an amicable settlement of the issue that left Canada alone.

Grant, Congress, and Republican Discord

The president deferred too much to Congress as congressional Republicans split on issues such as the protective tariff and the currency. The mainstream members of the party believed that a tariff policy to "protect" American industries against foreign competition helped business, workers, and the party itself. A minority of Republicans called the protective policy wrong economically and a potential source of corrupt influence from the affected industries. On the currency, eastern Republicans favored the gold standard and what was known as "hard money," where every dollar was backed by an equal amount of gold. Western Republicans advocated an expansion of the money supply through paper money, or "greenbacks," and, when necessary, even the issuance of dollars backed by silver as an alternative to gold. Civil service was another divisive issue. Since government was still small, who held coveted jobs became a question for public dispute. Some Republicans argued that the government should follow "civil service reform," a merit system of appointing its officials. Reformers maintained that competence and nonpartisanship were better ways to staff these positions.

Republicans who wanted to reduce the tariff, rely on the civil service, and treat the South with more leniency defected from the Grant administration. They formed **Liberal Republican** alliances with Democrats in such states as West Virginia and Missouri. In the 1870s, *liberal* meant someone who favored smaller government, lower tariffs, civil service, and, most important, an end to Reconstruction. If African Americans were the victims of southern violence, the liberal Republicans were willing to tolerate that result.

With his presidency under attack, Grant turned to Republican leaders in Congress who disliked the Liberal Republican program and its leaders. Grant knew that he could never satisfy the demands of the Liberals on Reconstruction or the civil service. Instead, he conciliated mainstream Republicans. He dismissed dissenting cabinet officers and aligned himself with party members willing to defend Congress and the White House. Officeholders who supported Liberal Republican candidates or Democrats were fired. Despite these actions, the 1870 elections went to Grant's opponents. Liberal Republicans won races in West Virginia and Missouri. The Democrats added forty-one seats to their total in the House and picked up another six seats in the Senate. The Republicans retained control of both houses, but their position was weakening. Grant's enemies even thought he might be defeated in 1872.

Liberal Republicans Organization formed in 1872 by Republicans who were not content with the political corruption and the policies of President Grant's first administration.

→ Violation of Tenure of office Act??

The Problem of the Ku Klux Klan

Mounting racial violence in the South added to the president's problems. By the summer of 1870, reports reached Washington of Klan violence against blacks and white Republicans across the South. The Klan and its offshoots, such as the Knights of the White Camelia, White Leagues, and the White Brotherhood, acted as the paramilitary arm of the Democratic Party to crush Republicanism through any means. In Tennessee a black Republican was beaten after he won an election for justice of the peace. His assailants told him "that they didn't dispute I was a very good fellow . . . but they did not intend any nigger to hold office in the United States." Four blacks died when the Klan attacked an election meeting in Alabama in October 1870. A "negro chase" in South Carolina left thirteen blacks dead. A wave of shootings and brutality undermined the chances of the Republican Party to survive and grow below the Mason-Dixon line.

Viewing the wreckage of their southern parties after the 1870 elections, Republicans recognized that the Klan's terror tactics had worked to intimidate voters and demoralize their leaders. Yet the party was divided about the right answer to terror in the South. As 1871 began, the Republicans had less stomach for sending troops to the South to affect politics. As an Illinois newspaper observed, "the negro is now a voter and a citizen. Let him hereafter take his chances in the battle of life." Republican leaders asked themselves whether the cost of maintaining party organizations in the South in the face of such resolute Democratic opposition justified the effort.

Still, the violence of the Klan presented a challenge that could not be ignored. Congress passed the Ku Klux Klan Act of 1871, outlawing conspiracies to deprive voters of their civil rights, and banned efforts to bar any citizen from holding public office. The government also received broader powers to fight the Klan through the use of federal district attorneys to override state laws. As a last resort, military force could also be employed. The Justice Department, established in 1870, argued that the threat the Klan posed to democratic

(The Granger Collection, New York)

In the 1870s, political cartoonist Thomas Nast brought attention to terror organizations like the Ku Klux Klan.

government amounted to war. Officials in Washington mobilized federal district attorneys and U.S. marshals to institute prosecutions against the Klan. The legal offensive in 1871 brought results; in state after state, Klan leaders were indicted. Federal troops assisted the work of the Justice Department in South Carolina. The Klan was discredited as a public presence in southern politics; its violence became more covert and less visible. Although the prosecutions of the Klan showed that effective federal action could compel southern states to comply with the rule of law, sentiment in the North for such stern measures began to recede.

Farmers and Railroads

The expansion of railroads posed new challenges for farmers in the South and West. Throughout the 1860s, two transcontinental railroads laid tracks across the country. The Union Pacific built westward while the Central Pacific started eastward from the West Coast. The two lines faced difficult obstacles of money and geography. The Central Pacific crossed the Sierra Nevada Mountains through rocky gorges and across treacherous rivers. Several thousand Chinese laborers did the most dangerous work: they tunneled into snowdrifts to reach their work sites and then toiled on sheer cliffs with picks and dynamite. On the Union Pacific side, more than ten thousand construction workers, many of them Irish immigrants, laid tracks across Nebraska and Wyoming. When the two lines met at Promontory, Utah, on May 10, 1869, railroad executives drove a golden spike into the ground with a silver sledgehammer: the transcontinental lines had become a reality.

Railroad construction accelerated. In 1869, railroad mileage stood at about 47,000 miles; four years later, the total had risen to 70,268 miles. The new railroad lines employed tens of thousands of workers and extended across a far larger geographical area than any previous manufacturing enterprise. American business was starting to become much larger than any previous endeavor in the nation; that development would have important consequences.

Farmers too enjoyed postwar prosperity with higher prices for wheat and other commodities. Beneath the surface, however, tensions between agrarians and the new industries grew. In late 1867, the Patrons of Husbandry, also known as the Grange, was formed to press the case for the farmers. The Grange complained about the high mortgages the farmers owed, the prices they paid to middlemen such as the operators of grain elevators, and the economic discrimination they faced in the form of higher charges at the hands of railroads in moving their goods to market. These grievances contributed to the turbulence of politics in the 1880s and 1890s.

To balance the power of the railroads, some states created railroad commissions. In Illinois, a new constitution in 1870 instructed the legislature to pass laws establishing maximum rates for the movement of passengers and freight. The legislature set up the Illinois Railroad Commission with wide powers. Neighboring states such as Iowa, Minnesota, and Wisconsin followed the Illinois example during the next several years. Railroad companies challenged some of these laws in court, but the U.S. Supreme Court upheld the authority of such commissions in *Munn v. Illinois* (1877) (see Chapter 16).

Indian Policies

The opening of the West to railroads and the spread of farmers onto the Great Plains meant that Native Americans had to once again, as in the 1830s and 1850s, resist an encroaching white presence. What had once been called the "Great American Desert" now beckoned as the home for countless farmers. The tribes that were living in the West and the Native Americans who had been displaced there in the 1830s and 1840s found their hunting grounds and tribal domains under siege.

Treatment of Native Americans after the Civil War mixed benevolence and cruelty. Grant brought more insight and respect to the issue of Native Americans than most previous presidents. His administration pursued what became known as the "peace policy." Although a majority of western settlers advocated the removal or outright extermination of the Indian tribes, advocates of the Indians convinced Grant that the hostile tribes should be located in Dakota Territory and the Indian Territory (now Oklahoma). The government would stop treating the entire West as a giant Indian reservation. Instead, specific areas would be set aside for the Native Americans. On these "reservations," the inhabitants would learn the cultural values of white society, be taught to grow crops, and be paid a small income until they could support themselves. (See Map 15.2.)

Grant appointed Ely Parker, a Seneca, as commissioner of Indian affairs. Congress appropriated $2 million for Indian problems and set up the Board of Indian Commissioners to distribute the funds. Indian agents would be chosen from nominees that Christian churches provided. The peace policy blended kindness and force. If the Indians accepted the presence of church officials on the reservations, the government would leave them alone. Resistance, however, would bring the army to see that Indians stayed on the reservations. To whites, the peace policy was humane. For Native Americans, it undermined their way of life.

MAP 15.2

Indian Reservations in the West

Following the end of the Civil War and the adoption of the peace policy of President Ulysses S. Grant, a network of Indian reservations spread across the West. This map shows how extensive the reservation system was.

(Copyright © Cengage Learning)

The 1870s brought increasing tensions on the frontier. The 1870 census reported more than 2.7 million farms; ten years later, that number had risen to more than 4 million. Competition for space and resources intensified. With millions of acres under cultivation and the spread of cattle drives across Indian lands, the tribes found themselves squeezed from their traditional nomadic hunting grounds.

The systematic destruction of the buffalo herds beginning in the 1860s dealt Indians another devastating blow. In the societies of the Plains tribes, the meat of the bison supplied food, and the hides provided shelter and clothes. Removal of these resources hurt the Indians economically, but the cultural impact was even greater because buffalo represented the continuity of nature and the renewal of life cycles. As railroads penetrated the West, hunters could send buffalo hides and other products to customers with relative ease. More than 5 million buffalo were slaughtered during the early 1870s, and by the end of the century, only a few of these animals were alive. Conservation eventually saved the buffalo from the near extinction.

During the mid-1870s, Native Americans tried a last effort to block the social and economic tides overwhelming their way of life. By that time, Grant's peace policy had faltered as corruption and politics replaced the original desire to treat the Indians in a more humane manner. The tribes that continued to hunt and pursue their nomadic culture found unhappy whites and a hostile military in their way. The Red River War, led by Cheyenne, Kiowas, and Comanches, erupted on the southern Plain, but Indian resistance ultimately collapsed when food and supplies ran out.

The discovery of gold in the Black Hills of Dakota brought white settlers into an area where the Sioux had dominated. The Indians refused to leave, and the government sent troops to protect the gold seekers. The Indian leaders, **Crazy Horse** and **Sitting Bull**, rallied their followers to stop the army. Near what the Indians called the Greasy Grass (whites called it the Little Bighorn), Colonel **George Armstrong Custer** led a force of six hundred men in 1876. With a third of his detachment, he attacked more than two thousand Sioux warriors. Custer and his soldiers perished. The whites called it "Custer's Last Stand." The Indian victory, shocking to whites, was only a temporary success, however. The army pursued the Indians during the ensuing months. By the end of the Grant administration, the Sioux had been conquered. Only in the Southwest did the Apaches successfully resist the power of the military. Native Americans now faced cruelty, exploitation,

Crazy Horse (1842?–1877) Native American Sioux leader who defeated George Custer in battle.

Sitting Bull (c. 1831–1890) Lakota Sioux Chief, he defeated George Custer in the Battle of Little Big Horn (1876).

Custer, George Armstrong (1839–1876) Lieutenant colonel famous for his defeat at Little Big Horn by the Sioux Indians.

Pima Indian Reservation School, 1870. The Peace Policy of the Grant administration moved Native Americans onto reservations like this one at Pima, Arizona.

(LC-USZC4-5613)/Library of Congress Prints and Photographs Division)

and oppression that extended through the rest of the nineteenth century and beyond 1900.

❖ Women in the 1870s

White women during this time did not have anything that approached social or political equality with men. Amid the male-dominated public life, women struggled for some political rights, a foothold in the new industrial economy, and a way to make their voices heard about social issues. But they faced significant barriers to any kind of meaningful participation in public affairs, a condition that continued into the early twentieth century.

The debates over the adoption of the Fifteenth Amendment underscored this problem. Women had hoped that they might share in the expansion of political rights. In fact, several major advocates of woman **suffrage**, including **Susan B. Anthony,** opposed the amendment because it left women out. In Anthony's mind, black and Asian men should be barred from voting unless women had the right of suffrage as well. That put her at odds with champions of black suffrage such as Frederick Douglass. (See *Doing History: Women's Rights and Black Suffrage During Reconstruction*.)

At a meeting of the Equal Rights Association in May 1869, two distinct groups of suffragists emerged. The National Woman Suffrage Association reflected the views of Susan B. Anthony and Elizabeth Cady Stanton that the Fifteenth Amendment should be shunned until women were included. The American Woman Suffrage Association, led by Lucy Stone and Alice Stone Blackwell, endorsed the amendment and focused its work on gaining suffrage in the states. Amid this dissension, the new territory of Wyoming granted women the right of suffrage in 1869. Nonetheless, their action represented a small step forward while the major suffrage groups feuded.

For women the decade of the 1870s offered both some opportunities and more reminders of their status as second-class citizens. On the positive side, educational opportunities expanded. The number of women graduating from high school stood at nearly nine thousand in 1870, compared with seven thousand men. Aware of these statistics, state universities and private colleges opened their doors to female students in growing numbers. By 1872, nearly one hundred institutions of higher learning admitted women, including Cornell University in Ithaca, New York. One of its first woman graduates was M. Carey Thomas, who received her B.A. in 1877. Five years later, she earned a Ph.D. at a German university. By the 1890s, she had become the president of Bryn Mawr, a women's college outside Philadelphia.

Obtaining a degree was not a guarantee of access to professions that males controlled. Myra Bradwell tried to become a lawyer in Illinois, but the state bar association rejected her application. She sued in federal court, and in 1873 the U.S. Supreme Court decided that the law did not grant her the right to be admitted to the bar. One justice wrote that "the paramount destiny and mission of woman are to fulfill the noble and benign offices of wife and mother." Although licensing of lawyers began in 1869, a year later there were only five female lawyers in the nation.

The Supreme Court also rebuffed efforts to secure woman suffrage through the courts. Virginia Minor, president of the Woman Suffrage Association of Missouri, tried to vote during the 1872 election, but the registrar of voters turned her away. She sued on the grounds that the action denied her rights as a citizen. In the case of *Minor v. Happersett* (1875), the Supreme Court unanimously concluded that suffrage was not one of the rights of citizenship because "sex has never been made one of the elements of citizenship in the United States." To gain the right to vote, women would have to amend the Constitution or obtain the right of suffrage from the states.

suffrage The right to vote, extended to African American men by the Fifteenth Amendment (1870). See also woman suffrage.

Anthony, Susan B. (1820–1906) Advocate of woman's suffrage and leader in the woman's rights movement along with Elizabeth Cady Stanton.

Doing History   Women's Rights and Black Suffrage During Reconstruction

One of the unexpected aspects of Reconstruction occurred during debates about the wisdom of extending the vote to black males but not to women in general. Out of these discussions would come the Fifteenth Amendment to the Constitution, which affirmed the right of citizens to vote without regard to their race, color, or status as former slaves. The amendment, however, said nothing about gender. Advocates of woman suffrage believed that women should be accorded the right to vote as well as men. The dispute divided African American men such as Frederick Douglass from champions of woman suffrage such as Elizabeth Cady Stanton. The divisions between Stanton and Douglass shed light on the interplay between race and gender that cut across American society in the nineteenth century.

The exchange of views between Stanton and Douglass that follows came at a meeting of the American Equal Rights Association in New York City during May 1867. George Downing was a black man who had asked Stanton about views on male suffrage for blacks and suffrage for all Americans.

Elizabeth Cady Stanton, 1867

WE DO NOT demand the right step for this hour in demanding suffrage for any class; as a matter of principle I claim it for all. But in a narrow view of the question as a feeling between classes, when Mr. Downing puts the question to me, are you willing to have the colored man enfranchised before the woman, I say no; I would not trust him with all my rights, degraded, oppressed himself, he would be more despotic with the governing power than even our Saxon rulers are.

Frederick Douglass, 1867

I champion the right of the Negro to vote. It is with us a matter of life and death, and therefore cannot be postponed. I have always championed woman's right to vote; but it will be seen that the present claim for the Negro is one of the most urgent necessity. The assertion of the right of women to vote meets nothing but ridicule; there is no deep seated malignity in the hearts of the people against her; but name the right of the Negro to vote, all hell is turned loose and the Ku-Klux and the Regulators hunt and slay the unoffending black man. The government of this country loves women. They are sisters, mothers, wives and daughters of our rulers; but the Negro is loathed.

Source: Both quotations are from Elizabeth Cady Stanton et al., *History of Woman Suffrage* (6 vols., New York: Flower and Wells, 1881–1922), 2: 214 (Stanton), 310–311 (Douglass), as cited in Rosalyn M. Terborg-Penn, "Afro Americans in the Struggle for Woman Suffrage" (Ph.D. dissertation, Howard University, 1977), 77 (Stanton), 79 (Douglass).

QUESTIONS for REFLECTION

1. What was Stanton's opinion of the capacity of black men to use the vote wisely?

2. How did Douglass see the issue as between black suffrage and votes for women?

3. In what ways did racial ideas and gender biases shape the debate about the Fifteenth Amendment?

The Rise of Voluntary Associations

Blocked off from politics, women carved out a public space through voluntary associations. Black churchwomen established missionary societies to work in both the United States and abroad. Clubs and literary societies sprang up among white women. In New York City, women created Sorosis, a club for women only, after the New York Press Club barred females from membership. In 1873, delegates from local Sorosis clubs formed the Association for the Advancement of Women. The New England's Women's Club, located in Boston, had local laws changed during the early 1870s to allow women to serve on the Boston School Committee. Later the club founded the Women's Education Association to expand opportunities in schools and colleges. During the two decades that followed, the women's club movement put down strong roots in all parts of the nation. Soon they also found ways to exert an influence on political and cultural issues.

Despite being turned away at the polls, women made their political presence felt, bringing energetic fervor to the **temperance movement** in particular. "The women are in desperate earnest," said a Missouri resident who witnessed a temperance campaign. In August 1874, a group of women active in the temperance cause met at Lake Chautauqua, New York, and set a national meeting that evolved into the Woman's Christian Temperance Union (WCTU). By the end of the 1870s, a thousand unions had been formed, with an estimated twenty-six thousand members. In 1879, Frances Willard became president of the WCTU, and she took the organization beyond its original goal of temperance and into broader areas of social reform such as woman suffrage and the treatment of children. As it had before the Civil War, the campaign against alcohol revealed some of the underlying social and cultural strains of society.

temperance movement Nineteenth century reform movement that encouraged the reduction or elimination of alcoholic beverage consumption.

Women at Work

The 1870s also brought greater economic opportunities for women in sales and clerical positions in the workplace. Sales of typewriters began in 1874. E. Remington and Sons, which produced the typewriter, said in 1875 that "no invention has opened for women so broad and easy an avenue to profitable and suitable employment as the 'Type-Writer.'" By 1880, women accounted for 40 percent of the stenographers and typists in the country.

The most typical experience of American women, however, remained toil in the fields and at home. Black women in the South labored in the open alongside their husbands who were tenant farmers or sharecroppers. In the expanding cities, women worked in textile factories or became domestic servants. Many urban women also took in boarders. Middle-class women with domestic servants had some assistance, but they still did a daunting amount of work. Preparing food, washing laundry by hand, keeping the house warm before electricity, and disposing of waste all demanded hard labor. In the daily rhythms of American society in this period, the often unpaid and unrecognized labor of women was indispensable to the nation's advancement.

American families faced challenges and changes during the postwar period. Divorce became an option in many states, and defenders of marriage moved to tighten the conditions under which marriages could be dissolved. Laws to limit the sale of birth control devices and restrict abortions reflected the same trend. The New York Society for the Suppression of Vice was formed in 1872 under the leadership of Anthony Comstock. It lobbied successfully for a national law barring information deemed obscene about birth control and abortion from being sent through the mails. Although women had made some gains after the Civil War, they remained second-class citizens within the masculine political order of the period. However, that brand of politics was also coming into question as voters prepared to decide whether President Grant deserved a second term.

❖ Political and Economic Turmoil

By 1872, many commentators and voters in the North were dismayed at the spectacle of national politics. "We are in danger of the way of all Republics," said one critic of the existing system. "First freedom, then glory; when that is past, wealth, vice and corruption." Restoring ethical standards was the goal of the Liberal Republicans who wanted to field a candidate against President Grant in 1872. These men, including Senator Carl Schurz, a Missouri Republican, and Charles Francis Adams, the son of former president John Quincy Adams, believed that only in that way could Reconstruction be ended and civil service reform achieved. They saw what happened in the South as an unwise experiment in racial democracy.

But Liberal Republicans did not have a good national candidate to run against Grant. Few party leaders were men with real stature. Schurz was a native of Germany and therefore ineligible to run. The race came down to Charles Francis Adams, Lyman Trumbull of Illinois, and **Horace Greeley,** editor of the *New York Tribune.* After six ballots, Greeley became the nominee. At the age of sixty-one, Greeley was an odd choice. He favored the protective tariff, unlike most reformers, and he was indifferent about the civil service. His main passion was ending Reconstruction. "That Grant is an Ass no man can deny," said one Liberal in private, "but better an Ass than a mischievous idiot."

Greeley, Horace (1811–1872) Grant's opponent in the 1872 election. Seen as a political oddball in the eyes of many Americans, the sixty-one-year-old editor favored the protective tariff and was indifferent to civil service reform. He was also passionate about vegetarianism and the use of human manure in farming.

The 1872 Election

Grant was renominated on a platform that stressed the need to preserve Reconstruction: voters in the North must safeguard what they had won during the Civil War. The Democrats were in a box: if they rejected Greeley, they had no chance to win; picking him, however, would alienate southern voters who remembered Greeley's passion against the Confederacy. In the end, the Democrats accepted Greeley as their only alternative. The Liberal Republican–Democratic nominee made a vigorous public campaign, while Grant observed the tradition that the incumbent did not take part in the race personally.

The Republicans made their appeal on the issues of the war. The black leader Frederick Douglass said of the impending contest: "If the Republican party goes down, freedom goes down with it." When the voters went to the polls, the outcome was a decisive victory for Grant and his party. There were still enough Republicans in the South to enable Grant to carry all but five of the southern states in one of the last honest elections the region would see for many years. The Democrats had reached a low point behind Greeley, who died in late November. The triumph was a mixed one for Grant: he remained in the White House, but scandals would soon plague his second term.

A Surge of Scandals

As the excitement of the 1872 election faded, allegations of corruption in Congress surfaced. The first controversy turned on the efforts of the Crédit Mobilier Company to purchase influence with lawmakers during the 1860s. The directors of the Union Pacific had established Crédit Mobilier to build the transcontinental line. Participants in the venture sold bonds that were marketed at a large profit to investors and insiders, but much of the money in effect came from the federal government through loans and guarantees. To avoid a congressional probe into the company, Crédit Mobilier's managers offered leading Republicans a chance to buy shares in the company at prices well below their market value. When the lawmakers sold their shares, they pocketed the difference, the equivalent of a bribe. A newspaper broke the story in late 1872, and an investigation ensued. The probe produced a few scapegoats but cleared most of the individuals involved. Nevertheless, the episode damaged the credibility of public officials.

Another embarrassing scandal occurred in February 1873. At the end of a congressional session, a last-minute deal gave senators and representatives a retroactive pay increase. The public denounced the action as the "Salary Grab." The *Chicago Tribune* said that it was "nothing more nor less than an act of robbery." When Congress reconvened in December 1873, repeal of the salary increase sailed through both houses as politicians backtracked. These two incidents produced widespread calls for reducing government expenditures and rooting out corruption.

Scandals persisted throughout Grant's presidency. Within the Treasury Department, the Whiskey Ring was exposed. Officials involved took kickbacks from liquor interests in return for not collecting federal excise taxes on whiskey. The administration also faced queries concerning the secretary of war, W. W. Belknap, whose wife had been receiving cash gifts from a man who sold supplies to the army. When these ties were revealed, a congressional committee sought to start impeachment proceedings, and Belknap resigned. Few doubted Grant's personal honesty, but his cabinet selections often seemed corrupt.

Humorist Mark Twain captured the spirit of the times in his novel *The Gilded Age*, published in 1873. The main character, Colonel Beriah Sellers, was an engaging confidence man who embodied the faith in progress and economic growth of the postwar years, along with a healthy amount of deceit that accompanied the rapid expansion of business. In time, the title of Twain's book came to be used for the entire era between the end of Reconstruction and the start of the twentieth century. During the Gilded Age, Americans grappled with issues of political corruption, social disorder, and economic inequities in ways that challenged older assumptions about the role of government in society.

Doing History Online

Grant and the Union Pacific Railroad

Go to the CourseMate website for this chapter and link to Primary Sources. After reading Edward Winslow Martin's account of the Crédit Mobilier scandal (Document 14), how do you think the scandals of the Grant era affected Reconstruction policy?

www.cengagebrain.com

The Panic of 1873 and Its Consequences

A sense of national crisis deepened in September 1873 when the banking house of Jay Cooke and Company failed. The bank, which had invested heavily in the Northern Pacific Railroad, could not pay its debts or return money to its depositors and had to close. As this important bank collapsed, others followed suit, businesses cut back on employment, and a downturn began. The problems rivaled similar panics that had occurred in 1819, 1837, and 1857; however, the panic of 1873 was the worst of them all. The panic of 1873 occurred because of a speculative post–Civil War boom in railroad building. When large railroads such as the Northern Pacific failed because of their overexpansion and inability to pay debts, the damage rippled through society. Economic activities that were dependent on the rail lines, such as car making, steel rail production, and passenger services, also fell off. Layoffs of employees and bankruptcies for businesses followed. More than ten thousand companies failed in 1878, the worst year of the depression.

The immediate effects of the problem lasted until 1879. Americans faced an economy in which falling prices placed the heaviest burdens on people who were in debt or who earned their living by selling their labor. An abundance of cheap unskilled labor proved a boon for capitalists who wanted to keep costs down. For the poor, however, it meant that they had little job security and could easily be replaced if they protested against harsh working conditions.

Americans out of work during the 1870s had no system of unemployment insurance to cushion the shock. In some cities, up to a quarter of the workforce looked for jobs without success. Laborers in the Northeast mounted a campaign called "Work for Bread" that produced large demonstrations in major cities. In January 1874, a demonstration at Tompkins Square in New York City pitted a crowd of seven thousand unemployed laborers against police. Many marchers were arrested; others were injured in the melee. Strikes marked 1874 and 1875.

In Pennsylvania the railroads used their control of police and strikebreakers to put down a protracted walkout of coal miners and their supporters. Conservatives feared that the nation was on the verge of revolution.

Discontent also flared in the farm belt. The price of wheat, which had stood at $1.16 a bushel in 1873, dropped to 95 cents a bushel a year later. The price of corn stood at 64 cents a bushel in 1874 but 42 cents in 1875. These changes meant substantial drops in farm income. As a result, farmers' land- and equipment-related debts posed an even greater burden. The Grange tried to use political pressure to press these issues, and its efforts reached Congress in 1873–1874, but little was accomplished for the next fifteen years.

The decline in consumer prices and the growing burden of debt on farmers and businessmen in the South and West created pressure for laws to put more money into circulation, which would make debts easier to pay. The Treasury Department's decision to end the coinage of silver aroused particular anger among southern and western advocates of inflation, who called it the "Crime of 1873." Proponents of the move argued that an overabundance of silver in the marketplace required the move to a gold standard. By coining silver into money at a price above its market levels, the government was subsidizing American silver production and cheapening the currency. Finally, an effort to inject a modest amount of inflation into the economy came in 1875. A currency bill cleared both houses of Congress, providing some $64 million in additional money for the financial system, but such intervention was controversial. President Grant ultimately decided to veto the bill in April 1875, and Congress sustained his action. The government would not intervene in the deepening economic crisis.

❖ The Failure of Reconstruction, 1875–1877

After the presidential election of 1872, the North's already weakened commitment to Reconstruction ebbed still more. The panic of 1873 distracted attention from the rights of black Americans. The Grant administration backed away from southern politics, and the Justice Department prosecuted fewer individuals for violations of the Ku Klux Klan Act and pardoned some of those who had earlier been convicted of terrorist activity. Liberal Republicans and northern Democrats spread racist propaganda to block the aspirations of southern blacks. The editor of *The Nation* said that black residents of South Carolina had an "average of intelligence but slightly above the level of animals." Northerners found it easier to believe that the South would be better off when whites were dominant.

A damaging setback to the economic hopes of African Americans came in 1874 with the failure of the Freedmen's Savings and Trust Company in Washington, D.C. Since its founding in 1865, the bank had managed the deposits of thousands of former slaves. It was supposed to provide lessons in thrift for its depositors. However, its manager sought larger returns by investing in speculative railroad projects. The panic of 1873 caused huge losses, and the bank failed a year later; most customers lost all of their money.

The Stigma of Corruption

Corruption among southern Republican governments became a favorite theme of critics of Reconstruction. There was no doubt that white governments that took over after Reconstruction also displayed lax political ethics; nevertheless, the corruption issue gave opponents of black political participation a perfect weapon. Of course, it would not have mattered if Reconstruction governments had lacked any moral flaws at all. Any government that represented a biracial community was unacceptable to white southerners.

Although participation of African Americans in southern politics increased dramatically during Reconstruction, their role in the region's public life never approached that of whites. Sixteen blacks served in Congress during the period, including two in the Senate, but it was not long before most were unseated by white opponents. Many more held offices in the state legislatures, but even there, their numbers were comparatively modest. In 1868, for example, the Georgia legislature had 216 members, of whom only 32 were black. In only one state, South Carolina, did blacks ever hold a majority in the legislature, and they did so in only one house. Six African Americans held the office of lieutenant governor in the states of Louisiana, Mississippi, and South Carolina. Thus, by the 1870s, blacks had made their presence felt in politics, but the decline of Reconstruction made that trend a short-lived one.

The Resurgence of the Democrats

Hard economic times arising from the panic of 1873 worked against the Republicans. Discontent farmers wanted the government to inflate the currency and raise prices on their crops. Factory workers clamored for more jobs to become available. In this setting, the fate of African Americans in the South became a secondary concern. In the 1874 congressional races, angry voters turned to the Democrats, who used the issue of Republican corruption to regain control of the House of Representatives for the first time in sixteen years. The Democrats added seventy-seven seats in the House and ten seats in the Senate, in what one happy party member called a "Tidal Wave."

In the South, the revitalized Democrats "redeemed," as they called it, several states from Republican dominance. They began with Texas in 1873, then won back Arkansas the next year, and elected most of the South's members in the U.S. House of Representatives. Louisiana saw the emergence of the White League, which was determined that "the niggers shall not rule over us." In September 1874, open fighting erupted in New Orleans between armed Republicans and more than three thousand White League partisans. President Grant sent in federal troops to restore calm, but this action angered northern Democrats and a growing number of northern Republicans. In Alabama, the Democrats also relied on violence and murder to oust the Republicans; seven blacks were killed and nearly seventy wounded. In view of the wide support for the Democratic Party among southern whites, honest elections would probably have produced similar results for that party at the polls; but intimidation and violence were key elements in the victories that the Democrats secured in the South in 1874.

The Democrats intended to use their control of the House of Representatives to roll back Reconstruction and prevent any further expansion of black rights. During the lame-duck congressional session of 1874–1875, Republicans, who were soon to lose power, enacted a path-breaking civil rights law that gave black citizens the right to sue in federal courts when they confronted discrimination in public accommodations such as a hotel or restaurant. However, it remained to be seen how federal courts would rule when black plaintiffs sued to enforce their rights. Without a national consensus behind civil rights and Reconstruction, the fate of black Americans lay in the hands of white southerners who were determined to keep African Americans in economic, political, and cultural subjugation. (See Map 15.3.)

The Centennial Year, 1876

As the nation's one hundredth birthday neared, the Centennial International Exhibition to be held in Philadelphia attracted public fascination. In May 1876, some 285 acres of fairgrounds held several hundred buildings crammed with

(Copyright © Cengage Learning)

MAP 15.3

Reconstruction in the South
This map shows the times at which the states of the former Confederacy reentered the Union and then saw the Democrats regain political control. Note how quickly this process occurred for most of the southern states. The relative brevity of Reconstruction is one of the keys to why more sweeping racial change did not take place.

Map legend:
- 1868 Date of readmission to the Union
- 1870 Date of reestablishment of conservative rule
- Military district commanding generals
  - 1 Gen. Schofield
  - 2 Gen. Sickles
  - 3 Gen. Pope
  - 4 Gen. Ord
  - 5 Gen. Sheridan

Map labels:
VA. Jan. 26, 1870 / Oct. 5, 1869 — Military District No. 1
N.C. Jun. 25, 1868 / Nov. 3, 1870 — Military District No. 2
S.C. Jun. 25, 1868 / Nov. 28, 1876
TENN. Jul. 24, 1866 / Oct. 4, 1869
ARK. Jun. 22, 1868 / Nov. 10, 1874 — Military District No. 4
ALA. Jul. 14, 1868 / Nov. 16, 1874
GA. Jul. 15, 1870 / Nov. 1, 1871
MISS. Feb. 23, 1870 / Jan. 4, 1876 — Military District No. 3
TEXAS Mar. 30, 1870 / Jan. 14, 1873 — Military District No. 5
LA. Jun. 25, 1868 / Jan. 2, 1877
FLA. Jun. 25, 1868 / Jan. 2, 1877

exhibits, specimens, and artifacts from thirty-seven nations. The doors opened on May 10 for two hundred thousand spectators, including both houses of Congress, who heard a welcoming address by President Grant. One of the most popular attractions was the huge Corliss steam engine, which stood 40 feet tall and weighed 700 tons. Equally alluring was the "harmonic telegraph" of Alexander Graham Bell, as the telephone was then called.

The complexity of American life in the 1870s was not depicted at the exhibit, however. African Americans had almost no representation. Native American cultures were displayed as "curiosities" consisting of totem poles, tepees, and trinkets. The Women's Pavilion stressed the joys of homemaking. That exhibit evoked a protest from Elizabeth Cady Stanton and Susan B. Anthony. On July 4, 1876, they read a "Women's Declaration of Independence" that contrasted their aspirations with the traditional attitudes toward women expressed at the fair. Their protest had little effect on public opinion, however.

Nearly 10 million Americans came to the fair during its run, which ended on November 10. The fair lost money, but nevertheless contributed to a growing sense of national pride and confidence. Those emotions would be tested during the bitter presidential election that dominated the second half of 1876.

The Race for the White House

A key test of the nation's institutions occurred during the disputed presidential election of 1876. As the election process commenced, the Democrats felt optimism about their chances to regain power for the first time since 1860. Difficult economic times in the East and Midwest made voters sympathetic to the Democrats. For its candidate, the party selected **Samuel J. Tilden,** the governor of New York. An opponent of corruption in his home state, he was also a corporate lawyer who believed in the gold standard, limited federal action, and restraints on spending. The Democratic platform spoke of a "revival of Jeffersonian democracy" and called for "high standards of official morality." Because Tilden was not in good

Tilden, Samuel J. (1814–1886)
Governor of New York and Democratic candidate for president in 1876. He narrowly lost what has been considered the most controversial election in American history.

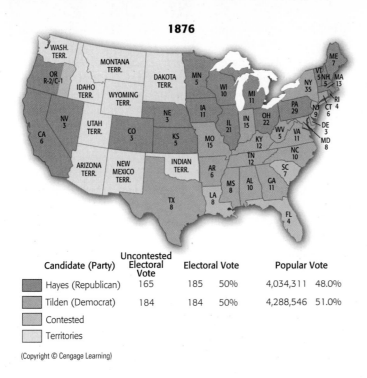

1876

Candidate (Party)	Uncontested Electoral Vote	Electoral Vote		Popular Vote	
Hayes (Republican)	165	185	50%	4,034,311	48.0%
Tilden (Democrat)	184	184	50%	4,288,546	51.0%
Contested					
Territories					

(Copyright © Cengage Learning)

MAP 15.4
The Election of 1876
The presidential election of 1876 between Samuel J. Tilden for the Democrats and Rutherford B. Hayes for the Republicans turned on the votes of Florida, Louisiana, and South Carolina to produce the narrow one-vote victory in the electoral college for Hayes.

health, the custom that presidential candidates did not campaign during that era worked to his advantage.

Among Republicans, the front-runner for the nomination was James G. Blaine, a former Speaker of the House of Representatives. With the nomination seemingly in his grasp, Blaine came under fire for financial dealings with an Arkansas railroad while he was in the House. His candidacy lost momentum at the national convention, where Republicans selected Governor **Rutherford B. Hayes** of Ohio. Hayes had the virtues of a good military record in the Civil War and a spotless record in public office. In the campaign, the Democrats stressed Republican corruption and Tilden's honesty. In response, the Republicans relied on Reconstruction and war memories, as they had in 1868 and 1872. This rhetoric became known as "waving the bloody shirt," in memory of a Republican speaker who had held up a bloodstained Union tunic and urged voters to remember the sacrifices of the Men in Blue.

When the election results rolled in, it seemed at first that Tilden had won. (See Map 15.4.) With most of the South in his column, the Democrat also carried New York, Connecticut, and New Jersey. The electoral vote totals indicated that Tilden had won 184 votes, one short of the 185 he needed to become president. Hayes had 165 electoral votes. Three southern states, Louisiana, Florida, and South Carolina, plus a disputed elector in Oregon, were still in doubt. If they all went for Hayes, he might prevail. Republican operatives moved to contest the outcome in the three undecided states. Telegrams to party members asked for evidence that African American voters had been intimidated. Honest returns from these states, Republicans argued, would show that Hayes had carried each one.

The Constitution did not specify how a contested presidential election was to be resolved. Each of the states in question was submitting two sets of election returns that claimed to be official and to reflect the will of the people. The House of Representatives had the responsibility for electing a president if no one won a majority in the electoral college. At the same time, the Senate had the constitutional duty to tabulate the electoral vote. With Republicans in control of the

Hayes, Rutherford B. (1822–1893) Nineteenth president of the United States (1877–1881), he won the most fiercely disputed election in American history.

Senate and with Democrats in control of the House, neither party could proceed without the support of the other.

To resolve the crisis, Congress created an electoral commission of fifteen members, ten from the Supreme Court. In a series of eight-to-seven votes along straight party lines, the electoral commission accepted the Republican returns from Louisiana, Florida, and South Carolina, and allocated the single disputed Oregon electoral vote to Hayes as well. The ruling declared that Hayes had received 185 electoral votes and Tilden 184. But who had really been elected president in 1876? Tilden had a margin of 250,000 popular votes over Hayes and had carried sixteen states. Hayes had won eighteen states in addition to the three contested southern states. In Louisiana, Florida, and South Carolina, Tilden had received a majority of the white vote, but black Republican voters had been intimidated and terrorized to such an extent that an honest count was in doubt. Essentially the election had ended in a tie.

Despite the decision of the electoral commission, the Democratic House still had to declare Hayes the winner. To prevent a crisis, complex negotiations began among leaders from both sides to put Hayes in the White House in return for Republican agreement to end Reconstruction. Democrats insisted that the South be freed from federal military intervention. After much discussion, an unwritten understanding, which later became known as the Compromise of 1877, along these lines led Congress to decide on March 2, 1877, that Republican Rutherford B. Hayes had been elected president of the United States.

Why Reconstruction Failed

The election of 1877 is often considered to have heralded the end of Reconstruction, but its failure is not so easily explained. Reconstruction failed to change American race relations because it challenged long-standing racist arrangements in both the North and South. The Civil War had called these traditions into question. In the years after the fighting ended, African Americans sought and to some degree succeeded in expanding their political role and taking charge of their collective destiny. Then the panic of 1873, the scandals of the Grant presidency, and waning interest in black rights led white Americans to back away from an expansion of racial justice.

To help the freed slaves overcome the effects of slavery and racial bias would have involved an expansion of national governmental power to an extent far beyond what Americans believed was justified during the nineteenth century. Better to keep government small, argued whites, than to improve the lot of the former slaves in the South. As a result, black Americans experienced segregation and deepening oppression. The political gains of the Reconstruction era, especially the Fourteenth and Fifteenth amendments, remained unfulfilled promises. That failure would be one of the most bitter legacies of this period of American history.

CHAPTER REVIEW, 1865–1877

SUMMARY

- The country embarked on an experiment in a multiracial democracy.

- African Americans in the South made a brave effort to participate in politics and economic life.

- Currents of racism and the opposition of white southerners doomed Reconstruction.

- Settlement of the West accelerated with the end of the Civil War and put pressure on Native American culture.

- Transcontinental railroads brought the nation together as a more cohesive economic unit.

- Although they were excluded from voting, women played a significant part in public life through voluntary associations.

- The panic of 1873 began a decade-long slump that brought protests from unhappy farmers and workers.

- By the nation's centennial in 1876, the disputed election between Hayes and Tilden marked the ebbing away of the issues of the Civil War and the eventual abandonment of Reconstruction.

IDENTIFICATIONS

Freedmen's Bureau
black codes
Ku Klux Klan
impeachment
Liberal Republicans
Crazy Horse
Sitting Bull
George Armstrong Custer
suffrage
Susan B. Anthony
temperance movement
Horace Greeley
Samuel J. Tilden
Rutherford B. Hayes

MAKING CONNECTIONS: LOOKING AHEAD ⅢⅢ➡

The next chapter takes up the process of industrialization and its effects on the economy and society. Elements in this chapter explain the rise of industrialism and set up the treatment of this issue in Chapter 16. Let's examine a few of them now.

1. What economic changes in the 1870s undercut Reconstruction and made industrialism seem more important?

2. How did the political system respond to the economic downturn of the 1870s, and how did these attitudes carry forward during the rest of the nineteenth century?

3. How did the political system then resemble modern alignments between Republicans and Democrats, and in what important ways were there differences?

RECOMMENDED READINGS

Edwards, Laura F. *Gendered Strife and Confusion: The Political Culture of Reconstruction* (1997). Looks at the role of women after the Civil War.

Fitzgerald, Michael W. *Splendid Failure: Postwar Reconstruction in the American South* (2007). A stimulating brief account of the successes and failures of Reconstruction.

Foner, Eric. *Reconstruction: America's Unfinished Revolution, 1863–1877* (1988). An excellent treatment of the whole period, especially the decline of Reconstruction.

Hahn, Steven. *A Nation Under Our Feet: Black Political Struggles in the Rural South from Slavery to the Great Migration* (2003). A prize-winning study of how African Americans built political institutions in the Reconstruction era.

Perman, Michael. *Emancipation and Reconstruction, 1862–1879*, 2nd ed. (2003). A good brief account of the issues and problems of Reconstruction.

Richardson, Heather Cox. *The Death of Reconstruction: Race, Labor, and Politics in the Post–Civil War North, 1865–1901* (2001). Considers how changing attitudes toward African Americans and labor undercut Reconstruction.

Simpson, Brooks D. *The Reconstruction Presidents* (1998). A treatment of Reconstruction from the perspective of the chief executives.

Smith, Jean Edward. *Grant* (2001). A full-scale, sympathetic biography of the general and president.

Wang, Xi. *The Trial of Democracy: Black Suffrage and Northern Republicans, 1860–1910* (1997). Discusses how voting issues shaped the adoption and then the abandonment of Reconstruction.

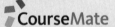 Go to the CourseMate website at www.cengagebrain.com for additional study tools and review materials for this chapter.

16 An Economy Transformed: The Rise of Big Business, 1877–1887

17 Urban Growth and Farm Protest, 1887–1893

18 A Troubled Nation Expands Outward, 1893–1901

19 Progressivism: Agendas for Change, 1901–1914

To white Americans during the late 1870s, the Civil War and Reconstruction seemed to be receding into history. That was a comforting illusion for them, but a misleading one. African Americans knew that the problem of race remained alive and painful for the entire society. At the same time, important forces were transforming the country. The national journey was leaving an agricultural, rural, underdeveloped economy and culture and heading toward an industrialized society. Out of these changes would come the modern United States.

Industry shaped the lives of more and more Americans during the years from the presidency of Rutherford B. Hayes (1877–1881) through the end of Theodore Roosevelt's administration in March 1909. The railroads appeared first and then, in rapid succession, steel, oil, machinery, telephones, and, after 1900, the automobile. Families moved from the country to the city. The look and the population of major urban centers were altered. Society kept pace to the rhythm of the machine and the factory.

Business leaders dominated the popular mind with their innovations and their faults. Reporters chronicled the doings of Andrew Carnegie, John D. Rockefeller, and J. P. Morgan in the way that they had written about politicians. Average Americans wondered and worried about their autonomy in the face of such concentrated economic power.

Industrialism brought material abundance for some and great want for many others. The ability of factories to provide cheaper, standardized goods such as canned foods, sewing machines, tools, and clothes pleased those who could afford to buy them. For those left behind or shut out from society's bounty, the riches of the new system seemed a mockery. Industry knit the country together in a shared experience as consumers in a national market; it alienated others who saw their hard work bringing no fair reward for themselves.

Immigration into the United States changed the shape of the nation's population and instilled an even richer diversity in the society. Older residents reacted with suspicion and hostility to the influx of newcomers from southern and eastern Europe, and ethnic tensions underlay voting decisions, residence patterns, and social conflict. The immigrants filled the nation's cities, tilled and settled the western plains, and did much of the work of the industrial sector. By the first decade of the twentieth century, pressures mounted for immigration restriction.

Politics hardly kept pace with accelerating change in the business sector. An even balance between Republicans and Democrats from 1877 to 1894 kept the national government passive and slow to react. An expansion of governmental power took place at the state level despite claims that the era favored noninvolvement in social policy. An economic depression during the 1890s destroyed the national stalemate, wounded the Democrats, and gave the Republicans a majority of the electorate. A third party, the Populists, failed to halt the erosion of the once powerful agricultural sector.

At the end of the 1890s, the United States stepped into the arena of international politics when it acquired an empire from Spain after a war over Cuba. The heyday of imperialism did not last; the consequences of overseas expansion endured. New responsibilities in the Atlantic and Pacific meant a growth in the power of the federal government to fulfill the world role. Currents of isolationism persisted to limit foreign adventures, but the movement toward world power continued.

The nation mixed confidence and doubt as the twentieth century opened. From the small nation of 1800 had emerged a continental giant, the world's largest internal free market, and a functioning experiment in political democracy. All that bred optimism by 1900. Social critics, however, pointed

Italian Immigrants in New York City. Immigrants from Italy as shown here were part of the larger experience of newcomers to the United States that included urbanization and industrialization in this period.

out the other side of the ledger. Too many in the United States—African Americans, Hispanics, Native Americans, immigrants, and women—did not share in all that the country offered. Progressive reformers at all levels of government began a vigorous period of change as the nation adjusted its institutions for the modern era. To Americans who lived through these times, electing Theodore Roosevelt, William Howard Taft, and Woodrow Wilson, it appeared that they had left the country better than they found it when they first addressed its problems during the 1870s. Their part in the American journey will be the underlying theme of the chapters that follow.

POLITICS AND DIPLOMACY

1877: Rutherford Hayes elected president
1878: Bland Allison Act
1879: Exoduster movement
1880: James A. Garfield elected president
1881: Garfield assassinated
Chester A. Arthur becomes president
1882: Chinese Exclusion Act
1883: *Civil Rights Cases*
Pendleton Civil Service Law
1884: Grover Cleveland elected president

1886: Haymarket Riot
Great Southwestern Strike
1887: Cleveland seeks tariff reform
1888: Benjamin Harrison elected president
1889: Oklahoma Territory opened
Hull House started
1890: Billion Dollar Congress is mentioned in text
Battle of Wounded Knee
Farmers' Alliance makes gains in elections
1891: Federal Elections bill killed
1892: Grover Cleveland elected president

1893: Sherman Silver Purchase Act repealed
1894: Coxey's army
Wilson-Gorman Tariff
1895: Venezuelan crisis
1896: William McKinley elected president
1897: Dingley Tariff is mentioned
1898: Hawaiian annexation
War with Spain
Philippines acquired
1899: Open Door policy enunciated

SOCIETY AND CULTURE

1877: New York YMCA offers typing course for women
1880: Metropolitan Museum of Art opens
1881: Helen Hunt Jackson, *A Century of Dishonor* published
Boston Symphony Orchestra established
1882: American Association of University Women founded
1883: Lester Frank Ward, *Dynamic Sociology* published
1884: Mark Twain, *Adventures of Huckleberry Finn* published

1885: William Dean Howells, *The Rise of Silas Lapham* published
1886: Emily Dickinson dies
Coca-Cola sold
Statue of Liberty
1888: Edward Bellamy, *Looking Backward* published
1889: Singer electric sewing machine
1890: Daughters of the American Revolution founded
1891: James Naismith invents basketball
1892: Ida Wells-Barnett launches anti-lynching campaign
Ellis Island opens

1893: Columbian Exposition
1894: Radcliffe College opens
1895: Atlanta Compromise of Booker T. Washington
1896: First commercial movie shown
1897: Introduction of Jell-O
1898: Condensed soups sold
1899: Edward Kennedy "Duke" Ellington born
"Maple Leaf Rag" published

ECONOMICS AND TECHNOLOGY

1877: Bell Telephone Company organized
Thomas A. Edison invents phonograph
1878: General Assembly of Knights of Labor
1879: Edison invents incandescent lamp
1879: Henry George, *Progress and Poverty* published
1880: George Eastman patents roll-film camera
1882: Standard Oil trust established
Labor Day first observed
1883: National time zones created
1884: Bureau of Labor established

1885: American Telephone and Telegraph Co. started
1886: American Federation of Labor (AFL) formed
Railroad tracks in South standardized
1887: Interstate Commerce Act
Electrical streetcar service in Richmond, Virginia
1888: Kodak hand camera perfected
1891: Edison receives radio patent
1892: Homestead Strike at Carnegie Steel

1893: Panic of 1893
1894: Pullman strike
1895: *U.S. v. E. C. Knight*
1896: Gold discovered in Yukon
1898: Mergers reflect industrial consolidation
1899: National Consumers League founded

1900	1907	1911
1900: McKinley reelected	**1907:** Gentleman's Agreement	**1912:** Republican party splits between
1901: McKinley assassinated	**1908:** William Howard Taft elected	Roosevelt and Taft
Roosevelt becomes president	president	Roosevelt forms Progressive Party
1902: *Northern Securities* case filed	**1909:** Taft inaugurated	Democrats nominate Wilson for
Anthracite Coal Strike	**1909:** Ballinger Pinchot controversy	president and he is elected
1903: Canadian boundary dispute	over conservation begins	**1913:** Wilson address Congress in
settled	**1910:** Roosevelt proclaims his New	person, breaking long-time
Panama Canal Zone acquired	Nationalism	precedent
1904: Theodore Roosevelt elected	Democrats regain control of	Underwood Tariff passed
president	House of Representatives	Sixteenth Amendment adopted
1905: Russo-Japanese war mediation		allowing income tax
discussed in text		**1914:** Clayton Antitrust law passed
1906: Hepburn Act		Vera Cruz incident leads to
Pure Food and Drugs Act		intervention in Mexico
Meat Inspection Act		World War begins in Europe

1900	1907	1911
1900: Olds Motor Works mass	**1907:** Electric clothes washer	**1911:** Harriet Quimby becomes first
produces cars	developed	licensed woman pilot
1901: Louis Armstrong born	**1908:** Model T automobile	**1912:** S.S. *Titanic* hits iceberg and sinks
1902: Teddy Bear toy marketed	Mother's Day observed	in North Atlantic
Muckrakers begin in journalism	Jack Johnson becomes	Children's Bureau established
1903: *Great Train Robbery* released to	heavyweight champion	Girl Scouts of America begins
audiences	**1909:** National Association for the	**1913:** Armory Show provides
1904: Ice cream cone marketed	Advancement of Colored	introduction to modern art
1905: *House of Mirth* by Edith	People founded	Massive suffrage march occurs in
Wharton	**1909:** Massachusetts forms first public	Washington, D.C., on March 3
1906: "Muckraking" journalism named	commission on aging	Brillo pads introduced
	Motion Picture Trust formed out	**1914:** Armory President Wilson
	of early movie companies	proclaims first national
	1910: Mann White Slave Traffic Act	Mother's Day
	passed to discourage	Margaret Sanger introduces term
	transportation of women	"birth control"
	across state lines for "immoral	
	purposes"	
	Jack Johnson defeats James	
	Jeffries ("the Great White	
	Hope") in heavyweight title	
	fight	
	Boy Scouts of America founded	

1900	1907	1911
1900: Gold Standard Act	**1907:** Panic of 1907	**1911:** Triangle Fire in New York City
1901: Creation of United States Steel	**1908:** *Muller v. Oregon*	produces regulation of
1902: National Women's Trade Union	**1909:** Payne-Aldrich Tariff	sweatshop conditions
League founded	**1909:** Payne Aldrich Tariff enacted	**1912:** Strike occurs in woolen mills,
1903: Department of Commerce and	International Ladies Garment	Lawrence, Massachusetts
Labor	Workers Union begins	**1913:** Federal Reserve Act passed and
Wright Brothers make first	prolonged strike in New York	system of twelve regional banks
airplane flight	City	created
1904: *Northern Securities Co. v. U.S.*	**1910:** Mann-Elkins Act to strengthen	**1914:** Ludlow, Colorado, strike leads to
1905: *Lochner v. New York*	railroad regulation passed	deaths of 21 people by state
1906: Bureau of Immigration created		militia
		Henry Ford introduces Five-Dollar
		Day for auto workers

16

An Economy Transformed: The Rise of Big Business

1877–1887

MAKING CONNECTIONS

⬅ LOOKING BACK

Reconstruction and its ultimate failure was the key theme of Chapter 15. Because the decision not to pursue racial justice had such long-range consequences for the United States, the substance of that chapter is central to an understanding of subsequent history. Before starting Chapter 16, you should be able to answer the following questions:

1. How did the Republicans intend to reconstruct the South after the Civil War? What obstacles did they encounter?

2. How did the election of Ulysses S. Grant help or hinder the Reconstruction effort?

3. Why did Reconstruction not succeed in the South? What obstacles did white southerners place in the way of black participation in politics?

4. What defects in the national political system between 1865 and 1877 helped derail the chances of Reconstruction?

5. Which groups fully participated in making decisions about the direction of society? Which groups were either not represented or ignored?

Railroads and a "Locomotive People"

The Railroad Business and Network
The Railroad as a Social and Political Issue
Regulating the Railroads

Big Business Arrives

John D. Rockefeller and the Emergence of Trusts
Andrew Carnegie and Steel
The Pace of Invention

Americans in the Workplace

The New Workforce
The Rise of Unions
Competing Unions
Social Darwinism

The Changing West

The Mining and Cattle Frontier
Farming on the Great Plains

The New South?

The Industrial South
Problems of Southern Agriculture
Segregation

American Life and Politics During the 1880s

Arts and Leisure in the 1880s
Political Life, 1877–1887

Doing History: Debating the Protective Tariff

The industrial growth that appeared in the United States after the Civil War severed American society from its agrarian past. Once the process of industrialization accelerated during the 1870s and 1880s, issues and problems emerged that would dominate American life for the next century. Few other issues have influenced the nation's history more than did the spread of industry and the rise of big business during this period.

Following the Civil War, industrialism and big business intensified as railroads, petroleum, steel, and other enterprises remade the economy. Although the extent of industrialization was spotty by 1900, the overall trend toward a capitalistic economy dominated by large integrated corporations was clear. Economic change proved a benefit to some sectors of the population and traumatic to others. During the 1880s, southern and western farmers, as well as urban workers, mobilized to protest the new order.

❖ Railroads and a "Locomotive People"

The belching, noisy, indispensable railroad stood as the symbol of industrialization. One British writer noted that "the Americans are an eminently locomotive people." The completion of the transcontinental railroads underscored the energetic pace of rail development. During the 1880s, the amount of track rose steadily, reaching 185,000 miles in 1890. By that time, the United States had a more extensive railroad network than all of the European countries combined, even with Russia included.

The Railroad Business and Network

Railroads crafted from iron and steel drew the nation together as bridges and tunnels swept away the obstacles of rivers and mountains. Another step toward unification was the implementation of a standard gauge, or width, for all tracks. Some railroads used the standard gauge of 4 feet 8.5 inches; others relied on tracks as much as 6 feet apart. Inconsistencies meant extra equipment, higher costs, and lost time. To put all railroads on the same set of working times, the railroads established four time zones across the country in 1883. Railroads could not operate effectively when times varied from state to state, as had been the case before. Standardized time zones promoted national cohesion.

Consistency streamlined the operation of the railroads, and innovations improved travel. Freight moved with greater ease through bills of lading (a statement of what was being shipped), which all lines accepted. Standard freight classifications appeared, and passenger schedules became more rational and predictable, especially after the establishment of standard time zones. With the enactment of the **Interstate Commerce Act (1887)** and the passage of other relevant legislation during the 1890s, all railroads adopted automatic couplers, air brakes, and other safety devices. The refrigerator car preserved food for distant consumers; George Pullman pioneered the sleeping car for passengers. The railroads built huge terminals through which millions of passengers and tons of freight moved each day. These structures, symbolic of industrialism, underlined the effect of the railroad on everyday life.

More than $4 billion had been invested in the railroad system by 1877. In contrast, the entire national debt of the United States government was just over $2.1 billion. To finance this huge commitment, the railroads drew on private investors in both the United States and Europe. An impressive amount, however,

Interstate Commerce Act (1887) Congressional legislation that set up the Interstate Commerce Commission (ICC) to supervise and regulate the nation's railroads.

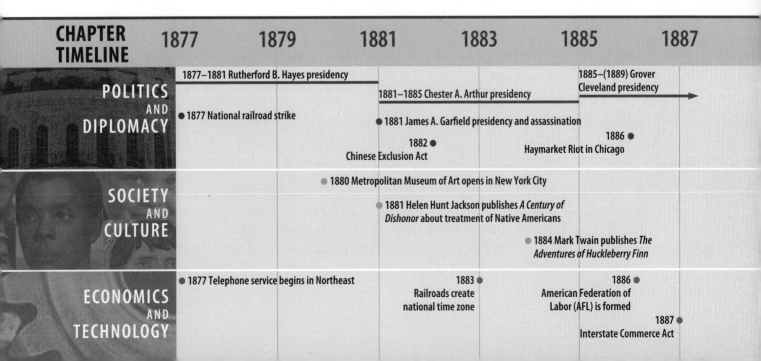

CHAPTER TIMELINE	1877	1879	1881	1883	1885	1887
POLITICS AND DIPLOMACY	1877–1881 Rutherford B. Hayes presidency • 1877 National railroad strike		1881–1885 Chester A. Arthur presidency • 1881 James A. Garfield presidency and assassination 1882 • Chinese Exclusion Act		1885–(1889) Grover Cleveland presidency 1886 • Haymarket Riot in Chicago	
SOCIETY AND CULTURE			• 1880 Metropolitan Museum of Art opens in New York City • 1881 Helen Hunt Jackson publishes *A Century of Dishonor* about treatment of Native Americans		• 1884 Mark Twain publishes *The Adventures of Huckleberry Finn*	
ECONOMICS AND TECHNOLOGY	• 1877 Telephone service begins in Northeast			1883 • Railroads create national time zone	1886 • American Federation of Labor (AFL) is formed	1887 • Interstate Commerce Act

came from government. Total federal land grants to railroads exceeded 130 million acres, and state and local governments added another 49 million acres. Other state aid included loans, tax reductions, and issuing of bonds. The total amount of all such assistance approached $500 million.

By 1880 the railroad network had assumed a well-defined shape, providing Americans with cheap, efficient transportation to accelerate industrialization. (See Map 16.1.) East of the Mississippi River to the Atlantic seaboard ran four trunk (main line) railroads that carried goods and passengers from smaller towns connected by feeder (subsidiary) lines. The transcontinental lines were the Union Pacific, Central Pacific, Northern Pacific, and Southern Pacific. During the 1880s and 1890s, southern railroads built five trunk lines, including the Southern Railway and the Louisville and Nashville Railroad.

Conducting their affairs on a grand scale, railroads became the first big business. For comparison, factories in a single location had fewer than a thousand workers; the railroads extended over thousands of miles and employed tens of thousands of workers. The railroads required an immense amount of equipment and facilities as well as new management systems. Executives set up clear lines of authority: separate operating divisions purchased supplies, maintained track and equipment, handled freight, dealt with passengers, and transmitted information. Local superintendents took care of day-to-day matters, general superintendents resolved larger policy issues, and railroad executives made the overall decisions.

Railroads stimulated and unified the national economy. From the late 1860s through the early 1890s, the railroads consumed more than half of the nation's output of steel. Railroads also used about 20 percent of coal production. The railroads' ability to move freight efficiently meant that similar goods and services were available to people throughout the nation, encouraging the growth of big business to meet consumer demand for canned goods, ready-made clothes, and industrial machinery. At the same time, the railroads allowed for more social and personal links among distant families and communities.

MAP 16.1

The Railroad Network, 1850–1900

The spread of the railroad network provided a unifying force for the nation as a whole during this decade of industrial expansion.

(Copyright © Cengage Learning)

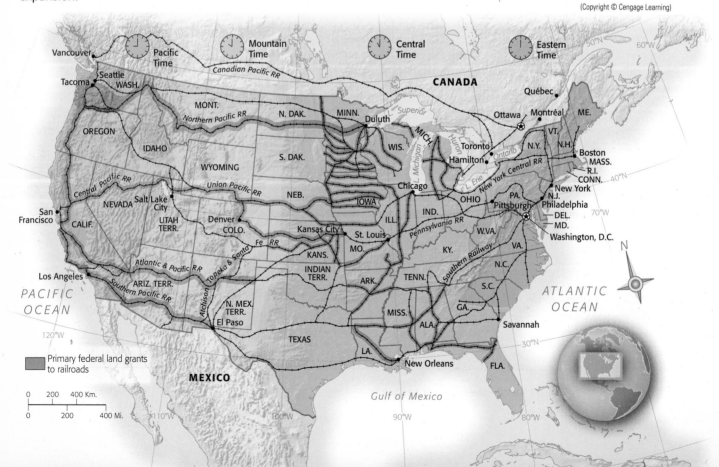

The Railroad as a Social and Political Issue

As they reshaped the economy, railroads raised concerns about their impact on government and society. Land grants affected numerous communities, and railroad executives provoked controversy. Cornelius Vanderbilt of the New York Central, Collis P. Huntington of the Southern Pacific, and Jay Gould of the Union Pacific, among others, employed ruthless methods against competitors. Their critics called them **robber barons,** a name that came to be applied to entrepreneurs from this period in general.

Railroad leaders disliked competition. Because a railroad ran constantly and had to maintain its equipment, facilities, and labor force on a continuing basis, its operating costs were inescapable, or "fixed." To survive, a railroad needed a constant flow of freight and passengers. One strategy was to build tracks and add lines in order to gain more business. Each new line, however, required additional business to pay off the cost of building it, so railroads waged a constant economic struggle for the available traffic. Another strategy was to lure customers, either openly or secretly, with reduced prices. From 1865 to 1900, railroad rates declined, partly due to a general deflation in prices and partly due to new efficiencies.

To maintain their share of the total available business, railroads relied on secret procedures. The rebate was a discount on published rates given to a favored shipper in cash payments. Other customers had to pay the listed rate or were charged more. When faced with potentially destructive competition, the railroads engaged in price wars or tried to acquire their rivals. Railroads (and other industries) also used the pool, a private agreement to divide the available business. Working together, the railroads hoped to maintain rates at a level that ensured profits for all members of the pool. But such secret procedures violated state laws against economic conspiracies, and weaker railroads cheated on the pool to obtain more business. By the mid-1880s, therefore, the larger railroads moved toward consolidation as the answer to too many railroads and too much competition.

robber barons Railroad industry leaders such as Cornelius Vanderbilt and Jay Gould who became renowned for their ruthless methods against competitors.

Regulating the Railroads

While rebates, pools, and consolidation made sense to the railroads, they angered those who traveled or shipped their goods by rail. Shippers who did not receive rebates complained. Railroads also posed dangers to the traveling public. In 1888 alone, some fifty-two hundred Americans were killed while traveling or working on the railroad, and another twenty-six thousand were injured.

Americans debated how society should treat the railroads. Few advocated government ownership to compete with private corporations. Using legislatures or courts to oversee the railroads was not popular either. The answer to the railroad problem was the regulatory commission. Ideally, such a body, created by the state legislature, was composed of experts who decided issues of rates, finance, and service in a neutral, nonpartisan way. There were twenty-eight such agencies by 1896. Some commissions, such as the one in Massachusetts, advised railroads of possible violations and publicized information about railroad operations. But critics claimed that such commissions were weak, because they could not set rates. Another kind of railroad commission was established in Illinois in 1871. It set rates and put them into effect in 1873. Because of this authority, which other Midwest states adopted, the Illinois model became known as the strong form of the railroad commission.

During the 1870s railroads challenged the authority of these state commissions, and one case reached the U.S. Supreme Court in 1876. The decision in *Munn v. Illinois* (1877) declared that the state could establish a commission to

Products manufactured in 20 largest cities

- Clothing
- Flour milling
- Food, beverage, and tobacco processing
- Foundry and machine shop products
- Iron and steel
- Printing and publishing
- Slaughtering and meatpacking
- Textiles
- Mixed or other

Natural resources

Ag	Silver	O	Oil (petroleum)
Au	Gold	Pb	Lead
C	Coal	Timber	Timber
Cu	Copper		
Fe	Iron ore		

States with 25% or more of employees in manufacturing

(Copyright © Cengage Learning)

MAP 16.2

Railroad Land Grants

To encourage the building of railroads across the West and, to a lesser degree, in the South, Congress and the states made sizable land grants in alternate sections to the rail lines. This map indicates how large these grants were and how they influenced patterns of settlement.

regulate railroad rates. Because Congress had not yet acted to regulate interstate commerce in railroad matters, the Court said, a state could make "such rules and regulations as may be necessary for the protection of the general welfare of the people within its own jurisdiction." Still, reservations about the effectiveness of state commissions grew. There was some corruption, and the process of regulation was often cumbersome. In 1886, in the case of *Wabash, St. Louis, and Pacific Railway Company v. Illinois*, the Supreme Court ruled that enforcement of the Illinois law infringed on interstate commerce. A national policy for regulating the railroads was needed.

In 1887, Congress passed the Interstate Commerce Act. This law set up an Interstate Commerce Commission (ICC), composed of five members that could investigate complaints of railroad misconduct or file suit against the companies. The law forbade rebates and pooling. The new regulatory agency was the first of its kind on the federal level. Despite a shaky start for the ICC in its first decade, commissions became a favored means of dealing with the problems of managing an industrial society.

❖ Big Business Arrives

The railroads were just one part of the process by which big business emerged. An acceptance of rapid change, an embrace of technology, and a growing dependence on industry became key characteristics of the United States (see Map 16.2). The days of farm and field, working by the sun and moving to the rhythm of the seasons, yielded to a faster paced, more hectic existence in which construction and destruction became the dominant social process.

Although the growth of the railroads laid the basis for further industrial expansion, the overall success of big business came during difficult economic times. The depression of the 1870s had ebbed by 1879, but the prosperity that followed was brief. From 1881 to 1885, there was another slowdown, with numerous business failures. Two years of good times preceded another recession during 1887 and 1888. Deflation brought about by increased productivity, a tight money supply, and an abundant labor force set the tone for business. Companies with high fixed costs, such as railroads, oil, and steel, faced intense, constant pressure to reduce competition. In a few industries, business leaders managed to escape competition altogether and establish monopolies.

John D. Rockefeller and the Emergence of Trusts

Competitive forces shaped the oil industry, and **John D. Rockefeller** of Standard Oil symbolized economic monopolization. Starting in the mid-1860s, he expanded from his base in Ohio and founded the Standard Oil Company in 1870. Despite his success in obtaining rebates from the railroads when he assured them of a dependable supply of oil to haul, Rockefeller still faced an industry with too many producers, so he set up Standard Oil to impose control on a chaotic business. Through rebates, other secret payments from railroads, and price cutting, he sought to dominate his business. By the end of the 1870s, he controlled about 90 percent of the nation's oil-refining capacity and had achieved a **horizontal integration** of the oil business.

Rockefeller next sought to resolve the legal barriers to his operations. Under state law, Standard Oil of Ohio could not legally own stock in other oil companies or conduct its business in other states. Yet registering to do business in other states could reveal aspects of the company's business to competitors and expose it to legal challenges. In 1882, a lawyer for Rockefeller, S. T. C. Dodd, formulated a new use for an old legal device, the trust. In the common law, trustees for a widow,

Rockefeller, John D. (1839–1937) Key figure in the development of the oil industry and the growth of large corporations.

horizontal integration A procedure wherein a company takes over competitors to achieve control within an industry.

(© Rycoff Collection/CORBIS)

Industrialization.
Industrialization was a major theme of American life in these years. This image of men working in the steel mill under intense heat and dangerous conditions captured the spirit of the decade.

orphan, or an estate had wider powers than a corporation, a point that Dodd and Rockefeller exploited. Standard Oil became the first example of the trust in American business. The forty-one stockholders of Standard Oil created a board of nine trustees who held the company's stock in trust and exercised "general supervision over the affairs of said Standard Oil Companies." In this way the trust escaped the restrictions of state laws everywhere. The term *trust* became a general label for the rise of big business.

In the late 1870s, several states passed laws that allowed corporations to own branches in other states, hold the stock of other corporations, and pursue a policy of consolidation to the extent that their industry and its conditions permitted. The "holding company" law, first enacted in New Jersey and later in Delaware, was more efficient than the trust approach. A large company simply held the stock of its subsidiaries. The spectacle of the trust swallowing up its rivals became ingrained in the popular imagination and produced calls on government for remedial action.

Andrew Carnegie and Steel

Almost as famous as Rockefeller was **Andrew Carnegie,** one of the few prominent businessmen of the era who rose from rags to riches. An immigrant from Scotland, he moved from telegraph clerk to private secretary of the president of the Pennsylvania Railroad. During the 1860s, he played the stock market through investments in railroading, oil, and telegraph company securities. By 1873, however, he had focused on steel. He summed up his philosophy: "Put all your good eggs in one basket, and then watch that basket."

In the 1870s, the technology of steelmaking relied on the Bessemer process of steel production in which air was blown across molten pig iron to remove impurities through oxidization. A flow of steel resulted in about fifteen to twenty minutes. Eventually, the open-hearth method of steelmaking proved better for heavy machinery, skyscraper beams, and other uses. In this method the iron ore was heated, and scrap metal was added to the mixture. By 1890, steel production had risen to 4.3 million tons annually; it would climb still more, to 10.2 million tons by 1900. (See Table 16.1.)

Carnegie became the dominant figure in steelmaking. Between 1873 and 1889, his operations cut the cost of steel rail from $58 a ton to $25 a ton. He poured money into new equipment and plowed profits back into the business. During the 1880s, his profits grew by over $1 million annually. Carnegie sought to achieve the **vertical integration** of his steel interests; this meant controlling all of the steps in the process of making steel. Carnegie acquired mines to ensure that he had raw materials, boats to move ore on rivers, railroads to carry it to his mills, and a sales force to market his many products.

Carnegie's innovations in steelmaking shaped the economy. The lower cost of steel spurred the mechanization of industry. In such industries as firearms, bicycles, and sewing machines, the use of machine tools spread technological innovations throughout the economy. Carnegie's and Rockefeller's managers broke work down into specific, well-defined tasks for each employee and made everyone in the workplace follow standardized procedures. Mass production and a continuous flow of resources into factories and of goods to the consumers were part of the larger process of industrialization.

The Pace of Invention

Inventive Americans poured out a flood of new ideas; an average of thirteen thousand patents were issued each year during the 1870s. In the next twenty years, the annual total climbed to about twenty-one thousand. Among the new devices

Carnegie, Andrew (1835–1919) Scottish-born industrialist and philanthropist, he played a major role in the evolution of the U.S. steel industry.

vertical integration A procedure wherein a company gains control of all phases of production related to its product.

TABLE 16.1
Steel Production (in tons), 1877–1890

1877	569,618
1880	1,247,335
1885	1,711,920
1886	2,562,503
1887	3,339,071
1890	4,277,071
1900	10,188,329

Source: *Historical Statistics of the United States,* p. 416.

were the phonograph (1877), the cash register (1879), the linotype in newspaper publishing (1886), and the Kodak camera (1888). The process of innovation led to such constructive changes as the twine binder, which made harvesting straw more efficient; time locks for bank vaults; and the fountain pen.

Alexander Graham Bell was a Scottish immigrant from Canada who wanted to transmit the human voice by electrical means. In 1876, he and his assistant, Thomas A. Watson, created a practical device for doing so: the telephone. By 1877, it was possible to make telephone calls between New York and Boston; New Haven, Connecticut, established the first telephone exchange. Soon President Hayes had a telephone installed at the White House. Long-distance service between some cities arrived in 1884.

An even more famous inventor was **Thomas Alva Edison**, the "Wizard of Menlo Park." Born in 1847, Edison was a telegrapher during the Civil War with a knack for making machines and devices. By the end of the 1860s, he had already patented some of his nearly eleven hundred inventions. In 1876, he established the first industrial research laboratory at Menlo Park, New Jersey. His goals, he said, were to produce "a minor invention every ten days and a big thing every six months or so." In 1877, he devised the first phonograph, although it would be another decade before he perfected it commercially. More immediately rewarding was the invention of the carbon filament incandescent lamp in 1879.

For the electric light to be profitable, it had to be installed in a system outside the laboratory. In 1882, Edison put his invention into operation in New York City. The area covered was about a square mile, and after a year in service there were five hundred customers with more than ten thousand lamps. Electric power caught on rapidly. Edison's system, however, relied on direct electric current for power. As the distance traveled by the current increased, the amount of usable electric power decreased. One of Edison's business rivals, George Westinghouse, discovered how to use a transformer to render electricity safe at the point where the consumer needed it. This device made possible alternating current, which could transmit higher amounts of electricity. Soon the United States was on the way to using more and more electricity.

Bell, Alexander Graham (1847–1922) His invention of the telephone in 1876 changed the nature of life in the United States.

Edison, Thomas Alva (1847–1931) The inventor of the phonograph, electric lights, and countless other products.

❖ Americans in the Workplace

Amid such astonishing economic change, Americans struggled to lessen the harmful effects of industrial growth. In 1877, there were 15 million nondomestic workers, more than half in agriculture and another 4 million in manufacturing. The economy was in the fourth year of a depression, stemming from the panic of 1873, and almost 2 million people were unemployed.

The labor force grew by more than 29 percent during the 1870s. One-fifth of the increase came from immigrants. Irish, Germans, British, and Scandinavians made up the bulk of the newcomers. On the West Coast, Chinese immigrants built railroads and did other work that native-born citizens shunned. The expansion of the transatlantic steamship business and the aggressive work of emigration agents in Europe helped persuade many to come to the United States; hard times in Europe impelled others to make the trip. The majority found work in the cities of the Northeast and Midwest, where distinctive ethnic communities soon grew up.

The New Workforce

Industrialization caused a rise in the need for unskilled and semiskilled employees. Technology replaced craft skills with machines, and market pressures led businesses to limit their dependence on trained artisans. Management became

(Library of Congress)

Lynn

Female Shoe Worker.   Women found new work in the industrializing economy, often in shops where their skills could be used at wages below those of men. This shoe worker was an example of this trend.

more of a hierarchy. Supervisors frowned on skilled workers who sought autonomy in doing their jobs. Government supported employers and restricted the ability of workers to organize. These new policies reduced the control artisans had once exerted in the workplace.

Women represented another new element in the labor force. They appeared in greater numbers as teachers and office workers, and as sales clerks in the expanding department stores. Eight thousand women worked in sales in 1880; a decade later the total was more than fifty-eight thousand. Many immigrant women toiled as domestic servants, but they also found work in the sweatshops of the textile trades. For the most part, the jobs open to women were lower paid, required fewer skills, and offered less opportunity than those open to men.

Real wages for workers increased as the prices of farm products and manufactured goods fell during the deflation that lasted until the late 1890s. The hours that employees worked declined from more than sixty-five hours a week in 1860 to under sixty by 1900. Gradual though they were, these changes represented real gains. But the industrial economy presented serious dangers to many employees. In the coal mines, steel mills, and factories, and on the railroads, work was hazardous and sometimes fatal. From 1880 to 1900, some 35,000 of the 4 million workers in manufacturing died in accidents each year and another 500,000 were injured.

Workers had almost no protection against sickness, injury, or arbitrary dismissal. For a worker who was fired during an economic downturn, there were no unemployment benefits, no government programs for retraining, and little private help. Old-age pensions did not exist, and there were no private medical or retirement insurance plans. Child labor reached a peak during this period. Almost 182,000 children under the age of sixteen were at work in 1880 with no health and safety restrictions to protect them. Workers had few ways to insulate themselves from the impact of harsh working conditions and often-cruel employers.

The Rise of Unions

During the 1860s and 1870s, skilled workers in cigar making, shoemaking, and coal mining formed unions. The National Labor Union (NLU), a coalition of trade unions, was established in 1866, but its influence eroded by the early 1870s. Other union organizers would soon try again.

Because of the number of workers they employed, railroads were the first business to confront labor issues on a national scale. The professional skills that engineers, firemen, brakemen, and others possessed made it more difficult for railroads to find replacements during a strike. Railroad workers joined unions based around these crafts such as the Brotherhood of Locomotive Firemen and the Brotherhood of Locomotive Engineers. "Unless labor combines," said one engineer, "it cannot be heard at all." The issue, according to one railroad executive, was, "Who shall manage the road?"

A bitter railroad strike erupted during the summer of 1877. On July 1, in the middle of an economic depression, the major eastern railroads announced a 10 percent wage cut. Facing their second pay reduction in a year, railroad employees launched an unplanned protest, disrupting train traffic across Pennsylvania, West Virginia, Maryland, and Ohio. A general strike spread to Chicago, St. Louis, and other large cities. The governors of the states with riots called out the militia, but some militia units refused to fire on their fellow citizens. As violence spread, the Hayes administration sent in the army. Deaths ran into the hundreds; many more were injured. Faced with the overwhelming force of the government, the unrest faded. Nevertheless, the strike had touched most of the nation.

Competing Unions

The strike increased support for a new national labor organization: the Noble and Bold Order of the **Knights of Labor.** The Knights combined fraternal ritual, the language of Christianity, and belief in the social equality of all citizens. While advancing the cause of labor through unions and strikes where necessary, the Knights sought "a system adopted which will secure to the laborer the fruits of his toil." By the mid-1870s, the union was established among coal miners in Pennsylvania. After the railroad strike, the Knights saw membership grow from nine thousand in 1879 to more than one hundred thousand by 1885, thanks to its inclusivity and message of worker solidarity. Terence V. Powderly was elected leader in 1879 and became the first national labor figure. Its ranks embraced workers from skilled craft unions, agricultural laborers in the South, and women who were new entrants into the workforce. The willingness of the Knights to include women and blacks set it apart from other unions.

> **Knights of Labor** Nineteenth-century labor organization that combined fraternal ritual, the language of Christianity, and a belief in the social equality of all citizens.

Success brought problems of internal strain and union discipline, however. In 1885, the Knights conducted a strike against a railroad owned by Jay Gould, one of the most hated of the rail executives. They struck his Wabash, Missouri Pacific, and other lines, and achieved a form of official recognition that allowed the order to represent the company's employees in relations with management. Because it appeared that the Knights had beaten Gould, the order's popularity exploded among workers. By 1886, there were more than seven hundred thousand members. A second walkout was called against Gould in February 1886, but this time the strike was broken through the use of police and violence against those who had walked out.

The **Haymarket Riot** in Chicago on May 4, 1886, in which anarchists were accused of throwing a bomb and sparking a deadly riot, shocked the nation. The incident grew out of a strike against the McCormick Company, which made reapers for farmers. A rally occurred, which was generally peaceful. Then, as police were dispersing the crowd, an explosion occurred in which eight police officers died. The police fired into the crowd, and eight more people died in the confusion. Police charged eight anarchists as having encouraged the bomb-thrower. The case was thin and the evidence weak. Convicted on perjured testimony and guilt by association, seven defendants received death sentences, four of which were carried out. The eighth defendant received life in prison.

> **Haymarket Riot** On May 4, 1886, workmen in Chicago gathered to protest police conduct during a strike at a factory of the McCormick Company.

As a result, the public support for labor's demands for an eight-hour workday and other concessions dried up as antiradical hysteria spread. The Haymarket episode gave new impetus to conservatives who believed that labor was tied to anarchism. Although the leadership of the Knights had questioned the wisdom of strikes, business leaders blamed them for the violence and unrest, and the union went into a permanent decline. To some workers, the failure of the Knights demonstrated the need for more violent action. The shift in emphasis that followed had important long-term consequences for the history of American labor.

One vigorous critic of the Knights of Labor was Samuel Gompers. Because a philosophy of "pure and simple unionism" had worked for his own Cigar

Makers International Union, he believed that only such an approach could help labor. The son of a British cigar maker, Gompers had come to the United States in 1863. During his years of employment in the cigar trade, he decided that labor should accept corporations as a fact of life, seek concrete and limited improvements in working conditions, and avoid political involvements. Late in 1886, Gompers and others organized the American Federation of Labor (AFL) whose participating unions had 150,000 members. An alliance of craft unions and skilled workers, the AFL did not try to organize the masses of industrial workers. The union opposed immigrant labor, especially of the Chinese on the West Coast, and was cool toward the idea of black members. Nevertheless, the AFL's membership rose to more than 300,000 during its first ten years, and it achieved considerable benefits for its members through judicious use of strikes and negotiations with employers.

Social Darwinism

To justify some of the harsher aspects of industrialized capitalism, a political doctrine emerged called **Social Darwinism.** Charles Darwin's famous work *On the Origin of Species*, published in 1859, explained why some species survived and others became extinct. Darwin contended that a process of "natural selection" occurred in nature that enabled the "fittest" animals and plants to evolve and develop. Advocates of Darwin's ideas, such as the English writer Herbert Spencer, applied them to human existence. If the doctrine of "survival of the fittest" operated in the natural world, Spencer argued, it governed human affairs as well. Since capitalists and the wealthy represented the "fittest" individuals, it was folly to interfere with the "natural" process that produced them.

Social Darwinism popped up in popular culture. The rags-to-riches novels of Horatio Alger, a popular writer of the day, spread these ideas. Alger argued that men of energy and determination (the "fittest") could triumph in the competitive system even against great odds. He wrote 106 books with such titles as *Brave and Bold* and *Paddle Your Own Canoe*. The central characters were impoverished young boys who used their natural talents to achieve riches and success. The public consumed millions of copies of Alger's books despite repetitive plots. They taught the lessons of self-reliance and personal commitment, though few corporate leaders (other than Andrew Carnegie) started at the bottom as Alger's characters did.

Despite the popularity of Social Darwinism, the impact of these ideas was limited. Although many Americans applauded Social Darwinism in theory, they also tolerated considerable government intervention in the economy and social relations. One of the most famous ardent critics of Social Darwinism was Henry George. A California newspaperman, George said that the gap between the wealthy and the poor was caused by the monopoly of land by the rich and the rents that landowners charged. He expressed his ideas in *Progress and Poverty* (1879), a book that sold more than 2 million copies in the United States and more abroad. Rent, he wrote, was "a toll levied upon labor constantly and continuously," and the solution for this social ill was a "single tax" on rising land values. George's writings enjoyed worldwide influence.

(The Granger Collection, New York)

Horatio Alger Book Cover. Horatio Alger's books, like this one in the "Luck and Pluck" series, won millions of readers with their tales of bright young boys rising through the economic system to achieve wealth and happiness.

Social Darwinism Nineteenth-century philosophy that argued that the social history of humans closely resembled Darwin's principle of "survival of the fittest." According to this theory, human social history could be understood as a struggle among races, with the strongest and the fittest invariably triumphing.

❖ The Changing West

The end of Indian resistance to white incursions and the economic development of the frontier brought the West into the political and social mainstream of the country (see Map 16.3). In so doing, they also contributed an enduring saga of the range cattle business and the cowboy to American folklore.

After the Battle of the Little Big Horn in June 1876, some sporadic Indian resistance continued. During 1877, the Nez Perce tribe in Oregon, led by Chief Joseph, resisted attempts to move them to a reservation. Through four months of running battles, Joseph led his band of 650 people toward Canada, but they were beaten before they could reach safety. The Nez Perces were sent to the Indian Territory in Oklahoma, where disease reduced their numbers before they were returned to reservations in the Northwest. Another famous example of Native American resistance was **Geronimo,** the Apache chief in New Mexico. With a small band of followers, he left the Arizona reservation where he had been living in 1881 and raided across the Southwest for two years. After brief periods of surrender he resumed his military forays. Finally, in September 1886, confronted with the power of the army, he was persuaded to surrender once again and was exiled to Florida.

As Native American resistance ebbed, the national government shaped policy for the western tribes. Many white westerners believed that the "Indian question" could be solved only when the tribes were gone. Easterners contended that Native Americans should be assimilated into white society. Organizations such as the Indian Rights Association lobbied for these policies, and a book by Helen Hunt Jackson, *A Century of Dishonor* (1881), publicized the plight of the Native

Geronimo (1829–1909)
Apache leader who resisted white incursions until his capture in 1886.

(Copyright © Cengage Learning)

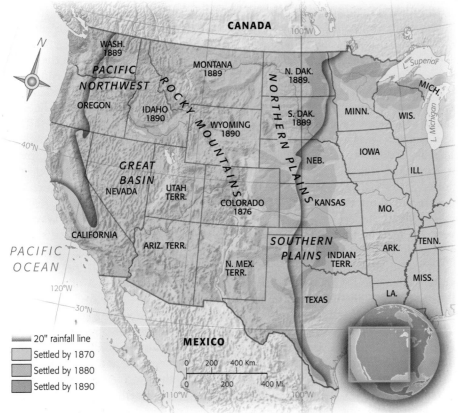

20" rainfall line
Settled by 1870
Settled by 1880
Settled by 1890

MAP 16.3
Settlement of the Trans-Mississippi West, 1870–1890
As this map indicates, the movement of people to the West occurred first on the coast and then filled up the interior states at the end of the nineteenth century.

Dawes Severalty Act (1887)
Congressional legislation that
distributed land to the Indians
so that it could eventually be sold
to whites.

Americans. Although the eastern policies were more benevolent than the westerners' destructive motives toward the Indians, their combined efforts devastated Indian culture.

Congress passed the **Dawes Severalty Act** in 1887. Named after Senator Henry L. Dawes of Massachusetts, the law authorized the president to survey Native American reservations and divide them into 160-acre farms. After receiving their allotment, Native Americans could not lease or sell the land for twenty-five years. Any Indian who adopted "habits of civilized life" became a U.S. citizen, but most Indians did not achieve citizenship. Any surplus land after this process was finished could be sold to white settlers. For the reformers, this law pushed Native Americans toward white civilization; for the western settlers, it made Indian land available. During the next fifty years, the total land holdings of Native Americans declined from 138 million to 47 million acres. By dividing up tribal land holdings and putting Indians at the mercy of white speculators, the Dawes Act undermined the tribal structure and culture of Native Americans and simultaneously helped allow whites to start mining and cattle ranching.

The Mining and Cattle Frontier

Mining booms drew settlers to a series of bonanzas, first of gold, later of silver, and eventually of copper in territories and states such as Colorado, Montana, and the Dakotas. The mining camps became notorious for their violence and frenzied atmosphere. More than 90 percent of their inhabitants were men; most of the women were prostitutes. During the 1870s, the western mining industry came to resemble other businesses. Individual miners gradually gave way to corporations that used industrial techniques such as jets of water under high pressure to extract the metal from the ground. The ravaged land left farmers with fouled rivers and polluted fields. Some corporations, such as the Union Pacific, brought in Chinese workers to operate coal mines and other projects. In September 1885, tensions between residents of Rock Springs, Wyoming, and these Asian laborers led to a violent confrontation, killing an estimated twenty-eight.

White settlement on the Great Plains during the 1880s started with the cattle ranchers, who dominated the open range in Wyoming, Colorado, and Montana. After the Civil War, ranchers in Texas found that their steers had multiplied during their absence. Enterprising cattlemen drove herds north to market at rail lines in Kansas and Nebraska. During the late 1870s and early 1880s, cattle raising shifted from Texas to areas nearer the railroads and the Chicago stockyards. The growth of the railroad network gave ranchers access to eastern and foreign markets. Improved breeding and slaughtering practices produced beef for consumers in both the United States and Europe, and the demand grew. With cattle easy to raise in the open spaces of the West and with an efficient transportation system, entrepreneurs in New York, London, and Scotland wanted to buy cattle cheaply in the West and resell them to eastern buyers at a profit. Money poured into the West and increased the number of cattle on the ranges of Montana and Wyoming.

Western development involved a subtle interaction of cultures that few whites understood. Cowboys worked fourteen-hour days. Much of what they did—riding the line, tending sick cattle, mending fences—consisted of grinding physical labor in a harsh environment. One of every seven was African American. Former slaves from ranches in Texas or fugitives from the oppression in the South, these black cowboys gained a living but were not granted social equality. Other cowboys included Hispanics and Native Americans, and they also faced discrimination. From the Hispanic *vaqueros* and the Native Americans, other cowboys learned the techniques of breaking horses and the complex skills of managing cattle.

(LC-USZ62-22483/Library of Congress Prints and Photographs Division)

Cowboys. The life of the cowboy on the lonely and desolate plains was far from romantic. Here some riders on the range in Wyoming show their skills with a rope for the camera.

The boom years did not last. As the ranges became overstocked in 1885 and 1886, prices for western cattle fell from thirty dollars a head to less than ten dollars. Then came the hard winter of 1886–1887 when thousands of cattle died in the blizzards. Before prices rose, investors from the East and Great Britain lost all they had. Ranchers in the West faced other challenges. Sheep raisers moved onto the range and discovered that sheep could graze more economically than cattle. Range wars between cattle and sheep growers over land and water broke out in Arizona and Wyoming. In the long run, sheep raising proved to be a viable business, and by 1900, there were some 30 million sheep on western ranges. Both sheep raisers and ranchers now faced competition from farmers who were moving westward.

Farming on the Great Plains

During the 1880s, hundreds of thousands of farmers swept onto the Great Plains. Advertising by the railroad companies, touting an abundance of land, water, and opportunity, drew them from midwestern states and northern Europe. The Homestead Act of 1862 gave farmers public land, which they could use and eventually own. In practice, however, the 160-acre unit of the Homestead Act was too small for successful farming; a serious settler had to purchase two or three times that acreage. Nor did the Homestead Act provide the money to go west, file a claim, and acquire the machinery required for profitable farming. Inevitably, land ownership began to be concentrated in the hands of those who had access to such resources. The Timber and Stone Act (1878) caused similar exploitation. Directed at lands that were "unfit for cultivation" in Washington, Oregon, California, and Nevada, it permitted settlers to acquire up to 160 acres at $2.50 per acre. Yet lumber companies used false entries to accumulate and gain title to valuable timber holdings.

Most settlers obtained their land from the railroads or land companies. Congress had granted the railroads every other 160-acre section of land along their rights of way. Large tracts were closed to settlement until the railroads sold the land to farmers. From 1862 to 1900, land companies acquired almost 100 million acres from railroads or the government. Other lands had been granted to eastern states to support their agricultural colleges under the Morrill Land-Grant Act of 1862. These western holdings went into the hands of speculators who purchased the lands, as did the land of Native Americans that had been sold off to white buyers. To buy the land, farmers borrowed from loan companies in the East and

Midwest, with interest rates on the resulting mortgages as high as 25 percent annually. As long as land values rose and crop prices remained profitable, the farmers made their payments. When prices fell, however, they faced economic ruin.

Industrial growth and technological advances made farming possible in the West. Joseph Glidden of Illinois devised the practical form of barbed wire in 1873. Soon Glidden's invention came to the attention of the Washburn and Moen Company of Massachusetts, which developed a machine to produce barbed wire. By 1880, some 80 million pounds had been produced, and the price of fencing stood at ten dollars per pound. Improved plows, the cord binder for baling hay, and grain silos also aided western farming. During the 1880s, steam-powered threshers for wheat and corn-husking machines were developed.

Machines alone could not provide enough water for farming. West of the ninety-eighth meridian, which ran through the Dakotas, Nebraska, Kansas, Oklahoma, and Texas, fewer than twenty inches of rain fell annually. Efforts to irrigate the land with the waters that ran from the Rocky Mountains worked in certain areas, but the region lacked adequate rivers. Ordinary wells did not reach the waters far below the surface. Windmills offered a possible solution, but the high cost of drilling and installing a windmill made it too expensive. The most practical technique was *dry farming*, that is, cultivation using water that the land retained after rainfall.

For farm families, and particularly for women, life on the western farms was a grind. With little wood available, shelter often consisted of a sod house made of bricks of dirt or dried sod. To keep warm in the winter, the farmers burned buffalo chips (droppings) or dried sunflower plants. Grasshoppers ruined crops, animals trampled fields, and rainfall was never reliable or enough to sustain profitable farming. Amid the endless spaces, women labored on small plots of land, sustained by a network of friends and neighbors. Some women achieved a degree of independence in the male-dominated West. They operated farms, taught school, ran boardinghouses, and participated in public life.

By the late 1880s, some of the western territories were ready for statehood. The territorial system had transferred eastern political ideas and values to the West and integrated settlers into the national political structure. In 1889 and 1890, Congress admitted the Dakotas, Montana, Washington, Idaho, and Wyoming into the Union.

Ranchers and settlers had overcome natural obstacles, political difficulties, and economic problems to create an elaborate economic and environmental system that linked the city and the country in mutually interdependent ways. By the end of the 1880s, however, the process of development stalled as farmers failed to achieve the anticipated prosperity. Crop prices fell, and settlers' debts rose. Farm protest stirred in the West even as the same sentiments were building in the southern states.

❖ The New South?

Reconstruction ended after the 1876 election. Democrats took over state governments in South Carolina, Louisiana, and Florida. In both the North and the South, the Democrats believed that white supremacy and limited government were the basic principles of political life. The bitter memories of Radical Reconstruction and the need to maintain the South as "a white man's country" made the Democrats dominant among white southerners. Southern Democrats believed that they had "redeemed" the region from the mistaken Republican experiment in multiracial politics. The Redeemers included plantation owners, a generous assortment of one-time Confederate officers, and aspiring capitalists who sought a more urban and developed South. This coalition dominated the politics of many southern states throughout the 1880s, though they could agree on only the most general (and vague) principles, especially white supremacy.

A key theme in the South was embodied in the phrase "the New South." Proponents of the New South argued that the region should welcome industrialization and economic expansion. An Atlanta newspaper editor named Henry Grady became the biggest backer of the idea. He thrilled northern audiences, anxious for markets and cheap labor, when he said, in 1886, that the South would soon have "a hundred farms for every plantation, fifty homes for every palace, and a diversified industry that meets the complex needs of this complex age." All over the region, steel mills, textile factories, and railroads arose.

The Industrial South

Manufacturing capacity in the South grew between 1870 and 1900. In the major cotton-producing states of South Carolina, Georgia, Alabama, Mississippi, and Louisiana, capital invested in manufacturing increased about tenfold between 1869 and 1889. Southern railroads expanded during the postwar period; by 1880, there were 19,430 miles of track, double the total in 1860. Other key industries grew during this decade as well. Southern forests fell to satisfy the growing national demand for lumber. Almost 3 million board feet of yellow pine were produced in 1879 by crews working under dangerous conditions for less than a dollar a day. The region's ample deposits of iron ore stimulated the expansion of the iron and coal industries. Production of iron ore rose from 397,000 tons in 1880 to almost 2 million tons twenty years later. Birmingham, Alabama, became a center of the burgeoning southern iron industry.

Before the Civil War, tobacco had been popular as something to chew, smoke in a pipe, or use as a cigar. During the war, northern soldiers tried the variety of bright leaf tobacco grown in North Carolina, and demand for Bull Durham and other products of the area increased. During the 1880s, James Buchanan Duke developed a practical cigarette-making machine, and as production costs fell rapidly, cigarette use skyrocketed. By the end of the 1880s, Duke's company was making more than 800 million cigarettes annually. Americans adopted smoking as an addictive habit.

New cities and towns sprang up in the expanding South. Although industrialism led to greater prosperity, not all southerners benefited. Workers in the factories and mills bore the burden of progress: wages that were often low and conditions crude. In the cotton mills, an average workweek might be more than sixty hours for wages that could be as low as fifteen cents a day, and hiring child laborers was common practice.

Problems of Southern Agriculture

Cotton was the money crop of the South, with 5.7 million bales produced in 1880. The crop rarely failed, caused less depletion of the soil, and brought a higher price per acre than any other alternative. World production of cotton was increasing, however, and when prices fell, cotton farmers became debt ridden and dependent.

Cheap labor became essential. Whites held most of the land, while blacks were forced to sell their labor. A system arose that combined **sharecropping**, tenant farming, and the "furnish merchant," who provided the farmers with the "furnish" (whatever was needed) to get them through the year. Sharecroppers received a proportion of their crops as their wage; the landlord controlled the crop until some of it was allocated to the sharecropper. Both tenants and "croppers" depended on local merchants for food, clothing, farm equipment, and crop supplies

sharecropping Labor system in the South after the Civil War. Tenants worked the land in return for a share of the crops produced, instead of paying cash rent. A shortage of currency in the South made this a common form of land tenure, and African Americans endured it because it eliminated the labor gangs of the slavery period.

until their harvests were completed. To safeguard the merchant's investment, southern states passed crop lien laws that gave the merchant a claim on the crop if a farmer could not pay his debt. Thus, the farmers in the South, both black and white, were in a cycle of debt first to the landlord and then to the "furnish" merchant. (Refer back to Map 15.1.) With interest rates as high as 50 percent, croppers and tenants were often in a situation that resembled slavery.

Southern farmers believed that they faced an economic conspiracy. Because the South had long lacked adequate capital, the furnish merchant represented the power of northern bankers, international cotton marketing companies, and industrialism. By the end of the decade, the problems of perpetual debt were becoming acute, and political discontent mounted. White southerners relied on one continuing advantage: they lived in a segregated society where blacks had been returned to a condition as close to slavery as the law would permit.

Segregation

Racial segregation evolved slowly but steadily across the South despite the national Civil Rights Act in 1875, which prohibited racial discrimination in public accommodations. In the *Civil Rights Cases* (1883), the Supreme Court ruled that under the Fourteenth Amendment, Congress could prohibit only state actions that violated civil rights. For individual acts of racial discrimination in restaurants, hotels, and other public places, it was up to the states to ban discrimination. Southern states chose instead to allow and encourage racial segregation as a preferred policy.

During this period, segregation lacked rigidity and legal power. In some southern states, black citizens used railroads and streetcars on a roughly equal basis with whites, but elsewhere in the region, travel facilities were segregated. Under the regimes of the Redeemers, black men voted in some numbers before 1890, retained the right to hold office, could be members of a jury, and were permitted to own weapons. But black men often found their choices at the polls limited to approved white candidates, and if too many African Americans sought to cast ballots, white violence erupted. By the end of the 1880s, growing numbers of white politicians believed that blacks should be barred from the electoral process.

The fifteen years after the end of Reconstruction began with hopeful signs for African Americans in the South. Black families wanted to rent farms and work land for themselves, and many believed that growing cotton in the Mississippi delta gave them a chance to participate in that region's expanding economy. The area saw an influx of blacks at the end of the 1880s as African American men competed for new jobs and the opportunity to acquire land. Sharecropping and tenant farming were also present, but in this part of the South for a brief period, there was a chance for black economic advancement. African Americans created networks of black churches and sought to educate their children. Booker T. Washington's leadership of the Tuskegee Institute in Alabama, which began in 1881, symbolized what education and training could do. Growing up with no direct experience of slavery, a new generation of southern blacks demanded their legal rights.

Some African Americans preferred to get out of the South if they could. At the end of the 1870s, rumors spread that Kansas offered a safer haven. During 1879, some twenty thousand blacks—known as Exodusters because they were coming out of bondage as the children of Israel had in the Exodus—arrived in Kansas. More settled in the cities than actually farmed on the prairie. Hundreds of thousands of other blacks also left the South during these years.

At the end of the 1880s, white spokesmen for the South boasted of the region's progress. The South produced more cotton than ever before, towns were growing throughout the region, industries had developed, and tens of thousands of black southerners had accumulated property. Yet there were danger signs. State legislatures wrote new laws to segregate first-class railroad passengers by race. Farmers who grew more cotton each year without getting ahead organized to oppose the power of merchants and railroads. Tenants and laborers of both races seemed restless and in constant motion. Racial violence reached unprecedented levels. Would the New South be any better than the Old?

❖ American Life and Politics During the 1880s

The daily rhythms of life were those of the country and the small town where most people, more than 70 percent in 1880, still resided. Of the nearly 10 million households in the nation, the most common family consisted of a husband, a wife, and their three children. The father worked the family farm or at a job in an office or at the factory. The mother stayed at home and did the endless rounds of cleaning, cooking, sewing, and shopping. The children attended schools near their home or, in less prosperous families, labored to bring home income.

Industrialism changed the way Americans ate. Millions of tin cans made vegetables and fruits available at the twist of a can opener. In large cities, fresh meats became more accessible as the Armour meat company moved beef in iced railroad cars. In 1886, an Atlanta druggist, **John Pemberton**, mixed syrup extracted from the cola nut with carbonated water and called it "Coca-Cola." A year later he sold out to Asa Candler, who made *Coca-Cola* a household word.

In the homes of city dwellers, gas and electricity provided new sources of power. People who had the money to afford the newer utilities no longer had to chop and gather wood, clean fireplaces, and maintain a multitude of candles and lamps. Running water replaced water drawn by hand. Refrigeration reduced the need for daily shopping; ready-made clothing relieved housewives of constant sewing chores.

Children were educated in schools that were designed to instill patriotism and moral values. "We went to school to work," remembered one student, "our playing was done elsewhere." City children attended school for some 180 to 200 days a year. In rural areas, however, the demands of farm work often limited school attendance to fewer than 100 days a year. For new immigrants, the school system taught the values of the dominant culture and prepared their children for citizenship. Although only a small percentage of students attended high schools and even fewer pursued a college degree, the late nineteenth century brought rapid growth for institutions of higher learning. Wealthy businessmen created private universities such as Johns Hopkins in Baltimore (1876), the University of Chicago (1890), and Stanford in California (1891). State universities expanded in the Midwest and were created in the South.

Arts and Leisure in the 1880s

Americans found an abundance of ways to entertain themselves. The first three-ring circus debuted in Manhattan in 1883, and P. T. Barnum, with his "greatest show on earth," became the entertainment equivalent of the giants of industry. During the same year, William "Buffalo Bill" Cody assembled a troupe of former Pony Express riders, stagecoach robbers, Indian warriors, and riding artists that toured the United States and Europe. Vaudeville, a form of entertainment consisting of a series of singers, comedians, and specialty acts, was a favorite of urban audiences. Baseball dominated sports. The National League, founded in 1876, entered an era of prosperity after 1880. In the 1880s, many new rules were

Pemberton, John (1831–1888) Atlanta druggist who in 1886 developed a syrup from an extract of the cola nut that he mixed with carbonated water and called "Coca Cola."

(Special Collections, Vassar College Libraries)

Vassar Women's Baseball Team. Baseball's popularity in the 1870s and 1880s spread to both the men and women's colleges of the era. The Vassar Resolutes baseball team posed for a picture in their caps and full-skirted uniforms.

adopted, including the format of three strikes and four balls, overhand pitching, and substitutions of players. Attendance figures rose, with as many as thirty thousand people turning out for games on Memorial Day.

Literate citizens found an abundance of reading. The magazines of the day, some thirty-three hundred in all, carried articles on every possible subject. Public libraries, funded in part by generous donations from Andrew Carnegie, provided easier access to the world of letters. Probably the most important literary work of the 1880s was *The Adventures of Huckleberry Finn*, written by Samuel L. Clemens ("Mark Twain") in 1884. In it, Clemens used an adventure in which a boy helps a runaway slave to create a chronicle of the nation's experience with slavery, freedom, the wonders of childhood, and the ambiguities of adult life. The most popular writer of his era, Twain captured the images of a vanishing America of Mississippi riverboats, small towns, and the social tensions that lay beneath the tranquil surface.

A symbol of the era was the Statue of Liberty in New York City, dedicated on October 28, 1886. The work of a French sculptor, FrÈdÈric-Auguste Bartholdi, it was sponsored by a public fund-raising effort in the United States; the statue was placed on Bedloe's Island, now called Liberty Island, at the entrance to New York Harbor. Out of the campaign to raise money came the celebrated poem by Emma Lazarus that promised the "golden door" of opportunity to Europe's "huddled masses yearning to breathe free."

Political Life, 1877–1887

In politics, both of the major parties sought to overcome an electoral stalemate. The Republicans won the presidency in 1876, 1880, and 1888; the Democrats triumphed in 1884 and 1892. Neither party controlled both houses of Congress on a regular basis. The Republicans had control twice, from 1881 to 1883 and 1889 to 1891; the Democrats only once, from 1893 to 1895. Outside the South, elections often were close and hard fought.

Moral and religious values shaped how people voted and helped define which party won their support. The prohibition of alcohol, the role of religious and sectarian education in the public schools, and the observance of the Sabbath were hotly contested questions. Republicans favored government intervention to support Protestant values; Democrats thought the government should keep out of such subjects.

The most prominent national issues involved the kind of money Americans used, how the government raised revenue, and who served in the government itself. Some Americans believed that for every dollar in circulation, an equal amount of gold should be stored in the Treasury or in banks. Others contended that the government should issue more money by coining silver into currency on an equal basis with gold. Debtors favored inflation, which made their loans easier to pay; creditors liked the deflation that raised the value of their dollars. Other major concerns were taxation and the protective tariff. There was no federal income tax; the government raised money from excise taxes on alcohol and tobacco, and customs duties (taxes) on imported goods. The protective tariff became a hot political issue. Those who favored it believed that high customs duties protected American industry, helped workers, and developed the economy. Republicans championed the protective system; Democrats countered that tariffs raised prices, hurt consumers, and made government too expensive. (See *Doing History: Debating the Protective Tariff*.)

Finally, there was the question of who should serve in government. Politicians preferred the "spoils," or patronage, system. Allocating government jobs to partisan supporters enabled them to strengthen their party. Critics of the patronage system called it a corrupt and inefficient way to choose government officials.

Doing History Debating the Protective Tariff

The protective tariff became a major dividing line between the two major parties in the 1880s. In the two addresses that follow, from a proponent of the tariff in William McKinley and an opponent in D. H. Chamberlain, the main points of contention are laid out. The two men differ about the impact of the protective policy on the economy and the average wage worker. The use of patriotism in McKinley's remarks was one key to the Republican appeal. Critics of the tariff such as Chamberlain stressed the economic arguments for free trade and international interdependence.

William McKinley, "What Protection Means to Virginia," 1885

WE DO NOT appeal to passions; we do not appeal to baser instincts; we do not appeal to race or war prejudices. We do appeal to our own best interests, to stand by a party that stands by the people. Vote the Republican ticket, stand by the protective policy, stand by American industry, stand by that policy which believes in American work for American workmen, that believes in American wages for American laborers, that believes in American homes for American citizens. Vote to maintain that system by which you can earn enough not only to give you the comforts of life but the refinements of life, enough to educate and equip your children, who may not have been fortunate by birth, who may not have been born with a silver spoon in their mouths, enough to enable them to educate and prepare their children for the great possibilities of life. I am for America because America is for the common people.

Source: William McKinley, "What Protection Means to Virginia," Petersburg, Virginia, October 29, 1885, in *Speeches and Addresses of William McKinley* (New York: D. Appleton, 1893), 194.

D. H. Chamberlain, "Tariff Aspects with Some Special Reference to Wage," 1888

A protective tariff is intended to shut out importations and keep the market for home productions. Keeping out foreign goods does not enrich but impoverishes a nation. If I am a farmer and want European goods which I can pay for with my farm products, if a tariff shuts them out, it likewise destroys the market for my products. I am just so much poorer for the tariff. My surplus farm products are worthless when what I desire to buy with them is shut out of my reach. My surplus crops go to waste, and I am so far impoverished and the country through me, and with me, and an impoverished many or country must pay lower wages than if rich and prosperous.

But a tariff which shuts out or hinders or reduces imports, so far deprives the community or nation on which it operates, of many opportunities and forms of labor. See how many laborers are employed in the strict work of importing foreign goods now. Whatever forbids, prevents or hinders such employments, obviously and necessarily deprives men of labor and reduces the demand for laborers and the wages of labor.

Source: D. H. Chamberlain, "Tariff Aspects with Some Special Reference to Wage: Speech of D. H. Chamberlain of New York City Before the Reform Club of New York, August 24, 1888" (New York: Albert King, 1888), 27–28.

QUESTIONS for REFLECTION

1. To what American values did each of the speakers appeal?

2. How does each speaker see the role of the worker in the economy and society?

3. How did the two political parties see the role of government in shaping economic policy and how are those views reflected in each of these statements?

They favored a civil service, in which individuals, chosen through competitive examinations, would administer government without being subject to partisan pressure. Civil service reformers urged Congress to write laws to reduce the power of patronage during the 1870s, but incumbents of both parties opposed such reform.

The Republicans began the period with Rutherford B. Hayes in the White House. He pushed for civil service reform and resisted pressure from Congress to base his appointments on candidates whom lawmakers favored. Hayes had promised to serve only one term. To succeed him, the Republicans nominated James A. Garfield of Ohio, and Chester Alan Arthur of New York as his running mate. The Democratic candidate was a former Civil War general named Winfield Scott Hancock. After an intense campaign that focused on the tariff issue, Garfield won by a narrow plurality in the popular vote and a larger margin in the electoral college.

On July 2, 1881, a crazed assassin shot Garfield. He died on September 19, and Chester Alan Arthur became president. Much to everyone's surprise, Arthur proved a competent chief executive. During his single term, Congress passed the Pendleton Act (1883), which created a civil service system, regulated campaign finance, and limited the practice of assessing campaign contributions from federal employees.

Arthur was a caretaker president. In 1884, the party selected its most popular figure, James G. Blaine of Maine, to run for the presidency. Questions raised about his political honesty, however, dogged him in the general election. To run against Blaine, the Democrats selected the governor of New York, Grover Cleveland, who offered an attractive blend of honesty, conservatism, and independence. His campaign suffered a setback when it was revealed that some years earlier, he had accepted responsibility for an illegitimate child in Buffalo. Cleveland acknowledged his part in the episode, however, and his candor defused the issue. Meanwhile, the issue of Blaine's public morality worked against the Republicans. Though the outcome of the election was very close, Cleveland carried the South, New York, New Jersey, Connecticut, and Indiana, receiving 219 electoral votes to Blaine's 182 (see Map 16.4). After twenty-four years in power, the Republicans had been defeated.

1884

Candidate (Party)	Electoral Vote		Popular Vote	
Cleveland (Democrat)	219	55%	4,874,985	48.5%
Blaine (Republican)	182	45%	4,851,981	48.3%
Territories				

(Copyright © Cengage Learning)

MAP 16.4

The Election of 1884

This map illustrates the tight presidential race between Grover Cleveland for the Democrats and James G. Blaine for the Republicans in 1884. Amid talk of scandal and corruption, the two parties battled to a virtual dead heat. Cleveland carried New York and eked out a narrow victory.

Cleveland took office on March 4, 1885. During his first term, he established that his party could govern, and his political opponents gave him grudging respect. For the Democrats, however, Cleveland proved to be a mixed blessing. He was slow to turn Republican officeholders out of office, and he alienated many Democrats with his patronage policies. Still, Republicans made few gains in the congressional elections of 1886, and Cleveland seemed to have good prospects for a second term in 1888.

In December 1887, hoping to establish an issue for his reelection campaign, the president devoted his annual message to Congress (known as the State of the Union message) to tariff reform. With a surplus in the Treasury, Cleveland believed that the tariff could be reduced, leading to lower prices for consumers. The Republican reaction to Cleveland's move was one of delight. Now the 1888 election could be fought on the issue that united the Republicans and divided the Democrats. In the 1890s, the rise of the American city would grow to be as important a force for change as industrialism had been in the years after 1877.

CHAPTER REVIEW, 1877–1887

SUMMARY

- Railroads emerged as the first big business.
- Initial efforts were made to regulate railroads through state railroad commissions.
- Standard Oil became a monopoly in the oil business, and a new form of business, the trust, was formed.
- Andrew Carnegie turned the steel industry into a major force for economic growth.
- The merits of Social Darwinism as an ideology were debated.
- The West was opened to mining and the range cattle industry.
- Industrialization spread through the South.
- The evenly divided party system produced few policies to address the issues of industrialism effectively.

IDENTIFICATIONS

Interstate Commerce Act
robber barons
John D. Rockefeller
horizontal integration
Andrew Carnegie
vertical integration
Alexander Graham Bell
Thomas Alva Edison
Knights of Labor
Haymarket Riot
Social Darwinism
Geronimo
Dawes Severalty Act
sharecropping
John Pemberton

MAKING CONNECTIONS: LOOKING AHEAD ⅢⅢ➡

Chapter 17 considers how cities developed in response to industrialism and looks at the ways in which the South and West reacted to the changes that agriculture was experiencing. Some of these shifts in thinking are anticipated in this chapter.

1. What pressures did industrialism place on farmers in the South and West?

2. How did the even balance of the political system prevent solutions to the economic changes of industrialism from being developed?

3. How did minorities fare during industrial growth?

RECOMMENDED READINGS

Ayers, Edward. *The Promise of the New South* (1992). A fine treatment of the South in the years after Reconstruction ended.

Calhoun, Charles W. *The Gilded Age: Essays on the Origins of Modern America* (2007). A valuable assortment of excellent essays about this period.

Cherny, Robert. *American Politics in the Gilded Age, 1868–1900* (1997). A good, brief introduction to the public life of the period.

Edwards, Rebecca. *New Spirits: Americans in the Gilded Age, 1865–1905* (2006). An energetic new synthesis of the post–Civil War decades.

Green, James. *Death in the Haymarket* (2006). A readable narrative about this pivotal protest and its effects on Gilded Age society.

Porter, Glenn. *The Rise of Big Business, 1860–1920* (1992). An excellent short introduction to the economic trends of the Gilded Age.

Saum, Lewis O. *The Popular Mood of America, 1860–1890* (1990). Considers how the nation responded to social change.

Schlereth, Thomas J. *Victorian America: Transformations in Everyday Life, 1876–1915* (1991). A good survey of the impact of the changes brought by industrialism on the lives of Americans.

Summers, Mark Wahlgren. *Rum, Romanism and Rebellion: The Making of a President 1884* (2000). A thoughtful study of a crucial election.

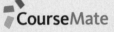 **CourseMate** Go to the CourseMate website at www.cengagebrain.com for additional study tools and review materials for this chapter.

17

Urban Growth and Farm Protest

1887–1893

The New Urban Society

  The Structure of the City
  The New Immigration
  The Urban Political Machine

The Diminishing Rights
of Minority Groups

  The Spread of Segregation

A Victorian Society

  The Rules of Life
  A Sporting Nation

Voices of Protest and Reform

Looking Outward: Foreign Policy
in the Early 1890s

  The Roots of Imperialism
  New Departures in Foreign Policy

Agrarian Unrest

  The Rise of the Farmers' Alliance

  Doing History: The Causes of
  Agrarian Discontent

  The Presidential Election of 1892

MAKING CONNECTIONS

◄▪▪▪ LOOKING BACK

Chapter 16 focused on the ways in which industrialism affected the United States between 1877 and 1887. The ramifications of the industrializing process would have large consequences for the subsequent course of American history. Particular attention was paid to how various groups in society, and specific regions of the country, responded to these new developments. Before starting Chapter 17, you should be able to answer the following questions:

1. What conditions in the previous decade made it possible for industrialism to take hold?

2. How did cost cutting and reducing labor expenses become a central effect of industrial growth?

3. How did the United States respond to the political problems arising from the spread of railroads?

4. In what ways was the country becoming more of a national market and economy?

5. What regions were left behind as industrialism grew?

As the United States approached its centennial in 1889, a burgeoning urban population posed growing social problems. Huge gaps between rich and poor marked the new cities. Americans sought to reconcile traditional rural values with the diversity and turbulence of the metropolis. The political system struggled to adjust to the new demands that the people of the cities posed.

The farm problems that had simmered during the early 1880s reached a crisis. In the South and West, angry farmers formed a new political organization, the People's Party. For Native Americans, African Americans, and Hispanics, the new decade emphasized their marginal status. The election of 1892 reflected such divisions as the nation found itself on the eve of a severe economic depression.

❖ The New Urban Society

After **Grover Cleveland** stressed tariffs in the 1888 election, the united Republicans rallied behind their candidate, **Benjamin Harrison**, and the doctrine of tariff protection for American industries. Cleveland won the popular vote, but Harrison won the electoral tally and became president. The Republicans also controlled both houses of Congress. With this hold on the government, the Republicans pushed an ambitious agenda of legislation, breaking the stalemated system that had existed since the end of Reconstruction.

During 1889 two events reflected the contrasting directions of the United States. Since the 1820s, the Five Civilized Tribes of Native Americans had lived in what is now Oklahoma. By the 1880s, however, pressure from white settlers proved irresistible in Congress. The Dawes Severalty Act of 1887 completed the process of stripping Indians of their rights. President Harrison announced that unoccupied land could be settled beginning April 22, 1889. One hundred thousand people rushed in. Within a few hours, the "Sooners," who entered the territory early, and the "Boomers" (a general name for eager settlers) had created towns and staked out farms. The Native Americans had to make do with land that whites did not occupy.

A few months later, in August 1889, Jane Addams and Ellen Gates Starr founded **Hull House**, a settlement home in a Chicago neighborhood. They sought solutions to poverty, disease, and political corruption in their new residence. Hull House and Addams became famous. Her experiment reflected the view that the concentration of population in cities was "the most remarkable social phenomenon" of the nineteenth century. Jane Addams and like-minded Americans wanted to make the new cities work.

Chicago symbolized urban America since the Civil War. In 1860, Chicago had a population of just under 109,000; thirty years later, its numbers had swelled

Cleveland, Grover (1837–1908) Twenty-second and twenty-fourth president of the United States (1885–1889 and 1893–1897), he was the first Democrat elected to the presidency after the Civil War.

Harrison, Benjamin (1833–1901) Twenty-third president of the United States (1889–1893), he lost the popular vote but won a majority of the electoral college.

Hull House Settlement house founded in Chicago in 1889 by Jane Addams and Ellen Gates Starr to help solve the troubling problems of city life.

(The Granger Collection, New York)

Hull House. Hull House, run by Jane Addams, was one of the many "settlement houses" that sought to bring social reform and economic improvement to the growing cities of the nation. Addams and her associates lived and worked with the people they helped, such as these Chicago children from the neighborhood.

CHAPTER TIMELINE	1887	1888	1889	1890	1891	1893
POLITICS AND DIPLOMACY	(1885)–1889 Grover Cleveland presidency (first term)		1889 Opening of Oklahoma Territory to non–Native American settlement	1890 National American Woman Suffrage Association is set up; 1890 Sherman Antitrust Act passes; 1890 Battle of Wounded Knee	1889–1893 Benjamin Harrison presidency	1892 Ellis Island opens in New York to receive immigrants; 1892 People's Party founded
SOCIETY AND CULTURE		1888 Edward Bellamy's *Looking Backward* becomes best-seller	1889 Jane Addams establishes Hull House in Chicago		1891 James Naismith invents basketball	1892 Ida Wells-Barnett begins campaigns against lynching; 1893 Columbian Exposition in Chicago
ECONOMICS AND TECHNOLOGY			1889 Electric sewing machine is developed; Thomas Edison received first U.S. radio patent		1891	1892 Homestead strike

to 1.1 million people. The major east-west railroads ran through the city. To the stockyards came beef cattle from the West, to its elevators grain from the prairies, and to its lumberyards wood from the forests of Wisconsin and Minnesota. After the great fire of 1871, which consumed the bulk of the city's buildings, Chicago had built the skyscrapers that gave it a distinct skyline and created the ethnic neighborhoods whose residents Hull House served. With so much economic opportunity in its streets and shops, Chicago's population boomed in the late nineteenth century. Elsewhere, especially in the Northeast and Midwest, urban population growth accelerated. Americans moved to the cities to escape the "hard work and no holidays" of rural life. Immigrants came from central and eastern Europe in increasing numbers as well.

The Structure of the City

After 1880 American cities boomed. The horsecar gave way to electric-power cable cars in San Francisco and other hilly cities. Relying on heavy cables running on the street, these devices were clumsy, inefficient, and expensive. Electric streetcars or trolleys, powered by overhead cables and moving at ten miles an hour, soon replaced the cable system. Across the nation, urban transit electrified. To avoid traffic jams, some cities ran streetcars on elevated tracks; others went underground to create subways. The older walking city disappeared. As their populations shifted away from their core areas, the cities used power granted by the state legislature to incorporate their suburbs into the larger metropolis. Within the center of the city, race and ethnicity determined where people lived. More affluent residents moved far from the center to avoid the lower classes.

Central business districts emerged. Railroads built terminals, banks and insurance companies located their main offices downtown, and department stores anchored shopping districts. Streetcars brought customers from the suburbs to Macy's in New York, Marshall Field's in Chicago, and Filene's in Boston. In these "palaces of consumption," middle-class women shopped for attractive products. Architects created the skyscraper for such districts. Louis Sullivan of Chicago developed building techniques that allowed builders to surpass the five to ten stories that had been the upper limits of structures. Passenger elevators and a framework of structural steel made it feasible to erect buildings of twenty to forty stories or more.

The numbers of people in the expanding cities strained the available living space. For the middle and upper classes, apartments were a practical answer, and apartment buildings replaced the single-family home. Poorer city residents lived in the tenement houses—six- or seven-story airless houses built on narrow lots. During the late 1870s, after legislation mandated that at least some ventilation be provided, "dumbbell tenements," with tiny indented windows along the sides, appeared. Dozens of people lived in small, dark rooms. From the outside, the buildings looked decent, but as the novelist William Dean Howells noted, "To be in it, and not have the distance, is to inhale the stenches of the neglected street and to catch the yet fouler and dreadfuller poverty-smell which breathes from the open doorways."

Inside the tenement or on the teeming sidewalks, the crush of people strained water and sanitation systems. The stench of manure, open sewers, and piled-up garbage filled nostrils. Smoke from the factories and grime from machinery were everywhere. City governments expanded their facilities to supply better services. New York City created a system of reservoirs that brought water from surrounding lakes and rivers to residents. Park building became a priority of urban political machines and reformers alike. Although most of the new parks appeared on the outskirts of the city, away from the poorer sections, the amount of parkland in larger cities doubled during the decade after 1888.

Doing History Online

Servicing the Urban Poor

Go to the CourseMate website for this chapter and link to Primary Sources. Read the articles by Richard Croker and Ray Stannard Baker. Political machines and political bosses were a source of controversy in the 1880s and 1890s. On what grounds does Baker attack them? How does Croker defend them? Whose argument do you find more persuasive, and why?

 www.cengagebrain.com

The New Immigration

For the twenty years after 1870, net immigration totaled more than 7.5 million people. Unlike the immigrants from northern and western Europe who had come during the first seventy-five years of the nineteenth century, these "New Immigrants" were mainly from southern and eastern Europe. Italians, Poles, Hungarians, Russian Jews, and Czechs brought with them languages, lifestyles, and customs that often clashed with those of native-born Americans or earlier immigrants. Marrying within their own ethnic group, speaking their own language, and reading their own newspapers, they created distinctive, vibrant communities within cities (see Map 17.1).

Many newcomers first saw the United States when they entered New York Harbor. They were processed at Castle Garden at the Battery in Lower Manhattan. By the end of the 1880s, these immigration facilities had become inadequate. They were closed in 1890, and a more extensive immigrant station was opened in 1892 on **Ellis Island** in the harbor.

The new arrivals labored for city construction gangs that built New York City's subways, the steel mills of Pittsburgh, and the skyscrapers of Chicago. Some men sold fruits and vegetables from pushcarts, others worked as day laborers, and increasing numbers built their own small businesses. Italian immigrant women "finished" garments for the clothing industry or made artificial flowers.

The cultural values and Old World experiences often dictated the jobs that men and women took. Italians preferred steady jobs with a dependable salary that

Ellis Island Immigration station in New York Harbor, opened in 1892, where new arrivals were given a medical examination and questioned about their economic prospects.

MAP 17.1

Immigration and Urbanization Immigrants concentrated in the nation's largest cities, swelling the population of these urban centers. This map shows where immigrants settled as the cities expanded.

(Copyright © Cengage Learning)

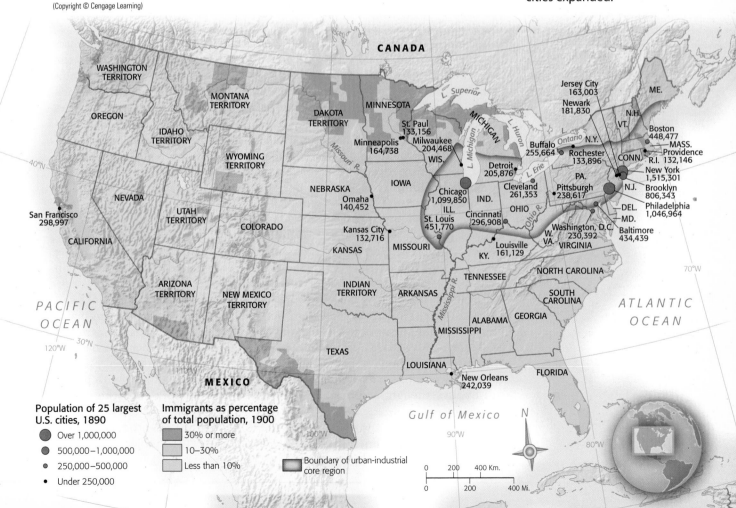

left time for family life. Greeks joined railroad gangs where they could work in the open. Jews became shopkeepers, merchants, and peddlers, the trades that had been open to them in the anti-Semitic world of eastern Europe. Ethnic neighborhoods appeared. In New York City, immigrants from Naples lived on Mott Street; Sicilians resided on Prince Street. Churches and synagogues shaped community life. Newcomers formed self-help societies to ease the transition for those who came after them: the Polish National Alliance, the Bohemian-American National Council, and the Hebrew Immigrant Aid Society, for example. They built theaters and concert halls, and created schools to educate their children. Some of the new arrivals moved away from their ethnic roots as they prospered; other immigrants soon replaced them. In the Tenth Ward of New York, the Jewish immigrant population in 1900 had a density of nine hundred people per acre, one of the highest in the world.

As the communities of immigrants grew, older residents worried about the impact of the newcomers on traditional values, and prejudice and religious intolerance flared. Editors of urban newspapers, speaking to the prejudices of their upper-class readers, called immigrants "the very scum and offal of the earth." During the 1880s, the anti-Catholic American Protective Association recruited those for whom the immigrants were a threat to Protestant religious values or a source of economic competition. Its members resolved to limit the role of Catholics in politics. Anti-Semitism also permeated American society, and quasi-scientific arguments arose to justify exclusion of Jews from universities and businesses. These sentiments that favored "native" Americans (hence "nativist") led to calls to restrict immigration through literacy tests for entrance into the United States or quotas based on national origin.

The Urban Political Machine

Politicians in the large cities grappled with ethnicity, race, and economic class divisions. Most cities had a mayor–council form of government in which the entire population elected the mayor, and council members represented individual districts or wards. Divided, ineffective government resulted as council members traded favors and blocked legislation that hurt their districts. The urban "political machine" led by the political boss developed in response. **Boss politics** consisted of an interlocking system of operations in each ward that delivered votes for their party at city and county conventions. The machine relied for its existence on the votes of the large inner-city population who turned out faithfully on election day to support the candidates whom the machine had designated.

Boss Politics Urban "political machines" that relied for their existence on the votes of the large inner-city population. The flow of money through the machine was often based on corruption.

The most notorious political machine of the era was the one connected to William Magear Tweed and the "Tweed Ring" of the late 1860s in New York City. Associated with the Democratic organization known as Tammany Hall (after the name of the clubhouse where its members met), Tweed used his influence to gain lucrative city contracts for his associates and supporters.

Democratic voters in New York applauded the ring as a source of jobs and patronage. Yet, Tweed's heyday was brief. He came under assault from major newspapers for corruption, but his most effective adversary was the cartoonist, Thomas Nast. Nast's drawings depicted Tweed as the leader of a band of criminals. Revelations about tainted contracts and crooked deals brought Tweed down in the early 1870s. The conditions that assisted his rise to power still existed, though, and machines flourished in New York and other major cities.

As the big cities grew, contracts were awarded to businesses to build streets, install sewers, lay gas lines, and erect elevated trains. These projects presented abundant chances for politicians to decide how money was spent. Judgments about who built streets, parks, and sewer connections depended on payoffs and graft to the boss and his associates. The flow of money, much of it based on corruption, enabled the machine to provide the social services that people wanted. Careful to keep their influence out of the spotlight, bosses rarely held office and managed affairs from behind the scenes through their control of the local Democratic Party. "Honest John" Kelly and Richard Croker of Tammany Hall were among the more celebrated of such leaders, but almost every major city had one. Their enemies depicted the bosses as unchallenged dictators of the city's destiny. In most cases, however, the bosses were shrewd politicians who balanced factions and interest groups in a constantly shifting political scene.

Members of the middle and upper classes, disturbed by the new power of the immigrants, attacked the boss and the machine as inefficient and wasteful. The boss and his allies often defeated the campaigns of the reformers because inner-city residents appreciated what the machine did for them. Reformers came and went, but the machine was always there, and on balance, they supplied reasonably good city government. Most cities had water, fire, and health services of a quality that compared with those found in the industrial nations of western Europe. In the city parks—Central Park in New York, the Boston park system, and the sprawling green spaces of St. Louis and Kansas City—the generation of the 1880s left a positive legacy to future urban residents.

The settlement houses that Jane Addams and others launched at the end of the decade improved city life. There were citizenship classes, training in cultural issues, and sports programs for local youth. At the same time, Addams and her colleagues conveyed a strong sense of moralistic paternalism to the people they sought to serve. Their goal was to "build a bridge between European and American experiences" over which the immigrants could pass toward integration into the dominant culture. Despite this condescending attitude, the settlement house movement softened the impact of the urban experience.

❖ The Diminishing Rights of Minority Groups

The rights of Native Americans, Mexican Americans, Chinese, and African Americans were at risk from repressive forces within white society. Possibilities narrowed for Americans who belonged to one of these distinct racial or ethnic minorities. In the case of Native Americans, the disastrous effects of the attitudes of whites played themselves out in tragedy.

The end of large-scale resistance to white expansion left few viable ways to protest policies that destroyed Native American traditions and confined natives to reservations or government schools. The appearance of a religious movement, the Ghost Dance, promised Plains Indians the return of their buffalo herds and an end to white domination. If the Indians performed the rituals of the dance, said a Paiute messiah named Wovoka, the Indian dead would be reborn and the whites would vanish for all time. But apprehensive whites saw the Ghost Dance as a portent of another Indian uprising.

When the army moved against the Sioux in December 1890, fighting occurred on Wounded Knee Creek on the Pine Ridge Reservation in South Dakota. Despite bitter hand-to-hand combat, the "battle" was no contest. The army's machine guns cut down the Indians; they suffered 146 dead and 51 wounded. Army losses were 25 killed and 39 wounded. The **Battle of Wounded Knee** was the last chapter in the Indian wars.

While the Indian conflicts were ebbing, social conflict involving Mexican Americans erupted in the territory of New Mexico. A major political issue was

Wounded Knee, Battle of (1890)
The last major chapter in the Indian wars, it was fought on the Pine Ridge Reservation in South Dakota.

the land grants that the Spanish Crown had made. Anglo lawyers acquired title to these properties in order to assemble large landholdings of their own. Hispanic residents had grazed their cattle on communal lands that all ranchers shared. Now Anglo ranchers and settlers divided up the land with fences and sold it among themselves. Spanish Americans tried to resist this trend by forming a secret vigilante organization, Las Gorras Blancas (the White Caps). In 1889, they cut fences and burned Anglo railroads, lumberyards, and other property.

Chinese immigrants came to the United States during the 1840s and 1850s to work the gold mines, and helped to construct the transcontinental railroads in the 1860s. But when jobs grew scarcer in the 1870s, whites in California felt threatened. Laws were passed that barred the Chinese from professions in which they competed with whites, and a movement to ban Chinese immigration grew. An 1868 treaty had guaranteed free access to Chinese immigrants to the United States, but twelve years later, Washington pressured the Chinese to change the treaty to allow the regulation of Chinese immigrants. As a result, the Chinese Exclusion Act of 1882 barred Chinese entry into the United States for ten years; it was extended in 1892 for another ten years. As prejudice against the 104,000 Chinese in the West became more intense, Congress moved to tighten restrictions on immigration. In 1889, the Supreme Court upheld the constitutionality of such laws and stated that such measures would help in "the preservation of our civilization there." By 1900, the number of Chinese living in the United States had fallen to 85,000.

The Spread of Segregation

The most elaborate and sustained policy of racial separation was aimed at African Americans in the South. As blacks tried to take part in politics and seek wealth and happiness, white southerners, believing that blacks were their inferiors, responded with a caste structure to ensure their continued dominance. Northern willingness to abandon the aims of the Civil War and Reconstruction was a key element in the rise of segregation.

With the tacit approval of the North, the white politicians of the South devised segregation laws to cover most spheres of human activity. Blacks were barred from white railroad cars and had to use the inferior and often shabby cars assigned to their race. Whites had their own hotels, parks, hospitals, and schools. Blacks had either to accept lesser facilities or do without them.

Laws removed blacks from the political process. They could not serve on juries in judgment of whites. They experienced harsher penalties when convicted of a crime than white offenders. In Mississippi, the 1890 constitutional convention required that voters demonstrate their literacy and pay a poll tax before they could cast a ballot. An illiterate man had to qualify to vote by demonstrating that he could "understand" a provision of the state constitution when it was read to him. Election judges allowed illiterate whites to vote; black voters faced complex questions about the state constitution. A poll tax had to be paid in advance and a receipt presented at the polls. In states like Mississippi and Louisiana, the number of registered black voters fell during the early 1890s; the number of white voters declined as well.

In addition to legal restrictions, blacks faced the constant possibility of violence. In the 1890s, an average of 187 black Americans were lynched annually. Blacks convicted of crimes were imprisoned in brutal circumstances in overcrowded penitentiaries or made to work on gangs that the state leased out to private contractors. The convict-lease system produced inmate death rates as high as 25 percent in some states.

Black leaders resisted to the extent they could. The remaining African American members of southern legislatures argued against discriminatory legislation, but they were easily outvoted. A Richmond, Virginia, Democrat boasted of the tactics used to exclude blacks from elections. "It was well understood that the blacks had to be beaten by hook or by crook—they knew what to expect and they knew who was putting the thing on them but they could not prevent it." By the mid-1890s, the South was as segregated as white leaders could make it. For most blacks the constitutional guarantees of the Fourteenth and Fifteenth amendments existed only on paper. The fate of minorities had a low priority in a society where racial stereotypes infused the mind-set of a Victorian society.

❖ A Victorian Society

In the late nineteenth century, the social customs embodied in the term *Victorian* shaped how most white Americans lived. Like their counterparts in Great Britain, where Queen Victoria ruled between 1837 and 1901, these Americans professed a public code of personal behavior that demanded restraint, sexual modesty, temperate habits, and hard work. They failed to see how much the minorities in the United States also exemplified these standards, and in their own lives, white Americans often fell well short of these ideals.

The Rules of Life

Victorian morality applied to every aspect of daily life. Relations between the sexes followed precise rules. Unmarried men and women were supposed to be chaperoned when they were together. A suitor asked a woman whether he might write to her before presuming to do so. A kiss resulted in an engagement or social disgrace. Premarital sex was taboo. People married for life, mourned a dead spouse for at least a year, and showed fidelity by not remarrying. Some people flouted these guidelines, of course, but many followed them and the social conventions that they represented.

Middle-class and upper-class men in Victorian society pursued careers out of the house, doing what a leading magazine took for its title: *The World's Work*. They spent their days at the factory or office, and the children saw them in the evening and on Sundays. Males displayed the right virtues in what was called their "character." In these classes, men might sow their "wild oats" before marriage, but after that were expected to adhere to their wedding vows. The rising number of divorces (fifty-six thousand by 1900), however, indicated that many did not do so. People looked the other way when men patronized prostitutes or had discreet sexual adventures outside wedlock. When it became known that a woman had followed such a course, she was disgraced.

A strict moral code governed the raising of Victorian children. Parents instilled character in their children, often by spanking or more intense physical abuse. Children were to be seen and not heard, and they were required to show respect to their elders. On Sundays, the middle-class family went to church. Religion permeated the nation of 63 million people. In 1890, there were 145 Christian denominations with nearly 22 million members. More than 8 million people were Roman Catholics. Presbyterians, Methodists, and Southern Baptists were the major Protestant denominations.

Although some mainline Protestant churches assimilated the teachings of Charles Darwin without protest, other denominations contended that evolution and religion could not coexist. "The human soul shrinks from the thought that it is without kith or kin in all this wide universe," concluded an observer of the intellectual currents of the decade. The struggle surrounding Darwinism continued over the course of the next century.

A Sporting Nation

While thinkers debated the impact of modern ideas on traditional religious verities, Americans sought relaxation and recreation in popular spectator sports. Among the upper and middle classes, football had emerged as second only to baseball in its appeal. The first intercollegiate football game occurred between Princeton and Rutgers in 1869; the modern game evolved as rules for scoring became established. Football appealed most to those who believed that young men should demonstrate commitment to a strenuous existence in a violent game that tested their masculine courage.

Boxing had a wider appeal to all classes of society, especially because it gave ethnic groups and immigrants a chance to advance in life. Irish American boxers dominated the sport, with **John L. Sullivan** the most famous champion. Some matches were held in secret and continued for as many as seventy-five bloody rounds. The contestants did not use gloves. Gloves and formal rules appeared during the 1880s. Sullivan lost his heavyweight crown in 1892 to James J. "Gentleman Jim" Corbett in the first gloved title fight. African American fighters appeared in interracial bouts in some divisions, but white heavyweight champions observed the "color line" before 1900.

Another popular diversion was bicycling, which became a craze after 1890. At first, cycling was a sport for those who could master the brakeless "ordinary" bikes with their oversize front wheels. Then in the 1880s, the "safety" bicycle, so called because of its brakes and inflated pneumatic tires, appeared. Technology had produced a bicycle that the average person could ride in relative comfort, and the fad was on. Some 10 million bikes were in use by 1900, but numbers declined with the advent of the automobile soon thereafter.

Sullivan, John L. (1858–1918)
Irish American boxing champion of the late nineteenth century.

❖ Voices of Protest and Reform

Bicycles were not the only craze that swept the nation at the end of the 1880s. **Edward Bellamy,** a former reporter turned novelist, published *Looking Backward: 2000–1887* in 1888. Its main character, Julian West, had gone to sleep in 1887 and woke in 2000. In the future he met Doctor Leete, who told him how the world had changed during the 113 years he had been asleep. In the new industrial order of "Nationalism," efficiency and discipline had replaced the chaos of the late nineteenth century. Citizens had purpose in their lives. Members of an industrial army, they served the state, which in turn provided them with material rewards. Bellamy had hit a nerve in a society that was restive about industrialism. His evocation of community and cooperative action resonated in a competitive, capitalist society.

Religion offered one answer to the social ills of industrialism. Many clergymen had defended the inequalities of wealth and status in society. But this harsh response offended younger members of the ministry, who sought to improve society rather than to save individual souls. They rebelled against the tenets of Social Darwinism and the idea that the ills of society were the results of natural selection. Walter Rauschenbusch, a Baptist clergyman in Rochester, New York, had seen firsthand the hardship and despair that slum dwellers experienced. He believed that it was necessary to "Christianize" the social order to bring it "into

Bellamy, Edward (1850–1898)
Reporter and novelist, the author of the popular utopian novel *Looking Backward* (1888).

harmony with the ethical convictions which we identify with Christ." Rauschenbusch's ideas came to be known as the Social Gospel. He and other ministers went into the city to preach the Gospel to poor slum dwellers. The Social Gospel contributed to the reform impulses that extended through the 1890s.

Middle-class women were leaders in the reform efforts of the 1890s. The Woman's Christian Temperance Union (WCTU) expanded its role under Frances Willard, its president from 1879 to 1899. It pursued missions to the urban poor, constructive changes in the situation of prison inmates, and protests against male-dominated politics. Prohibition thus became more than just the restriction of alcohol; for the WCTU it included a spectrum of ideas to improve society.

Women who had gained leisure time during the 1880s transformed their literary and discussion clubs into campaigns with a more ambitious agenda. A leading feminist, Charlotte Perkins Gilman, saw clubs as "the first timid steps toward social organization of these so long unsocialized members of our race." In 1890 the General Federation of Women's Clubs was founded, with a core membership of two hundred clubs and some twenty thousand women on its rolls. It sponsored cultural and educational activities for working women and homemakers.

The campaign to achieve woman suffrage had remained divided after the National Woman Suffrage Association and the American Woman Suffrage Association split over the Fifteenth Amendment and African American voting rights. The rift was healed through the efforts of Lucy Stone Blackwell. In 1890, the **National American Woman Suffrage Association (NAWSA)** appeared. The president was Elizabeth Cady Stanton; Susan B. Anthony succeeded her in 1892. Progress toward suffrage was slow: by the mid-1890s, only four states (Wyoming, Utah, Colorado, and Idaho) allowed women to vote.

Other reform goals attracted the support of committed women. Josephine Shaw Lowell animated the Charity Organization Society, which sent "friendly visitors" into urban slums to instruct residents and "in great measure prevent the growth of pauperism." Homes were established for the impoverished mother and prostitute where she could obtain "Friends, Food, Shelter and a HELPING HAND by coming just as she is." Florence Kelley of Hull House carried the ideas of the settlement movement into the more ambitious Illinois Women's Alliance in 1892. The New York City Working Women's Society protested harsh working conditions in that city in 1890; its activities led to the formation of consumers' leagues in other cities. These diverse examples of social criticism and constructive action taught lessons about the effects of industrialism that would shape the experience of the coming generation.

National American Woman Suffrage Association (NAWSA) This association was formed in 1890 through the efforts of Lucy Stone Blackwell, and its first president was Elizabeth Cady Stanton.

❖ Looking Outward: Foreign Policy in the Early 1890s

After decades of internal development, the nation sought a larger role in world affairs. The campaign for an expansionist foreign policy moved slowly in the face of persistent isolationism. In 1889, the United States was a weak military and diplomatic force. The army was small, with fewer than twenty-five thousand men who served in isolated posts in the West. The navy was equally insignificant. One congressman called the fleet "an alphabet of floating washtubs." Sails and wooden vessels were the rule until the 1880s when four steel ships were built.

One apparent source of support for expansion was the interest in overseas markets. In 1890, the Census Bureau announced the official closing of the frontier with the disappearance of a clear line of unsettled territory. Any desired future expansion would have to be international. Noting the size of the nation's industrial output, business leaders and farmers worried whether the home market could consume everything that factories and farms produced. The United States still imported more than it exported; in 1887, exports stood at $810 million, imports at $967 million. By the mid-1890s, the nation was exporting more than it imported.

The zeal for overseas markets helped feed a general enthusiasm for expansion, but the direct impact on policy was less certain. The percentage of the gross national product devoted to exports remained low. The official economic policy toward foreign trade was protectionist. Proponents of tariffs resisted efforts to lower trade barriers in order to expand overseas commerce. As a result, the sentiment for imperialism in the United States had an economic component, but the real drive for an international role had different causes.

The Roots of Imperialism

European powers scrambling to expand their empires had a powerful impact on American attitudes. As Africa and Asia became colonies and protectorates of Great Britain, Germany, France, and other countries, Americans worried about being left behind. Applying the doctrines of Social Darwinism to foreign nations, advocates of empire said that a nation that did not expand would not survive.

One expansionist leader was Captain Alfred T. Mahan of the U.S. Navy. Mahan's research into naval history led to his most important work, *The Influence of Seapower on History, 1660–1783*, published in 1890. Mahan wanted his country to seek global greatness through sea power. Only through naval bases, a powerful battleship fleet, and an aggressive foreign policy could the United States compete in a world of empires. He told policy makers that the United States should expand its foreign commerce, construct a strong navy, and acquire overseas bases. Of particular concern was a canal across Central America.

The notion of Anglo-Saxon supremacy fed the new interest in foreign affairs. The Protestant minister Josiah Strong contended in *Our Country: Its Possible Future and Its Present Crisis* (1885) that "God, with infinite wisdom and skill, is training the Anglo-Saxon race for an hour sure to come in the world's future." The popular author John Fiske gave lectures on "manifest destiny." In them he predicted that "every land on the earth's surface" that was not already civilized would become "English in its language, in its religion, in political habits and traditions, and a predominant extent in the blood of its people." These statements helped make expansionism seem aligned with the nation's future.

New Departures in Foreign Policy

The gradual movement toward a greater international role continued under Presidents Chester Arthur and Grover Cleveland. Secretary of State Frederick T. Frelinghuysen pursued treaties for trade reciprocity with Mexico, Santo Domingo, and Colombia. Frelinghuysen believed that these treaties would unite the interests of those countries with those of the United States. Congress, however, declined to act on the pacts. Under Cleveland, the process slowed as the administration showed less enthusiasm for a canal across Central America or a greater American presence worldwide. Still, the size of the navy grew during the Cleveland years. When James G. Blaine became secretary of state under Benjamin Harrison in 1889, he promoted an expansionist policy.

Blaine sent out invitations for a conference to Latin American countries, and delegates from nineteen nations assembled in Washington on October 2, 1889, for the first International American Conference. Blaine urged the delegates to set up mechanisms for freer trade among themselves and to work out procedures for settling their regional conflicts. Unwilling to accept what seemed to be the dominance of the United States, the conference declined to pursue these initiatives. Instead, it established the International Bureau of the American Republics, which became the Pan-American Union in 1910.

Blaine persuaded his Republican colleagues in Congress to include language allowing for reciprocity treaties in the McKinley Tariff Act of 1890. A number of products were placed on the free list, including sugar, molasses, coffee, and tea; the president could impose tariffs on such items if Latin American countries did not grant the United States similar concessions on its exports. Blaine used the reciprocity clause of the McKinley Tariff Act to negotiate treaties with such South American countries as Argentina. U.S. exports increased, disproving the claims of critics who warned that it would stifle trade with other nations.

The Harrison administration followed a more aggressive foreign policy, particularly in Asia and the Pacific. Secretary of the Navy Benjamin F. Tracy urged Congress to appropriate money for a battle fleet that would not only protect the coastline of the United States but also engage enemies across the oceans. With their eyes on potential markets for produce and crops, business leaders said that the Hawaiian Islands seemed a logical steppingstone to the Orient. Missionaries had been preaching in the islands since the 1820s; their reports fed American fascination with Hawaii. Trade relations between the United States and Hawaii had grown stronger since the reciprocity treaty, signed in 1875, gave Hawaiian sugar and other products duty-free entry into the United States. In exchange, Hawaii agreed not to grant other countries any concessions that threatened the territorial or economic independence of the island nation. The relationship was strengthened in 1887 when the treaty was renewed and the United States received the exclusive right to use the superb strategic asset of Pearl Harbor.

Within Hawaii, white immigrants and the native rulers clashed. The Hawaiian monarch, King Kalakua, had been inclined to accept closer ties between the United States and his nation. He died in 1891, bringing to power his sister, Queen Liliuokalani. She resented the American presence in Hawaii and believed that the white minority should not dominate. Hawaiian politics became more complex after the McKinley Tariff Act removed the duty-free status of Hawaiian sugar and granted bounties to American cane growers in Louisiana and beet sugar growers in the Rocky Mountain states. As the Hawaiian sugar industry slumped, economic conditions on the islands worsened. Calls for annexation arose from Americans in Hawaii and Congress in Washington.

During 1892, the Hawaiian legislature and queen argued over the presence and role of foreigners in the country. As the new year began, the queen dismissed the legislature and put in place a constitution that stripped white settlers of many of the powers they had enjoyed under the previous document. Proponents of annexation launched a revolt and called on the U.S. minister (the official representative of the United States to the islands) and the U.S. Navy. With the aid of 150 U.S. Marines, the coup succeeded. The queen capitulated and a provisional government was created. The United States agreed to a treaty of annexation with the pro-American and predominantly white rebels on February 14, 1893. It looked as if Hawaii would become a possession of the United States. Then the incoming president, Grover Cleveland, said that the treaty should not be ratified until the new administration took office. The fate of Hawaii remained in limbo.

(The Granger Collection, New York)

Queen Liliuokalani. When America endeavored to bring the Hawaiian Islands under United States control, Queen Liliuokalani led the native Hawaiians in efforts to forestall the end of their independence. Her resistance led the Cleveland administration to block Hawaiian annexation for most of the 1890s.

Despite this temporary pause, American expansion during the Harrison administration was striking. The navy had grown and its mission broadened. The ties to Latin America had been extended, and the fate of Hawaii seemed to be linked to that of the United States. Harrison and Blaine had launched the nation on a path of greater overseas involvement that would continue through the 1890s. For the moment, however, internal ferment captured the nation's attention as social and political unrest flared in the heartland of the United States.

❖ Agrarian Unrest

Of all the groups that found themselves at odds with the direction of American society between 1887 and 1893, the unhappy farmers of the South and West had the greatest impact on the nation and its political system.

The election of Benjamin Harrison in 1888 and Republican control of Congress had allowed the majority party to enact a wide-ranging program of legislative activism. The key measures included the McKinley Tariff Act, the **Sherman Antitrust Act,** and the Sherman Silver Purchase Act. The tariff law raised rates, and the Sherman Act on silver provided for limited government purchases of the white metal. The antitrust act outlawed "combinations in restraint of trade" without providing much means to enforce the new law.

In the election of 1890, the Democrats capitalized on unhappiness with these national Republican policies, as well as a backlash against the Grand Old Party over local issues such as prohibition and laws requiring the closing of businesses on the Sabbath. The new McKinley Tariff Act proved unpopular in the North, and in the South, Democrats used racial issues against their political rivals. The result was a Democratic victory that gave the opposition control of the House of Representatives.

The Rise of the Farmers' Alliance

In the 1890 election, candidates identified with the **Farmers' Alliance** made impressive gains in the South and West. Alliance candidates won nine seats in the House and elected two U.S. senators. Their candidates dominated several southern state legislatures, where a crisis in agriculture had been building for decades, and they showed strength as well in Kansas, Nebraska, South Dakota, and Minnesota.

Farmers had many grievances. When farm prices declined, western farmers found that the debts they had run up during the 1880s were now more difficult to pay. For southern farmers, whether sharecroppers or tenants, the slide in prices meant that their debts to the "furnish merchant" also mounted up. Railroads were also resented: high rates cut into the farmers' profits, and there were complaints that the rail lines favored manufacturers and middlemen over agrarians.

The prevailing perception among farmers in the South and West was that the system took no heed of their needs or interests. The system of money and banking drew scorn. Every dollar in circulation had to have an equal amount of gold bullion behind it to keep the nation's currency on "the gold standard." Gold was stored in banks and at the U.S. Treasury. Because international gold production was static, the amount of money in circulation did not keep up with the growth in the population. The currency became deflated as the value of the dollar rose. Wheat farmers on the Plains and cotton farmers in the South had to work harder to maintain the same level of income. The thoughts of many farmers turned to ways in which the currency might be inflated—that is, ways of putting more dollars into circulation.

Sherman Antitrust Act (1890) Federal legislation designed to curb the growth of large monopolistic corporations.

Farmers' Alliance First started as local groups of angry farmers in Texas during the 1880s, these alliances spread across the South and West and eventually formed into the Farmers' Alliance and Industrial Union in 1889. The Alliance was a forerunner of Populism.

The complaints of the farmers were genuine, but workable solutions were another matter. Farm prices were low because of expanding acreage under cultivation. One long-term solution was the consolidation of small farms into larger, more efficient agricultural businesses, a process that would occur later in the nation's history. But at the end of the nineteenth century, it ran counter to the widely held belief in the importance of small landowners to the health of a democratic society.

Angry farmers organized into alliances and associations that expressed their grievances. They came up with proposed solutions in a three-stage process. During the first phase, southern and western farmers looked toward cooperative action. A leader in this effort was Charles Macune, who became president of the Texas Alliance in 1886. He envisioned alliances and cooperative exchanges across the South. These institutions could provide farmers with supplies and equipment at a cost below what local merchants and retailers charged. The farmers would gain more control over the marketplace. To spread the creed of the cooperatives, the alliance sent out "lecturers" who fanned out across the region. But cooperatives proved easier to organize than to sustain, because farmers lacked the money and influence to make such a scheme work. Nonetheless, the ideology of cooperative action appealed to isolated farm families. The alliance meetings brought farmers together to hear speeches, enjoy entertainment, and share experiences. The alliance thus built on collective emotion among farmers as the 1890s began.

Some members of the alliance saw African American farmers as potential allies. The Colored Farmers' National Alliance and Cooperative Union was formed in 1886. The interaction between the black alliance and its white counterpart was uneasy. Whites were usually landowners, even if impoverished ones; blacks tended to be either tenants or farm laborers. In 1891, the Colored Alliance sought to get higher wages for picking cotton. A strike for that purpose, organized by a black leader named Ben Patterson in Lee County, Arkansas, was met with violence. Fifteen of the strikers, including Patterson, were lynched, and the Colored Alliance vanished.

As farm conditions worsened during years of drought and falling crop prices, branches of the alliance gained members in the Dakotas, Nebraska, and especially Kansas. Representatives of these various organizations met in St. Louis in December 1889 to form the Farmers' Alliance and Industrial Union. The delegates agreed to leave out the word *white* from the organization's requirements, although state organizations in the South could exclude black members. Three key northern states, Kansas and the two Dakotas, joined the national organization.

Charles Macune offered the most important policy proposal of the conference, the subtreasury plan. Macune recognized that the major problem that confronted cotton and wheat farmers was having to sell their crops at harvest time when supplies were abundant and prices low. To surmount this obstacle, he envisioned a system of government warehouses or subtreasuries where farmers could store their crops until prices rose. To bridge the months between storage and selling, the farmers would receive a certificate of deposit from the warehouse for 80 percent of the crop's existing market value. The charge for this service would be a 1 or 2 percent annual interest rate. Farmers would wait, sell their crops for higher prices, repay the loans, and keep the resulting profits.

If a majority of wheat or cotton farmers waited until prices rose and then sold their crops, the market glut would force prices down again. The certificates that the farmers would have received for storing their crops at the subtreasury warehouses would represent another form of paper money that would fluctuate in value. Beyond that, the idea involved a large expansion of government power in an era when suspicion of federal power was still strong. To its agrarian advocates, the subtreasury seemed to be a plausible answer to the harsh conditions they confronted.

Doing History The Causes of Agrarian Discontent

The Populist platform in 1892 was written by Ignatius Donnelly and consisted of a stinging indictment of the political system. The two other quotations that appear here were published in a popular magazine of the day, The Forum, and a government report from the Department of Agriculture. They reflected eastern attitudes toward the emerging farm discontent that culminated in the emergence of the People's Party. The gap in understanding among these perspectives was typical of how American society in the 1890s reacted to the political tensions that populism represented.

Populist Party Platform, *1892*

The conditions which surround us best justify our cooperation; we meet in the midst of a nation brought to the verge of moral, political, and material ruin. Corruption dominates the ballot box, the Legislatures, the Congress, and touches even the ermine of the bench. The people are demoralized, most of the States have been compelled to isolate the voters at the polling places to prevent universal intimidation and bribery. The newspapers are largely subsidized or muzzled, public opinion silenced, business prostrated, homes covered with mortgages, labor impoverished, and the land concentrated in the hands of capitalists. The urban workmen are denied the right to organize for self-protection, imported pauperized labor beats down their wages, a hireling standing army, unrecognized by our laws, is established to shoot them down, and they are rapidly degenerating into European conditions. The fruits of the toil of millions are boldly stolen to build up colossal fortunes for the few, unprecedented in the history of mankind; and the possessors of these, in turn, despise the Republic and endanger liberty. From the same prolific womb of government injustice we breed two great classes—tramps and millionaires.

C. Wood Davis, "Why the Farmer Is Not Prosperous," *April 1890*

The working force in the United States is about 23,000,000 persons, of whom 10,000,000 are engaged in agricultural pursuits, employing a capital of $16,000,000,000 invested in farms and their equipment. That the greater part of this host of workers and of this immense capital is unprofitably employed is beyond question; and this state of unthrift has progressed so far as to discourage great numbers of those so unemployed.

This state of affairs is not due to any lack of industry or frugality on the part of the farmer. Nor can it be attributed to crop failures, as is evident from the increasing quantities of products put upon the markets of the world at prices ever growing less. Indeed, our farms are so numerous and productive as to reduce the returns of American agriculture to a point far below a reasonable profit, and to lessen the values of the farms and farm products of Canada, Great Britain, and western Europe.

J. R. Dodge, "Agricultural Depression and Its Causes," *March 1890*

During the last ten years more than two million workers in agriculture, armed with improved implements, have been added to the seven million that were making corn and wheat and cotton; and shall they still insist on the same limited range of effort, walk in the same furrows their farmers turned, and seek to live and die in the same overdone and profitless routine? If so agricultural depression will become chronic and intensified to a degree unknown at present. Shall farmers hug the chains of their dependence, limit the range of their industry, refuse to strike out into new paths, and sink into comparative idleness and poverty? There are millions of them too intelligent and enterprising and ambitions to co-operate in any such scheme of self-degradation.

QUESTIONS for REFLECTION

1. How are the Populists reacting to the rise of industrialism and the commercialization of agriculture?

2. How do all three authors respond to the changes that occurred in American life as discussed in Chapter 16 and this chapter?

3. Despite their differences, are there areas of agreement about the nature of the farm problem at this time?

During the 1890 election, the protest movement poured its energy into speeches. In Kansas it represented an entirely new party. At a time when women took little direct part in politics, the alliance allowed female speakers to address audiences. Mary Elizabeth Lease proved one charismatic attraction with her urging to the farmers to raise "less corn and more hell." Another female attraction was Annie Diggs, who rivaled Lease in her appeal to Kansas voters.

The success of the Farmers' Alliance in the South and West led their leaders to consider mounting a third-party campaign during the next presidential election. They gathered in Ocala, Florida, in early December 1890, and their platform was known as the Ocala Demands. Their goals included the subtreasury program, abolition of private banks, regulation of transportation facilities, and the free and unlimited coinage of silver into money at a fixed ratio with gold. The issue of a third party was put off until February 1892 to allow the legislatures that had been elected with alliance support to see what they could accomplish.

As the two major parties, and especially the Democrats, fought back against the alliance, the idea of a third party gained in appeal. At a meeting of the alliance in February 1892 in St. Louis, the delegates decided to create a third party under the name the People's Party, or the Populists. They would hold their first national convention in Omaha, Nebraska, on July 4, 1892. They even had a candidate, Leonidas L. Polk of North Carolina, who was popular enough to satisfy both northern and southern farmers. When Polk died a month before the convention, the Omaha Convention chose James B. Weaver, a long-time third-party politician from Iowa, as its presidential candidate.

The party's platform took a stern view of the state of the nation. It proclaimed, "We meet in the midst of a nation brought to the verge of moral, political, and material ruin. Corruption dominates the ballot box, the legislature, the Congress, and touches even the ermine of the bench." The specific planks endorsed the subtreasury, other reform proposals, and a new idea that was dominating the dialogue among the Populists: the free coinage of silver. (See *Doing History: The Causes of Agrarian Discontent.*)

By 1892, the subtreasury plan was going nowhere in Congress. As that proposal faded, the idea that inflation could be promoted by coining silver into money gained support. To expand the currency, raise prices, and reduce the weight of debt on those who owed money, silver was, the Populists argued, the best solution. The nation would base its money on two metals, gold and silver. If silver were coined into money at a ratio of 16 to 1 with gold, there would soon be ample money in circulation.

The country needed controlled inflation. However, the market price of silver stood at closer to 25 to 1, relative to gold. A policy of free coinage would lift the price of the white metal in an artificial way. If that happened, people would hoard gold, silver would lose value, and inflation would accelerate.

The **Populist Party** rejected these arguments, maintaining that "money can be created by the government in any desired quantity, out of any substance, with no basis but itself." The idea of crop supports underlying the subtreasury plan and the manipulation of the money supply through the free coinage of silver would become common ideas during the twentieth century. But in 1892 they seemed radical to many Americans.

Populist Party Also known as the People's Party, the Populists held their first national convention on July 4, 1892. The party platform took a stern view of the state of the nation, with planks endorsing the subtreasury, free coinage of silver, and other reforms.

The Presidential Election of 1892

Republicans and Democrats noticed the Populist challenge, but for the presidential election of 1892, the familiar routines of political life went on. The elections of 1890 had shown Republicans that President Harrison was not a strong candidate for reelection, but despite a last-minute challenge by

(© Bettmann/ CORBIS)

Homestead Strike. The Homestead strike brought violence between the steelworkers who had left their jobs and the troops sent in to break the walkout. This contemporary illustration depicts the violence that resulted.

Homestead strike (1892) Labor uprising of workers at a steel plant in Homestead, Pennsylvania, that was put down by military force.

James G. Blaine, Harrison was renominated. Confidently, the Democrats nominated Grover Cleveland and promoted a platform promising lower tariffs and an end to the government spending they associated with the Republicans. Although he favored the gold standard, Cleveland kept his real views muted to placate Democrats who favored inflation. In some western states, the Democrats and the Populists struck deals and "fused" their two tickets, with Cleveland getting the electoral vote and the Populists electing state candidates.

During the election year, one event seemed to embody the tensions between capital and labor that industrialism had fostered. For workers at Andrew Carnegie's Homestead steelworks outside Pittsburgh, Pennsylvania, the summer of 1892 was a time of misery and violence. The manager of the plant, Henry Clay Frick, cut wages and refused to negotiate with skilled workers who had unionized their craft. A strike resulted, and violence broke out when detectives hired by management stormed through the town of Homestead to allow strikebreakers to retake the mills. Detectives and workers died in the ensuing battle, and state troops came in to restore order. Although the **Homestead strike** was broken, the walkout helped the Democrats in their appeal to labor voters disillusioned with Republicans.

The Populists tried to make the same argument about the struggle between agriculture and capital. James B. Weaver drew big crowds, but Democrats in the South pelted him with rotten eggs and tomatoes when he appeared. Thomas E. Watson, a Populist leader, saw his own reelection campaign fail when the Democrats stuffed the ballot boxes against him. Other Populist candidates were counted out when the Democrats controlled the election process. When the votes in the South had been tallied, the Democrats had carried the region for Cleveland.

On the national level, Cleveland gained a second term by a decisive margin. His plurality over Harrison was almost four hundred thousand votes, and he won in the electoral tally with 277 votes to 145 for the Republicans. The Democrats secured control of both houses of Congress for the first time since the Civil War.

(Chicago Historical Society)

The Columbian Exposition.
The Columbian Exposition of 1892–1893 marked the 400th anniversary of the landing of Christopher Columbus. The "Great White City" in Chicago symbolized the progress of the nation and its technological accomplishments. The outbreak of the Panic of 1893 dulled the luster of the occasion for many Americans.

Weaver carried four states and won electoral votes in three additional states for a total of 22 electoral votes. His popular vote total stood at just over 1 million.

The American economy was heading for trouble at the beginning of 1893, but a large popular spectacle in Chicago distracted the public from gloom. The World's Columbian Exposition commemorated the arrival of Columbus in "The New World" four hundred years earlier. Architect Daniel Burnham and his coworkers created a series of exhibition buildings that became known as "The Great White City."

To commemorate the exposition, the American Historical Association held its annual meeting in Chicago in 1893. There a young historian from the University of Wisconsin, Frederick Jackson Turner, offered a new interpretation of how the United States had changed and the challenges it faced in the immediate future. In his paper, "The Significance of the Frontier in American History," Turner stressed that the availability of free land and the presence of the frontier had played a significant part in the development of democracy in the nation. He inquired about what would happen to the nation now that the possibility of free land and a new life in the West was vanishing. Turner's "frontier thesis" became a powerful and controversial explanation of how the nation had developed.

Like many other Americans, Turner was groping to comprehend the changes that had occurred in American life since the Civil War. Industrialism, the rise of the city, and the strains of farm life all contributed to the sense of crisis that gripped the country during the 1890s. The United States was leaving its agrarian past for the uncertain rewards of a more industrialized, more urbanized, and more international future. Troubling signs of economic difficulties made citizens wonder if prosperity might disappear and the hard times of the 1870s return. Their fears were realized when the panic of 1893 changed the direction of American life.

CHAPTER REVIEW, 1887–1893

SUMMARY

- Urban growth accelerated as big cities appeared in the wake of industrialism.

- Poverty and wealth made the city a place of contrasts and social problems.

- Urban machines arose to provide services to residents and opportunity for capitalists.

- Victorian ideas shaped middle-class attitudes as Americans sought certainty in an unstable decade.

- The nation looked outward as overseas expansion became a popular cause.

- Southern and western farmers joined together to battle low prices and the burden of debt through the Populist Party.

- The election of 1892 brought Grover Cleveland back to the White House amid growing concerns about the direction of the economy.

IDENTIFICATIONS

Grover Cleveland

Benjamin Harrison

Hull House

Ellis Island

Boss politics

Wounded Knee, Battle of

John L. Sullivan

Edward Bellamy

National American Woman Suffrage Association (NAWSA)

Sherman Antitrust Act

Farmers' Alliance

Populist Party

Homestead strike

MAKING CONNECTIONS: LOOKING AHEAD ⅢⅢ➡

Chapter 18 looks at the peak of the farm protest during the economic depression of the 1890s. To understand what made the issues of the agrarian sector so explosive requires a good understanding of the roots of the unrest. Consider to what extent this chapter helps anticipate these issues.

1. What assumptions did Americans share about the role of government in this period? How do these premises differ (if they do) from contemporary attitudes?

2. How well equipped was the political sector to deal with the issues the Populists were advocating?

3. What attitudes about farm and city life in this period are still present in modern society?

RECOMMENDED READINGS

Calhoun, Charles. *Conceiving a New Republic: The Republican Party and the Southern Question, 1869–1900* (2006). A perceptive look at the failure of Republican efforts to remake the South after Reconstruction.

Clanton, O. Gene. *A Common Humanity: Kansas Populism and the Battle for Justice and Equality, 1854–1903* (2004). An excellent look at how populism emerged in one of its key states.

Crapol, Edward P. *James G. Blaine: Architect of Empire* (2000). An interpretive biography of one of the moving spirits behind American expansionism.

Cronon, William. *Nature's Metropolis: Chicago and the Great West* (1991). An interesting treatment of how Chicago grew and interacted with the region it dominated.

Duis, Perry R. *Challenging Chicago: Coping with Everyday Life, 1837–1920* (1998). An insightful book about how Americans lived their lives in the industrial cities.

Perman, Michael. *Struggle for Mastery: Disfranchisement in the South, 1888–1908* (2001). A thorough synthesis of the way blacks were excluded from politics in the South.

Schneirov, Richard. *Labor and Urban Politics: Class Conflict and the Origins of Modern Liberalism in Chicago, 1864–1894* (1998). Examines the impact of urban industrial growth on politics in a major American city.

Sklar, Kathryn Kish. *Florence Kelley and the Nation's Work: The Rise of Women's Political Culture, 1830–1900* (1995). An excellent biography of an urban reformer in Chicago in the 1890s.

Williams, R. Hal. *Years of Decision: American Politics in the 1890s* (1993). A fine introduction to the decade.

CourseMate Go to the CourseMate website at www.cengagebrain.com for additional study tools and review materials for this chapter.

18

A Troubled Nation Expands Outward

1893–1901

The Panic of 1893
  Economic Downturn
  1894: A Significant Election
The 1890s Depression
  Reshaping the Economy
  The Reform Campaigns
  Substantive Due Process and Its Critics
  Pragmatism and Realism
  African Americans and Segregation
  Doing History: Lynching and the Rights of African Americans, 1898–1900

Foreign Policy Challenges
  The Cuban Crisis, 1895–1896
  The Battle of the Standards: 1896
  Bryan and the Cross of Gold
The War with Spain and Overseas Expansion, 1898–1900
  Spain and Cuba
  The Sinking of the *Maine:* February 15, 1898
  The Spanish-American War, 1898
  The 1900 Election and a New Century

MAKING CONNECTIONS

◀▬III LOOKING BACK

The problems that urban and rural Americans faced in the period 1887–1893 grew out of the achievements of industrialism during the preceding decade. Chapter 17 discussed the consequences of rapid economic change and how Americans sought to use existing institutions to respond to these developments. Before starting Chapter 18, you should be able to answer the following questions:

1. In what ways did the growth of cities test the capacities of local governments?

2. Was the urban machine a constructive or destructive response to the changes that metropolitan areas experienced?

3. What causes underlay the economic hard times in the South and West for the nation's farmers?

4. Why was inflation a priority for those who joined the Farmers' Alliance?

5. What forces produced interest in overseas expansion around 1890? What assumptions about the world did the enthusiasm for empire reflect?

During the 1890s, social problems that had been building since the Civil War reached crisis proportions. An economic depression began in 1893, and Americans struggled with its effects for four years. With millions unemployed and faith in national institutions eroding, the major political parties confronted unhappy voters. With the majority Democrats in disarray and the Populists not a viable third party, the Republicans emerged. The election of 1896 brought William McKinley, the architect of Republican success, to the White House. He revitalized the presidency after its eclipse since the death of Abraham Lincoln. The events of these years established patterns that affected the early decades of the twentieth century.

As the economy improved at the end of the 1890s, Americans sought an empire in the Caribbean and the Pacific. A war with Spain brought territorial gains and a debate about whether overseas possessions meant fundamental change. American institutions and leaders faced the challenge of the new responsibilities of world power, particularly in Europe and Asia.

❖ The Panic of 1893

Grover Cleveland's second term began on March 4, 1893. In May 1893, the weakened economy collapsed into the panic of 1893. After years of growth, investors turned cautious in the early 1890s, worried about the soundness of the banking system and the stability of the currency. Banks began to fail as depositors withdrew their funds and hoarded cash. A decline in export trade further strained the economy. Business activity slowed, workers were laid off, and firms cut back on production.

By the end of 1893, some six hundred banks had failed. Court-appointed receivers ran 119 bankrupt railroads. Another fifteen thousand businesses had closed. The stock market lost hundreds of millions of dollars. Most important, by early January 1894, 2.5 million people were unemployed and were without the safety net of insurance payments or government benefits. The economy was functioning at only three-quarters of its capacity.

Economic Downturn

The depression fell hardest on average workers and their families. In New York City, daily newspapers distributed food, clothing, and fuel to the needy. Charitable organizations in Boston, New York, and Chicago coordinated volunteer efforts. Most well-off Americans still believed the federal government should not intervene to alleviate a depression. As a result, people slept in the parks, camped out in railroad stations, and sought food at the soup kitchens that appeared in the big cities. Angry poor people called the soup kitchens "Cleveland Cafés."

In August 1893, Cleveland called a special session of Congress to repeal the Sherman Silver Purchase Act, arguing that the law produced inflation, undermined business confidence, and caused investors to take money out of the nation's gold reserve at the Treasury Department. His own party was split: northeastern party members believed in the gold standard with religious fervor. In the South and Far West, Democrats contended that the nation needed the free and unlimited coinage of silver into money at the fixed ratio of silver to gold of 16 to 1. By asking his party to repeal the Sherman Act, Cleveland caused a Democratic uproar. Over the protests of his party and with no tolerance of compromise, he won the battle with the aid of Republican votes. The bill repealing the Sherman Act was signed into law on November 1, 1893.

CHAPTER TIMELINE	1893	1895	1897	1899	1901
POLITICS AND DIPLOMACY	1893–1897 Grover Cleveland presidency (second term)	1896 ● Supreme Court upholds segregation in *Plessy v. Ferguson*	1897–1901 William McKinley presidency	● 1898 Spanish-American War	
SOCIETY AND CULTURE	1894 ● Radcliffe College for Women opens in Cambridge, Massachusetts	● 1895 Booker T. Washington proposes Atlanta Compromise ● 1895 Stephen Crane publishes *The Red Badge of Courage* ● 1896 First commercial movie showing			
ECONOMICS AND TECHNOLOGY	1893–1897 Economic depression started by panic of 1893 ● 1894 Pullman strike			● 1900 Gold Standard Act 1901 ● United States Steel created as first billion-dollar corporation	

Coxey's Army. Members of Coxey's Army on their way to Washington during the spring of 1894.

Pullman, George (1831–1897)
Developer of the railroad sleeping car and creator of a model town outside Chicago for his employees.

Pullman strike (1894) Strike by railway workers that led to nationwide unrest.

Having blamed the Sherman Act for the depression, Cleveland waited for an economic turnaround. Although confidence in the dollar grew and the flow of gold out of the country eased, prosperity did not return. By 1894, every indicator headed downward. More railroads failed, more businesses closed, and more people were laid off to join the millions who were already unemployed.

In the 1892 campaign, the Democrats had promised to lower tariff rates, but with only narrow control in their chamber, Senate Democrats wrote a tariff bill that appealed to only certain states. Congress finally passed the Wilson-Gorman Tariff Act in August 1894. It reduced rates on wool, copper, and lumber, and raised duties on many other items. The measure repealed the reciprocal trade provisions of the McKinley Tariff Act, which had aimed at opening up markets and easing the political costs of protection. To make up for lost revenues, the Wilson-Gorman bill added a modest tax on personal incomes. Disgusted with the outcome, Cleveland let the bill become law without his signature.

Outside Washington, as the hard times lingered, some of the unemployed took their grievances to Washington. In the Midwest, those out of work formed "Coxey's army," uniting behind Jacob S. Coxey, a businessman from Massillon, Ohio. On Easter Sunday 1894, he left for Washington with three hundred supporters to petition for a program of road building paid for by $500 million of paper money. Coxey and his son, "Legal Tender Coxey," headed the procession, which included more than forty reporters. The climax for Coxey and his followers came on May 1, 1894, when they reached Capitol Hill and tried to present their demands to Congress. But police intercepted Coxey, clubbed him, and then arrested him for trespassing and "walking on the grass." The soldiers were discouraged and dispersed, but the protests undermined the political credibility of the Cleveland administration.

Even more devastating was a major railroad strike. **George Pullman**, the developer of the railroad sleeping car, had created a model town outside Chicago where his employees lived and worked. When he laid off employees and trimmed wages for others, Pullman did not reduce the rents that his workers paid. As a result, in May 1894 the workers struck. They asked railroad workers across the nation not to handle Pullman's cars to help the walkout. By late June, the American Railway Union's president, Eugene Victor Debs, started a sympathetic boycott.

At its height, the **Pullman strike** involved 125,000 men representing twenty railroads. The commerce of the nation stalled as freight shipments backed up. On July 2, 1894, President Cleveland and the Justice Department obtained a court injunction to bar the strikers from blocking interstate commerce. Federal troops were ordered to Chicago. Violence erupted as angry mobs, irate at the action of the federal government, destroyed railroad property and equipment. The strikers were not to blame for the episode; the rioters were local people. Police and National Guard troops put down the disturbance, but the public gave Cleveland and the federal government the credit.

Debs went to jail for violating the court's injunction, and the U.S. Supreme Court confirmed his sentence in *In re Debs* (1895). By doing so the Court gave businesses a potent way to stifle labor unrest. If a strike began, management could seek an injunction from a friendly federal judge, jail the union leaders, and break the strike. As a result, union power stagnated throughout the rest of the decade.

Politically, the strike divided the Democrats. The governor of Illinois, John P. Altgeld, had protested Cleveland's actions. When the president overruled him, the governor resolved to oppose the administration in 1896. Across the South and West, bitterness against the president became even more intense. Hate mail flooded into the White House, warning him of death if he crossed the Mississippi River.

1894: A Significant Election

Approaching the congressional elections of 1894, the Democrats were demoralized and divided. For the Populists, however, these elections offered an excellent chance to establish themselves as a credible challenger to the two major parties. The Republicans assailed the Democrats for failing to restore prosperity and urged a return to the policy of tariff protection. Party leaders, such as **William McKinley,** the governor of Ohio, crisscrossed the Midwest speaking to enthusiastic audiences.

The Republicans prevailed in one of the most decisive congressional elections in the nation's history. The Democrats lost 113 seats in the largest transfer of power from one party to another in the annals of the two-party system. The Republicans regained control of the House of Representatives by a margin of 244 to 105. There were twenty-four states in which no Democrat won a federal office; six other states elected only one Democrat. In the Midwest, 168 Republicans and only 9 Democrats were elected to Congress. The stalemated politics of the late nineteenth century had ended in an election that changed the nation's politics and foreshadowed a Republican victory in the presidential contest in 1896.

The Populists were disappointed with the outcome of the 1894 election. Although the total vote for the Populists had increased over 1892, much of that rise occurred in the South where the Democrats then used their control of the electoral machinery to deny victory to Populist candidates. The Populist delegation in Congress went from eleven members to seven. By 1894, the Populists were identified with the free coinage of silver, which appealed to the debt-burdened South and West but seemed less attractive to urban industrial workers who had to survive on a fixed or declining income. The Populists' failure to mount a significant challenge to the major parties during the 1894 election signaled the end of their assault on the two-party system.

McKinley, William (1843–1901) Twenty-fifth president of the United States (1897–1901), he won by the largest majority of popular votes since 1872.

❖ The 1890s Depression

The economic impact of the depression of the 1890s was profound and far reaching. By 1894, the economy operated at 80 percent of capacity. Total output of goods and services was down by some 13 percent. Unemployment ranged between 17 and 19 percent of the workforce. As the amount of money in circulation dropped, the nation experienced severe deflation. For people with money, their dollars bought more goods. Among those out of work and without funds, however, lower prices were little comfort when they had no money to pay for the necessities of life.

With their husbands, fathers, and sons laid off, women joined the workforce in greater numbers during the decade. During the 1890s, the total number of women with jobs rose from 3.7 million to just under 5 million. They gained employment in the expanding clerical fields, where they mastered typing and stenography, as well as teaching and nursing. Other women worked in factories, earning essential income for the survival of their families. When the male wage earner brought home only $300 per year, and rents for a tenement dwelling were as much as $200 annually, the contributions of a daughter or wife were vital. However, the wages paid to women were as much as 40 percent below what men earned in industrial jobs.

The depression also brought young children back into the workforce. During the 1880s, the percentage of employed children between the ages of ten and fifteen had fallen from 17 percent to 12 percent. In the next decade, the percentage rose to 18 percent. By 1900, 1.75 million children were employed. By the end of the century, thirty states had passed child labor laws, but these were often ineffective.

Reshaping the Economy

In the economy as a whole, the depression brought important changes. As a result of the downturn, the number of bankrupt businesses grew, revealing an obvious economic need for reorganization. In railroads, for example, major systems such as the Union Pacific were in receivership. The investment banker J. P. Morgan refinanced many of these rail lines and consolidated them to raise profits and increase efficiency. Thirty-two railroads, capitalized at more than $100 million, controlled nearly 80 percent of the nation's rail mileage. Shippers complained that these railroads gave larger customers unfair advantages in the form of rebates. By the end of the decade, there were increasing pleas from the South and Midwest to revive and strengthen the Interstate Commerce Commission, whose power to oversee railroad rates had been reduced by court decisions.

In the 1890s, "finance capitalists" like Morgan challenged the dominance of the "industrial capitalists" of the 1870s and 1880s who had built large enterprises in steel, oil, and railroads. These financiers launched a wave of corporate mergers that began in 1895 and continued for a decade. In New York a market for industrial stocks enabled bankers to raise capital. In the case of *U.S. v. E. C. Knight* (1895), the Supreme Court ruled that the Sherman Antitrust Act applied only to monopolies of interstate commerce and not to those solely of manufacturing. This decision made it more difficult to enforce the antitrust laws, and as a result, the government took little action against any of the mergers that occurred during the 1890s.

Many citizens became angry about the power a few men or businesses wielded over single industries. Indeed, the depression of the 1890s aroused fear and apprehension across the country. Writers questioned whether the government should simply promote economic expansion and then allow fate to decide who prospered and who did not. In 1894, Henry Demarest Lloyd published *Wealth Against Commonwealth*, a book that detailed what he believed the Standard Oil Company had done to monopolize the oil industry and corrupt the nation. Lloyd called for public ownership of many transportation and manufacturing firms. For the first time, many argued that government should regulate the economy in the interest of social justice. In discussion groups in Wisconsin, at rallies of farmers in Texas, and on the streets of New York and Boston, citizens wondered whether their governments at all levels should do more to promote the general welfare.

The Reform Campaigns

In states such as Illinois and New York, bands of women joined together as consumers pushed for better working conditions in factories and fair treatment of employees in department stores. Social workers and charity operatives decided that the plight of the poor was not simply the fault of those in need. Better government and more enlightened policies could uplift the downtrodden. As one settlement worker put it, "I never go into a tenement without longing for a better city government."

Doing History Online

Fixing the Blame for Hard Times

Go to the CourseMate website for this chapter and link to Primary Sources. Read Eugene Debs's address to the American Railway Union and Henry Demarest Lloyd's article, "Wealth Against Commonwealth." Where do Debs and Lloyd lay the blame for the state of the nation's economy during the depression of the 1890s?

www.cengagebrain.com

Women's participation in the process of change was significant. Julia Lathrop and Florence Kelley worked in Illinois improving state charitable institutions and inspecting factories. Mary Church Terrell led the National Association of Colored Women, founded in 1896, in making the women's clubs in the black community a more effective force for change. **Ida Wells-Barnett** rallied African American women against lynching from her first editorials in 1892 and then joined Terrell in further campaigns against these illegal executions. The suffrage movement and the women's clubs among white middle-class women and their black counterparts slowly established the basis for additional reforms after 1900.

A leading voice for a new role for women was **Charlotte Perkins Gilman**, whose major work, *Women and Economics*, was published in 1898. Gilman advocated that women should seek economic independence. The home, she argued, was a primitive institution that should be transformed through modern industrial practices lest it impede "the blessed currents of progress that lead and lift us all." Housework should be professionalized and homes transformed into domestic factories; women would then be free to pursue their own destinies, which could include social reform. Gilman's work influenced a generation of women reformers as well as future feminists.

The renewed emphasis on reform during the 1890s also affected the long-standing campaign to control the sale and use of alcoholic beverages. In 1895, the Reverend H. H. Russell established the Anti-Saloon League in Oberlin, Ohio. Its organization relied on a network of local Protestant churches throughout the nation. The prohibition campaigns in the South brought black women and white women together in a brief alliance to cripple what they both regarded as an important social evil. In some parts of North Carolina, for example, white women organized chapters of the Woman's Christian Temperance Union (WCTU) among black women. When white volunteers did not visit black neighborhoods, however, black women took over and set up their own organizations. Even as racial barriers rose in the South, black women and white women continued to work together to curb drinking until the end of the 1890s, when deteriorating race relations made it politically impossible to do so.

To counter the drive for prohibition, brewers and liquor producers created lobbying groups to match the Anti-Saloon League and the persistent militance of the WCTU. Brewing associations appeared in battleground states such as Texas to coordinate strategies in local option elections and to get "wet" voters to the polls. Antiprohibition sentiment flourished among Irish Americans and German Americans in the cities and towns of the Northeast and Midwest.

As the depression revealed social problems and political injustices, efforts at reform were made in the cities. In Detroit, Hazen Pingree had been elected mayor in 1889. During the depression, he decided to construct his own political machine to pursue social justice through lower utility rates and expanded government services. That brought him into conflict with the streetcar companies and utilities that dominated Detroit politics. In Chicago, a British editor, William T. Stead, visited the city for the Columbian Exposition in 1893. What he saw in the slums led him to write *If Christ Came to Chicago* in 1894. Stead's exposure of urban corruption and decadence led to the formation of the Chicago Civic Federation, which sought to control gambling, clean up the slums, and promote fair rates for

(LC-USZ62-106490)/Library of Congress Prints and Photographs Division)

Charlotte Perkins Gilman.
Charlotte Perkins Gilman's writings challenged the traditional roles that women occupied in the household. She became an important advocate for a new kind of thinking about how women should function in society.

Wells-Barnett, Ida B. (1862–1931) African American journalist and leader of an anti-lynching campaign.

Gilman, Charlotte Perkins (1860–1935) Feminist who advocated that women should seek economic independence; author of *Women and Economics* (1898).

public transportation and services. By the mid-1890s, these examples of urban reform sparked ideas that would flourish during the Progressive era a decade later.

As the depression worsened, citizens looked to their state governments for answers and instead found political and social problems that rivaled the plight of the cities. In Wisconsin a Republican politician, Robert M. La Follette, built a political following by attacking the entrenched organization within his own party. He called for primary elections to choose candidates for office rather than leave the decision to the politicians and their rigged meetings.

The work of reform governors and their supporters in the states led to greater reliance on experts and nonpartisan commissions in making decisions about public policy. Railroad commissions, public utility commissions, and investigative boards to oversee key industries were formed. By the end of the decade, however, observers believed that meaningful reform would come only when the federal government shaped national legislation to curb railroads and trusts engaged in interstate commerce.

Substantive Due Process and Its Critics

Among the most powerful obstacles to reform were judges who upheld business interests. The doctrine of substantive due process gave state and federal judges a way to block legislative attempts to regulate economic behavior. According to this doctrine, the due process clause of the Fourteenth Amendment did not apply only to the issue of whether the procedure used to pass a law had been fair. Judges might consider how the substance of the law affected life, liberty, and property. They had the right to decide whether a law regulating business enterprise was fair to the corporation being supervised.

Judges also interpreted federal laws in ways that limited efforts to curb corporate power. The same year (1895) that the Court issued the *E. C. Knight* decision, which constrained the scope of the Sherman Antitrust Act, it also ruled in *Pollock v. Farmers' Loan and Trust Co.* that the income tax provisions of the Wilson-Gorman Tariff Act were unconstitutional because they were a direct tax that the Constitution prohibited. In labor cases, courts imposed injunctions to bar unions from boycotts and strikes.

A few jurists and lawyers, however, had doubts about this philosophy of favoring corporations. In Massachusetts, Oliver Wendell Holmes, Jr., had published *The Common Law* in 1881. Holmes contended that "the life of the law has not been logic; it has been experience." By this he meant that judges should not base their rulings on abstract premises and theories such as freedom of contract, but should consider the rational basis of a law in judging whether it was constitutional or not.

Conservative himself, Holmes was ready to defer to the popular will in legislative matters. If the Constitution did not prohibit a state from building a slaughterhouse or regulating an industry, his response was, "God-dammit, let them build it." In Nebraska, Roscoe Pound was evolving a similar reality-based approach to legal thinking that became known as sociological jurisprudence. Louis D. Brandeis of Massachusetts was gaining a reputation as the "People's Lawyer" who believed that the legal system should serve small businesses and consumers as well as large corporations.

Pragmatism and Realism

The philosopher William James of Harvard University developed an explanation for what political and legal reformers were trying to do: *pragmatism*. James believed that truth is more than an abstract concept. Truth must demonstrate its value in the real world. To James, pragmatism meant "looking away from first things, principles, 'categories,' supposed necessities; and of looking towards last things, fruits, consequences, facts." He divided the world into tough-minded people, who based their actions on facts and pragmatic truths, and tender-minded people, who were swayed by abstractions. His philosophy emphasized self-reliance and gritty reality. It appealed to a generation of reformers who sought practical solutions to the problems they saw in their communities and the nation as a whole.

Another spokesman for reform was a University of Chicago teacher and philosopher named John Dewey. In his major work, *The School and Society* (1899), Dewey contended that schools should undertake the task of preparing students to live in a complex, industrial world. The public school must do more than transmit academic knowledge for its own sake. As an institution, it should be a means of instilling democratic values and usable skills. Education, Dewey wrote, "is the fundamental method of social progress and reform." During the 1890s, writers and artists turned to the world around them. They preached the doctrine of realism and tried to capture the complexity of a natural world in which science, technology, and capitalism were challenging older values. **Stephen Crane** depicted the ways in which the city exploited and destroyed a young woman in *Maggie: A Girl of the Streets* (1893). Two noteworthy practitioners of literary naturalism were Frank Norris and Theodore Dreiser. Norris wrote about California railroads in *The Octopus* (1901) and about the wheat market in Chicago in *The Pit* (1903). In his Darwinian world, humanity was trapped in the impersonal grip of soulless corporations. In *Sister Carrie* (1900), Dreiser described how a small-town girl went to work in Chicago and was consumed by its temptations. These novels reached a large audience, and their depiction of characters caught in an amoral universe intensified the sentiment for reform.

By the 1890s, then, the currents that would come together as the Progressive movement of the 1900–1920 period were forming. Urban reformers, believers in the Social Gospel, politically active women, candidates angry with the established powers in their state's dominant party—all of these groups shared a pervasive discontent with the state of society. The volatile domestic and international events of the 1890s would prepare the ground for a generation of reform.

Crane, Stephen (1871–1900) American naturalist writer, author of *Maggie: A Girl of the Streets* (1893) and *The Red Badge of Courage* (1895).

African Americans and Segregation

In addition to experiencing the economic deprivations affecting the country as a whole during the 1890s, African Americans confronted the ever-tightening grip of segregation in the South. Although blacks had made great strides in building viable communities and economic institutions since Reconstruction, white southerners disliked their advancement. A spokesman for blacks emerged in **Booker T. Washington,** who argued that African Americans should emphasize hard work and personal development rather than rebelling against their condition.

Washington believed that African Americans must demonstrate their worthiness for citizenship through their own achievements. In 1895, he reached a national audience when he spoke at the Cotton States and International Exposition in Atlanta. His **Atlanta Compromise** told white Americans what they wanted to hear about black citizens. Accordingly, what Washington said made him the leading black figure in the United States for a generation. "In all the things that are purely social, we can be separate as the fingers," Washington proclaimed, "yet one as the hand in all things essential to mutual progress." To his fellow blacks he said, "Cast down your bucket where you are"

Washington, Booker T. (1856–1914) Educator, founder of Tuskegee Institute. He argued that African Americans should emphasize hard work and personal development rather than agitating for social reform.

Atlanta Compromise (1895) Speech by Booker T. Washington outlining a program for African American self-help, industrial education, and acceptance of white supremacy.

(© CORBIS)

Booker T. Washington.
Booker T. Washington was a captivating speaker who preached that African Americans must demonstrate to whites their capacity to achieve progress.

Plessy, Homer A. (1863–1925)
In a test of an 1890 law specifying that blacks must ride in separate railroad cars, this one-eighth-black man boarded a train and sat in the car reserved for whites. When the conductor instructed him to move, he refused and was arrested.

Plessy v. Ferguson **(1896)** Supreme Court decision that approved racial segregation.

and be "patient, law-abiding and unresentful." Any "agitation of questions of social equality" would be "the extremest folly."

Washington's white audience gave him an enthusiastic response, and white philanthropists funded his school, the Tuskegee Institute, generously. Behind the scenes, Washington dominated the political lives of blacks and he secretly funded court challenges to segregation. In public, however, he came to symbolize an accommodation with the existing racial system.

The Supreme Court put its stamp of approval on segregation as a legal doctrine a year later. On June 7, 1892, **Homer A. Plessy,** who was one-eighth black, had been arrested in Louisiana for riding in a railroad car reserved for whites. He appealed his case all the way to the Supreme Court, which heard oral arguments in April 1896 and rendered its judgment five weeks later. By a vote of seven to one in the case of ***Plessy v. Ferguson***, the justices upheld the Louisiana law and, by implication, the principle of segregation. Writing for the majority, Justice Henry Billings Brown said that the Fourteenth Amendment "could not have been intended to abolish distinctions based on color, or to enforce social, as distinguished from political equality, or a commingling of the two races upon terms unsatisfactory to either." He rejected the argument that "the enforced separation of the races stamps the colored race with a badge of inferiority." In a dissenting opinion, Justice John Marshall Harlan responded that "our Constitution is color-blind, and neither knows nor tolerates classes among citizens." The *Plessy* ruling determined the legal situation of African Americans for more than half a century.

As the political rights of blacks diminished, white attacks on them increased. During the North Carolina elections of 1898, race was a key issue that led to a Democratic victory over the Populists, Republicans, and their African American allies. Once whites had won, they turned on the black-dominated local government in Wilmington, North Carolina. Several hundred whites attacked areas where blacks lived in December 1898, killing eleven people and driving residents from their homes. Lynchings in the South continued at a rate of more than one hundred per year. (See *Doing History: Lynching and the Rights of African Americans, 1898–1900*.)

Although black Americans faced daunting obstacles in the 1890s, they made substantial progress toward improved living conditions in ways that showed that they were more than simply the victims of white oppression. They founded colleges in the South, created self-help institutions in black churches, and developed pockets of well-off citizens in cities such as Washington, Boston, Baltimore, and Philadelphia. The National Association of Colored Women sought to become, in the words of its president, Mary Church Terrell, "partners in the great firm of progress and reform." African American resistance to segregation shaped the 1890s as much as did the white drive to subjugate blacks in the South and the North.

Doing History Lynching and the Rights
of African Americans, 1898–1900

*Lynching of blacks in the South persisted throughout the 1890s, and effective federal
action to stop this cruel practice did not occur. In 1898, Ida Wells-Barnett was one
of a number of white and black politicians who asked President William McKinley
to punish those responsible for killing an African American postmaster, by the name
of Baker, in Lake City, South Carolina. The statement she made, which appears
below, laid out her reasons for seeking federal action. Although he was not
responding directly to Wells-Barnett and this case, Senator Benjamin R. Tillman
offered a justification for lynching to the U.S. Senate in 1900 that represented the
southern rationale for extralegal murders. Their contrasting statements follow.*

Ida Wells-Barnett, 1898

For nearly twenty years lynching crimes, which
stand side by side with Armenian and Cuban
outrages, have been committed and permitted by
this Christian nation. Nowhere in the civilized
world save the United States of America do men,
possessing all civil and political power, go out in
bands of 50 and 5,000 to hunt down, shoot, hang
or burn to death a single individual, unarmed and
absolutely powerless. Statistics show that nearly
10,000 American citizens have been lynched in the
past twenty years. To our appeals for justice the
stereotyped reply has been that the governor could
not interfere in a state matter. Postmaster Baker's
case was a federal matter, pure and simply. He died
at his post of duty in defense of his country's honor,
as truly as did ever a soldier on the field of battle.
We refuse to believe this country, so powerful to
defend its citizens abroad, is unable to protect its
citizens at home.

Source: *Cleveland Gazette*, April 9, 1898, in Herbert Aptheker, ed.,
A Documentary History of the Negro People in the United States, vol. 2
(New York: Citadel Press, 1970), 798.

Benjamin R. Tillman, Congressional Speech on Segregation

We did not disfranchise the negroes until 1895. Then
we had a constitutional convention convened which
took the matter up calmly, deliberately, and
avowedly with the purpose of disfranchising as many
of them as we could under the fourteenth and
fifteenth amendments. We adopted the educational
qualification as the only means left to use, and the
negro is as contented and as prosperous and as well
protected in South Carolina today as in any State of
the Union south of the Potomac. He is not meddling
with politics, for he found that the more he meddled
with them the worse off he got. As to his "rights"—
I will not discuss them now. We of the South have
never recognized the right of the negro to govern
white men, and we never will. We have never
believed him to be the equal of the white man, and
we will not submit to his gratifying his lust on our
wives and daughters without lynching them. I would
to God the last one of them was in Africa and have
none of them had ever been brought to our shores.
But I will not pursue the subject further.

Source: U.S. Senate, *Congressional Record*, 56 Cong., 1. Sess.
(March 23, 1900), 3223–3224.

QUESTIONS for REFLECTION

1. How did the views of Ida Wells-Barnett and Benjamin R. Tillman differ on the issue of the rights of
   African Americans? Did they have a contrasting opinion about what it meant to be an American citizen?

2. What were the dominant motives behind Tillman's justification of lynching? How does Wells-Barnett
   regard this practice, and what arguments, religious and humanitarian, does she raise in attacking it?

3. To what extent did Tillman and his constituents accept the constitutional amendments that resulted
   from Reconstruction?

❖ Foreign Policy Challenges

Amid the political turmoil of the second Cleveland administration, the nation stood on the verge of becoming a world power. National leaders debated how to respond to increasing competition with powerful international rivals and the upsurge of nationalism among colonial peoples.

The first pressing issue was Hawaii. Grover Cleveland was not convinced that the revolution that had occurred in 1893 represented the will of the Hawaiian people (see Chapter 17), and dispatched a special commission to investigate conditions. Believing that the native population backed Queen Liliuokalani, he refused to send the treaty to the Senate and asked for restoration of the native government. The revolutionary government declined to yield power, however, and in 1894 the administration granted it diplomatic recognition.

Another foreign policy crisis occurred in 1894 when a dispute arose between Great Britain and Venezuela over the precise boundary line that separated Venezuela and British Guiana. The Cleveland administration concluded that the controversy was also a test of the Monroe Doctrine, which barred European influence in the Western Hemisphere. In 1895, the new secretary of state, Richard Olney, sent a diplomatic note to London that asserted that the United States was "practically sovereign on this continent, and its fiat is law upon the subjects to which it confines its interposition." The British initially rejected the argument, but in the end they decided to arbitrate their quarrel with Venezuela through a joint Anglo-American-Venezuelan commission to resolve the dispute, and the crisis passed.

The Cuban Crisis, 1895–1896

The most dangerous foreign policy issue that confronted Cleveland stemmed from the revolution that Cubans launched against Spanish rule in February 1895. The Wilson-Gorman Tariff Act had increased import duties on Cuban sugar, damaging the island's economy, which depended on sugar. Rebels took to the battlefield in February 1895 seeking to oust the Spanish. Unable to defeat the rebels in direct combat, the Spanish drove the civilian population into cities and fortified areas. The "reconcentration" camps where these refugees were housed were disease ridden and overcrowded.

The American public took a close interest in the Cuban situation. Investments in the island, totaling about $50 million, were threatened by the conflict. Religious denominations saw the brutality and famine of the rebellion as cause for concern and perhaps direct intervention. Sensational newspapers, known as the "yellow press" because one of them carried a popular comic strip about "The Yellow Kid," printed numerous stories about atrocities in Cuba. **William Randolph Hearst**, publisher of the *New York Morning Journal*, and Joseph Pulitzer of the *New York World* were the most sensational practitioners of this kind of "**yellow journalism.**" Concern about Cuba was a significant element in the nation's foreign policy during the mid-1890s.

President Cleveland did not recognize the Cubans as belligerents, and he informed the Spanish that they might count on the good offices of the United States in negotiating an end to the fighting. This position suited Spain, which followed a policy of procrastination to quell the revolt before the United States intervened. By the end of his administration, the president was pressing Spain to make concessions to the Cubans, but he never challenged Spain's right to exercise its sovereignty over the island, despite entreaties from Congress.

Hearst, William Randolph (1863–1951) The most celebrated publisher of yellow journalism.

yellow journalism A type of journalism that stressed lurid and sensational news to boost circulation.

The Battle of the Standards: 1896

The foreign policy problems of the Cleveland administration stemmed in part from the weakened political situation after the 1894 elections. Preferring to work alone and wary of threats on his life, Cleveland increased the number of guards around the White House and rarely ventured out to meet his fellow citizens. The reserves of gold were still shrinking, despite the repeal of the Sherman Silver Purchase Act in 1893. To bolster the reserves and bring in gold, the White House sold government bonds.

As the 1896 election approached, the Republicans, after their sweep of the 1894 election, wanted a candidate who could cash in on their likely victory. The front-runner was William McKinley of Ohio, a veteran of the Civil War, former member of Congress, and governor of Ohio from 1892 to 1896. A popular speaker, he was identified with the protective tariff. With the aid of his close friend Marcus A. Hanna, an industrialist from Ohio, McKinley became the favorite for the Republican nomination. His campaign slogan proclaimed him as the "Advance Agent of Prosperity."

McKinley won on the first ballot at the Republican National Convention in St. Louis in June 1896. The only difficult issue was gold and silver. Eastern Republicans wanted the party to endorse the gold standard. The key plank contained that language, but it also placated pro-silver Republicans with a promise to seek wider international use of silver. The Republicans expected to wage a tariff-centered campaign against a nominee saddled with the unpopularity of Cleveland.

Bryan and the Cross of Gold

The Democratic convention took an unexpected turn. After the elections of 1894, the free silver wing of the party dominated the South and West. By 1896, a young politician from Nebraska named William Jennings Bryan emerged as an articulate spokesman for the silver cause. At the Democratic National Convention in Chicago in July 1896, he arranged to be the final speaker on behalf of free silver. Bryan had a clear, musical voice that could be heard across the convention hall. The speech he gave, entitled the "Cross of Gold," became a classic moment in American political oratory. He asked the delegates whether the party would stand "upon the side of the idle holders of capital, or upon the side of the struggling masses?" His answer was simple. To those who wanted a gold standard, the Democrats would say: "You shall not press down upon the brow of labor this crown of thorns, you shall not crucify mankind upon a cross of gold." His audience was enthralled.

The next day the convention nominated Bryan for president on a free silver platform. A wave of support for Bryan swept the country, and the Republicans found their careful plans for the campaign suddenly at risk. Since the Democrats could not raise much in the way of campaign funds, Bryan decided to take his message to the voters. He prepared for an extensive nationwide campaign tour to speak on behalf of the common man, a rural nation, and the older agrarian virtues.

Bryan's nomination left the Populist Party in disarray. The Populists had delayed their national convention until after the two major parties had named their candidates, and they now faced a dilemma: if they failed to select Bryan as their candidate, they would be accused of depriving silver of any chance of victory; yet if they went along with Bryan's nomination, there would be no need for their party.

(LC-USZC4-1329/Library of Congress Prints and Photographs Division)

William McKinley: The First Modern President. William McKinley's use of his power as commander in chief, his improved relations with the press, and his mastery of Congress helped make him the first modern president.

With some reluctance, they ultimately decided to name Bryan as the presidential nominee and picked Thomas E. Watson as their vice-presidential choice. The Democrats refused to accept this awkward compromise; all that Watson's selection did was to confuse voters about which Bryan slate of elections they should pick.

Bryan, thirty-six years old, pursued the presidency with youthful energy. He traveled eighteen thousand miles and gave more than six hundred speeches; his audiences, estimated at a total of 3 million people, turned out to see the "Boy Orator of the Platte River." To counter Bryan, the Republicans raised between $3.5 million and $4 million from fearful corporations. The Democrats charged that the Republicans and their business allies were coercing workers to vote for McKinley.

The key to the Republican campaign was McKinley, who stayed home in Canton, Ohio, and let the voters come to him. As the weeks passed, more than 750,000 people stood in McKinley's yard to hear his speeches about the dangers of free silver. "If the free coinage of silver means a fifty-three cent dollar, then it is not an honest dollar," McKinley said. By mid-September, the tide turned against Bryan, and there were signs that the Republicans would win in November.

The result was the most decisive outcome since the 1872 presidential contest. McKinley had a margin of six hundred thousand popular votes and won 271 electoral votes to 176 for Bryan (see Map 18.1). Bryan ran well in the South, the Plains states, and the Far West. McKinley dominated in the Northeast, the mid-Atlantic states, and the Midwest. Despite his appeals to the labor vote, Bryan ran poorly in the cities. Free silver might lead to inflation, an idea that had little appeal to workers on fixed incomes. McKinley's argument that the tariff would restore prosperity also took hold in the more industrialized areas of the country. Bryan and the Populists had suggested that government should play a larger regulatory role; the voters had chosen instead to accept the economic nationalism of the Republicans as embodied in the tariff and the gold standard.

MAP 18.1

The Election of 1896

The election of 1896 was a climax to the upheavals of the mid-1890s. Note the sectional alignment that divided the nation between the agrarian South and West, which supported William Jennings Bryan, and the industrialized East and Midwest, where William McKinley and the Republicans were strong.

(Copyright © Cengage Learning)

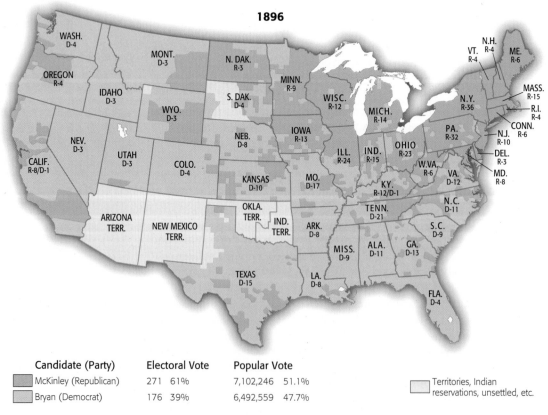

1896

Candidate (Party)	Electoral Vote		Popular Vote	
McKinley (Republican)	271	61%	7,102,246	51.1%
Bryan (Democrat)	176	39%	6,492,559	47.7%

Territories, Indian reservations, unsettled, etc.

❖ The War with Spain and Overseas Expansion, 1898–1900

When Grover Cleveland departed in March 1897, he left a weakened presidency. McKinley improved relations with the press, which Cleveland had ignored; he traveled extensively to promote his policies; and he used experts and commissions to strengthen the operation of the national government.

In domestic policy, McKinley persuaded Congress to enact the Dingley Tariff Act of 1897, which raised customs rates. He also sought, without success, to convince European nations to agree to wider use of silver through an international agreement. As a result, when the Republicans gained control of both houses of Congress after the 1898 election, the Gold Standard Act of 1900 reaffirmed that gold, and only gold, was the basis of the nation's currency. Gold discoveries in South Africa and Alaska inflated the currency by making more gold available. Returning prosperity relieved the agricultural tensions of the decade.

Spain and Cuba

The Cuban rebellion of 1895 extended into McKinley's tenure as president and the crisis was continuing to grow. McKinley wanted Spain to withdraw from Cuba if its forces could not suppress the rebellion quickly. Any solution must be acceptable to the Cuban rebels. Since they would accept nothing less than the end of Spanish rule, there was little basis for a negotiated settlement. During 1897, however, McKinley tried to persuade Spain to agree to a diplomatic solution.

At first it appeared that the president's policy might work. In the fall of 1897 the Spanish government moved toward granting the Cubans some control over their internal affairs. Foreign policy, however, was to remain in Spanish hands. The practice of moving Cubans into reconcentration camps was abandoned. However, the situation worsened during the early months of 1898 as the rebellion persisted. On January 12, 1898, pro-Spanish elements in Cuba rioted against the autonomy program. To monitor the situation, the White House sent a warship to Havana. The battleship U.S.S. *Maine* arrived there on January 25. On February 1, Spain insisted that its sovereignty over Cuba must be preserved even if it meant resisting foreign intervention.

On February 9, 1898, newspapers in the United States published a letter written by the Spanish minister to the United States, Enrique Dupuy de Lôme, to a friend; Cuban rebels had intercepted the letter. In it, de Lôme described McKinley as "weak and a bidder for the admiration of the crowd." These insulting remarks led to de Lôme's recall and resignation. The minister's other statements revealed, however, that Spain was playing for time in its negotiations with Washington in hopes that the Americans might change their mind or that pressure from European countries would lead them to do so.

The Sinking of the *Maine*: February 15, 1898

On February 15, the U.S.S. *Maine* exploded in Havana Harbor, killing 260 men. The cause of the blast, according to modern research, was spontaneous combustion in a coal bunker. In 1898, however, the public believed that Spain had either caused an external explosion or had failed to prevent it. McKinley established a naval board of inquiry to probe the disaster. The deadline for its report was mid-March 1898. While he waited, McKinley made military preparations and explored unsuccessfully the idea of buying Cuba from Spain.

On March 17, a Republican senator who had visited Cuba, Redfield Proctor of Vermont, told the Senate that conditions in the country were horrible. Two days later, McKinley learned that the naval board had concluded, on the basis of the science of the time and the physical evidence, that an external explosion had caused the destruction of the *Maine*. When the report went to Congress, public pressure on the president to intervene in Cuba mounted.

McKinley pushed Spain to agree to an armistice in the fighting that still raged in Cuba or to permit American mediation that would end in Cuban independence. However, the Spanish were opposed to independence for Cuba in any form. Still, McKinley was able to hold off Congress until Spain had another chance to consider its options. When a negative answer arrived from Spain on March 31, 1898, McKinley prepared to put the issue before Congress. There was one last flurry of diplomatic activity, but the Spanish still refused to yield on the key demands of the United States.

McKinley sent his message to Congress on April 11, requesting presidential authority to end the fighting in Cuba through armed force if necessary. Over the following week, Congress debated the president's request. To show that the United States had no selfish motives, the lawmakers adopted an amendment offered by Senator Henry M. Teller, a Colorado Democrat. The Teller Amendment stated that the United States did not intend to control Cuba or annex it. Yet Congress also declined to extend official recognition to the Cuban rebels to preserve freedom of action for the United States. For McKinley, the important result was a resolution authorizing him to act; this was passed on April 19, and the president signed it the following day. Spain immediately broke diplomatic relations with the United States; it declared war on April 24.

The Spanish-American War, 1898

The war between the United States and Spain began with a stunning naval victory. On May 1, 1898, Commodore George Dewey and the Asiatic naval squadron defeated the Spanish navy at Manila Bay in the Philippine Islands. The U.S. unit was in the waters of the Philippines because of war plans that had been developed in 1895 and updated as relations with Spain worsened. The goal was to hit the Spanish hard in the Philippines and thus pressure them to surrender Cuba. The triumph at Manila Bay made Dewey a national hero, but it confronted the president with new opportunities and problems in foreign policy.

To follow up on Dewey's success, the McKinley administration dispatched troops to the Philippines. The president wanted the option of acquiring the islands as a result of the war. He thought that a port in the Philippines might be enough, but he intended to maintain flexibility.

With the Philippines at stake, the Hawaiian Islands gained in strategic value. A treaty of annexation had been worked out during 1897, but the pact stalled in Congress. After the war began, the president and congressional leaders turned to a strategy of annexation by means of a legislative resolution that needed only a simple majority from Congress. Through presidential persuasion, the required votes for the resolution were obtained in July 1898, and Hawaii was annexed.

Meanwhile, U.S. policy toward the Philippines and their possible acquisition became a source of tension with Filipino leaders, notably Emilio Aguinaldo, who wanted independence. The administration instructed army and navy officers not to have any formal dealings with the Filipinos. The buildup of military strength continued, and the ambitions of the Filipinos were seen as an obstacle to American policy rather than as a legitimate expression of nationalism.

The main combat of the war took place in Cuba (see Map 18.2). The U.S. Army numbered 25,000 men, so the nation turned to volunteers. In the first wave

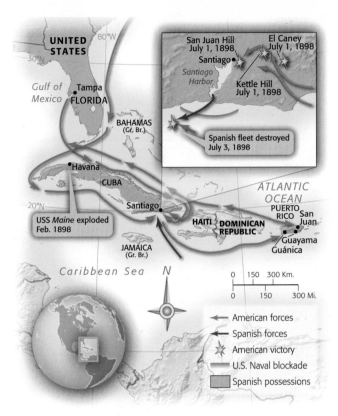

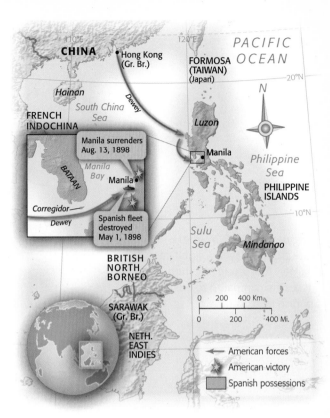

(Copyright © Cengage Learning)

MAP 18.2

The Spanish-American War, 1898

The main fighting in the war with Spain was on the island of Cuba and in the Caribbean. This map shows the movement of American and Spanish naval forces toward the decisive battles in the vicinity of Santiago de Cuba, as well as the capture of Puerto Rico.

of national enthusiasm, there were 1 million volunteers, far more than the army could handle. Eventually about 280,000 men saw active duty. In the regular army, an important part of the force that fought the Spanish were the four regiments composed of African American soldiers, or the "Smoked Yankees," as the Spanish troops described them. Seasoned fighters against Indians, the black soldiers were ordered to move south and prepare to invade Cuba. On their way through the southern states, they encountered scorn, segregation, and threats.

The African American soldiers did not endure such treatment quietly. When they boarded segregated railroad cars, they sat wherever they pleased. If they saw signs that barred their presence, they took down the signs. Violence broke out between white troops and black troops in Florida, and men were killed and wounded in the exchanges of gunfire. Seeing all this, one soldier asked poignantly: "Is America any better than Spain?" Once the black regiments reached Cuba, their military contribution was significant. They earned numerous decorations for bravery, and five of them won the Congressional Medal of Honor.

In late June, the U.S. Navy found the Spanish fleet in the harbor of Santiago de Cuba, and army detachments went ashore to engage the Spanish forces holding the city. On July 1, the army, commanded by General William R. Shafter, defeated the Spanish defenders at the Battle of San Juan Hill. Theodore Roosevelt and his volunteer regiment of Rough Riders took part in the battle, receiving timely support from their black comrades. On July 3, the navy destroyed the Spanish fleet when it tried to escape from Santiago Harbor. Negotiations for an armistice began. McKinley insisted that Spain relinquish Cuba and Puerto Rico and that the fate of the Philippines be discussed at the peace conference. Spain did not like these terms, but it had no choice but to accept them, which it did on August 12, 1898.

(The Granger Collection New York)

African American Soldiers. Black troops played a significant, if largely forgotten, role in the successful campaign to oust the Spanish from Cuba.

John Hay, soon to be McKinley's secretary of state, called it "a splendid little war." Victory had been achieved at a low cost in terms of combat deaths: 281 officers and men. However, malaria, yellow fever, and other diseases killed more than 2,500 others. A public outcry arose after the war about the condition of the army, and McKinley named a commission to investigate the leadership of the War Department and the way the war had been conducted. The commission's report led to reforms such as general staff shakeups and improved organization that strengthened the future fighting ability of the army. The war also strengthened the power of the presidency because of McKinley's expansive use of his role as commander in chief of the armed forces.

The peace conference with Spain was held in Paris. McKinley appointed a commission that included several senators who would ultimately vote on any treaty that they negotiated. The president was aware that Germany and Japan had an interest in the Philippines, and he intended for the United States to retain control of the islands. American officials did not believe that the Filipinos could determine their own destiny; the islands would fall into the hands of another power.

To build support for American control of the Philippines, McKinley made effective use of the powers of his office. During October, he toured the Midwest. Ordinarily presidents did not take part in congressional election campaigns. However, though billed as a nonpartisan event, McKinley's tour helped Republican candidates in the 1898 congressional contest. It also gave the president an opportunity to state the case for a more expansive foreign policy. In a typical address, he told an Iowa audience that "we do not want to shirk a single responsibility that has been put upon us by the results of the war."

The Philippines were the most divisive issue at the peace conference. On October 25, 1898, the president's commissioners asked him for instructions. On October 28, he responded that he could see "but one plain path of duty, the acceptance of the archipelago." In the peace treaty signed on December 10, 1898, the United States gained the Philippines, Guam, and Puerto Rico (see Map 18.3). Spain gave up its claims to Cuba and received a payment of $20 million for what it had lost. The United States obtained legal sovereignty over the Philippines but would soon face challenges from the island's inhabitants. Opponents of the treaty, calling themselves anti-imperialists, aroused public sentiment against the

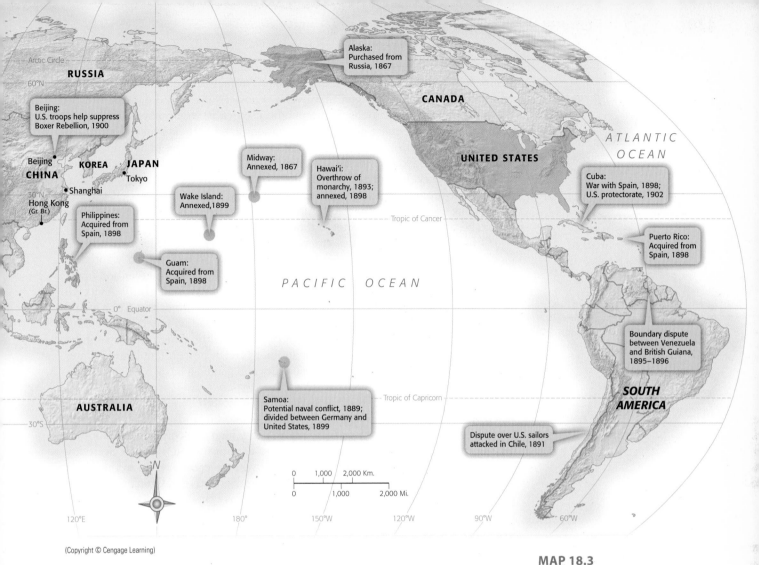

Alaska:
Purchased from
Russia, 1867

RUSSIA

Beijing:
U.S. troops help suppress
Boxer Rebellion, 1900

Beijing
KOREA
JAPAN
CHINA
Tokyo
Shanghai
Hong Kong
(Gr. Br.)

Philippines:
Acquired from
Spain, 1898

Wake Island:
Annexed,1899

Midway:
Annexed, 1867

Hawai'i:
Overthrow of
monarchy, 1893;
annexed, 1898

Guam:
Acquired from
Spain, 1898

CANADA

UNITED STATES

ATLANTIC
OCEAN

Cuba:
War with Spain, 1898;
U.S. protectorate, 1902

Tropic of Cancer

Puerto Rico:
Acquired from
Spain, 1898

PACIFIC OCEAN

Equator

Boundary dispute
between Venezuela
and British Guiana,
1895–1896

SOUTH
AMERICA

AUSTRALIA

Samoa:
Potential naval conflict, 1889;
divided between Germany and
United States, 1899

Tropic of Capricorn

Dispute over U.S. sailors
attacked in Chile, 1891

0   1,000   2,000 Km.

0   1,000   2,000 Mi.

(Copyright © Cengage Learning)

MAP 18.3

U.S. Overseas Expansion, 1867–1899

For four decades after the Civil War the United States expanded, slowly at first and then with a rush in the 1890s. This map shows what the nation acquired and when it did so. It also indicates where the United States was involved with Latin American nations and in some instances the great European powers.

administration. In the end, believing that the Democrats would benefit if the issue was settled before the 1900 elections, William Jennings Bryan endorsed the treaty. That action divided the opposition at a key point. The Senate approved the Treaty of Paris on February 6, 1899, by a vote of 57 to 27, one more than the necessary two-thirds.

As the Senate voted, the nation knew that fighting had erupted in the Philippines between U.S. soldiers and the Filipino troops that Aguinaldo commanded. Relations between the two sides had worsened during December 1898 as it became clear that the United States did not intend to leave the islands. Although the president asserted that his nation had "no imperial designs" on the Philippines, anti-imperialists and the Filipinos were not convinced. For Aguinaldo and his supporters, it seemed that they had ousted the Spanish only to replace them with another imperial master, the United States.

During 1899, the U.S. Army defeated the Filipinos in conventional battles, and the administration sent out a commission to work out a civil government under U.S. sovereignty. However, the Filipinos turned to guerrilla tactics. Their soldiers hit selected targets and then blended back into the population. Faced with this new threat, the U.S. Army responded by killing some Filipino prisoners and torturing others to gain information. With revelations of these misdeeds, enthusiasm for further imperialistic adventures ebbed.

During the last two years of McKinley's first term, imperialism became a heated issue. An Anti-Imperialist League, created in November 1898, united the opposition against McKinley's foreign policy. Critics of expansionism, including

Doing History Online

President McKinley Learns of the Philippine Insurrection

Go to the CourseMate website for this chapter and link to Primary Sources. Based on your reading of the text and the excerpt from the diary of George B. Cortelyou, answer the following questions: Why had the Filipinos attacked the U.S. forces near Manila? What was the peace treaty to which President McKinley referred? When did the Senate approve the treaty and what part might these events have played in senatorial deliberations?

www.cengagebrain.com

steelmaker Andrew Carnegie, House Speaker Thomas B. Reed, and the longtime reformer Carl Schurz, charged that overseas possessions would damage the nation's democratic institutions. Some people used racist arguments to block the acquisition of lands where nonwhite populations lived. Others evoked moral concern about imperialism. Advocates of empire adapted the ideas of Social Darwinism and Anglo-Saxon supremacy to justify the acquisition of other countries. Theodore Roosevelt, Henry Cabot Lodge of Massachusetts, and their allies contended that the nation could not escape the world responsibilities that the war with Spain had brought. By 1900, Americans believed that the gains of empire should be retained and protected but not increased.

Other foreign policy issues emerged after the war. The Teller Amendment blocked the annexation of Cuba, but the McKinley administration wanted to ensure that the island did not become a target of European intervention, most notably from Germany. A military government ran Cuba during 1899. As a civil government developed, the United States insisted on guarantees that Cuba would retain political and military ties with the country that had liberated it. The result of this process was the Platt Amendment of March 1901, which barred an independent Cuba from allying itself with another foreign power. The United States had the right to intervene to preserve stability and gained a naval base at Guantanamo in Cuba.

The acquisition of the Philippines heightened interest about the fate of China, where European powers sought to establish economic and political spheres of influence. Worried about the nation's trade with China and concerned about preserving that country's territorial integrity, the administration, through Secretary of State John Hay, issued in September 1899 what became known as the Open Door Notes. The messages asked European countries active in China to preserve trading privileges and other economic rights that gave the United States a chance to compete for markets there. The replies of the powers were noncommittal, but Hay announced in March 1900 that the other nations had accepted the U.S. position in principle. The Open Door Notes became a significant assertion of U.S. interest in China.

When antiforeign sentiment in China, especially against Western missionaries, led to the Boxer Rebellion during the summer of 1900, an important test of the Open Door principle occurred. Secret associations known as the Righteous and Harmonious Fists (hence Boxers) launched a series of attacks on Westerners in China. Europeans who had taken refuge in Beijing (Peking) were rescued by an international force that included twenty-five hundred U.S. soldiers. President McKinley justified sending the troops into a country with which the United States was at peace as a legitimate use of his war power under the Constitution. Secretary Hay reaffirmed the U.S. commitment to the Open Door policy in a diplomatic circular to the powers that he issued on July 3, 1900. McKinley withdrew the troops rapidly after their rescue mission had been completed.

The Spanish-American War and the expansion of American commitments in the Pacific demonstrated the need for a waterway that would link the two oceans and enable the navy to conduct its growing worldwide responsibilities. The McKinley administration laid the groundwork for a canal across Central America when it renegotiated the Clayton-Bulwer Treaty of 1850 with Great Britain. That document prohibited both nations from exercising exclusive control over any future waterway. After extended negotiations with the British, a treaty was worked out in the summer of 1901.

The 1900 Election and a New Century

By 1899, McKinley's reelection seemed assured: prosperity had returned, and the conflict in the Philippines was being won. McKinley's vice president, Garret A.

Hobart, died in November 1899. Theodore Roosevelt, the popular young governor of New York, became McKinley's running mate. To oppose McKinley, the Democrats again turned to William Jennings Bryan. Bryan attacked imperialism as a threat to the nation's institutions, and accused the Republicans of being the tools of the trusts and the business community. The Democratic candidate also renewed his pleas for a free silver policy.

Because in that era incumbent presidents did not make speeches, McKinley allowed Theodore Roosevelt to do most of the campaigning. Bryan made so many criticisms that his campaign lacked a clear theme. McKinley increased his margin in the popular vote over what he had achieved four years earlier. The result in the electoral college was 292 for McKinley and 155 for Bryan.

McKinley gained further victories in foreign policy. Congress set up a civilian government for the Philippines when the insurrection had ended, which occurred shortly after the capture of Emilio Aguinaldo in March 1901. On May 27, 1901, the Supreme Court ruled in the *Insular Cases* that the Philippines and Puerto Rico were properly possessions of the United States but that their inhabitants had not become citizens of the country. The decision upheld McKinley's colonial policy and provided legal justification for imperialism.

Meanwhile, the president was turning his attention to two major domestic issues: the growth of big business and the issue of high tariffs. By 1901, McKinley was persuaded that some action was necessary to enforce the Sherman Antitrust Act of 1890. He had also modified his earlier support for the protective tariff and now believed that reciprocal trade treaties should be adopted that would lower duties on products entering the United States. As he had done to secure ratification of the treaty with Spain in 1898, McKinley planned to travel extensively during 1901 to raise the trade issue with the American people. That decision would bring him to Buffalo, New York, in September 1901 to make a speech about free trade and reciprocal tariff treaties. It was there that an anarchist named Leon Czolgosz, who saw the president as the embodiment of political corruption, shot him on September 6. McKinley died a week later, leaving the presidency in the hands of his vigorous young vice president, Theodore Roosevelt.

As the new century began, McKinley had revived the power of the presidency after the decades of congressional supremacy that followed the Civil War. He had expanded the size of the president's staff, begun to involve the press in the coverage of White House affairs, and personalized the office through his travels. In many respects, McKinley was the first modern president.

The nation saw the arrival of the twentieth century on December 31, 1900, with a mixture of confidence about what the United States had accomplished and apprehension about what the future held. The depression of the 1890s remained a vivid memory for most citizens, even with the return of prosperity after 1897. The shift in attitudes toward government and its role that had occurred during the hard times led many people to advocate for programs of social reform.

Although the often-anticipated social revolution of the 1890s had not occurred, influential leaders such as Theodore Roosevelt worried about the potential for violence and upheaval if moderate reforms did not take place. In addition, the nation faced the problems of segregation, the future of Native Americans, and the place of immigrants in American society. Americans turned to these questions with an energy that made the twenty years between 1900 and 1920 famous as an age of political reform and government regulation.

CHAPTER REVIEW, 1893–1901

SUMMARY

- The country faced the challenge of a serious economic depression.
- Labor unrest and social dislocation proliferated.
- The Democratic Party split into competing factions and lost national power.
- The Populists failed to become a viable third party.
- The Republicans gained a national majority in the 1894 and 1896 elections.
- William McKinley revitalized the presidency.
- Tension with Spain over Cuba led to war in 1898.
- The United States had acquired an overseas empire by 1900.

IDENTIFICATIONS

George Pullman
Pullman strike
William McKinley
Ida Wells-Barnett
Charlotte Perkins Gilman
Stephen Crane
Booker T. Washington
Atlanta Compromise
Homer A. Plessy
Plessy v. Ferguson
William Randolph Hearst
yellow journalism

MAKING CONNECTIONS: LOOKING AHEAD ⅲ▶

In the next chapter, Theodore Roosevelt takes the stage as one of the leaders of the Progressive movement of political reform. In what ways does this chapter foreshadow these developments?

1. How did attitudes change during the 1890s about the proper role of government?

2. What problems did imperialism leave to be solved after 1900?

3. How did Americans see themselves and their country as the twentieth century opened?

4. What was the position of the United States in the world in 1900?

RECOMMENDED READINGS

Beatty, Jack. *Age of Betrayal: The Triumph of Money in America, 1865–1900.* (2007). A new, very critical analysis of the late nineteenth century.

Campbell, W. Joseph. *Yellow Journalism: Puncturing the Myths, Defining the Legacies* (2001). A skeptical look at the sensational journalism and the war with Spain.

Gilmore, Glenda. *Gender and Jim Crow: Women and the Politics of White Supremacy in North Carolina, 1896–1920* (1996). An excellent study of the ways in which black and white women interacted during the era of segregation.

Offner, John L. *An Unwanted War: The Diplomacy of the United States and Spain over Cuba, 1895–1898* (1992). Valuable for the interplay of Cubans, Spaniards, and Americans as the war drew near.

Perez, Louis A. *The War of 1898: The United States and Cuba in History and Historiography* (1998). Offers an insightful, sympathetic look at the war from a perspective that takes Cuba into account.

Postel, Charles. *The Populist Vision* (2007). Looks at the impact of the farmers' revolt on American history.

Richardson, Heather Cox. *West from Appomattox: The Reconstruction of America after the Civil War* (2007). Considers the 1890s in the light of the aftermath of the Civil War and Reconstruction.

Smith, Joseph. *The Spanish-American War: Conflict in the Caribbean and the Pacific, 1845–1902* (1994). A good one-volume account of the military history of the war.

Traxel, David. *1898: The Birth of the American Century* (1998). An interpretive survey of the war with Spain and its consequences for the nation.

Williams, R. Hal. *Years of Decision: American Politics in the 1890s* (1993). The best narrative account of this important decade.

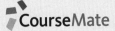 **CourseMate** Go to the CourseMate website at www.cengagebrain.com for additional study tools and review materials for this chapter.

19

Progressivism: Agendas for Change

1901–1914

Theodore Roosevelt and Modern America

Social Changes
A Nation of Consumers
Theodore Roosevelt in Power
Controlling Big Business and the Trusts
Labor and Race Relations in the
 Roosevelt Era
Roosevelt and Foreign Policy
The Election of 1904

**Progressive Campaigns to Reform
the Nation**

Currents of Reform
The Muckrakers
Women and Progressive Reform
Reform in the Cities and States

Roosevelt, Taft, and the Modern Presidency

The Expansion of Regulation

Doing History: Theodore Roosevelt
 and the Regulation of Business

Roosevelt and World Politics
Roosevelt's Domestic Policies
The 1908 Presidential Election
Taft's Conservative Presidency

The Battle over Conservation
Roosevelt's Return

Progressive Victories

Woman Suffrage and Prohibition
Restriction of Immigration
Saving Children
Reforming the Workplace
Varieties of Labor Protest

**Republican Discord and Democratic
Opportunity**

The Struggle Between Roosevelt
 and Taft
The Democratic Opportunity
Woodrow Wilson and the
 1912 Election

**Reform and Social Change During
the Wilson Years**

Tariff Reform
The Federal Reserve System
Wilson and the Progressive Agenda
Modern Technology and Mass Markets
Artistic and Social Ferment
The New Leisure

MAKING CONNECTIONS

◀▥▥ LOOKING BACK

The events that dominated American life in the 1890s stemmed from problems that had been accumulating since the Civil War. Chapter 18 discussed the political and economic systems as they confronted the effects of a major depression and the country's increasing presence on the world stage. Before starting Chapter 19, you should be able to answer the following questions:

1. What were the options open to the government when an economic collapse occurred?

2. Why did President Grover Cleveland face the political blame for problems with business and finance that he inherited?

3. Why did the Republicans become the big winners in the politics of the 1890s?

4. How did American social commentators react to the panic of 1893 and its effects on the nation?

5. Should the United States have intervened in Cuba in 1898?

On September 6, 1901, President William McKinley was shot in Buffalo, New York. A week later he died, and Vice President Theodore Roosevelt became president, launching what became known as the Progressive era. Responding to the social and economic impacts of industrialism, Americans endeavored to curb the power of large businesses, improve conditions for consumers, and reform the political parties. The issues that Americans debated at the turn of the twentieth century would dominate the agenda of domestic policy for decades.

When Theodore Roosevelt left office in March 1909, progressivism entered a phase of partisan upheaval. The Democrats moved toward a more active role for the national government and away from states' rights, while Socialists mounted a vigorous challenge from the left. Political ferment revealed reform tensions: campaigns for woman suffrage, the prohibition of alcohol, restriction of immigration, and social justice created new coalitions that sometimes followed party lines and at other times disrupted them. In the process, progressivism provoked a conservative reaction that limited the possibilities for reform.

The social and economic forces creating a consumer society also gathered strength. Henry Ford's low-priced automobile gained greater popularity, while other products of industrialism attracted more customers. Women found more opportunities for employment. For minorities, however, these years saw continuing tension and racial strife, while international developments forced Americans to reckon with thorny foreign policy challenges.

❖ Theodore Roosevelt and Modern America

In 1901, Americans balanced confidence about the future in a new century with worries about the direction of their society. The population stood at 76 million, up from 63 million ten years earlier. Immigrants accelerated the population growth, with new arrivals coming at a prodigious rate: 488,000 in 1900, 688,000 in 1902, and more than 1.1 million in 1906 (see Table 19.1). Though a majority of immigrants settled in cities, most Americans still lived in rural areas or small towns with fewer than twenty-five hundred residents. Not for another twenty years would the population become more urban than rural. As the cities expanded, tensions between rural and urban areas mounted.

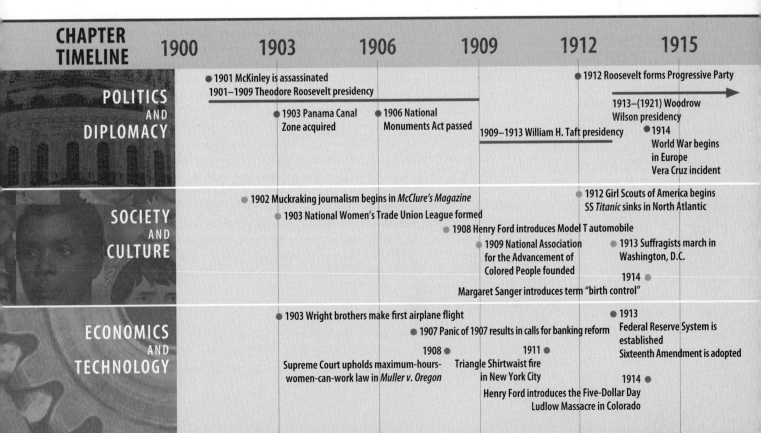

CHAPTER TIMELINE   1900   1903   1906   1909   1912   1915

POLITICS AND DIPLOMACY
- 1901 McKinley is assassinated
- 1901–1909 Theodore Roosevelt presidency
- 1903 Panama Canal Zone acquired
- 1906 National Monuments Act passed
- 1909–1913 William H. Taft presidency
- 1912 Roosevelt forms Progressive Party
- 1913–(1921) Woodrow Wilson presidency
- 1914 World War begins in Europe / Vera Cruz incident

SOCIETY AND CULTURE
- 1902 Muckraking journalism begins in *McClure's Magazine*
- 1903 National Women's Trade Union League formed
- 1908 Henry Ford introduces Model T automobile
- 1909 National Association for the Advancement of Colored People founded
- 1912 Girl Scouts of America begins / SS *Titanic* sinks in North Atlantic
- 1913 Suffragists march in Washington, D.C.
- 1914 Margaret Sanger introduces term "birth control"

ECONOMICS AND TECHNOLOGY
- 1903 Wright brothers make first airplane flight
- 1907 Panic of 1907 results in calls for banking reform
- 1908 Supreme Court upholds maximum-hours-women-can-work law in *Muller v. Oregon*
- 1911 Triangle Shirtwaist fire in New York City
- 1913 Federal Reserve System is established / Sixteenth Amendment is adopted
- 1914 Henry Ford introduces the Five-Dollar Day / Ludlow Massacre in Colorado

TABLE 19.1 **Immigration into the United States, 1901–1909**	
The influx of newcomers into the United States in the first years of the twentieth century caused a dramatic transformation in politics, economics, and culture.	
1901	487,918
1902	687,743
1903	857,046
1904	812,870
1905	1,026,499
1906	1,100,735
1907	1,285,349
1908	782,870
1909	751,786

Source: *The Statistical History of the United States* (1965), p. 56.

National Women's Trade Union League (1903–1950) Labor organization founded by women. It campaigned for better working conditions, protective labor laws, minimum wage regulation, and a ban on child labor.

Social Changes

Immigration, improved medical care and diets, and other influences caused demographic growth and change at the turn of the century. People lived longer in 1900, a trend that accelerated throughout the twentieth century, but on average, the population was young in 1900: the median age was twenty-three. The death rate for the entire population was 17 per thousand in 1900, and fell to 13 per thousand by 1920. For infants in the Progressive era, the prospects were less encouraging. In 1915, the first year for which there are accurate numbers, almost 61 deaths were recorded for every 10,000 births; the infant mortality rate reached more than 68 deaths per 10,000 births in 1921. For nonwhite babies the picture was even worse: almost 106 deaths per 10,000 live births in 1915. Still, as more and more mothers gave birth in hospitals rather than at home, improved medical techniques helped reduce the incidence of infant mortality.

American families and children faced new challenges and new opportunities. In 1900, more than 1.75 million children between the ages of ten and fifteen worked in the labor force. In the South, children worked in cotton mills, which reformers decried as "the poorest place in the world for training citizens of a democracy." Abolishing child labor was a major goal of reform campaigns after 1900. In families whose children did not have to work, child rearing became more organized and systematic. The federal government held conferences on child rearing and issued booklets about infant care. Improved methods of contraception led to smaller families. In 1900, the average mother had 3.6 children, compared with 7.0 children in 1800.

The status of women also changed after 1900. Some younger women delayed marriage to attend college, yet opportunities for women to enter law, medicine, or higher education remained limited. In 1910, there were only nine thousand women doctors, about 6 percent of all physicians. While nursing and social work were more accessible, women still faced exclusion from many professional fields. Working-class women in factories, mills, and garment sweatshops saw little improvement in their condition as the new century began. Their workday was ten hours long, and six- and seven-day weeks were common. When labor unions regarded women as competitors for jobs held by men, women set up their own unions, such as the **National Women's Trade Union League**, established in 1903. They also formed the backbone of the International Ladies Garment Workers Union, which led strikes in New York City in 1910 and 1911.

Social trends altered the status of women. Their clothes became less confining and cumbersome as petticoats and corsets disappeared after 1900. In dance halls and restaurants, young people danced the turkey trot and the bunny hug to the rhythms of ragtime. These changes affected the institution of marriage. Fewer marriage ceremonies used the word *obey*. Women asked more of their husbands, including companionship and sexual pleasure. Divorce was easier, more common, and less denigrated than in the past. About four marriages out of every thousand ended in divorce in 1900, but in the ensuing years, the divorce rate increased three times faster than the rate of population growth. There were 56,000 divorces in 1900 and 100,000 in 1914.

A Nation of Consumers

In 1900, 76 million people in the United States owned 21 million horses. During the next decade, however, Henry Ford of Dearborn, Michigan, developed mass production techniques to sell an automobile called the Model T to middle-class

Americans. In 1908, 5,986 Model T's were sold; by 1912, the total was 78,611. The mass-produced automobile promoted mobility and was a key element in the evolution of the consumer society during the Progressive era.

Standardized food products also gained popular acceptance. Asa Candler's Coca-Cola became more available when the parent company licensed bottling plants throughout the nation. There were 241 bottlers by 1905, 493 by 1910, and 1,095 a decade later. Other famous brands, such as Kellogg's Corn Flakes and Kodak cameras, relied on mass advertising, billboards, and mail flyers to create demand for these new and convenient consumer goods.

Advertising and the active marketing of products and services soon permeated American culture. Men were urged to buy Gillette razors because "You Ought to Shave Every Morning." Toothbrush ads proclaimed that Americans should "keep their teeth and mouths clean." Sears, Roebuck and Company led in consumer marketing. Founded in 1893, the company was the brainchild of Richard Warren Sears, who created an annual catalog and spent lavishly on advertising—over $1.5 million in 1902—promising low prices, product guarantees, and the opportunity to order merchandise without prepaying. "Send No Money" was the Sears slogan. Volume sales at low prices built a market for Sears; the company sent out more than 1.5 million catalogs in 1902. For rural Americans, the Sears catalog became their link to the expanding world of consumer products.

A British visitor said that the standard of American life had reached a height "hitherto unrealized in a civilized society." National income stood at $17 billion; the average American's annual per capita income of $227 was the highest in the world. Innovations promised further abundance to a prosperous population. Despite these positive trends, however, citizens worried about the nation's future. The growth of big business, the spread of labor organizations, the corruption in politics, the decline of the individual in a bureaucratic society—all of these trends prompted fear that older values and attitudes were under assault.

(The Granger Collection, New York)

Sears Catalogue Cover. The mail-order services of Sears, Roebuck and Company became a familiar part of countless American households as the new century began. In this *Consumers Guide,* Sears is instructing its customers about comparing the prices of local shopkeepers with the less expensive goods that can be obtained through the mail.

Theodore Roosevelt in Power

The president during these dramatic changes in American life was Theodore Roosevelt who, at age forty-two, was the youngest chief executive up to that point. During the war with Spain, his volunteer regiment of Rough Riders had charged up Kettle Hill in Cuba against a fortified Spanish position. A national hero, he was elected governor of New York in 1898. When he criticized corporate abuses, Republican leaders exiled him to the vice presidency, thrusting him into the presidency upon McKinley's assassination. The youthful and vigorous Roosevelt made news in fresh ways. He changed the official name of the president's residency to the White House and infused energy into its daily routine. His large family—he had six children—captivated the nation. The spread of newspapers and the emergence of motion pictures enabled Americans to follow the nation's leader with greater attention than ever before.

Roosevelt decided that the president should be the "steward" of the general welfare. As long as the Constitution did not prohibit executive action, the president should stretch the limits of what was possible, including protecting the

(The Granger Collection, New York)

Theodore Roosevelt.
Theodore Roosevelt imparted his energy and enthusiasm to the first decade of the twentieth century. Here he sits astride a horse during one of his frequent trips around the United States. His intense smile became one of the trademarks of his public image.

nation's natural resources. Like a preacher in church, he called the White House his "bully pulpit," using it to give sermons to the country about morality and duty. By using the power of his office in this way, he strengthened the presidency for future challenges. The new president wanted to limit the power of big business to avoid more radical reforms from the Democrats or Socialists. As a result, he left the protective tariff alone and cooperated with the conservative Republicans who dominated Congress during his first term. Later, when he exerted stronger presidential power, his relations with Capitol Hill worsened.

Controlling Big Business and the Trusts

Morgan, J. P. (Pierpont) (1837–1913) U.S. financier. He purchased Carnegie Steel Company in 1901 for $480 million from Andrew Carnegie, creating United States Steel, which controlled 60 percent of the steel industry's productive capacity.

On February 19, 1902, the Department of Justice announced a suit under the Sherman Antitrust Act (1890) against the Northern Securities Company. That firm, created in late 1901, merged major railroads in the Northwest, including the Great Northern, the Northern Pacific, and the Chicago, Burlington, and Quincy Company. The key leaders of this large company were James J. Hill and E. H. Harriman; their financing came from **J. P. Morgan**, the investment banker who had restructured the railroad network in the 1890s, and the steel companies that he represented. The merger sought to reduce destructive competition among warring railroads and stabilize railroad rates, but farmers and business operators in the Upper Midwest feared that a giant railroad would raise rates and limit their profits. They urged their governors to file suit against the new company in federal court.

Another highly publicized merger that symbolized big business was the merger between the Carnegie Steel Company and J. P. Morgan's steel companies, which was made public on March 3, 1901. The half-billion dollars that Carnegie received for his holding—probably more than $50 billion in modern terms—was a staggering sum in an era when there was no federal income tax, no capital gains tax, and low inflation. The new company, United States Steel, was capitalized at $1.4 billion. It had 168,000 employees and controlled 60 percent of the steel industry's productive capacity. Workers in steel now faced a powerful employer that could fix wage levels in any way it chose. "We have billion dollar combines," said one editor, "maneuvered by a handful of men who have never been in a plant and think of a factory as just another chip in a gigantic financial poker game."

Theodore Roosevelt saw business consolidation as inevitable, but he believed the federal government should not just stand by. Firms that were socially beneficial should be encouraged; those that misbehaved should be regulated. A good firm, in Roosevelt's mind, paid its workers a decent wage, avoided labor strife, did not overcharge the public, and did not corrupt the political process. Bad corporations failed to follow these precepts. At first Roosevelt thought that publicizing the activities of corporations would be enough regulation. He soon concluded that he must establish the power of the federal government to intervene in the economy. The Northern Securities Company was unpopular, so the president acted.

In 1904, the Supreme Court ruled 5 to 4 that the Northern Securities Company violated the Sherman Act. The case reestablished the power of the national government to use the Sherman Act, which had been called into question in the 1895 case of *U.S. v. E. C. Knight*. The American public saw Roosevelt as a **trustbuster**, willing to curb the power of big business. Having established that the government was supreme, the president used trustbusting sparingly against "bad" trusts and sought to assist "good" trusts with policies that rewarded their positive behavior.

trustbuster Term applied to Theodore Roosevelt's efforts to enforce the Sherman Act.

Labor and Race Relations in the Roosevelt Era

One of Roosevelt's most important first-term actions was his intervention in a coal strike during the autumn of 1902. The 140,000 members of the United Mine Workers had walked off their jobs in the anthracite (hard coal) fields of Pennsylvania, asking for a pay hike and for the railroads and coal operators to recognize their union. Having lost an earlier strike in 1900, management wanted to break the strike and the union. As the walkout stretched into autumn, fears grew of winter coal shortages. If voters were cold in November, the Republicans faced political losses in the 1902 congressional elections. As the crisis worsened, Roosevelt brought both sides to the White House in early October.

Throughout a day of talks, Roosevelt urged the workers and owners to settle. The panel granted the miners a 10 percent pay increase, but the union was not recognized. Unlike Grover Cleveland during the Pullman strike, Roosevelt wielded presidential power to treat capital and labor on an equal basis. Roosevelt called his approach the **Square Deal.** Other reforms he championed included the Elkins Act, which would outlaw the rebates railroads gave to favored customers, and the creation of the Department of Commerce. One of the agencies of this new department would be the Bureau of Corporations, which would publicize corporate records and indicate which businesses were behaving in the public interest. Roosevelt now had the weapons he sought to distinguish between businesses that he deemed socially good and those that behaved improperly.

Square Deal Theodore Roosevelt's policy of treating capital and labor on an equal basis.

Roosevelt also sought to portray himself as a friend to African Americans. On October 16, 1901, Booker T. Washington, the director of the Tuskegee Institute in

Alabama and the leading African American in the United States, dined with the president and his family at the White House. Since he had emerged as a leading advocate for African Americans during the 1890s, Washington had built a political machine among black Republicans in the South. Southerners were not happy to learn that a black man had eaten with the president. A Tennessee newspaper editor called the occasion "the most damnable outrage that has ever been perpetrated by any citizen of the United States." Needing the votes of black delegates to win the Republican nomination, Roosevelt defended his more tolerant approach, appointing African Americans to post offices and customs houses. But Roosevelt did not challenge the system of racial segregation that now permeated the nation.

Morris, "Bill" (d. 1901) Black man burned at the stake in Balltown, Louisiana, for allegedly robbing and raping a white woman; no trial was held.

For the majority of African Americans in the first decade of the twentieth century, bigotry and violence were everywhere. Eight days after Washington and Roosevelt sat down to dinner, a black man named **"Bill" Morris,** who had allegedly robbed and raped a white woman, was burned at the stake in Balltown, Louisiana. Apprehended by a mob, Morris was "taken back to the scene of his crime." No trial occurred. Instead, "pine knots and pine straw were heaped about him and over this kerosene was poured and the whole set on fire." Between seventy and eighty black citizens of the United States were lynched during each year of Roosevelt's presidency.

Economic, social, and political conditions had worsened since the passage of segregation laws in the South during the 1880s and 1890s. Nine million southern blacks lived in rural poverty. Black wage workers received much less per day and per hour than their white counterparts in the same trade. "The white man is the boss," said one man. "You got to talk to him like he is the boss." Facilities for the races were supposed to be "separate but equal," but this was rarely the case in practice. In addition, African Americans had been effectively disenfranchised by 1900, no longer voting in significant numbers. The bitter comment of one African American politician summed up the situation: "The Negro's status in Southern politics is dark as Hell and smells like cheese."

Du Bois, W. E. B. (1868–1963) Initially a supporter of Booker T. Washington's education policy, he later criticized Washington's methods as having "practically accepted the alleged inferiority of the Negro."

While Booker T. Washington demonstrated to other African Americans that he could deliver the support of white politicians, he also implicitly accepted segregation and the racist system it represented. By the time Roosevelt became president, more militant blacks charged that Washington's methods had failed. Their leader was **W. E. B. Du Bois,** who had received a doctoral degree from Harvard and taught sociology at Atlanta University, a black institution. After initially supporting Washington's policy, Du Bois decided that blacks had to confront segregation. In *The Souls of Black Folk* (1903), he criticized Washington's method as having "practically accepted the alleged inferiority of the Negro." In June 1905, Du Bois led a delegation of twenty-nine blacks to Niagara Falls, New York, where they called for political and social rights. The meeting denied that "the Negro American assents to inferiority, is submissive under oppression and apologetic before insult." The Niagara Conference laid the basis for more protests about the worsening situation of African Americans.

Du Bois, Washington, and blacks in general found Roosevelt less sympathetic to their needs in his second term when he was no longer a candidate for the presidency. He made no public statement about a 1906 race riot in Atlanta, Georgia, in which four blacks were killed and many others injured. As Roosevelt abandoned African Americans, their plight worsened. In August 1908, whites rioted against blacks in Springfield, Illinois, where two blacks were lynched. A tide of bigotry swept the nation that neither the president nor the national government did anything to quell.

In 1909, prominent white reformers such as Oswald Garrison Villard (grandson of the abolitionist William Lloyd Garrison), Mary White Ovington, and William E. Walling met with Du Bois, Ida Wells-Barnett, and other African Americans to form the **National Association for the Advancement of Colored People (NAACP)**. They sought an end to segregation, voting rights for blacks, and equal education for all children. In an era of ethnocentrism and a struggle among the Western powers to subdue colonial peoples, this appeal for racial justice went unheeded.

National Association for the Advancement of Colored People (NAACP) Civil rights organization founded in 1909 to fight racial injustice.

Roosevelt and Foreign Policy

In foreign policy, Theodore Roosevelt wanted to complete the work left over from the Spanish-American War. Because the world was increasingly dangerous, military preparedness was a key goal. "There is a homely adage which runs," the president said, "Speak softly and carry a big stick; you will go far." By 1905, he had added ten battleships to the navy and improved its gunnery. But Roosevelt always remembered the public's caution about overseas adventures. Except in the Philippines, where guerrilla war sputtered on, Roosevelt sent no American forces into armed combat during his presidency.

He did act in places where the power of the United States was dominant. In 1902, Germany and Great Britain used their navies to collect debts that Venezuela owed them; Roosevelt sent the U.S. Navy into the region to limit foreign involvement. Similar problems with the Dominican Republic and its debts two years later led him to pronounce the **Roosevelt Corollary** as a natural extension of the Monroe Doctrine. In his annual message in 1904, he said that the "chronic wrongdoing or impotence" of Latin American nations in paying their debts might lead the United States "to the exercise of an international police power." After 1905, the United States controlled customs revenues and tax services in the Dominican Republic.

Roosevelt Corollary (1904) Theodore Roosevelt's extension of the Monroe Doctrine to Latin American states and the right to supervise their behavior.

A key strategic interest of Roosevelt's was the building of a canal across Central America. Recognizing that better relations with Great Britain were necessary to achieve the goal, Roosevelt sought and won a diplomatic resolution of disputed territory in the Yukon region, where gold had been discovered. In the Hay-Pauncefote Treaty (1901), Great Britain gave up its rights to a canal, and in 1902, congressional leaders pursued the Panama isthmus through a treaty with Colombia, of which Panama was then a part. The pact called for a six-mile-wide canal zone, running forty miles from ocean shore to ocean shore, under American control, with a ninety-nine-year lease. The Colombians would receive a $10 million payment and $250,000 per year in rent. The U.S. Senate ratified the treaty, but when the Colombian Senate resisted, Roosevelt tacitly encouraged a mounting spirit of Panamanian nationalism that led to an uprising in November 1903. The presence of American naval vessels discouraged the Colombians from putting down the rebellion, so the United States recognized the new Panamanian government, as did other European and Latin American nations.

In November 1903, discussions with the representative of Panama, a Frenchman named Philippe Bunau-Varilla, led to the Hay–Bunau-Varilla Treaty, which created a ten-mile-wide zone across Panama in exchange for a $10 million payment and $250,000 annual rent. Within the Canal Zone, the United States could act as a sovereign nation, a provision that subsequent Panamanian governments resented. Construction of the canal proceeded slowly until Roosevelt put the U.S. Army in charge. Roosevelt visited Panama himself in 1906, thus becoming the first president to leave the continental United States while in office.

Building the Panama Canal cost more than $350 million, or the equivalent of several billion dollars in modern funds. Almost six thousand workers died of disease and accidents during construction. The official opening took place on August 15, 1914. Theodore Roosevelt regarded the canal as the greatest achievement of his presidency. His infringement on Colombian sovereignty, however, left bitter feelings in Latin America.

The Election of 1904

Roosevelt's domestic and foreign policy triumphs made him the favorite in the 1904 election. The Democrats turned to Alton B. Parker, a dull, conservative New York state judge. Despite last-minute Democratic charges that big business was behind the Republican campaign, Roosevelt received more than 56 percent of the vote, compared with Parker's 38 percent. The number of Americans who voted, however, was more than four hundred thousand below the 1900 figure. On election night, Roosevelt said that he would not be a candidate for another term in 1908. In his 1904 annual message, Roosevelt asked legislators to strengthen the power of the Interstate Commerce Commission to regulate the railroads. Sensing where public opinion was going, Roosevelt caught the spirit of change that came to be called the Progressive movement. In his second term, he put the power of the modern presidency behind the new agenda for reform.

❖ Progressive Campaigns to Reform the Nation

Responding to the growth of cities, the problems of industrialism, and fears about the nation's future, some American citizens called for political and societal reforms. The movement, termed **progressivism,** sought to expand the power of government and make politics more democratic.

Currents of Reform

Progressivism occurred during a period of prosperity in which Americans saw themselves more as consumers than producers. A sense of well-being allowed middle-class citizens to address the social and economic problems that had emerged during the depression of the 1890s. After the deflation of the late nineteenth century, rising prices aroused concern about the high cost of living. Equally strong were fears of the effects of business consolidation on the smaller companies for which so many people worked. In 1909, 1 percent of firms accounted for 45 percent of manufactured goods. Progressives also focused on the quality and safety of the products they bought and used.

The movement for progressive reform drew on forces that had been gathering strength for two decades. Despite their diversity of goals and approaches, shared assumptions united most people who called themselves progressives. One assumption was that government at all levels could promote a better society, and the state had a duty to relieve the ills that were a result of industrial growth. To achieve a better democracy, progressives promoted *more* democracy. The voters themselves should have the right to decide public issues in referenda, propose laws in initiatives, and remove or recall officials or judges whose decisions offended majority sentiment in a city or state. Another strand of progressivism sought order and efficiency: efforts were made to improve the structure of cities and states to make them work with more economy and less confusion. Regulatory agencies like the Federal Trade Commission and the **Interstate Commerce Commission,** staffed with experts on the industries they supervised, would see that the marketplace operated in an orderly way without partisan influences.

Some reformers sought programs that emphasized social control of groups and individuals. Prohibition of the use of alcohol, restriction of immigration into the United States, and efforts to shift political power in cities away from the poor and unorganized reflected a desire to compel correct behavior or restrict

progressivism Reform movement from 1890 to 1920 that sought to make state and national politics more democratic and government more efficient. The administrations of Theodore Roosevelt and Woodrow Wilson carried out many progressive reforms.

Interstate Commerce Commission First federal regulatory agency, established by the Interstate Commerce Act (1887). It had the power to investigate complaints of railroad misconduct and file suit against the companies. The Hepburn Act (1906) gave the commission the authority to establish maximum rates and to review the accounts and records of the railroads.

democracy to native-born white Americans and the "respectable" classes. While these coercive aspects of reform became less attractive to later generations, progressivism did cause constructive changes. The men and women who joined the crusades for change during the era of Theodore Roosevelt wanted to improve their country, not to revolutionize it.

The Muckrakers

A group of journalists who exposed corruption and weaknesses in American society were important progressive figures. They published their revelations in numerous monthly and weekly magazines. Samuel S. McClure, publisher of *McClure's Magazine*, helped launch the popular literature of exposure. By 1902, his monthly journal had attracted a wide middle-class audience for its appealing blend of fact and fiction. McClure sent one of his star reporters, **Ida Tarbell**, to look into the Standard Oil Company. After Tarbell's articles ran in the autumn of 1902, McClure published another that reporter Lincoln Steffens had written about municipal corruption in St. Louis. That essay, "Tweed Days in St. Louis," led to a series on city government in the magazine that was published under the title "The Shame of the Cities" (1904). Other magazines soon followed McClure's.

In April 1906, Theodore Roosevelt, unhappy with press attacks on the Republican party and conservative senators, used the label "muckrakers" to refer to investigative journalists. He was comparing them to a character in John Bunyan's *Pilgrim's Progress* who spent all of his time raking the muck on the floor and therefore could not see heaven above him. While their influence lasted, **muckrakers** gave progressivism much of its momentum. One journalist, Samuel Hopkins Adams, exposed fraud in patent medicines; his series contributed to the passage of the Pure Food and Drugs Act of 1906.

Women and Progressive Reform

Women were the crucial foot soldiers of progressive reform. With Jane Addams of Chicago's Hull House at its forefront, the settlement house movement attracted young women who were interested in social service. These institutions gave female reformers a supportive environment and a foundation on which to base their role in society. Other women sought reform in other arenas: Florence Kelley guided the National Consumers League; Julia Lathrop supported child labor legislation and in 1912 became the first director of the federal Children's Bureau. In garden clubs and women's improvement clubs, women criticized the spread of billboards, dirty streets, and neglected parks in efforts they called "municipal housekeeping." Women joined the Audubon Society, the Women's National Rivers and Harbors Congress, and the Sierra Club. They saved species of birds from extinction, fought against dams and destructive logging in the West, and campaigned for more national parks.

The campaign for woman suffrage again took center stage, but the movement faced substantial challenges. Carrie Chapman Catt, president of the National American Woman Suffrage Association, said that "the enfranchisement of women will be the crowning glory of democratic government." But in Congress, southern Democrats opposed suffrage because it might lead to votes for African Americans, and liquor interests feared that suffrage would help the prohibitionists. By 1910, the strategy of pursuing a constitutional amendment at the federal level had stalled, so suffragists turned to the states, where they organized campaigns that appealed to a majority of male voters. The result was a string of victories in western states.

Doing History Online

Tainted Food and Drugs

Go to the CourseMate website for this chapter and link to Primary Sources. Which group played a more important role in safeguarding the nation's food and drug supply: progressive reformers or the Congress?

 www.cengagebrain.com

Tarbell, Ida (1857–1944) Preeminent crusading journalist, she exposed the abuses of the oil trust in *A History of the Standard Oil Company* (1904).

muckrakers The name given to investigative reporters in the early 1900s.

Reform in the Cities and States

Progressive political reformers made their first important impact in the nation's cities. Two Ohio mayors, Samuel "Golden Rule" Jones of Toledo (1897–1903) and Tom L. Johnson of Cleveland (1901–1909), pushed for safer, cleaner cities and fought corruption. Some cities, such as Milwaukee, Syracuse, and Minneapolis, elected Socialist mayors during the Progressive era who demonstrated that Socialist politicians could govern responsibly. But more typical of urban reform across the country were efforts to change the structure of city government itself. In September 1900, a devastating hurricane hit Galveston, Texas. As they buried their seven thousand dead and surveyed the wreckage of their city, residents decided to change their form of government. The reforms became known as the commission form of city government, or in more popular use, the "Galveston Idea."

Individual commissioners, elected from the city at large rather than from geographically based wards, conducted the affairs of the police, fire, and utility departments. In that way, the influence of local politics and ward bosses was reduced. Refined in Des Moines, Iowa, in 1908, commission government was in place in 160 cities by 1911. Later, the commission form gave way to the city manager idea because a single, professionally trained executive was thought to be more efficient even than a group of commissioners. Smaller and medium-sized municipalities began instituting the city manager form around 1908.

Urban reform achieved positive results in many cities. Reduction of political influence and limits on the role of partisanship did produce better government in some instances if a lack of corruption and efficiency were the only ruling criteria. However, what "better government" meant always depended on the class, ethnicity, or social perspective from which these changes were viewed. Middle-class reformers pursuing change often did so at the expense of residents of poorer areas of the city, who now found it harder to get a hearing from city hall. Stressing the interest of the city as a whole did not always translate into fair treatment for the less advantaged and less powerful.

As urban reformers tried to improve their cities, they often confronted barriers within state government. Frustrated reformers saw state governments as obstacles to change. When progressives looked at the state level, they saw corruption and business influence that resembled those they had fought locally. They favored the initiative, referendum, and recall because these practices gave less authority to established political figures and institutions. The initiative and referendum first appeared in South Dakota in 1898; other western states adopted them before 1908. The direct primary spread across most of the nation by 1916; it was popular because it gave the power to make nominations to the voters.

Greater emphasis on the regulatory power of state government accompanied these procedural reforms. State government attracted popular and effective leaders during the twenty years after 1900. Theodore Roosevelt was a forceful executive for New York during his one term as governor. Also in New York, Charles Evans Hughes became famous for his probe of insurance companies, which gained him the governorship in 1906. Woodrow Wilson, elected governor of New Jersey in 1910, limited the power of corporations in that state. But the leading symbol of state reform was **Robert M. La Follette**, a Wisconsin Republican elected governor in 1900. During his two terms, he established the direct primary, regulated Wisconsin's railroads, and levied higher taxes on corporations. He forged a close relationship between the state government and faculty members at the University of Wisconsin who advised him about policy. This reliance on academic experts was called the "Wisconsin Idea."

By 1905, progressivism was moving on to the national stage. The issues that reformers faced in the states and cities now seemed to require action by the federal government. Corporations were interstate in character; only Washington

La Follette, Robert M. (1855–1925) Progressive governor (1900–1906) and senator (1906–1925) from Wisconsin; Progressive Party candidate for president in 1924.

could regulate them. To solve the problems of political parties, the Constitution had to be changed. To create a more moral society, progressives contended, the national government had to grant women the vote, regulate the consumption of alcohol, and limit immigration into the United States.

The changes that sought to make the political process more democratic sometimes had unexpected results. Conservative groups used the initiative and referendum for their own ends. Well-funded pressure groups could employ the ballot to pursue an issue such as lower taxes or to attack an unpopular idea or group. The initiative could also reduce the electorate to deciding such issues as how long the lunch hour of a fire department might last. The direct primary did not mean that good candidates replaced bad candidates: a wealthy but less-qualified candidate could circumvent the party and achieve success in the primary. A major result of progressivism was more opportunity for organized groups to shape public policy.

The direct election of U.S. senators, mandated through the Seventeenth Amendment in 1913, took the power of choice away from the state legislatures and gave it to the voters in each state. Candidates had to raise larger amounts of money for their campaigns, which gave an advantage to wealthy men. Meanwhile, lobbying groups simply found new channels for improper influence. One unexpected consequence of these changes was the declining popular interest in voting that became evident in the 1904 presidential election and later contests. Political parties, for all their weaknesses, had mobilized voters to come to the ballot box. The progressives never found a replacement for that function of the parties.

During the spring of 1905, however, reform was still fresh. Advocates of change believed that limited and gradual measures could improve society. With Roosevelt in the White House, they had a president who also believed that moderate reform was necessary to avoid radical transformations.

❖ Roosevelt, Taft, and the Modern Presidency

In his second term, Theodore Roosevelt traveled to promote his programs, built up the bureaucratic machinery of the national government, and pushed Congress to consider a wide range of social problems, from child labor to increased taxation of the wealthy. Under Roosevelt the nation's capital became the focus of news.

The Expansion of Regulation

Roosevelt began his reform campaign with the railroad rate regulation he had promised in his 1904 annual message. Customers of railroads as well as the president thought that the Interstate Commerce Commission (ICC) should have the power to review railroad rates to ensure that they were reasonable. (See *Doing History: Theodore Roosevelt and the Regulation of Business.*)

In 1905, the Department of Justice launched well-publicized probes to find out whether railroads were still giving rebates in violation of the 1903 Elkins Act. Roosevelt dangled the threat of revising the tariff to sway Republican leaders in the House to favor his approach. He shared information about railroad misdeeds with sympathetic reporters.

Still, getting a bill that the White House wanted through Congress was not easy. While matters went smoothly in the House, the Senate was the main obstacle. A long struggle ensued between Roosevelt and the conservative Republican leader, Nelson W. Aldrich of Rhode Island. The issue was whether the courts should have broad power to review the ICC's rulings. If courts had such authority, they could water down the law. The Senate won some victories on the issue, but the Hepburn

Doing History   Theodore Roosevelt and the Regulation of Business

During 1905–1906, in the debates over the Hepburn Act to strengthen the power of the Interstate Commerce Commission, the political process dealt with the issue of government regulation of the economy. On the one side was President Theodore Roosevelt, who believed in the need for such supervision of corporate power. On the other were members of the business community, who took a different view. One such critic of government intervention in the economy was Charles E. Perkins, president of the Burlington Railroad. Perkins wrote to Senator William Boyd Allison of Iowa to express his dissent. In their contrasting views, they reflected a division of opinion over regulation and its effects that has continued to the present time.

Charles E. Perkins to William Boyd Allison, February 23, 1906

I do not believe any question more important to the country than this Rate question was ever before you, because Government rate making means pretty soon Government ownership and the political as well as commercial consequences must to say the least be serious. It is not a Railroad question. Transportation by Rail is either a "business" or it is not. That is the question. It cannot for long be both "business" and "not business"; it must be one or the other. If not business it is politics, and if so decided by the Senate, the man on horseback will soon come to stay. We do not know perhaps what the commercial consequences of Government rate making may be, but we can see, it seems to me, what the political consequences must be. Both will undoubtedly be bad enough.

I sometimes wonder if the current which carries us along may not bring us up against practical socialism ending in some kind of a revolution before so very long—not in our day but soon. Or will the common sense of the people get tired of the actors and charlatans who are now in the saddle and return to sound first principles? Does the current of human affairs admit of that?

Source: Charles E. Perkins to William Boyd Allison, February 23, 1906, William Boyd Allison Papers, Iowa State Department of History and Archives, Des Moines, Iowa.

Theodore Roosevelt, "Legislative Actions and Judicial Decisions," 1906

A similar extension of the national power to oversee and secure correct behavior in the management of all great corporations engaged in interstate business will in similar fashion render far more stable the present system by doing away with those grave abuses which are not only evil in themselves but are also evil because they furnish an excuse for agitators to inflame well-meaning-people against all forms of property and to commit the country to schemes of wild would-be remedy which would work infinitely more harm than the disease itself. The government ought not to conduct the business of the country; but it ought to regulate it so that it shall be conducted in the interest of the public.

Perhaps the best justification of the course which in the National Government we have been pursuing in the past few years, and which we intend steadily and progressively to pursue in the future, is that it is condemned with almost equal rancor by the reactionaries—the Bourbons—on one side, and by the wild apostles of unrest on the other.

Source: Theodore Roosevelt, "Legislative Actions and Judicial Decisions," Address at the Dedication of the New State Capitol Building, Harrisburg, Pennsylvania, October 4, 1906, *The Works of Theodore Roosevelt: American Problems*, 20 vols. (New York: Charles Scribner's Sons, 1906), XVI, 73.

QUESTIONS for REFLECTION

1. What does Charles E. Perkins mean by "socialism," and how does he think Roosevelt's policies will lead to that result?

2. How would Roosevelt define the public interest, and why does he believe that the national government can best represent that interest?

3. In what areas of American life are the issues that Perkins and Roosevelt raise still being debated and decided?

Act was passed in late June 1906. The Hepburn Act gave the ICC the power to establish maximum rates and to review the accounts and records of the railroads. It also showed how a strong president could achieve a major legislative goal by summoning public opinion to support a popular cause.

There was more to Roosevelt's regulatory program than railroads. Muckrakers had revealed that patent medicines sold over the counter were usually ineffective and sometimes dangerous. Led by Dr. Harvey Wiley of the Department of Agriculture, the government conducted experiments on the purity of food that revealed that toxic chemicals made many food products unsafe. By early 1906, the clamor for reform had led to the introduction of a bill in Congress to restrict the sale of impure or adulterated food and drugs. The measure was passed by the Senate but stalled in the House of Representatives. Then, during the winter of 1906, thousands of Americans read *The Jungle*, a novel about the meat-packing industry in Chicago. Written by a young socialist named **Upton Sinclair**, the book depicted shocking conditions in the plants, outraging readers who learned that filth endangered their meat supply.

President Roosevelt was angered as well. If the government did not take action, he feared that the socialism Sinclair favored might gain followers. The White House supported an amendment to the Agricultural Appropriation Act of 1906 that set up a federal program for meat inspection. The meat-packing industry tried to water down the bill, but the law represented a significant advance in regulatory power. The controversy over meat inspection cleared the way for House action on the Pure Food and Drugs Act. As a result, that measure was passed on June 30, 1906. A happy president called the three regulatory laws "a noteworthy advance in the policy of securing Federal supervision and control over corporations."

To achieve that control, Roosevelt placed less emphasis on breaking up large corporations. Having decided which businesses and corporate leaders met his standards of morality in the marketplace, he made private agreements with International Harvester and United States Steel. In return for letting the government examine their financial records, these companies would not be subjected to antitrust prosecutions. Firms that Roosevelt disliked, including Standard Oil, would be disciplined by federal lawsuits. Presidential power, mixed with administrative discretion, would control corporate misdeeds.

Upton Sinclair, *The Jungle.* Upton Sinclair's *The Jungle* provided graphic information about conditions in the meatprocessing plants that supplied so much of the nation's food. These revelations spurred on a regulatory campaign to make meat products more reliable and safe for the consumer.

Sinclair, Upton (1878–1968) Progressive era writer whose novel *The Jungle* exposed abuses in the meat-packing industry.

Roosevelt and World Politics

Roosevelt displayed equal energy in the conduct of foreign affairs. He carried on secret negotiations without Congress's knowledge, broadened the nation's activities in Asia and Europe, and tried to educate the American people to accept a new role as a world power.

Early in 1904, war broke out when the Japanese launched a surprise attack on Russia to seize territory on the Asian mainland and dominate Manchuria. Roosevelt sympathized with Japan because he regarded the Russians as a threat to the Open Door policy in China, and he acted as an intermediary when the two parties began negotiations. Roosevelt summoned the combatants to a peace conference held in Portsmouth, New Hampshire, in August, and the two nations agreed to end the conflict; the Treaty of Portsmouth was signed in September 1905. Meanwhile the Roosevelt administration recognized the supremacy of Japan over its neighbor,

Korea. In turn, Japan pledged that it had no aggressive designs on the Philippines. In 1906, Roosevelt received the Nobel Peace Prize for his achievement.

In Europe, Roosevelt sought to reduce the growing tension between Germany and the other major powers, France and Great Britain, over Berlin's ambitions to play a larger role on the continent. Roosevelt sympathized with Britain and France, and he wanted Germany and its leader, Kaiser Wilhelm II, to be reasonable. During 1905, the Germans made a major issue of French dominance of Morocco. The kaiser wanted a conference to determine Morocco's status. Roosevelt convinced Britain and France to accept a conference rather than go to war over the fate of the North African country, helping to preserve an uneasy European peace for the remainder of the decade.

Later in 1906, the lingering problems in Japanese-American relations flared up again. Japan resented the nativist immigration policies of the United States that discriminated against Japanese newcomers. On the West Coast, the increasing number of Japanese workers and residents intensified nativist and racist sentiments. When the San Francisco school board segregated children of Japanese ancestry, Japan reacted angrily. Washington and Tokyo eventually worked out the "Gentlemen's Agreement" of 1907. The order of the school board was revoked, and Japan agreed to limit the number of immigrants who left that country for the United States.

To increase funding for the navy from an economy-minded Congress, Roosevelt sent the American navy's "Great White Fleet" on an around-the-world tour from 1907 to 1909. When the vessels stopped in Japan in October 1908, the reception was enthusiastic and friendly. A month later, the two nations negotiated the Root-Takahira Agreement, which called for the open door in China, the independence of that country, and preservation of the status quo in the Pacific. Indeed, when he left office in March 1909, Roosevelt expressed pride that the United States was "at absolute peace" with the rest of the world.

Roosevelt's Domestic Policies

As the congressional elections of 1906 approached, the still-dominant Republican Party faced challenges from Democrats as well as more radical voices. The Democrats had a new asset to help them against the Republicans: organized labor. With a membership of nearly 1.7 million by 1904, Samuel Gompers of the American Federation of Labor (AFL) called for the defeat of Republican candidates due to a dispute over using federal courts to block strikes through injunctions.

In addition to the opposition of the AFL, Roosevelt worried about the growing power of the Socialist Party and the most radical wing of the labor movement, the Industrial Workers of the World (IWW). Founded in 1905, the IWW, nicknamed the "Wobblies," criticized the AFL as timid and called for the overthrow of capitalism. The Socialist Party, under the leadership of Eugene V. Debs, also gained strength at the polls. In 1904, Debs won four hundred thousand votes. Roosevelt believed that his reforms were necessary to stave off more sweeping social change.

Despite Roosevelt's efforts, the Republicans lost twenty-six seats in the elections, but the campaign of the AFL to unseat Republicans did not do as much damage as Gompers had promised. Nevertheless, the results revealed that the Republicans had significant problems. The protective tariff divided the party: midwesterners wanted lower duties, whereas Republicans in the East would tolerate no tariff revision. Roosevelt's regulatory policies alienated party conservatives who became angry when Roosevelt regulated railroads, watched over the quality of food products, and attacked large corporations.

Conservatives believed that one branch of the government could withstand the temptations to follow Roosevelt. The judiciary, composed of judges who were usually appointed rather than elected, often ruled in a conservative manner to strike down progressive laws. In the case of *Lochner v. New York* (1905), for example, the Supreme Court overturned a New York law that limited the hours employees could work in a bakery. The Court ruled that the law infringed on the right of the bakers under the Fourteenth Amendment to get the best reward for their labor. But sometimes the justices made an exception and supported progressive laws. For example, in the 1908 case of **Muller v. Oregon**, influenced by a brief submitted by Louis D. Brandeis, they upheld an Oregon statute that limited the hours women could work. In other decisions that same year, however, the Court invalidated the Employers Liabilities Act of 1906 and curbed the power of labor unions in the Danbury Hatters' case (*Loewe v. Lawlor*).

Roosevelt's campaign for the conservation of natural resources also reflected his presidential activism. He created refuges for wild birds, preserved the Grand Canyon against intrusion from development, and set aside national parks. During his first term, he worked for passage of the Newlands Reclamation Act (1902), which established a system of irrigation reservoirs in the West financed through the sale of public lands. Roosevelt worked closely with Gifford Pinchot of the U.S. Forestry Service to formulate conservation policy. Both men thought that the national parks, coal lands, oil reserves, water-power sites, and national forests in the West should be managed by trained experts from the federal government to achieve the maximum amount of effective use.

Roosevelt had alerted Americans to a serious national problem. He raised important issues about the future of timber, water, wildlife, and mineral resources. He created national parks, including Mesa Verde and Crater Lake, and established four national game preserves, fifty-one bird reservations, and 150 national forests (see Map 19.1). He could be proud of the National Monuments Act (1906),

Muller v. Oregon **(1908)** Case in which the Supreme Court upheld limits on working hours for women.

(Copyright © Cengage Learning)

MAP 19.1

Theodore Roosevelt: National Parks and Monuments

Theodore Roosevelt, as a conservationist president, established national parks and monuments to preserve the nation's heritage. This map shows what he accomplished in both categories. Several of the national monuments later became national parks and thus have the date when Roosevelt established them and the date that their status changed to a park.

which put some important national treasures beyond the reach of development and destruction. He also convened the 1908 Governors Conference on Conservation that looked into social issues relating to natural and human resources. The president had alerted the nation to these pressing concerns in an innovative way. However, in the West there was much resentment of programs that Washington had devised without much local support and implemented over the protests of the westerners themselves.

The 1908 Presidential Election

Roosevelt remained popular with the American people during the waning years of his administration. Among conservative Republicans, however, unhappiness with the president mounted. On Capitol Hill, party members in the House and Senate balked at Roosevelt's assertiveness. When problems in the banking industry led to the panic of 1907, a momentary collapse of the financial system and a brief recession followed. Roosevelt's Republican opponents blamed the economic troubles on his regulatory policies.

Hoping to see his progressive policies carried on, the president decided to support his secretary of war, William Howard Taft, whom he regarded as his natural successor. Taft advanced toward the Republican nomination at the national convention in June, where he won on the first ballot. In their platform, the Republicans promised to revise the protective tariff at a special session of Congress shortly after the new president was inaugurated. The public assumed that any change in the tariff would lead to lower rates.

The Democrats nominated William Jennings Bryan for the third time and were optimistic about his chances. After all, Roosevelt was not a candidate, and Taft had not been tested at the polls. In the early days of the campaign, Bryan ran well, but when Roosevelt supported Taft, the Republicans won again: Taft garnered 321 electoral votes to Bryan's 162. The election was marked by ticket splitting: voters cast ballots for Taft for president and Democrats for other offices. The partisan allegiances and loyalties of the late nineteenth century were breaking down.

Taft's Conservative Presidency

Taft, William Howard (1857–1930) Twenty-seventh president of the United States (1909–1913), who split with Theodore Roosevelt once in office. He served as Chief Justice of the United States Supreme Court (1921–1930).

Soon after **William Howard Taft** took office on March 4, 1909, Theodore Roosevelt left for his hunting safari in Africa. The hope on Wall Street, ran a joke of the day, was that a lion would do its duty. The issues of regulation, social justice, and corporate power with which Roosevelt had struggled were also on the agenda for his successor.

The new president became torn between Republican conservatives, who expected him to slow the movement toward reform, and party progressives, who wanted him to expand Roosevelt's legacy. A native of Cincinnati, Ohio, fifty-one-year-old Taft had been a lawyer and a federal judge before heading the Philippine Commission in 1900. As secretary of war under Roosevelt, Taft acted as troubleshooter for the administration. Roosevelt looked forward to a continuation of his policies under his successor, but Taft did not agree with Roosevelt's expansive view of presidential power. Taft believed that the president should act within the strict letter of the law and the constitutional boundaries of his office, a philosophy that was bound to disappoint Roosevelt and the progressive Republicans.

When the issue of revising the tariff arose, Taft confronted the consequences of Roosevelt's postponement of the issue. Progressive Republicans favored reductions in customs duties and a move away from protectionism. Conservatives like Senate majority leader Nelson Aldrich, however, regarded the tariff as the cornerstone of Republicanism and felt that high rates were justified. Once Congress assembled in March 1909, Taft asked for a new tariff law that would, as he had said in his inaugural address, "permit the reduction of rates in certain schedules and will require the advancement of few, if any." In April, the House passed a tariff bill that lowered rates on sugar, iron, and lumber. It placed lumber, coal, and cattle hides on the free list. The measure was named the Payne bill after its author, Sereno E. Payne, chairman of the Ways and Means Committee.

In the Senate, tariff reform faced a fight. Among the Senate Republicans, there were seven to ten midwesterners, such as Robert La Follette of Wisconsin, Albert J. Beveridge of Indiana, and Jonathan P. Dolliver of Iowa, who wanted to see lower tariffs as well as limits on majority leader Aldrich's power. On the other side of the debate, senators from the East and Far West insisted that goods from their states must be protected against foreign competition. Aldrich had the Senate Finance Committee write a bill with eight hundred amendments, half of which raised rates back toward those of the Dingley Tariff Act. That move outraged progressive Republican senators. During the summer of 1909, Dolliver, La Follette, and Beveridge attacked Aldrich's bill, but it finally passed in early July by a vote of 45 to 34. As a House–Senate conference committee hammered out the final version of the bill, President Taft obtained some concessions, such as lower duties on gloves, lumber, and cattle hides, but he failed to gain reductions on wool, cotton, and industrial products. Convinced that he had achieved all he could, Taft signed the Payne-Aldrich Tariff Act in early August 1909, but the battle split the Republicans because the tariff had not fulfilled the promises of the 1908 party platform.

Wilson and Taft at the 1913 Inauguration. On March 4, 1913, President Taft and President-Elect Wilson posed for photographers. The jovial Taft had accepted his defeat with grace and he made the transition to Wilson as smooth as possible. His smile reflected his relief at laying down the burdens of his difficult presidency.

The Battle over Conservation

Taft also found himself engaged in a battle over conservation that threatened to disrupt his friendship with Theodore Roosevelt. Taft disliked Roosevelt's principal aide, Gifford Pinchot, and doubted whether the conservation policies Roosevelt had pursued were legal. Taft and his secretary of the interior, Richard A. Ballinger, adopted conservation policies that conformed to existing laws and allowed less room for presidential initiative. When Ballinger opened lands for development that Pinchot had closed off to settlers and businesses, Pinchot struck back. He accused Ballinger of acting as an agent for J. P. Morgan and a syndicate trying to sell valuable coal lands in Alaska. After looking into the charges, Taft sided with Ballinger, brought the dispute to the press, and ultimately fired Pinchot for insubordination. In the ensuing controversy, a congressional probe revealed that Taft and Ballinger had not done what Pinchot had charged. Still, Roosevelt in Africa received letters from friends saying that Taft was betraying him.

The congressional session in the spring of 1910 compounded Taft's problems. In a rebuke to the White House, Progressive Republicans joined with Democrats to hold up legislation. Some constructive measures emerged from the session: railroad legislation broadened the power of the Interstate Commerce Commission; the navy was given more money; and progressives enacted a law to encourage private citizens to use federal banks. But Taft got little credit for these improvements.

Roosevelt's Return

Meanwhile, Theodore Roosevelt had returned to the United States in June 1910, determined to get the Republican Party back on the right course. He received a hero's welcome when his ship entered New York Harbor, and a crowd of a hundred thousand people cheered him as he rode up the streets. At first, Roosevelt refrained from public quarrels with the president, but the Republicans' internal warfare intensified. Taft used his appointment power once again against the midwestern progressives in his party; their candidates were not nominated for positions in the federal government. Taft went even further, trying to organize loyal Republicans against reform leaders such as Dolliver, La Follette, and Beveridge. These moves failed, and the president's inability to rally support within his own party emphasized his weakness.

Roosevelt began to attack his successor in a series of speeches during the summer of 1910. He called his program the **New Nationalism** and said the "rules of the game" should be "changed so as to work for a more substantial equality of opportunity and reward for equally good service." He called for an income tax, inheritance taxes on large fortunes, workmen's compensation laws, and legislation to "regulate child labor and work for women." Roosevelt was advocating the modern regulatory state.

In the congressional elections of 1910, the Democrats gained control of the House of Representatives when the Republicans lost fifty-eight seats. In the Senate, the Republicans dropped ten seats. They still had a ten-seat majority, but progressive Republicans often voted with the Democrats. Republicans suffered their biggest losses in the industrial East, where twenty-six Republican House members were defeated. Stressing inflation and the high cost of living, Democrats won governorships in New York, New Jersey, Ohio, and Indiana.

New Nationalism Theodore Roosevelt's far-reaching program that called for a strong federal government to stabilize the economy, protect the weak, and restore social harmony.

❖ Progressive Victories

Between 1910 and 1913 progressivism intensified, as the movement for social change gathered momentum. The reformers seemed to have public opinion behind them, and conservatives in both parties were on the defensive. The forces of reform pushed forward to achieve their policy goals.

Woman Suffrage and Prohibition

In April 1910, the National American Woman Suffrage Association (NAWSA) presented Congress with a petition that more than four hundred thousand people had signed. The document sought a constitutional amendment allowing women to vote. Although Congress refused to act, one suffrage worker, surprised by the number of signers of the petition, said that her cause "is actually fashionable now." Under the leadership of Anna Howard Shaw, NAWSA's membership grew. In Washington (1910), California (1911), and Arizona, Kansas, and Oregon (1912), **woman suffrage** triumphed. However, referenda to give women the vote failed in Ohio, Wisconsin, and Michigan. Within the movement, younger women, eager for results, urged the older leaders to concentrate on obtaining a constitutional amendment.

Alice Paul led the radical wing of the suffrage movement that aimed to change the Constitution. She had fought for the vote in England and now wanted to apply tactics of picketing and civil disobedience to the United States. Other women joined her, including Lucy Burns and Harriot Stanton Blatch, daughter of Elizabeth Cady Stanton. For a few years, Paul and her allies worked on NAWSA's congressional committee. NAWSA stressed that female voting meant purer and

Doing History Online

Votes for Women a Practical Necessity

Go to the CourseMate website for this chapter and link to Primary Sources. Read the articles on woman suffrage. How have other progressive reform movements influenced the woman suffrage movement?

www.cengagebrain.com

woman suffrage The right of women to vote, which they achieved in 1919–1920 after an intense struggle in congress.

Paul, Alice (1885–1977) A main figure in the radical wing of the woman suffrage movement in the early twentieth century.

more honest politics. The organization also played down the argument that women should have equal political rights and instead contended that woman suffrage would offset the votes of immigrants and racial minorities in large cities. Thus, suffragists would be protecting traditional values against "alien" assaults. Eventually frustrated at the cautious tactics of NAWSA, Paul and Burns left the organization in early 1914 to form the Congressional Union.

Efforts to restrict the use and sale of alcohol also prospered. Since the 1890s, the Anti-Saloon League had held a dominant position among prohibitionist organizations by using interest group politics that focused on specific, targeted legislative goals. The league sought to limit the power of the liquor industry to sell its product. At first the league sought elections to give voters in a county or state the "local option" to ban the sale of alcohol. By 1906, impatient with the slowness of the local option, the league turned to statewide elections to get the job done more quickly.

Oklahoma adopted Prohibition in 1907. By 1914, eight other states had banned the sale of alcohol. Militant prohibitionists found the state-by-state process discouraging. In 1913, prohibitionists in Congress passed the Webb-Kenyon Act, which outlawed the shipment of alcohol into dry states. Skeptical of Prohibition as a social cause, President Taft vetoed the bill, but Congress overrode him. The Anti-Saloon League's next goal was a constitutional amendment to ban the sale of alcohol in the United States.

Restriction of Immigration

As the flow of newcomers from southern and eastern Europe persisted, the effort to restrict immigration into the United States accelerated. There were more than 1 million immigrants in 1910, nearly 2 million in 1913, and over a million more in 1914, before the outbreak of World War I. In addition, revolutionary upheavals in Mexico drove thousands of Hispanic immigrants into the Southwest.

Nativist and racist feelings fueled the opposition to immigration. Workers on the West Coast wanted to keep out Chinese and Japanese immigrants; in the East, Protestants wanted to keep out Catholic and Jewish newcomers. Progressive reform offered some support for such prejudices. Because businesses favored a loose immigration policy, opposition to immigration was portrayed as a way to help workers already in the United States. A feeling that cultures from southern and eastern Europe threatened traditional values led some progressives to endorse restriction. By 1913, a bill to impose a literacy test on immigrants had passed both houses of Congress. President Taft, however, vetoed the measure, and Congress was unable to override it.

Saving Children

Americans worried about their children's future as mass entertainment, the lure of the city, and looser attitudes about sex offered new temptations. Three organizations sprang up to address these concerns. In 1910–1911, the Boy Scouts of America, modeled on the British precedent created by Robert Baden-Powell, began offering young men instruction in "the military virtues such as honor, loyalty, obedience, and patriotism." For young women, there were the Girl Scouts and the Campfire Girls, which prepared American girls for future domestic responsibilities. "The homemaker of tomorrow," said one Girl Scout leader, "must be made efficient in her task and happy in it."

(The Granger Collection New York)

Despite such obstacles as the Chinese Exclusion Act of 1882, Chinese immigrants continued to move to the United States and prosper, inspiring resentment in some white Americans.

The struggle against child labor overshadowed all other drives to improve the condition of children. In 1910, some two hundred thousand youngsters below the age of twelve labored in mills and factories. Attempts to limit child labor in textile firms in the South brought meager results. In 1912, the reformers succeeded in establishing the Children's Bureau within the federal government, but Congress failed to pass any legislation that directly addressed the child labor problem.

Reforming the Workplace

Despite the many obstacles that progressive reformers faced, many believed that the nation was making genuine gains. Yet conflicts between workers and employers continued to rage, notably among the garment unions of New York, the textile workers of Massachusetts, and in the coal mines of Colorado. American laborers risked violent and bloody confrontations to improve harsh conditions in the workplace.

As industrialization spread, factories and businesses expanded. In Chicago during these years, the Marshall Field's department store had five thousand salespeople in its many store departments. The meat-packing firm of Swift and Company employed twenty-three thousand people in its seven plants by 1903. The Amoskeag Company textile mills in Manchester, New Hampshire, dominated the lives of its seventeen thousand employees with welfare programs and company organizations.

The nature of large corporations changed as relationships between employers and workers became more structured and routinized. To control costs and ensure steady production, companies set up procedures for regular reporting on expenditures, centralization of purchasing and maintenance, and measurement of worker productivity.

Out of these innovations came a new way to run the factory and workplace. Frederick Winslow Taylor developed scientific management. As a mechanical engineer in the steel industry, Taylor believed that careful study of each individual task would lead to efficiency. Once the maximum amount of time to do a specific job was established, workers could be instructed on how to complete the task without any wasted motion. Stopwatches measured the speed of work down to the split second. As a concept, Taylorism enjoyed great popularity among businesspeople, but workers resented practices that made them perform repetitive, routine movements all day long.

Some corporations revived paternalism through welfare and incentive programs. Lunchrooms and toilet areas were cleaned up, recreational facilities established, and plans devised for pensions and profit sharing. Yet most American workers saw only marginal improvement. Businesses used a variety of techniques to block unions and prevent workers from improving their condition. When strikes occurred, employers used nonunion labor (strikers called them "scabs") to end the walkouts. Court injunctions limited the ability of strikers to picket and organize. Violent clashes between workers and police accompanied many strikes.

Varieties of Labor Protest

The working classes in the cities faced the ravages of inflation as prosperity and an increasing supply of gold contributed to a rising price level for consumers. Although wages rose, prices of consumer products accelerated at a faster rate. Most workers faced dangerous conditions in their factories and sweatshops. Laborers turned to strikes and unions. In New York City and Philadelphia from 1909 to 1911, the International Ladies Garment Workers Union organized workers within the shirtwaist (a woman's blouse) manufacturing business. Twenty

(National Archives)

Triangle Fire Mourners. The many deaths in the Triangle Fire and the funerals that followed emphasized the impact of this workplace tragedy on the minds of New York legislators and the public.

thousand female strikers took to the streets to demonstrate their solidarity. They wrested some concessions from their employees in the form of union shops and improved working conditions, but not enough to avert disaster. In March 1911, a fire erupted at the Triangle Shirtwaist Company on New York City's Lower East Side. As the workers fled the flames, they found locked doors and no fire escape routes. The conflagration claimed 146 lives, many of them killed when they jumped to the pavement below. The **Triangle Shirtwaist fire** spurred reform efforts among politicians in the New York legislature.

Labor unions grew between 1900 and 1914. The American Federation of Labor, led by Samuel Gompers, had several million members. The politics of the AFL had not changed since the end of the nineteenth century, and the union was still unfriendly to women.

The Industrial Workers of the World (IWW) appealed to the unskilled masses. Its ultimate goal was still a social revolution that would sweep away industrial capitalism. To the IWW's leadership, including William D. "Big Bill" Haywood and Elizabeth Gurley Flynn, violent strikes seemed the best way to promote industrial warfare.

The IWW gained national attention during a strike in the textile mills of Lawrence, Massachusetts, in mid-January 1912. After the textile companies announced substantial wage reductions, the workers walked out. Haywood came to Lawrence to support the strike. On March 1, the companies granted the workers a pay hike. Female strikers were key participants in the victory. As one of their songs put it, they sought "bread and roses," or a living wage and a life with hope. Despite this local success, the IWW did not build a strong following in the East.

In Colorado, the United Mine Workers struck against the Colorado Fuel and Iron Company in September 1913, complaining about low wages and company camps with brutal guards. John D. Rockefeller, who controlled the coal company, asked the governor to call in the National Guard. Confrontations between soldiers and miners ended in the "Ludlow Massacre" of April 20, 1914,

Triangle Shirtwaist fire (1911) Fire at the Triangle Shirtwaist Company in New York that killed 146 female workers and spurred reform legislation regulating factories and protecting workers.

in which troops fired on miners in a tent city at Ludlow. Five strikers and one soldier were shot, and two women and eleven children died in the flames that broke out in the tents. Federal inquiries followed, and the workers obtained some concessions. Yet later in 1914 they were forced to end the strike without gaining union recognition.

Despite the valiant efforts of protesters, changes in the workplace during the Progressive period benefited the employers far more than they improved the lot of workers. Unlike Great Britain or Germany, the United States still did not provide social insurance when a worker became unemployed, pension benefits for old age, or equal bargaining power on the job. The absence of these benefits fed the political passions that surged through the nation during the years that Taft was president. Whether it was in his view of labor relations, his attitude toward progressivism, or his conduct of foreign policy, Taft seemed out of touch with the nation's mood.

❖ Republican Discord and Democratic Opportunity

dollar diplomacy Term for Secretary of State Philander C. Knox's foreign policy under President Taft, which focused on expanding American investments abroad, especially in Latin America and China.

In foreign affairs, the Taft administration followed the broad outlines of what Roosevelt had done, but with some new labels for the effort to spread American influence in Asia and Latin America. William Howard Taft and his secretary of state, Philander C. Knox, adopted the policy of **dollar diplomacy** toward Latin America and Asia. When U.S. corporations traded and invested in underdeveloped areas of the world, peace and stability increased. Instead of military force, the ties of finance and capital would instruct countries in the wise conduct of their affairs. Latin America offered an ideal location for applying the principles of dollar diplomacy. In 1909, Taft and Knox induced bankers to loan money to Honduras to prevent British investors from achieving undue influence. In 1911, they compelled the government of Nicaragua to accept another loan from U.S. investors, but some Nicaraguans regarded the scheme as an intrusion, and they rebelled against the government that had made the deal. The Taft administration sent U.S. Marines to Nicaragua; the resulting U.S. military presence continued for several decades, and a lasting feeling of bitterness marked relations with Latin America.

Taft and Knox also applied dollar diplomacy to China. The government wanted American capitalists to support a railroad in China, first to develop the country and then to offset Japan's influence in China. Roosevelt had recognized Japanese dominance in the region; Knox challenged it economically. A syndicate of nations would lend China money to purchase existing railroads in Manchuria. The plan collapsed when the British, Russians, and Japanese rejected the idea in early 1910. Instead of promoting stability in China, the Knox initiative sparked resentment in Japan, and relations between that country and the United States remained tense. Dollar diplomacy proved to be an ineffective way to achieve world influence.

A foreign policy problem closer to home emerged in 1911. Porfirio Dìaz had ruled Mexico for almost forty years. American investment came because he had maintained apparent calm and stability. In fact, however, his dictatorial rule eventually erupted in a revolution. Francisco I. Madero, the leader of the rebels, came to power hoping to transform the nation. But he aroused the opposition of conservative forces, including the military, large landowners, and the Roman Catholic church. Shortly before Taft's term ended in 1913, Madero was overthrown and murdered. Mexico remained in revolutionary ferment.

The Struggle Between Roosevelt and Taft

Following Republican losses in the elections of 1910, Taft and Roosevelt agreed not to attack each other during the first half of 1911. To placate progressives, Taft eased Ballinger out of the cabinet and named two supporters of Roosevelt as secretary of the interior and secretary of war. But his troubles with Congress persisted. He negotiated a trade agreement with Canada based on reciprocal concessions on tariffs, which neither the Democrats nor the progressive Republicans liked because it lowered import duties on products that affected their districts. Taft pushed the agreement through Congress in mid-1911, but when Canadian voters rejected the government that had supported it, another Taft initiative died.

Next, the president's fragile friendship with Roosevelt collapsed. Unlike Roosevelt, Taft really believed in "busting" the trusts, and his Justice Department attacked large corporations. In October 1911, carrying out Taft's policy views about the wisdom of competition, the Department of Justice filed an antitrust suit against United States Steel. One of the practices that violated the law, according to the indictment, was the company's acquisition of the Tennessee Coal and Iron Company during the panic of 1907. Since Roosevelt had approved the merger, the indictment held him up to ridicule, and he was furious. By the early part of 1912, he decided to challenge Taft for the Republican nomination. "My hat is in the ring, the fight is on, and I am stripped to the buff," he said in February 1912.

Throughout the spring of 1912, a bitter battle for the Republican nomination raged. For the first time, a few states held primary elections to choose delegates to the Republican convention, favoring the still-popular Roosevelt. Taft, however, ran strongly among the party regulars who controlled the nominating conventions. As the Republican National Convention opened in Chicago, neither man had a clear majority. Several hundred delegates were contested, but the Republican National Committee awarded most of them to Taft. Roosevelt denounced Taft and promised to fight on. For the next two months, Roosevelt prepared to run as a third-party candidate.

The Democratic Opportunity

To exploit the disarray of their opponents, the Democrats needed a credible presidential candidate. One attractive newcomer was the governor of New Jersey, **Woodrow Wilson,** who had carried that staunchly Republican state by a sizable majority in 1910. Woodrow Wilson was fifty-six years old in 1912. Born in Virginia, he grew up in the South and shared its racial views. He attended Princeton University in New Jersey, later joining the faculty and becoming university president in 1902. In 1910, Wilson won the New Jersey governorship in his first try at elective office.

Wilson, Woodrow (1856–1924) Twenty-eighth president of the United States (1913–1921), he was an advocate for the New Freedom and the League of Nations.

Woodrow Wilson and the 1912 Election

Although he was an educational innovator, Wilson had long been a conservative Democrat; political opportunity led him to champion such reform ideas as the direct primary, the initiative, and the referendum. Some Democrats preferred the moderate and less inspiring leadership of the Speaker of the House, James Beauchamp "Champ" Clark of Missouri, who endorsed lower tariffs and not much else. When the national convention met in Baltimore in late June, Wilson gained strong backing among the delegates as a fresh candidate all Democrats could agree to endorse. After forty-six ballots, Wilson was nominated. The hopes for victory looked bright in November.

Once again the Socialist party selected Eugene V. Debs as its candidate. Debs had run in every election since 1900, and his total vote had increased each time. He knew that he would not be elected, but in his mind he was preparing the way for a nation that would in time turn to socialism. Seven hundred thousand voters supported Socialist candidates in 1910, and the following year Socialist mayors or city officials were chosen in seventy-four cities. Socialism gained followers because the party spoke to the grievances of the agricultural and working poor. "Comrades," Debs cried, "this is our year."

Republicans who supported Roosevelt formed the Progressive Party, also known as the "Bull Moose" Party, behind his banner and prepared to hold their first national convention. The atmosphere of the convention, which met in Chicago in August 1912, mixed the fervor of a revival meeting with the traditional backroom bargaining of other conventions. To woo the white South, the delegates excluded African Americans from the convention. Roosevelt defended the protective tariff and attacked reciprocity with Canada. The main financial support for the new party came from wealthy newspaper publishers and corporate executives, who liked Roosevelt's belief that big business should be accepted as a fact of economic life and regulated as he had during his presidency.

At its core, however, the Progressive Party's endorsement of expanded social justice legislation made it more forward looking than either the Republican or Democratic parties. Jane Addams and other social justice reformers joined Roosevelt's crusade for that reason. The party supported woman suffrage, limits on child labor, and a system of "social insurance." The centerpiece of Roosevelt's New Nationalism was the proposal for an "administrative commission" that would "maintain permanent, active supervision over industrial corporations engaged in interstate commerce." Roosevelt continued his policy of distinguishing between "good trusts" that served the public interest and "bad trusts" that harmed society. Roosevelt's position in 1912 anticipated the regulatory and welfare state that emerged later in the twentieth century. Critics at the time warned that in the wrong hands, this increased national power could threaten individual liberty.

At first Woodrow Wilson did not plan to campaign much. As Roosevelt laid out his program, however, the Democratic nominee soon decided to confront his major rival. Wilson told the voters that only a Democratic president could govern effectively with the Democratic Congress that was certain to be elected. He then offered a program of his own to counter Roosevelt's New Nationalism. He called it the New Freedom and emphasized the need for greater competition to control monopolies and called for stricter enforcement of the antitrust laws. Rather than relying on trusts and large corporations to act in a socially responsible manner, as Roosevelt contended, the government should create conditions in which competition could flourish.

As for social justice, Wilson said that he supported the goals of eliminating child labor, improving wages for women, and expanding benefits for employees, but he questioned whether the federal government should supply these benefits. In that way he appealed to progressives but also prevented southern Democrats from opposing him as an enemy of states' rights (and segregation). Throughout the campaign, Wilson stressed that the tariff should be reduced to lower prices and break the link between the government and big business that the Republicans had established. The New Freedom was, like most other campaign slogans, broad and vague. It gave Wilson a mandate for action without tying his hands.

The 1912 election was turbulent down to election day. From the outset of the campaign, it was clear that the Democrats had the electoral advantage over the divided Republicans and Progressives. Wilson received 435 electoral votes to 88 for Roosevelt and 8 for Taft. The Democrats swept Congress: they had fifty-one

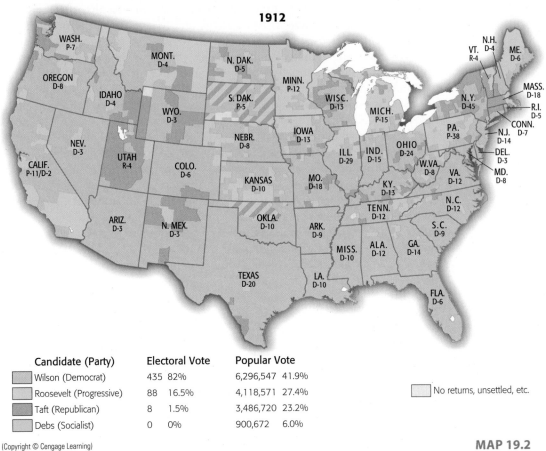

1912

Candidate (Party)	Electoral Vote		Popular Vote	
Wilson (Democrat)	435	82%	6,296,547	41.9%
Roosevelt (Progressive)	88	16.5%	4,118,571	27.4%
Taft (Republican)	8	1.5%	3,486,720	23.2%
Debs (Socialist)	0	0%	900,672	6.0%

No returns, unsettled, etc.

(Copyright © Cengage Learning)

MAP 19.2

The Election of 1912

Because Democrat Woodrow Wilson faced a divided opposition in the presidential election of 1912, the result was a landslide victory in the electoral vote. Theodore Roosevelt's Progressive Party ran second, and William Howard Taft's Republicans were a distant third.

seats in the Senate to forty-four for the Republicans, and their margin in the House was 291 to 127 (see Map 19.2). Nevertheless, Wilson was a minority president, receiving about 42 percent of the popular vote. Despite the electoral drama, turnout for the election was lower than it had been in 1908.

❖ Reform and Social Change During the Wilson Years

In the White House, Woodrow Wilson was a brilliant speaker whose moral rhetoric spoke of lofty ideals. Even more than Roosevelt, he had the capacity to articulate national values in effective and moving language. But Wilson could also be stubborn and reluctant to accept unwelcome advice. His righteousness and sense of personal virtue caused his political enemies to develop an intense dislike of his methods and tactics. However, when the tide of events ran with Wilson, as they did during his first term, he was a powerful leader.

Tariff Reform

Wilson soon demonstrated his intention to be a strong president. He picked **William Jennings Bryan,** the leading Democrat in the country other than Wilson himself, to be secretary of state in recognition of Bryan's leadership of the party after 1896. Wilson first asked Congress to take up the issue of the tariff, which

Bryan, William Jennings (1860–1925) Democratic presidential candidate in 1896, 1900, and 1908. Named secretary of state by President Wilson, he pursued world peace through arbitration treaties.

symbolized the links between Republicans and big business. He called the law-makers into a special session in April 1913, and to dramatize the problem, he decided to deliver his message to Congress in person. No president had done so since Jefferson had abandoned the practice in 1801, but the move proved to be an important step in expanding presidential influence on Capitol Hill and in the nation at large.

Wilson urged the House and Senate to reduce import duties. The Democratic House responded with a measure to lower tariffs, named after Oscar W. Under-wood, the chairman of the Ways and Means Committee. The Underwood bill cut duties on raw wool, sugar, cotton goods, and silks. To compensate for the revenue that would be lost, the new tariff imposed a small tax on annual incomes over $4,000 with rates increasing for those who made more than $20,000 a year. Progressives had secured ratification of the **Sixteenth Amendment** in February 1913, which made the income tax constitutional. Democrats in the Senate stuck together, and a modified version of the bill passed both houses in October. Wilson signed the Underwood Tariff Act into law on October 3, 1913. The president and his party had demonstrated that they could provide positive leadership.

Sixteenth Amendment (1913)
Constitutional amendment that made a federal income tax constitutional.

The Federal Reserve System

Building on his momentum, Wilson turned to banking in June 1913. Since the panic of 1907, there had been a clear need for reform of the nation's banking system. A modern economy could not function efficiently without a central bank with the capacity to control the currency, meet the monetary needs of different sections of the country, and ensure that the money supply was adequate to the demands of the growing economy. The issue became whether private banking interests or the national government should be in charge of the central bank. Wilson agreed with Secretary of State Bryan, who insisted that the government must control the reserve banks.

After six months of negotiations, Congress passed a bill in mid-December, and Wilson signed the Federal Reserve Act on December 27. This act was one of the most important pieces of economic legislation of the first half of the twentieth century. It established the Federal Reserve Board, whose members the president appointed, and created a structure consisting of twelve reserve banks located around the country. The Federal Reserve was given the power to determine the amount of money in circulation, expand or contract credit as needed, and respond to some degree to changes in the business cycle. That has proved to be an indispens-able weapon for the government in managing the economy ever since that time.

Wilson and the Progressive Agenda

Wilson had now fulfilled his campaign pledges to reduce the tariff and reform the banking system. Early in 1914, the president asked Congress to deal with the trust issue. Some of the legislation passed in that year followed the principles that Wilson had outlined in his campaign. The Clayton Antitrust Act (1914) endeav-ored to spell out the business practices that restricted competition and then to prohibit them.

As time passed, Wilson came to favor the creation of a trade commission that would respond to business practices as they evolved, an idea that resembled what Theodore Roosevelt had proposed in 1912. The Federal Trade Commission was established during fall 1914. A delighted Wilson said that he had almost com-pleted the program he had promised in his 1912 presidential campaign.

The president's statements disappointed progressives who wanted social jus-tice legislation. Wilson did not yet believe that Washington should support the demands of progressive interest groups. He was particularly reluctant to address the persistent issue of racial inequality; when supporters of woman suffrage sought Wilson's backing in 1913 and 1914, he refused to provide it. He also opposed federal aid for rural credits, restrictions on child labor through congressional action, and Prohibition. Worsening economic conditions during the spring and summer of 1914 reinforced Wilson's belief that his administration should remain conservative on social and labor issues. His style of presidential progressive governance differed significantly from Roosevelt's.

Modern Technology and Mass Markets

While politicians worked out Wilson's New Freedom programs during 1913 and 1914, social and cultural transformations proceeded. When Wilson went to his inauguration on March 4, 1913, he drove in an automobile, the first time a president-elect had traveled to his swearing-in by car. This action symbolized the vast changes that were making the people of the United States more mobile in their daily lives and more eager for the consumer products of an industrial society. In particular, Henry Ford's innovations in both production and marketing were bringing cars within the reach of the average middle-class American.

To fulfill his dream of building "a motor car for the great multitude," Ford borrowed the concept of the assembly line from the meat-packing industry, and his engineers adapted it to making cars. The Ford plant covered more than sixty-five acres in Highland Park, Michigan. It featured a large belt, fed by smaller belts that brought the chassis of the car and its windshields, tanks, batteries, and other parts together in a smoothly functioning operation. By 1920, the cars were coming off the line at the rate of one per minute. In 1914 the Model T cost under $500 and Ford produced more than 260,000 cars.

On January 5, 1914, Ford proclaimed that he would pay his workers five dollars for an eight-hour day—about three times that of the average manufacturing worker. The announcement made headline news across the country, and Ford became a national hero. He understood that people needed to earn enough money in wages to be able to afford the cars he was making; Ford also recognized the need to head off potential unrest among Ford workers. Ford developed a

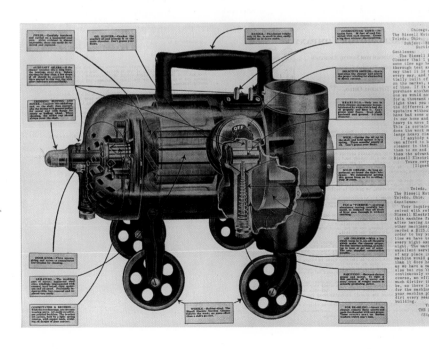

Advertisement for Vacuum Cleaner. This advertisement for a vacuum cleaner that could be used conveniently in the home was part of the growing market for consumer appliances that reshaped American domestic life.

"Sociological Department" to instill in employees the values required for efficient mass production. Workers who were productive and cooperative received higher wages. Those who were not were discharged.

Another sign of progress was the spreading reliance on electricity. Average annual use of electricity doubled during the twenty years after 1912. New products offered homemakers the chance to ease the dull routines of domestic work. General Electric introduced the Radiant Toaster in 1912, which promised "Crisp, Delicious, Golden-Brown Toast on the Breakfast Table." Newer stoves and washing machines also came into use, and women could buy ready-made clothes from garment factories instead of sewing their own.

Other technological developments were still in their early stages. The Wright brothers had made the first powered flight in 1903, and technological progress in flying accelerated during the decade that followed. Meanwhile, the use of wireless telegraphy in marine navigation expanded. The disaster of the SS *Titanic*, which hit an iceberg in April 1912 and sank with the loss of hundreds of passengers, underlined the need for reliable radio communications for all vessels. Congress enacted a bill mandating the navy to promote radio usage. Within a few years tentative steps would be taken toward broadcasting voices over the airwaves.

Artistic and Social Ferment

In 1913, the International Exhibit of Modern Art took place at the 69th Regiment Armory in New York City. Quickly dubbed "the Armory Show," it displayed the works of such European painters as Pablo Picasso and Henri Matisse. The modernist paintings, abstract and challenging, offended many critics, but one predicted, "American art will never be the same again."

The period also produced innovative literary figures who would become even more famous during the 1920s. Reporters and novelists clustered in New York's Greenwich Village. Among them were Max Eastman, publisher of *The Masses*, a magazine that assailed conventional values and the established political system;

New York City, 1913. The American painter George Bellows records the teeming life of New York City in 1913 in his painting that reflects the newer currents of art at the time of the Armory Show and the onset of World War I.

(George Bellows, *The Cliff Dwellers*, 1913. Los Angeles County Museum of Art, Los Angeles)

Eugene O'Neill, a playwright; and John Reed, a radical journalist. Outside New York City, Theodore Dreiser was continuing a literary career that included *The Financier* (1912), a novel depicting a ruthless tycoon; Sherwood Anderson was a short-story author who criticized middle-class life in the nation's heartland.

Women sought to gain greater rights and share the freedoms that men enjoyed. In 1912, women in Greenwich Village founded a club called Heterodoxy, whose only demand was that its members "not be orthodox" in their views. In their discussions and in the public meetings they sponsored, they called their doctrine "feminism," which they defined as an attempt on the part of women to be "our whole big human selves." Cultural changes occurred even for those who did not call themselves feminists. Women's skirts had become several inches shorter since the beginning of the century, when they had reached down to the ankle. Bobbed hair became fashionable, and more women smoked openly in public. The years between 1910 and 1920 saw greater opportunities for women in employment and cultural affairs than would occur in the 1920s.

The New Leisure

The ways in which Americans used their leisure time reflected a trend toward mass entertainment and sports. Boxing was a major sport. When Arthur John **"Jack" Johnson** became the first African American heavyweight champion in 1908, the white-controlled media clamored for a "white hope" to reclaim the title. Jackson defeated each of his white challengers in the ring, but fled the country when the government accused him of transporting women across state lines for immoral purposes. In 1915, an aging Johnson lost the heavyweight title. Meanwhile, baseball attained new heights of popularity, and the World Series had become an annual fall ritual to decide the "world's champion." The public avidly absorbed the ample news coverage that baseball received.

Johnson, "Jack" (1878–1946)
First African American heavyweight boxing champion, taking the title in 1908.

During the time Wilson was president, motion pictures were challenging the dominance of vaudeville. Movies were evolving from short features into stories of an hour or more. The places where patrons saw films were upgraded, while the price of admission remained reasonable. Within a decade, movies emerged as the mass entertainment of the nation. They were lively and up to date and conveyed a sense of modern life and spontaneity that made nineteenth-century ideas appear even more dated and obsolete.

With the advent of World War I in August 1914, the nineteenth century would soon seem even more of a vanished age.

CHAPTER REVIEW, 1901–1914

SUMMARY

- During Theodore Roosevelt's presidency, he launched a program of government regulation, attacked the trusts, and expanded the role of the United States in the world.

- The Progressive movement was a grassroots effort that began with reform in the nation's cities and expanded to deal with state issues.

- Progressivism became a national force under Roosevelt's leadership and addressed such social problems as woman suffrage, child labor, and conservation of natural resources.

- In general, Progressives sought greater democracy and social efficiency.

- Labor unions continued to struggle against corporate interests, winning improvements in workplace safety and prompting some employers to offer modest benefits known as corporate welfare.

- When the presidency of William Howard Taft faltered, the Republican Party split between Taft and Roosevelt, leading to Roosevelt's creation of the Progressive Party in 1912.

- The Democrats made a comeback under Woodrow Wilson, who enacted New Freedom reforms as president.

- Consumer culture emerged as cars and movies changed social patterns, and cultural ferment led to new trends in art and writing.

IDENTIFICATIONS

National Women's Trade Union League

J. P. Morgan

trustbuster

Square Deal

"Bill" Morris

W. E. B. Du Bois

National Association for the Advancement of Colored People (NAACP)

Roosevelt Corollary

progressivism

Interstate Commerce Commission

Ida Tarbell

muckrakers

Robert M. La Follette

Upton Sinclair

Muller v. Oregon

William Howard Taft

New Nationalism

woman suffrage

Alice Paul

Triangle Shirtwaist fire

dollar diplomacy

Woodrow Wilson

William Jennings Bryan

Sixteenth Amendment

"Jack" Johnson

MAKING CONNECTIONS: LOOKING AHEAD ⫸

The next chapter considers what happened when progressives encountered the effects of the war raging in Europe beginning in 1914. The outbreak of the conflict called into question the progressive conviction that human beings were basically good. When the United States entered the war in April 1917, some reforms were pushed forward, and some progressive issues suffered. The international problems that came out of World War I set the pattern for future disputes in the Middle East and Asia.

1. How did Woodrow Wilson view the U.S. role in the rest of the world, especially in Latin America?

2. How much of a world power was the United States in 1914?

3. What kind of presidential leadership did Woodrow Wilson offer to the Democrats?

RECOMMENDED READINGS

Cooper, John Milton, Jr. *Woodrow Wilson* (2009). An excellent recent biography of the president.

Cordery, Stacy. *Theodore Roosevelt: In the Vanguard of the Modern* (2002). A newer, brief biography of Roosevelt that provides a good look at his historical impact.

Gould, Lewis L. *Four Hats in the Ring: The 1912 Election and the Birth of Modern American Politics* (2008). A fast-paced account of this important election.

Gould, Lewis L. *The Presidency of Theodore Roosevelt* (1991). Reviews the president's achievements in office.

McGerr, Michael. *A Fierce Discontent: The Rise and Fall of the Progressive Movement in America, 1870–1920* (2003). A new interpretation of the reform movement and its results.

Miller, Char. *Gifford Pinchot and the Making of Modern Environmentalism* (2001). Places one of the leaders of the progressive conservation movement in a broader context.

Sanders, Elizabeth. *Roots of Reform: Farmers, Workers, and the American State, 1877–1917* (1999). Provides insights into how reform legislation fared in Congress.

Unger, Nancy. *Fighting Bob La Follette: The Righteous Reformer* (2000). A biography of the Wisconsin senator who challenged Roosevelt for progressive leadership.

CourseMate Go to the CourseMate website at www.cengagebrain.com for additional study tools and review materials for this chapter.

20 Over There and Over Here: The Impact of World War I, 1914–1920

21 The Age of Jazz and Mass Culture, 1921–1927

22 The Great Depression, 1927–1933

Progress seemed everywhere on the eve of World War I. Aviators crossed the English Channel for the first time, wireless communication linked ships at sea with their destinations. At home, Americans took to the open road in their new Ford automobiles. In such a heady climate of advancing technology and growing economic abundance, writers spoke of an end of war as nations talked out their disputes at the conference table rather than settling them on the battlefield. The path of history seemed well lit and clear toward a bright future of hope and peace.

By the winter of 1933, the United States lay in the grip of a severe economic depression. Banks had closed, unemployment had soared, and the homeless and destitute roamed the land. Newspapers and magazines ran articles that speculated on whether democracy had failed. To a minority of Americans, the opposing ideologies of communism and fascism seemed alluring. As the nation faced the prospect of a potential social revolution, its citizens looked back with nostalgia to the early years of the century and wondered what had happened to destroy that optimistic and confident world.

The outbreak of a world war in the summer of 1914 did the most to unhinge the sense of progress that then permeated the United States. If advanced nations could ravage each other on European battlefields, who could any longer believe in the perfectibility of humanity? Americans first tried to stay out of the conflict, but by 1917 they entered the war on the side of France and Great Britain.

In less than two years, the experience of World War I accelerated trends toward a more powerful federal government, a more bureaucratic society, and a nation in which large corporations exercised an even greater role. At the same time, the bitter national and ideological conflicts of Europe spilled over into American life. Racial, ethnic, and sectional tensions produced social unrest and group hatreds that raged between 1917 and 1933.

During the war, however, some aspects of prewar reform reached completion. Women gained the vote in 1920 after three generations of struggle. Their ballots did not transform national politics in the years that followed, but women's presence in the process ended centuries of a male monopoly of the elective system. The war years also achieved the temperance dream of a national prohibition of alcohol. Despite this reform success, the nation remained divided over its attitude toward liquor, a condition that raised problems for enforcing the new constitutional amendment.

In the aftermath of World War I, Americans rushed forward to embrace the new world of consumer goods and economic affluence. Automobiles, appliances, and installment buying reshaped attitudes about frugality and the future. The spread of mass media and big-time sports brought shared cultural experiences to many Americans. The decade seemed vibrant with the wailing of jazz, the roar of the metropolis, and the excitement of flaming youth.

Not all Americans shared in the prosperity or endorsed the headlong embrace of the modern world. Farmers never experienced the prosperity of the 1920s, and they encountered economic downturns sooner than did their city counterparts. Rural values remained strong even when transplanted to an urban setting. Some dislocated citizens sought the missing sense of community in an organization such as the Ku Klux Klan, which promised ritual, controversy, and social change in equal measure. Many Americans found that fundamentalist religious denominations spoke to their spiritual needs in ways that the modernist churches did not. Strains between the city and country showed themselves in politics in the 1928 presidential election when the urban, Catholic background of Democrat Al Smith

Aftermath of World War I.
The flamboyant young woman depicted on the cover of *Life* Magazine symbolized the sense of liberation and daring that moved many American females in the years between 1909 and 1933.

turned many in his party toward the Republican nominee, Herbert Hoover.

Throughout the 1920s, the confidence that the economy would move ever upward sustained people even when they lacked wealth themselves. By the end of the decade, however, the prosperity that consumers had built and corporations relished began to totter. Poor distribution of income, corporate excesses, weaknesses in the banking structure, and mounting problems with international finance led to a stock market crash in 1929 and a depression that grew steadily worse during the early 1930s.

A generation raised on the prospect of burgeoning prosperity found itself confronted with want, destitution, and despair. Organized charity seemed inadequate to the task of relief, and government at all levels failed to address the economic problems in effective ways. By the winter of 1932, the nation was experiencing a tightening spiral of gloom and fear. The sunny days of progressivism and reform were only a grotesque echo of an age that had disappeared. In the American passage, the early 1930s seemed as close as any citizen wished to get to the valley of the shadow.

POLITICS AND DIPLOMACY

1914: Clayton Antitrust law passed
Vera Cruz incident leads to intervention in Mexico
World War begins in Europe
1915: *Lusitania* sunk
Leo Frank lynched in Georgia
1916: Germany makes Sussex Pledge about submarines
Americans intervene in Mexico to attempt capture of Pancho Villa
Wilson defeats Hughes in presidential election

1917: Zimmerman Telegram released
United States declares war on Germany
1918: Wilson announces Fourteen Points
Armistice ends World War I
Democrats are defeated and Wilson repudiated in congressional elections
1919: Wilson attends Peace Conference, but League of Nations is defeated in Senate
Prohibition adopted

1920: Woman suffrage adopted
Harding defeats Cox and is elected president
1921: Harding inaugurated
United States signs separate peace with Germany
1922: Washington Naval Conference
Democrats make gains in congressional elections

SOCIETY AND CULTURE

1914: President Wilson proclaims first national Mother's Day
Margaret Sanger introduces term "birth control"
New Republic magazine begins publication
1915: *Birth of a Nation* becomes hit movie
Support for woman suffrage grows
Charlie Chaplin becomes movie star
Great Migration of African Americans to north begins
1916: First birth control clinic opens in Brooklyn, New York
National Woman's Party founded

1917: Frozen food processing developed
Woman suffrage advocates jailed for picketing White House
1918: Influenza epidemic sweeps the globe and kills 21 million people
First granulated soap ("Rinso") introduced
1919: Dial telephones introduced
Red Scare about Bolsheviks occurs

1920: Edith Wharton wins Pulitzer Price for her novel *The Age of Innocence*
Miss America beauty pageant begins
Marcus Garvey's United Negro Improvement Association claims more than 2 million members
1921: Immigration laws set quotas for Eastern Europeans
Shepard-Towner Maternity and Infancy Protection Act passed
1922: Sinclair Lewis's *Babbitt* is published
Radio gains in popularity as stations spread
Reader's Digest begins publication

ECONOMICS AND TECHNOLOGY

1914: Ludlow, Colorado, strike leads to deaths of 21 people by state militia
Henry Ford introduces Five-Dollar Day for auto workers
1915: Preparedness movement and war orders revive American economy
1916: Federal Farm Loan Act passed
Adamson Act creates eight-hour day for railroad workers

1917: Production and use of food is regulated through food administration
War Industries Board created
1918: Webb-Pomerene Act passed to promote foreign trade
National War Labor Board established
1919: Economy reverts to peacetime status with little government supervision
Strikes and labor disputes occur nationwide
Inflation becomes a problem

1920: Esch-Cummins Act passed to return railroads to private control and broaden powers of Interstate Commerce Commission
Woman's Bureau created in Department of Labor
1921: Nation experiences business recession as intense deflation occurs
1922: Fordney-McCumber Tariff Act passed

1923: Teapot Dome scandal breaks Harding dies of heart attack Calvin Coolidge becomes president **1924**: Miriam Amanda Ferguson and Nellie Tayloe Ross elected as first woman governors Democratic convention takes 103 ballots to nominate John W. Davis Coolidge defeats Davis and third-party candidate Robert M. La Follette **1925**: Scopes trial on evolution in Dayton, Tennessee **1926**: United States membership in World Court fails Democrats make gains in congressional elections	**1927**: President Coolidge says he will not run in 1928 Sacco and Vanzetti executed **1928**: Hoover defeats Smith in presidential election **1929**: Hoover becomes president **1930**: London Naval Conference on disarmament Democrats erase most of Republican House majority in elections	**1931**: Depression deepens Hoover declares moratorium on war debts **1932**: Bonus Marchers dispersed in Washington Roosevelt defeats Hoover in election **1933**: Roosevelt inaugurated president as Depression hits bottom
1923: *Time* magazine is launched Blues singers such as Alberta Hunter and Bessie Smith become popular **1924**: Kleenex is introduced **1925**: Red Grange becomes national football hero and signs professional contract Publication of F. Scott Fitzgerald's *The Great Gatsby* Harlem Renaissance at height in New York City *New Yorker* magazine starts publication **1926**: Publication of Ernest Hemingway's *The Sun Also Rises* Gertrude Ederle becomes first woman to swim English Channel	**1927**: Babe Ruth hits sixty home runs Charles Lindbergh flies across the Atlantic alone Al Jolson makes talking pictures popular in *The Jazz Singer* **1928**: Walt Disney releases his first cartoon, "Plane Crazy" Eugene O'Neill's play *Strange Interlude* wins Pulitzer Prize **1929**: Sales of processed baby food begin Museum of Modern Art founded in New York City The first Blue Cross health insurance group starts in Dallas **1930**: *Amos 'n' Andy* radio show becomes nationally popular Sliced bread introduced commercially First supermarket opens	**1931**: Southern Commission on the Study of Lynching formed Empire State Building, world's tallest, opens in New York City Al Capone, leading mobster, sentenced to jail for tax evasion **1932**: Charles Lindbergh's son kidnapped and found dead Amelia Earhart makes first solo transatlantic flight by a woman Radio City Music Hall opens in New York City **1933**: Prohibition ends
1923: Supreme Court in *Adkins v. Children's Hospital* invalidates law providing for minimum wage for women in Washington, D.C. **1924**: McNary-Haugen Bill to help farmers is introduced **1925**: Florida land boom flourishes **1926**: Revenue Act produces substantial tax reduction Florida land boom collapses	**1927**: Henry Ford introduces Model A car **1928**: Federal Reserve raises interest rates to curb speculation **1929**: Stock Market crash occurs in September and October **1930**: Great Depression begins Smoot-Hawley Tariff enacted	**1931**: Hoover administration relief measures address condition of unemployed but do not bring upturn in economy **1932**: Reconstruction Finance Corporation created to deal with bank and corporate failures during Depression Revenue Act cuts government spending **1933**: Depression hits bottom as Franklin D. Roosevelt takes office

20

Over There and Over Here: The Impact of World War I

1914–1920

MAKING CONNECTIONS

◄◄▮▮▮ **LOOKING BACK**

The Taft–Roosevelt split that devastated the Republicans had its origins amid the issues discussed in Chapter 19. The basis for the division had been created during the last years of Roosevelt's presidency. Before starting Chapter 20, you should be able to answer the following questions:

1. Was Theodore Roosevelt as good a politician as he thought he was?

2. How did Roosevelt and Taft differ in their view of what a president should do?

3. How did the New Nationalism represent a culmination of Roosevelt's political philosophy as president?

Staying Neutral in a World Conflict

New Freedom Diplomacy
War's Outbreak in Europe
The War and American Public Opinion
The *Lusitania* Crisis

Social Change During the Period of Neutrality

Enduring Racism
The Rise of the Movies
Shifting Attitudes Toward Sex
The Persistence of Reform
A Hazardous Neutrality

The 1916 Presidential Election

Mediation and Intervention
The Outbreak of Hostilities

A Nation at War

Managing the Wartime Economy
Black Americans in the War

Women's Issues in the Great War
Civil Liberties and the Limits
of Dissent

The Road to Victory

Wilson's Peace Program
The Paris Peace Conference
The Shadow of Bolshevism
Wilson and the Treaty of Versailles

Doing History: The League of Nations
Debate, 1919

The Senate and the League
of Nations

From War to Peace

The Waning Spirit of Progressivism
The Struggles of Labor
Harding and "Normalcy"

Americans wanted to keep out of the European war. Yet events in the conflict influenced domestic politics, altered the Progressive movement, and changed the fortunes of women, African Americans, and socialists. The nation's traditional values came under repeated attack as the war continued. U.S. entry into the war in April 1917 transformed the country in an even more striking fashion.

World War I brought several campaigns for social change, most notably Prohibition and woman suffrage, to national success. Yet by the time these results occurred, the movement for reform had stalled. The nation rejected an activist government, expensive programs, and efforts to improve society. When Woodrow Wilson left the White House on March 4, 1921, he gave way to Warren G. Harding, who promised a return to older values and a respite from moral uplift.

❖ Staying Neutral in a World Conflict

Throughout the Progressive era, domestic political and economic concerns dominated. Newspapers covered international news, and readers could follow the unfolding of European diplomacy if they wished. Isolated from the tensions of world affairs by two vast oceans, Americans allowed their elected leaders to conduct foreign policy as long as the general policies of isolation and noninvolvement with Europe were observed.

New Freedom Diplomacy

Early in 1913, Woodrow Wilson remarked to a friend that it "would be the irony of fate if my administration had to deal chiefly with foreign affairs." Despite his lack of experience, Wilson proactively addressed diplomatic problems in Asia and Latin America that trained him for the greater trials he would face in World War I. The president appointed peace advocate William Jennings Bryan as secretary of state. In foreign affairs, Woodrow Wilson believed that the United States should set an example for the rest of the world because of the nation's commitment to democracy and capitalism. "Morality and not expediency is the thing that must guide us," he said in 1913.

Wilson's foreign policy decisions departed from those of his Republican predecessors in some ways. In Asia, the Wilson administration recognized the Republic of China, which had come into power following the 1911 revolution that ousted the Manchu dynasty. Wilson and the Democrats put the Philippine Islands on the road toward independence, but their efforts to counter the rise of Japanese influence in Asia proved less successful. In Latin America, Wilson sought a policy that was less intrusive and less dominant than Roosevelt's had been. To that end, he worked out a treaty with Colombia that apologized for Roosevelt's actions in helping to foment the Panamanian revolution in 1903–1904. The pact outraged Roosevelt, and the Senate did not approve the treaty while Wilson was

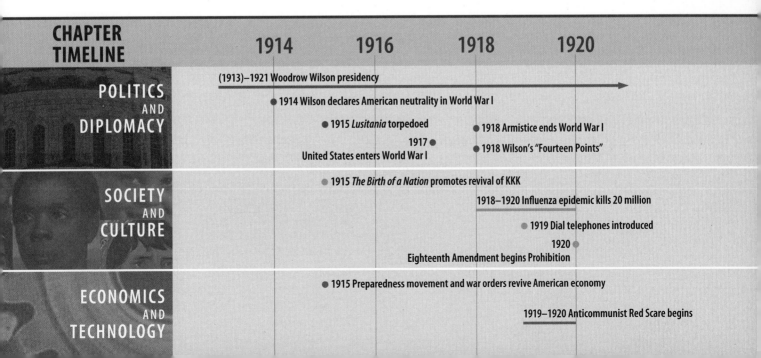

CHAPTER TIMELINE	1914	1916	1918	1920

POLITICS AND DIPLOMACY

(1913)–1921 Woodrow Wilson presidency

● 1914 Wilson declares American neutrality in World War I

● 1915 *Lusitania* torpedoed

1917 ● United States enters World War I

● 1918 Armistice ends World War I

● 1918 Wilson's "Fourteen Points"

SOCIETY AND CULTURE

● 1915 *The Birth of a Nation* promotes revival of KKK

1918–1920 Influenza epidemic kills 20 million

● 1919 Dial telephones introduced

1920 ● Eighteenth Amendment begins Prohibition

ECONOMICS AND TECHNOLOGY

● 1915 Preparedness movement and war orders revive American economy

1919–1920 Anticommunist Red Scare begins

Huerta, Victoriano (1854–1916)
Mexican general and president
(1913–1914). The United States
did not recognize Huerta's
government, and President Wilson
ordered U.S. military intervention
in support of his rival, Venustiano
Carranza.

in office. But some interventions were unavoidable: Wilson kept troops in Nicaragua and extracted further concessions from that country. Other military detachments went to Cuba, Haiti, and the Dominican Republic.

In Mexico, Wilson confronted a revolution. Just before Wilson was inaugurated in March 1913, the Madero government, which had taken over from Porfirio Díaz in 1911, was ousted by General **Victoriano Huerta**. Although most European nations quickly recognized Huerta's government, the United States did not.

Wilson instead threw the weight of the United States behind Venustiano Carranza, a rebel against the Huerta government, but Wilson's offers of cooperation were not accepted. If Carranza agreed to Wilson's insistence on some U.S. presence in Mexico, he would have been regarded as pro-American, a fatal weakness to the Mexican populace.

To block the flow of munitions into Mexico from the United States and Europe, Wilson had sent the navy to patrol the Gulf of Mexico. When American sailors went ashore at Tampico on April 9 without permission, Mexican authorities arrested them. Released quickly and without further incident, they returned to their ship, but the American admiral on the scene nonetheless demanded that the Mexican authorities apologize. Huerta's government refused.

The president asked Congress for authority to use force at a time when a German vessel was unloading arms on the Mexican shore. Wilson ordered troops to occupy the port of Vera Cruz. In the heavy fighting that erupted, more than a hundred Mexicans and nineteen Americans died. All of the warring parties in Mexico denounced the United States. The two countries seemed on the edge of outright war until Wilson drew back and accepted mediation. The negotiations led to the evacuation of Vera Cruz on November 14. Dependent on outside funds to pay his army, Huerta left office when his money ran out in July 1914. Carranza took power, and Wilson promptly recognized his government.

Revolutionary upheavals in Mexico produced an increase in immigrants from that country into the United States after 1910. Although many of those immigrants returned to Mexico after working in the United States for several months, some thirty-five thousand to seventy-five thousand Hispanic immigrants stayed on each year, finding work from Texas to California. Throughout these years, the spread of irrigation, agriculture, railroads, and mining in the Southwest increased the demand for inexpensive labor. The closing off of Japanese immigration after 1907 made Mexican laborers an attractive option for Anglo businesses.

Major centers of Hispanic life emerged in the southwestern cities. Ethnic communities sponsored mutual aid societies and established Spanish-language newspapers to ease the immigrants' adjustment to a new culture. Prejudice remained strong, however. When Mexican immigrants settled in San Bernadino, California, one long-time resident warned that he "might use a shotgun on these aliens if necessary." In Texas and California, segregation and poverty limited the opportunities open to Mexican Americans. By 1915, a violent cultural conflict that claimed hundreds of lives was in progress in south Texas. As a result of these struggles, Mexican Americans lost much of the land they held in the area.

War's Outbreak in Europe

By 1914, the major European nations were on edge. Because of secret alliances, if one country found itself at war with another, all the other powers could be drawn into the struggle. (See Map 20.1.) On one side stood Germany; its powerful industries and efficient army worried neighbors France and Russia. Led by the expansionist Kaiser Wilhelm II, Germans sought the international respect they believed to be their rightful due, building up a large navy that fueled tensions with Great Britain. The Germans had treaty links to the sprawling and turbulent nations of Austria-Hungary and the even more ramshackle regime of the Ottoman Turks. Italy had been part of the so-called **Triple Alliance** with Germany and Austria-Hungary, but these ties were frayed by 1914.

Against the Germans stood the French (who coveted territory they had lost in the Franco-Prussian War of 1871), the Russians, and, if the Germans attacked France, the British. The Russian Empire was in decay, with revolutionary sentiments just below the surface. The French feared another defeat at the hands of Germany, and the British eyed the growing German navy warily. All the powers had elaborate plans for mobilization in a general crisis. Once these timetables went into effect, the relentless pressure of military events would frustrate efforts at a diplomatic resolution.

World War I began in the Balkans. On June 28, 1914, the Austrian archduke, **Franz Ferdinand,** and his wife were murdered by Serbian terrorists in the town of Sarajevo in Bosnia, a province of the Austro-Hungarian Empire. The Austrians made harsh demands on Serbia, supported by the Germans, with the result that the Russians came to the defense of the Serbs. By early August 1914, all of the European countries had been drawn into the conflict. Germany, Austria-Hungary, and Turkey, known as the Central Powers, were fighting Great Britain, France, and Russia, now called the Allies. Italy remained neutral. Soon the guns of August began a conflagration that lasted four years and consumed a generation.

The sudden outbreak of fighting in Europe surprised Americans. Although the arms race among the great powers had seemed potentially dangerous, it had been a century since a major war had involved all of the major European countries. Faith in progress and the betterment of humanity, so much a part of the

Triple Alliance Pre–World War I alliance between Germany, Austria-Hungary, and Italy, established in 1882.

Franz Ferdinand (1863–1914) Austrian archduke murdered along with his wife in Sarajevo, Bosnia. Austria's ultimatum to Serbia led to the outbreak of World War I.

MAP 20.1

Europe on the Eve of World War I

In the summer of 1914, when World War I erupted, Germany and Austria-Hungary dominated the center of the European land mass. France, Great Britain, and Russia counterbalanced the Central Powers. Once the fighting began, the system of alliances drew most of Europe into the conflict.

(Copyright © Cengage Learning)

1. **June 28**
   Assassination at Sarajevo

2. **July 28**
   Austria-Hungary declares war on Serbia

3. **July 30**
   Russia begins mobilization

4. **August 1**
   Germany declares war on Russia

5. **August 3**
   Germany declares war on France and invades Belgium

6. **August 4**
   Great Britain declares war on Germany

7. **August 6**
   Russia and Austria-Hungary at war

8. **August 12**
   Great Britain declares war on Austria-Hungary

Central Powers (Triple Alliance— except Italy—and allies)

The Allies (Triple Entente and allies)

Neutral nations

Progressive era's creed, made war unthinkable. The world war came at a time of emotional distress for Wilson: his wife, Ellen, had died on August 6, 1914. On the domestic political scene, the Democrats expected serious losses in the congressional elections. The Republicans had won back some of the Progressive voters who had followed Roosevelt in 1912. Until war broke out, it seemed as if politics might be returning to something resembling its normal patterns.

The War and American Public Opinion

President Wilson in August 1914 asked his fellow citizens to "be neutral in fact as well as in name" and "impartial in thought as well as in action." Long an admirer of British government and culture, Wilson himself had more sympathy for the Allies than for Germany and its wartime partners. In conducting foreign policy, however, he was as even-handed toward the two sides as any president could have been. The initial results of Wilson's neutrality decisions came in national politics. In the congressional elections of 1914, the Republicans picked up sixty-three seats in the House, but the Democrats retained control. In the Senate, the president's party actually added five seats.

The British had inherent advantages in their financial ties with the United States. Economic links with Great Britain were strong, and they intensified as the war progressed. Exports to Britain and France totaled $754 million in 1914; in 1916, they stood at $2.75 billion. Meanwhile, trade with Germany, which had totaled $190 million in 1914, virtually ceased because of the British blockade. The United States could have embargoed all trade with belligerent powers, as many American supporters of Germany recommended, but that strategy would have devastated the economy. Over the course of the neutrality period, the British gained in their efforts to influence American thinking.

But Germans also had strong support in the United States. The more than 5 million German Americans, most numerous in the Midwest, represented a sizable bloc of votes that usually favored Republicans. The 3 million–plus Irish Americans hated England and cheered for its enemies. Germany conducted an expensive propaganda campaign of pamphlets and newspaper advertisements. Money directed through the German-dominated brewing industry paid for the campaign. Undercutting their public relations image, however, the Germans also used espionage and sabotage to cripple the British war effort and hamper American assistance to the Allies.

These strategies hurt the Germans' cause with Americans. In the opening days of the fighting, the German army violated Belgium's neutrality, crossing that nation's borders to invade France. Confronted with a British naval blockade designed to strangle its capacity to wage war, Germany turned to a new weapon, the submarine, early in 1915. In contrast to surface ships, the submarine relied on surprise attacks based on its ability to submerge. Germany declared that enemy vessels would be sunk on sight, a policy many Americans regarded as a violation of the civilized rules of war. The use of the submarine put Germany in direct conflict with the United States.

The *Lusitania* Crisis

Lusitania British liner sunk by a German torpedo in May 1915. Among the nearly 1,200 passengers who died were 128 Americans.

On May 7, 1915, when a German submarine fired a torpedo into the British liner **Lusitania** off the Irish coast, the huge vessel sank quickly. Among the nearly 1,200 passengers who died were 128 Americans. To most people, this event was an atrocity, not an inescapable by-product of modern warfare. Wilson had said that Germany would be held to "strict accountability" for submarine attacks on Americans. However, three days after the *Lusitania* incident, Wilson said that "there is such a thing as a man being too proud to fight. There is such a thing as a nation being so right that it does not need to convince others by force that it is right." Allied sympathizers denounced Wilson's words, but the president's readiness to negotiate was generally approved.

Wilson sought an apology and a pledge to limit submarine warfare. His diplomatic response was strong enough, however, that his anti-war Secretary of State William Jennings Bryan, fearful that war might result, resigned in protest in June 1915. He was replaced by Robert Lansing, a pro-Allied diplomat. During the remainder of the summer, the Germans kept the negotiating process going without apologizing or yielding on any point. In August, they torpedoed a British liner, the *Arabic*, wounding two Americans. Under pressure from Wilson, Berlin offered a conditional pledge not to make unannounced attacks on passenger liners, which defused the situation briefly. In the following year, the Germans sank thirty-seven unarmed liners.

Birth of a Nation, The (1915) Racist movie portrayal of the Reconstruction period in the South that depicted African Americans as ignorant and that glamorized the Ku Klux Klan.

The neutrality issue forced Americans to consider the nation's future role in a warring world. Many groups wanted the United States to maintain its traditional posture of noninvolvement. German Americans and Irish Americans saw no need to help the British. Progressive reformers regarded war and foreign commitments as the death of reform. In the Midwest and on the Pacific Coast, peace sentiments were widespread. The other side, mainly northeastern Republicans, called for military "preparedness" in the event of ultimate American entry into the war. Army and navy officials knew that they would have to expand their forces if they were to play any significant role on the Allied side. By the summer of 1915, Wilson began to seek a larger army and navy. He promised a navy "second to none" and more troops for the regular army. In early 1916, the president made a speaking tour to arouse popular support for his policy.

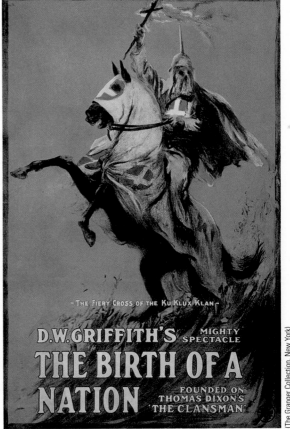

(The Granger Collection, New York)

❖ Social Change During the Period of Neutrality

During 1915, Americans flocked to theaters to see a new motion picture that depicted sensational events in the nation's past. David Wark Griffith's **The Birth of a Nation** was based on a racist novel by Thomas Dixon, *The Clansman*. An artistic triumph because it used new techniques such as flashbacks and close-ups, the movie twisted history to glamorize the Ku Klux Klan and demonize African Americans. Audiences were enthusiastic and attendance broke box office records, while efforts by African Americans to have the film banned were largely unsuccessful. Inspired by the film's portrayal of the Klan, a group of white men burned a cross at Stone Mountain, Georgia, to symbolize their resurgence as a racist order.

The Birth of a Nation.
D. W. Griffith's film *The Birth of a Nation* was an artistic triumph with a racist theme. This poster advertising the film depicts the Ku Klux Klan as akin to medieval knights in the garb of chivalry. White audiences ignored the Klan's violent reality for African Americans.

Enduring Racism

The political prospects for improved rights for blacks remained bleak during the war. The Wilson administration and the Democratic Party resisted efforts to reduce racism. After protests from blacks and a few progressives, the White House retreated from efforts to enforce segregation in the federal government, but that was a minor victory. The Supreme Court did, however, rule in the case of *Guinn v. United States* (1915) that the grandfather clause that Oklahoma used to exempt whites from a literacy test for voting was unconstitutional. Oklahoma found other ways to register whites and restrict blacks, but the decision foreshadowed future progress for minority rights.

For African Americans in the South, life was still painful and burdensome. Southern agriculture experienced crippling problems. Natural disasters hit the region in the form of floods and droughts. The boll weevil, an insect that destroys cotton, undermined the farm economy. Blacks began leaving the South for cities in the North. The **Great Migration** started slowly around 1910 and then accelerated between 1914 and 1920, when more than six hundred thousand African Americans moved north (see Map 20.2). The outbreak of the war played a key role in this process: as immigration from Europe ended, the labor market for unskilled workers in the North expanded. Blacks who came to the North secured work in the coal mines of West Virginia, the stockyards of Chicago, and the steel mills of Pittsburgh. Sixty thousand blacks moved to Chicago between 1916 and 1920, a 148 percent increase in its African American population. Similar percentage increases occurred in Pittsburgh, Cincinnati, and Detroit (see Table 20.1).

As their population in the North grew, blacks encountered discrimination in housing and public services, including from long-standing residents of African

Great Migration A massive movement of blacks leaving the South for cities in the North that began slowly in 1910 and accelerated between 1914 and 1920. During this time, more than six hundred thousand African Americans left the South.

(Copyright © Cengage Learning)

MAP 20.2
The Great Migration, 1930
This map shows how the Great Migration of blacks from the South flowed northward into cities and states where significant African American communities arose.

African-American migration

TABLE 20.1
Migration of African Americans to Five Northern Cities, 1910–1920

	New York	Chicago	Philadelphia	Baltimore	Detroit
1910	91,709	44,103	84,459	84,749	5,741
1920	152,467	109,458	134,229	108,322	40,838
Percentage rise	66.3	148.2	58.9	27.8	611.3

Source: Robert B. Grant, *The Black Man Comes to the City* (Chicago: Nelson-Hall, 1972).

American communities in northern cities who looked down on the new arrivals. Nevertheless, southern blacks continued to move north in an historic population shift that reshaped the politics and culture of the nation's largest cities.

The Rise of the Movies

In 1914, a young British comedian began appearing in films for the Keystone company, a filmmaking venture in Los Angeles. Although most of his thirty-five pictures were very short, one film, *Tillie's Punctured Romance,* ran for thirty minutes. Audiences asked about the funny actor in the derby hat and little tramp costume. By 1915, the whole nation was talking about Charlie Chaplin. Other "stars" created by the studios during the silent movie era included Mary Pickford, who became "America's Sweetheart" in a series of roles that depicted a demure damsel in acute distress, and the swashbuckling Douglas Fairbanks, who starred in *American Aristocracy* (1916) and *Wild and Woolly* (1917).

After a shaky start at the beginning of the century, motion pictures had arrived as mass entertainment. There were more than ten thousand nickelodeon theaters by 1912, and up to 20 million Americans went to the movies regularly. Because of its mild climate, Hollywood, California, emerged as the center of the picture industry, where studios like Vitagraph and Paramount dominated the making and marketing of films. Most moviegoers lived in cities where the large theaters were located. Immigrants found that they could learn about American life at the movies. Parents worried when their children saw such films as *Women and Wine* or *Man and His Mate.* Reformers clamored for censorship boards to screen films for scenes that showed lustful images or suggested that criminals profited from their crimes.

Shifting Attitudes Toward Sex

The nation's family and sexual values faced challenges as norms of sexual behavior moved away from the restrictions of the Victorian era. In 1916, one of every nine marriages ended in the divorce courts. Meanwhile, family size was decreasing. By 1920, two or three children were born to the average mother; in 1860, the average had been five or six. For women born around 1900, the rate of sexual intercourse before marriage was twice as high as it had been for women born a decade earlier.

Despite the changes in sexual practices, the official attitudes of the nation remained restrictive. Homosexual relationships were outlawed, even though some college-educated women maintained "partnerships" or "Boston marriages." Laws governing the dissemination of information about birth control discouraged the use of contraception. A federal statute, the Comstock Law of 1873, barred the making, selling, distribution, or importation of contraceptives, as well as any

Sanger, Margaret (1883–1966)
Social reformer and birth control pioneer. As a public health nurse in New York, she saw women suffering from disease and poverty because of the large number of children they bore. In 1914 she coined the term *birth control* and in 1915 she opened a clinic in Brooklyn. In 1921 she founded the American Birth Control League, which became Planned Parenthood in 1942.

Catt, Carrie Chapman (1859–1947)
Woman suffrage leader; president of the National American Woman Suffrage Association (1900–1906).

(© Bettmann/CORBIS)

Woman Suffrage Picketer.
Militant proponents of woman suffrage picketed the White House in 1917–1918 to move President Wilson to support their cause. Their presence embarrassed the president and several of the picketers went to jail for their beliefs.

transmission of birth control information through the mails. The only ground on which abortions were permitted was to save the life of the mother.

Margaret Sanger, a home nurse and radical activist living in Greenwich Village in New York City, saw women suffering from disease and poverty because of their large number of children. In 1914, she coined the term *birth control* and began publishing a periodical, *Woman Rebel*. Women, she wrote, "cannot be on an equal footing with men until they have full and complete control over their reproductive function." She founded a clinic in a poor neighborhood of Brooklyn that distributed information about contraception to the female residents. The police soon closed the clinic down, and Sanger went to jail. When the case was appealed, a higher court affirmed the right of doctors to prescribe birth control devices. Sanger then organized the Birth Control League to promote her cause.

The Persistence of Reform

Besides Sanger's crusade, other progressive reform campaigns pressed ahead. Prohibition capitalized on anti-German sentiment to reduce the political power of the brewing industry. The end of the flow of immigrants from Europe enabled advocates of immigration restriction to gain support for tighter laws. Supporters of woman suffrage also used the war as a way of mobilizing women behind their cause.

Woman suffrage gained strength after 1914 despite serious divisions among the movement's leaders. Alice Paul and the militant Congressional Union pressed for a constitutional amendment. Their tactics included demonstrations and a direct challenge to the Democrats as the party in power. In contrast, the National American Woman Suffrage Association (NAWSA), led by **Carrie Chapman Catt** after 1915, emphasized nonpartisanship and state-by-state organization. Paul and her allies formed the National Woman's Party to defeat Wilson and the Democrats. The momentum for suffrage seemed to be building. (See Map 20.3.)

The drive for Prohibition, the second major cultural reform campaign, intensified. In 1914, the Anti-Saloon League pressed for a constitutional amendment to ban the sale of alcohol. At the same time, efforts to make the states liquor-free went forward, with notable success. In 1913–1914, more than a dozen states adopted Prohibition legislation or held referenda in which the voters adopted Prohibition. Nine more states adopted such laws in 1915.

After 1914, progressive reformers looked to the federal government for help with the agenda of social change. In the light of the results of the 1914 congressional elections, Wilson understood that he must move left to win four more years in office. During the months before the election campaign began, Wilson came out for laws to restrict child labor, promote federal loans to farmers, provide federal aid for highway construction, and cover federal employees with workers' compensation laws. When a national railroad strike threatened in August 1916, Wilson compelled Congress to pass the Adamson Act, which mandated an eight-hour work day for railroad employees. Labor responded with strong support for Wilson's reelection bid. Meanwhile, the improving economy, driven by orders from the Allies for American products and foodstuffs, helped the Democrats.

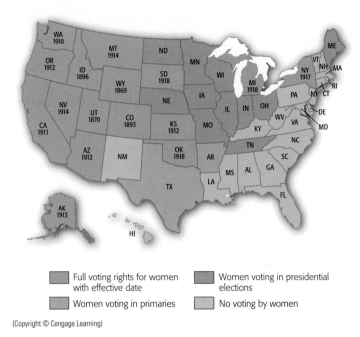

MAP 20.3
The March of Woman Suffrage
This map tracing the progress of woman suffrage gives an excellent sense of the sectional split over the issue with the West and Middle West in favor and the South and East in opposition.

One notable step that Wilson took was to nominate Louis D. Brandeis to the U.S. Supreme Court in January 1916. Brandeis had advised Wilson on the New Freedom, and he had won renown as the "People's Lawyer" and as a foe of consolidated business enterprise. Since Brandeis was a longtime champion of reform causes and a prominent Jew, his appointment aroused intense, often anti-Semitic, feelings among conservatives. In the end he was confirmed, and Wilson's strong endorsement of him convinced progressives that the president was on their side.

A Hazardous Neutrality

Wilson's reelection chances hinged on the uneasy neutrality he had maintained toward the Germans and the British throughout 1916. By the end of 1915, he had obtained a German apology and indemnity for the dead Americans of the *Lusitania*. After the sinking of the *Arabic*, the Germans had also pledged not to attack passenger liners without warning. Then the United States suggested an arrangement in which the Germans would limit submarine warfare and the Allies would not arm merchant ships. When this proposal collapsed, Germany resumed submarine attacks on armed shipping in February 1916.

On March 24, 1916, a German submarine attacked an unarmed steamer, the *Sussex*, in the English Channel. American passengers on board were injured, and another diplomatic crisis ensued. Wilson told Berlin that continued attacks on unarmed merchant vessels without warning would lead to a breaking of diplomatic ties, a prelude to U.S entry into the war. With hopes of a victory on land still alive, the Germans pledged that they would not conduct attacks on merchant vessels without warning. The so-called Sussex Pledge gave Wilson a major diplomatic success because it had staved off a war that most Americans dreaded.

During the first half of 1916, Wilson emerged as a forceful national leader. His speaking tour calling for preparedness swung public opinion behind his program to provide more weapons and personnel for the army and navy. When Congress sought to assert itself through resolutions warning Americans not to travel on the ships of the warring powers, the president pressured Congress to have the resolutions defeated on the grounds that they interfered with his power to conduct foreign policy.

In the spring of 1916, the issue of Mexico once again grabbed the nation's headlines. The Mexican civil war had continued after the American intervention at Vera Cruz in 1914. Although Wilson did not like the regime of Venustiano Carranza, he extended diplomatic recognition to it when it became clear that Carranza had emerged as the nation's effective leader. Then a rebel named Pancho Villa raided towns in New Mexico and Texas in 1916, killing and wounding numerous Americans. The U.S. Army under General John J. Pershing pursued him across the Rio Grande. Mexicans were outraged at this intrusion on their sovereignty, but Wilson negotiated a diplomatic settlement. Nevertheless, American troops remained in Mexico for two years, placing a continued strain on relations between the two nations.

❖ The 1916 Presidential Election

The Democrats approached the 1916 election with confidence. The president's program of progressive domestic legislation was moving through Congress, the international situation appeared to have vindicated Wilson's leadership, and the economy was prosperous because of the war orders that the British and French had placed for munitions, food, and industrial products. The Democrats' slogan for the campaign was "He kept us out of war."

Theodore Roosevelt hoped to be the Republican nominee, but the Republicans turned to Supreme Court Justice **Charles Evans Hughes.** He had been a progressive governor of New York, was not scarred with the wounds of 1912, and had said little about foreign policy. A remnant of the Progressive Party nominated Roosevelt, but he declined, and the party soon disappeared. The Republicans offered assurances that they favored some domestic reforms and carefully straddled the more controversial questions of preparedness, neutrality, and loyalty of ethnic groups such as the German Americans.

Hughes, Charles Evans (1862–1948) Governor of New York (1907–1910), Supreme Court justice (1910–1916), and Republican candidate for president in 1916, when he was defeated by Woodrow Wilson. He served as secretary of state under Presidents Harding and Coolidge (1921–1925) and returned to the Supreme Court as Chief Justice in 1930.

In the campaign that followed, Wilson employed the themes of peace, progressivism, and prosperity in his speeches. Hughes, in contrast, had difficulty finding a way to appeal to Republicans who shared Roosevelt's position and to the German American voters who wanted the nation to stay out of the conflict. Hughes also proved to be an ineffective campaigner. To win, the Democrats assembled a coalition of voters in the South and West, the peace vote, women (who could vote in western and middle western states), and midwestern farmers who were happy with wartime prosperity. Wilson won one of the closest elections in the nation's history. He gained 277 electoral votes from thirty states, and Hughes won 254 electoral votes from eighteen states. The president amassed a little more than 49 percent of the vote, polling six hundred thousand more popular votes than Hughes did.

Mediation and Intervention

Wilson now pressed for a negotiated settlement of the war. Relations with the British had soured during 1916 because of the way the Royal Navy and the British Foreign Office interfered with American shipping in enforcing their blockade against Germany. Meanwhile, the British were becoming more dependent on American loans and credits to pay for the supplies that they had been buying since 1914. Under the circumstances, the president believed, London might be receptive to an American mediation effort. The president also knew that pressure was rising within the German military for unrestricted use of submarines.

On December 18, 1916, Wilson asked the warring countries to state their terms for a negotiated peace. Both the British and the Germans rejected the president's offer; the solution would have to come on the battlefield. In response, Wilson addressed the U.S. Senate on January 22, 1917, in a speech that called for a "Peace Without Victory." He argued that "only a peace among equals can last," and set out a program that included plans to create a league of nations. The attitude of the warring powers was skeptical. The idea of a league of nations to prevent future wars also aroused opposition in the Senate.

Aware that their military position in the conflict was deteriorating, the German high command decided on January 9, 1917, that only the submarine could win the war before the United States sent troops to Europe. Unrestricted submarine attacks would be resumed on February 1 to choke off supplies to Great Britain. Wilson learned of the German decision on January 31 and realized that Berlin had not been negotiating in good faith. He broke diplomatic relations on February 4. The submarine campaign began as scheduled, and American lives were lost. On February 26, the president asked Congress for authority to arm U.S. merchant ships, but with peace sentiment still strong on Capitol Hill, the administration faced a tough fight.

An unexpected revelation about German war aims then happened. British intelligence had intercepted and decoded a secret German diplomatic telegram to its ambassador in Mexico. The **Zimmerman telegram**, named after the German foreign minister Arthur Zimmerman, dangled the return to Mexico of Arizona, New Mexico, and Texas as bait to entice the Mexicans to enter the war on the German side. Wilson released this diplomatic bombshell to the public on March 1, and the House promptly passed the bill to arm merchant ships. Although the bill was filibustered in the Senate, Wilson armed the ships on his own authority on March 9.

The Outbreak of Hostilities

One stumbling block to American support for the Allied cause had always been the presence of Russia on the side of the British and French. Alliance with that autocratic monarchy mocked the notion that the Allies were fighting for

Zimmermann telegram (1917) Secret German diplomatic telegram to the German ambassador in Mexico that was intercepted and decoded by the British. It dangled the return to Mexico of Arizona, New Mexico, and Texas as bait to entice the Mexicans to enter the war on the side of Germany.

Navy Recruiting Poster. With the American entry into World War I, the armed forces sought recruits through volunteers and the draft. This poster of a Navy gun crew in action was designed to appeal to the patriotism of potential enlisted men. The government felt impelled to make such arguments because substantial portions of society did not share the fervor for the war.

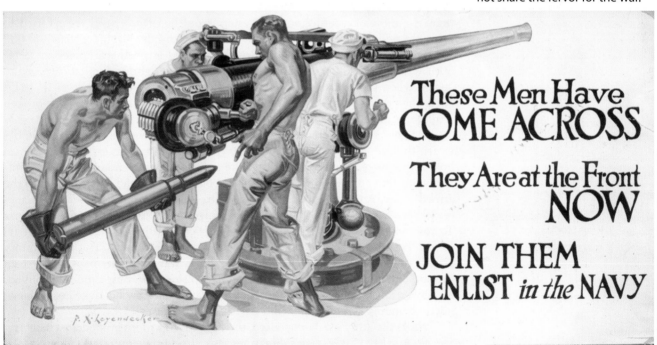

These Men Have
COME ACROSS
They Are at the Front
NOW

JOIN THEM
ENLIST *in the* NAVY

democratic values. When the outbreak of revolution in Russia toppled the regime of Tsar Nicholas II, it seemed to offer some hope for reform. Meanwhile, the Germans sank three American ships on March 18 with large losses. Wilson called Congress into special session on April 2 to ask for a declaration of war against Germany. "The world must be made safe for democracy," he told them. "It is a fearful thing to lead this great peaceful people into war, into the most terrible and disastrous of all wars, civilization itself seeming to be in the balance. But the right is more precious than peace."

Congress declared war on Germany on April 6, 1917. Although the votes were overwhelming (82 to 7 in the Senate; 373 to 50 in the House), the nation was divided. In large parts of the South and West, the public felt no need to become involved in European quarrels or to benefit eastern business interests that might profit from the fighting. Opposition to the war remained high among German Americans and Irish Americans. Dedicated reformers and Socialists saw the war as a betrayal of reform ideals. For Wilson himself, involvement in the war seemed to be the price the nation had to pay to influence the peace settlement. His lofty rhetoric encouraged Americans to believe that a better world could be obtained through the use of military force.

❖ A Nation at War

During World War I, the power of the federal government increased in response to the need to mobilize the populace for war. Average citizens found that they had to respond to government programs and directives in strange and unfamiliar ways, such as accepting bureaucratic rules for their businesses, listening to government propaganda, and changing their eating habits.

By April 1917, the battlefields of Europe had developed into two brutal fronts. Gigantic battles occurred on the "eastern front" between the Russians, on the one hand, and the Germans and their Austrian allies, on the other. On the "western front," where the Allies and the Germans confronted each other in France, the two sides fought in elaborate trenches from which soldiers fired at each other or mounted attacks against well-fortified positions. Dug-in artillery and machine guns gave the advantage to the defense. The French suffered more than 1.4 million casualties on the western front in 1915. The Germans tried to break the will of the French at Verdun in 1916; both sides lost more than 300,000 men in the ensuing struggle. The British attacked in northern France in 1916; 60,000 men were killed or wounded in a single day's fighting. Similar carnage occurred when the British renewed their offensive on the Somme River in 1917. After the French went on the attack in 1917 with heavy casualties, their broken armies mutinied against further slaughter.

In May 1917, Congress adopted the Selective Service Act, whereby men between the ages of twenty-one and thirty had to register for the draft with local boards that were set up to administer the program. By the end of the war 24 million young men had been registered, and about 3 million had been called into the armed forces. Another 340,000 men tried to evade the draft and became "slackers." There were also 65,000 men who claimed exemptions for religious reasons. To command the American Expeditionary Force (AEF), Wilson selected General John J. Pershing, who had pursued Pancho Villa into Mexico. The U.S. military was ill prepared: the army had no plans for a war with Germany in western Europe, and it lacked the rifles and machine guns necessary for a modern conflict. Moreover, its staff structure was loaded with old officers who lacked experience in commanding large numbers of men.

While the army was being raised, the navy faced a more immediate challenge. During April 1917, German submarines sank almost nine hundred thousand tons of Allied shipping. At that rate, half the oceangoing shipping available to the British would disappear by the end of 1917. The American naval commander in Europe, Admiral William S. Sims, turned to convoys to escort vulnerable merchant ships across the Atlantic. American destroyers on escort duty became a key part of the strategy that eventually ended the submarine threat, and troops began to move toward Europe. The Germans did not regard troop ships as significant targets because of their belief that American soldiers lacked fighting ability. Two million men were shipped to France before the armistice was signed, and they provided the margin for an Allied victory.

Training the troops for warfare often reflected progressive ideals. The government endeavored to maintain the purity of troops with extensive programs to limit excessive drinking and venereal disease. The army also provided an optional opportunity to acquire inexpensive life insurance, which increased popular interest in such programs after the war. The pace of mobilization was slow. It was not until more than a year after the entry into the war that American troops reached France in substantial numbers.

The government raised a third of the money for the war, some $9 billion, through increased taxes. The remainder came from citizens who purchased **Liberty Bonds** from the government. These interest-bearing securities brought in more than $15 billion. Those who were unwilling to contribute were told that failure to buy bonds was unpatriotic and helped the Germans. The total cost of the war to the United States exceeded $35 billion. The United States loaned more than $11.2 billion to the Allies, most of it never repaid. Yet Washington had no choice. In June 1917, one British official told his government that "if loan stops, war stops." President Wilson counted on the Allies' financial dependence on the United States as a weapon to use in achieving the goals of his postwar diplomacy.

Liberty Bonds Thirty-year government bonds sold to individuals with an annual interest rate of 3.5 percent. They were offered in five issues between 1917 and 1920, and their purchase was equated with patriotic duty.

The Allies also needed food. To mobilize the agricultural resources of the United States, Congress passed the Lever Act, which established the Food Administration. Wilson selected Herbert Hoover to head this new agency. A mining engineer from California, Hoover had gained international fame through his work to feed the starving people of Belgium. Hoover asked Americans to observe "wheatless days" and "meatless days" because "wheatless days in America make sleepless nights in Germany." Women and children planted "war gardens" to raise fruits and vegetables. Higher prices induced farmers to expand their production. The wheat crop was 637 million bushels in 1917; a year later, it stood at 921 million bushels.

The campaign to conserve food boosted the effort to restrict the sale and use of alcoholic beverages. Scarce grain supplies had to be reserved for soldiers in the field and Allied populations overseas. As a wartime slogan put it, "Shall the many have food or the few have drink?" Prohibitionists argued that drink impaired the fighting ability of the armed forces and those working in defense plants. The connection of the brewing industry with German Americans also worked in favor of the prohibitionist cause. In December 1917, lawmakers approved the **Eighteenth Amendment,** which banned the production and sale of alcoholic beverages. All that remained was to ensure ratification of the amendment by the required number of states, a task that the Anti-Saloon League was well equipped to handle.

Eighteenth Amendment (1919) Constitutional amendment that barred the production and sale of alcoholic beverages. Its adoption represented the national high point of the prohibition movement.

Managing the Wartime Economy

The president used his power to expand the bureaucracy required to manage production of war supplies and oversee their shipment to the Allies. Wilson did not seek to have government take over business: he hoped that a business–government partnership would develop naturally. However, much government encouragement and direction were needed before the business community fully joined the war effort.

The eventual record of mobilization was mixed. The United States tried to build ships and planes under the direction of government agencies. Those efforts produced at least one British-designed plane that used American-built engines, and large numbers of merchant ships were constructed in American shipyards. But Pershing's men used British and French artillery and equipment. The government had more success with expanding the production of coal, the major source of residential heating and industrial power, through the Fuel Administration. Coal prices were raised to stimulate production, and "daylight savings time" was established to reduce the use of fuel for nonmilitary purposes. To facilitate mobilization, the government took over the railroads in January 1918, placing the secretary of the treasury, William G. McAdoo, in charge of operations. McAdoo raised the wages of railroad workers, dropped inefficient routes, and allowed the lines to raise their rates.

The War Industries Board (WIB) was established to make sure that the purchasing and allocation of supplies for the armed forces followed rational programs. Wilson placed Bernard Baruch, a Wall Street speculator and contributor to the Democratic Party, at the head of the WIB. Baruch and his aides attacked needless waste in production. They standardized products, established priorities for the shipment of important goods, and set prices to encourage factories to turn out goods quickly. Simply by altering bicycle designs, the WIB saved two thousand tons of steel for war goods. Baruch had to compromise with the powerful automobile and steel industries to induce them to abandon peacetime production in favor of handling wartime orders. In the process, the industries made significant profits from their government contracts. As one steel executive put it, "We are all making more money out of this war than the average human being ought to."

The American Federation of Labor and its president, Samuel Gompers, threw their support behind the war. In return for the government's agreement to allow unions to participate in economic policy making, Gompers and the AFL promised not to strike or to press for union shops in factories. Between 1917 and 1920, the AFL gained more than 2 million members. Nonunion workers also benefited from the government's wartime policies. The National War Labor Board, headed by former president William Howard Taft, set standards for wages and hours that were far more generous and enlightened than those private industry had provided. A minimum wage was mandated, as were maximum hours and improved working conditions. The government also created housing for war workers and began a system of medical care and life insurance for federal employees.

Black Americans in the War

While some blacks wanted no part of the European conflict because they considered it a conflict among their white oppressors, most African American leaders agreed with W. E. B. Du Bois that they should "forget about special grievances and close our ranks shoulder to shoulder with our own fellow white citizens." Some 367,000 black soldiers served during the war; 42,000 of them saw combat in France. Most of the African American servicemen, however, were assigned to labor battalions and supply duties. The War Department moved very slowly to commission black officers; at the end of the war there were only 1,200.

Several African American units fought bravely. Others were given inadequate training and equipment, but when they performed poorly in combat, the blame was placed on their supposed inferiority. African American troops stationed in the United States faced familiar dangers. In August 1917, in Houston, Texas, black soldiers reacted to segregation and abuse by the police with attacks on the police and on white citizens that left sixteen whites and four soldiers dead. The army indicted 118 soldiers, of whom 110 were convicted by courts-martial. Nineteen black soldiers were hanged.

Racial tensions intensified elsewhere in the nation as whites and blacks confronted each other when northern cities experienced an influx of African Americans. During the summer of 1917, race riots in East St. Louis, Illinois, resulted in the deaths of forty blacks and nine whites. Forty-eight lynchings occurred in 1917 and sixty-three in 1918. Facing discrimination and violence, blacks responded with a heightened sense of outrage. Marches were held to protest the race riots. Banners called on President Wilson to "Bring Democracy to America Before You Carry It to Europe."

During the war the black migration to northern cities continued. As the African American communities in Chicago, New York, Philadelphia, and other northern cities grew, black newspapers published articles about the **"New Negro"** who did not "fear the face of day. The time for cringing is over." The repressive actions of the Wilson administration in such episodes as the Houston riot and the failure to act against lynching fed the new currents of militance among black Americans.

"New Negro" A term associated with the Harlem Renaissance of the 1920s that involved a proud assertion of the value of African American culture.

Women's Issues in the Great War

The leaders of the National American Woman Suffrage Association decided that identification with the war offered the surest and fastest road to achieving their goal. Carrie Chapman Catt argued that giving women the vote would enable them to offset disloyal elements at home. "Every slacker has a vote," said Catt, a vote that newly enfranchised women could counter. Members of NAWSA appeared at rallies and proclaimed that suffrage should be a "war measure" that would repay women for their contributions to the war. The National Woman's Party picketed the White House to embarrass Wilson for failing to support woman suffrage. The combined impact of these tactics led to the passage of the woman suffrage amendment in the House of Representatives in January 1918. Wilson came out in favor of the amendment just before the congressional elections of that year. The Senate still had to act, but the war had made possible the eventual victory of the campaign to give women the vote.

Beyond the success of woman suffrage, however, the war did not produce lasting changes in the condition of American women. Only about four hundred thousand more women joined the labor force; more than twenty thousand women served in the military. In industry, women were hired as drivers, farm workers, and secretaries. As soon as the war ended, though, they were expected to relinquish these jobs to returning servicemen. As a Chicago woman complained, "During the war they called us heroines, but they throw us on the scrapheap now."

Civil Liberties and the Limits of Dissent

The Wilson administration mobilized public opinion to offset potential opposition to the conflict. As a result, the White House mounted a campaign of laws, agencies, and popular spirit to arouse support for the war and to quell dissent. In doing so, however, Woodrow Wilson and the men around him abused and restricted the civil liberties of many Americans.

The government created the Committee on Public Information (CPI) on April 13, 1917, and President Wilson named George Creel, a former newspaperman, as its head. Creel called his task "the world's greatest adventure in advertising"; he saw his role as one of fusing Americans into "one white-hot mass . . . with fraternity, devotion, courage, and deathless determination." To spread its message, the CPI used pamphlets, billboards, and motion pictures such as *The American Indian Gets into the War Game*. Seventy-five thousand speakers, known as "Four-Minute Men" because of the length of their talks, spoke to audiences throughout the nation to promote unity.

Doing History Online

The Propaganda War

Go to the CourseMate website for this chapter and link to Primary Sources. Study the documents online, and read the section "A Nation at War" in the textbook. How did America's involvement in the war alter the relationship between the federal government and the people of the nation?

www.cengagebrain.com

The Wilson administration and Congress placed legislative limits on the ability of Americans to criticize the government or the war effort. The Espionage Act of 1917 curbed espionage and sabotage, and made its definitions so sweeping that they embraced even public criticism of the war and its conduct. A person who violated the law could be sentenced to twenty years in prison. The Trading with the Enemy Act, passed in October 1917, authorized the postmaster general to suspend the mailing privileges of foreign-language periodicals and newspapers that he deemed offensive to the government. Postmaster General Albert S. Burleson used that law and the Espionage Act to bar from the mails publications that he considered treasonous or seditious. In 1918, Congress passed the Alien Act, which gave the government broad powers to deport any noncitizen who advocated revolution or anarchism. Most sweeping was the Sedition Act of 1918, which prohibited "uttering, printing, writing, or publishing any disloyal, profane, scurrilous, or abusive language" about either the government or the armed forces.

These laws were vigorously enforced. Burleson pursued critics of the administration relentlessly. The Socialist magazine *The Masses* was barred from the mails for carrying articles claiming that "this is Woodrow Wilson's and Wall Street's War." The Justice Department was equally vigilant. People were sent to prison for saying, "Wilson is a wooden-headed son of a bitch" or remarking that this was "a rich man's war." Eugene V. Debs, the perennial Socialist candidate for president, received a ten-year prison sentence for opposing the draft and the war. The American Protective League, a volunteer organization designed to locate draft evaders, became a vigilante branch of the Justice Department that used wiretapping, illegal searches, and other lawless techniques to find "slackers" and other opponents of the war.

The zeal of the government to stamp out dissent was matched by private hysteria toward Germans. Sauerkraut became "liberty cabbage," hamburgers reemerged as "Salisbury steak," and some cities gave up pretzels. Speaking the German language in public was banned in half of the states by 1918, and German literary works vanished from libraries. Editorials warned: "YOUR NEIGHBOR, YOUR MAID, YOUR LAWYER, YOUR WAITER MAY BE A GERMAN SPY." Radicals, too, were the victims of mob violence. Frank Little, an organizer for the Industrial Workers of the World (IWW), was hanged from a railroad trestle in Montana for denouncing the war at a labor rally.

The government had legitimate reason to be concerned about German espionage, but the repression of civil liberties during the war was excessive. President Wilson did not order cabinet officials to engage in such conduct, but he failed to keep them in check when he learned about what they were doing. The government's campaign against radicals and progressives, key areas of Wilson's coalition in 1916, undermined support for the president in domestic politics. In his eagerness to win the war, Wilson had allowed his government to destroy part of his own political base.

❖ The Road to Victory

During the late winter of 1918, as American troops arrived in France, the Allies faced a dangerous military crisis. In November 1917, the Communist revolution in Russia had taken that nation out of the Allied coalition and enabled the Germans to move troops to the western front. Berlin hoped to achieve victory before the Americans could reinforce the Allies. The German attack came on March 21, 1918, and it made impressive gains until the Allies held. When further attacks were made against the French in April and May, American reinforcements helped stop the assault. At battles near Chateau-Thierry and in Belleau Wood in early June, the men of the American Expeditionary Force (AEF) endured frightful losses but halted the Germans. (See Map 20.4.)

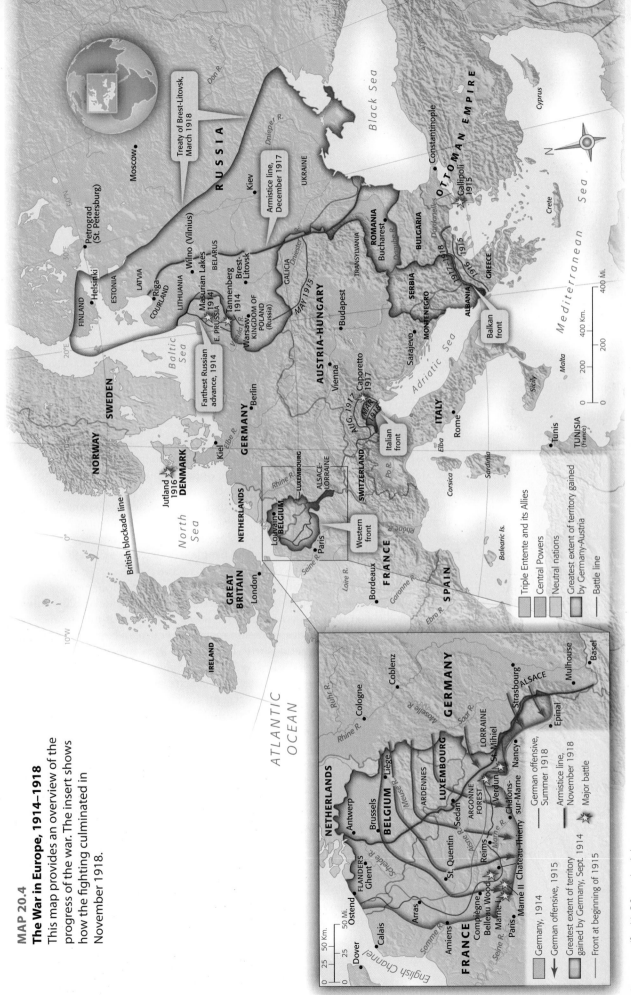

MAP 20.4

The War in Europe, 1914–1918

This map provides an overview of the progress of the war. The insert shows how the fighting culminated in November 1918.

(Copyright © Cengage Learning)

American Troops in France.
American troops, like the ones shown here in France, provided vital manpower to turn the tide against the Germans and impel the Allies to victory in 1918.

The Germans made one more offensive thrust in mid-July, and the British, French, and Americans repelled that advance as well. Counterattacks moved the Germans backward, a retreat that continued until the end of the war. In September 1918, the American army went on the offensive at the town of Saint-Mihiel in France near the southern end of the trenches. At the end of the month, Americans launched another thrust toward the Meuse River and the Argonne Forest. Their casualties were heavy, but the AEF pierced the German defenses to threaten key supply routes of the enemy.

Wilson's Peace Program

Wilson had set out his views on peace in a major address to Congress on January 8, 1918. Using the archives of the tsarist government, the Russian Communists had released secret treaties that the Allies had made before 1917 dividing up Europe and the Middle East once victory was achieved. These documents cast doubt on Allied claims that they were fighting for unselfish reasons. Wilson endeavored to shape the Allied answer and regain the diplomatic initiative.

To present the American cause in a better light, Wilson offered a peace program that became known as the Fourteen Points. Among the key provisions were freedom of the seas, free trade, and more open diplomacy. Freedom of the seas would prevent a repetition of the submarine threat the United States had faced before entering the war. Wilson believed that secret treaties and balance-of-power diplomacy had helped bring about the war itself. The president advocated national self-determination for all nations. He meant that the borders of countries should reflect the national origins of the people who lived in a particular area. He also advocated an "association of nations" to keep the peace.

The Fourteen Points would not be easy to achieve. After four years of slaughter, Britain and France wanted to punish Germany and cripple its ability to wage war. They disliked Wilson's criticism of their war aims and his interference with European policies. For the desperate Germans, the Fourteen Points seemed much more appealing than negotiations with London and Paris. In early October, a civilian government in Germany asked Wilson to arrange an armistice based on the Fourteen Points. Wilson used the threat of a separate settlement with the Germans to induce the British and French to accept the Fourteen Points and attend the peace conference. The fighting ended on November 11, 1918, at 11:00 A.M. Woodrow Wilson had achieved a diplomatic triumph, but his success proved to be temporary.

Even as Wilson prepared to lead the American delegation to Paris, his domestic political base was eroding. Throughout the conflict, President Wilson kept the Republicans at arm's length and treated the conflict as a war for Democrats only. He did not bring Republicans into his government at the highest levels, and he attacked Republicans who opposed his policies. Meanwhile, during the 1918 elections, his enemies capitalized on the unhappiness of farmers and workers over the administration's domestic programs. Progressives who had supported Wilson in 1916 recoiled from the administration's repressive tactics toward dissenters. In late October 1918, Wilson tried to stave off defeat with an appeal to the American people to elect a Democratic Congress. But when the results showed that both the House and the Senate would have Republican majorities, the president faced trouble ahead.

The Paris Peace Conference

In a break with the tradition that presidents did not travel outside the country, Wilson attended the peace conference despite Republican criticism. But his selection of delegates to accompany him showed his continuing insensitivity to bipartisanship. The five men he chose were his close allies, with only one nominal Republican among them. Wilson did not send any senators to Paris. Had he done so, he would have had to include Senator Henry Cabot Lodge of Massachusetts, the next chairman of the Foreign Relations Committee. Wilson and Lodge hated each other. If Wilson did not take Lodge, he could not invite any other senators either. (See *Doing History: The League of Nations Debate, 1919.*)

Europeans greeted Wilson with rapturous applause. When he arrived in Paris, 2 million people cheered him as he rode up the Champs-Elysées. They called him "Wilson le Juste (the Just)" and expected him to fulfill their desires for a peaceful world and for revenge against the Germans. To them, the Fourteen Points were a rhetorical device, not a statement of Wilson's real position on issues. The other major figures at the conference were David Lloyd George, the prime minister of Great Britain, and Georges Clemenceau, the premier of France. Both men were hard-headed realists who did not share Wilson's idealism. "God gave us the Ten Commandments, and we broke them," said Clemenceau. "Wilson gives us the Fourteen Points. We shall see." Along with the prime minister of Italy, Vittorio Orlando, Wilson, Clemenceau, and Lloyd George made up the "Big Four" who directed the peace conference.

The Shadow of Bolshevism

Four years of war had left the world in disorder, and nations large and small came to Paris to have their fate decided. A striking absentee was the new Soviet Union, the Communist nation that the Russian Bolsheviks had established after their successful revolution. Civil war raged in Russia between the "Reds" of communism and the "Whites," who wanted to block Bolshevik control of the nation. Meanwhile, the Bolsheviks' authoritarian leader, Vladimir Ilyich Lenin, and his colleagues wished to extend Communist rule beyond Russia's borders.

In 1919, national leaders worried that the infection of communism might spread into western Europe, and they had not recognized the government in Moscow. The French and British had tried to strangle the new regime by providing financial support for its enemies and intervening militarily in some areas of Russia. Helping its allies and trying to undermine bolshevism, the United States had dispatched small detachments of troops to Siberia and Vladivostok in 1918 and 1919. The American presence in Russia became a long-standing grievance for the Soviet regime that emerged from the Bolshevik victory.

Wilson and the Treaty of Versailles

The negotiations about the terms of peace with Germany produced both victories and defeats for Wilson. He had to accept the inclusion in the treaty of a clause that assigned Germany "guilt" for starting the war in 1914. That language proved to be a source of discontent for a resurgent Germany in the 1920s and 1930s. The Germans were also assessed severe financial penalties in the form of reparations that eventually amounted to $33 billion, a provision that fueled their resentment in the 1930s.

Wilson achieved partial success in his efforts to establish self-determination in the peace settlement. He accepted Italian desire for control of the city of Fiume on the Adriatic Coast, could not block Japan from territorial gains in China, and

Doing History The League of Nations Debate, 1919

In the debate over American membership in the League of Nations, Woodrow Wilson confronted the strong opposition of a group of senators known as the "irreconcilables," led by William E. Borah of Idaho. These two excerpts, from speeches given by Wilson and Borah, portray the clash of opinions over this heated foreign policy issue. In the end, Borah prevailed, and the Treaty of Versailles was not approved. The issues raised in this controversy have echoed in American history ever since.

Woodrow Wilson, Speech to Congress, *1919*

Our isolation was ended twenty years ago, and now fear of us is ended also, our counsel and association sought after and desired. There can be no question of our ceasing to be a world power. The only question is whether we can refuse the moral leadership that is offered us, whether we shall accept or reject the confidence of the world.

The war and the conference of peace, now sitting in Paris, seem to me to have answered that question. Our participation in the war established our position among the nations, and nothing but our own mistaken action can alter it. It was not an accident or a matter of sudden choice that we are no longer isolated and devoted to a policy which has only our own interest and advantage for its object. It was our duty to go in, if we were, indeed, the champions of liberty and of right.

We answered to the call of duty in a way so spirited, so utterly without thought of what we spent of blood or treasure, so effective, so worthy of the admiration of true men everywhere, so wrought out of the stuff of all that was heroic that the whole world saw, at last, in the flesh, in noble action, a great ideal asserted and vindicated by a nation they had deemed material and now found to be compact of the spiritual forces that must free men of every nation from every unworthy bondage. It is thus that a new role and new responsibility have come to this great nation that we honor and which we would all wish to lift to get higher levels of service and accomplishment.

Source: Woodrow Wilson speech to Congress, *New York Times*, July 11, 1919.

Senator William E. Borah, Speech to the Senate, *1919*

Senators, even in an hour so big with expectancy, we should not close our eyes to the fact that democracy is something more, vastly more, than a mere form of

was unable to prevent several groups of ethnic and national minorities in eastern Europe from being left under the dominance of other ruling groups, as in the case of Germans in the new nation of Czechoslovakia.

Wilson's main goal was establishment of the League of Nations. The league consisted of a general assembly of all member nations; a council made up of Great Britain, France, Italy, Japan, and the United States, with four other countries that the assembly selected; and an international court of justice. For Wilson, the "heart of the covenant" of the League of Nations was Article X, which required member nations to preserve each other's independence and take concerted action when any member of the league was attacked.

In February 1919, Wilson returned to the United States for the end of the congressional session. Senator Lodge then circulated a document, signed by thirty-seven senators, that stated that the treaty must be amended or they would not vote for it. The president attacked his critics publicly, further intensifying partisan animosity, but did make concessions to the other nations at the Peace Conference when he returned to Europe. These included the imposition of reparations on Germany, the war guilt clause, and limits on Germany's ability to rearm. In return, Wilson obtained provisions that protected the Monroe Doctrine from league action, removed domestic issues from the league's proceedings, and government by which society is restrained into a free and orderly life. It is a moral entity, a spiritual force, as well. And these are things which only and alone in the atmosphere of liberty. The foundation upon which democracy rests is faith in the moral instincts of the people. Its ballot boxes, the franchise, its laws, and constitutions are but the outward manifestations of the deeper and more essential thing—a continuing trust in the moral purposes of the average man and women. When that is lost or forfeited your outward forms, however democratic in terms, are a mockery. Force may find expression through institutions democratic in structure equal with the simple and more direct processes of a single supreme ruler. These distinguishing features of a real republic you can not commingle with the discordant and destructive forces of the Old World and still preserve them. You can not yoke a government whose fundamental maxim is

that of liberty to a government whose first law is that of force and hope to preserve the former. These things are in eternal war and must ultimately destroy the other. You may still keep for a time the outward form, you may still delude yourself, as others have done in the past with appearances and symbols, but when you shall have committed this Republic to a scheme of world control based upon force, upon the combined military forced of the four great nations of the world, you will have soon destroyed the atmosphere of freedom, of confidence in the self-governing capacity of the masses, in which along a democracy may thrive. We may become one of the four dictators of the world, but we shall no longer be masted of our own spirit.

Source: William E. Borah, speech to the Senate, November 10, 1919, *Congressional Record* (November 10, 1919).

QUESTIONS for REFLECTION

1. How does President Wilson view the experience of World War I as far as the United States is concerned? In what ways did participation in the conflict, in his mind, prepare the nation to join the League of Nations?

2. How do Borah and Wilson differ over the responsibilities of the United States after the war had been concluded?

3. How do the conceptions of democracy diverge in the speeches of Borah and Wilson?

4. In what ways have the views of Borah and Wilson continued to affect American foreign policy even to the present day?

allowed any nation to leave the world organization with two years' notice. The final version of the Treaty of Versailles was signed on June 28, 1919, in the Hall of Mirrors at the Palace of Versailles outside Paris. For all of its problems and weaknesses, the treaty was the closest thing to a reasonable settlement that Wilson could have obtained, yet he still had to get the Senate to ratify it. (See Map 20.5.)

The Senate and the League of Nations

The Republicans now controlled the Senate 49 to 47, so the president could not win the necessary two-thirds majority without the votes of some of his political opponents. Some Republicans were opposed to the treaty as an infringement on American sovereignty, no matter what it said. The president could count on about thirty-five of the forty-seven Democrats in the Senate. Assuming that some of the mild reservationists would support the treaty, the Democrats had to find twenty Republican votes to gain the necessary sixty-four votes to approve the treaty. In the political battle that ensued, Senator Lodge focused on Article X and the issue of whether Congress should be able to approve any American participation in the league's attempts to prevent international aggression. Lodge also played for time,

MAP 20.5

Europe After the Peace Conference, 1920

The Treaty of Versailles attempted to contain Germany against future aggressive behavior. Note the number of new states created out of the old Russian and Austro-Hungarian empires. Nonetheless, Germany remained a major force in Central Europe.

hoping that public opinion would turn against the treaty. He had the lengthy treaty read aloud to the Senate. Meanwhile, Wilson insisted that the treaty be approved without changes or "reservations."

By September 1919, with the treaty in trouble, Wilson decided to take his case to the American people. Despite audience approval of his speeches, Wilson's health broke under the strain. The circulatory problems that had bothered him for years erupted. He was rushed back to Washington, where he suffered a massive stroke on October 2, 1919. His left side was paralyzed, seriously impairing his ability to govern. The president's second wife and his doctors did not reveal how sick Wilson was. The first lady screened his few visitors and decided what documents her husband would see. As for the nation's chief executive, Wilson was only a shell of a president, and the government drifted.

The Senate voted on the treaty on November 19, 1919, with reservations that Lodge had included in the document. Lodge would have required Congress to approve any sanctions imposed by the league on an aggressor. When the

Democratic leader in the Senate asked Wilson about possible compromises, he replied that changing Article X "cuts the very heart out of the Treaty." The Senate rejected the treaty with reservations by a vote of 39 to 55. Then the lawmakers voted on the treaty without reservations. It lost, 38 in favor and 53 against. In the end, the decision about a possible compromise with Lodge was Wilson's to make. He told Senate Democrats: "Let Lodge compromise."

❖ From War to Peace

Meanwhile the nation experienced domestic upheaval. Citizens grappled with labor unrest, a Red Scare (fear of Communist or "Red" subversion), a surge in prices following the end of the war, and an influenza epidemic. The postwar period was one of the most difficult that Americans had ever experienced.

The influenza epidemic began with dramatic suddenness at the end of 1918 and spread rapidly through the population. No vaccines existed to combat it; no antibiotics were available to fight the secondary infections that resulted from it. More than 650,000 Americans died of the disease in 1918 and 1919. The number of dead bodies overwhelmed the funeral facilities of many major cities; coffins filled a circus tent in Boston.

The influenza pandemic receded in 1920, leaving a worldwide total of 20 million people dead. The pandemic had sapped the strength of the Allied armed forces to enforce the peace treaty, had diverted attention from important social problems, and illustrated how vulnerable humanity was to these infectious diseases.

The League of Nations. Cartoonists in the United States found Wilson's League of Nations and the political battle that ensued a natural subject.

The Waning Spirit of Progressivism

By 1919, the campaigns for Prohibition and woman suffrage were nearing their goals. Enough states had ratified the Eighteenth Amendment (the Prohibition amendment) by January 1919 to make it part of the Constitution. In October 1919, Congress passed the Volstead Act, named after its congressional sponsor, Andrew J. Volstead of Minnesota, to enforce Prohibition. Wilson vetoed the measure as unwarranted after the war had ended, but Congress passed it over his objection. The United States became "dry" on January 15, 1920. Prohibitionists expected widespread compliance and easy enforcement.

After the House passed the Nineteenth Amendment (the woman suffrage amendment) in 1918, it took the Senate another year to approve it. Suffrage advocates then lobbied the states to ratify the amendment. When the Tennessee legislature voted for ratification in August 1920, three-quarters of the states had approved woman suffrage. Women would now "take their appropriate place in political work," said Carrie Chapman Catt.

The Struggles of Labor

After the Armistice, the nation shifted from a wartime economy to peacetime pursuits with dizzying speed. The government declined to manage the changeover from a wartime to a peacetime economy. High inflation developed as prices were freed from wartime controls, and unemployment rose as returning soldiers sought jobs. The government's cost of living index rose nearly 80 percent above prewar levels in 1919, and it went up to 105 percent a year later. Unemployment reached nearly 12 percent by 1921.

Unions struck for higher wages. Seattle shipyard workers walked off their jobs, and the Industrial Workers of the World called for a general strike to support them. When sixty thousand laborers took part in the protest, the mayor of Seattle, Ole Hanson, responded with mobilization of police and soldiers that made him, in the eyes of those who agreed with him, "the Saviour of Seattle." Newspapers depicted the strike as a prelude to a Communist revolution.

The largest industrial strike of the year occurred in the steel industry. The American Federation of Labor tried to organize all steelworkers to end the seven-day week and the twelve-hour day. In September, 350,000 steelworkers left the mills. The steel manufacturers refused to recognize the union and hired strike-breakers from the ranks of unemployed blacks, Hispanics, and immigrants. The steel companies kept their factories running while they waited for the strike to be broken through police harassment and internal divisions within the unions. Conservatives attacked the radical background of one of the strike organizers, William Z. Foster. Although the strikers remained united for several months, they could not withstand the accumulated financial and political pressure from management. This first effort at a strike by an entire workforce failed in early 1920. Other strikes of the year included a walkout by coal miners and a strike by police in Boston.

Racial tensions also flared up in the turbulent postwar atmosphere. There were frequent lynchings in the South. In the North, the tide of African American migration produced confrontations with angry whites. Rioting against blacks occurred in Washington, D.C., in June 1919. During the same summer a young black man was stoned and killed when whites found him on a Chicago beach from which African Americans had been excluded. Angry blacks attacked the police who had stood by while the killing occurred. Five days of violence followed in which thirty-eight people, most of them black, were killed and another five hundred were injured. Violent episodes roiled two dozen other cities during what one black leader called "the red summer." Racism and antilabor sentiments fed on each other during these months.

Searching for a cause of the social unrest that pervaded the nation, Americans blamed radicalism and communism. The emotions aroused by the government's wartime propaganda fueled the Red Scare of 1919–1920. About seventy thousand people belonged to one of the two branches of the Communist Party. However, the radicals' reliance on violence and terrorism inflamed popular fears. When several mail bombs exploded on May 1, 1919, and dozens of others were found in the mail, the press and the public called for government action.

Attorney General A. Mitchell Palmer established a division in the Justice Department to hunt for radicals; the division was headed by J. Edgar Hoover, who later became director of the Federal Bureau of Investigation. In November 1919, Palmer launched raids against suspected radicals, and a month later he deported three hundred aliens to the Soviet Union. In the process, the legal rights of these suspects were violated, and they were kept in custody, away from their families and attorneys. Throughout the country, civil liberties came under assault. Communist parties were outlawed, antiradical legislation was adopted, and Socialists were expelled from the New York legislature. Suspected members of the IWW and other groups were subjected to vigilante violence and official repression.

The U.S. Supreme Court upheld the constitutionality of most of the laws that restricted civil liberties during the war and the Red Scare. Justice Oliver Wendell Holmes, Jr., devised a means of testing whether the First Amendment had been violated. In *Schenck v. United States* (1919), he asked whether words or utterances posed "a clear and present danger" of interference with the government, the war effort, or civil order. The answer was that they had. The Court also sustained the conviction of Eugene V. Debs for speaking out against the war.

By 1920, the Red Scare lost momentum. Palmer had forecast a violent uprising on May 1, 1920, and when it did not occur, his credibility suffered. Some government officials, especially in the Department of Labor, opposed Palmer's deportation policies. Other public figures, such as Charles Evans Hughes, denounced New York's efforts against socialist lawmakers. Despite the waning Red Scare hysteria, it was during this period that police in Massachusetts arrested two anarchists and Italian aliens, Nicola Sacco and Bartolomeo Vanzetti, for their alleged complicity in a robbery and murder at a shoe company in South Braintree, Massachusetts. In a case that attracted international attention, the two were convicted and eventually executed (see Chapter 21).

Harding and "Normalcy"

In March 1920, with Wilson ill and the government leaderless, the Senate once again took up the Treaty of Versailles with reservations. On March 19, the treaty received forty-nine votes in favor and thirty-five against, seven short of the number needed to ratify it. Wilson had said that he would not approve the pact with reservations, but the vote showed that a compromise could have been reached. Wilson hoped that the election would be a "solemn referendum" on the treaty, but that did not happen.

The Republicans had expected that Theodore Roosevelt would be their nominee in 1920, but he died on January 6, 1919, of circulatory ailments and heart problems. The Republicans turned to Senator Warren G. Harding of Ohio. A first-term senator, Harding was not a smart man, but he looked like a president and had made few enemies. He had been engaged in an illicit love affair in his home town of Marion, Ohio, but that information was carefully repressed. To run with him, the convention named Governor Calvin Coolidge of Massachusetts. Harding emphasized a return to older values, which he labeled "normalcy."

For the Democrats the nominee was Governor James M. Cox of Ohio, a moderate progressive from the party's antiprohibitionist wing, and his running mate was Franklin D. Roosevelt of New York. The Democratic candidates supported the League of Nations; the Republicans generally dodged the subject until the end of the campaign, when Harding advocated rejection of the treaty. The issue did not have much effect. Voters wanted to turn the Democrats out of office because of anger at big government, high taxes, and labor unrest. Harding received 16 million votes to 9 million for Cox.

In the wake of World War I, the nation briefly contemplated a more active role in the world but then drew back. Woodrow Wilson's League of Nations, building on wartime idealism, seemed less attractive in the harsh light of the postwar disillusionment with attempts to make the world safe for democracy. Although there was no going back to isolation, Americans thought they could let the Old World grapple with the consequences of its mistakes.

CHAPTER REVIEW, 1914–1920

SUMMARY

- The nation grappled with how to remain neutral in a world experiencing political upheaval.

- Southern blacks moved to northern cities in what came to be known as the Great Migration.

- The movies emerged as mass entertainment.

- Woodrow Wilson was reelected in 1916.

- The United States entered the world war in April 1917.

- Government power expanded during wartime.

- The American military contributed to the Allied victory.

- The Senate debated and then rejected the League of Nations.

- The country passed through postwar trauma including the Red Scare.

- Warren G. Harding was elected president in 1920.

IDENTIFICATIONS

Victoriano Huerta

Triple Alliance

Franz Ferdinand

Lusitania

The Birth of a Nation

Great Migration

Margaret Sanger

Carrie Chapman Catt

Charles Evans Hughes

Zimmerman telegram

Liberty Bonds

Eighteenth Amendment

"New Negro"

MAKING CONNECTIONS: LOOKING AHEAD Ⅲ➡

In the 1920s, Americans would reject many of the accomplishments of the Progressive era and repudiate much of what reformers had contributed to government and politics. The next chapter explores whether these conservative trends went too far. What remained of value in the Progressive legacy?

1. Why did the United States adopt Prohibition as an answer to the problems of alcohol?

2. Why did woman suffrage not produce the fundamental changes in American society that its proponents expected?

3. How did Americans feel about their place in the world after the experiences of the First World War I and the struggle over the League of Nations?

RECOMMENDED READINGS

Auchincloss, Louis. *Woodrow Wilson* (2000). A brief, readable life of this important president.

Chambers, John Whiteclay. *The Tyranny of Change: America in the Progressive Era, 1890–1920* (2000). A helpful synthesis of this whole period.

Clements, Kendrick. *The Presidency of Woodrow Wilson* (1992). Offers a thorough guide to the accomplishments of Wilson in office.

Cooper, John Milton. *Breaking the Heart of the World* (2002). An excellent examination of the fight over the League of Nations.

Davis, Donald E., and Trani, Eugene P. *The First Cold War: The Legacy of Woodrow Wilson in U.S.–Soviet Relations* (2002). Considers the impact of Wilson's policies on these two nations.

Graham, Sally Hunter. *Woman Suffrage and the New Democracy* (1996). Describes how women obtained the vote during World War I and afterward.

Levin, Phyllis Lee. *Edith and Woodrow: The Wilson White House* (2001). Looks at the effect of Wilson's illness on his presidency.

Saunders, Ronald M. *In Search of Woodrow Wilson: Beliefs and Behavior* (1998). A very critical account of the president and his record.

Schaffer, Ronald. *America in the Great War: The Rise of the War Welfare State* (1991). An informative text about woman suffrage and race.

Trotter, Joe William, ed. *The Great Migration in Historical Perspective* (1991). An excellent collection of essays about the movement of African Americans to northern cities.

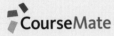 **CourseMate** Go to the CourseMate website at www.cengagebrain.com for additional study tools and review materials for this chapter.

21

The Age of Jazz and Mass Culture

1921–1927

MAKING CONNECTIONS

◀—ⅲ LOOKING BACK

The problems that reformers encountered after 1914 had their roots in the record of the first years of the twentieth century. Looking back on the era of Theodore Roosevelt, William Howard Taft, and the early years of Woodrow Wilson's presidency, you can see the assumptions about human nature and the role of government that foreshadowed the later problems that weakened the hold of progressivism on the American people. Before starting Chapter 21, you should be able to answer the following questions:

1. How deeply rooted was the progressive spirit? What groups did it include, and which ones did it leave out?

2. How far did the presidents in this period want to go in changing American society?

3. Why did World War I have such a devastating effect on progressive assumptions about humanity and the world?

An Urban Nation

Immigration Restricted
The Sacco-Vanzetti Case
White and Black Militance
Dry America: The First Phase
Harding as President

The New Economy

The Car Culture
Electrical America
1920s Movies and Advertising
Troubled Farmers and Workers
The Harding Scandals
Keep Cool with Coolidge
The Discordant Democrats

Modern Cultural Currents

The Harlem Renaissance
The Sound of Jazz

An Age of Artistic Achievement
Youth Culture and Sports

Fundamentalism and Traditional Values

The Fundamentalist Movement

Doing History: Bryan Versus Darrow:
The Scopes Trial

The Scopes Trial
Prohibition in Retreat

New Roles for Women

Women in Politics
The New Woman

Coolidge in the White House

Coolidge's Foreign Policy
Diplomacy and Finance in the 1920s
Lucky Lindy and Retiring Cal

During the 1920s the United States became modern as the automobile and other technological developments reshaped the economy and society. The shared experiences of Americans made the nation more cohesive as citizens encountered movies, radio, and sports in common. Social attitudes toward sex and family life moved away from Victorian restraints. Young people emerged as a distinct group. Advertising made public relations a significant characteristic of the period.

After a postwar depression, the economy rebounded from 1922 to 1927. The Republican administrations of Warren G. Harding and Calvin Coolidge lowered income taxes and encouraged private enterprise. Issues of culture and morality shaped politics more than did questions of economic reform. Prohibition and the Ku Klux Klan split the Democrats.

In foreign affairs, the decade was officially a time of isolation after the rejection of the League of Nations in 1919–1920. Government policy reinforced perceptions that the United States was aloof from the world. Yet the reality was more complex and subtle. Although involvement in world affairs increased more slowly than in prior decades, the United States maintained a significant stake in the postwar European and Asian economies.

❖ An Urban Nation

The census of 1920 indicated the country was on an important new course. For the first time, the government reported that more Americans lived in towns and cities with twenty-five hundred or more residents than in the countryside. The small-town and rural experience still dominated the lives of most citizens, but more than 10 million Americans lived in cities with 1 million people or more in 1920; that figure rose to more than 15 million by 1930. Such places as New York, Detroit, and Los Angeles saw large increases in their populations. Some 19 million people left the country for the city during these ten years, including millions of African Americans. The percentage of blacks listed as urban residents rose by nearly 10 percent between 1920 and 1930, compared with a rise of about 5 percent for whites.

For the young people who flocked to Chicago, New York, and Los Angeles, city life offered excitement and energy that farm life could not match. Within the concrete canyons and electric avenues, visitors found theaters, dance halls, and vaudeville artists that they could never hope to see in a small town. Many Americans resented the temptations of the city and associated them with foreign influences and assaults on traditional values.

Immigration Restricted

After the war, more than 430,000 people sought entry to the United States in 1920, and another 805,000 came in 1921. In response, advocates of immigration restriction renewed their campaign to shut off the flow of entrants from southern and eastern Europe, arguing that the immigrants lacked the qualities of successful American citizens. Madison Grant, one of the leading advocates of immigration restriction, said that "these immigrants adopt the language of

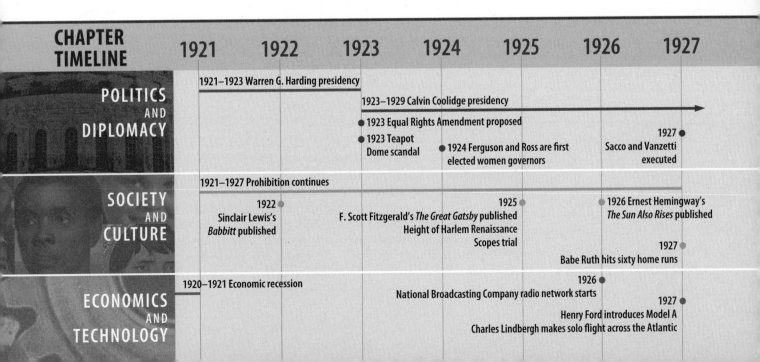

CHAPTER TIMELINE	1921	1922	1923	1924	1925	1926	1927
POLITICS AND DIPLOMACY	1921–1923 Warren G. Harding presidency		1923–1929 Calvin Coolidge presidency				
			● 1923 Equal Rights Amendment proposed				1927 ● Sacco and Vanzetti executed
			● 1923 Teapot Dome scandal	● 1924 Ferguson and Ross are first elected women governors			
SOCIETY AND CULTURE	1921–1927 Prohibition continues						
		1922 ● Sinclair Lewis's *Babbitt* published	F. Scott Fitzgerald's *The Great Gatsby* published Height of Harlem Renaissance Scopes trial		1925 ●	● 1926 Ernest Hemingway's *The Sun Also Rises* published	
							1927 ● Babe Ruth hits sixty home runs
ECONOMICS AND TECHNOLOGY	1920–1921 Economic recession		National Broadcasting Company radio network starts			1926 ●	
							1927 ● Henry Ford introduces Model A Charles Lindbergh makes solo flight across the Atlantic

the [native-born] American, they wear his clothes, they steal his name, and they are beginning to take his women, but they seldom adopt his religion or understand his ideals." The American Federation of Labor, which feared the use of aliens as strikebreakers, added its weight to the campaign for immigration restrictions.

In 1921, Congress enacted an emergency quota law that limited immigration from Europe to 600,000 people annually. Great Britain and Germany received the highest quotas. Three years later, the lawmakers passed the National Origins Quota Act, which reduced annual legal immigration from Europe to about 150,000 people, gave preference to entrants from northern European countries, and blocked Asian immigrants entirely. The quota of immigrants from each country was determined by the number of residents from these countries counted in the 1890 census.

Despite their racist premises, the new laws did not end immigration during the 1920s. After 1924, the recorded number of immigrants totaled about three hundred thousand annually until the Great Depression. Legal immigrants from Canada and Mexico accounted for much of that total. Five hundred thousand Mexicans arrived during the 1920s, settling mostly in Texas and California. However, the impact on people who wished to emigrate from southern and eastern Europe was dramatic. For example, ninety-five thousand immigrants had come into the United States from Poland in 1921; for each of the next three years, the annual total of immigrants from that country was only about twenty-eight thousand.

The Sacco-Vanzetti Case

The widespread tension about immigration played a significant part in the fate of two Italian immigrants whose criminal trial became a major controversy. In 1920 a murder and robbery took place in South Braintree, Massachusetts. Nicola Sacco and Bartolomeo Vanzetti were arrested for the crime, and their trial began in June 1921. Despite allegations that authorities had framed the two men for the crime because of their anarchist beliefs, a jury found them guilty. The case soon became a focus for liberals and intellectuals convinced that **Sacco and Vanzetti** had not received a fair trial because of their foreign origin.

During the next several years, the attorneys for the convicted defendants filed a series of appeals to overturn the verdict. The lawyers challenged the conduct of the jury, attacked the quality of the evidence against the two men, and questioned the accuracy of the identifications that various witnesses had made. None of this changed the mind of the presiding judge. By 1927, the appeals process had run its course. With a worldwide campaign under way to save Sacco and Vanzetti, pressure intensified on Massachusetts officials to review the case. The governor appointed a special commission to look into the trial. After flawed and biased proceedings, the panel decided to affirm the convictions, and Sacco and Vanzetti were executed on August 23. The outcome convinced many radicals of the inherent unfairness of the American legal system.

White and Black Militance

The pressures of immigration from abroad and the movement of Americans from the country to the city produced intense social strains. The most sensational and violent of these developments was the reappearance of the Ku Klux Klan. Revitalized after 1915 in the South, the Klan gained followers slowly, spouting racism, anti-Catholicism, and anti-immigrant views to acquire converts. The hooded order spread into northern states as well, with a particularly large presence in Indiana. The Klan claimed that it had 3 million members in the early 1920s. Masks, sheets,

Sacco, Ferdinando Nicola (1891–1927), and Vanzetti, Bartolomeo (1888–1927) Italian immigrants tried for murder in Massachusetts in 1921. The trial attracted worldwide attention because of allegations of bias due to their anarchist beliefs. After exhausting their appeals, they were executed in 1927.

Ku Klux Klan. The Ku Klux Klan was on the march with its message of bigotry in the early 1920s. This picture shows members of the hooded order as they paraded in Washington, D.C. The tensions that the Klan represented echoed through the entire decade.

and secret rituals added to the Klan mystique: members read the Kloran and dedicated themselves to "Karacter, Honor, Duty."

The Klan's program embraced opposition to Catholics, Jews, blacks, Asians, violators of the Prohibition laws, and anyone else who displeased local Klansmen. In many states, its members lynched people they disagreed with; tortured blacks, Catholics, and Jews; and made a mockery of law enforcement. They also went into politics: in 1922, its members elected a senator in Texas and became a powerful presence in the legislatures of that state and others in the Southwest. In Indiana, members of the order dominated the police of the state's major cities. The Klan also wielded significant influence in the Rocky Mountain states and the Pacific Northwest. But that influence peaked around 1923. As the Klan sought greater political power, the two major parties, especially the Democrats, absorbed some of the Klan's appeal and weakened its hold on the public.

African Americans asserted their identity and independence in these years. Sacrifices during World War I had made blacks impatient and resentful of the indignities of segregation. Yet white-on-black violence, such as a brutal attack on the African American area of Tulsa, Oklahoma, in 1921, persisted. A growing spirit of assertiveness and militancy appeared in the art and literature of black intellectuals. A poet named Claude McKay issued his rallying cry in 1922: "If we must die, let it not be like hogs / Hunted and penned in an inglorious spot." Instead, he concluded, "Like men we'll face the murderous, cowardly pack, / Pressed to the wall, dying, but—fighting back."

For the African Americans who crowded into the large northern cities during the Great Migration, the promise of America seemed illusory. They lived in substandard housing, paid higher rents for their apartments than whites did, and could obtain only menial jobs. The Harlem neighborhood of New York City might be "the greatest Negro city in the world," as author James Weldon Johnson called it, but it was also a place where every day, blacks saw how white society discriminated against them.

This atmosphere of dissatisfaction greeted **Marcus Garvey**, a young black man who immigrated to the United States in 1916. Garvey preached a doctrine of Pan-Africanism and promised to "organize the 400,000,000 Negroes of the World into a vast organization to plant the banner of freedom in the great continent of Africa." He worked through the Universal Negro Improvement Association (UNIA) to establish societies that were not controlled by imperialist nations. He founded his campaign on international shipping lines and newspapers that would enable blacks to travel to Africa and communicate among themselves. Rallies and conventions in New York and other cities drew up to twenty-five thousand people and raised funds for the UNIA.

Ultimately, Garvey's business ventures failed, he upset members of the NAACP by calling its political agenda too cautious, and perhaps most controversially, he met with a Klan leader. Black opponents sent damaging information about Garvey's finances to the Department of Justice, and the government indicted him for mail fraud. He was convicted and went to prison in 1925. The important legacy of Garvey and the UNIA was the idea that urban blacks could band together to wield economic and political power.

Dry America: The First Phase

The initial impact of Prohibition on the lives of Americans achieved much of what its proponents had predicted. The national consumption of alcohol declined from about two gallons per capita during the war years annually to around three-fourths of a gallon in 1921 and 1922 (Table 21.1). Alcohol use rose again during the rest of the decade but remained below prewar levels. Alcoholism as a medical problem became less prevalent. Contrary to later legend, Prohibition did affect drinking habits in the United States.

Yet the extent of compliance with Prohibition was spotty. The upper classes expected the working poor to obey the Prohibition law, but they resisted any change in their own drinking practices. Some people made their own liquor; instructions for doing so were easily obtained. In centers of "wet" sentiment, like San Francisco and Boston, the law was never enforced. Believing that compliance ought to be voluntary, Congress appropriated inadequate funds to the Treasury Department's Prohibition Bureau, so there were never enough federal men to cover the nation adequately. Even when agents acted decisively, the rising number of arrests led to huge backlogs in the federal court system.

Although enterprising individuals brought in shipments of illegal alcohol to supply the market, Prohibition did not create organized crime. Nor were the 1920s a decade of rising crime rates. The nation became more aware of crime as a social problem, because of the well-publicized activities of gangsters like **Alphonse "Al" Capone** and Johnny Torrio in Chicago. Capone devoted himself to gaining control of gambling, prostitution, and bootlegging in the Chicago area. In New York, other mobsters built up networks of criminal enterprises to provide the same services. "Rum runners" and **bootleggers** sold their wares at illegal saloons or "speakeasies" where city dwellers congregated in the evenings.

Garvey, Marcus (1887–1940)
Jamaican immigrant who promised to "organize the 400 million Negroes of the World into a vast organization to plant the banner of freedom in the great continent of Africa."

TABLE 21.1 Estimated Alcohol Consumption in the United States, 1920–1930 (Gallons per Capita)	
1920	N/A
1921	0.54
1922	0.91
1923	1.07
1924	1.05
1925	1.10
1926	1.18
1927	1.12
1928	1.18
1929	1.20
1930	1.06

Source: Derived from Joseph R. Gusfield, "Prohibition: The Impact of Political Utopianism," in *Change and Continuity in Twentieth-Century America: The 1920s*, ed. John Braeman, Robert H. Bremner, and David Brody (Columbus, OH: Ohio State University Press, 1968), 275.

Capone, Alphonse "Al" (1899–1947) Chicago gangster; devoted to gaining control of gambling, prostitution, and bootlegging.

bootleggers Enterprising individuals who moved alcohol across the border into the United States from Canada and the Caribbean during Prohibition. Their wares were sold at illegal saloons or "speakeasies" where city dwellers congregated in the evenings.

Harding as President

Because of the scandals associated with his administration, Warren G. Harding once was depicted as the worst president in American history. During his brief term, however, he was very popular. He surrounded himself with what he called the "Best Minds," as his selection of Charles Evans Hughes as his secretary of state, banker Andrew Mellon as secretary of the treasury, and Herbert Hoover as secretary of commerce attested. After years in which the presidency had seemed separated from the people, Harding and his wife, Florence, opened up the White House to tourists and greeted visitors from the public with evident pleasure. Throughout the country, Harding was a well-regarded president whose speeches appealed to a desire for a calmer, less activist chief executive.

The new administration pressed for a legislative program that combined some constructive reforms with a return to older Republican trade policies. The 1921 Budget and Accounting Act gave the government a more precise sense of how the nation's funds were being spent. It established an executive budget for the president, the General Accounting Office for Congress, and the Bureau of the Budget in the executive branch. The Republicans rebuilt tariff protection in an emergency law of 1921 and then wrote the Fordney-McCumber Tariff law a year later. Reflecting the party's suspicion of a powerful national government, Treasury Secretary Mellon pushed for lower income tax rates, particularly for individuals with higher incomes.

The Harding administration stayed aloof from the League of Nations. Since the failure to ratify the Treaty of Versailles left the nation in a technical state of war with Germany, the two countries negotiated a separate peace treaty in 1921. Throughout the 1920s, Washington withheld recognition from the new Soviet Union because of fears that diplomatic relations with the Communist government might spread the bacillus of subversion. Harding's administration reduced the nation's military role in Latin America, withdrawing marines from Haiti, the Dominican Republic, and Nicaragua. Meanwhile, trade and investment expanded south of the border.

The Far East claimed a large amount of attention as Japan expanded its power in China. The United States wanted to preserve the Open Door policy and restrain Japanese influence, and it relied on diplomacy and economic pressure as its main weapons. Both nations were, however, increasing the size of their navies at this time. Congress and the administration called for a conference in which representatives of Great Britain, Japan, and the United States would meet to discuss naval issues and peace in the Far East. The Washington Naval Conference began in 1921 and resulted in the Five-Power Treaty, which provided a fixed ratio for warship construction. For every five ships the United States built, the British could also build five, and the Japanese could build three. The Japanese were not happy with the five-five-three arrangement, but in return they secured an American pledge not to construct defenses in such U.S. possessions as Guam and the Philippines. For a time, the naval arms race in the Pacific slowed, but the episode fueled Japanese–American tensions.

The Washington Conference also resulted in two other pacts: the Four-Power Treaty and the Nine-Power Treaty. The Four-Power Treaty ended a long-standing (since 1902) alliance between Great Britain and France, and committed the United States, France, Great Britain, and Japan to respect each country's territorial possessions. In the Nine-Power Treaty, the signatory nations agreed to avoid interference with China's internal affairs. The Washington Conference ended without the United States having to make commitments that entailed the risk of force or greater international involvement. In diplomacy as in domestic policy, the Harding administration seemed attuned to the desires of the country.

❖ The New Economy

The postwar recession dogged the first two years of the Harding administration, and the hard times contributed to substantial Republican losses in the 1922 congressional elections. The Democrats gained seventy-four seats in the House and six in the Senate. Yet the long-range news proved beneficial for Republicans. The economy slowly picked up in 1922 and 1923, productive output returned to its 1918 levels, and employment rose.

The improvement in the economy's performance during 1922 began a period of unprecedented prosperity. The gross national product soared almost 40 percent, increasing from nearly $76 billion in 1922 to $97.3 billion in 1927. The per capita income of Americans went up about 30 percent during the same period. Real earnings for wage workers rose more than 20 percent, whereas hours worked declined slightly. The unemployment rate fell from 12 percent of the labor force in 1922 to 4 percent in 1927.

The Car Culture

The number of cars registered in 1920 totaled 8.25 million, while the number of trucks was 1.1 million (Table 21.2). By 1927, there were more than 20 million cars on the roads, along with more than 3 million trucks and buses. For the traveler on the road, motels offered accommodations, billboards advertised attractions, and roadside restaurants provided food and diversion. The Federal Highways Act of 1921 left road construction to the states, but set national standards for concrete road surfaces and access to roads. The size of the road network grew from seven thousand miles at the end of the war to fifty thousand miles in 1927. Gasoline taxes brought in revenues for the states, enabling them to build more roads, which in turn fostered the development of suburbs distant from the old city centers.

Cars consumed a large chunk of the working family's income as Americans readily took to the practice of buying their cars on the installment plan. The car began to change social patterns and norms. For many African Americans in the South, owning a car gave them at least some mobility and escape from a segregated life. The enclosed car, initially a prestigious model, soon became standard on the road; by 1927, 83 percent of cars were of this type.

As the decade began, Henry Ford was still the most famous carmaker in the nation. His showplace was the huge factory on the Rouge River near Detroit. Sprawling across two thousand acres, the Rouge River plant employed seventy-five thousand workers to turn out the reliable, familiar Model T car. In 1921, Ford made more than half of the automobiles produced in the United States, turning out a new vehicle every ten seconds. A car cost less than $300.

The Model T was a popular car, but not an attractive one. The joke was that you could get a Model T in any color, as long as it was black. Ford's failure to develop different car models opened a competitive opportunity to General Motors (GM). Under the leadership of Alfred P. Sloan, Jr., GM introduced self-starters, fuel gauges, reliable headlights, and other features that consumers liked. The constant flow of new models induced customers to want a fresh vehicle every few years. The General Motors Acceptance Corporation made it easy to acquire a car on the installment plan.

By the mid-1920s, Ford's sales fell as those of General Motors rose. Ford dealers switched to General Motors, and the used-car market undercut Ford at the other end of the price scale. In response, Henry Ford ended production of the Model T and turned to the development of a new car. On December 1, 1927, the company unveiled the Model A. Like General Motors, Ford marketed the

TABLE 21.2
Automobile Registrations, 1921–1929

1921	9,212,158
1922	10,704,076
1923	13,253,019
1924	15,436,102
1925	17,481,001
1926	19,267,967
1927	20,193,333
1928	21,362,240
1929	23,120,897

Source: *The Statistical History of the United States* (New York: Fairfield Press, 1965), 462.

Model A through a huge advertising campaign. It also created a credit corporation, again modeled on what General Motors had done, to enable buyers to obtain cars on credit. The combined efforts of Ford and Sloan gave the automobile business in the 1920s the structure and style that would dominate until the start of World War II.

Electrical America

Electricity also stimulated the economy during the 1920s. By 1928, electricity drove 70 percent of factory equipment. Two-thirds of the families in towns and cities had electricity in their homes as well, stimulating demand for the electrical appliances that industry was turning out in abundance. Homemakers bought some 15 million electric irons and another 7 million vacuum cleaners. Advertisers appealed to women with descriptions of the all-electric kitchen "Where Work Is Easy!" Sales of consumer appliances were one of the major economic stimulants of the decade. The electric power industry expanded rapidly, as did the firms that made equipment for the power plants.

The diffusion of electricity facilitated the growth of radio. The first station, KDKA in Pittsburgh, went on the air in 1920. There were only four in 1922; a year later, 566 were in operation. In 1923, a New York station, WBAY, began selling time to anyone who would pay for it. Commercial radio caught on quickly; by 1923, there were radios in four hundred thousand households. Three years later, the Radio Corporation of America (RCA), led by its president, David Sarnoff, established the first national network of stations, the National Broadcasting Company (NBC). Programming was diverse, and commercial sponsors oversaw the content of such programs as *The Maxwell House Hour* and the *Ipana Troubadours*. Radio was another element in the creation of a mass culture during the decade.

1920s Movies and Advertising

Each week, 100 million people went to see movies at one of the twenty thousand theaters that showed silent pictures. Ticket prices were relatively low and stable, usually about fifty cents. As one college student recalled, "You learn plenty about love from the movies." Pictures shaped how young people kissed on dates, what they wore, and what they said.

From their uncertain beginnings at the turn of the century, motion picture studios had developed into large enterprises employing hundreds of people. Studio heads like Adolph Zukor of Paramount Pictures and Louis B. Mayer of Metro-Goldwyn-Mayer (MGM) controlled chains of theaters, to which they allocated the pictures they made on a rigidly controlled basis. Motion picture stars like Charlie Chaplin and Rudolph Valentino were the bedrock of the business. By the end of the decade, silent films began to be replaced with sound pictures. The first such film, **The Jazz Singer,** was produced by one of the smaller studios, Warner Brothers, and it starred Al Jolson, who specialized in rendering popular tunes in blackface.

The advertising business boomed during the 1920s as advertisers developed new and effective ways to persuade Americans to acquire the products coming out of the nation's factories and workshops. Before World War I, the total amount spent on advertising stood at about $400 million annually. It soared to $2.6 billion

(Bettmann/Corbis)

Radiola Advertisement.
The spread of mass entertainment through radio made the 1920s the first decade when Americans could experience simultaneously the same programs and stars. The product advertised here, the Radiola Super-Heterodyne, was designed for portability: "Under a tree, on a mountain top—tune in."

Jazz Singer, The (1927) One of the first motion pictures with sound, it starred Al Jolson who specialized in rendering popular tunes in blackface.

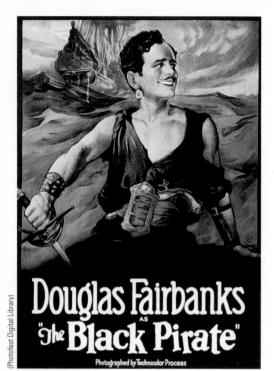

(Photofest Digital Library)

Douglas Fairbanks Sr. in
The Black Pirate.   Douglas
Fairbanks, Sr., shown here in "The
Black Pirate," used his athletic
skills to create stunts that thrilled
audiences during the 1920s.

Doing History Online

Automotive Advertising, 1923

Go to the CourseMate website for
this chapter and link to Primary
Sources. According to the ads
online, what are some of the
ways in which the automobile
reshaped Americans' lives?

    www.cengagebrain.com

---

by 1929. Radios brought advertising into the home, and billboards attracted the attention of millions of motorists. Advertising, said one of its practitioners, "literally creates demand for the things of life that raise the standard of living, elevate the taste, changing luxuries into necessities." Among the products that advertising promoted was Listerine, which was said to eliminate halitosis, the medical term for bad breath. Other consumers were urged to ingest yeast at least twice a day to fight constipation and skin problems.

The most celebrated advertising man of the decade was Bruce Barton, who wrote a biography of Jesus Christ in order to demonstrate that advertising went back to biblical times. In *The Man Nobody Knows* (1925), Barton retold the New Testament in terms that Americans of the 1920s could easily grasp. Jesus, wrote Barton, "recognized the basic principle that all good advertising is news." The twelve disciples were a model of an efficient business organization, and Jesus himself was a master salesman. "He was never trite or commonplace; he had no routine." Barton's book became a national best-seller.

Troubled Farmers and Workers

Not all segments of society shared equally in the return of good times. The postwar depression hit the farm sector with devastating force. Farmers had never benefited from the upturn that marked the cities. For labor also, this was a time of retreat.

The United States still relied on farming as a key element in the economy. The 7 million families who lived on farms in 1920 did not generally enjoy the modern conveniences and appliances that had appeared in the cities. Overproduction of crops drove down prices and led to massive harvests that could not be marketed. In the South, for example, the price of cotton was 40 cents a pound in 1920 but slid to 10 cents a pound in 1921. The postwar recovery of agriculture in Europe meant that overseas markets were smaller as well. The per capita income of most farmers did not rise substantially after 1919, and there was a widening gap between what farmers earned and what city dwellers made. To improve their lot, farmers sought higher tariff duties on imported products. They also revived the idea of farm cooperatives to market more effectively.

In 1921, a plow manufacturer named George Peek proposed that American farmers ship surplus products overseas and dump them on the world market at whatever price they could obtain. The government would buy farm products at the market price and then sell them abroad. Taxes on the processing of crops would cover the cost to the government and the taxpayer. The chairs of the House and Senate Agriculture Committees introduced a bill to enact such a program in January 1924. Known as the McNary-Haugen Plan, it gained much support in the Midwest and soon commanded national attention. Critics called it price fixing at government expense.

Other workers did not receive even modest assistance; instead, government and business threw up numerous obstacles to labor's interests. The U.S. Supreme Court struck down minimum wages for women in Washington, D.C., and when railroad industry strikes occurred in 1922, the Harding administration obtained harsh court orders that effectively ended the walkouts. Businesses used less repressive tactics as well. Some of the bigger and more enlightened firms provided what became known as welfare capitalism. General Electric, International Harvester, and Bethlehem Steel represented companies that sought to appease workers with recreational facilities, benefit plans, and sometimes even profit-sharing opportunities. Estimates indicated that as many as 4 million workers received such rewards. After the middle of the decade, however, these programs stalled as the lack of labor militancy removed the incentive to make concessions to workers.

The Harding Scandals

By early 1923, Harding's presidency was mired in rumors of scandal. Attorney General Harry Daugherty was a political ally of the president, but his loose direction of the Justice Department allowed corruption to flourish. Scandals also festered in the Veterans Bureau and the Office of the Alien Property Custodian. The most serious wrongdoing involved the secretary of the interior, Albert B. Fall. Federal oil reserves at Elk Hills, California, and Teapot Dome, Wyoming, were leased to private oil companies. Fall received $400,000 in loans from friends in the industry in what many interpreted as payoffs for his leasing decisions. The Teapot Dome scandal emerged in 1923–1924 after Harding had died, but it established his administration's reputation as one of the most corrupt in American history.

A weak president and a poor judge of people, Harding allowed cronies and crooks to infest his administration. By 1923, he knew about the ethical problems in the Veterans Bureau, and he suspected that scandals lurked in the Department of the Interior and the Justice Department as well. During a tour of the Pacific Northwest in July 1923, the president fell ill. He died in San Francisco on August 2 of heart disease.

Keep Cool with Coolidge

Harding's successor was Calvin Coolidge, the former governor of Massachusetts. Coolidge came to be viewed in Washington as a stereotypical New Englander, a man of few words. In fact, Coolidge was quite talkative in the regular press conferences that he held twice a week. His wife, Grace, brought glamour and a sense of fun to the White House, offsetting her husband's dour personality.

Coolidge was much more committed to the conservative principles of the Republicans than Harding had been. He proclaimed that "the business of America is business," and he endorsed policies designed to promote corporate enterprise. He extended the tax-cutting policies of Treasury Secretary Mellon and appointed pro-business individuals to head the regulatory agencies and departments that the progressives had established a generation earlier. The president used modern public relations techniques to bolster his image as an embodiment of old-time virtues of morality and frugality.

The Discordant Democrats

The Democrats hoped that the Teapot Dome scandal and other revelations of wrongdoing in the Harding years would be their ticket back to the White House. But when the Teapot Dome scandal could not be linked to anyone in the White House, the issue faded away.

Prohibition had split the Democrats between the dry faithful of the South and West, who wanted strict enforcement of the Volstead Act, and the wet residents of the large cities of the North and Midwest, who saw Prohibition as a foolish experiment. The two leading candidates for the Democratic Party nomination reflected this regional tension. William G. McAdoo represented the progressive, prohibitionist wing. Governor Alfred E. Smith of New York was a Roman Catholic who opposed Prohibition. The Democratic National Convention left the party with almost no chance of defeating President Coolidge as McAdoo and Smith deadlocked through dozens of ballots. Finally, the exhausted delegates chose a former member of Congress and Wall Street lawyer named John W. Davis.

Senator Robert M. La Follette of Wisconsin, who had been seeking the presidency for many years, became the champion of what remained of the progressive spirit and the anger of the midwestern farmers. Although he was nominated for president at a convention of the Progressive Party, he did not attend the meeting or identify himself with the party. The American Federation of Labor and the railroad unions backed La Follette, but with little money or enthusiasm.

The Republicans ignored Davis and concentrated on the alleged radicalism of La Follette and his supporters. The choice, they said, was "Coolidge or Chaos." Coolidge polled more than 15.7 million votes, more than the combined total of his two rivals. Although the Republicans retained firm control of both houses of Congress, beneath the surface, electoral trends were moving toward the Democrats. In the northern cities the party's share of the vote grew during the 1920s. If a candidate appeared who could unite the traditionally Democratic South with the ethnic voters of the Northeast, Republican supremacy might be in jeopardy.

❖ Modern Cultural Currents

While politics followed a conservative path during the 1920s, the nation's cultural life experienced a productivity and artistic success that would be unrivaled during the rest of the twentieth century. In music, drama, and literature, the decade brought forth a rare assembly of first-rate talents.

The Harlem Renaissance

African American intellectual life centered in New York City. There, authors and poets lived in the black section known as Harlem. The "Harlem Renaissance" owed much to W. E. B. Du Bois's encouragement of African American writing in *The Crisis*, the journal of the National Association for the Advancement of Colored People (NAACP). In the New York of the early 1920s, the ferment associated with Marcus Garvey, the exciting nightlife, the relative relaxation of racial bigotry, and the interest of wealthy white patrons enabled a few black writers to pursue literary careers.

The Harlem Renaissance reached its peak in 1925, when a national magazine ran an article titled "Harlem: Mecca of the New Negro." In the same year, **Alain Locke's** book *The New Negro* was published. Locke argued that African Americans' "more immediate hope" depended on the ability of blacks and whites to evaluate "the Negro in terms of his artistic endowments and cultural contributions, past and prospective." Other major figures in the Renaissance were the poets Langston Hughes ("The Weary Blues"), Countee Cullen ("Do I Marvel"), **Zora Neale Hurston** (the play *Color Struck*), and Claude McKay (*Harlem Shadows*), as well as the memoirist and songwriter James Weldon Johnson (*God's Trombones*). Although these writers' artistic merit was undeniable, the Harlem Renaissance did little to alter the segregationist laws and customs that restricted the lives of most African Americans.

The Sound of Jazz

After World War I, the improvised music that came to be called jazz became a unique American art form, bringing together black musicians and a few white players in Kansas City, Chicago, and New York. The major innovators of jazz

Locke, Alain (1885–1954) African American poet and an important member of the Harlem Renaissance.

Hurston, Zora Neale (1901–1960) African American novelist who embodied the creative and artistic aspirations of the Harlem Renaissance in the 1920s.

Louis Armstrong's Hot Five,
     Exclusive Okeh Record Artists.

(Frank Driggs Collection/Getty Images)

Louis Armstrong and His "Hot Five."   Louis Armstrong and his "Hot Five" demonstrated what a cohesive small band could do in creating complex improvisations in the new "hot jazz" style.

included trumpeter **Louis Armstrong** and tenor sax player Coleman Hawkins, who took the new music beyond its roots in New Orleans toward a more sophisticated style. Blues artists such as Bessie Smith and Ma Rainey sold "race records" to black and white audiences. Edward Kennedy "Duke" Ellington and Fletcher Henderson led larger orchestras that showed what jazz could accomplish in a more structured setting. The rhythms and sounds of jazz gave the 1920s its enduring title: the Jazz Age.

Armstrong, Louis (1901–1971)
A trumpeter and a major innovator of jazz.

An Age of Artistic Achievement

Writers looked at the postwar world in a critical spirit that grew out of European ideas and a skepticism about older values. The most popular novelist of the early 1920s was Sinclair Lewis, whose books *Main Street* (1920) and *Babbitt* (1922) examined with unsparing honesty small-town life in the Midwest. Young people devoured the work of the acidic essayist and social critic Henry L. Mencken, who wrote for the *American Mercury*. Mencken was a Baltimore newspaperman who had little time for the sacred cows of middle-class culture. He characterized democracy as "the worship of jackals by jackasses" and said that puritanism was "the haunting fear that somebody, somewhere may be happy." Aimed more at the middle-class audience was *Time* magazine, started in March 1923 by Briton Hadden and Henry Luce. *Time* sought to present the week's news in readable and sprightly prose.

The list of important authors during the 1920s was long and distinguished. It included such artistic innovators as T. S. Eliot, who lived in Great Britain and whose poems such as "The Waste Land" (1922) influenced a generation of poets on both sides of the Atlantic. Novelists such as John Dos Passos, Sherwood Anderson, Edith Wharton, Willa Cather, and William Faulkner produced a body of work that delved into the lives of aristocratic women (Wharton), prairie pioneers (Cather), the working poor and middle class (Dos Passos), the residents of small towns (Anderson), and the Deep South (Faulkner).

Fitzgerald, F. Scott (1896–1940)
Jazz Age novelist; author of *The Great Gatsby* (1925). He and his wife Zelda embodied the free spirit of the Jazz Age.

The most influential fiction authors of the decade were Ernest Hemingway and F. Scott Fitzgerald. Hemingway's terse, understated prose in bestsellers such as *The Sun Also Rises* (1926) and *A Farewell to Arms* (1929) spoke of the pain and disillusion that men had suffered during the fighting in World War I. Like Hemingway, **F. Scott Fitzgerald**, along with his wife, Zelda, captured attention as the embodiment of the free spirit of the Jazz Age. In *The Great Gatsby* (1925), he chronicled the story of young Jay Gatsby, who sought to recapture a lost love among the aristocracy of the Long Island shore. In Gatsby's failure to win his dream, Fitzgerald, like other authors of the Jazz Age, saw the inability of Americans to escape the burdens of their own pasts.

The theater witnessed the emergence of the Broadway musical in the work of Richard Rodgers and Lorenz Hart (*Garrick Gaieties*), George and Ira Gershwin (*Lady, Be Good*), Jerome Kern and Oscar Hammerstein II (*Showboat*), and Cole Porter (*Paris*). The great age of the American popular song, inspired by the musicals, began in the 1920s. Serious drama drew on the talents of the brooding Eugene O'Neill as well as Elmer Rice and Maxwell Anderson.

In architecture, the innovative work of Frank Lloyd Wright had given him a reputation for artistic daring before 1920, but commercial success eluded him. American architects designed planned, suburban communities modeled on historical models from England or the Southwest. Skyscrapers and city centers such as Rockefeller Center in New York City embodied a building style that emphasized light and air. Amid the prosperity and optimism of the 1920s, it seemed that the possibilities for a lively and vibrant culture were limitless.

Youth Culture and Sports

During the 1920s, changes in the family gave youth more importance. Women stopped having children at a younger age, and they thus had more time to devote to their own interests. Divorce gained favor as a way of ending unhappy marriages; in 1924, one marriage in seven ended in divorce, a large increase since the turn of the century. The emphasis shifted to making marriages more fulfilling for both partners. As the nature of marriage changed, the role of children in the household was also transformed. One major influence on how American children were raised was the work of the behavioral psychologist John B. Watson. He taught that by manipulating the stimuli that a child experienced, the parents could create the kind of adult they wanted. Children, he said, "are made, not born."

The ability of parents to decide what their children should read and think came under attack from the growing consumer culture, however. Young people were bombarded with alluring images of automobiles, makeup, motion pictures, and other attractions. Since children no longer were so important to the wage-earning power of the family, they were given greater freedom and leisure time. Adolescence came to be seen as a distinct phase in the development of young Americans in which they sought fun, excitement, and novelty. Dating became a ritualized form of courting behavior carried on at movies, dances, and athletic events, as well as in automobiles.

More young Americans attended high school during the 1920s than ever before, and the percentage of those who went to college increased. Middle and upper class college women could smoke in public, go out on dates, and engage in the latest trends in sexual activity, "necking and petting." Male students with enough income joined fraternities, drank heavily, and attended athletic contests and dates. The college experience for students from lower-class families, different religious backgrounds, or minority groups was less comfortable. Informal quotas limited the numbers of Jewish students admitted to Yale, Columbia, and Harvard. In the South, African Americans of college age were restricted to predominantly black institutions that struggled with fewer resources. Poorer students at state universities and private colleges worked their way through, often performing the menial tasks that made life pleasant for their affluent peers.

During the 1920s, college football grew into a national obsession as money was poured into the construction of stadiums, the coaching staffs, and in many instances, the players themselves. Large stadiums sprang up on the West Coast and in the Midwest. The most famous football player of the era was Harold "Red" Grange of the University of Illinois. When he scored four touchdowns in twelve minutes against the University of Michigan in 1924, his picture appeared on the cover of the new *Time* magazine. After he left college, Grange joined the newly formed National Professional Football League and received $12,000 per game at the start. In contrast, the average worker in 1925 made 65 cents an hour.

Although the popular sport of boxing attracted millions of followers, baseball best symbolized the excitement and passion of the 1920s. A new kind of player in the person of **George Herman "Babe" Ruth** emerged. Ruth was a pitcher for the Boston Red Sox when they sold him to the New York Yankees for $400,000 in 1918. Ruth was the first of the celebrity sluggers; he belted out fifty-four home runs during the 1920 season, and fans flocked to see him perform. The Yankees decided to construct Yankee Stadium ("the House that Ruth built") to accommodate the fans who wanted to be there when Ruth connected. The 1920s saw baseball reach its peak in 1927 when Babe Ruth hit sixty home runs and the New York Yankees captured the American League pennant and the World Series in four games. Commentators speculated that his record would stand for decades. The feat summed up the allure of a sports-crazy decade. Professional baseball remained a white man's game, however; talented black players such as Josh Gibson labored in obscurity in the Negro leagues.

Ruth, George Herman ("Babe") (1895–1948) Boston Red Sox pitcher who was sold to the New York Yankees in 1918 for $400,000. He belted out fifty-four home runs during the 1920 season, and fans flocked to see him play.

❖ Fundamentalism and Traditional Values

For most Americans, the literary and artistic ferment of the 1920s was part of a broader set of challenges to the older lifestyles with which they had grown up. Residents of small towns and newcomers to the growing cities sought to find reassurance in the older ways that they fondly remembered. The currents of religious and social conservatism remained dominant.

The Fundamentalist Movement

Amid the social ferment that accompanied the rise of the Ku Klux Klan, the tensions over nativism, and the reaction against modern ideas, American Protestantism engaged in a passionate debate over the proper position of Christians toward science, the doctrine of evolution, and liberal ideas. Conservative church leaders in northern Baptist and Presbyterian pulpits spoke of the dangers to faith from a society that had moved away from the Bible and its teachings. In 1920, a minister called the movement "fundamentalism" because it sought to reaffirm precepts of the Christian creed such as the literal truth of the Bible and the central place of Jesus Christ in saving humanity. In California, evangelist Aimee Semple McPherson fused fundamentalism with modern media techniques and achieved national fame.

Fundamentalism had a political and social agenda as well as a religious message. The doctrine of evolution became a special target of fundamentalist wrath. William Jennings Bryan emerged as a leading champion of the crusade. "It is better to trust the Rock of Ages," he said, "than to know the age of rocks." In a dozen state legislatures, lawmakers introduced bills to ban the teaching of evolution in

Doing History Bryan Versus Darrow: The Scopes Trial

The cultural clashes of the 1920s included the sensational trial of John T. Scopes, a Tennessee schoolteacher accused of instructing his students in evolution, which put him in violation of a state law against teaching the subject. His trial on the charges brought great publicity to the small town of Dayton, Tennessee, where the proceedings were held. William Jennings Bryan appeared to assist the prosecution in convicting Scopes of the charges against him. Defending Scopes was the celebrated criminal lawyer Clarence Darrow. The defense called Bryan to the witness stand as an expert in the issues of fundamentalism, the biblical teachings on creation, and the criticism of evolution that Bryan articulated. The ensuing cross-examination between Bryan and Darrow illustrated the cultural divide of the 1920s and the divergent ways in which these two men, and the cultural views they represented, saw the world.

Darrow Cross-Examines Bryan

Darrow: You have given considerable study to the Bible, haven't you, Mr. Bryan?

Bryan: Yes, sir, I have tried to.

Darrow: Then you have made a general study of it?

Bryan: Yes, I have. I have studied the Bible for about fifty years, or sometime more than that, but of course I have studied it more as I have become older than when I was but a boy.

Darrow: You claim that every-thing in the Bible should be literally interpreted?

Bryan: I believe every-thing in the Bible should be accepted as it is given there; some of the Bible is given illustratively. For instance: "Ye are the salt of the earth." I would not insist that man was actually salt, or that he had flesh of salt, but it is used in the sense of salt as saving God's people.

Darrow: But when you read that Jonah swallowed the whale—or that the whale swallowed Jonah—excuse me please, how do you literally interpret that?

Bryan: When I read that a big fish swallowed Jonah—it does not say whale. . . . That is my recollection of it. A big fish, and I believe it, and I believe in a God who can make a whale and can make a man and make both what He pleases.

Darrow: Now, you say, the big fish swallowed Jonah, and there remained how long—three days—and then he spewed him upon the land. You believe that the big fish was made to swallow Jonah?

public schools. The Anti-Evolution League hoped to amend the Constitution to bar the teaching of evolution anywhere in the nation. In 1924, Tennessee passed a law that prohibited the spending of public money "to teach any theory that denies the story of the Divine Creation of man as taught in the Bible."

The Scopes Trial

In 1925, a schoolteacher named John T. Scopes taught evolution in Dayton, Tennessee. The local authorities indicted Scopes, and his case came to trial. William Jennings Bryan agreed to help prosecute Scopes, and the American Civil Liberties Union brought in the noted trial lawyer Clarence Darrow for the defense. The **Scopes trial** attracted national attention, and the trial became a media circus. The judge refused to let Darrow call in scientists to defend evolution.

Darrow summoned Bryan as an expert witness on the Bible. The two men sparred for several days. Bryan defended the literal interpretation of the Bible, but to the reporters covering the trial, he seemed to wither under Darrow's

Scopes trial (1925) Trial of biology teacher John Thomas Scopes in Dayton, Tennessee, for teaching evolution. The jury found him guilty and assessed a small fine.

Bryan: I am not prepared to say that; the Bible merely says it was done.

Darrow: You don't know whether it was the ordinary run of fish, or made for that purpose?

Bryan: You may guess; you evolutionists guess. . . .

Darrow: You are not prepared to say whether that fish was made especially to swallow a man or not?

Bryan: The Bible doesn't say, so I am not prepared to say.

Darrow: But you do believe He made them—that He made such a fish and that it was big enough to swallow Jonah.

Bryan: Yes sir. Let me add. One miracle is just as easy to believe as another.

Darrow: Just as hard?

Bryan: It is hard to believe for you, but easy for me. A miracle is a thing performed beyond what man can perform. When you get within the realm of miracles; and it is just as easy to believe the miracle of Jonah as any other miracle in the Bible.

Darrow: Perfectly easy to believe that Jonah swallowed the whale.

Bryan: If the Bible said so; the Bible doesn't make extreme statements as evolutionists do.

Source: See Scopes Trial, University of Missouri, Kansas City, School of Law at www.law.umkc.edu/faculty.projects.ftrials/scopes/day7.html.

This exchange, like the others between Bryan and Darrow, changed few minds in the controversy over evolution. As the contemporary debate over evolution indicates, the differences that existed in the 1920s have persisted to the present. In that sense the 1920s were a precursor of debates over social and cultural issues that have not disappeared with the passage of decades.

QUESTIONS for REFLECTION

1. How did Bryan and Darrow differ in their views of the Bible and its relation to science?

2. What assumptions about the world and nature did each man bring to this encounter?

3. How did Bryan and Darrow illustrate some of the contrasting ways in which progressives of the first two decades of the century had responded to the intellectual and cultural currents of the 1920s?

cross-examination. (See *Doing History: Bryan Versus Darrow: The Scopes Trial.*) Sophisticated Americans regarded Bryan as a joke, but in rural America, he remained a hero. The jury found Scopes guilty and assessed him a small fine. Bryan died shortly after the trial. Although Scopes lost, to many Americans the Scopes trial signaled the end of fundamentalism, but it would remain a potent element in American culture.

Prohibition in Retreat

By the mid-1920s, the Prohibition experiment was faltering. Enforcement and compliance waned. The spread of bootlegging and its ties with organized crime meant that state and federal authorities faced an ever-growing challenge in attempting to stop the movement of illegal liquor across the Canadian border or from ships that gathered near major U.S. ports. The brewing and liquor interests called for a campaign to repeal the Eighteenth Amendment, and the Association Against the Prohibition Amendment became a strong lobbying force.

Doing History Online

. . . And Its Discontents

Go to the CourseMate website for this chapter and link to Primary Sources. Who or what groups are represented in this online section? What do some of them have in common?

 www.cengagebrain.com

Consumption of alcohol rose to more than one gallon annually per capita by 1923 and reached almost one and one-quarter gallons three years later. With the national law on the books, the Anti-Saloon League lost some of its intensity during the 1920s. When the problems associated with drinking declined, its urgency as a social issue receded. The consensus that had brought Prohibition into existence during World War I was crumbling as the 1928 presidential election approached.

❖ New Roles for Women

After the achievement of woman suffrage, most people expected the newly enfranchised voters to produce a genuine change in politics. It soon became apparent that women cast their votes much as men did. The possibility of a cohesive bloc of female voters evaporated. Yet while women did not change politics, they found that their place in society underwent significant transformations.

Women in Politics

National Woman's Party Created by Alice Paul, this organization pushed for the Equal Rights Amendment during the 1920s.

Having achieved the vote, the more militant wing of the suffragists, identified with Alice Paul and the **National Woman's Party**, advocated the equal rights amendment (ERA). The amendment stated that "men and women shall have equal rights throughout the United States and every place subject to its jurisdiction." Other female reformers, such as Florence Kelley and Carrie Chapman Catt, regarded the ERA as a threat to the hard-won legislation that protected women in the workplace on such issues as maximum hours, minimum wage, and safer conditions. Despite the efforts of the National Woman's Party and the support of the Republicans, the ERA was not adopted.

Two states, Wyoming and Texas, elected female governors. Nellie Tayloe Ross of Wyoming was chosen to fill out the unexpired term of her husband after he died in office. Miriam Amanda Ferguson of Texas won election in 1924 because her husband, a former governor, had been impeached and barred from holding office in the state. She became his surrogate. Eleven women were elected to the House of Representatives, many of them as political heirs of their husbands. Many more won seats in state legislatures or held local offices. Eleanor Roosevelt, the wife of a rising Democratic politician in New York, built up a network of support for her causes and career among women in her party.

Social causes enlisted women who had started their careers in public life years earlier. Margaret Sanger continued to be a staunch advocate of birth control. She founded the American Birth Control League, which became Planned Parenthood in 1942. Sanger capitalized on a popular interest in "eugenics," a quasi-scientific movement to limit births among "unfit" elements of the population. The racist implications of the theory stirred only modest controversy before the rise of Nazi Germany in the 1930s. Sanger found increased support for birth control among doctors as the 1920s progressed. The greatest effect of the campaign was seen in middle-class women. The poor and minorities turned to older, less reliable methods of avoiding pregnancy and often resorted to abortions when pregnant.

The New Woman

Social feminism confronted the influence of the mass media in shaping the attitudes of women during the 1920s. In their relations with men, young women of the 1920s practiced a new sexual freedom. Among women born after 1900, the rate of premarital intercourse, while still low by modern standards, was twice as high as it had been among women born a decade earlier.

Women joined the workforce in growing numbers. At the beginning of the decade, 8.3 million women, or about 24 percent of the national workforce, were employed outside the home. Ten years later, the number stood at 10.6 million, or 27 percent. A few occupations accounted for 85 percent of female jobs. One-third of these women worked in clerical positions, 20 percent labored as domestic servants, and another third were employed in factory jobs. The median wage for women usually stood at about 55 percent of what men earned for comparable jobs. At the same time, women entered new professions and became celebrities. Amelia Earhart, for example, was the first female pilot to cross the Atlantic, and emerged as the most famous female flier of the era.

For the majority of women, however, the barriers to advancement and opportunity remained high. Poor white women in the South often worked at dead-end jobs in textile mills or agricultural processing plants. Black women found it difficult to secure nondomestic jobs in either the North or the South. Labor unions rarely addressed the situation of female workers. When strikes did occur, as in New Jersey and Massachusetts during the middle of the decade, employers sometimes granted concessions—and then moved their factories to the South, where labor was cheaper and unions were weaker.

Career women faced formidable obstacles. When a woman schoolteacher married, many school districts compelled her to resign. College faculties, the medical profession, and the law had more women members than in the past, but they made it difficult for women to advance in these careers. In government, men received favorable treatment. Although many women worked outside the home out of economic necessity, they were expected to juggle their careers and domestic responsibilities.

❖ Coolidge in the White House

The inauguration of President Coolidge on March 4, 1925, was the first to be broadcast over the radio. The administration's policy goals were modest. In 1926, Coolidge asked Congress for a cut in taxes. The lawmakers responded with a measure that lowered the surtax on people who made more than $100,000 annually, reduced the estate tax to 20 percent, and eliminated the gift tax. Few married couples earned more than the $3,500 exemption, and only about 4 million Americans filed tax returns during this period. The changes in the law affected only the most affluent in the society.

The president also supported laws to oversee the expansion of the new airline industry and regulate the growing radio business. Coolidge vetoed a bill to develop the electric power potential of the Tennessee River at Muscle Shoals, Alabama, for public purposes. When Congress twice passed the McNary-Haugen Plan to assist agriculture, Coolidge vetoed it on the grounds that trying to raise crop prices through government intervention was both expensive and wrong.

Coolidge's Foreign Policy

Although the United States remained out of the League of Nations and proclaimed that it would remain aloof from foreign involvements, it was not in fact an isolationist country during the 1920s. The Coolidge administration participated in foreign relations in ways that would have seemed impossible a decade earlier. The government encouraged the expansion of American business around the world, and Washington used corporate executives as ambassadors and in framing monetary policy. Americans applauded U.S. policy in Latin America, Asia, and Europe because it did not involve the use of force. Sentiment for peace remained strong.

In Latin America, troubled relations with Mexico, especially over control of oil reserves, persisted. The administration sent an emissary, Dwight Morrow, who mediated an agreement to protect American oil companies from further expropriation. Marines were withdrawn from Nicaragua in 1925 but were sent back a year later when civil war erupted again. American efforts to instruct the Nicaraguans in what Washington said were democratic procedures did not produce the desired results by the time the Coolidge presidency ended.

Diplomacy and Finance in the 1920s

After the decision not to join the League of Nations, U.S. interest in Europe became chiefly financial. American bankers and investors played a large part in providing the reparation payments required of Germany in the Treaty of Versailles. Because of the size of the sums they had to pay, the Germans were unable to meet their obligations without American help. In 1924, the Coolidge administration endorsed a plan that scaled back German reparations and loaned that country money to meet its debts. During the next four years, Germany borrowed almost $1.5 million from the United States. European nations in turn used the money paid to them by the Germans to buy American farm and factory products.

The Coolidge administration continued the policy of nonrecognition of the Soviet Union, but it did not object when business interests, including those of Henry Ford, made substantial investments there. Americans also sent large amounts of aid and food when the Soviets faced famine during the early 1920s. In China, the U.S. government watched apprehensively as revolution and civil war wracked that nation. Washington extended de facto recognition to the government of the Nationalist leader, Chiang Kaishek, a stance that reflected the general policy of encouraging positive developments overseas without assuming any direct obligations. A symbol of that sentiment came in American support for the idea of outlawing war altogether. When the French foreign minister, Aristide Briand, proposed a mutual security agreement between his country and the United States, the State Department, under Frank B. Kellogg, proposed instead a multilateral agreement to have signatory nations renounce war. Peace groups supported the idea, and the Kellogg-Briand Pact was signed in 1928 and ratified a year later.

Lucky Lindy and Retiring Cal

Lindbergh, Charles A. (1902–1974) His solo flight across the Atlantic Ocean in 1927 made him an international hero.

In 1927, two surprising events riveted the attention of Americans. The first came in May when **Charles A. Lindbergh** flew alone across the Atlantic Ocean from New York to Paris. Lindbergh did not make the first nonstop flight across the ocean; two British aviators had accomplished that feat eight years earlier, flying from Ireland to Newfoundland in 1919. By 1926, however, a $25,000 prize was offered for the first nonstop flight between New York and Paris, a distance of thirty-six hundred miles. Charles Lindbergh had been an army flier and was working as an airmail pilot for the government when he heard about the contest. He raised money from local leaders in St. Louis and other cities. He called his monoplane the *Spirit of St. Louis*. On May 10, a tired Lindbergh (he had not slept the night before) took off from Roosevelt Field in New York on his way to Paris. When he landed in the French capital thirty-six hours later, he was a worldwide

(The Granger Collection, New York)

The Heroic Lindbergh. This picture of Charles A. Lindbergh after his historic flight to Paris captures the fascination that people of the 1920s had with celebrity, science, and the cult of the individual.

celebrity. He received a ticker tape parade in New York City, medals from foreign nations, and a lifetime in the public eye. To the generation of the 1920s, Lindbergh's feat symbolized the ability of a single person to bend technology to his will and overcome nature.

Calvin Coolidge could easily have sought another term in 1928. But he may have sensed the weaknesses in the economy that would become evident two years later. While vacationing in the Black Hills of South Dakota during the summer of 1927, the president gave reporters a simple statement: "I do not choose to run for president in 1928." This surprise announcement opened up the race for the Republican presidential nomination to other potential contenders, including the secretary of commerce, Herbert Hoover.

As 1927 ended, there were some signs that the economy was not as robust as it had been. A slight recession occurred in which wholesale prices fell nearly 4.5 percent. Production slowed, and consumer spending also dropped. Despite these warning signs, the banking system continued to expand credit, and stock market speculation persisted. For the average American, there was little concrete evidence that the boom years might be coming to a close. Calvin Coolidge was going out of public life on top with prosperity still a sure thing in the minds of most Americans with money to spend and invest.

In retrospect, these years would come to be seen as a time of isolation from the cares and problems of the postwar world. The United States was involved overseas with its destiny linked to the economies of Europe and Asia. The American people did not, however, believe that they would have to be militarily committed to the fates of people beyond the two oceans that protected the continent. In the 1930s, that confidence would decrease as dangerous new powers arose to challenge democracy in western Europe and the Pacific. Soon the 1920s would come to be regarded as a time of lost innocence.

CHAPTER REVIEW, 1921–1927

SUMMARY

During the 1920s, the United States became more modern because of:

- The rise of a consumer society
- The growing popularity of automobiles
- The development of radio and the motion picture industry
- The expanding use of electricity
- Greater opportunities for women in the economy.

Resisting the trends toward a mass society and culture were:

- The effort to enforce Prohibition
- The rise of the Ku Klux Klan
- The growing tension between secular forces and religious fundamentalism
- Continuing discrimination against minorities.

IDENTIFICATIONS

Sacco and Vanzetti
Marcus Garvey
Alphonse "Al" Capone
bootleggers
The Jazz Singer
Alain Locke
Zora Neale Hurston
Louis Armstrong
F. Scott Fitzgerald
George Herman "Babe" Ruth
Scopes trial
National Woman's Party
Charles A. Lindbergh

MAKING CONNECTIONS: LOOKING AHEAD Ⅲ➡

The key elements of the 1920s were economic prosperity, cultural change toward a more urban and cosmopolitan society, and the underlying problems that caused the Great Depression at the end of the decade. As you read the following chapters, be alert for the ways in which these forces interacted to make the 1920s so important in shaping the rest of the century.

1. Although the 1920s were prosperous, not all sectors of American life shared in the bounty. Why was the depressed state of agriculture so important?

2. How solidly based was the consumer culture of the decade in economic terms?

3. How was income distributed, and what government tax policies affected that issue under Harding and Coolidge?

4. What accounted for the flowering of the arts and culture during this period? What traces of the 1920s can still be found in mass entertainment now?

RECOMMENDED READINGS

Brophy, Alfred I., and Kennedy, Randall. *Reconstructing the Dreamland: The Tulsa Race Riot of 1921* (2002). A case study of racial violence in the decade.

Coben, Stanley. *Rebellion Against Victorianism: The Impetus for Cultural Change in 1920s America* (1991). Discusses how Americans in the 1920s reacted against the ideas and values of an earlier time.

Douglas, Ann. *Terrible Honesty: Mongrel Manhattan in the 1920s* (1995). A cultural history of the decade from the perspective of events in New York City.

Dumenil, Lynn. *The Modern Temper: American Culture and Society in the 1920s* (1995). An excellent analysis of the major trends of the period.

Ferrell, Robert H. *The Strange Deaths of President Harding* (1996). Explodes many of the sensational myths about Harding's career.

Ferrell, Robert H. *The Presidency of Calvin Coolidge* (1998). Provides a good survey of what Coolidge did as president.

Goldberg, David J. *Discontented America: The United States in the 1920s* (1999). A thoughtful narrative about the main currents of this period.

Larson, Edward J. *Summer for the Gods: The Scopes Trial and America's Continuing Debate over Science and Religion* (1997). A prize-winning look at the celebrated trial about evolution.

Leinwand, Gerald. *1927: High Tide of the Twenties* (2001). Considers the year that defined the spirit of the decade.

Matthew Avery Sutton, *Aimee Semple McPherson and the Resurrection of Christian America* (2007). An insightful treatment of an important figure in the development of religion during the 1920s.

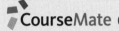 **CourseMate** Go to the CourseMate website at www.cengagebrain.com for additional study tools and review materials for this chapter.

22

The Great Depression

1927–1933

The Stock Market Crash of October 1929

Causes of the Crash
Underlying Economic Weaknesses

Brother, Can You Spare a Dime:
The Great Depression

The Depression Takes Hold
Hoover's Programs to Fight the
Depression
Everyday Life During the
Depression
Mass Culture During the Depression

A Darkening World

A Challenge to the League of Nations
Germany Moves Toward the Nazis

A Political Opportunity for the Democrats

A New Deal

Doing History: 1932: The Clash
of Philosophies

The Economy in Distress
The Bonus March
The 1932 Election
Hoover Defeated

MAKING CONNECTIONS

◀━▮▮▮ LOOKING BACK

The 1920s owed much to the way the economy made the transition from war to peace between 1918 and 1921. The political effects of the same period prepared the way for Republican dominance throughout the decade. Unhappiness with the League of Nations also shaped American foreign policy. Before starting Chapter 22, you should be able to answer the following questions:

1. What problems did Warren G. Harding confront when he took office in March 1921?

2. How did the failure of the League of Nations to gain Senate approval affect foreign policy under Harding and Coolidge?

3. What were the roots of the cultural tensions of 1920s as reflected by anti-immigration, the Ku Klux Klan, and the revolt against the city?

As the end of the 1920s approached, some well-off Americans viewed the future with confidence. Accepting the Republican presidential nomination in 1928, Herbert Hoover proclaimed: "We in America today are nearer to the final triumph over poverty than ever before in the history of any land."

Then came the shocks: first, the stock market crash in October 1929, then a severe economic depression that worsened during the early 1930s. The good times of the 1920s were replaced with breadlines, soup kitchens, and the wandering homeless. The administration of President Herbert Hoover took unprecedented actions to relieve the crisis, but nothing seemed to work. Resentment against the president, the economic system, and the wealthy grew. The specter of social revolution arose. Pressures for political change led to the election of **Franklin D. Roosevelt** in 1932.

By 1933, the Great Depression, as it came to be called, affected almost everyone in American society. It worsened the already difficult situation of the nation's farmers. For African Americans, Hispanics, and the poor, it meant even more misery and suffering than they usually faced. A generation of Americans looked to the federal government for answers to the social and economic problems they confronted.

❖ The Stock Market Crash of October 1929

At the time of the **stock market crash of 1929**, the incumbent president was Herbert Hoover. Elected in 1928 after a divisive campaign against the Democratic candidate, Governor Alfred E. Smith of New York, Hoover brought to the White House the knowledge gained from a successful career in the mining business and in government as secretary of commerce under Warren G. Harding and Calvin Coolidge. For the Republicans, he was the natural front-runner in 1928 once Coolidge decided not to run. In the election contest, Hoover benefited from Americans' suspicion of Smith, a Roman Catholic, which permeated the heavily Protestant South and Midwest. Now the question was whether "the Great Engineer," as Hoover was dubbed, could become a successful president.

To the average American, the economic signs during the summer of 1929 seemed encouraging. The prices of stocks traded on the New York Stock Exchange were reaching ever-higher levels. Radio Corporation of America stock shot up

Roosevelt, Franklin D. (1882–1945) Thirty-second president of the United States (1933–1945), he assumed the presidency at the depth of the Great Depression and helped the American people regain faith in themselves. He brought hope with his inaugural address in which he promised prompt, vigorous action and asserted that "the only thing we have to fear is fear itself."

stock market crash of 1929 The collapse of stock prices that ended the speculative boom of the 1920s and is associated with the onset of the Great Depression.

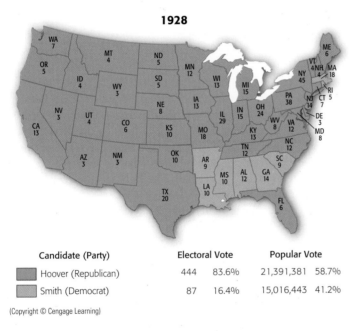

1928

Candidate (Party)	Electoral Vote		Popular Vote	
Hoover (Republican)	444	83.6%	21,391,381	58.7%
Smith (Democrat)	87	16.4%	15,016,443	41.2%

(Copyright © Cengage Learning)

MAP 22.1
The Election of 1928
In the election of 1928, Herbert Hoover achieved an electoral landslide and cracked the "Solid South" for the first time since Republican successes in Reconstruction. Alfred E. Smith did carry Massachusetts and Rhode Island, whose heavily Roman Catholic populations supported him. Those victories anticipated Democratic gains in the 1930s.

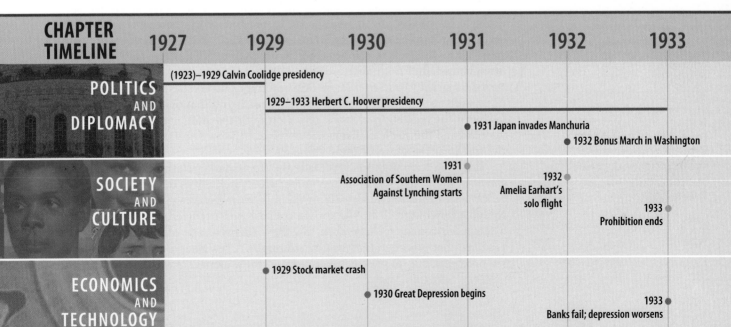

CHAPTER TIMELINE	1927	1929	1930	1931	1932	1933
POLITICS AND DIPLOMACY	(1923)–1929 Calvin Coolidge presidency	1929–1933 Herbert C. Hoover presidency		1931 Japan invades Manchuria	1932 Bonus March in Washington	
SOCIETY AND CULTURE			1931 Association of Southern Women Against Lynching starts		1932 Amelia Earhart's solo flight	1933 Prohibition ends
ECONOMICS AND TECHNOLOGY		1929 Stock market crash	1930 Great Depression begins			1933 Banks fail; depression worsens

from $85 a share to $420 a share during 1928. DuPont's stock price went from $310 to $525. A poem appeared in a popular magazine:

> Oh, hush thee, my babe, granny's bought some more shares,
> Daddy's gone out to play with the bulls and bears,
> Mother's buying on tips, and she simply can't lose,
> And baby shall have some expensive new shoes!

These giddy investors would be brought up short when the market's rise came to a shuddering halt.

Causes of the Crash

What dire alignment of negative economic forces triggered the calamity of October 1929? The decade of the 1920s had seen a wild investment fever that led all too many gullible investors into risky ventures for the allure of quick profits. In the sunshine state of Florida, where dreams of riches blossomed in the humid atmosphere, there had been an epic land boom in the middle part of this ten-year span. Asking prices for some of the most favored lots, those near the balmy waters of the subtropical Atlantic Ocean, rose to $15,000 or $20,000 a foot for acreage on the shore. When a devastating hurricane in 1926 deflated these dreams, land prices collapsed.

By 1927, the stock market seemed the ideal place to acquire the fast buck that Americans pursued. The issuance of Liberty Bonds during World War I had shown citizens the potential upside of stock purchases. Corporations increasingly relied on stock offerings to bring in the cash to finance the growth of their businesses. In addition, during the go-go years of the Harding and Coolidge presidencies, generous government tax policies allowed the very wealthy to retain money that they then invested in stock purchases. The richest Americans, by legal means, sometimes paid no income taxes at all.

One tempting device for smaller investors was to buy stocks in what was called then, as it is now, "margin" trading. An investor purchased a stock on credit, putting up only 10 or 15 percent of the actual price. Because Wall Street sentiment believed that stock prices were headed toward even higher levels in the future, a person, according to this rosy scenario, could sell the stock at a higher price, pay off the broker, and still pocket a substantial profit. People borrowed money to buy on margin. In this way, a tiny investment could be used to make a commitment to buy several thousand dollars worth of stock.

Investors with inside knowledge manipulated a stock's price up and down in order to fleece the unwary public or, in the phrase of the market, "shear the sheep." A firm called Kolster Radio had no earnings in 1929, but insiders drove the value up to $95 before the price collapsed back to $3 a share. New companies often consisted of nothing more than schemes to issue stock on the assumption that the market would rise. These firms produced no goods; they were paper empires with no real value, such as Ivar Kreuger's International Match Company. Government regulation of stock issues on both the state and federal levels was very lax, and the stock exchanges themselves had few requirements for revealing the true financial status of these companies.

Rosy statistics and forecasts made the stock market crash of October 1929 a shock. The problem began in September after stock prices reached record levels. Stock prices then declined early in the month, regained some strength, and resumed a downward drift. No abrupt collapse had occurred, and many on Wall Street, their confidence unshaken, saw these events as one of the temporary "corrections" that preceded further upward surges. A few people warned of impending problems, but they were dismissed as chronic naysayers who had been wrong before. President Hoover told his financial broker to sell off some of his holdings because "possible hard times are coming." He did not say that to the public. Most owners of stock simply waited for the rise in prices to begin again.

Then on October 24, 1929, which became known in Wall Street lore as **Black Thursday,** traders began selling stocks and found that there were few buyers. Prices collapsed, and the total number of shares traded reached 13 million, then an all-time record. Stockholders absorbed, by some estimates, a $9 billion loss in the value of their equities. During the afternoon, a banking syndicate, led by J. P. Morgan, Jr., urged investors to be calm. The syndicate bought stocks, and the market seemed to quiet. Over the weekend, the hope was that normal trading might recover.

The blow fell on October 29, when selling of stocks resumed at an even more intense rate. More than 16 million shares changed hands in a single day. Prestigious stocks such as American Telephone and Telegraph and General Electric recorded declines that wiped out large parts of their equity value. Fistfights occurred on the trading floor, and rumors of suicides swept through the exchange. The story went that when one trader checked into a hotel and asked for a room, the clerk inquired: "For sleeping or jumping, sir?" The naive optimism of the 1920s was evaporating as harsh reality came home to Wall Street.

The consequences of the stock market's decline were striking. The prices of individual stocks underwent a sustained downward slide. Within a few months, such a high-flying issue as General Electric had dropped from $403 a share to $168. Standard Oil shares fell from $83 to $48. One index of stock prices had gone to 469.5 in September and was at 220.1 by November. During the next twelve months, the gross national product sank from nearly $88 billion down to $76 billion. The economy was slumping into a prolonged depression.

Underlying Economic Weaknesses

Although the stock market crash represented a serious setback for the nation's economic health, the Great Depression of the 1930s that followed arose from causes more deeply rooted than just the decline in stock values of October 1929.

Black Thursday October 29, 1929; the day the spectacular New York stock market crash began.

Breadline. In the wake of the Great Depression, breadlines became a common occurrence in the United States. This one was formed under the Brooklyn Bridge in New York City as desperate people waited for food.

Despite the apparent prosperity of the 1920s, the United States faced serious structural problems that combined to cause the prolonged economic downturn.

The most pervasive dilemma that the U.S. economy faced had to do with the distribution of income during the 1920s. By 1929, the 5 percent of Americans at the top income level were receiving one-third of the total annual personal income. Those who made up the lowest 40 percent of the population received about one-eighth of the available income. For an economy that depended on the purchase of consumer goods for its expansion, there were not enough people with money to buy the products that industry was turning out.

Wealth was also concentrated in the hands of those with the highest incomes. More than 21 million families, or 80 percent of the national population, did not have any savings at all. The 2.3 percent of families with incomes above $10,000 a year, however, possessed two-thirds of the available savings. A consumer society had emerged, but the bulk of the consumers were unable to participate fully in the economic process. The disparities of the late 1920s contributed to the onset of the Depression.

Instead of using the profits that their businesses gained from selling goods during the mid-1920s to invest in new factories or a better paid workforce, industry leaders had put their gains into the stock market or speculative ventures. Loans to New York stockbrokers, for example, went from $3.5 billion in July 1927 to $8.5 billion in September 1929. By 1927, the market for new cars and new houses began to weaken, indicating falling demand for consumer goods.

Another chronic weakness of the economy was in agriculture, a sector that never shared in the general prosperity of the 1920s. The problem of overproduction of farm goods had not been addressed, and as prices fell at the beginning of the Depression, farmers felt the effects. At the beginning of 1931, cotton stood at nine to ten cents per pound; when farmers brought in their crop in the fall, the price had skidded to under six cents a pound. When farmers could not pay off their mortgages, rural banks soon failed. The ripple of banking failures strained a banking system that the stock market crash had weakened.

The world economy was also fragile. The settlement of World War I had imposed heavy reparation payments on the defeated Germans. Because the Germans could not pay these sums, they borrowed from investors and banks in the United States. In that way Americans financed the German debt payments to the victorious British and French. Those countries, in turn, could use the funds to pay off their war debts to the United States.

In 1924, the United States had reduced the burden of German war debts, and in 1929, another plan was offered that cut back further on the amount that Germany owed while establishing a payment schedule that extended the length of time for retiring the debt. These concessions alleviated the situation to some degree, but the basic problem persisted. This intricate and interlocking process hinged on the strength of the American economy. The United States, however, created tariff barriers that discouraged European imports and steered American capital toward internal economic development. When the European economies experienced difficulties themselves after 1929, the weakened structure of debts and loans soon collapsed, further damaging the economy of the United States.

❖ Brother, Can You Spare a Dime: The Great Depression

In 1929–1930, the United States lacked many of the government programs to lessen the cumulative effects of a depression. There was no government insurance of bank deposits. Individual banks were vulnerable to sudden demands by depositors to withdraw their money. Many banks had invested in the stock market and thereby placed their assets at risk. Other prominent bankers had embezzled some of the funds under their control to finance their investing. Among banks in general, there was little cooperation when a crisis occurred. To save themselves, stronger banks called in loans made to smaller banks, thus worsening the condition of weaker banks. (See Table 22.1.)

For an individual employee thrown out of work, there was no unemployment insurance. Old age pensions were also rare. Conventional economic thinking taught that the government should play a minimal role during hard times. Many people believed that the natural forces of the economy must work themselves out without the government intruding into the process. Secretary of the Treasury Andrew Mellon told President Hoover that "a panic was not altogether a bad thing" because "it will purge the rottenness out of the system."

The Depression Takes Hold

For some months after the disaster on Wall Street, it seemed as though the economy might rebound without much assistance from Washington. President Hoover endeavored to strike an encouraging note when he said in late 1929, "The fundamental business of the country is sound." He conferred with leading business figures about measures to maintain public confidence, especially programs to bolster prices and wages. He asked the Federal Reserve System to facilitate business borrowing. During the first several months of 1930, stock market prices recovered from their 1929 lows. In 1930, Congress enacted the Smoot-Hawley Tariff Act, which raised customs duties to high levels. Republicans believed that tariff protection would enable American agriculture and industry to rebound. The bill passed the Senate by a narrow margin, and despite some reservations, Hoover signed the measure on June 17, 1930. The Smoot-Hawley law has been blamed for the worsening of the worldwide economic crisis because it made it more difficult for European business to sell goods in the United States. By the middle of 1930, the effects of the downturn began to be felt.

TABLE 22.1
Bank Suspensions, 1927–1933

1927	669
1928	499
1929	659
1930	1352
1931	2284
1932	1458
1933	4004

Source: *Historical Statistics of the United States, 1985* (New York: Cambridge University Press, 1985), 536.

(LC-US262-94394)/Library of Congress Prints and Photographs Division)

Herbert Hoover. President Herbert Hoover kept up a jaunty public demeanor during the Depression. In this image he accepts a large pumpkin from a delegation that came to the White House for this public occasion. Over time, Hoover's image deteriorated as the Depression worsened.

TABLE 22.2
Unemployment, 1927–1933

Year	Number Unemployed	Percentage of Labor Force
1927	1,890,000	4.1
1928	2,080,000	4.4
1929	1,550,000	3.2
1930	4,340,000	8.7
1931	8,020,000	15.9
1932	12,060,000	23.6
1933	12,830,000	24.9

Source: *Historical Statistics of the United States, 1985* (New York: Cambridge University Press, 1985), 73.

During the 1930s and afterward, many Americans would place the responsibility for the Great Depression on President Hoover and his policies. But more than any previous chief executive, Hoover endeavored to use the power of his office to address the economic crisis. He favored reduction of taxes, easing of bank credits, and a modest program of public works to provide jobs. Some members of Congress opposed these ideas as too activist; others said that Hoover proposed too little. When the stock market turned upward briefly in 1930, the president told the nation: "I am convinced we have passed the worst and with continued effort shall rapidly recover."

But as 1930 continued, it was clear that the Depression was not going away. Bank failures soared from 659 in 1929 to 1,350 a year later. Businesses were closing, investment was declining, and corporate profits were falling off. Industrial production was 26 percent lower at the end of 1930 than it had been twelve months earlier. By October 1930, 4 million people were without jobs (almost 9 percent of the labor force), and the trend worsened as each month passed. Within a year, nearly 16 percent of the labor force was out of work. (See Table 22.2.) To encourage confidence, Hoover exhorted businesses to keep prices up and employees at work. Conferences with industry leaders at the White House were covered extensively in the press, but corporate executives continued to trim payrolls and reduce costs.

Hoover's Programs to Fight the Depression

President Hoover sought to apply his principles of voluntary action to keep the banking system afloat. In October 1931, he persuaded bankers to set up the National Credit Corporation, a private agency that would underwrite banks that had failed and safeguard their depositors. Unfortunately, the management of the banks proved reluctant to acquire the assets of their failed competitors, and the experiment was a disaster.

The president believed that the traditional self-reliance and volunteer spirit of the American people provided the most dependable means of ending the economic slump. His policies promoting economic recovery and providing relief for the unemployed stemmed from that fundamental conviction. He asked Americans who had jobs to invest more in their neighbors, to spend something extra to ensure that everyone could work. He set up presidential committees to coordinate volunteer relief efforts for the unemployed. One of those committees was the President's Organization of Unemployment Relief (or POUR). Yet none of these efforts alleviated the misery that Americans faced every day as the Depression intensified.

The programs that Hoover put forward were inadequate for the size of the unemployment situation. By 1931, 8 million people were on the jobless rolls and overwhelming the resources of existing charitable agencies. The POUR program coordinated relief agencies and urged people to help their neighbors, but these efforts did little to deal with the mass unemployment that gripped the country. Yet when politicians clamored for action by the national government, Hoover remained resolutely opposed.

A symbolic event underscored the president's political ineptitude in dealing with the Depression and its effects. When drought struck the Midwest in 1930 and 1931, Congress proposed to appropriate $60 million to help the victims of the disaster buy fuel and food. Hoover accepted the idea of allocating money to feed animals, but he rejected the idea of feeding farmers and their families. One member of Congress said that the administration would give food to "jackasses . . . but not starving babies." The spectacle of the president being more solicitous for animals than starving citizens was another testimony to Hoover's inability to empathize with his fellow Americans.

Everyday Life During the Depression

For most Americans after 1929, there was no single decisive moment when they knew that the economy was in trouble. A husband might find his pay reduced or his hours of work cut back. Soon families were making changes in their lifestyle, postponing purchases, and sending children out to find jobs. When a person lost a job, savings helped tide the family over until another job could be found. But as time passed and no jobs appeared, savings ran out, and the family home was put up for sale or the mortgage was foreclosed. Beggars and panhandlers became a common sight.

For those who were at the bottom of the economy even during boom times, the Depression presented still greater challenges. "The Negro was born in depression," said one African American. "It only became official when it hit the white man." In the South, whites seeking work took over the low-paying service jobs that African Americans had traditionally filled. Some black workers in the South encountered violence when whites compelled them to leave their jobs. Elsewhere, white laborers went on strike, insisting that African American workers be dismissed.

Women were told that they too should relinquish their jobs to men to end the unemployment crisis. Some corporations fired all their married women employees, and school districts in the South dismissed women teachers who were married. Because women did the domestic and clerical tasks that men did not care to do even in hard times, the number of women employed did not decline as fast as the number of men. Nevertheless, the Depression retarded the economic progress of women.

For Native Americans, the hard times perpetuated a legacy of neglect that had endured for decades. The Bureau of Indian Affairs (BIA) did not address the many social problems that the people under its jurisdiction confronted. Nearly half the Indians on reservations had no land; the other half subsisted on poor-quality land. Poverty pervaded Indian society along with a rate of infant mortality that far exceeded the rate for the white population. Criticism of the BIA mounted, but, despite a rhetorical commitment to reform, the Hoover administration accomplished little to improve Native American life.

On the nation's farms, abundant crops could not find a market, so the produce rotted in the fields. Mortgages were foreclosed, and many former landowners fell into the status of tenant farmers as the Depression wore on. In 1929, President Hoover had persuaded Congress to pass the Agricultural Marketing Act, which created the Federal Farm Board whose purpose was to stabilize farm prices. When farm surpluses around the world swamped grain markets in 1930, it proved impossible to prevent commodity prices from falling. Talk of strikes and protests was common among farmers during 1931 and 1932.

In the Southwest, the Hoover administration, faced with growing unemployment in that region, endeavored to reduce the number of people looking for jobs by creating a program to send Hispanic workers and their families back to Mexico and other Latin American countries. Some eighty-two thousand Mexicans were deported, and another half-million immigrants crossed the border out of fear that they would be sent back under duress. For Hispanic Americans who stayed in the United States, relief from the government was often hard to find because of a belief that it should be limited to "Americans."

As the Depression deepened, the homeless and unemployed took to the roads and rails, looking for work or better times. Migratory workers moved through the agricultural sections of California, picking figs and grapes for whatever they could earn. Others went from city to city, finding inadequate meals at relief stations, shuffling through a breadline in some cities, stealing or begging for food in others. The homeless lived in shantytowns outside cities that were dubbed **Hoovervilles.** Soon derogatory references to the president spread throughout the nation. A pocket turned outward as a sign of distress was "a Hoover flag."

Hoovervilles Makeshift "villages" usually at the edge of a city with "homes" made of cardboard, scrap metal, or whatever was cheap and available and named for President Hoover who was despised by the poor for his apparent refusal to help them.

By 1931, a sense of despair and hopelessness pervaded many segments of society. People who had been out of work for a year or two had lost the energy and inner resources to rebound even if a job was available. Others began to question the nation's values and beliefs. Bread riots occurred in several cities, the Communist Party forecast that the system was toppling, and the nation's political leaders seemed out of touch with the downward trend of economic events. A popular song caught the nation's angry, restless mood:

Once I built a railroad, made it run
Made it race against time.
Once I built a railroad, now it's done
Brother, can you spare a dime?

The Depression did not touch every American in the same way. Despite the economic disruptions, daily life in much of the nation went on as it always had. Families stayed together with the father holding a job, the mother running the home, and their children growing up and attending school. There might be less money to spend, but in many regions, poverty had not yet become entrenched. Nevertheless, the economic uncertainty that gripped so many people contributed to a general sense of unease and doubt that permeated the early 1930s.

Mass Culture During the Depression

Amid the hardships of the Depression, Americans found diversions and amusements in the mass media and popular entertainment that had emerged during the 1920s. Radio's popularity grew despite the hard times. Sales of radio sets in the United States reached $300 million annually by 1933. The habit of listening to a favorite program was an integral part of the daily lives of many families. Programming appealed to popular tastes and sought the largest available audience. Listeners preferred daytime dramas such as *One Man's Family* and *Mary Noble, Backstage Wife,* quickly dubbed "soap operas" after the detergent companies that sponsored them. The most popular radio program of the Depression years was **Amos 'n' Andy,** which portrayed the lives of two African American men in Harlem as interpreted by two white entertainers, Freeman Gosden and Charles Correll. Performed in heavy dialect, the show captured a huge audience at seven o'clock each evening. The tales of black life appealed to white stereotypes about African Americans, but they also gained an audience among blacks because the characters' experiences were comparable to those of minority listeners.

Amos 'n' Andy The most popular radio program of the Depression years, it portrayed the lives of two African American men in Harlem as interpreted by two white entertainers, Freeman Gosden and Charles Correll.

With ticket prices very low and audiences hungry for diversion from the trials of daily life, Hollywood presented a wide choice of films between 1929 and 1932. Sound movies had replaced the silent pictures of the 1920s, and escapist entertainment dominated movie screens across the country. Audiences laughed at the Marx Brothers in *Cocoanuts* (1929) and *Monkey Business* (1931). Musicals found a ready audience, and there was a vogue for gangster films such as *The Public Enemy* (1931) with James Cagney. During the early 1930s, Hollywood pressed the limits of tolerance for sexual innuendoes and bawdy themes with stars such as Mae West.

Despite the economic and social limits of the economic downturn, the cultural flowering that had begun during the preceding decade continued. In Kansas City and other midwestern cities, African American musicians were developing a new jazz style that would become known as "swing" when white musicians smoothed its hard edges to make it appealing to their audiences. The hardships of the era evoked artistic creativity and a vibrant popular culture that would dominate the entertainment scene for half a century.

❖ A Darkening World

With the economies of the democratic nations weakened and the structure of international relations tottering, authoritarian forces around the world asserted themselves against the existing order. The democracies and the Hoover administration seemed powerless to alter the trend of events.

Herbert Hoover entered the White House with well-formulated ideas about the national role in foreign affairs. Since future wars were unlikely, he believed, it was time to pursue disarmament and let the force of world opinion maintain peace. In Latin America, the president proclaimed the **good neighbor policy.** He promised not to repeat previous U.S. interventions in the region and withdrew marines from Nicaragua and Haiti. In 1930, the State Department renounced the Roosevelt Corollary of 1904, which had asserted an American right to intervene in nations to the south. Despite outbreaks of revolutions in South America during his term, Hoover kept his word and left Latin American nations alone.

good neighbor policy A new Latin American policy wherein Hoover withdrew the Marines from Nicaragua and Haiti, and in 1930 the State Department renounced the Roosevelt Corollary of 1904.

Drawing on his Quaker heritage, Hoover thought that wars were senseless and disarmament imperative. A naval conference in 1927 had brought Great Britain, Japan, and the United States to the diplomatic table but failed to generate any resolutions. Hoover reassembled the major naval powers in London in 1930, generating a modest contribution to peace. To reduce military spending, the provisions of the Washington Conference pacts were extended for five years. The United States won parity with Britain in all naval vessels, and the Japanese gained the same result for submarines. Japan remained the dominant power in the Pacific, but there was little that the Hoover administration could do to change that reality.

As the U.S. economy deteriorated, the effects spread to Europe and further undermined the power of the democratic nations. With less money to invest, American capitalists could not lend to European governments, especially in Germany. The Smoot-Hawley tariff made it more difficult for Europeans and other importers to sell their products in the United States. International trade stagnated, and production in all industrial companies declined. In 1931, the entire structure of international banking stood on the brink of disaster.

(The Granger Collection, New York)

Japanese Invasion of Manchuria. When Japan invaded Manchuria in 1931, it violated a number of international agreements that it had signed. This cartoon provides an American commentary on these actions. The depiction of Japanese militarism would be a running theme in the United States throughout the 1930s and 1940s.

Hoover decided that the only answer was a moratorium on the payment of war debts to give the European countries time to regain their financial stability. He declared on June 21, 1931, that the United States would observe an eighteen-month moratorium on the collection of its foreign debts. The French held back for two weeks, putting further strain on German banks. In the end, all the countries involved agreed to Hoover's initiative. Unfortunately, the moratorium came too late to stop the erosion of the international financial system. A few months later, Great Britain devalued the pound when it could no longer maintain the gold standard. (That meant that the British would no longer buy gold at a fixed price and would allow the value of the pound to fall relative to other currencies.) This step reduced the price of British products and made them more competitive in world markets. However, as other nations soon followed this course, prices began to fall worldwide as production slowed, people took money out of circulation, and economic activity began to halt.

The weakening of the democracies provided an opening for authoritarian powers eager to challenge the existing order. The first test came in the Far East. In September 1931, Japanese troops detonated a weak explosive charge under a Japanese-owned railroad in Manchuria and blamed the episode on the Manchurians. The Japanese military had fabricated the incident as an excuse for attacking Chinese positions in Manchuria. During the weeks that followed, the Japanese army invaded Manchuria and advanced deep into the countryside. They then bombed Chinese cities to deter any opposition to their effort to occupy all of Manchuria. Frustrated by the power of the Western countries and desperate for raw materials, Japan and its military wanted to expel the foreign countries that had achieved a political and economic presence in China and the Far East. Desire for political and economic supremacy in the Pacific drove the Japanese agenda.

A Challenge to the League of Nations

Japan's attack on Manchuria posed a threat to the League of Nations. It also confronted the United States with the problem of what to do about a clear violation of policies and treaties to which Washington was a party, such as the Open Door policy and the Nine-Power Treaty. Yet the American army was no match for Japan's, and the administration had not maintained naval strength at the levels allowed in the various treaties that had been signed during the preceding decade. In addition, Congress would not have been sympathetic to U.S. intervention in a remote foreign quarrel. For the same reason, Washington could not look to European countries. Secretary of State Henry L. Stimson issued statements to China and Japan that proclaimed the unwillingness of the United States to recognize territorial changes in China produced by aggressive actions. This policy of nonrecognition became known as the Stimson Doctrine, but it was ignored by the Japanese.

The League of Nations criticized the Japanese policy, and Japan responded by withdrawing from the organization early in 1933. The United States and Japan were now embarked on a course that would lead to ever more bitter encounters and ultimately to all-out war.

Germany Moves Toward the Nazis

In Germany, resentment about the Treaty of Versailles had grown during the Depression. Germans listened to the nationalistic ravings of the National Socialist Party under Adolf Hitler. Hitler's message of national power and fanatical hatred of the Jews proved intoxicating to the German people, and in 1932, he stood on the brink of obtaining power. Some Americans, insensitive to Hitler's ideology of racial oppression, even admired the policies of Hitler and the Italian dictator Benito Mussolini because they apparently offered decisive action to deal with the economic crisis. The situation of democratic governments, on the other hand, was perilous as the United States entered the third year of the Depression.

❖ A Political Opportunity for the Democrats

At the beginning of 1932, the Hoover presidency was in dire political trouble. By 1932, the limits of the president's voluntary approach had become evident even to him. During the winter he supported a congressional initiative to establish the

Reconstruction Finance Corporation (RFC). Congress authorized this agency to loan up to $2 billion in tax money to save banks, insurance companies, and railroads from financial collapse. The law that set up the RFC repudiated the principle of voluntary action that Hoover had been following since the Depression began. It put the federal government behind the effort to achieve economic recovery and signaled that Washington could no longer take a passive role when the economy turned downward.

Republican problems meant opportunity for the Democrats, even though they offered few economic remedies. A deep split persisted within the party over the proper role of government in dealing with the Depression. In the 1930 elections, the Democrats picked up eight seats in the Senate. The Republicans retained control of the upper house by only a single vote. In the House, the Democratic gain was forty-nine seats, not enough to give the Democrats a majority, although their total of 216 members put them close. Whether the Democrats could unite behind a coherent program remained an open question in Washington as the presidential election neared.

When Congress reassembled late in 1931, the Democrats had gained several other seats because of the death or retirement of four Republicans. As a result, **John Nance "Cactus Jack" Garner** of Texas became the new Speaker of the House. A crusty conservative with no fresh ideas, Garner's major proposals seemed likely to make the Depression even worse. His answer to the growing budget deficit that the Depression produced was to offer a national sales tax. Such a proposal would have hurt lower-income Americans and, by taking money out of the economy, would also have been deflationary at a time when the economy needed stimulation. Before the bill could pass the House, angry rebels in both parties killed the sales tax idea. The Democrats in Congress seemed as bereft of ideas as the Republicans for fighting the Depression.

The front-runner for the Democratic prize in 1932 was Franklin D. Roosevelt, from a wealthy branch of his family that lived on the Hudson River in Hyde Park, New York. After attending the aristocratic Groton School and Harvard University, he had studied law in New York City. In 1910, he won a seat in the New York state senate and three years later became assistant secretary of the navy in the Wilson administration. Seven years in Washington had given him a thorough introduction to the politics of that city.

Although Franklin D. Roosevelt was only a distant cousin of Theodore, his wife, Eleanor, was the former president's niece. His connection to a famous name

Garner, John Nance "Cactus Jack" (1868–1967) Speaker of the House in 1931 whose answer to the growing budget deficit was to offer a national sales tax. He ran against Roosevelt for the Democratic nomination for president but released his delegates and was in turn rewarded with the vice presidential nomination.

(The Granger Collection, New York)

Franklin D. Roosevelt with His Wife and Daughter in Warm Springs, Georgia. Franklin D. Roosevelt conveyed a smiling, optimistic image in 1932. As he traveled with his wife and members of his family, Roosevelt's enthusiasm conveyed itself to voters eager for change during the Depression.

helped Roosevelt secure the Democratic vice-presidential nomination in 1920. Although the Democrats lost, the race gave Roosevelt valuable national exposure. But in 1921, Roosevelt was stricken with polio and lost the use of his legs. For the rest of his life, he could not walk without crutches and usually used a wheelchair. The public knew of his disability, but the press did not stress his condition. Counted out of politics because of his illness, Roosevelt worked his way back into Democratic affairs during the mid-1920s and in 1928 was elected governor of New York by a narrow margin. Two years later, he won reelection by a huge majority.

Roosevelt shared many of the ideas of the mainstream of the Democratic Party. He believed in balanced budgets, the gold standard, and capitalism. Yet he also had an instinctive rapport with people in all segments of society, and he relished the exercise of power. His progressive views on the role of government separated him from conservatives in his party, who longed for a return to the pre-Wilsonian traditions of small government, states' rights, and minimal government involvement with the economy.

Roosevelt's 1932 presidential campaign got off to a strong start. As a source of ideas for his campaign, Roosevelt turned to the academic community in the Northeast. He recruited several professors from Columbia University in New York to write speeches and formulate concepts for his programs. These scholars were promptly named the **brain trust.** In his speeches, Roosevelt talked of "the forgotten man at the bottom of the economic pyramid" who was suffering from the effects of the Depression. The answer, Roosevelt said, was "bold, persistent experimentation." (See *Doing History: 1932: A Class of Philosophies.*)

brain trust Group of prominent academics recruited as a source of ideas for the Franklin Roosevelt presidential campaign.

As Roosevelt's campaign gathered strength, it became clear from newspaper surveys, crude polls, and the sense that the administration was faltering, that Hoover was going to lose. Other Democrats challenged the front-runner. Still angry over his 1928 defeat, which he blamed on religious bigotry, and no longer friendly with Roosevelt, Al Smith wanted another chance at the White House. He became a more active candidate as the weeks passed, and his strength in the Northeast made him a serious rival to Roosevelt. Roosevelt was clearly the choice of a majority of the Democrats, but party rules mandated that a nominee receive two-thirds of the votes of the convention delegates. If Garner and Smith teamed up against him and their delegates stood firm, Roosevelt could not win.

The Democratic National Convention opened in Chicago on June 20, 1932. The Roosevelt forces faced many difficulties during the days that followed. But when it came to the actual balloting, his opponents could not rally around anyone else. In the end, Speaker Garner decided to release his delegates to Roosevelt; his reward would be the vice-presidential nomination, which he said was "not worth a pitcher of warm piss." At the same time, the California delegation swung its support to Roosevelt on the fourth ballot.

A New Deal

In a dramatic break with the political tradition that barred candidates from appearing at a convention to accept a nomination, Roosevelt boarded a plane and flew to Chicago through stormy weather. There he delivered his speech in which he used a phrase that would become the trademark of his presidency: "I pledge you, I pledge myself to a new deal for the American people." The candidate seemed poised and self-assured, and he radiated optimism. The convention band played the new Democratic theme: "Happy Days Are Here Again." Meanwhile, the gloomy Republicans nominated Hoover and braced for defeat.

Doing History 1932: The Clash of Philosophies

In the 1932 election, Franklin D. Roosevelt, the Democratic candidate for president, argued that the government must do more to fight the Depression. His position put him at odds with President Herbert Hoover, who contended that Roosevelt's programs meant regimentation and the end of American democracy. The voters elected Roosevelt in November 1932, but the debate that the two men waged has continued to shape politics to the present time.

Roosevelt articulated his position about government's role in a speech in September 1932 to the Commonwealth Club in San Francisco. In his remarks he mentions the electric utility financier, Samuel Insull, whose corporate empire had collapsed:

"This implication is, briefly, that the responsible heads of finance and industry, instead of acting each for himself, must work together to achieve the common end. They must, where necessary, sacrifice this or that private advantage; and in reciprocal self-denial must seek a general advantage. It is here that formal government—political government, if you choose—comes in.

"Whenever in the pursuit of this objective the lone wolf, the unethical competitor, the reckless promoter, the Ishmael or Insull whose hand is against every man's, declines to join in achieving an end recognized as being for the public welfare and threatens to drag the industry back to a state of anarchy, the government may properly be asked to apply restraint. Likewise, should the group ever use its collective power contrary to the public welfare, the government must be swift to enter and protect the public interest.

"The government should assume the function of economic regulation only as a last resort, to be tried only when private initiative, inspired by high responsibility, with such assistance and balance as government can give, has finally failed. As yet there has been no final failure, because there has been no attempt; and I decline to assume that this nation is unable to meet the situation."

President Hoover, noting that Roosevelt had promised also to use the power of the government to provide more jobs for the unemployed, went on the attack against this program, as well as his opponent's view of government, in a speech in New York in late October 1932. The *New York Times* covered the event: "If Mr. Roosevelt undertook to make good his promise to a constituent to support measures for inaugurating self-liquidating projects to provide work for all," Mr. Hoover declared, it would mean "the total abandonment of every principle on which this government and the American system is founded." Continuing, he said:

"The stages of this destruction would be first the destruction of government credit, the value of government securities, the destruction of every fiduciary trust in our country, insurance policies and all. It would pull down the employment of those who are still at work by the high taxes and demoralization of credit upon which their employment is dependent. It would mean the pulling and hauling of politics for projects and measures, to favoring of localities, sections and groups. It would mean the growth of a fearful bureaucracy which, once established, could never be dislodged. If it were possible, it would mean one third of the electorate with government jobs earnest to maintain this bureaucracy and to control the political destinies of the country."

The promises and measures advocated by leaders of the Democratic Party and until now not disavowed by Governor Roosevelt, Mr. Hoover said, would mean the "growth of bureaucracy such as we have never seen in our history." They would "break down the savings, the wags, the equality of opportunity among our people, and lead to further centralization of government," he asserted.

Source: The New York Times, September 24, 1932 (Roosevelt); The New York Times, November 1, 1932 (Hoover).

QUESTIONS for REFLECTION

1. How do Hoover and Roosevelt differ in their views of government power and its impact on the economy?

2. What contrasts can be made between Roosevelt's view of the business community and what Hoover believes about the same issue?

Cartoon from 1932 by John McCutcheon.   The spreading bank failures during 1932 led even conservative cartoonists such as John T. McCutcheon to suggest that there were flaws in the system that led to the collapse.

The Economy in Distress

As the politicians prepared for battle, the economy remained on a downward path. To deal with the growing budget deficit, Congress imposed new taxes in the Revenue Act of 1932. The sales tax idea had been dropped, but other levies on corporations, estates, and incomes made this the greatest peacetime increase in taxes in the nation's history. At a time when the economy needed fiscal stimulus, the tax measure drew funds out of the hands of consumers. Raising taxes in an election year added to Hoover's growing unpopularity.

The weakening of the Hoover administration and the increasing power of the Democrats led to an important change in labor policy during 1932. The Norris-LaGuardia Act of 1932 extended to workers "full freedom of association" in unions and labor representation, restricted the use of injunctions, and barred reliance on "yellow-dog" contracts, which prevented workers from joining unions.

As the Depression worsened during its third year, the plight of unemployed Americans deteriorated well beyond the ability of cities and states to provide aid. Congress became restive as the Reconstruction Finance Corporation extended loans to large corporations and the White House resisted legislation to help the needy and distressed. Bills were introduced to provide direct assistance to the unemployed, but a coalition of Republicans and southern Democrats blocked their passage. As news spread about how much money businesses had received from the RFC, pressure intensified for Congress to do something. The result was the Emergency Relief and Construction Act of 1932, which required states to attest that they could not raise any money themselves before federal funds were allocated to them. The law limited the kinds of construction projects that could be funded, but it represented at least a symbolic step toward a greater federal role in meeting the needs of desperate Americans.

The Bonus March

During the summer of 1932, other desperate citizens sought immediate relief from the government in the form of cash. After World War I, Congress had promised war veterans cash bonuses in the form of paid-up life insurance to be disbursed in 1945. During the Hoover presidency, the needs of veterans as a group had been generously funded, but as the Depression worsened the veterans clamored for early access to their "bonus" money. Hoover vetoed a proposal to allow veterans to borrow against the value of their bonuses in 1931, and during spring 1932, Congress decided not to authorize early payment of the bonuses.

To make their presence felt, thousands of veterans organized the Bonus Expeditionary Force, or the **Bonus Army,** which came to Washington during the summer of 1932 to listen to Congress debate the bonus proposal. They camped out in tarpaper dwellings and tents on the banks of the Anacostia River; some slept in government buildings. The authorities in Washington generally cooperated with the veterans, but Hoover ignored them. In July 1932, the Hoover administration urged the Bonus Army to leave Washington and even allocated $100,000 to pay for the cost of sending the men home. But many stayed on, hoping for a change in government policy.

On July 28, the secretary of war ordered the police to remove marchers from government buildings. When the police moved in, the veterans resisted, and fighting broke out. A police pistol went off, other officers began shooting, and soon two Bonus Marchers lay dead. The president ordered the federal troops in Washington, commanded by General Douglas MacArthur, to restore order. The general

Bonus Army Thousands of veterans, determined to collect promised cash bonuses early, came to Washington during the summer of 1932 to listen to Congress debate the bonus proposal.

took his men, armed with tanks and machine guns, across the Anacostia River into the main camp of the Bonus Army. The veterans fled in terror as the soldiers approached. Tear gas canisters were hurled, tents were burned, and the crowd dispersed in a panic. Motion picture cameras caught MacArthur in full military regalia directing the attack, and moviegoers across the nation saw newsreels of American soldiers ousting the Bonus Army from its camp. Many Americans were shocked. "If the Army must be called out to make war on unarmed citizens," said a newspaper editor, "this is no longer America."

The 1932 Election

The economic devastation produced by the Great Depression offered groups outside the two-party system a promising chance to win votes for more radical solutions to the nation's problems. The Communists, for example, organized Unemployed Councils to stage protests against high rents and evictions of tenants. Socialists and other left-wing groups cooperated with the Communists in protest marches and petitions for relief. The Communists wooed African American support when they defended the **Scottsboro boys**, a group of young black men who had been unjustly accused of raping two white women in Alabama in 1931. In 1932, some prominent intellectuals endorsed the Communist presidential campaign or supported the Socialist candidate, Norman Thomas.

For the majority of Americans who were still aligned with the two-party system, however, the only real choice lay between Roosevelt and Hoover. Many of Roosevelt's advisers told him that he did not have to campaign to win the race. Roosevelt saw the matter differently. If he ran a passive, traditional campaign, he would not persuade the voters who were looking for a change. So Roosevelt crisscrossed the country, making speeches that assailed the Republican leadership and attacked Hoover's record. His campaign speeches took a variety of contradictory positions: at times he seemed to be calling for a more activist federal government, while on other occasions he attacked Hoover's budget deficits and wasteful government spending. Most of Roosevelt's appeal came down to hope, confidence, and the promise of political change.

The incumbent president knew he was going to lose, but he campaigned doggedly. Hoover told the voters that the nation faced a choice between "two philosophies of government," with freedom and individual initiative the philosophy of the Republicans and socialism and regimentation the aim of the Democrats. Abandoned by many of his fellow Republicans and unpopular with the voters, Hoover staggered through his lifeless campaign.

Hoover Defeated

On election day, the Democratic candidate won overwhelmingly in the popular vote and scored a 472-to-59 triumph in the electoral college. His party secured almost 57 percent of the popular vote and made significant gains in Congress: ninety seats in the House and thirteen in the Senate. The election proved a major disappointment to both the Socialists and the Communists. Norman Thomas, running on the Socialist ticket, received fewer than 1 million votes. William Z. Foster, the Communist candidate, gained just over 100,000 ballots.

By 1932, politicians realized that the four-month period between the time that a president was elected and the inauguration was too long for a modern industrialized nation. A quicker transition to the incoming administration was imperative. A constitutional amendment moving the date of the inauguration to January 20 was under consideration, but the **Twentieth Amendment** would not go into effect until 1937. Meanwhile, the country faced a worsening economic crisis.

Scottsboro boys Nine black youths convicted by an all-white jury in 1931 on charges of raping two white women in Alabama. The case became a source of controversy and the focus of civil rights activism in the early 1930s.

Twentieth Amendment (1933) Constitutional amendment that moved the presidential inauguration date from four months after the election to January 20.

During these four months, the Depression reached its lowest point. One-quarter of the workforce could not find jobs, and the relief system had failed. The gross national product, which had stood at more than $103 billion in 1929, slid to $58 billion by 1932. Wheat sold for 30 cents a bushel compared with the $3 a bushel it had brought in 1920. In December, hunger marchers came to Washington to ask for government aid. The growing numbers of failing banks presented a dire threat: 1,453 banks shut their doors in 1932. Neither Hoover nor Roosevelt was able to deal with these growing problems.

Meanwhile, a crisis of confidence in banks gripped the country. Alarm about the banking system had been spreading since October 1932. During that month, the governor of Nevada proclaimed a twelve-day bank "holiday" to end depositor runs on banks. The news spurred depositors in other states to remove funds from their local banks. Hoover tried to persuade business leaders to place deposits in the troubled banks, but most were unwilling. The governor of Michigan intervened and declared a bank holiday on February 14. Depositors in other states, fearing that their deposits would be frozen, tried to withdraw their money from local banks. Governors in nine other states were forced to announce bank holidays.

Hoover pressed the incoming president for immediate joint action. Roosevelt was reluctant to tie his own hands before he took office. The days passed as February ended with no agreement on either side to do anything about the banking crisis. The two men held one last awkward business meeting on March 3 but came to no positive decisions. As the transition of power neared, general apprehension increased. By the morning of March 4, banks in New York City, the nation's financial capital, were shutting their doors. A weary Hoover concluded in a moment of personal despair: "We are at the end of our string." Shortly before eleven o'clock, the outgoing president joined Franklin Roosevelt in a waiting limousine, and the two men drove off toward the Capitol. Roosevelt waved to well-wishers in the crowd as Hoover sat in silence. A nation mired in the worst depression in its history waited to hear what the new president would say.

CHAPTER REVIEW, 1927–1933

SUMMARY

- The stock market collapsed in October 1929.

- Confidence in the economy eroded quickly.

- President Hoover's efforts to restore public confidence did not succeed.

- Existing programs to provide relief to the unemployed proved inadequate.

- Economic decline helped fuel the rise of authoritarian governments in Europe and Asia.

- By 1932 President Hoover's administration had lost political credibility.

- The election of 1932 brought the election of Franklin D. Roosevelt and the arrival of the New Deal.

- The economy stood at a low point when Roosevelt took office in March 1933.

IDENTIFICATIONS

Franklin D. Roosevelt
stock market crash of 1929
Black Thursday
Hoovervilles
Amos 'n' Andy
good neighbor policy
John Nance "Cactus Jack" Garner
brain trust
Bonus Army
Scottsboro boys
Twentieth Amendment

MAKING CONNECTIONS: LOOKING AHEAD ⅢⅢ➡

Nothing had prepared Americans for the Great Depression, and the effects proved to be long-lasting in all aspects of life. Debate still continues over what caused the downturn and why it lasted so long. Chapter 23 focuses on what made this period so traumatic for so many citizens.

1. Why would the Depression prove to be so hard to end?

2. What structural weaknesses in the American economy did the Depression reveal?

3. Herbert Hoover said that the 1932 election presented the United States with a fundamental choice between liberty and regimentation. What did he mean by that statement?

4. Why was Hoover, who was so successful in bringing relief to millions in Belgium and the Soviet Union, unable to do the same in the United States?

5. Which deeply held beliefs of Hoover did the Depression challenge?

RECOMMENDED READINGS

Clements, Kendrick. *Hoover. Conservation and Consumerism: Engineering the Good Life* (2000). Offers a probing study of the president's attitude toward nature and society.

Cook, Blanche Wiesen. *Eleanor Roosevelt, 1884–1933* (1992). The first volume of a biography of the important first lady.

Doherty, Thomas. *Pre-Code Hollywood: Sex, Immorality, and Insurrection in American Cinema, 1930–1934* (1994). Considers the role of popular entertainment during the Depression.

Finan, Christopher M. *Alfred E. Smith: The Happy Warrior* (2002). An engaging biography of the Democratic candidate in 1928.

Houck, Davis W. *Rhetoric as Currency: Hoover, Roosevelt, and the Great Depression* (2001). Examines how Hoover's speaking style affected his presidency.

Kennedy, David M. *Freedom from Fear: The American People in Depression and War, 1929–1945* (1999). Provides a prize-winning discussion of the Depression and its impact.

Liebovich, Louis. *Bylines in Despair: Herbert Hoover, the Great Depression, and the U.S. News Media* (1994). Looks at the troubled relations between Hoover and the press.

McElvaine, Robert S. *The Depression and the New Deal: A History in Documents* (2000). A well-chosen collection of revealing documents about the economic crisis.

Parrish, Michael E. *Anxious Decades: America in Prosperity and Depression, 1920–1941* (1992). An excellent synthesis of the interwar period.

Watkins, T. H. *The Great Depression: America in the 1930s* (1993). Offers a popular account of the events of the Depression decade.

CourseMate Go to the CourseMate website at www.cengagebrain.com for additional study tools and review materials for this chapter.

PASSAGES 1933 to 1960

23 The New Deal, 1933–1939
24 The Second World War, 1939–1945
25 Postwar America, 1946–1953
26 The Eisenhower Years, 1953–1960

Americans who grew up in the Great Depression served their country during World War II, and ushered in the enormous prosperity of the 1950s and beyond have been celebrated in recent books and movies as "the greatest generation." There are good reasons for such praise. In no other period except the Civil War and Reconstruction was America as severely tested, its direction as radically changed. The 1930s saw the worst economic catastrophe in modern history. Banks collapsed, farms failed, factories closed, bread lines formed in the cities. Yet what truly defined the nation in this decade was its passionate response to misfortune—the way Americans mixed protest, innovation, and reform. Dramatic changes occurred. The Great Depression not only increased the social responsibilities of government, it also opened the political process to millions of "forgotten Americans," who exercised power by joining labor unions, switching political parties, and migrating to places where they could vote and be represented. In contrast to the violent ideologies that gripped much of Europe and Asia in the 1930s, the United States witnessed a remarkable expansion of the democratic principles it held so dear.

Although the Great Depression would linger until World War II, the federal government provided Americans with food and employment, optimism and hope. Furthermore, the vast public works projects of that era—the roads, dams, bridges, tunnels, schools, hospitals, post offices, airports, parks, and playgrounds—created a physical infrastructure that tied the nation together while it spurred its future success. World War II brought on new challenges and opportunities. Battling on two fronts, the nation resolutely mobilized a superb U.S. fighting force and a masterful home front effort in which almost everyone took part. The war provided better employment for minorities and for women, although discrimination in wages and skilled jobs remained. So too did segregation in the armed forces—a hypocrisy that did not end until 1948. Nevertheless, Americans stood shoulder-to-shoulder against the villainy of fascism, Pearl Harbor, and Nazi genocide.

The enormous prosperity following World War II quickly pushed fears of economic depression aside. What remained in place, however, were the structural reforms that made banks safer, capitalism stronger, and people more secure. Postwar Americans strongly supported an active government role in domestic and foreign affairs. There was little opposition to expanding the social security system, increasing the defense budget, or providing hefty benefits to veterans of the war. Soldiers came home and picked up their lives. The marriage rate soared, a baby boom followed, and young families rushed to the suburbs. Peacetime consumption replaced wartime production as the key to national prosperity, with the sale of new homes, automobiles, and appliances reaching record heights.

The prosperity and good feelings generated by World War II, however, were not equally shared. Employment opportunities for women fell dramatically after the veterans returned. Racial prejudice remained a national disgrace. The South still required segregation by law, while other regions discriminated more subtly in housing, education, and jobs. Furthermore, growing fears about Soviet expansion and domestic communism dissolved the political unity, or bipartisanship, that had marked American foreign policy throughout the war. As Russian troops established an "iron curtain" across Eastern Europe and the pro-American government of Chiang Kaishek fell to the Red army of Mao Zedong on mainland China, Americans began to see the expansion of communism in much the same way they had viewed the spread of nazism a decade before. In 1949, the Russians successfully tested an atomic bomb, ending America's nuclear monopoly

Troops Returning Home.   More than twelve million American men and women were discharged from military duty following Japan's surrender in 1945. Their return created temporary problems in the job market and the housing market, but led to an era of unprecedented prosperity in the United States.

and creating fears of a nuclear confrontation in the future. A year later, U.S. and UN troops were battling Communist forces in Korea. The resulting Red Scare, fueled by opportunistic politicians like Senator Joseph R. McCarthy, challenged America's most cherished ideals.

Still, the nation prospered and grew. The 1950s saw the spread of a powerful civil rights movement and the demise of Senator McCarthy. Breakthroughs in medicine and technology ended the nightmare of polio, fueled the space race, and brought the miracle of television into almost every American home. The economic boom continued, raising living standards and national confidence to even greater heights. As 1960 approached, the nation appeared content and comfortable—thanks in large part to "the greatest generation," now approaching middle age.

POLITICS AND DIPLOMACY

1932: Franklin Roosevelt elected president
1933: Adolph Hitler becomes chancellor of Germany
Congress passes Agricultural Adjustment Act
U.S. recognizes the Soviet Union
1935: Congress passes Social Security
Senator Huey Long assassinated
1936: Spanish Civil War
1937: Court packing defeated
1939: Nazi forces invade Poland

1940: Roosevelt wins unprecedented third term
Congress enacts first peacetime draft
1941: Japanese bomb Pearl Harbor
1942: Incarceration of Japanese-Americans
1943: German army crushed at Stalingrad
1944: Normandy invasion
1945: Germany surrenders
Nazi death camps liberated
Atomic bombs dropped on Hiroshima and Nagasaki
Japan surrenders
United Nations founded

1946: Cold War emerges
1947: Truman Doctrine and Marshall Plan implemented
1947: HUAC investigates Hollywood
1948: Truman defeats Dewey
Alger Hiss indicted for perjury
1949: Communists triumph in China

SOCIETY AND CULTURE

1933: Prohibition ends
1935: Congress of Industrial Organizations formed
1936: Jesse Owens dominates the Berlin Olympics
1938: "War of the Worlds" radio dramatization spurs national panic
1939: John Steinbeck publishes *The Grapes of Wrath*
Marian Anderson sings at Lincoln Memorial

1941: A. Philip Randolph threatens March on Washington
1942: Women enter war industries in record numbers
1943: Race riot in Detroit
1944: GI Bill passed
1945: 12.5 million Americans in uniform

1946: Dr. Spock published *Common Sense Book of Baby and Child Care*
1947: Jackie Robinson breaks baseball's color line
1948: Kinsey Report
1949: Sears, Roebuck catalog advertises television set

ECONOMICS AND TECHNOLOGY

1932: Unemployment reaches 25 percent
Thousands of banks close
1933: Federal Deposit Insurance Corporation created
Tennessee Valley Authority created
1937: Severe recession
1938: Fair Labor Standards Act bans most child labor

1940: Military production ends unemployment
1942: Manhattan Project begins
Penicillin enters market as wonder drug
1943: Ford Willow Run plant turns out a warplane every sixty-three minutes
1945: United States produces more than half the world's manufactured goods

1946: Reconversion
1947: First suburban Levittown opens
1949: Soviet Union tests atomic bomb

1950: Senator Joseph McCarthy raises
　　　Communist issue
1951: Twenty-Second Amendment
　　　passes, limiting president to
　　　two terms in office
1952: Dwight Eisenhower elected
　　　president
1953: Cease-fire in Korea
　　　Stalin dies
1954: U.S. Senate censures Joseph
　　　McCarthy
　　　Brown v. Board of Education

1956: Eisenhower reelected
　　　Hungarian Revolution
　　　Suez crisis
1957: Federal troops sent to Little
　　　Rock, Arkansas

1958: Democrats sweep congressional
　　　elections
1959: Soviet Premier Khrushchev visits
　　　United States
　　　Alaska becomes forty-ninth and
　　　largest state
　　　Cuban Revolution

1950: Diner's Club introduces first
　　　credit card
1951: Alan Freed hosts rock 'n' roll
　　　radio show
1955: Montgomery bus boycott

1956: Elvis Presley appears on *Ed
　　　Sullivan Show*
1957: Brooklyn Dodgers move to Los
　　　Angeles
　　　Jack Kerouac publishes *On
　　　the Road*

1958: Elvis Presley drafted into army
1959: Vice President Nixon and Premier
　　　Khrushchev engage in Moscow
　　　Kitchen Debate
　　　TV quiz show scandal

1951: Televised coverage of Kefauver
　　　crime hearings draws
　　　25 million viewers
1954: IBM markets business computer
1955: Salk polio vaccine

1956: Federal Highway Act
1957: *Sputnik* launched

1958: U.S. manned space
　　　program begins
1959: Fifty million homes
　　　have television sets

23 The New Deal
1933–1939

MAKING CONNECTIONS

◀ ▪▪▪ LOOKING BACK

Chapter 22 discussed the causes of the Great Depression, which were rooted in the period of World War I and projected forward into the developing economy of the 1920s. When reviewing the causes of the economic collapse, look for signs of problems that were discussed in the preceding chapter. Before starting Chapter 23, you should be able to answer the following questions:

1. Why was the stock market crash of 1929 an important element in the nation's economic problems and yet not a decisive cause of the Depression?

2. Why was more not done to prevent the weaknesses in the economy that became apparent after 1929?

3. Why was Herbert Hoover elected in 1928? What political assets did he have that became liabilities once the Depression began?

Taking Charge of the Crisis, 1932–1933

The Banking Crisis
Extending Relief
Conservation, Regional Planning, and Public Power
Agricultural Recovery
Tenants and Landowners
Centralized Economic Planning

New Deal Diplomacy, 1933–1934

The Soviet Question
The Good Neighbor

Critics Right and Left, 1934–1935

The American Liberty League and the 1934 Election
"Every Man a King"
The Radio Priest and the Pension Doctor

The Second New Deal, 1935–1936

Jobs, Jobs, Jobs
Social Security
"Class Warfare"

The Fascist Challenge

Hitler and Mussolini
The Neutrality Acts

Doing History: The Battle over Neutrality

The American People in Transition

The 1936 Election
African Americans and the New Deal
Popular Culture in the Depression

Losing Ground, 1937–1939

Union Struggles
Fascists on the Rise
An End to Reform

On March 4, 1933, Franklin Roosevelt took the presidential oath of office in a steady, chilling rain. "Only a foolish optimist can deny the dark realities of the moment," he told the huge crowd and the millions who listened on radio. Roosevelt's voice radiated confidence and concern. "This nation asks for action, and action now," he declared. Comparing the Depression to an all-out war of survival, he vowed to ask Congress for the "broad executive power . . . that would be given to me if we were in fact invaded by a foreign foe."

Roosevelt offered few specifics. His objective was to convince a dispirited people to have faith in him and in themselves. Standing erect in his cumbersome leg braces, Roosevelt stressed four major themes: sacrifice, discipline, compassion, and hope. "The only thing we have to fear," he assured the nation, "is fear itself."

❖ Taking Charge of the Crisis, 1932–1933

This fear was understandable. The winter of 1932–1933 was a time of intense suffering and despair. Unemployment reached a staggering 25 percent. Banks were failing everywhere. Food prices had collapsed, forcing farmers from their land. Roosevelt understood how deeply the Depression had shaken the country and sapped its confidence. "I have [seen] the faces of thousands of Americans," he confided to a friend. "They have the frightened look of children. . . . They are saying, 'We are caught in some thing we don't understand; perhaps this fellow can help us out.'" No peacetime president ever faced a tougher challenge, or a greater opportunity. Respected commentators were predicting the end of capitalism if the Depression hung on much longer.

Roosevelt possessed neither a comprehensive plan to end the Depression nor a rigid set of economic beliefs. What he did have was the willingness to experiment, act decisively, and use the government as a powerful weapon in the struggle for economic recovery. "Take a method and try it," he liked to say. "If it fails admit it frankly and try another." Roosevelt surrounded himself with men and women of talent, accomplishment, and wide-ranging views. His closest advisers included Republicans and Democrats, agricultural theorists and urban planners, college professors and political pros. The **New Deal** attracted thousands of young people to Washington, drawn by the opportunity to do something meaningful—and perhaps historic—with their lives.

The Banking Crisis

More than five thousand banks had failed in the United States between 1930 and 1932, wiping out countless savings accounts and stalling the nation's credit. Panicked depositors, unable to tell a good bank from a bad one, lost faith in them

Mar. 4, 1933 · THE · Price 15 cents
NEW YORKER

(The Granger Collection, New York)

Hoover and Roosevelt. This *New Yorker* cartoon, sketched well before the inauguration, accurately predicted feelings of both men—the glum Hoover and the exuberant Roosevelt—as they rode down Pennsylvania Avenue together on March 4, 1933.

CHAPTER TIMELINE	1933	1935	1937	1939
POLITICS AND DIPLOMACY	1933–(1945) Franklin Delano Roosevelt presidency			
	● 1933 "First hundred days" of New Deal			
	● 1933 TVA established	● 1935 "Second New Deal" emerges		
	● 1933 Adolf Hitler becomes chancellor of Germany			● 1938 Munich Agreement appeases Hitler
SOCIETY AND CULTURE		1936 ● Jesse Owens dominates Berlin Olympics		1939 ● Marian Anderson gives concert at Lincoln Memorial
				1939 ● John Steinbeck publishes *The Grapes of Wrath*
ECONOMICS AND TECHNOLOGY	1934 ● Labor violence erupts in major American cities	● 1935 Labor leaders break with AFL to form CIO	● 1937 Severe economic recession begins	
				● 1938 Fair Labor Standards Act

New Deal Term for the domestic programs and reforms instituted by President Franklin D. Roosevelt and his administration in response to the Great Depression of the 1930s.

all, and an avalanche of withdrawals resulted. By the time Roosevelt took office, nineteen states had declared "bank holidays" (or closings) to head off a full-scale collapse.

On March 6, 1933, the president called Congress back into special session and proclaimed a national "bank holiday." Three days later, his emergency banking proposal was enacted in a matter of hours. The new law provided for the federal inspection of all banks. Those with liquid assets would be allowed to reopen with a license from the Treasury Department; the others would be reorganized, if possible, or closed for good.

On March 12, Roosevelt addressed the nation in the first of his "fireside chats." About half of America's homes had radios in 1933, and the president's audience that Sunday evening was estimated at 60 million people. "I want to talk for a few minutes about banking," he began, assuring everyone that the system was now safe. The listeners believed him. In the following days, as the stronger banks reopened, deposits greatly exceeded withdrawals. By the end of March, almost $1 billion had been returned from mattresses to bank vaults. The crisis was over.

Roosevelt's handling of the bank emergency revealed his essential pragmatism. In the midst of such turmoil, he could easily have taken a more radical approach—by nationalizing the banks, for example, or instituting much tighter controls. Instead, he demonstrated that his primary mission would be to preserve capitalism by reforming its institutions with substantial federal aid. The president also showed himself to be a master communicator. His ability to reach people in the radio age, to win their confidence, was perhaps his greatest gift. He would use it often in the coming years as the nation faced the twin crises of economic hardship and global war.

Extending Relief

The special session of Congress lasted from March 9 to June 16, 1933, a period known as "the first hundred days." In that time, more than a dozen major bills proposed by the White House were enacted. With both the House and the Senate now under firm Democratic control, Roosevelt had little trouble getting his legislation passed. As the banking crisis ended, he moved quickly to help those too desperate to help themselves. The problem was daunting. By conservative estimates, more than 30 million Americans were now living in family units with no income at all.

Roosevelt believed that relief efforts should be a local responsibility. He worried about the cost of funding such efforts and about the consequences of giving people money that they hadn't actually earned. Yet there seemed to be no alternative. It was essential, said one of Roosevelt's advisers, to pursue "long-run" economic growth. The problem, he added, is that "people don't eat in the long run—they eat every day."

On March 21, the White House sent two major relief proposals to Capitol Hill. The first one created the **Civilian Conservation Corps (CCC).** Based on a program that Roosevelt had implemented as governor of New York, the CCC combined the president's enthusiasm for nature with his belief in national service for the young. It provided government conservation jobs to "city boys," ages seventeen to twenty-four, in isolated camps run by the U.S. Army. More than half a million recruits cleaned beaches, built wildlife shelters, fought forest fires, and stocked rivers and streams. The pay was thirty dollars a month, with twenty-two dollars going directly to the worker's family. The CCC was both popular and successful. It eased unemployment a bit, lowered crime rates in the cities, and kept countless families off relief.

Civilian Conservation Corps (CCC) One of the New Deal's most popular programs, it took unemployed young men from the cities and put them to work on conservation projects in the country.

Roosevelt's second relief measure was the Federal Emergency Relief Administration (FERA), which had a budget of $500 million to assist individual states in their efforts to help the unemployed. Hoping to spend the money as quickly and humanely as possible, Roosevelt chose **Harry Hopkins**, a former social worker who had directed New York's relief effort, to run the FERA. With boundless energy and an ego to match, Hopkins personified the New Deal's activist, free-wheeling style. He became Roosevelt's closest adviser.

Hopkins convinced the president to approve a federal work relief program for the unemployed. The **Civil Works Administration (CWA)** hired more than 4 million people in a matter of months, creating jobs and restoring self-respect by handing out pay envelopes instead of relief checks. The CWA spent much of its $1 billion budget on projects of lasting value. Its workers built airports and paved roads; they ran nursery schools, immunized children, served hot school lunches, and collected garbage. Yet Roosevelt ended the CWA experiment after only four months, citing its spiraling costs. He expected federal job programs to be short-term experiments, nothing more. Otherwise, he warned, they will "become a habit with the country."

Conservation, Regional Planning, and Public Power

In the spring of 1933, FDR appeared to be governing the nation by himself. His proposals were so sweeping, and so easily enacted, that Congress seemed to have no independent function of its own. Never before had the White House taken such initiative on domestic legislation; never before had it been so successful.

At Roosevelt's behest, Congress created the Securities and Exchange Commission (SEC) to oversee the stock and bond markets. It established the Federal Deposit Insurance Corporation (FDIC) to insure bank deposits up to five thousand dollars. It provided funds to refinance one-fifth of the nation's home and farm mortgages. And it effectively ended Prohibition by permitting the sale of beer and wine with an alcoholic content of 3.2 percent. (The Eighteenth Amendment would be repealed on December 5, 1933.)

Some of Roosevelt's early proposals had personal roots. The Civilian Conservation Corps was one example; the **Tennessee Valley Authority (TVA)**, created in May 1933, was another. Like many other progressives, Roosevelt had a deep interest in the related issues of conservation, regional planning, and public power. Believing that poverty could be eradicated through the careful development of natural resources, he turned the Tennessee Valley (see Map 23.1) into a laboratory for his most cherished ideas.

Covering seven states and forty thousand square miles, the Tennessee Valley was America's poorest region. Most of its 4 million people—mainly small farmers and sharecroppers—lived in isolated communities, without electricity, medical care, proper schooling, or paved roads. The TVA transformed this region in fundamental ways. Within a decade, sixteen huge dams and hydroelectric plants were in operation along the Tennessee River, providing flood control; cheap, abundant power; and thousands of jobs. Per capita income rose dramatically. Electric power gave local residents what millions of other Americans already took for granted: radios and refrigerators, plumbing, lights in houses and barns. Despite some criticism, the TVA was widely viewed as one of the New Deal's greatest achievements.

Agricultural Recovery

With the bank crisis over and federal relief flowing to those most desperately in need, the Roosevelt administration turned to the long-term issue of providing a structure for the nation's economic recovery. In agriculture, which accounted for

Hopkins, Harry (1890–1946)
Roosevelt's choice to run the Federal Emergency Relief Administration. He eventually became Roosevelt's closest adviser.

Civil Works Administration (CWA)
The agency tasked with creating jobs and restoring self-respect by handing out pay envelopes instead of relief checks. In reality, workers sometimes performed worthless tasks, known as "boondoggles," but much of the $1 billion budget was spent on projects of lasting value including airports and roads.

Tennessee Valley Authority (TVA)
Created in 1933 during the New Deal's first hundred days, it was a massive experiment in regional planning that focused on providing electricity, flood control, and soil conservation to one of the nation's poorest regions, covering seven states in the Tennessee Valley.

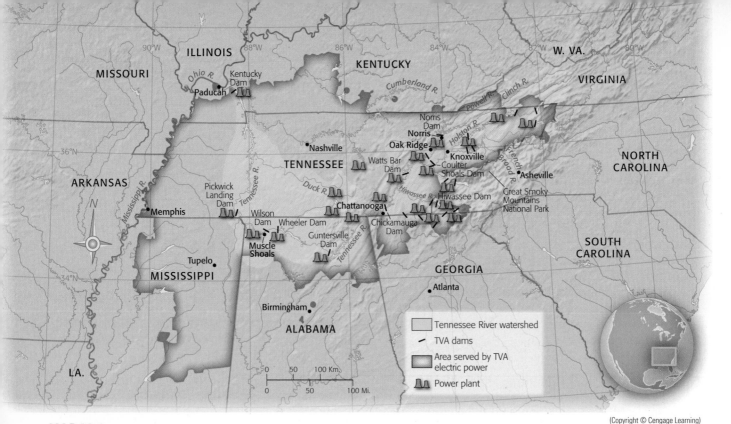

(Copyright © Cengage Learning)

MAP 23.1

The Tennessee Valley
The Tennessee Valley Authority, acclaimed as the most visionary model of government planning in the New Deal era, brought electric power, flood control, and employment to one of the nation's most impoverished regions.

Agricultural Adjustment Act (AAA) (1933) Created under Roosevelt's New Deal program to help farmers, its purpose was to reduce production of staple crops, thereby raising farm prices and encouraging more diversified farming.

one-quarter of all American jobs, the problems were severe. Most farmers had been slumping badly since the 1920s. The introduction of tractors and high-grade fertilizer had made them more productive than ever before. Yet their share of the world market had declined because of high tariff walls and tough foreign competition. Farmers in 1932 were earning less than one-third of their meager 1929 incomes. As food prices collapsed, there was talk of open rebellion in the heartland.

Passed in May 1933, the **Agricultural Adjustment Act (AAA)** confronted the problems of overproduction and mounting surpluses that had conspired to erode farm income over the years. The act also created the Agricultural Adjustment Administration to raise farm prices by encouraging farmers to produce less. The idea was no longer to win back world markets, but rather to limit domestic output in order to achieve "parity," or fair price levels, within the United States. The act compensated farmers who voluntarily removed acreage from production. It funded these payments through a tax on farm processors—such as flour millers, meatpackers, and cotton gin operators.

Problems quickly arose. Because spring planting was already under way, the Agricultural Adjustment Administration encouraged farmers to plow under a large portion of their crops. Producing less food while millions were going hungry was difficult for people to understand, but destroying food seemed particularly senseless and cruel. Still, within a year, more than 3 million farmers had signed individual contracts with the Agricultural Adjustment Administration, and the early results were encouraging. Cotton, wheat, and corn production fell significantly as farmers cultivated fewer acres and cashed their government checks. Farm income shot up almost 60 percent between 1932 and 1935—the result of rising food prices and generous loans to those who stored their surpluses in government warehouses.

Nature played a role as well. During the 1930s, the American farm belt experienced record highs in temperature and record lows in rainfall. The Great Plains were hardest hit. Terrifying dust storms swept through Kansas, Nebraska,

Colorado, Oklahoma, Texas, and the Dakotas like a black blizzard, packing gale-force winds and stripping nutrients from the soil. Cornfields were turned into sand dunes and cattle were buried alive. "This is the ultimate darkness," a Kansas woman wrote in her diary. "So must come the end of the world."

The **Dust Bowl** disaster (see Map 23.2) triggered one of the largest internal migrations in the nation's history. More than 3 million people abandoned their Dust Bowl farms in the 1930s, with Oklahoma, Kansas, and South Dakota losing huge chunks of population. Many set out for California, where the "fortunate" among them found work picking fruit, boxing vegetables, and baling hay. Living in hellish squatter camps, enduring disease and discrimination ("Negroes and Okies Upstairs," read a local theater sign), they moved from field to orchard in the San Joaquin and Imperial Valleys, earning pitiful wages and "going on relief."

Dust Bowl The name given to areas of the prairie states that suffered ecological devastation in the 1930s and then again to a lesser extent in the mid-1950s.

Dust Storm in Kansas. Dust storms turned daylight into darkness in towns throughout Kansas, the epicenter of the Dust Bowl.

MAP 23.2
The Dust Bowl, 1936–1940
The immense dust storms that blew through the high plains in the 1930s covered nearly 100 million acres in the hardest hit states of Texas, Oklahoma, Kansas, Colorado, and New Mexico. The great Dust Bowl tragedy caused terrible economic hardship and a mass migration from the High Plains, with tens of thousands of displaced farmers heading west to California.

(Copyright © Cengage Learning)

Tenants and Landowners

The AAA helped countless farm families and ignored countless others. The large farmers got the biggest subsidies. Yet the system barely touched those at the bottom: the tenants and sharecroppers, almost one-half of the nation's white farm families and three-quarters of the black farm families. Most of them lived in desperate poverty, working the cotton fields of the rural South. Under AAA regulations, these tenants were supposed to get a fair share of the acreage reduction payments, but this rarely occurred. Few landlords obeyed the rules, and some evicted their tenants in order to take even more land out of production.

In response, tenants and sharecroppers formed their own organization, the Southern Tenant Farmers' Union (STFU), to fight for their rights. "The landlord is always betwixt us, beatin' us and starvin' us," complained a black sharecropper from Arkansas. "There ain't but one way for us to get him where he can't help himself and that's for us to get together and stay together." But tenants who joined the union were evicted from their shacks, blacklisted by employers, and denied credit at banks and stores. Union organizers were beaten and jailed, and the SFTU soon collapsed.

Conditions were no better in the Southwest and Far West, where destitute Mexican farm workers struggled to survive. Many had been brought north by American ranchers and growers seeking cheap labor in better times. Now, as the demand for workers decreased, and job competition with poor whites (including the Dust Bowl refugees) intensified, their desperation grew. Because most of these farm workers were not U.S. citizens, local governments often denied them relief. Between 1930 and 1935, moreover, the federal government deported at least two hundred thousand Mexicans, some of whom were longtime residents of Texas, Arizona, and California; a larger number returned to Mexico on their own. In 1936, author John Steinbeck reported on a strike of Mexican lettuce workers near his home in Salinas, California. "The attitude of the employer," he wrote, "is one of hatred and suspicion, his method is the threat of the deputies' guns."

The AAA revolutionized American agriculture. Never before had the federal government been as deeply involved in the affairs of American farmers; never before had it encouraged its citizens to produce fewer goods, not more. Although key elements of the AAA would be struck down by the Supreme Court in *United States v. Butler* (1936), the concept of federal farm subsidies continues to dominate America's agricultural policy to the present day.

Centralized Economic Planning

National Industrial Recovery Act (NIRA) Enacted on June 16, 1933, this emergency measure was designed to encourage industrial recovery and help combat widespread unemployment.

The Roosevelt administration had an equally ambitious plan to revive the economy, reopen idle factories, and put people back to work. On June 13, 1933, Congress passed the **National Industrial Recovery Act (NIRA)** amid a flood of optimistic projections. Modeled on the industrial mobilization during World War I, the NIRA was designed as a vehicle for centralized economic planning. Roosevelt himself viewed it as the primary weapon in his crusade against the Depression. The act, he boasted, "is the most important and far reaching legislation ever enacted by the American Congress."

The NIRA created two more federal agencies: the Public Works Administration (PWA) and the National Recovery Administration (NRA). The former, with a budget of $3.3 billion, was supposed to "prime the economic pump" by providing jobs for the unemployed and new orders for the factories that produced steel, glass, rubber, cement, and heavy equipment. What made the PWA so appealing was its emphasis on private employment: workers were to be hired and paid by individual contractors, not by the federal government. Roosevelt selected

Secretary of the Interior Harold Ickes, a veteran progressive, to run the PWA. No one brought more honest efficiency to government than Harold Ickes. Under his leadership, the PWA constructed schools, hospitals, post offices, and sewage systems. It built the Golden Gate Bridge in San Francisco and the Triborough Bridge in New York City, the Grand Coulee Dam in Washington State, and the Boulder Dam in Colorado.

The key to Roosevelt's recovery program, however, was the NRA. Under the flamboyant leadership of General Hugh S. Johnson, the NRA encouraged representatives of business and labor to create codes of "fair practice" designed to stabilize the economy through planning and cooperation. In return for the suspension of antitrust laws that had dogged them for years, business leaders agreed to significant labor reforms. Each NRA code featured a maximum hour and minimum wage provision (usually forty hours and dollars per week). Child labor was forbidden, and Section 7A of the NIRA guaranteed labor unions the right to organize and bargain collectively.

General Johnson barnstormed the country by airplane, giving speeches and lining up support. With a patriotic symbol (the blue eagle) and a catchy slogan ("We Do Our Part"), Johnson signed up the big industries—coal, steel, oil, autos, shipbuilding, chemicals, and clothing—before going after the others. By the end of 1933, the NRA had 746 different agreements in place. Before long, however, the program was in trouble. Small businessmen complained that the codes encouraged monopolies and drowned them in paperwork. Labor leaders charged that employers ignored the wage and hour provisions, while cracking down on union activity. Consumers blamed the NRA for raising prices at a time when their purchasing power was extremely low. Because the codes were voluntary, they carried no legal weight; large companies obeyed them when it was in their interest to do so and ignored them when it wasn't.

In 1934, General Johnson suffered a nervous breakdown, leading Roosevelt to replace him with a five-member executive board. The president seemed relieved when the Supreme Court, in *Schechter Poultry Company v. United States* (1935), struck down the NRA on the grounds that Congress had delegated too much legislative authority to the executive branch. "It has been an awful head-ache," Roosevelt confided to an aide. "I think perhaps NRA has done all it can do."

Doing History Online

John L. Lewis on the NRA, 1934

Go to the CourseMate website for this chapter and link to Primary Sources. Based on your reading of the document online and the "Taking Charge of the Crisis, 1932–1933" section of this chapter, what were the benefits and disadvantages of the NRA for organized labor?

 www.cengagebrain.com

❖ New Deal Diplomacy, 1933–1934

Foreign affairs were not high on President Roosevelt's agenda. His riveting inaugural address had devoted one sentence to the entire subject. "In the field of world policy," he declared, "I would dedicate this nation to the policy of the good neighbor"—a theme already sounded by outgoing president Herbert Hoover. The United States was in turmoil, struggling through the worst economic crisis in its history. "I favored as a practical policy," said Roosevelt, "the putting of first things first."

The Soviet Question

FDR was no isolationist. He believed deeply in the concepts of international cooperation and global security, as Americans would shortly discover. One of his first diplomatic initiatives, in November 1933, was to extend formal recognition to the Soviet Union. The move was opposed by many Americans who viewed the Soviet Union as a godless, totalitarian society bent on exporting the "Communist revolution" throughout the world. But Roosevelt believed that the United States could no longer afford to ignore the world's largest nation. The move did not pay quick dividends to either side, but relations between the United States and the Soviet Union would slowly improve in the 1930s and early 1940s as ominous world events drew them closer together.

The Good Neighbor

The Roosevelt administration showed a growing interest in Latin America, where U.S. companies had billions of dollars invested in the production of foodstuffs like coffee and sugar and in raw materials such as copper and oil. With fascism rising in Europe and in Asia, the need for inter-American cooperation was essential. Along with efforts to increase trade in this region, the United States extended the Good Neighbor Policy by affirming at the 1933 Pan-American Conference in Uruguay that no nation "has the right to intervene in the internal or external affairs of another." Shortly after, the Roosevelt administration recalled several hundred U.S. Marines stationed in Haiti and signed a treaty with Panama recognizing the responsibility of both nations to operate and defend the Panama Canal.

There were exceptions, however. In Cuba, a nation of vital economic and strategic importance to the United States, intervention was a way of life. In 1934, the State Department helped bring an "acceptable" government to power in Havana, more sympathetic to North American business interests. With the new regime in place, led by Sergeant Fulgencio Batista, the United States agreed to renounce direct intervention under the Platt Amendment in return for permission to keep its huge naval base at Guantánamo Bay.

The Good Neighbor Policy faced its sternest test even closer to home. In 1934, President Lázaro Cárdenas of Mexico began a national recovery program much like FDR's New Deal. Pledging "Mexico for the Mexicans," Cárdenas attempted to nationalize the agricultural and mining properties of all foreign corporations, as required by the Mexican Constitution of 1917. Though Cárdenas promised "fair compensation" for these holdings, American and British companies demanded far more than the Mexicans were willing to pay—$262 million. Over the objections of many businessmen, the Roosevelt administration convinced Mexico to pay $40 million in compensation for foreign-owned lands it had seized and another $29 million for the oil fields.

❖ Critics Right and Left, 1934–1935

By 1934, the Depression seemed to be easing. Although enormous problems remained, there was less talk about the dangers of starvation, violent upheaval, or complete economic collapse. The New Deal had injected a dose of confidence into the body politic. Yet as things got better, people inevitably wanted more. The shared sense of hardship and struggle began to dissolve.

The American Liberty League and the 1934 Election

The first rumblings came from the political right. In the summer of 1934, a group of conservative business leaders formed the American Liberty League to combat the alleged "radicalism" of the New Deal. They believed that Roosevelt was leading the country down "a foreign path" by attacking free enterprise, favoring workers over employers, and increasing the power of the federal government. The league generously supported Roosevelt's political opponents in the 1934 congressional elections. But instead of losing ground—the normal pattern for the majority party in midterm elections—the Democrats picked up nine seats in the Senate and nine in the House. Few pundits could recall a more lopsided election; as publisher William Allen White put it, Roosevelt had been "all but crowned by the people."

In reality, the election results were a mixed blessing for the Democrats. Most Americans approved of the New Deal. Their main criticism was that it had not gone far—or fast—enough to end the Depression. In Minnesota, for example, Governor Floyd Olsen was reelected on an independent "Farmer-Labor" ticket that advocated state ownership of utilities and railroads. In California, Upton Sinclair, author of *The Jungle*, ran for governor on a program called EPIC (End Poverty in California), which promised to hand over idle factories and farmland to the poor and unemployed. Sinclair received almost nine hundred thousand votes in a bitter, losing effort—a sign of things to come.

"Every Man a King"

The most serious challenge to Roosevelt's leadership was offered by Louisiana's **Huey P. Long.** Known as the "Kingfish," after a strutting, smooth-talking character on the popular radio program *Amos 'n' Andy*, Long combined a gift for showmanship with ruthless ambition. A superb orator and a master storyteller, he understood the value of the spoken word in a state where few people owned radios, read newspapers, or traveled far from home. As governor of Louisiana, Long pushed his unique brand of southern populism, revising the tax codes to make corporations and wealthy citizens pay more, while providing more services to the masses. At the same time, he built a political machine of almost totalitarian proportions. When Long vacated the governor's chair to enter the U.S. Senate in 1932, he controlled the legislature, the courts, and the civil service system of Louisiana.

"I came to the United States Senate," Long wrote, "to spread the wealth of the land among all of the people." As a Democrat, he campaigned hard for Roosevelt in 1932 and supported much of the early New Deal. But as time passed, he grew restless with the slow pace of reform. In 1934, Long proposed his own agenda, promising to "make every man a king." Under Long's plan, no one would be allowed to earn more than $1.8 million per year or to keep a personal fortune in excess of $5 million. After confiscating this surplus, the government would provide each family with a house, a car, a radio, and an annual income of at least twenty-five hundred dollars.

Most economists were appalled. They knew that there weren't nearly enough millionaires around to finance Long's proposal. According to one study, the government would have had to confiscate all yearly incomes above $3,000—not $1.8 million—to provide each family with $2,500. Nonetheless, by 1935, Long's "Share Our Wealth Society" claimed 8 million members nationwide.

The Radio Priest and the Pension Doctor

Long did not lack for competitors. In Royal Oak, Michigan, a working-class suburb of Detroit, Father Charles Edward Coughlin was busy leading a protest movement of his own. As the pastor of a small Catholic church, Shrine of the Little Flower, Coughlin became a towering figure in the 1930s by mixing prayer with politics in a way that touched millions—and frightened millions more.

Coughlin could be heard every Sunday on seventeen CBS radio outlets nationwide. An early Roosevelt supporter, he compared the New Deal to "Christ's Deal." Like Huey Long, Coughlin deplored the fact that too much

Long, Huey P. (1893–1935)
Populist but dictatorial governor of Louisiana (1928–1932), he instituted major public works legislation; as a U.S. senator (1932–1935), he proposed a national "Share the Wealth" program.

wealth was concentrated in too few hands. Unlike Long, however, he blamed this evil on a tight money supply, manipulated by international bankers in London and New York.

Coughlin believed that "free silver"—the old Populist nostrum—would solve this problem and bring prosperity to all. His attacks on British bankers won him strong support in the Irish-Catholic community, and his call for monetary reform appealed to debt-ridden farmers and merchants in America's small towns. Before long, Coughlin's radio show, *Golden Hour of the Little Flower*, had an estimated 40 million listeners. By 1934, the "Radio Priest" was souring on the New Deal. Angered by Roosevelt's disinterest in his "silver solution," he formed the National Union for Social Justice to challenge the president's leadership. "I glory in the fact that I am a simple Catholic priest," Coughlin declared, "endeavoring to inject Christianity into the fabric of an economic system woven upon the loom of the greedy."

A third protest movement, led by Francis E. Townsend, a retired physician living in California, proposed a measure to revive the economy by meeting the specific needs of older Americans. It guaranteed a pension of two hundred dollars per month to those over the age of sixty who promised to stay out of the job market and spend the two hundred dollars by month's end. The pensions would be funded by a 2 percent sales tax on all "business transactions." According to Townsend, his plan would create jobs for the young, increase the country's purchasing power, and provide security for the elderly. But his plan, known as Old Age Revolving Pensions Limited, was impossibly expensive. By most estimates, Townsend needed a sales tax approaching 70 percent in order to properly fund his proposal. By 1935, more than 10 million Americans had signed petitions supporting Townsend's idea, and public opinion polls showed strong support for a government-sponsored pension plan. Townsend had unleashed a powerful new interest group, the elderly, and American politics would never be the same again.

❖ The Second New Deal, 1935–1936

Although national income in 1935 was a full 25 percent above the 1933 level, millions were still living on handouts, without much hope of a permanent job. Inside the White House, Roosevelt's key advisers were nudging him further to the left. "Boys—this is our hour," said the opportunistic Harry Hopkins. "We've got to get every-thing we want—a works program, social security, wages and hours, every-thing—now or never." In the spring of 1935, Roosevelt presented Congress with a "must" list of reforms, the so-called second New Deal.

Jobs, Jobs, Jobs

The president requested—and received—$4.8 billion in work relief for the unemployed, the largest single appropriation in the nation's history. After allocating generous shares to his favorite projects, such as the CCC, Roosevelt established yet another agency, the Works Progress Administration (WPA), with Hopkins in charge, to create "jobs, jobs, jobs!"

In that task, it was very successful. At its height in 1936, the WPA employed 25 percent of the nation's entire work force. Many of these jobs, however, were low-paying and temporary so as to avoid competition with private enterprise. Concentrating on small construction projects, the WPA built schools and playgrounds, repaired countless bridges and landing fields, and improved 650,000 miles of roads. Its National Youth Administration, inspired by Eleanor Roosevelt, provided part-time work to several million high school and college students.

(© Morton Beebe/CORBIS)

The New Deal and the Arts. Among the Works Progress Administration's programs was Federal One, which provided government funding for a variety of arts projects around the country.

Social Security

The president's "must" list included a social welfare plan that challenged the cherished concepts of voluntarism and individual responsibility. At the urging of Labor Secretary Frances Perkins, the nation's first woman cabinet member, Roosevelt proposed legislation to create a national pension fund, an unemployment insurance system, and public assistance programs for dependent mothers and children, those with physical disabilities, and those in chronic need. The pension was financed by a payroll tax to begin in 1937. Benefits were purposely modest—about twenty to thirty dollars per month—because Roosevelt did not intend "social security" to be the main source of personal retirement income.

The Social Security Act of 1935 had numerous defects. It excluded millions of vulnerable wage earners, such as domestics, farm workers, and the self-employed, from the pension fund. It taxed all participants at a fixed rate, forcing those with the lowest incomes to pay a far greater share of their wages into the system. Over time, the Social Security fund emerged as the country's most important and expensive domestic program.

"Class Warfare"

Roosevelt had never been a strong supporter of organized labor. He felt uneasy about the tactics of labor leaders such as **John L. Lewis,** head of the United Mine Workers, who had tripled his membership (from 150,000 to almost 500,000) with an aggressive organizing campaign that declared, "The president wants you to join a union!" Roosevelt worried that labor's militant new spirit would accelerate the violent confrontations of 1934, when pitched battles erupted between striking workers and police on the streets of Minneapolis, San Francisco, and Detroit.

In the wake of these disturbances, Senator Robert Wagner of New York authored a bill to protect the rights of workers to organize and bargain collectively. His legislation filled a dramatic void, because the Supreme Court had just declared parts of the NIRA—including Section 7A regarding labor union rights—to be unconstitutional. Passed in 1935, the National Labor Relations Act

Lewis, John L. (1880–1969) U.S. labor leader; president of the United Mine Workers of America (1920–1960) and the Congress of Industrial Organizations (1935–1940).

FIGURE 23.1

Unemployment, 1925–1945
This chart shows the two great peaks of unemployment—the first in 1933, as FDR took office; the second (and smaller one) during the recession of 1938, when federal spending was reduced. The chart also shows the enormous impact of World War II in bringing unemployment—and the Great Depression itself—to an end.

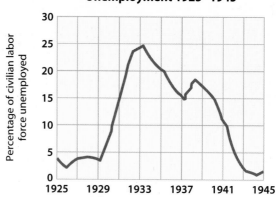

Unemployment 1925–1945

FIGURE 23.2

The Statistics of Hard Times
This chart shows the close correlation between the nation's economic productivity and its personal income. Both indicators dropped dramatically in the years between 1929 and 1933—the depth of the Great Depression—but rose even more dramatically between 1940 and 1945, as the nation prepared for, and entered, World War II.

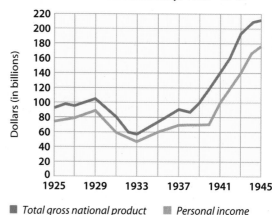

The Decline and Recovery of the U.S. Economy, 1925–1945

■ *Total gross national product* ■ *Personal income*

Doing History Online

National Labor Relations Act, 1935

Go to the CourseMate website for this chapter and link to Primary Sources. Read the document online. According to the act, why is this legislation needed? What is significant about this reasoning?

www.cengagebrain.com

prohibited employers from engaging in a wide range of "unfair labor practices," such as spying on their workers. The law also created the National Labor Relations Board (NLRB) to supervise union elections and determine the appropriate bargaining agents.

The Wagner Act revealed deep divisions within the union movement. At the American Federation of Labor's (AFL's) annual convention in 1935, John L. Lewis pleaded with fellow leaders to begin serious membership drives in the steel mills, automobile plants, and rubber factories, but most AFL leaders were unmoved. As representatives of skilled craftsworkers, such as masons and carpenters, they had little interest in organizing industrial unions composed largely of African Americans and ethnic groups from eastern and southern Europe. Indeed, after Lewis finished his emotional plea to the AFL convention, Carpenters' president "Big Bill" Hutcheson called him a "bastard." Lewis floored Hutcheson with a solid right to the jaw and stormed out of the convention.

Shortly after, Lewis joined with like-minded labor leaders to form the Congress of Industrial Organizations (CIO). Their goal was to create powerful unions in the larger mass production industries such as automobiles and steel. Labor's "civil war" had begun.

❖ The Fascist Challenge

As the 1936 presidential election approached, Americans watched events in Europe with growing apprehension. From the Soviet Union came stories about a regime that was brutalizing its people in an attempt to "collectivize" the society and stamp out internal dissent. In Germany and Italy, powerful dictators emerged, preaching race hatred and vowing to expand their nation's borders.

Hitler and Mussolini

Adolf Hitler became the German chancellor in January 1933, a few months before FDR was sworn in as president. Born in Austria in 1889, Hitler had moved to Bavaria as a young man and fought in the German army during World War I. Wounded and jobless, he helped form the National Socialist (Nazi) Party, one of the many extremist groups that thrived in the economic chaos of war-battered Germany. In 1923, Hitler was arrested in Munich for staging an unsuccessful coup against the Weimar government. From his prison cell, he wrote *Mein Kampf* ("My Struggle"), a rambling account of his racial theories, plans for Germany, and hatred of Jews.

As the Weimar government collapsed during the Depression, the Nazis gained strength. Millions welcomed their promise to create jobs, restore German glory, and avenge the "humiliation" of Versailles. Nazi representation in the Reichstag (parliament) rose from 12 in 1928 to 230 by 1932. A year later, Hitler became chancellor of Germany. The results were alarming. Constitutional rights were suspended and competing political parties banned. Nazi supporters held mass book-burning rallies, drove Jews from universities, boycotted their businesses, and attacked them in the streets. "Hitler is a madman," President Roosevelt told a French diplomat.

Under the Nazis, the state increased its control over industry, while leaving it in private hands. This allowed Hitler to begin a massive rearmament program, which produced badly needed jobs. By 1934, German factories were producing tanks and military aircraft. A year later, Hitler proposed a 500,000-man army and instituted the draft. In 1936, Nazi forces marched into the Rhineland—a clear violation of the Versailles treaty—and reoccupied it without firing a shot. "Today Germany," the Nazis chanted, "tomorrow the world."

Hitler had modeled himself, to some degree, after Italian dictator Benito Mussolini, the father of fascism in modern Europe. Born in 1883, Mussolini had served in the Italian army during World War I. Playing on the social unrest and economic turmoil of the postwar era, he seized national power in 1922 and proclaimed Fascismo, a merging of state and business leadership under the banner of extreme nationalism. As the supreme leader, or Duce, he destroyed labor unions, censored the press, abolished all political parties but his own, and relied on a secret police force to silence his critics. In 1935, Italian forces invaded Ethiopia as a way of restoring Italy's ancient glory. The fighting in Ethiopia was brutal and one sided, pitting Italian tanks and machine guns against local defenders armed with little more than spears and bows and arrows. At the League of Nations, Ethiopian Emperor Haile Selassie pleaded for support. The league responded by branding Italy the aggressor but sent no military help. After annexing Ethiopia in 1936, Mussolini signed a pact of friendship with Hitler, known as the Rome-Berlin Axis.

The Neutrality Acts

Americans did not want to become involved in European squabbles as they had in the past. They were determined that history must not repeat itself—that American blood must not be shed again on foreign soil. There was only one way

Doing History   The Battle over Neutrality

No other foreign policy issue proved more divisive than the ongoing debate over American neutrality, which began with the rise of Nazi and fascist aggression in Europe and Africa in the mid-1930s and continued until the Japanese attack on Pearl Harbor in December 1941. The first Neutrality Acts, passed overwhelmingly by Congress in 1935 and 1936, had reflected the American public's understandable fear of being pulled into another world war. Though President Roosevelt had signed these Neutrality Acts, he did not believe that they allowed him the leeway he needed to support the nations that were threatened by German, Italian, and Japanese aggression. In his famous Quarantine Speech of October 5, 1937, Roosevelt spoke out for the first time about the dangers posed by strict neutrality.

Among the president's strongest critics was famous aviator Charles A. Lindbergh. A true national hero and a dedicated isolationist, Lindbergh was a leading spokesman for the America First Committee, which opposed all attempts to intervene in the European war. In various speeches, Lindbergh praised the German military, brushed off reports of Nazi atrocities, and claimed that American Jews were responsible for pushing the nation toward war. In this speech, he warned Americans that support for England against the Nazis would drag the United States into a conflict it couldn't win.

President Franklin D. Roosevelt, Senate Document No. 188, 77th Congress, 2d Session

The political situation in the world, which of late has been growing progressively worse, is such as to cause grave concerns and anxiety to all peoples and nations who wish to live in peace and amity with their neighbors. . . .

Innocent people, innocent nations, are being cruelly sacrificed to a greed for power and supremacy which is devoid of all senses of justice and humane consideration. . . .

If [these] things come to pass in other parts of the world, let no one imagine that America will escape, that America may expect mercy, that this Western Hemisphere will not be attacked and that it will continue tranquilly and peacefully to carry on the ethics and arts of civilization.

Source: "Addresses and Messages of Franklin D. Roosevelt," Senate Document No. 188, 77th Congress, 2d Session, 21–24.

Colonel Lindbergh, "We Cannot Win This War for England," 1941

I know I will be severely criticized by the interventionists in America when I say we should not enter a war unless we have a reasonable chance of—winning. . . . And I know that the United States is not prepared to wage war in Europe successfully at this time. . . .

In time of war, truth is always replaced by propaganda. I do not believe we should be too quick to criticize the actions of a belligerent nation. There is always the question whether we, ourselves, would do better under similar circumstances. But we in America have a right to think of the welfare of America first. . . .

There is no better way to give comfort to any enemy than to divide the people of a nation over the issue of foreign war. There is no shorter road to defeat than by entering a war with inadequate preparation. . . .

The United States is better situated from a military standpoint than any other nation in the world. Even in our present condition . . . no foreign power is in a position to invade us today. If we concentrate on our own defenses and build the strength that this nation should maintain, no foreign army will ever attempt to land on American shores.

Source: Charles A. Lindbergh, "We Cannot Win This War for England," *Vital Speeches*, May 1, 1941, 424–426.

QUESTIONS for REFLECTION

1. What are the key arguments and issues represented by President Roosevelt and Colonel Lindbergh?

2. Were the arguments that Roosevelt and Lindbergh put forth unique to American intervention in World War II, or do they continue to have relevance today?

to avoid another war, most people believed, and that was to remain truly neutral in world affairs. (See *Doing History: The Battle over Neutrality*.)

Although this sentiment had deep historical roots, running all the way back to George Washington, the key to understanding America's anxiety in the early 1930s was the legacy of World War I. In 1934, the U.S. Senate set up a committee, chaired by isolationist Gerald P. Nye of North Dakota, to investigate the reasons for America's involvement in that conflict. The Nye committee highlighted a series of well-known facts: large banks and corporations had made huge profits during World War I by giving loans and selling arms to the various combatants. The press dubbed such bankers and businessmen "merchants of death." Blaming business interests ignored the rather tangled reality of American intervention—from submarine warfare to the Zimmermann Telegram, from President Wilson's rigid morality to the defense of neutral rights. Yet the Nye committee findings enjoyed wide popular support.

The isolationist impulse was particularly strong in the Great Plains and Upper Midwest, where populist suspicions of Wall Street and international bankers went back a long way. It attracted many Americans of German descent, who remembered their treatment during World War I; of Irish descent, who opposed aid to Great Britain in any form; and of Italian descent, who viewed Mussolini as a hero in these years. Isolationism and pacifism also appealed to clergy, peace groups, and college students.

Congress responded to this public mood with legislation designed to avoid the "entanglements" that had led to American participation in World War I. The two Neutrality Acts, passed in 1935 and 1936, circumscribed the actions of both the president and business leaders during foreign wars. President Roosevelt did not like these bills, yet he signed them into law for political reasons. He believed that absolute neutrality favored powerful aggressor nations by forcing the United States to treat all sides equally, but he knew that a veto of the popular legislation would give strong ammunition to the Republicans in the coming presidential campaign.

❖ The American People in Transition

As the 1936 election approached, FDR had reason for concern. Although personal income and industrial production had risen dramatically since he took office in 1933, millions were still unemployed. In addition, more than 80 percent of the nation's newspapers and most of the business community remained loyal to the Republican Party, meaning that Roosevelt's major presidential opponent could count on strong editorial and financial support.

The 1936 Election

In June, the Republicans gathered in Cleveland to nominate their presidential ticket. Herbert Hoover, anxious for another crack at Roosevelt, received a thunderous ovation, but the convention delegates chose Kansas governor Alfred M. Landon to head the Republican ticket, and Frank Knox, a Chicago publisher, to be the vice-presidential nominee. Landon, a political moderate, promised "fewer radio talks, fewer experiments, and a lot more common sense." His problem was that he radiated little of the compassion and confidence that made the president so popular with the masses.

Roosevelt also faced presidential challenges from the left. Both the Communists and the Socialists ran spirited campaigns in 1936, demanding more federal aid for the poor. But Roosevelt's most serious concern—a political merger involving Coughlin, Townsend, and Long—was effectively eliminated in September 1935, when an assassin's bullet killed the Louisiana senator in Baton Rouge. To replace the charismatic Long, these dissident forces nominated William "Liberty Bill" Lemke, an obscure North Dakota congressman, to be their presidential candidate on the new Union Party ticket.

Roosevelt's political strategy differed markedly from 1932. In that campaign, he had stressed the common hopes and needs that bound people together; in 1936, he emphasized the class differences that separated those who supported the New Deal from those who opposed it. Time and again, Roosevelt portrayed the election as a contest between common people and privileged people, between compassion and greed. In his final campaign speech in New York, he declared that the "forces of selfishness" had "met their match" in the Roosevelt administration. "They are unanimous in their hatred of me," the president thundered, "and I welcome their hatred."

On November 3, FDR crushed Landon and Lemke in the most one-sided election since 1820. The final totals showed Roosevelt with 27,752,869 popular votes, Landon with 16,674,665, and Lemke with 882,479. (The Socialist and Communist party candidates polled fewer than 300,000 votes between them.) Roosevelt won every state except Maine and Vermont, and the Democratic Party added to its huge majorities in both houses of Congress. A few days after the election, Father Coughlin announced his retirement from the radio.

African Americans and the New Deal

Roosevelt's landslide victory signaled a dramatic shift in American politics. A new majority coalition had emerged. In the farm belt, Roosevelt won over longtime Republicans with federal subsidies and price supports. In the cities, he attracted workers grateful for welfare benefits and WPA jobs. And he appealed to ethnic minorities by filling many White House positions, cabinet posts, and federal judgeships with Catholics and Jews. Adding to the president's strength was the support he received from the CIO. Describing Roosevelt as "the worker's best friend," the industrial unions campaigned tirelessly for him.

The most striking political change, however, occurred within the nation's African American community. The steady migration of blacks to northern cities, where they could vote, increased their political power. Historically, most blacks supported the Republican Party, an allegiance that dated back to Abraham Lincoln and the Civil War. With the New Deal, however, a massive switch took place. In large part, African Americans became Democrats because the Roosevelt administration provided jobs and welfare benefits to all Americans, regardless of race. This federal assistance was especially welcome in black communities, where poverty and discrimination had long been facts of life.

African Americans Voting.
Although few blacks voted in the South during the 1930s, their growing numbers in northern cities like Chicago and New York increased their political influence within the New Deal coalition.

By 1933, black unemployment had reached 50 percent. Fortunately, the two New Deal administrators most responsible for creating jobs were sympathetic to minority needs. At the PWA, Harold Ickes insisted that blacks receive equal pay on all construction projects. Although local officials often ignored these rules, the PWA provided thousands of jobs for African Americans, while building black schools and hospitals throughout the segregated South. At the WPA, blacks received a generous share of work in northern cities—a testimony to both their joblessness and political clout. Many blacks welcomed an administration that showed some interest in their struggle, and they particularly admired the efforts of first lady **Eleanor Roosevelt,** who served as the White House conscience on matters pertaining to minority rights.

Eleanor Roosevelt had a passion for public service and a deep commitment to the poor. Her interest in civil rights had been fueled in large measure by her friendship with prominent African Americans such as **Mary McLeod Bethune,** founder of Bethune-Cookman College in Florida. In 1936, Eleanor Roosevelt recommended Bethune to head the National Youth Administration's Office of Negro Affairs. As the New Deal's highest ranking black appointee, Bethune presided over the administration's "black cabinet," which advised the White House on minority issues. In an age of rigid segregation, Eleanor Roosevelt visited black colleges, spoke at black conferences, and socialized with black women. When the Daughters of the American Revolution refused to allow **Marian Anderson,** a gifted black contralto, to perform at Washington's Constitution Hall, Eleanor Roosevelt resigned from the organization. A few months later, Harold Ickes arranged for Anderson to sing at the Lincoln Memorial on Easter Sunday, 1939. An integrated audience of seventy-five thousand gathered to hear her.

Yet the good work of Eleanor Roosevelt and others could not mask larger New Deal failures in the field of civil rights. Throughout his presidency, for example, Franklin Roosevelt never attempted to challenge southern racial customs. He made no effort to break down segregation barriers or enable blacks to vote. And he remained on the sidelines as federal anti-lynching bills were narrowly defeated in Congress. Roosevelt argued that he could not support civil rights legislation without alienating southern Democrats, who controlled the most important committees in Congress. "They will block every bill I [need] to keep America from collapsing," Roosevelt said. "I just can't take that risk." The president's position did not prevent blacks from supporting him in 1936. Roosevelt received 76 percent of their votes—the same total that Herbert Hoover had won four years before.

Roosevelt, Eleanor (1884–1962)
Diplomat, writer, and First Lady of the United States (1933–1945) as the wife of President Franklin D. Roosevelt. A delegate to the United Nations (1945–1953 and 1961–1962), she was an outspoken advocate for human rights. Her written works include *This I Remember* (1949).

Bethune, Mary McLeod (1875–1955) An educator who sought improved racial relations and educational opportunities for black Americans, she was part of the U.S. delegation to the first United Nations meeting (1945).

Anderson, Marian (1897–1993) Opera singer and human rights advocate, she performed on the steps of the Lincoln Memorial before a crowd of seventy-five thousand after being denied the use of Constitution Hall by the Daughters of the American Revolution. She helped focus national attention on the racial prejudice faced by African Americans in all facets of national life.

Popular Culture in the Depression

The economic struggles of the 1930s shaped not only the politics of American life but the culture as well. Hard times encouraged federal participation in the arts and triggered a leftward tilt among many intellectuals and writers. A flurry of "proletarian literature" emerged in the early Depression years, emphasizing the "class struggle" through stories about heroic workers resisting the exploitation of evil employers. Several important black writers—including Ralph Ellison, Richard Wright, and Langston Hughes—identified with the Communist Party because it appeared to actively support civil rights. For most intellectuals, however, the fascination with communism was fleeting. As free thinkers, they could not adjust to the party's rigid conformity or its blind support of the Soviet dictator, Joseph Stalin.

By the 1930s, the motion picture was the leading form of popular culture in the United States. Most Americans attended at least one movie a week; many followed the lives of their favorite stars in gossip columns and fan magazines. In the larger cities, movie theaters were transformed into fantasy palaces, with thick carpets, winding staircases, ushers in tuxedoes, and the twinkling lights of chandeliers. For millions, the theater became a temporary escape from the bleak realities of the Depression.

Doing History Online

Letters from the "Forgotten Man" to Mrs. Roosevelt, 1934

Go to the CourseMate website for this chapter and link to Primary Sources. Read the letters online. Why did ordinary people write to Mrs. Roosevelt?

 www.cengagebrain.com

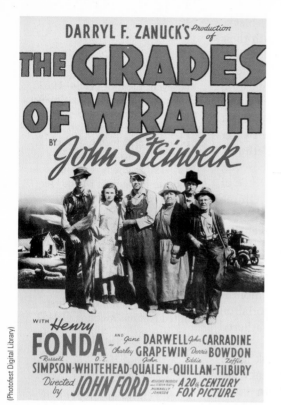

(Photofest Digital Library)

The Grapes of Wrath. John Steinbeck's extraordinary novel about the struggle of working families during the Great Depression was made into a highly successful movie, attracting even more attention to their plight.

Grapes of Wrath, The (1939) Novel by John Steinbeck depicting the struggle of ordinary Americans in the Great Depression, following the plight of the Joad family as it migrated west from Oklahoma to California.

Hollywood mirrored the changing attitudes of the 1930s. It was no accident that the most popular movie of 1932, the year America hit rock bottom, was Mervyn LeRoy's *I Am a Fugitive from a Chain Gang*, the story of a decent man, unjustly convicted of a crime, who escapes from a brutal southern penal farm. The public's fascination with criminal activity reached a peak in these years with the romanticizing of bank robbers (and cold-blooded murderers) like John Dillinger, Bonnie Parker and Clyde Barrow, Baby Face Nelson, and Ma Barker. All died in shoot-outs with local police or the FBI.

The evolving optimism of the 1930s—the promise of better times—was apparent in Hollywood films. The 1930s saw Fred Astaire whirling Ginger Rogers across the nightclub dance floor; Mickey Rooney courting Judy Garland in the blissfully innocent "Andy Hardy" movies; and Walt Disney raising the animated cartoon to an art form in his feature film *Snow White and the Seven Dwarfs* (1937). The moral dramas of director Frank Capra, including *Mr. Deeds Goes to Town* (1936), starring Gary Cooper, and *Mr. Smith Goes to Washington* (1939), with Jimmy Stewart, represented the virtues of heartland America. Common people could be fooled by greedy bankers and selfish politicians, but life got better when "good folks" followed their instincts.

The most memorable films of this era, *Gone with the Wind* and **The Grapes of Wrath,** showcased Hollywood's ability to transform best-selling fiction into successful movies, seen by millions who had read the novels of Margaret Mitchell and John Steinbeck—and millions more who had not. Both films related the epic struggle of families in crisis, trying desperately to survive. *The Grapes of Wrath*, set in the Depression, depicts marginal people confronting economic injustice.

Like the movie boom, the rapid growth of radio in the Depression encouraged the spread of popular culture. Politicians and public figures such as President Roosevelt and Father Coughlin used radio to great effect. So did companies seeking to mass-market their products. Organized along commercial lines in the 1920s, radio continued firmly down that path in the 1930s, with two giant firms—the National Broadcasting Company (NBC) and the Columbia Broadcasting System (CBS)—dominating the nation's airwaves. In the evenings, as entire families gathered around the radio, the entertainment broadened to include quiz shows, talent contests, and adventure programs like *Inner Sanctum* and *The Green Hornet*. Radio carried sporting events, political conventions, and the news. Millions followed the 1936 Berlin Olympics, where Jesse Owens, the African American track star, embarrassed Adolf Hitler by winning four gold medals.

Perhaps nothing better demonstrated the power of radio than the infamous "War of the Worlds" episode. On Halloween eve, 1938, actor Orson Welles, star of CBS's *Mercury Theater*, did a powerful reading of the H. G. Wells novel, *War of the Worlds*, presenting it as a simulated newscast in which violent aliens from Mars land in the New Jersey town of Grovers Mills. "I can see the thing's body," sobbed a "roving reporter" at the scene. "It's large as a bear and it glistens like wet leather. That face . . . the black eyes and saliva dripping from its rimless lips." Although Welles repeatedly interrupted the program to explain what he was doing, national panic nevertheless ensued. Traffic came to a halt in parts of the Northeast; bus and train stations were jammed; churches overflowed with weeping families. Newspaper headlines screamed: "Radio War Terrorizes U.S." and "Panic Grips Nation as Radio Announces 'Mars Attacks World.'" When the furor died down, President Roosevelt invited Welles to the White House. "You know, Orson," he joked, "you and I are the two best actors in America."

❖ Losing Ground, 1937–1939

In his second inaugural address, FDR emphasized the New Deal's unfinished business. "I see one-third of a nation ill-housed, ill-clad, ill-nourished," he declared. The election had provided him with a stunning popular mandate and with huge Democratic majorities on Capitol Hill. To Roosevelt's thinking, only one road-block lay in his path: the Supreme Court.

A confrontation seemed inevitable. The Supreme Court was dominated by elderly, conservative justices, appointed in the Harding–Coolidge years, who despised the New Deal and worked zealously to subvert its legislation. In Roosevelt's first term, the Court had struck down the NRA, the AAA, and a series of social welfare laws. In the coming months, it would be reviewing the National Labor Relations Act and the Social Security Act, two of the New Deal's most precious accomplishments.

Roosevelt struck first. In February 1937, without consulting Congress, he un-veiled sweeping legislation to reorganize the federal court system. Under his plan, fifty new judgeships would be created by adding one judge for each sitting justice over the age of seventy who refused to retire. The Supreme Court would get a maximum of six new members, raising its total to fifteen. The plan was legal. The Constitution sets no limits on the size of the Supreme Court; indeed, the number of justices, determined by Congress, had fluctuated between six and ten in the previous century. Roosevelt assumed that his overwhelming reelection in 1936 had given him a mandate—but he was mistaken. Many Americans worried that his "Court-packing" plan would undermine judicial independence and threaten the balance of power among the three branches of government. As the opposition grew stronger, aides urged Roosevelt to withdraw the bill.

In the spring of 1937, the Supreme Court changed course. By votes of 5 to 4, with one moderate justice switching sides, it upheld both the Wagner Act and the Social Security Act. Then, one by one, the old conservatives decided to retire. This allowed Roosevelt—the only president in American history to make no Supreme Court appointments during his first four-year term—to fill five vacancies in the next three years. The justices he chose—especially Hugo Black, Felix Frankfurter, and William O. Douglas—would steer a more liberal course for decades to come. Nevertheless, the Court battle emboldened Roosevelt's opponents by proving that the president could be beaten. "The New Deal," wrote one observer, "would never be the same."

Union Struggles

Away from Washington, new battles raged in the automobile plants of Michigan, the textile mills of North Carolina, and the coal fields of Kentucky as industrial workers demanded union recognition under the banner of the CIO. In perhaps the most spectacular episode, autoworkers at a General Motors plant in Flint, Michigan, went on strike inside the factory, refusing to leave. Their spontaneous technique, known as the "sit-down," spread quickly to other sites. In February 1937, GM recognized the CIO's United Automobile Workers (UAW) as the bar-gaining agent for its employees. Chrysler came to terms a few months later. The victory at GM forced other employers into line, including Firestone, General Electric, and RCA, and even U.S. Steel, an old enemy of organized labor.

There were some holdouts. Henry Ford hired an army of thugs to rough up union organizers and disrupt strikers on the picket lines. Republic Steel of Chicago stockpiled more weapons than did the city police department. The worst violence occurred outside Republic's South Chicago mill on Memorial Day 1937. There heavily armed police battled rock-throwing strikers on the picket line. Before it ended, ten workers had been killed by gunfire, and dozens more had been injured. Under pressure from the National Labor Relations Board, Ford and Republic Steel gradually accepted industrial unionism as a legitimate force in American life. With a membership approaching 3 million, the CIO had come a long way since its break with the conservative, craft-oriented American Federation of Labor a few years before.

The Court battle and the sit-down strikes slowed the political momentum that followed FDR's reelection landslide in 1936. Further problems loomed in Europe, where fascism continued to gain strength, and in the United States, where a serious recession in 1937 eroded public confidence in the New Deal. For President Roosevelt, the road ahead appeared even more menacing than before.

Fascists on the Rise

Late in 1936, civil war broke out in Spain. A group of military officers, led by General Francisco Franco, attempted to overthrow the recently elected government. Because Franco represented the Falangist, or fascist elements in Spain, he received military aid from Hitler and Mussolini. On the other side, Joseph Stalin aided the government (or "loyalist") forces, which contained a large Socialist and Communist contingent. The war itself was brutal, with extreme cruelty on both sides. Before it ended, more than six hundred thousand people had been killed.

The Spanish Civil War triggered strong emotions in the United States. Some Americans praised Franco as a bastion against communism and a strong supporter of the Catholic Church. Others condemned him as a fascist thug, determined to overthrow a popularly elected government by force. Several thousand Americans went to Spain as part of the Abraham Lincoln Brigade, organized by the Communist Party, to fight on the loyalist side. As Ernest Hemingway said of Franco, "There is only one way to quell a bully and that is to thrash him."

In central Europe, Hitler marched boldly toward war. Vowing to unite all German-speaking people, he moved on Austria in 1938, adding 6 million "Germans" to the Third Reich. Then he demanded the Sudetenland, a region in western Czechoslovakia where 3 million ethnic Germans lived. The Czechs possessed both a well-trained army and a defense treaty with France. As central Europe's only remaining democracy, Czechoslovakia looked to the French and British for support against the Nazi threat. That support never came. Neither France nor England wanted a showdown with Germany. France had lost half of its male population between the ages of twenty and thirty-two during World War I. Antiwar feeling was so strong that a kind of diplomatic paralysis set in.

The result was the Munich debacle of 1938. At Munich, Prime Minister Neville Chamberlain of England and Premier Edouard Daladier of France agreed to Hitler's demand for the Sudetenland. In return the German leader promised not to take any more territory. Daladier then pressured the Czechs to accept this dismal bargain, while Chamberlain congratulated everyone—Hitler included—for bringing "peace in our time."

The news from inside Germany was even worse. Early in 1938, the Nazis torched Munich's Great Synagogue and began the initial deportation of Jews to the infamous concentration camp at Buchenwald. On the evening of November 9—known as Kristallnacht, the "night of broken glass"—Nazi mobs burned synagogues, looted stores, and attacked Jews in cities throughout Germany. Dozens were murdered, and hundreds beaten and raped. Then the Nazis passed new laws to confiscate Jewish property, bar Jews from meaningful employment, and deprive them of ordinary liberties such as attending school and driving a car.

When word of these events reached the United States, President Roosevelt was furious. "I myself could scarcely believe that such things could occur in a twentieth century civilization," he told reporters. Roosevelt immediately called a conference of thirty-two nations to discuss plans for accepting desperate Jewish refugees from Germany, Austria, and Czechoslovakia. But no country, with the exception of small and densely populated Holland, showed a willingness to help. In the United States, a combination of anti-Semitism, isolationist sentiment, and hard times kept the "golden door" tightly shut.

The result was disastrous. At a time when many Jews could have fled from Hitler, there was almost no place for them to go. Between 1935 and 1941, the United States took in an average of eighty-five hundred Jews per year—a number far below the annual German quota of thirty thousand set by the National Origins Act of 1924. Among those allowed to enter were "high-profile" Jewish refugees such as the physicist Albert Einstein.

An End to Reform

Until 1937, the American economy had been making steady, if uneven, progress. National income and production finally reached 1929 levels, stock prices were climbing, and profits were up. Roosevelt now hoped to slow government spending as the business picture improved, seeking to balance the federal budget and cut the mounting national debt.

The president knew that national recovery had been fueled by the New Deal's farm subsidies, relief programs, and public works. He was familiar with the writings of British economist John Maynard Keynes, who advocated a policy of deficit spending in hard times to spur economic growth. Yet Roosevelt had never been fully comfortable with government's expanding role. He feared that the growing national debt would generate inflation, and he worried about the effect of federal welfare programs on the recipients' initiative and self-respect.

In 1937, Roosevelt slashed funding for both the PWA and WPA, cutting almost 2 million jobs. At the same time, the new Social Security payroll tax took effect, removing billions of dollars of purchasing power from the economy. The result was recession—the most serious economic plunge of the Roosevelt years. As unemployment rose and production plummeted, the nation slipped back toward the nightmare of 1933, with breadlines and soup kitchens dotting the landscape.

In October, Roosevelt called Congress into special session. Within weeks, a $5 billion expenditure was approved for federal relief and public works. The economy responded, showing the impact of government spending once again. But the recession further weakened Roosevelt's image as a forceful leader in perilous times.

By 1938, the New Deal had clearly lost momentum. Harry Hopkins claimed that the public was "bored with the poor, the unemployed, the insecure." Facing a more combative Congress—Republicans and conservative Democrats made significant gains in the 1938 elections—Roosevelt decided to "tread water" for a while. Among his few legislative achievements that year was passage of the Fair Labor Standards Act, which abolished child labor in most industries, and provided a minimum hourly wage and maximum workweek (forty hours). Almost a million Americans had their wages raised immediately by this law, and countless millions had their work hours shortened as well.

Still, when the New Deal ended in 1939, more than 8 million Americans were still unemployed. It would take a world war, and the full mobilization that followed, to put them permanently back to work.

CHAPTER REVIEW, 1933–1939

SUMMARY

- The United States hit rock bottom economically as banks collapsed and millions lost their jobs.

- Congress enacted emergency legislation to provide needed relief during the "first hundred days."

- The nation slowly recovered, leading to Roosevelt's landslide reelection in 1936.

- The New Deal laid the foundation for a welfare state with programs such as Social Security and unemployment insurance.

- Unions won recognition following successful strikes against employers in the automobile, steel, and other industries.

- Drought and dust storms caused great damage in parts of Kansas, Nebraska, Oklahoma, Texas, and Colorado and forced tens of thousands of people to leave the region.

- Fascist aggression and Japanese militarism led to a bitter national debate regarding America's role in the world.

IDENTIFICATIONS

New Deal

Civilian Conservation Corps (CCC)

Harry Hopkins

Civil Works Administration (CWA)

Tennessee Valley Authority (TVA)

Agricultural Adjustment Act (AAA)

Dust Bowl

National Industrial Recovery Act (NIRA)

Huey P. Long

John L. Lewis

Eleanor Roosevelt

Mary McLeod Bethune

Marian Anderson

The Grapes of Wrath

MAKING CONNECTIONS: LOOKING AHEAD ⅢⅢ➡

Chapter 24 examines the impact of World War II on American society. Following the Japanese attack on Pearl Harbor, isolationist sentiment would end, the nation would mobilize its defenses, and 15 million men and women would serve in the armed forces against the Axis powers of Germany, Italy, and Japan.

1. What impact would the coming of World War II have on the economic problems facing Americans in the 1930?

2. What would happen to the powerful isolationist movement of this era?

3. Given the darkening world situation, would President Roosevelt decide to break with political precedent and run for a third presidential term?

RECOMMENDED READINGS

Brinkley, Alan. *Voices of Protest: Huey Long, Father Coughlin, and the Great Depression* (1982). A revealing account of Depression era dissidents.

Cohen, Lizabeth. *Making a New Deal: Industrial Workers in Chicago* (1990). Examines working-class protest and culture during the Depression.

Cooke, Blanche Wiesen. *Eleanor Roosevelt* (1992). Follows the life of the nation's most active first lady.

Egan, Timothy. *The Worst Hard Time* (2006) A powerful narrative of those who experienced the great American Dust Bowl.

Goodman, James. *Stories of Scottsboro* (1994). Vividly recreates the most important civil rights trial of the 1930s.

Leuchtenburg, William. *The Supreme Court Reborn: The Constitutional Revolution in the Age of Roosevelt* (1995). Studies the conflicts and changes that altered the Supreme Court in the 1930s and beyond.

Margolick, David. *Beyond Glory: Joe Louis, Max Schmeling, and a World on the Brink* (2005). A gripping account of the heavyweight championship fight that captured world attention.

McElvaine, Robert S. *The Great Depression* (1984). An excellent survey of American life and politics during the New Deal era.

Terkel, Studs. *Hard Times* (1970). Views the Depression through the oral histories of those who lived through it.

Ware, Susan. *Holding Their Own: American Women in the 1930s* (1982). Explores the role of women in America's worst economic crisis.

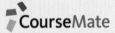 **CourseMate** Go to the CourseMate website at www.cengagebrain.com for additional study tools and review materials for this chapter.

24

The Second World War

1939–1945

MAKING CONNECTIONS

◀▥▥ LOOKING BACK

Chapter 23 considered the impact of the Great Depression on the social, economic, and political structure of the United States. Among the key issues was the new relationship between the federal government and the average citizen. Before starting Chapter 24, you should be able to answer the following questions:

1. What were the most pressing problems facing the Roosevelt administration when it came to power, and how did it address them?

2. Who were President Roosevelt's major critics, and how did they propose to deal with the Great Depression?

3. What impact did the Great Depression have on the realignment of the major political parties?

4. How did the American people view international relations in the 1930s, and what factors were responsible for the perceptions of America's role in the world?

War in Europe, 1939–1940
Blitzkrieg
A Third Term for FDR

The End of Neutrality, 1940–1941
Lend-Lease
The Road to Pearl Harbor
Early Defeats
War Production
Making Do on the Homefront

Opportunity and Discrimination
Women and the War Effort
The "Double V" Campaign
Internment of Japanese Americans, 1942–1945

The Grand Alliance
North Africa, Stalingrad, and the Second Front, 1942–1943
The Normandy Invasion, June 1944
Facing the Holocaust

The Pacific War, 1942–1945
Doing History: Bombing the Death Camps
Turning the Tide, May–June 1942
Closing in on Japan

A Change in Leadership, 1944–1945
The Yalta Accords
Truman in Charge
The Atomic Bombs, August 1945

Prime Minister Neville Chamberlain's "peace in our time" lasted fewer than six months. In March 1939, the Germans marched into central Czechoslovakia. To the south, Franco's forces won a final victory in the Spanish Civil War, and Mussolini's army annexed neighboring Albania. Throughout the summer months, Nazi threats multiplied. "So long as Germans in Poland suffer grievously, so long as they are imprisoned away from the Fatherland," warned Hitler, "Europe can have no peace."

President Roosevelt declared neutrality, reflecting the clear sentiment of the American people. At the same time, he worked to mobilize the nation's defense effort and shape public opinion against the growing Nazi menace.

❖ War in Europe, 1939–1940

In August 1939, Hitler and Stalin stunned the world by signing a nonaggression pact. Both dictators were buying time for an inevitable showdown between their armed forces. And both had designs on Polish territory, which they secretly divided in their agreement. On September 1, German ground troops and armored divisions stormed into Poland from the west, backed by their powerful air force (Luftwaffe). Two weeks later, Soviet troops attacked from the east, reclaiming the territory that Russia had lost to Poland after World War I.

Blitzkrieg

Hitler's Blitzkrieg (lightning strike) into Poland shattered the lingering illusions of Munich. Having pledged themselves to guarantee Poland's borders, England and France reluctantly declared war on Germany. The British sent a small, ill-equipped army to defend western Europe against further Nazi aggression, while the French reinforced their "impregnable" Maginot Line facing Germany. An eerie calm settled over Europe as all sides prepared for battle.

That six-month calm, known as the "phony war," ended in April 1940 when the Nazis overran Denmark and Norway. In May, they invaded Belgium, Holland, Luxembourg—and France itself. From the skies, the Luftwaffe strafed fleeing civilians and flattened cities such as Rotterdam. On the ground, German troops and armor swept through the Ardennes Forest, skirting the Maginot Line. The huge French army collapsed in disarray. Within weeks, German units reached the French coastline, trapping the British army at Dunkirk, with its back to the sea. In early June, a flotilla of small ships from England—tugs, pleasure craft, and naval vessels—ferried 330,000 soldiers to safety. It was both a defeat and a deliverance for the British forces.

In mid-June, as Paris fell to the advancing Nazi army, Mussolini attacked France from the south. Following the French surrender on June 22, the German Luftwaffe attacked England day and night, dropping bombs on cities in an attempt to break civilian morale. Day and night, the British Royal Air Force rose up to meet the Luftwaffe, with devastating effect. By early fall, Nazi air losses forced Hitler to abandon his invasion plans. "Never in the field of human conflict," said England's new prime minister, **Winston Churchill**, of the brave pilots who fought the Battle of Britain, "was so much owed by so many to so few."

Churchill, Sir Winston (1874–1965) British politician and writer. As prime minister (1940–1945 and 1951–1955) he led Great Britain through World War II. He published several books, including *The Second World War* (1948–1953), and won the 1953 Nobel Prize for literature.

A Third Term for FDR

Events in Europe shattered America's isolationist facade. If England fell to the Nazis, Roosevelt believed, the United States would become an isolated fortress, vulnerable to attack from the air and the sea. Most Americans felt the same way. A national poll found 83 percent hoping for a British victory, 16 percent neutral, and only 1 percent supporting the Nazis.

The German Blitzkrieg increased American concerns about defense. In August 1940, President Roosevelt and Congress worked to fashion the first

CHAPTER TIMELINE 1939 1940 1941 1942 1943 1944 1945

POLITICS AND DIPLOMACY
(1933)–1945 Franklin Delano Roosevelt presidency
1944 Normandy Invasion
1939 Germany invades Poland, starting World War II
1945 Roosevelt dies; Harry Truman becomes president
1941 Japan attacks Pearl Harbor
1942 Internment of Japanese Americans begins
1945 U.S. drops atomic bombs on Hiroshima and Nagasaki; Japan surrenders, ending World War II

SOCIETY AND CULTURE
1943 Race riots in Detroit and Los Angeles
1944 G.I. Bill passes

ECONOMICS AND TECHNOLOGY
1942 Manhattan Project begins
1945 U.S. produces more than half the world's manufactured goods

peacetime draft in American history, the Selective Service Act, as well as a $10.5 billion appropriation for defense. With factories now open around-the-clock to build tanks, war planes, and naval vessels, unemployment virtually disappeared. The Great Depression was over.

Building a strong defense was one thing; aiding the Allies quite another. As Michigan senator Arthur Vandenberg, a leading isolationist, put it: "I do not believe that we can become an arsenal for one belligerent without becoming a target for another." With a presidential election on the horizon, FDR would have to answer this charge.

However, no American president had ever served a third term—a taboo that reflected the public's deep suspicion of entrenched federal power. By 1940, with World War II raging, the idea of tested presidential leadership took on added appeal. Hoping to defuse the third-term issue, Roosevelt allowed himself to be "drafted" by the Democratic National Convention in Chicago, thus appearing reluctant but dutiful in the public's mind. Roosevelt selected the enigmatic Henry Wallace to be his vice-presidential running mate. The Republicans, meeting in Philadelphia, nominated **Wendell Willkie** of Indiana for president and Senator Charles McNary of Oregon for vice president. A Wall Street lawyer and the head of a large utilities corporation, Willkie held two positions almost guaranteed to make the voters suspicious. He had never run for public office before or held an appointive government position.

The 1940 campaign was dominated by foreign affairs. Although Willkie shared Roosevelt's views about the dangers of Nazi aggression, he attacked the president for moving too quickly on the European stage. Among Willkie's complaints was a controversial decision by FDR to supply England with "over-age" destroyers. In September 1940, at Churchill's request but without consulting Congress, the president sent fifty old but serviceable warships to England in return for long-term leases to British military bases throughout the Western Hemisphere. The agreement outraged isolationists, who viewed it as a clear violation of American neutrality. In response, Roosevelt made a public promise he would not be able to keep. "I have said this before, but I shall say it again and again and again," he told a cheering crowd in Boston. "Your boys are not going to be sent into any foreign wars."

Roosevelt defeated Willkie with ease—27 million votes to 22 million, 449 electoral votes to 82. He carried all of America's major cities, piling up impressive totals among blacks, Jews, ethnic minorities, and union members.

Willkie, Wendell (1892–1944)
Wall Street lawyer who ran against Franklin D. Roosevelt in his bid for a third consecutive term, which Roosevelt won.

❖ The End of Neutrality, 1940–1941

Shortly after the election, Roosevelt learned that England could no longer afford the supplies it needed to fight the Nazi war machine. He responded by asking Congress for the authority to sell or lease "defense material" to any nation he judged "vital to the defense of the United States." Roosevelt supported his **Lend-Lease** proposal by arguing that the British desperately needed tanks, guns, and planes to extinguish the raging inferno of Nazism. "We must be the great arsenal of democracy," Roosevelt declared.

Lend-Lease (1941) Passed in 1941, this act forged the way for the United States to transfer military supplies to the Allies, primarily Great Britain and the Soviet Union.

Lend-Lease

Lend-Lease set off a furious national debate. In 1940, FDR's opponents organized the America First Committee to keep the nation "neutral" by defeating Lend-Lease. Supported by Henry Ford and Charles Lindbergh, it appealed to the isolationist notion that America should be prepared to defend its own territory, leaving Europe's wars to the Europeans. But by 1941, Roosevelt gained the upper hand.

Public opinion moved sharply against isolationism as Hitler became a more ominous threat. In March, a $7 billion Lend-Lease bill sailed through Congress.

In June 1941, Hitler shattered the recent Nazi-Soviet Pact by invading the Soviet Union with more than 2 million troops. Roosevelt responded by offering Stalin immediate Lend-Lease support. The idea of aiding a Communist dictator was hard for Americans to accept. But Roosevelt stood firm, believing that wars made strange bedfellows and that Hitler must be stopped at all costs. At his insistence, the Soviets received $12 billion in aid over the next four years.

With Lend-Lease in place, Roosevelt abandoned all pretense of neutrality. To ensure that American goods reached England, he instructed the navy to protect merchant shipping in the North Atlantic sea lanes. In August 1941, Roosevelt and Churchill met aboard the USS *Augusta*, off the Newfoundland coast, to discuss their mutual aims and principles. The result was a communiqué known as the **Atlantic Charter**, which called for freedom of the seas, freedom from want and fear, and self-determination for all people. The charter would become the blueprint for the United Nations following World War II.

In the fall of 1941, Roosevelt armed America's merchant fleet and authorized U.S. destroyers to hunt German U-boats (or submarines) under a policy known as "active defense." That October, a German submarine sank a U.S. destroyer off Iceland, with the loss of a hundred American lives.

War would come shortly, but not where Roosevelt expected.

The Road to Pearl Harbor

As Hitler swept relentlessly though Europe, another power was stirring halfway around the globe. Like Germany and Italy, Japan had become a militarist state controlled by leaders with expansionist ideas. In the 1930s, the Japanese had invaded China, routing its army, terror-bombing cities, and brutalizing civilians in the infamous "rape of Nanking," where thousands died at the hands of rampaging Japanese troops. The United States barely protested. With his focus on the Nazis, Roosevelt sought to avoid a crisis with Japan, even after its planes bombed an American gunboat, the *Panay*, on the Yangtze River in 1937, killing three sailors and injuring forty-three more.

In 1938, the Japanese unveiled their plan for empire, known as the "Greater East Asia Co-Prosperity Sphere." Viewing themselves as superior to their

Atlantic Charter (1941)
Composed during a meeting between President Franklin Roosevelt and British Prime Minister Winston Churchill, it listed eight principles for a better world, such as freedom from fear and want, self-determination for all people, and the disarming of aggressor nations. Many see the Atlantic Charter as a guiding force behind the establishment of the United Nations following World War II.

(© Bettmann/CORBIS)

Pear Harbor. The Japanese attack on Pearl Harbor—December 7, 1941—destroyed eighteen warships, killed twenty-four hundred Americans, and plunged the nation into World War II.

neighbors, they aimed to rule their region by annexing European colonies in Southeast Asia and the Western Pacific. Only one obstacle stood in the way—the United States. Japan purchased the bulk of its steel, oil, heavy equipment, and machine parts from U.S. suppliers. To help prevent further Japanese expansion, the Roosevelt administration placed an embargo on certain strategic goods to Japan and moved the Pacific Fleet from San Diego to **Pearl Harbor.** The Japanese responded by negotiating a defense treaty (the so-called Tripartite Pact) with Germany and Italy. Relations steadily declined between the United States and Japan. When France and Holland were unable to defend their Asian colonies, Japan moved against Indochina in April 1941. Roosevelt retaliated by freezing all Japanese assets in the United States and blocking shipments of scrap iron and aviation fuel to Japan.

Pearl Harbor Site of a U.S. naval base on the southern coast of Oahu, Hawaii, which the Japanese attacked on Sunday, December 7, 1941; the United States entered World War II the following day.

Both sides prepared for war. Military analysts expected Japan to move southwest, toward the Dutch East Indies and British Malaya, in search of needed rubber and oil. Instead, on November 26, 1941, a huge Japanese naval fleet, led by Admiral Chuichi Nagumo, headed due east into rough Pacific waters. The armada included six aircraft carriers with four hundred warplanes, two battleships, two cruisers, nine destroyers, and dozens of support vessels. Traveling under complete radio silence, the fleet was destined for Pearl Harbor, Hawaii, five thousand miles away.

On Sunday morning, December 7, 1941, Admiral Nagumo's fleet reached its takeoff point, 220 miles north of Pearl Harbor. At 7:40 A.M., the first wave of Japanese warplanes appeared. The battleship *Arizona* suffered a direct hit and went up in flames. More than twelve hundred crew members were killed. The *Oklahoma* capsized after taking three torpedoes, trapping four hundred men below deck. A second Japanese assault at 9:00 A.M. completed the carnage. All told, eighteen warships had been sunk or were badly damaged, three hundred planes had been lost, and twenty-four hundred Americans had died.

Why was Pearl Harbor so woefully unprepared? By the fall of 1941, the United States had broken the Japanese diplomatic code, known as MAGIC. American planners knew that war was coming. On November 27, Army Chief of Staff George C. Marshall sent a warning to all American military outposts in the Pacific. "Japanese future action unpredictable," it said, "but hostile action possible at any moment." Yet Pearl Harbor was not viewed as the likely point of attack. It was thousands of miles from Japan and supposedly well defended. The very idea of a Japanese fleet sailing so far without detection seemed utterly fantastic.

On December 8, Congress declared war against Japan. Only Montana's representative, Jeanette Rankin, dissented. (A longtime peace activist, she also had voted against President Wilson's war message in 1917.) On December 11, Germany and Italy honored the Tripartite Pact by declaring war on the United States. Almost instantly, Americans closed ranks. As Roosevelt's former enemy Senator Burton Wheeler put it, "The only thing to do now is lick the hell out of them."

Early Defeats

The attack on Pearl Harbor began one of the bleakest years in American military history. In the North Atlantic, allied shipping losses reached almost a million tons per month. On the Eastern front, Nazi forces approached the outskirts of Moscow, where Soviet resistance was fierce. In Egypt, German General Erwin Rommel's elite Afrika Korps threatened the Suez Canal.

The news from Asia was grimmer still. Following Pearl Harbor, Japan moved quickly against American possessions in the Pacific, overrunning Guam, Wake Island, and Malaya. Burma, Hong Kong, Singapore, Malaya, and the Dutch East Indies fell like dominoes to Japanese invaders. For Americans, the most galling defeat occurred in the Philippines, where one hundred thousand U.S. and Filipino troops surrendered to the Japanese after a bloody six-month struggle. The military campaign had actually been lost on December 8, 1941, when the Japanese successfully bombed Clark Field, destroying dozens of planes based there to defend the islands. Lacking air cover, the defenders retreated to the jungles of the **Bataan Peninsula,** just north of Manila. As food ran out, they ate snakes, monkeys, cavalry horses, plants, and grass.

In March 1942, President Roosevelt ordered the commanding officer, **General Douglas MacArthur,** to slip out of the Philippines, leaving his troops behind. The trapped defenders made their stand at Corregidor, a fortress-like island in Manila Bay. After two months of constant bombardment, General Jonathan Wainwright surrendered to the Japanese. His diseased and starving men were brutalized by their captors on the infamous Bataan Death March, an event that further fueled America's boiling hatred of Japan.

War Production

The United States had begun to mobilize for World War II before the attack on Pearl Harbor. In 1940, following the Nazi invasion of Western Europe, Congress had enacted the first peacetime draft in American history. When war came a year later, the draft was extended for the length of the conflict. Six million men volunteered for military service between 1942 and 1945 and another 10 million were drafted. The Selective Service System permitted those who opposed war on religious grounds to register as conscientious objectors, a status that permitted them to fulfill their obligation by doing nonmilitary tasks in the Army Medical Corps or by working in civilian hospitals or on selected public works projects.

On the home front, Americans vowed to outproduce their enemies and sacrifice for the "boys" at the front. "Our great strength," said a defense worker from San Diego, "is that we're all in this together." FDR named Donald Nelson of Sears, Roebuck to run the newly created War Production Board (WPB). Nelson's main job was to oversee the transformation of American factories—to get companies such as Ford and General Motors to make tanks and warplanes instead of automobiles. To accomplish this, the federal government offered generous incentives. Antitrust laws were suspended so military orders could be filled quickly without competitive bidding. Companies were given low-interest loans to retool and "cost-plus" contracts that guaranteed them a profit. As the war progressed, America's top one hundred companies increased their percentage of the nation's total production from 30 to 70 percent. Ford, for example, began construction of a huge new factory in 1941, named Willow Run, to build B-24 Liberator bombers. In the next four years, it turned out 8,685 airplanes—one every sixty-three minutes.

Between 1940 and 1945, the nation's gross national product doubled, and the federal budget reached $95 billion, a tenfold increase. In the first half of 1942, the government placed more than $100 billion in war orders, requesting more goods than American factories had ever produced in a single year. The list included 60,000 planes, 45,000 tanks, 20,000 antiaircraft guns, and 8 million tons of merchant shipping. The orders for 1943 were even larger. By war's end, military spending exceeded $300 billion.

Roosevelt hoped to finance this effort without dramatically raising the national debt. Congress passed the Revenue Act in 1942, adding millions of new taxpayers to the federal rolls and dramatically raised the rates paid by Americans in higher income brackets. Along with increases in corporate and inheritance rates, taxation provided about 45 percent of the war's total cost—less than Roosevelt wanted, but far more than the comparable figures for World War I or the Civil War.

Bataan Peninsula U.S. and Filipino World War II troops surrendered this peninsula in western Luzon, Philippines, to the Japanese in April 1942 after an extended siege; U.S. forces recaptured the peninsula in February 1945.

MacArthur, Douglas (1880–1964) U.S. general. He served as chief of staff (1930–1935) and commanded the Allied forces in the South Pacific during World War II. Initially losing the Philippines to the Japanese in 1942, he regained the islands and accepted the surrender of Japan in 1945. He commanded the UN forces in Korea (1950–1951) until a conflict in strategies led to his dismissal by President Truman.

Borrowing accounted for the rest. The national debt reached $260 billion in 1945, six times higher than that in 1941. The government relied on banks and brokerage houses for loans, but common people did their share. "There are millions who ask, 'What can we do to help?'" said Treasury Secretary Henry Morgenthau in 1942. "The reason I want a [war bond campaign] is to give people an opportunity to do something." Hollywood stars promoted war bonds, organizing "victory tours" through three hundred communities. Factory workers participated in payroll savings plans by putting a percentage of their earnings into government bonds.

By 1942, the problem was no longer finding enough work for the people; it was finding enough people for the work to be done. Factories stayed open around the clock, providing new opportunities to underemployed groups such as women, blacks, and the elderly. Seventeen million new jobs were created during World War II. Wages and salaries more than doubled, due in large part to the overtime that people put in. Per capita income rose from $373 in 1940 to just over $1,000 by 1945. As a result, the United States experienced a rare but significant redistribution of wealth, with the bottom half of the nation's wage earners gaining a larger share of the pie.

Making Do on the Homefront

Though Americans took home bigger paychecks than ever before, they found less and less to spend them on. In 1942, Congress created the Office of Price Administration (OPA) to ration vital goods, preach self-sacrifice to the public, and control the inflation caused by too much money chasing too few goods. Gas, tires, sugar, coffee, meat, butter, alcohol—all became scarce. Pleasure driving virtually ended, causing thousands of restaurants and drive-in businesses to close. As manufacturers cut back on cloth and wool, women's skirts got shorter, two-piece swimsuits (midriff exposed) became the rage, and men's suits no longer had cuffs.

Changes on the home front could be seen through "the prism of baseball," the national game. Many wanted major league baseball suspended during the war, but Roosevelt disagreed, claiming that it built up American morale. The 1941 season had been one of the best ever, with Ted Williams batting over 400 and Joe DiMaggio's fifty-six-game hitting streak. The next year was very different indeed. Night games were banned because of air-raid blackouts. Ballparks held blood drives and bond drives, and soldiers in uniform were admitted free of charge. In 1942, Detroit Tigers slugger Hank Greenberg became the first major leaguer to be drafted into the armed forces. By 1943, most of the stars were gone, replaced by men who were too old or physically unfit for duty, such as Pete Gray, a one-armed outfielder for the St. Louis Browns.

❖ Opportunity and Discrimination

In many respects, World War II produced a social revolution in the United States. The severe labor shortage caused an enormous migration of people from rural areas to cities, from South to North, and especially to the West Coast, where so many war industries were located. With defense factories booming and 15 million people in the armed forces, Americans were forced to reexamine long-held stereotypes about women and minorities in the workplace and on the battlefield. The war provided enormous possibilities for advancement and for change. It also unleashed prejudices that led to the mass detention of American citizens on largely racial grounds.

Women and the War Effort

The war brought new responsibilities and opportunities for American women. During the Depression, for example, women were expected to step aside in the job market to make way for unemployed men. A national poll in 1936 showed an overwhelming percentage of both sexes agreeing that wives with employed husbands should not work. The war brought instant changes. More than 6 million women took defense jobs, half of whom had not been previously employed. They worked as welders and electricians, on assembly lines and in munitions plants. More than three-quarters of these women were married, and most were over thirty-five years old—a truly remarkable change. Because the government and private industry provided little child care assistance, absenteeism and job turnover among younger women were extremely high.

The symbol of America's new working woman was **Rosie the Riveter,** memorialized by Norman Rockwell on the cover of the *Saturday Evening Post* with her overalls, her work tools, and her foot planted on a copy of *Mein Kampf,* helping to grind fascism to dust.

> All the day long whether rain or shine—
> She's a part of the assembly line—
> She's making history working for victory—
> Rosie the Riveter.

Although this work paid well, wage discrimination was rampant in the defense industries, where women earned far less than did men in the same jobs. Employers and labor unions rationalized such inequities by noting that men had seniority, put in more overtime, and did the "skilled" work. In 1945, female factory workers averaged thirty-two dollars per week compared with fifty-five dollars for men.

Women also were told that their work would end with the war's completion, when defense spending dropped and the veterans came home to reclaim their old jobs. Many women welcomed a return to domesticity after four years of struggle, but a survey of female defense workers in 1944 showed that most of them hoped to continue in their jobs. This was not to be. Although more women than ever before remained in the labor force following World War II, the bulk of them were

Rosie the Riveter Symbol of the new breed of working women during World War II.

(LC-USW361-128)/Library of Congress Prints and Photographs Division)

Women Workers. The labor shortages of World War II created new employment opportunities for women, most of whom were married and over thirty-five. More than six million women worked in defense industries across the country, including shipyards, munitions plants, and aircraft factories.

pushed back into lower-paying "feminized" work. Still, a foundation had been laid. As a riveter from Los Angeles recalled, "Yeah, going to work during the war made me grow up and realize I could do things. . . . It was quite a change."

The "Double V" Campaign

For millions of American blacks, the war against racist Germany and Japan could not be separated from the ongoing struggle to achieve equal rights. The *Pittsburgh Courier*, an influential African American newspaper, demanded a "Double V" campaign from the Negro community: "victory over our enemies at home and victory over our enemies on the battlefields abroad."

One problem was the small number of blacks employed in high-paying factory jobs. "The Negro will be considered only as janitors," stated North American Aviation, one of the nation's leading military contractors. "Regardless of their training as aircraft workers, we will not employ them." In 1941, A. Philip Randolph, president of the Brotherhood of Sleeping Car Porters, an all-Negro labor union, proposed a "March on Washington" to protest job discrimination in the defense industries and segregation of the armed forces. Fearing the negative publicity, President Roosevelt convinced the organizers to call off their march in return for an executive order (8802) declaring that "there shall be no discrimination in the employment of workers because of race, creed, or national origin." To facilitate the order, Roosevelt appointed the Fair Employment Practices Committee (FEPC) to "investigate complaints" and "redress grievances." With a tiny budget and no enforcement powers, the FEPC held public hearings, preached equality in the workplace—and was largely ignored.

Still, the desperate need for labor provided new opportunities for minorities. More than a million blacks migrated to the North and West during World War II, taking factory jobs in New York and California, Michigan and Illinois. The percentage of African Americans in the war industries reached 7.5 percent by 1944—less than their share of the population but a vast improvement over 1941. The work itself was often menial, such as cleaning factory bathrooms and sweeping the floors. But thousands of African Americans took semiskilled positions on the assembly line, which meant higher wages than ever before. By war's end, about four hundred thousand black females had left domestic work for the defense plants. "The war made me live better, it really did," recalled an aircraft worker who moved from rural Texas to Los Angeles. "My sister always said that Hitler was the one that got us out of the white folks' kitchen."

Where racial barriers were crossed, however, violence often followed. In Mobile, Alabama, the promotion of eleven black welders led white shipyard workers to go on a rampage through the African American community, severely beating dozens of residents. The worst racial violence flared in Detroit, the nation's leading war production center. With good jobs available on the assembly lines of Chrysler, General Motors, and Ford, Detroit's area-wide labor force grew from four hundred thousand in 1940 to almost nine hundred thousand by 1943. In 1942, an angry mob in Detroit kept several black families from moving into a public housing project in a white neighborhood. The following year, a fight between whites and blacks at a municipal park sparked a race riot involving huge mobs with guns, knives, and clubs. Detroit's poorly trained police force did little to stop the carnage. By the time federal troops established calm in the city, thirty-five people were dead and more than seven hundred wounded. The police shot seventeen "looters" during the riot, all of them black.

Mob violence on the West Coast involved other victims. In California, a hate campaign led by local politicians and the press blamed Mexican Americans for an alleged rise in drugs, crime, and gang warfare. In June 1943, white sailors from surrounding naval bases roamed the Mexican districts of Los Angeles, Long Beach, Pasadena, and other cities looking for "zooters"—young Mexican Americans in ducktail haircuts wearing long jackets with wide pleated pants, pegged at the cuff. Cheered on by white crowds, the sailors became a vigilante mob—stripping the young men of their "zoot suits," cutting their hair, and beating them senseless. The zoot suit violence had roots in the so-called *bracero* (contract labor) program, launched in 1942, in which several hundred thousand Mexicans were brought to the United States to plant and harvest crops. In cities like Los Angeles, where African American and Hispanic workers arrived at a rate of ten thousand per month, crowding and competition bred resentment and fear.

To many residents of southern California, the "zooters" came to represent the Hispanic community as a whole. Rumors flew that Mexican Americans were hindering the war effort by evading the draft. In fact, the reverse was true: Mexican Americans served in numbers far greater than their percentage of the general population—350,000 out of 1.4 million—and seventeen were awarded the Congressional Medal of Honor.

Mexican Americans were integrated in the armed forces during World War II; African Americans were not. All branches except the tiny Coast Guard practiced race discrimination as a matter of course. More than 500,000 African Americans served in the army, which placed them in segregated divisions that were commanded by white officers. The marines did not take blacks until 1943, when twenty thousand were recruited to unload supplies and munitions during the amphibious Pacific landings—an extremely hazardous duty that subjected them to withering artillery and sniper fire from dug-in Japanese defenders. The navy segregated blacks by occupation, with most working as food handlers, stevedores, and "mess-boys." In July 1944, a huge explosion at an ammunition depot in Port Chicago, California, killed 250 black sailors from a segregated work unit. When 50 survivors refused an order to return to work, claiming they had been singled out for these dangerous jobs on account of race, they were court-martialed, convicted of mutiny, and sentenced to prison. Following an intense publicity campaign in the Negro press, the black sailors were returned to duty.

Only one black army division saw significant combat—the 92nd Infantry in Italy. When questioned about this, Secretary of War Henry Stimson claimed that "Negroes have been unable to master efficiently the techniques of modern weapons." But when given the opportunity, black units performed superbly. The 99th Air Force Fighter squadron, known as the Tuskegee Airmen, earned two Distinguished Unit Citations and shot down a dozen Nazi planes during the Anzio invasion of 1943. Escorting American bombers over Germany in 1944 and 1945, pilots of the 99th compiled a perfect record: not a single bomber under their protection was lost to enemy fire.

Such treatment fueled anger, protest, and pride. The Negro press became more assertive in the drive for equal rights. America's leading black organization, the National Association for the Advancement of Colored People (NAACP), increased its wartime membership from seventy thousand to five hundred thousand. In 1942, young activists, black and white, formed the Congress of Racial Equality to challenge segregated restaurants in Washington and Baltimore, chanting, "We die together. Let's eat together." A powerful civil rights movement was slowly taking shape.

Internment of Japanese Americans, 1942–1945

President Roosevelt was determined to avoid a recurrence of the federal repression and vigilante activity that had marred the home front during World War I. Yet the years between 1942 and 1945 witnessed the most glaring denial of civil liberties in

Japanese American Family Facing Internment. In one of the most egregious violations of civil liberties in American history, the federal government rounded up 120,000 people of Japanese ancestry on the West Coast and sent them to isolated internment camps in California, Arkansas, and parts of the Southwest.

Nisei A person born in the United States of parents who emigrated from Japan.

American history. The victims included people of Japanese ancestry—citizen and noncitizen alike—living mainly on the West Coast of the United States.

On December 8, 1941, Roosevelt issued a standard executive order requiring enemy aliens to register with local police. Before long, the president lifted the enemy alien designation for Italians and Germans in the United States, but not for the Japanese. The attack on Pearl Harbor, the Bataan Death March, the fall of Hong Kong and Singapore, Wake Island, and the Philippines—all sent shock waves across the United States. Although J. Edgar Hoover saw no evidence of a Japanese "threat" to American security, the public thought otherwise. *Time* magazine published an article after Pearl Harbor entitled, "How to Tell Your Friends from the Japs." Henry McLemore, a columnist for the *San Francisco Examiner*, wrote, "I am for the immediate removal of every Japanese on the West Coast to a point in the interior. Herd 'em up, pack 'em off, and give 'em the inside room in the badlands. . . . Personally, I hate the Japanese. And that goes for all of them."

More than 90 percent of the 125,000 Japanese Americans lived in California, Oregon, and Washington. Two-thirds were citizens, or **Nisei**, born in the United States; the rest were noncitizens, or Issei, born in Japan and ineligible for naturalization under the Immigration Laws of 1882 and 1924. Few in number, politically powerless, and less well assimilated than European ethnic groups, the Japanese in America made perfect targets. Military leaders raised the dangers of allowing them to live so close to aircraft plants and naval bases. Patriotic groups linked them to the atrocities committed by the Japanese armed forces eight thousand miles away. Local farmers and fishermen resented the economic success of these hard-working people. All wanted their removal from the West Coast.

President Roosevelt capitulated. In February 1942, he issued Executive Order 9066, giving Secretary of War Stimson the authority to designate military zones inside the United States "from which any or all persons may be excluded." A few days later, the army interpreted that order to include the entire West Coast and all people of Japanese extraction. "A Jap's a Jap," said General John DeWitt, head of the West Coast Defense Command. "It makes no difference whether he is an American citizen or not." In March, the president issued Executive Order 9102, establishing the War Relocation Authority. Japanese internment camps were set up in the deserts of California and Arizona, the mountains of Wyoming, and the scrublands of Utah and Colorado (see Map 24.1). Japanese Americans on the West Coast were given a few weeks to sell their belongings, get their affairs in

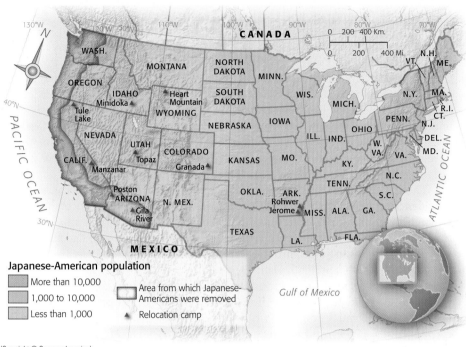

Japanese-American population

More than 10,000
1,000 to 10,000
Less than 1,000

Area from which Japanese-Americans were removed
▲ Relocation camp

MAP 24.1

Japanese American Relocation, 1942–1945

The 120,000 Japanese Americans removed from the West Coast during World War II were sent to internment camps in six states, run by the newly established War Relocation Authority. The relocation order did not affect the small number of Japanese Americans living elsewhere in the United States or the large Japanese population living in Hawaii.

order, and report to "processing centers." By June, 120,000 men, women, and children, most of them American citizens, reached the internment camps.

Conditions in the camps were harsh but not brutal. Families lived together in spartan army barracks with little privacy and poor sanitation. Most worked as farm laborers. "All of Manzanar was a stockade, actually—a prison," wrote a young Japanese American woman of her California camp. "We were in jail. There was barbed wire all around, there were great big watch towers in the corners, and there were spotlights turned on during the night."

The Supreme Court did not intervene in Japanese internment; it took almost forty years for a measure of justice to prevail. In *Hirabayashi v. United States* (1943) the court upheld a curfew ordinance against Japanese Americans in Seattle on the grounds that wartime conditions sometimes justified measures that "place citizens of one ancestry in a different category from others." The Court also ruled (*Korematsu v. United States*, 1944) that the evacuation of Japanese Americans was appropriate, but added (*Endo v. United States*, 1944) that the War Relocation Authority should attempt to separate "loyal" internees from "disloyal" ones, and set the loyal free. It wasn't until 1981 that a congressional panel concluded the internment program had resulted from a combination of race prejudice, war hysteria, and the failure of political leadership. In 1988, Congress awarded each survivor of the internment camps $20,000 in "reparations."

❖ The Grand Alliance

Most Americans saw Japan as the primary villain of World War II. Opinion polls showed the public overwhelmingly in favor of concentrating the war effort in the Pacific against a "barbaric" and "treacherous" foe. Yet President Roosevelt and his military advisers believed that American power should be directed against the stronger enemy—Germany. Roosevelt viewed the Nazis as the real threat to world peace, and Europe as the key battleground.

Doing History Online

Civil Liberties in Wartime

Go to the CourseMate website for this chapter and link to Primary Sources. Read the section on internment and refer back to the World War I section on the propaganda war (in Chapter 20). Evaluate the following statement: The federal government restricted civil liberties more during World War II than during World War I.

www.cengagebrain.com

North Africa, Stalingrad, and the Second Front, 1942–1943

America's two major allies had conflicting strategies, interests, and concerns. The British had a far-flung empire to defend; they did not believe in confronting Hitler with immediate, massive force. Their strategy was to strike at "the soft underbelly" of the Axis in North Africa and the Mediterranean rather than to confront Hitler directly in France. The Russians strongly disagreed: they wanted the United States and Britain to open a "second front" in western Europe so as to relieve German pressure on them in the east. That meant a major Allied invasion of France. As one American diplomat said of Soviet Foreign Minister V. M. Molotov, "He knows only four words of English—'yes,' 'no' and 'second front.'"

Though America's top military advisers leaned toward the Russian strategy, President Roosevelt favored the British approach. At present, he realized, the United States was unprepared for a full-scale invasion of Europe; a smaller operation against Nazi forces in North Africa, as the British proposed, had the benefit of getting the United States into the war quickly on the proper scale. To make this possible, the United States had to gain control of the ocean. In the first three months of 1942, German submarines sank almost 1 million tons of Allied shipping. The so-called wolf packs were so close to American shores that bathers on the New Jersey and Virginia coasts watched in horror as merchant ships were torpedoed. By 1943, however, technological advances in antisubmarine warfare turned the tide. The use of sonar, radar, and powerful depth charges made German U-boats more vulnerable. More than 900 of the 1,162 German submarines commissioned during World War II were sunk or captured.

In November 1942, American troops under the command of **General Dwight D. Eisenhower** invaded the French North African colonies of Morocco and Algeria in an operation code-named TORCH. At virtually the same moment, British forces badly mauled General Rommel's army at El Alamein in Egypt, ending Nazi hopes of taking the Suez Canal. Though Hitler rushed reinforcements to North Africa, the Allies prevailed, taking enemy-held territory for the first time in the war.

In the Soviet Union, the Russians were fighting two hundred German divisions along an enormous two-thousand-mile front. The pivotal battle occurred at Stalingrad, a vital transportation hub on the Volga River, in the bitter winter of 1942–1943. As the Germans advanced, Stalin ordered his namesake city held at all costs. The fighting was block-to-block, house-to-house, and finally hand-to-hand. Hitler would not let his forces retreat, even after they ran out of fuel and food. Surrounded by Russian forces, overwhelmed by starvation, exposure, and suicide, the German commander surrendered on February 2, 1943.

Stalingrad marked the turning point of the European war. The myth of German invincibility was over. The Russians were advancing steadily in the east, aided by a stream of tanks, planes, food, and clothing from the United States under Lend-Lease. Now Stalin expected an Allied thrust from the west—the long-promised second front.

Churchill had other ideas. At a meeting with Roosevelt in Casablanca, he convinced the president to put off a cross-channel invasion in favor of an assault on Axis troops across the Mediterranean in Italy. Roosevelt attempted to pacify Stalin by promising to open a second front the following year and to accept nothing less than Germany's unconditional surrender. But the Soviets, having sacrificed more troops at Stalingrad than the United States would lose in the entire war, were suspicious and displeased.

The Italian campaign began in the summer of 1943. Sicily fell in a month, and Mussolini along with it. Overthrown by antifascist Italians, the Duce fled to Nazi lines in the north. (In April 1945, antifascists captured Mussolini, killed him, and strung him up by his heels.) The battle for Italy dragged on for almost two years, draining troops and resources for the planned invasion of France. Suspicions

Eisenhower, Dwight D. (1890–1969) U.S. general and thirty-fourth president of the United States (1953–1961). As supreme commander of the Allied Expeditionary Force in World War II, he launched the invasion of Normandy (June 6, 1944) and oversaw the defeat of Germany in 1945.

between Stalin and his wartime allies deepened as Roosevelt and Churchill set the terms of Italy's surrender without consulting the Soviet leader. In addition, postponement of the second front gave Stalin the opportunity to gobble up much of central Europe as his troops pushed toward Germany from the east.

The three Allied leaders met together for the first time in November 1943 at the Tehran Conference in Iran. Roosevelt and Churchill promised to launch their cross-channel invasion the following spring. The future of Germany and need for a United Nations were also discussed. "We are going to get along fine with Stalin and the Russian people," Roosevelt declared.

The Normandy Invasion, June 1944

By 1944, the Allies were in complete control of the skies over western Europe and in command of the seas. Their amphibious landings in North Africa and Italy had provided valuable experience for the job that lay ahead. In April and May, General Eisenhower assembled his huge invasion force in England—3 million men, 2.5 million tons of supplies, and thousands of planes, landing craft, and escort vessels. Meanwhile, Allied aircraft pounded the Atlantic Wall, a line of German fortifications stretching hundreds of miles along the coast of France and the Low Countries.

Despite meticulous preparation, Eisenhower faced enormous risks. The Nazis had fifty-five divisions in France. To keep them dispersed and guessing, Allied intelligence spread false information about the planned invasion sites. The deceptions worked: Hitler and his generals put their strongest defense at Pas de Calais, the English Channel's narrowest point. The massive D-Day invasion— **Operation OVERLORD**—began on the morning of June 6, 1944. Before the men left, Eisenhower told them: "You are about to embark upon the Great Crusade, toward which we have striven these many months. The eyes of the world are upon you."

The invasion succeeded. With overwhelming air cover, Allied forces assaulted Normandy and dropped paratroopers behind enemy lines. The heaviest fighting took place at Omaha Beach, where U.S. Rangers scaled sheer cliffs under withering fire to silence Nazi gunners. By nightfall, 150,000 men were ashore; others

Operation OVERLORD (1944)
Code name for the Allied invasion of Normandy launched on D-Day, June 6, 1944.

(dpa/CORBIS)

D-Day Invasion. On June 6, 1944, Allied troops stormed the beaches of Normandy. By nightfall, more than 150,000 troops were ashore and others quickly followed, beginning the long-awaited "second front" that sealed Hitler's fate.

(Copyright © Cengage Learning)

MAP 24.2

The War in Europe

The U.S. military effort against German and Italian forces in World War II began in North Africa, moved to Italy, and culminated in the D-Day invasion of France in 1944. With the aid of England and other nations, the Allied forces reached Germany from the west in 1945. Meanwhile, following a tenacious defense of their homeland, Russian troops pushed deep into Germany from the east, destroying the bulk of Nazi fighting forces and playing a key role in the German surrender.

quickly followed. Within two months, more than a million Allied troops were in France—liberating Paris in August and reaching the German border by September (see Map 24.2). With the Soviets pressing from the east, a Nazi surrender seemed only weeks away.

But the Germans counterattacked in December 1944, taking British and American forces by surprise. The Battle of the Bulge was Hitler's last gasp—a failed attempt to crack Allied morale. U.S. troops took heavy casualties but stood firm. Germany lost one hundred thousand men and the will to fight on. Hitler committed suicide in his Berlin bunker on April 30, 1945, with Russian soldiers a few miles away. Germany surrendered a week later. The Thousand-Year Reich had lasted a dozen murderous years.

Facing the Holocaust

In the spring of 1945, Allied troops liberated the Nazi concentration camps in Poland and Germany. Ghastly pictures of starving survivors and rotting corpses flashed around the world, recording the almost inconceivable horror in which 6 million European Jews and 4 million others (including Poles, gypsies, homosexuals, and political dissidents) were exterminated during World War II.

(United States Holocaust Memorial Museum)

Concentration Camp Survivors. The liberation of Nazi concentration camps offered undeniable proof of Nazi genocide. The question of whether the United States and its allies could have done more to prevent it has been a matter of great controversy ever since.

To American leaders, these photos of the Holocaust produced shock but hardly surprise. Evidence of the death camps had reached the United States in 1942, yet the government had paid scant attention to the consequences. The State Department, well known for its anti-Semitism in that era, made it virtually impossible for refugees fleeing the Nazis to enter the United States. An applicant for a wartime visa had to provide the names of two American sponsors before submitting six copies of a form that measured four feet in length. As a result, only 10 percent of America's immigration quotas were met during World War II, leaving almost two hundred thousand slots unfilled.

President Roosevelt did not seriously intervene. His only acknowledgment of the impending disaster came in 1944, when he created the War Refugee Board, which helped finance the activities of Raoul Wallenberg, the courageous Swedish diplomat who prevented thousands of Hungarian Jews from being deported to the death camps. Had it been formed earlier and supported more firmly by the White House, the War Refugee Board might have played a major role in saving innocent lives. The United States could have also bombed the rail lines leading to the death camps, as well as the gas chambers and crematoria that lay inside. The War Department avoided these targets, claiming they were too dangerous and too far away. This clearly was not true. In 1944, Allied bombers flew hundreds of missions within a thirty-five-mile radius of Auschwitz. (See *Doing History: Bombing the Death Camps*.)

When liberation came to the concentration camps, the vast majority of prisoners were dead. One survivor at Dachau recalled the very moment the American troops arrived. "We were free. We broke into weeping, kissed the tank. A Negro soldier gave us a tin of meat, bread, and chocolate. We sat down on the ground and ate up all the food together. The Negro watched us, tears in his eyes."

❖ The Pacific War, 1942–1945

The war against Japan would be fought differently from the war against Germany. In the Pacific, the United States would do the great bulk of the Allied fighting; in Europe, that burden was shared by others, including Great Britain, and, most important, the Soviet Union. In Europe, armor and artillery were essential to the Allied victory; in the Pacific, it would be aircraft carriers and submarines. By war's

Doing History Bombing the Death Camps

One of the most controversial aspects of the Allied war effort in Europe was the failure of American and British warplanes to bomb the rail lines leading to the Nazi death camp at Auschwitz, Poland, where tens of thousands of European Jews were being murdered in gas chambers. When British Prime Minister Winston Churchill urged such bombings in 1944 to prevent "probably the greatest and most horrible crime ever committed in the whole history of the world," he was told by his air force commanders that only the United States had the resources to get the job done.

To this day, it is unclear whether President Roosevelt seriously considered the possibility of bombing Auschwitz and its surrounding rail lines. For years, Assistant Secretary of War John J. McCloy insisted that the president had not been briefed on this matter because military planners were convinced that such bombings would divert crucial resources from the larger war effort. But shortly before his death in 1989, McCloy claimed that he did speak to Roosevelt about this matter and that the president had opposed bombing Auschwitz on grounds that it would kill innocent Jewish victims without doing any real harm to their German oppressors.

In November 1944, John H. Pehle, director of the War Refugee Board, wrote to McCloy urging the immediate bombing of Auschwitz and other death camps.

I send you herewith copies of two eye-witness descriptions of the notorious . . . extermination camps. . . . No report of Nazi atrocities received by the Board has quite caught the gruesome brutality of what is taking place in these camps of horror as have these sober, factual accounts of conditions at Auschwitz and Birkenau. I earnestly hope you will read these reports.

The destruction of large numbers of people apparently is not a simple process. The Germans have been forced to devote considerable technical ingenuity and administrative know-how in order to carry out murder on a mass production basis. . . . If [these] elaborate murder installations . . . were destroyed, it seems clear that the Germans could not reconstruct them for some time. . . .

---

end, the United States would lose 128 combatant vessels to Japanese warships and aircraft but only 29 to German fire. The Japanese surrender in 1945 would end the largest naval war in history.

Turning the Tide, May–June 1942

The Japanese hoped to create an impregnable defense line in the Pacific. Their strategy included new conquests, such as Australia, and a naval thrust against the U.S. carrier fleet. Yet two key engagements in the spring of 1942 shattered their illusions about American will power and naval strength. On May 7, a task force led by two American carriers—the *Lexington* and *Yorktown*—held its own against a larger Japanese force at the Battle of the Coral Sea, just north of Australia (see Map 24.3). Though the "Lady Lex" was sunk, heavy Japanese losses saved Australia from invasion or certain blockade.

A month later, the two sides clashed again. Admiral Isoroku Yamamoto brought a huge fleet to **Midway Island**, a thousand miles west of Hawaii, to flush out and destroy the American carrier fleet. But the U.S. Navy, having broken the Japanese military code, was well aware of his intentions. In a three-day battle, brilliantly commanded by Rear Admiral Raymond A. Spruance, the Americans sank four Japanese carriers (losing the *Yorktown*) and shot down 320 planes. Japan would never fully recover from this beating at Midway.

Midway Island Location of 1942 decisive World War II naval battle, in which land and carrier-based U.S. planes defeated a Japanese fleet.

I am convinced that the point has now been reached where such military action is justifiable if it is deemed feasible by competent military authorities.

McCloy responded to Pehle ten days later:

The Operations Staff of the War Department has given careful consideration to your suggestion that the bombing of these camps be undertaken. In consideration of this proposal the following points were brought out:

Positive destruction of the camps would necessitate precision bombing . . . by low flying or dive bombing aircraft, preferably the latter.

The target is beyond the maximum range of [such aircraft] located in United Kingdom, France or Italy.

Use of heavy bombardment from United Kingdom bases would necessitate a hazardous round trip flight unescorted of approximately 2000 miles over enemy territory.

. . . The positive solution to this problem is the earliest possible victory over Germany, to which end we should exert our entire means.

Despite McCloy's claims, there is little doubt that the U.S. Air Force, sending hundreds of bombers over German cities and military targets in 1944, could have easily spared the planes required to destroy Auschwitz and the surrounding rail lines. Whether innocent lives would have been saved by these missions will never be known. What is certain, however, is that McCloy was well aware of the horrors that were occurring in these death camps and of the increasingly desperate pleas for help.

Source: John H. Pehle to John J. McCloy, November 8, 1944; McCloy to Pehle, November 18, 1944, War Refugee Board Records, Franklin D. Roosevelt Library, cited in Richard D. Polenberg, *The Era of Franklin D. Roosevelt, 1933–1945* (New York: St. Martin's, 2000), 222–223.

QUESTIONS for REFLECTION

1. What is the key argument put forth in favor of, and in opposition to, the bombing of the Nazi death camps?

2. What information should have been provided to President Roosevelt in order for him to have made an informed decision about these bombings?

3. Even if no lives had been saved, was it important for the Allies to have destroyed these death camps as a way of expressing their horror at the genocide that was unfolding?

Closing in on Japan

After Midway, the United States followed a two-pronged plan of attack. Admiral Chester Nimitz was to move west from Hawaii toward Formosa, while General Douglas MacArthur was to come north from Australia toward the Philippines, with their forces combining for an eventual assault on Japan. The Pacific theater would see no massed land battles like Stalingrad or the Bulge. The fighting would be sporadic but brutal, involving air attacks, naval duels, and amphibious landings by U.S. Marines on selected Japanese-held islands. It would be "a war without mercy."

The first American offensive occurred at Guadalcanal, a small tropical island in the Solomons, off New Guinea, in August 1942. For six months, American marines waged a desperate campaign in swamps and jungles, battling intense heat, malaria, dysentery, infection, and leeches, as well as the Japanese. When the island was finally secured in February 1943, General MacArthur began a "leapfrog" campaign across New Guinea to the Philippines, attacking some islands while bypassing others. By 1944, Manila was in his sights.

In the central Pacific, Admiral Nimitz was moving west, ever closer to Japan. In November 1943, the marines assaulted Tarawa, a tiny strip of beach in the Gilbert Islands, incurring three thousand casualties in a successful three-day assault. Next came the Marshall Islands; the Marianas—Guam, Tinian, and Saipan—followed. Control of the Marianas, only twelve hundred miles from Tokyo, placed

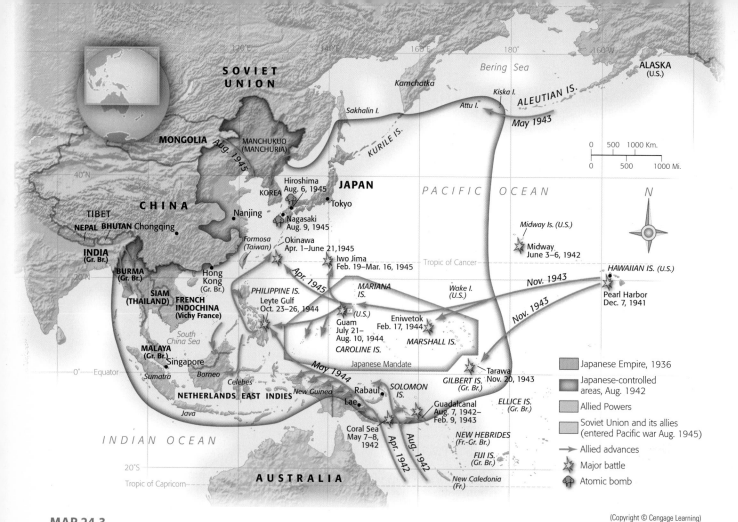

MAP 24.3

The War in the Pacific

Following Pearl Harbor, the Japanese attempted to set up an impregnable defense line across the Pacific. But the stunning American naval victory at Midway Island in 1942 allowed U.S. forces to move west toward Japan, successfully clearing Japanese-held islands in brutal combat. By 1944, the American bombing campaign against Japan itself was fully under way. The dropping of two atomic bombs in August 1945 helped bring the war to a close.

(Copyright © Cengage Learning)

major Japanese cities within range of America's new B-29 bombers. The battle for Saipan raged through June and July 1944. The Japanese defenders fought, quite literally, to the last man. Worse, thousands of Japanese civilians on the island committed suicide—a preview, some believed, of what lay ahead in Japan.

The end seemed near. In October 1944, MacArthur returned to the Philippines in triumph, while an American naval force destroyed four Japanese carriers at the Battle of Leyte Gulf, outside Manila. To the north, American troops took the island of Iwo Jima in brutal combat and then attacked Okinawa, less than four hundred miles from Japan. Admiral Nimitz assembled a huge force for the invasion—180,000 troops, most of his carriers, and eighteen battleships. The Japanese had an army of 110,000 on Okinawa, the final barrier to the homeland itself.

The battle took three months, from April through June 1945. Waves of Japanese kamikaze (suicide) planes attacked the Allied fleet, inflicting terrible damage. American troops suffered a casualty rate of 35 percent, the highest of the war. Seven thousand were killed on land and five thousand at sea, and forty thousand were wounded. The Japanese lost fifteen hundred kamikazes and virtually all of their soldiers. These appalling losses would be a factor in America's decision to use atomic weapons against Japan.

❖ A Change in Leadership, 1944–1945

In November 1944, the American people reelected Franklin Roosevelt to an unprecedented fourth presidential term. Roosevelt defeated Republican Thomas Dewey, the moderate forty-two-year-old governor of New York. Roosevelt campaigned as the war leader, urging voters "not to change horses in midstream." To bolster his chances, Democratic Party leaders removed the increasingly un-popular Vice President Henry Wallace from the ticket and replaced him with **Senator Harry S Truman** of Missouri.

The Yalta Accords

When Truman visited the White House to plan campaign strategy with Roosevelt, he was appalled by the president's feeble condition. In February 1945, with Germany near collapse, an exhausted FDR met with Churchill and Stalin at Yalta, in southern Russia, to lay the groundwork for peace and order in the postwar world. On several issues, agreement came easily. The Russians promised to enter the Pacific war after Germany's defeat in return for territorial concessions in the Far East. The three leaders also blessed the formation of a new international body, to be known as the United Nations.

But agreement on the larger issues proved elusive. The Soviet Union had suf-fered staggering losses at German hands. At least 20 million Russians were dead or wounded; thousands of towns, factories, and collective farms had been destroyed. From Stalin's perspective, the Soviets deserved more than simple grati-tude for their role in defeating the great bulk of Hitler's army. He hoped to ensure Soviet security through the permanent partition of Germany and demanded huge reparations from the Germans, with Russia getting half. Furthermore, Stalin had no intention of removing Soviet troops from the lands they now controlled in eastern Europe. In both world wars, Germany had marched directly through Poland to devastate the Russian heartland. Stalin would not let this happen again.

Roosevelt and Churchill had other ideas. Both men viewed a healthy, "de-Nazified" Germany as essential to the reconstruction of postwar Europe, and both feared the expansion of Soviet power into the vacuum created by Hitler's defeat. The British also claimed a moral stake in Poland, having declared war on Germany in 1939 to help defend the Poles from the Nazi assault. To desert them now—to permit a victorious Stalin to replace a defeated Hitler—smacked of the very appeasement that had doomed Allied policy a decade before. Few believed that the Polish people would pick Stalin or communism if given a free choice.

The **Yalta Conference** created a legacy of mistrust. The parties agreed to split Germany into four "zones of occupation"—American, Russian, British, and French. Berlin, deep inside the Soviet zone, also was divided among the Allies. Yet the vital issue of reparations was postponed, as were plans for Germany's even-tual reunification. At Roosevelt's urging, Stalin accepted a "Declaration for a Liberated Europe" that promised "free and unfettered elections" in Poland and elsewhere at some unspecified date.

However, in the weeks following Yalta, Roosevelt's optimism about Soviet–American relations seemed to fade. The Yalta Accords did not prevent Stalin from ordering the murder of political dissidents in Romania and Bulgaria and the arrest of anti-Communist leaders in Poland. His ruthlessness seemed to highlight the unpleasant truth that America had little or no influence in the nations now occupied by Soviet troops. "We can't do business with Stalin," FDR complained privately. "He has broken every one of the promises he made at Yalta."

Truman in Charge

On April 12, 1945—less than two months into his fourth term—FDR died of a massive stroke at his vacation retreat in Warm Springs, Georgia. The nation was shocked. Roosevelt had been president for twelve years, leading the people through the Great Depression and World War II. "He was the one American who

Truman, Harry S (1884–1972) Thirty-third president of the United States (1945–1953), he took office following the death of Franklin D. Roosevelt. Reelected in 1948 in a stunning political upset, Truman's controversial and historic decisions included the use of atomic weapons against Japan, desegregation of the U.S. military, and dismissal of General MacArthur as commander of U.S. forces during the Korean War.

Yalta Conference (1945) World War II conference where Franklin Roosevelt, Winston Churchill, and Joseph Stalin attempted to establish the political future of a liberated Europe. Though Stalin agreed that Soviet forces would enter the war against Japan within three months of Germany's surrender, his determination to dominate Eastern Europe effectively ended the so-called Grand Alliance.

knew, or seemed to know, where the world was going," wrote *Life* magazine. "The plans were all in his head."

The new president was largely unknown. Born on a Missouri farm in 1884, Harry Truman had served as an artillery officer in World War I before jumping into local politics in Kansas City. Elected to public office in the 1920s with the help of a crooked party boss, Truman walked a fine line between efficient service to his constituents and partisan loyalty to a corrupt political machine. Fair and honest himself, Truman went about the business of improving public services while ignoring the squalor of those who put him in office. But his political experience did not inspire immediate confidence. Small in stature, with thick glasses and a high-pitched midwestern twang, Truman seemed thoroughly ordinary to all but those who knew him best. As vice president, he was largely excluded from the major discussions relating to foreign policy and the war. After taking the presidential oath of office, Truman turned to reporters and said, "Boys, if you ever pray, pray for me now."

Truman received conflicting advice on how to end the war. A number of FDR's confidants, including Henry Wallace, urged him to keep the wartime alliance alive by accommodating Russia's economic needs and security demands. But others, such as Averell Harriman, U.S. ambassador to the Soviet Union, prodded Truman to demand Russia's strict compliance with the Yalta Accords. The new president did not want a confrontation with Stalin, yet the more Truman learned about events in Poland and eastern Europe, the angrier he became. Ten days after taking office, he confronted Soviet Foreign Minister V. M. Molotov at the White House, claiming that Russia had ignored the Yalta Accords and warning him that economic aid to Russia would never get through Congress so long as this attitude persisted. When Truman finished, Molotov told him, "I've never been talked to like that in my life." "Carry out your agreements," Truman shot back, "and you won't get talked to like that."

In July 1945, Truman left the United States aboard the USS *Augusta* for his first face-to-face meeting with Stalin and Churchill at Potsdam, near Berlin. The three leaders agreed on a number of important issues, including the terms of peace for defeated Germany and public trials for Nazi war criminals. Then, the conference was halted for several days by the stunning defeat of Winston Churchill's Conservative Party in the British parliamentary elections. Churchill returned to England, replaced by the new Labour prime minister, Clement Attlee. When the talks resumed, Stalin brushed aside Truman's concerns about Poland

The Potsdam Conference, July 1945. Winston Churchill, Harry Truman, and Joseph Stalin clasp hands at the Potsdam Conference in July 1945. The good feeling did not last long, as Churchill's ruling party was defeated at the polls in England, and relations between the United States and the Soviet Union moved swiftly downhill.

(CORBIS)

and eastern Europe, and Truman rebuffed Stalin's attempt to claim reparations from the western zones of occupation in Germany. The conference ended on a chilly note.

The Atomic Bombs, August 1945

One of Truman's first decisions concerned the use of atomic weapons. As the United States took control of the island chains east of Japan in 1944, a ferocious bombing campaign of the Japanese home islands took place. In March 1945, three hundred American B-29s led by Major General Curtis LeMay firebombed Tokyo, killing one hundred thousand people, leaving 1 million homeless and destroying much of the city. These raids were particularly devastating because Japan had few planes left to defend its densely populated areas. In the following months, bombings pounded Japan's major cities.

Shortly after taking office, President Truman was told about the atomic bomb by Secretary of War Stimson, who called it "the most terrible weapon ever known in human history." The decision to build this bomb had been made by President Roosevelt in response to reports from refugee scientists, such as Germany's Albert Einstein, that the Nazis were already at work on one. The American effort, known as the Manhattan Project, included top-secret facilities in Hanford, Washington; Oak Ridge, Tennessee; and Los Alamos, New Mexico; to design and construct this bomb, and produce the fissionable material for an atomic explosion.

At President Truman's direction, an Interim Committee was formed to advise him about the bomb. Chaired by Henry Stimson, the committee recommended the use of atomic weapons against Japan, without warning, as soon as they became available. Another group, the Target Committee, chose four major cities—Hiroshima, Kokura, Niigata, and Nagasaki—based on their strategic importance and the fact that each of them, unlike Tokyo, was untouched by war. On July 16, 1945, the atomic bomb was successfully tested near Alamogordo, New Mexico.

(© CORBIS)

Atomic Bomb Destruction of Hiroshima. The atomic bomb dropped on Hiroshima on August 6, 1945, killed at least 100,000 people. Since that time, a debate has raged over the atomic bombings of Hiroshima and Nagasaki—in particular, their role in ending the war.

The explosion, equivalent to fifteen thousand tons of dynamite, was visible two hundred miles away. Truman learned of the test while attending the Allied Summit meeting in Potsdam. He immediately issued a public ultimatum to the Japanese, calling on them to surrender unconditionally or face "prompt and utter destruction." This prompted a number of top scientists and military officials to beg the president not to use it against Japan.

But Truman held firm, believing that the bomb would save American and Japanese lives by ending the war quickly. On the morning of August 6, 1945, a B-29 named *Enola Gay* dropped an atomic bomb over Hiroshima, incinerating the industrial city and killing at least one hundred thousand people. Thousands more would die later of radiation effects, a problem poorly understood by scientists at that time. Three days later, a B-29 named *Bock's Car* dropped a second atomic bomb on Nagasaki, with much the same effect. On August 14, the Japanese asked for peace.

Though Americans overwhelmingly supported these bombings, the decision remains controversial to this day. Some believe that Truman dropped the bomb to scare the Russians in Europe; others think the decision was based on racism and revenge. For all the controversy, however, one inescapable fact remains: Japanese leaders could not bring themselves to surrender until two atomic bombs had been dropped.

World War II formally ended on September 2, 1945, when the Japanese signed the document of surrender aboard the battleship *Missouri* in Tokyo Bay. More than 25 million soldiers and civilians died in the struggle (see Table 24.1). Speaking from the deck of the Missouri that day, General MacArthur issued a warning for the new atomic age. "We have had our last chance," he said. "If we do not devise some greater and more equitable system, Armageddon will be at our door."

Enola Gay The B-29 bomber, named after the mother of pilot Colonel Paul W. Tibbets, that dropped the first atomic bomb on the Japanese city of Hiroshima on August 6, 1945, killing more than one hundred thousand people.

TABLE 24.1
World War II Casualties

Country	Battle Deaths	Wounded
U.S.S.R.	6,115,000	14,012,000
Germany	3,250,000	7,250,000
China	1,324,516	1,762,006
Japan	1,270,000	140,000
Poland	664,000	530,000
United Kingdom	357,116	369,267
United States	291,557	670,846
France	201,568	400,000
Italy	149,496	66,716

Source: *Information Please Almanac* (Boston: Houghton Mifflin Co., 1988).

CHAPTER REVIEW, 1939–1945

SUMMARY

- Nazi Germany invaded Poland on September 1, 1939, unleashing World War II.

- Roosevelt won an unprecedented third term in 1940 by vowing to keep the country out of war.

- The Japanese attack on Pearl Harbor plunged the nation into World War II.

- Heavy war production brought the Great Depression to an end.

- Married women joined the labor force in record numbers, taking jobs normally reserved for men.

- Allied forces in the North Atlantic Theater stormed the beaches of France in 1944, following heavy fighting in North Africa and in Italy.

- Roosevelt, Stalin, and Churchill met at Yalta in 1945 to map strategy for the postwar world.

- Vice President Harry S Truman became president following the death of FDR in April 1945.

- Germany surrendered a month later, following the suicide of Adolf Hitler and the Allied assault on Berlin.

- Japan surrendered in August 1945, following the dropping of two atomic bombs.

IDENTIFICATIONS

Winston Churchill
Wendell Willkie
Lend-Lease
Atlantic Charter
Pearl Harbor
Bataan Peninsula
General Douglas MacArthur
Rosie the Riveter
Nisei
General Dwight D. Eisenhower
Operation OVERLORD
Midway Island
Harry S Truman
Yalta Conference
Enola Gay

MAKING CONNECTIONS: LOOKING AHEAD ⅢⅢ➡

Chapter 25 looks at American society following World War II, tracing the impact of the war on foreign and domestic affairs, from the Cold War to the baby boom to the growth of suburbia.

1. What decisions were made, or avoided, during World War II that had a direct impact on the diplomatic problems facing the United States and the Soviet Union in the coming years?

2. How difficult would it be for America's 15 million veterans to readjust to civilian life following the war?

3. Would the tremendous wartime prosperity in the United States be maintained once the conflict was over?

RECOMMENDED READINGS

Asahina, Robert. *Just Americans: How Japanese Americans Won a War at Home and Abroad* (2006). Shows the experiences of Japanese Americans in internment camps and on the battlefield.

Birdwell, Michael. *Celluloid Soldiers* (1999). Carefully examines Hollywood's war effort against the Nazis.

Bradley, James. *Flags of Our Fathers* (2000) A dramatic account of the marines who raised the flag at Iwo Jima.

Dower, John. *War Without Mercy: Race and Power in the Pacific War* (1986). Explores the racial attitudes of the United States and Japan in the brutal Asian conflict.

Hartmann, Susan. *The Homefront and Beyond: American Women in the 1940s* (1982). Documents the extraordinary impact of World War II on women at home and in the workplace.

Jeffries, John. *Wartime America* (1996). Concentrates on the home front during World War II.

Keegan, John. *The Second World War* (2005). The best single-volume military account of World War II.

Kennett, Lee. *G.I.: The American Soldier in World War II* (1997). Describes the day-to-day order of life of the average American soldier in the training camps, in combat, and in victory.

Walker, J. Samuel. *Prompt and Utter Destruction: Truman and the Use of Atomic Bombs Against Japan* (1997). Offers a balanced account of the factors leading to the president's fateful decision.

Wyman, David S. *The Abandonment of the Jews* (1984). Examines the failure of American policy makers, the press, and the larger public to provide a sanctuary for victims of the Holocaust.

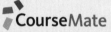 Go to the CourseMate website at www.cengagebrain.com for additional study tools and review materials for this chapter.

25

Postwar America

1946–1953

MAKING CONNECTIONS

◀━━Ⅲ **LOOKING BACK**

Chapter 24 examined both the way in which the United States fought World War II and the great changes that occurred in domestic and international affairs. Before starting Chapter 25, you should be able to answer the following questions:

1. How did America mobilize for war? What changes took place on the home front that aided the war production?

2. How lasting and substantial were the gains made by women and minorities during the war?

3. How well did the Grand Alliance work, what strategies were employed to keep it together, and what problems arose regarding the interests of the different parties?

Affluence and Anxiety

Economic Reconversion
Lurching Toward Prosperity
The Postwar American Family
Suburbia

The Soviet Threat

Containment
The Truman Doctrine and
the Marshall Plan

Liberalism in Retreat

The Cold War at Home
The Domestic Agenda

Breaking the Color Line
Man of the People

The Cold War Intensifies, 1949–1953

The Fall of China and the Creation of
NATO, 1949
War in Korea, 1950–1953

McCarthyism and the Election of 1952

The Rise of Joe McCarthy
"I Like Ike"

Doing History: Senator Smith
Confronts Senator McCarthy

Henry R. Luce was a man of grand visions and powerful views. One rival dubbed him "Lord of the Press" because his publishing empire included *Time*, *Life*, and *Fortune*, among other mass circulation magazines. In February 1941, Luce composed an editorial prodding the American people to accept their new role as citizens of "the strongest and most vital nation in the world." The time had come, he insisted, to exert "the full measure of our influence, for such purposes as we see fit" in the dawning "American Century."

The belief in America's destiny was as old as the country itself. Yet the challenges of World War II had turned this rhetoric into reality by placing the United States at the very center of the international stage. Old empires lay in ruins; an atomic era had begun. Only the United States seemed to possess the combination of military strength, economic resources, and political stability to rebuild a world battered by war.

❖ Affluence and Anxiety

The United States faced two major problems following World War II. The first concerned relations with the Soviet Union. Would the two nations be able to maintain the Grand Alliance, or would their obvious differences about the shape and direction of postwar Europe degenerate into conflict, and possibly war? The second problem related to the domestic economy. Many Americans feared that the Great Depression might return after World War II as defense spending dropped and factory jobs disappeared. In the months following Japan's surrender, the federal government cancelled more than $30 billion in military contracts, forcing eight hundred thousand layoffs in the aircraft industry alone. Could the United States handle the difficult reconversion from a wartime to a peacetime economy? Or would it slip back into the dark days of joblessness, poverty, and despair?

Economic Reconversion

President Truman's first job was to bring the soldiers home. Twelve million Americans were still in uniform in 1945, most of them young men, ages eighteen to thirty-four, who had experienced the dual hardships of economic depression and war. For many GIs, the homecoming was difficult. The divorce rate shot up dramatically in 1945, reflecting the tensions of readjustment to civilian life. A major housing shortage, brought on by the absence of home building during World War II, made things even worse. Washington, D.C., reported twenty-five thousand homeless veterans, Chicago more than one hundred thousand. North Dakota veterans took to living in converted grain bins. One serviceman complained: "You fight a damn war and you finally come home and everybody slaps you on the back and tells you what a wonderful job you did . . . but when it comes to really doing something, then nobody's home."

In fact, assistance for returning veterans had received careful attention from the wartime Congress, which passed the popular Servicemen's Readjustment Act in 1944. Known as the GI Bill, it provided almost $20 billion for various programs in the decade following World War II. The social and economic effects of this legislation were enormous. The GI Bill fueled a nationwide construction boom by providing long-term, low-interest mortgages to veterans, plus a two thousand dollar bonus toward the purchase of a new home. Furthermore, it allowed former soldiers to fulfill the dream of a college degree, thereby expanding the system of higher education as never before. Determined to make up for lost time, they formed the nucleus of America's expanding white-collar workforce in the prosperous years ahead.

CHAPTER TIMELINE	1946	1947	1948	1949	1950	1951	1952

POLITICS AND DIPLOMACY

(1945)–(1953) Harry S Truman presidency

● 1947 Truman Doctrine proposed
● 1947 Marshall Plan enacted
● 1950 Korean War begins
● 1951 General Douglas MacArthur relieved of command in Korea

SOCIETY AND CULTURE

● 1946 Dr. Spock publishes *Common Sense Book of Baby and Child Care*
● 1947 Jackie Robinson breaks baseball's color line
1948 ● *Kinsey Report* on sexual behavior published
● 1949 Sears, Roebuck catalogue advertises television sets

ECONOMICS AND TECHNOLOGY

● 1946 Reconversion to a peacetime economy takes place
● 1947 Levittown opens
● 1949 Soviet Union successfully tests atomic bomb

Lurching Toward Prosperity

The fear of another economic depression in the United States did not last long. The increase in federal spending for veterans helped to offset the decrease in defense spending. And a surge of consumer demand held out the promise of prosperity based on peace. For the past five years, Americans had worked overtime in offices and factories, banking their paychecks, buying savings bonds, and dreaming of the day when cars, appliances, prime beef, and nylon stockings would reappear in the nation's stores and showrooms. Between Pearl Harbor and the Japanese surrender, the public had accumulated an astonishing $140 billion in savings and liquid securities, and the average weekly wage had almost doubled, from $24.20 to $44.30. "I'm tired of ration books and empty shelves," said one factory worker. "I'm ready to spend."

But factories could not change from fighter planes to automobiles overnight. Reconversion took time. With the demand for consumer goods far outpacing the supply, President Truman hoped to keep inflation in line by extending wartime price controls. His plan met strong opposition from the business community, which lobbied hard to "strike the shackles from American free enterprise." In June 1946, controls were lifted and prices shot up. The cost of meat doubled in two weeks.

Not surprisingly, the labor movement took a militant stance. Since higher prices meant a drop in real wages, the United Automobile Workers (UAW) demanded an average pay hike of 33 cents an hour from General Motors in 1946, from $1.12 to $1.45. When the corporation offered a 10-cent hourly raise, the union struck for 113 days, eventually settling for 18 cents. Shortly after, the UAW and the auto companies agreed to a cost-of-living adjustment (COLA) clause in future contracts.

The country was soon plagued by a wave of strikes. When two railroad brotherhoods threatened a work stoppage designed to shut down the country's rail service, President Truman signed an executive order seizing the railroads. A few weeks later, the United Mine Workers (UMW) went on strike, forcing power stations and factories to close for lack of fuel. In response, President Truman went on the radio to demand that the miners return to work at once. They did, coaxed along by a federal court injunction that led to $3.5 million in damages against the UMW. For Truman, these victories came at a heavy cost. Not only did he offend large parts of the labor movement, he also appeared incapable of governing a nation wracked by consumer shortages, labor strife, soaring inflation, and an approaching cold war.

In November 1946, the Democratic Party suffered a crushing defeat at the polls. Campaigning against the ills of reconversion ("Had Enough?") and the president's alleged incompetence ("To Err Is Truman"), the Republicans gained control of the Senate and the House for the first time since 1928. When the Truman family returned to Washington from a campaign trip on election eve, no one showed up to greet them. The train station was deserted. "Don't worry about me," the president told his daughter, Margaret. "I know how things will turn out and they'll be all right."

The Postwar American Family

The pain and sacrifice of the Great Depression and World War II led most Americans to yearn for both emotional security and material success. As expected, the family grew in importance, providing a sense of comfort and stability to people after years of separation and loss. Along with the focus on families came a thriving middle-class culture, based on suburban living, a **baby boom,** an emphasis on more traditional sex roles, and an explosion of consumer goods.

baby boom (1946–1964)
Increased numbers of births in the years after World War II.

Beginning in 1946, the United States experienced a surge in marriage rates and birthrates, following record lows in the Depression decade. The young adults (ages eighteen to thirty) of this era became the most "marrying" generation in American history, with 97 percent of the women and 94 percent of the men taking marriage vows. The baby boom was equally dramatic. The number of children per family in the United States jumped from 2.6 in 1940 to 3.2 by decade's end. Birthrates doubled for a third child and tripled for a fourth, as the American population grew by 20 million in the 1940s. At a time when access to birth control information was rapidly increasing, U.S. population growth rivaled not England's but rather India's.

These spiraling marriage rates and birthrates went hand in hand with a shift back to more traditional sex roles following World War II. One of the most popular wartime advertisements showed a mother in overalls about to leave for the factory. She is at the door when her little daughter asks: "Mother, when will you stay home again?" And she responds: "Some jubilant day, mother will stay home again doing the job she likes—making a home for you and daddy when he gets back." Quite naturally, this emphasis on family life strengthened long-held prejudices against married women holding full-time jobs outside the home. As a result, the gains made in female employment during World War II largely disappeared. Returning veterans reclaimed millions of factory jobs held by women and minorities. The female labor force dropped from a wartime high of 19 million in 1945 to less than 17 million by 1947.

The social pressures on women were enormous. A host of "experts" asserted that women belonged in the home for their own good as well as the good of society—that women needed to be housewives and mothers in order to be fulfilled. In their 1947 best-seller, *Modern Women: The Lost Sex*, Marynia Farnham and Ferdinand Lundberg noted that "all mature childless women are emotionally disturbed" and that "the pursuit of a career is essentially masculine." Furthermore, these experts claimed that returning veterans needed special love and attention after so many years away from home.

The concept of mothering as central to the postwar family was further popularized by Dr. Benjamin Spock, whose *Common Sense Book of Baby and Child Care* (1946) became the standard reference for parents of the baby boom generation. While most reviewers noted Spock's relaxed, more permissive attitude toward child rearing, another message came through as well. Women must be the primary caregivers, Spock insisted. It was their role to shape the infant into a normal, happy adult. For Spock and countless others, a man's success was measured by his performance in the outside world, a woman's success by her skills in raising well-adjusted children. As feminist author Betty Friedan recalled, "Oh, how Dr. Spock could make me feel guilty!"

The emphasis on traditional sex roles also affected female education. World War II had opened up new opportunities for women in science, engineering, and medicine. For the first time in history, women constituted a majority of the nation's college graduates. But the return of male veterans, combined with the educational benefits provided them by the GI Bill, reversed these temporary gains. The percentage of college women who graduated fell from 40 percent during World War II to 25 percent by 1950. The steepest declines occurred in professional education. Female enrollments in medical schools dropped from a high of 15 percent during World War II to 5 percent by 1950. A study of medical students in this era showed deep prejudice among men and self-limiting attitudes among women. On campuses across the nation, educators struggled to find the proper curriculum for female students. The ideal, said one college president, was to enable women "to foster the intellectual and emotional life of her family and community"—to fill the American home with proper moral values and good cooking.

See for yourself!
All you want in your dream kitchen IS HERE!

Youngstown Kitchens

(Peter Newark's American Pictures/Bridgeman Art Library)

Advertisement for the "Dream Kitchen." A surge of consumer spending after World War II quickly erased fears that America would slip back into economic depression.

Levittown An unincorporated community of 53,286 people in southeast New York on western Long Island, which was founded in 1947 as a low-cost housing development for World War II veterans.

Before long, the postwar American woman became the nation's primary consumer. Between 1946 and 1950, Americans purchased 21 million automobiles, 20 million refrigerators, 5.5 million electric stoves, and more than 2 million dishwashers. This consumer explosion resulted from a combination of factors: the baby boom, the huge savings accumulated during World War II, the availability of credit, and the effectiveness of mass advertising in creating consumer demand. The average American now had access to department store charge accounts and easy payment plans with almost no money down. In 1950, the Diner's Club introduced America's first credit card. "Buy Now, Pay Later," urged General Motors, and most people obliged.

Ironically, this new consumer society led millions of women back into the labor force. By 1950, more women were working outside the home than ever before. The difference, however, was that postwar American women returned to low-paying, often part-time employment in "feminine" positions such as clerks, salespeople, secretaries, waitresses, telephone operators, and domestics. Working to supplement the family income and help finance the automobile, the kitchen appliances, the summer vacation, the children's college tuition, American women earned but 53 percent of the wages of American men in 1950—a drop of 10 percent since the heady years of "Rosie the Riveter" during World War II.

Suburbia

No possession was more prized by the postwar American family than the suburban home. In 1944, fewer than 120,000 new houses were built in the United States, a figure that rose to 900,000 by 1946 and 1.7 million by 1950. More than 80 percent of these new houses were built in suburban areas surrounding established cities. The rush to suburbia was accelerated by a flood of federal mortgage money through the GI Bill and a revolution in the building of affordable, single-family homes. Leading the way were builders like William Levitt, who purchased several thousand acres of farmland in Hempstead, New York, twenty-five miles east of Manhattan, for the mass production of private homes.

Levitt modeled his operation after Henry Ford's automobile assembly plants. His building materials were produced and precut in Levitt factories, delivered by Levitt trucks, and assembled by Levitt work crews, each performing a single task such as framing, pouring concrete, or painting window shutters. In good weather, Levitt workers put up 180 houses a week. The typical dwelling—a solid, two-bedroom Cape Cod style, with a kitchen–dining room, living room with fireplace, single bath, and expansion attic—sold for $7,900. When completed, **Levittown**, Long Island, contained 17,000 houses, plus dozens of parks, ball fields, swimming pools, churches, and shopping areas for the 82,000 residents. Levitt followed his Long Island venture with similar towns in Pennsylvania and New Jersey.

City dwellers were attracted by Levittown's good schools, safe streets, and open space. The idea of owning one's home, moreover, was a central part of the American dream. But what stood out to others was the sameness of Levittown—a place where people lived in similar houses, accumulated similar possessions, and conformed to similar rules. Levitt salesmen restricted their communities to white applicants, who then signed pledges saying they would not resell their homes to blacks. As late as the 1960s, the percentage of African Americans living in the three Levittown developments was well below 1 percent, a figure that represented most suburban areas nationwide. Furthermore, Levittown appeared to reinforce the traditional family roles of postwar America, with mothers caring for their children while fathers commuted long distances to work.

❖ The Soviet Threat

Meanwhile, relations between the United States and the Soviet Union were moving swiftly downhill. The failure to find common ground on a host of vital issues—from "free elections" in Poland to the German payment of reparations—raised anger and suspicion on both sides. Soviet leaders now viewed the United States as largely indifferent to the security needs of the Russian people, and American leaders increasingly portrayed the Soviet Union as a belligerent force in the world, bent more on expanding its empire than on defending its territory. Relations would worsen in the coming years, as the Soviets tightened their grip in Eastern Europe and successfully tested an atomic bomb in 1949. The Grand Alliance was over; the Cold War had begun.

Containment

In February 1946, Stalin delivered a major address predicting the collapse of capitalism and the dawn of a Communist world. The following month, with Truman at his side, former Prime Minister Churchill told an audience at Westminster College in Missouri that Russia had drawn an **Iron Curtain** across Europe. The West must unite against Soviet expansion, Churchill said, adding that "God had willed" the atomic bomb to Britain and America so as to ensure their ultimate triumph over this totalitarian foe.

A more compelling rebuttal to Stalin's speech came from a forty-two-year-old foreign service officer stationed at the U.S. embassy in Moscow. In an eight-thousand-word telegram, George F. Kennan laid out the doctrine of **containment** that would influence American foreign policy for the next twenty years. According to Kennan, Russia was an implacable foe, determined to expand its empire and undermine Western democratic values. America must define its vital interests and then be prepared to defend them through "the adroit and vigilant application of counterforce at a series of constantly shifting geographical and political points."

Kennan's "long telegram" arrived in Washington at the perfect time. Poland and Eastern Europe were now lost causes; there seemed little that the United States could do to change their dismal fate. The objective, Truman believed, was to block Communist expansion into new areas vulnerable to Soviet influence and control. "Unless Russia is faced with an iron fist and strong language another war is in the making," he predicted. "I am tired of babying the Soviets."

The Truman Doctrine and the Marshall Plan

The new trouble spot appeared to be the Mediterranean, where the Soviet Union was demanding territorial concessions from Iran and Turkey, and where Communist-led guerrillas were battling the Greek government in a bloody civil war. Early in 1947, Great Britain, the traditional power in that area, informed the United States that it could no longer provide military and economic assistance to Greece and Turkey. Exhausted by World War II, Britain urged the United States to maintain that aid in order to prevent further Soviet expansion.

Doing History Online

The Six Thousand Houses That Levitt Built, 1948

Go to the CourseMate website for this chapter and link to Primary Sources. Read the article online along with the *Suburbia* section in the textbook. Imagine that you are a newly married World War II veteran or someone married to a soldier just returned from the war in 1947. Would you want to live in Levittown? Why or why not?

   www.cengagebrain.com

Iron Curtain Military, political, and ideological barrier established between the Soviet bloc and Western Europe from 1945 to 1989.

containment U.S. national security doctrine during the Cold War. Attributed to State Department officer George Kennan, containment came to define America's political-military strategy for confronting Soviet expansion.

Marshall, George C. (1880–1959)
U.S. general and statesman. As secretary of state (1947–1949), he organized the European Recovery Plan, often called the Marshall Plan, for which he received the 1953 Nobel Peace Prize.

Truman Doctrine (1947)
Reflecting a tougher approach to the Soviet Union following World War II, President Truman went before Congress in 1947 to request $400 million in military aid for Greece and Turkey, claiming the appropriation was vital to the containment of communism and to the future of freedom everywhere.

Marshall Plan Post–World War II U.S. economic aid program, also known as the European Recovery Plan. The plan, costing about $13 billion, helped restore economic confidence throughout Western Europe, raise living standards, curb the influence of local Communist parties, and increase U.S. trade and investment on the European continent.

At a White House meeting six days later, General **George C. Marshall**, the new secretary of state, presented the case for American aid to congressional leaders from both parties. When Marshall's soft-spoken approach failed to rally the meeting, his assistant, Dean Acheson, took over. In sweeping terms, Acheson portrayed the future of Greece and Turkey as a test case of American resolve against Soviet aggression. If Greece fell to the Communists, Acheson warned, other nations would follow "like apples in a barrel infected by one rotten one." When he finished, Republican Senator Arthur Vandenberg of Michigan summed up the feeling in the room. "Mr. President," he said, turning to Harry Truman, "if you will say that to Congress and the country, I will support you and I believe most members will do the same."

On March 12, 1947, the president offered his **Truman Doctrine** before a joint session of Congress and a national radio audience. In the current crisis, he began, "every nation must choose between alternative ways of life." One way guaranteed "individual liberty" and "political freedom," the other promoted "terror" and "oppression." In a world of good and evil, Truman declared, it "must be the policy of the United States to support free peoples who are resisting attempted subjugation by armed minorities or by outside pressures." Although some critics worried that the Truman Doctrine would lead the United States into an expensive, open-ended crusade, most Americans supported Truman's position, and Congress allocated $400 million in military aid for Greece and Turkey.

On June 5, 1947, at the Harvard University commencement, Secretary of State Marshall unveiled a far more ambitious proposal known as the European Recovery Plan, or the **Marshall Plan.** The danger seemed clear: without massive economic aid, European governments might collapse, leaving chaos in their wake. "Our policy is not directed against any country or doctrine," Marshall said, "but against hunger, poverty, desperation, and fear."

Several weeks later, seventeen European nations, including the Soviet Union, met in Paris to assess their common needs. But the Soviets walked out after a few sessions, forcing nations like Poland and Hungary to leave as well. The Soviets balked at the idea of divulging critical information about their economy to outsiders. And they surely feared that massive American aid would tie them and the nations they now controlled to a capitalist orbit that might undermine the Communist system.

Truman was not sorry to see them leave. He realized that Congress would not look favorably on the prospect of spending billions of dollars to reconstruct a country that seemed so brutal to its neighbors and so threatening to the United States. With the Russians and their satellites out of the picture, the remaining European nations prepared an agenda for economic recovery that came to $27 billion, a huge sum. After six months of bitter debate, Congress reduced that figure by about half. The largest expenditures went to Britain, Germany, and France.

The Marshall Plan proved a tremendous success. By creating jobs and raising living standards, it restored economic confidence throughout Western Europe and curbed the influence of local Communist Parties in Italy and France. Furthermore, the Marshall Plan increased American trade and investment in Europe, opening vast new markets for U.S. goods. As President Truman noted, "Peace, freedom, and world trade are indivisible."

The rising prosperity in Western Europe was matched by growing repression in the East. Stalin moved first on Hungary, staging a rigged election backed by Russian troops. Next came Czechoslovakia, where the Soviets toppled a coalition government led by Jan Masaryk, a statesman with many admirers in the West. A few days later, Masaryk either jumped or was pushed to his death from an office window in Prague. Against this ominous background, President Truman proposed legislation to streamline the nation's military and diplomatic services. Passed as the National Security Act of 1947, it unified the armed forces under a single Department of Defense, created the National Security Council (NSC) to provide foreign policy information to the president, and established the Central Intelligence Agency (CIA) to coordinate intelligence gathering abroad. While providing the White House with vital information in a number of Cold War crises, the CIA would face criticism in the coming years for illegally spying on American citizens and attempting to overthrow governments viewed as hostile to the United States.

❖ Liberalism in Retreat

In foreign affairs, President Truman could count on strong bipartisan support, but the president had no such luck on domestic issues. For one thing, the widening rift with Russia produced a growing concern about the influence of Communists and their "sympathizers" inside the federal government. For another, the president's attempt to extend the liberal agenda through ambitious social and economic legislation—known as the "Fair Deal"—met with stiff resistance in Congress after 1946. As one Republican leader put it: "We have to break with the corrupting idea that we can legislate prosperity, legislate equality, legislate opportunity."

The Cold War at Home

The Iron Curtain that descended on Europe had a tremendous psychological impact on the United States. Americans were fearful of communism and frustrated by the turn of global events: the defeat of fascism had not made the world a safer place. The result was an erosion of public tolerance for left-wing activity, spurred on by prominent government officials in the administration and Congress. In fact, the American Communist Party was far weaker in 1947 than it had been a decade before, and its numbers were dwindling by the day. Yet that did not stop President Truman from establishing a Federal Loyalty-Security Program for the first time in American history. The congressional assault on domestic subversion was led by the **House Un-American Activities Committee (HUAC).** Formed in the 1930s to investigate Nazi propaganda in the United States, HUAC had been revived after World War II as a watchdog against Communist propaganda. Among its more visible members was a young congressman from Southern California named Richard M. Nixon.

In 1947, HUAC launched a spectacular investigation of the motion picture industry, alleging that "flagrant Communist propaganda films" had been produced during World War II on the specific orders of President Roosevelt. The committee subpoenaed a number of pro-Communist writers and directors, who angrily refused to answer questions about their political beliefs and associations. Known as the "Hollywood Ten," these individuals were cited for contempt, sent to jail, and "blacklisted" from working in the entertainment industry, a practice that became increasingly common in the late 1940s and 1950s. In 1948, a witness named Whittaker Chambers, then a senior editor for *Time* magazine, claimed to have once been part of a "Communist cell" in Washington that included Alger Hiss, a former government official who had advised President Roosevelt in foreign affairs. Hiss denied Chambers's allegations in testimony before HUAC a few days later. When Chambers repeated the charge on a national radio broadcast, Hiss sued him for libel.

Chambers struck back hard, producing dozens of classified State Department documents from the 1930s that, he claimed, Hiss had stolen and passed on to the Russians. Suddenly the ground had shifted to espionage, a more serious charge. The evidence—known as the "Pumpkin Papers" because Chambers had

House Un-American Activities Committee (HUAC) Formed in the 1930s as a watchdog against Nazi propaganda, HUAC was revived after World War II as a watchdog against Communist propaganda.

briefly hidden it in a pumpkin patch on his Maryland farm—included five rolls of microfilm and summaries of confidential reports Hiss had written in longhand or typed on a unique typewriter he once owned. In December 1948, a federal grand jury indicted Hiss for perjuring himself before HUAC. (The ten-year statute of limitations on espionage had just run out.) The first trial ended in a hung jury; the second one sent Hiss to jail. The guilty verdict sent shock waves through the nation.

The Domestic Agenda

The Republican landslide of 1946 appeared to signal the decline of American liberalism. In the following months, the Republican Congress brushed aside President Truman's proposals for national health insurance and federal aid to education, and passed major legislation, known as the Taft-Hartley Act, to curb the power of organized labor. Taft-Hartley generated strong public support, given the crippling strikes of the previous year. In 1947, organized labor was at the height of its influence, with 15 million members nationwide. To counter such power, Taft-Hartley gave the president authority to impose an eighty-day "cooling-off" period to prevent strikes that threatened the national interest. More important, the bill outlawed the closed shop, a device that forced workers to join a union at the time they were hired, and it encouraged the states to pass "right-to-work" laws that made union organizing more difficult. Although Truman strongly opposed Taft-Hartley, the Republican Congress easily overrode his veto.

Truman also confronted the issue of racial discrimination by forming a special task force on civil rights. Its final report included a series of bold recommendations, such as the desegregation of the armed forces and the creation of a special division within the Justice Department devoted solely to civil rights. Truman endorsed these recommendations. Addressing the NAACP's national convention in 1947—the first American president to do so—Truman spoke out strongly against prejudice and hate. "The only limit to a [person's] achievement," he declared, "should be his ability, his industry, and his character."

Breaking the Color Line

Truman's statement seemed particularly appropriate in 1947. On April 15, Major League baseball broke its long-standing "color line" in an opening day game at Brooklyn's Ebbets Field. "History was made here Tuesday afternoon," reported the *Pittsburgh Courier*, an African American newspaper, "when smiling **Jackie Robinson** trotted out on the green-swept diamond with the rest of his Dodger teammates."

Baseball had been all-white for generations. Blacks played in the so-called Negro Leagues. Poorly paid, they often barnstormed from town to town, taking on local teams in exhibitions that combined great baseball with crowd-pleasing entertainment. The vast majority of Major League owners opposed integration, but Branch Rickey of the Brooklyn Dodgers was an exception. Mixing deep religious values with shrewd business sense, Rickey insisted that integration was good for America, for baseball, and for the Dodgers. "The Negroes will make us winners for years to come," he said, "and for that I will happily bear being called a bleeding heart and a do-gooder and all that humanitarian rot."

To break the color line, Rickey selected Jack Roosevelt Robinson, twenty-seven years old, a man of tremendous talent and pride. The son of sharecroppers and the grandson of slaves, Robinson moved from rural Georgia to Pasadena, California, where his athletic skills earned him a scholarship to UCLA. Drafted into the army during World War II, Robinson fought bigotry at every turn. As a second lieutenant in a segregated tank unit, he was court-martialed for insubordination, but acquitted,

Doing History Online

Jackie Robinson and the Negro Leagues, 1948

Go to the CourseMate website for this chapter and link to Primary Sources. Read the documents online. How does the document on *The Decline of the Negro Leagues, 1948,* relate to the others in this unit?

www.cengagebrain.com

Robinson, Jackie (1919–1972)
First African American player in the Major Leagues in the twentieth century, he was a second baseman for the Brooklyn Dodgers, had a lifetime batting average of .311, and was inducted into the Baseball Hall of Fame in 1962.

after refusing to move to the rear of an army bus. Honorably discharged in 1944, he joined the Kansas City Monarchs, a Negro League team, as a shortstop at four hundred dollars a month.

Rickey met secretly with Robinson in the fall of 1945. Talent was not an issue; what most concerned Rickey was Robinson's temper. How would he react to racial slurs, pitches thrown at his head, runners sliding into him spikes first? For three hours, Rickey grilled Robinson about the need for absolute self-control. "Do you want a ballplayer who's afraid to fight back?" Robinson asked. "I want a ballplayer with enough guts not to fight back," Rickey answered. "You will symbolize a crucial cause. One incident, just one incident, can set it back twenty years." "Mr. Rickey," Robinson replied, "if you want to take this gamble, I will promise you there will be no incident." Robinson kept his word, enduring segregated hotels, racial insults, even death threats against his family. His pioneering effort caught the public's fancy, and huge crowds followed him everywhere. By season's end, Robinson had led the Dodgers to the National League pennant and won designation as Rookie of the Year.

But the struggle was far from over. It would be another decade before all Major League teams accepted integration. Yet the efforts begun by Branch Rickey and Jackie Robinson helped change the face of America by democratizing its "National Game." Looking back on the events of 1947, sportswriter Jimmy Cannon recalled a side of Robinson that captured both his courage and his pain. He was, said Cannon, "the loneliest man I have ever seen in sports."

Jackie Robinson. Breaking the color line in Major League baseball in 1947, Jackie Robinson led the Brooklyn Dodgers to six pennants and a World Series victory in his brilliant career.

(AP/Wide World Photos)

Man of the People

As the 1948 presidential election approached, Harry Truman seemed a beaten man. His relations with Congress were stormy and unproductive, especially in domestic affairs. The press, remembering the elegant and fatherly FDR, portrayed Truman as too small for the job. In December 1947, a band of left-wing Democrats formed the Progressive Citizens of America, with an eye toward the coming election. Their leader was Henry Wallace, the former vice president and secretary of commerce whom Truman had fired for criticizing the administration's firm stance toward the Soviet Union. Though Wallace had no hope of winning the presidential election in 1948, his Progressive Party seemed likely to split the Democratic vote.

Some urged Truman not to run. A number of Democratic leaders suggested other presidential candidates, including General Dwight D. Eisenhower. The *New Republic*, a favorite of liberals, ran the front cover headline: "Harry Truman Should Quit." The Democrats convened in Philadelphia, where the heat was oppressive and tempers grew short. When word reached the convention that Eisenhower was unavailable, the delegates nominated Truman for president and Alben Barkley, the popular but aging Senate majority leader from Kentucky, for vice president. Barkley had strong ties to the South. Yet even he could not prevent the convention from dividing along sectional lines when northern liberals, led by Mayor Hubert Humphrey of Minneapolis, demanded the endorsement of Truman's civil rights initiatives. "The time has arrived," said Humphrey, "for the Democratic party to get out of the shadow of states' rights, and walk forthrightly into the bright sunshine of human rights."

The passage of a strong civil rights plank led many southern Democrats to walk out of the convention. Two days later, waving Confederate flags and denouncing Harry Truman, they formed the States' Rights (Dixiecrat) party at a gathering in Birmingham, Alabama. The Dixiecrats chose governors Strom

Thurmond of South Carolina and Fielding Wright of Mississippi to be, respectively, their presidential and vice-presidential candidates. Their platform demanded "complete segregation of the races."

Divided into three camps, the Democratic Party appeared hopelessly overmatched. Not only did President Truman face Henry Wallace on his left and Strom Thurmond on his right, but the national Republican ticket of New York Governor Thomas E. Dewey for president and California Governor Earl Warren for vice president was the strongest in years. Truman's campaign strategy was to portray himself as a common people's president, protecting the voters and their hard-earned New Deal benefits from a heartless Republican assault.

Truman also emphasized his international leadership. He showed support for the new state of Israel by offering it political recognition and economic assistance. He issued his promised executive order desegregating the armed forces. And he forcefully confronted Stalin in a showdown over Germany and Berlin. In June 1948, Russian troops blockaded West Berlin to protest the merging of the French, British, and American occupation zones into the unified nation of West Germany. The city lay deep inside Soviet-controlled territory. Truman ruled out force to break the blockade because American troops were greatly outnumbered. Instead, he and his advisers decided to supply West Berlin from the air. In the coming months, American and British pilots made close to three hundred thousand flights into the city, delivering food, fuel, and medical supplies. By the time the Russians called off their blockade, Berlin had become the symbol of resistance to Communist oppression.

Truman could see his fortunes rising as the 1948 campaign progressed. Crisscrossing the nation by train, he drew huge, friendly crowds at each whistle stop. To shouts of "Give 'em hell, Harry!" he ripped into the "do-nothing" Republican Congress and its "plans" to dismantle Franklin Roosevelt's work. "This is a crusade of the people against the special interests," Truman repeated, "and if you back me up we're going to win."

On election eve, the staunchly Republican *Chicago Tribune* carried the now-famous mistaken headline: "Dewey Defeats Truman." In fact, Truman won the closest presidential contest since 1916, collecting 24.1 million votes to Dewey's 22 million, and 303 electoral votes to Dewey's 189 (see Map 25.1). Strom

MAP 25.1

The Election of 1948

The presidential election of 1948 is considered one of the greatest upsets in American political history. Because there were four significant candidates, two running on third-party tickets, the victor, President Truman, captured a majority of the electoral votes without actually winning a majority of the popular vote.

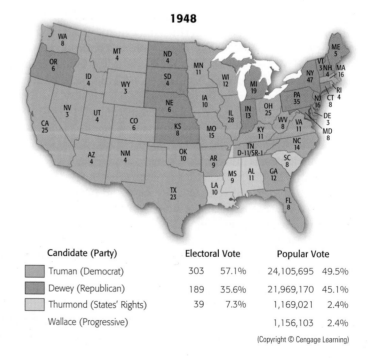

1948

Candidate (Party)	Electoral Vote		Popular Vote	
Truman (Democrat)	303	57.1%	24,105,695	49.5%
Dewey (Republican)	189	35.6%	21,969,170	45.1%
Thurmond (States' Rights)	39	7.3%	1,169,021	2.4%
Wallace (Progressive)			1,156,103	2.4%

(Copyright © Cengage Learning)

Thurmond captured 1.1 million votes and four southern states under the Dixie-crat banner, and Henry Wallace won no states and barely a million votes. Ironically, the three-way Democratic split appeared to help Truman: the people chose his frank, common appeal over Dewey's stiff, evasive demeanor. The New Deal coalition had held for another election.

❖ The Cold War Intensifies, 1949–1953

Truman had little time to savor his victory. In the summer of 1949, an American spy plane returned from a flight over the Soviet Union with evidence of radioactive activity: the Russians had exploded an atomic device. Combined with alarming new developments in Asia, the loss of America's atomic monopoly served to heighten global tensions in the coming months while dramatically increasing the fear of communism at home.

The Fall of China and the Creation of NATO, 1949

President Truman broke the news in a one-sentence statement to the press: "We have evidence an atomic explosion occurred in the USSR." Ever since Hiroshima, Americans had been taught to depend on nuclear superiority in the Cold War and to believe that Russia, a supposedly backward nation, could not possibly develop an atomic bomb before the mid-1950s, if ever. That could mean only one thing: espionage. The Soviets, it appeared, had stolen the biggest secret of all.

The news from China was equally grim. Following World War II, Chiang Kai-shek and his Nationalist (Kuomintang) forces had renewed their offensive against the Communist forces of Mao Tse-tung. Chiang counted heavily on American support. But the president and his advisers were far less interested in Asia than they were in Western Europe. They were not about to be trapped into an open-ended commitment in the Far East. From 1946 to 1949, the United States gave Chiang's government about $2 billion in military aid.

As civil war raged in China, Chiang's forces met defeat after defeat. Much of the American weaponry that fleeing Nationalist troops discarded ended up in Communist hands. In August 1949, the State Department issued a 1,054-page "White Paper on China," conceding that the world's largest country was about to fall to the Communists. "The unfortunate but inescapable fact," said Dean Acheson, the new secretary of state, "is that the ominous result of the civil war in China was beyond [our] control." Americans were bewildered. How well did "containment" really work when more than 600 million people were "lost" to communism?

Determined to prevent further Communist expansion elsewhere, the United States joined with eleven West European nations to create the **North Atlantic Treaty Organization (NATO)** in 1949. The treaty was extremely significant; in promising to support fellow NATO members in the event of Soviet attack, it formally ended America's long tradition of avoiding entangling alliances abroad. A year later, Secretary of State Acheson and Paul Nitze, his deputy, produced a secret document known as National Security Council Paper 68 (NSC 68), which advocated the use of military force to stop Communist aggression throughout the world. According to NSC 68, the United States should act in concert with other nations wherever possible, but alone if need be. The document called for an unprecedented peacetime increase in military spending—from $13 billion to $50 billion per year—and for the construction of a huge new "thermonuclear device," the hydrogen bomb. Though Truman never showed this document to Congress, it shaped America's defense policy in the coming years profoundly.

North Atlantic Treaty Organization (NATO) Military alliance, founded in 1949, between the United States and eleven other nations to protect Western Europe from invasion. It was a leading force in the Cold War struggle to contain Soviet aggression, expanding to include new nations over the years.

War in Korea, 1950–1953

On June 25, 1950, troops from Communist North Korea invaded anti-Communist South Korea with infantry, armor, and artillery in a massive land assault (see Map 25.2). Korea had been arbitrarily divided by Russian and American troops at the end of World War II. In 1948, an election to unify Korea had been cancelled when the Soviets refused to allow United Nations (UN) observers north of the dividing line at the thirty-eighth parallel. A stalemate thus developed, with Kim Il Sung, the Communist dictator of North Korea, and Syngman Rhee, the anti-Communist dictator of South Korea, making daily threats to "liberate" each other's land.

The North Korean attack put great pressure on President Truman. His administration had treated the Rhee government with indifference, removing American combat troops from Korea in 1949 and implying that Korea itself was not vital to the free world's security. Yet here was a classic case of aggression, Truman believed. He also feared looking "soft" on communism. Thus, Truman moved quickly, proposing a UN resolution that offered "such assistance to South Korea as may be necessary to repel armed attack." (The Russians, boycotting the Security Council to protest the UN's refusal to seat Communist China, were unable to cast a paralyzing veto.) A week later, without consulting Congress, Truman dispatched ground troops to South Korea.

Following two months of backward movement, UN forces under the command of General Douglas MacArthur took the offensive. In September 1950, MacArthur outflanked the enemy with a brilliant amphibious landing at Inchon, on South Korea's west coast. By October, UN troops had crossed the thirty-eighth parallel in pursuit of the routed North Korean army. As the public listened in amazement, MacArthur spoke of having his men "home before Christmas."

There were ominous signs, however. First, by sending troops into North Korea, President Truman and the United Nations had gone beyond their original mandate to defend South Korea from outside aggression. Second, General MacArthur appeared oblivious to the possibility that Communist China might enter the war. As UN forces drove north, they captured scores of Chinese Communist troops near the Yalu River that divided North Korea and Manchuria. On November 5, the Chinese attacked—three hundred thousand strong—pushing MacArthur's startled army back toward the thirty-eighth parallel. In the following weeks, American army and marine units fought their way through mountain blizzards and a wall of Chinese infantry to form a defense line just south of the thirty-eighth parallel. (See Map 25.3.) Although disaster had been averted, the nation was shocked by what *Time* magazine described as "the worst military setback the United States has ever suffered."

By March 1951, the Communist offensive had stalled. UN forces pushed ahead to the thirty-eighth parallel, where the two sides faced each other in a bloody standoff. Not surprisingly, General MacArthur called for an escalation of the war. Believing in the concept of total victory, MacArthur recommended a naval blockade of China's coast, massive bombing of its factories and power plants, and an invasion of the Chinese mainland by the forces of Chiang Kai-shek.

(© Bettmann/CORBIS)

Soldiers in Korea. Fighting under command of the United Nations, American soldiers fought courageously to defend South Korea from an invasion by Communist North Korea in 1950.

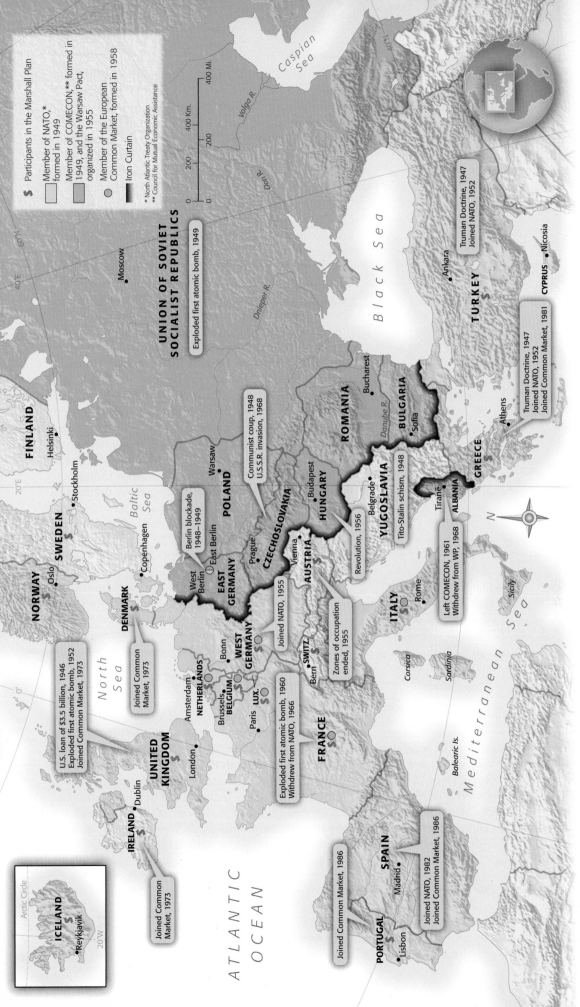

MAP 25.2

Cold War Europe, 1945–1989

The Cold War in Europe, lasting almost fifty years, marked one of the great ideological struggles of the twentieth century. By the time communism collapsed, the nations of Western Europe, bolstered by American economic and military support, had risen from the ashes of World War II to become prosperous political democracies, unlike their Soviet-controlled neighbors behind the Iron Curtain.

(Copyright © Cengage Learning)

Participants in the Marshall Plan

Member of NATO,* formed in 1949

Member of COMECON,** formed in 1949, and the Warsaw Pact, organized in 1955

Member of the European Common Market, formed in 1958

Iron Curtain

* North Atlantic Treaty Organization
** Council for Mutual Economic Assistance

UNION OF SOVIET SOCIALIST REPUBLICS

Exploded first atomic bomb, 1949

Moscow

FINLAND
Helsinki

NORWAY
Oslo

SWEDEN
Stockholm

Copenhagen

DENMARK

POLAND
Warsaw

Berlin blockade, 1948–1949

East Berlin

West Berlin

EAST GERMANY

Prague

CZECHOSLOVAKIA

Communist coup, 1948
U.S.S.R. invasion, 1968

Budapest

HUNGARY

Vienna

AUSTRIA

Zones of occupation ended, 1955

ROMANIA
Bucharest

Danube R.

BULGARIA
Sofia

Belgrade

YUGOSLAVIA

Tito-Stalin schism, 1948

Revolution, 1956

Tiranë

ALBANIA

Left COMECON, 1961
Withdrew from WP, 1968

GREECE

Truman Doctrine, 1947
Joined NATO, 1952

Athens

TURKEY

Ankara

Truman Doctrine, 1947
Joined NATO, 1952
Joined Common Market, 1981

CYPRUS • Nicosia

Black Sea

Caspian Sea

Volga R.

Don R.

Dnieper R.

NETHERLANDS
Amsterdam

Bonn

WEST GERMANY

Joined NATO, 1955

Brussels

BELGIUM

LUX.

Paris

SWITZ.

Bern

ITALY
Rome

Joined Common Market, 1973

U.S. loan of $3.5 billion, 1946
Exploded first atomic bomb, 1952
Joined Common Market, 1973

UNITED KINGDOM

London

IRELAND
Dublin

Exploded first atomic bomb, 1960
Withdrew from NATO, 1966

FRANCE

Joined Common Market, 1986

SPAIN
Madrid

Joined NATO, 1982
Joined Common Market, 1986

PORTUGAL
Lisbon

Joined Common Market, 1986

Corsica

Sardinia

Balearic Is.

Sicily

Mediterranean Sea

ATLANTIC OCEAN

North Sea

Baltic Sea

ICELAND
Reykjavik

Joined Common Market, 1973

Arctic Circle

20W

20E

40E

40N

60N

0
200
400 Km.

0
200
400 Mi.

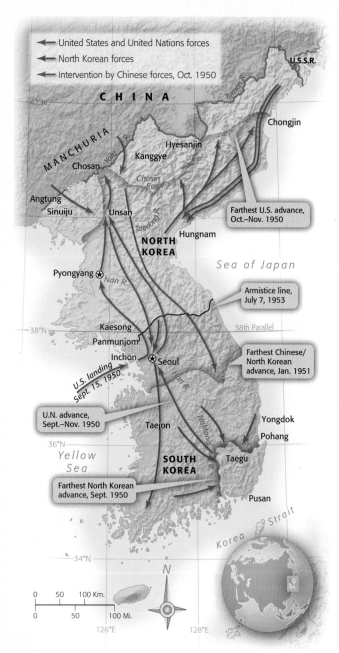

MAP 25.3

The Korean War
This map shows the main offensive thrusts: the North Korean attack into South Korea in June 1950; the Inchon Landing of September 15, 1950; the UN offensive in fall 1950; and the Communist Chinese counteroffensive beginning in November 1950. The war ended in stalemate, with the final truce line almost identical to the previous division of Korea into North and South at the thirty-eighth parallel.

The president saw things differently. Any attempt to widen the war, he realized, would alarm other UN participants and perhaps bring Russia into the conflict. The Soviets might send troops to the Asian front or put pressure on Western Europe. Furthermore, Russia's involvement raised the threat of nuclear attack. MacArthur's strategy was the very opposite of the one proposed by President Truman and the Joint Chiefs of Staff. Despite repeated warnings from the president, MacArthur refused to keep his views to himself. The final blowup came in April 1951 when Republicans in Congress released a letter that MacArthur had sent them from the battlefield that criticized Truman's refusal to meet force "with maximum counterforce," and ended with the oft-quoted phrase: "There is no substitute for victory." Furious at such insubordination, the president relieved MacArthur of his command.

MacArthur returned to the United States a genuine folk hero, a man who symbolized old military values in a world complicated by the horrors of nuclear war. Cities across the nation burned President Truman in effigy. Letters to the White House ran twenty-one to one against MacArthur's firing. On Capitol Hill, angry representatives placed some of the telegrams they received into the *Congressional Record:* "Impeach the Imbecile" and "We Wish to Protest the Latest Outrage by the Pig in the White House." Meanwhile, the Korean War escalated Americans' fear of communism. Air raid drills became the order of the day, with schoolchildren taught to dive under their desks and shield their eyes against atomic blasts. In New York City, school officials distributed metal "dog tags." "If a bomb gets me in the street," a first-grader explained, "people will know what my name is."

❖ McCarthyism and the Election of 1952

On a bleak February evening in 1950, a little-known politician delivered a speech about "Communist subversion" in the federal government to a Republican women's club in Wheeling, West Virginia. "I have here in my hand," Senator **Joseph R. McCarthy** of Wisconsin told his audience, "a list of 205 Communists that were made known to the secretary of state and who are still working and shaping the policy of the State Department." The message was clear: America, the strongest nation on earth, was losing the Cold War to the evil forces of communism because the U.S. government was filled with "traitors" like **Alger Hiss** who wanted the Communists to win.

The Rise of Joe McCarthy

Wisconsin's junior senator was an erratic politician, known for his reckless ambition and raucous behavior. He knew little about Communists in government or anywhere else. But the newspapers printed his charges, and the public was aroused. McCarthy had struck a nerve in the country, rubbed raw by Soviet aggression in Europe, the Communist victory in China, the Alger Hiss case, and the news of the Russian atomic bomb. As Americans searched for explanations, McCarthy provided the simplest answer of all. The real enemy was not in Moscow, he thundered, but rather in Washington, D.C.

McCarthy's charges of treason in high places made him an instant celebrity. Prominent Republicans, sensing the political benefits of the "Communist issue," rallied to his side. Soon, McCarthy's attacks grew bolder. As the 1952 presidential campaign approached, he called George C. Marshall a traitor, mocked Dean Acheson as the "Red Dean of fashion," and described President Truman as a drunkard, adding, "the son-of-a-bitch ought to be impeached." Yet party colleagues continued to encourage McCarthy, viewing him as the man who could turn public anxiety and distrust into Republican votes. (See *Doing History: Senator Smith Confronts Senator McCarthy*.)

"I Like Ike"

By 1952, Harry Truman's public approval rating had dropped to 23 percent—the lowest ever recorded by an American president. The *New Republic* called him "a spent force politically" and urged him to withdraw from the coming presidential campaign. In March, Truman announced he would not seek reelection.

The most impressive Democratic candidate, Governor Adlai Stevenson of Illinois, had earned a reputation as a liberal reformer. Eloquent and witty, he appealed to both party regulars and the liberal intelligentsia, much as FDR had. The Democrats nominated him for president on the third convention ballot. Senator John Sparkman of Alabama, a Fair Dealer and a segregationist, was given the vice-presidential nod.

The battle for the Republican presidential nomination was in many ways a battle for control of the Republican Party. The moderate wing, represented by Governor Thomas Dewey of New York and Senator Henry Cabot Lodge, Jr., of Massachusetts, was committed to internationalism and to many New Deal reforms. The conservative wing, led by Senator Robert Taft of Ohio, was suspicious of the New Deal and wary of America's expanding global commitments, especially the defense and reconstruction of Europe. Senator Taft, the son of former President and Chief Justice William Howard Taft, had earned the respect of his colleagues and the plaudits of Washington reporters, who voted him "best senator" in 1949.

Only one man stood between Taft and the Republican nomination: General Dwight D. Eisenhower. In 1948, the leaders of both major political parties had begged him, unsuccessfully, to enter their presidential primaries. Eisenhower, sixty-one years old, was raised in Abilene, Kansas, and won an appointment to the U.S. Military Academy at West Point in 1911. After graduating, Eisenhower married Mamie Dowd, the daughter of a Denver businessman, and began his swift climb through the ranks of the military. In the 1930s, he served as chief aide to General Douglas MacArthur, recalling: "Oh, yes, I studied dramatics under him for seven years." In 1941, he moved to the War Department and helped plan the D-Day invasion of France. His work was so outstanding that President Roosevelt named him Commanding General, European Theater of Operations, a promotion that jumped him over hundreds of officers with greater seniority.

It turned out to be one of the best decisions of World War II. Eisenhower commanded history's most successful coalition force—American, British, French, Polish, and Canadian troops—with courage, diplomacy, and skill. He was brilliant at handling people and reconciling the most diverse points of view. In the following years, Eisenhower served as army chief of staff, president of Columbia University, and commander of NATO forces.

McCarthy, Joseph R. (1908–1957) U.S. senator from Wisconsin (1947–1957), he presided over the permanent subcommittee on investigations and held public hearings in which he accused army officials, members of the media, and public figures of being Communists. These charges were never proved, and he was censured by the Senate in 1954.

Hiss, Alger (1904–1996) State Department official accused of espionage at the height of the Cold War, he was convicted of perjury in 1950 in a controversial case.

Doing History Online

Undercover in the Communist Party, 1951

Go to the CourseMate website for this chapter and link to Primary Sources. Read the article online along with the section on McCarthyism in the textbook. Why did the Communist Party target the steel industry, as Mary Markward said it did in her congressional testimony?

 www.cengagebrain.com

Doing History   Senator Smith Confronts Senator McCarthy

On February 9, 1950, Republican Senator Joseph R. McCarthy gave one of the most famous—and inflammatory—speeches in modern American political history. In it, he charged that the Truman administration was riddled with traitors who had helped to deliver much of the world to the Communist enemy. The speech turned McCarthy into a national celebrity, seen by millions as a truthful patriot, and by millions of others as a dangerous fraud.

The reason why we find ourselves in a position of impotency is not because [the] enemy has sent men to invade our shores . . . but rather because of those . . . who have had all the benefits that the wealthiest nation on earth has to offer—the finest homes, the finest college education, and the finest jobs in government we can give.

This is glaringly true in the State Department. There the bright young men who were born with silver spoons in their mouths are the ones who have been the worst. . . . While I cannot take the time to name [them], I have in my hand 205 cases of individuals who would appear to be either card carrying members or certainly loyal to the Communist Party, but who nevertheless are still helping to shape our foreign policy.

One thing to remember in discussing the Communists in our government is that we are not dealing with spies who get thirty pieces of silver to steal the blueprints of a new weapon. We are dealing with a far more sinister type of activity because it permits the enemy to guide and shape our policy.

Margaret Chase Smith of Maine, the Senate's only woman, became the first Republican to speak out against Senator Joseph McCarthy's controversial crusade against domestic subversion.

The Republican convention nominated Eisenhower on the first ballot. Most delegates did not believe he would make a better president than Taft, simply a better candidate. Eisenhower defused the bitter feelings of conservatives by selecting Richard Nixon to be his running mate and accepting a party platform that accused the Democrats of shielding traitors in high places and bungling the Korean War. On the campaign trail, General Eisenhower talked about leadership and morality. At every stop, he introduced Mamie, praised America, bemoaned the "mess in Washington," and promised to clean it up.

The Republican ticket faced a challenge on September 28, 1952, when the *New York Post*, a pro-Democratic newspaper, broke the biggest story of the campaign: "Secret Rich Men's Fund Keeps Nixon in Style Far Beyond His Salary." The Nixon fund of eighteen thousand dollars had, however, never been a secret.

McCarthy's speech caused a furor in the U.S. Senate, which began an immediate investigation of his charges. For months afterward, McCarthy's Republican colleagues either supported him or remained silent. But on June 1, 1950, Senator Margaret Chase Smith of Maine, the Senate's lone woman, spoke out against him without actually mentioning him by name. She called her speech a "Declaration of Conscience."

I speak as a Republican. I speak as a woman. I speak as a United States Senator. I speak as an American.

The United States Senate has long enjoyed worldwide respect as the greatest deliberative body in the world. But recently that deliberative character has too often been debased to the level of a forum of hate and character assassination sheltered by the shield of congressional immunity. . . .

I think it is high time for the United States Senate and its members to do some soul-searching—for us to weigh our consciences—on the manner in which we are performing our duty to the people of America—on the manner in which we are using or abusing our individual powers and privileges. . . .

Those of us who shout the loudest about Americanism in making character assassinations are all to frequently those who, by our own words and acts, ignore some of the basic principles of Americanism:

The right to criticize;
The right to hold unpopular beliefs;
The right to protest;
The right of independent thought. . . .

The American people are sick and tired of being afraid to speak their minds lest they be politically smeared as "Communists" or "Fascists" by their opponents. Freedom of speech is not what it used to be in America. It has been so abused by some that it is not exercised by others.

Source: *Congressional Record*, February 12, 1950 (McCarthy); June 1, 1950 (Smith).

QUESTIONS for REFLECTION

1. What events were responsible for Senator McCarthy's rise from obscurity?

2. What made McCarthy's charges seem believable to so many Americans?

3. Why did Senator Smith call her speech a "Declaration of Conscience"? What point was she trying to make?

Donated by a group of California supporters, it had been used for routine political expenses and it was similar to the funds of other politicians. Nixon responded by blaming the "Reds" for his troubles. "The Communists, the left-wingers, have been fighting me with every smear," he declared.

The campaign ground to a halt. On September 23, Nixon went on national television to explain his side of the story. To an audience estimated at 55 million, he spoke about his boyhood, his family, his war record, his finances, and his admiration for General Eisenhower. He explained how the fund worked, asked the American people to support him, and then described the one gift he would never return. It was, said Nixon, "a little cocker spaniel dog and our little girl named it Checkers. And you know the kids love that dog and I just want to say that we're going to keep it." The reaction was volcanic. More than 2 million phone calls and telegrams poured into Republican offices across the country. They were followed by millions of letters, running 300 to 1 in Nixon's favor. The "Checkers speech" saved Nixon's career.

It also demonstrated the emerging power of television in national affairs. In the campaign's final weeks, the Republican Party ran dozens of twenty-second TV

"We Like Ike." America liked Ike, who won a smashing victory at the polls in 1952, ending twenty years of Democratic party rule.

spots for Eisenhower, who used the ads to soothe voter anxiety about his views on popular New Deal welfare programs. "Social security, housing, workmen's compensation, unemployment insurance—these are things that must be kept above politics and campaigns," he said. "They are rights, not issues." The general also vowed that if elected, he would visit Korea "to help serve the American people in the cause of peace." On November 4, Eisenhower overwhelmed Stevenson—33.9 million votes to 27.3 million and 442 electoral votes to 89. Eisenhower became the first Republican in decades to crack the Solid South; he also did well in cities, where ethnic voters, concerned about the rise of communism in Europe, deserted the Democrats in droves. Nearly 25 percent of Eisenhower's total came from men and women who had supported Harry Truman in 1948.

Some observers spoke of a new Republican era, but this was not the case. Almost everywhere, Eisenhower ran well ahead of his ticket. Although the Republicans managed to gain a slim majority in Congress, they did so by riding the general's coattails to victory. Following two decades of economic depression, world war, and cold war, Americans wanted a leader who would steer a moderate course in domestic and foreign affairs: a leader who would heal partisan wounds without turning back the clock and who would end the conflict in Korea without widening it or compromising the nation's honor. In 1952, Dwight D. Eisenhower seemed to be the one.

CHAPTER REVIEW, 1946–1953

SUMMARY

- The United States moved from a wartime to a peacetime economy.

- Returning veterans received generous education and housing benefits under the GI Bill.

- A tremendous surge in marriage rates and birthrates spurred a rush to suburbia.

- Soviet–American relations deteriorated as the Iron Curtain descended over Eastern Europe.

- A symbolic step toward racial justice occurred with the integration of Major League baseball in 1947.

- The Alger Hiss case heightened fears of Soviet espionage in the United States.

- Harry Truman's surprise reelection in 1948 kept the New Deal coalition intact.

- The Korean War raised fears of a widening conflict with Communist China and a nuclear confrontation with the Soviet Union.

- Dwight Eisenhower's victory in 1952 ended two decades of Democratic control of the executive branch.

IDENTIFICATIONS

baby boom

Levittown

Iron Curtain

containment

George C. Marshall

Truman Doctrine

Marshall Plan

House Un-American Activities Committee (HUAC)

Jackie Robinson

North Atlantic Treaty Organization (NATO)

Joseph R. McCarthy

Alger Hiss

MAKING CONNECTIONS: LOOKING AHEAD ▮▮▮➡

Chapter 26 examines the United States in the 1950s, a time of continued economic prosperity and material comfort, on the one hand, and a time of enduring Cold War tensions and momentous racial stirrings, on the other.

1. What were the major problems Dwight Eisenhower would face in assuming the presidency?

2. Was it possible that a new administration in Washington would be better able to deal with international problems than the old one, especially problems relating to the Cold War?

3. Would the prosperity of the early postwar era last into the future, and would it expand to include the poorest groups in society?

RECOMMENDED READINGS

Ackerman, Marsha. *Cool Comfort* (2002). Describes how air-conditioning changed the way middle-class Americans lived and worked in this new age of affluence.

Bennett, Michael. *When Dreams Came True* (1996). Studies the impact of the GI Bill on the making of modern America.

Boyer, Paul. *By the Bomb's Early Light* (1985). Considers the impact of atomic weaponry on American society in the early Cold War years.

Grossman, Andrew. *Neither Dead Nor Red* (2001). Focuses on the often bizarre plans of American officials to fight and survive a nuclear war.

Hamby, Alonso. *Man of the People* (1995). Examines the personal life and political career of President Harry Truman.

Jackson, Kenneth. *Crabgrass Frontier* (1985). Analyzes the suburbanization of America, especially after World War II.

Spock, Dr. Benjamin. *Common Sense Book of Baby and Child Care* (1946). The book that has had a lasting impact on child rearing and gender roles in the United States.

Tanenhaus, Sam. *Whittaker Chambers* (1997). Tells the absorbing story of the man who helped ignite the nation's anti-Communist crusade in the late 1940s.

Tygiel, Jules. *Baseball's Great Experiment* (1983). A fine account of Jackie Robinson and the integration of Major League baseball.

CourseMate Go to the CourseMate website at www.cengagebrain.com for additional study tools and review materials for this chapter.

26

The Eisenhower Years

1953–1960

A New Direction, 1953

Modern Republicanism
A Truce in Korea

The Cold War at Home and Abroad, 1953–1954

The Hunt for "Subversives"
Brinksmanship and Covert Action

The Civil Rights Movement, 1954–1955

Brown v. Board of Education

Doing History: The Long Reach of *Brown*

The Montgomery Bus Boycott

American Families at Mid-Century

The Golden Age of Television
A New Kind of Music
The Beat Generation

Crises and Celebration, 1955–1956

Conquering Polio
Interstate Highways
Hungary and Suez

A Second Term, 1957–1960

Confrontation at Little Rock
Sputnik and Its Aftermath
End of an Era
The Election of 1960

MAKING CONNECTIONS

◄▬▬ LOOKING BACK

Chapter 25 looked at the United States in the post–World War II years, following one of the defining moments in its history. Key points were the baby boom, the growth of suburbia, and the beginning of the Cold War. Before starting Chapter 26, you should be able to answer the following questions:

1. What accounted for the worsening of relations between the Soviet Union and the United States?

2. Why did the wartime prosperity continue, and greatly increase, following World War II? What factors accounted for this?

3. Why did Harry Truman defeat Thomas Dewey for the presidency in 1948? Why did so many pundits think Dewey would win?

4. What impact did the case of Alger Hiss have on the rise of Senator Joseph R. McCarthy? What else was responsible for the popular support that McCarthy received?

The United States at the middle of the twentieth century was far different from the nation we live in today. The **Cold War** was at its height, U.S. soldiers were dying in Korea, and communism seemed a formidable foe. The American population of 153 million contained a small and declining number of people who were foreign born, the result of strict immigration quotas installed in the 1920s. Most blacks still lived in the South, where racial segregation was the law. Blue-collar workers outnumbered white-collar workers, and labor unions, led by charismatic figures like John L. Lewis and Walter Reuther, were at the height of their power. There were no supermarkets or shopping malls, no motel chains or ballpoint pens. Television was just beginning, rock music still a few years away.

Marriage rates were at an all-time high, and divorce rates kept declining. In 1954, *McCall's* magazine used the term *togetherness* to describe American family life, with shared activities such as Little League, car rides, and backyard barbecues. Though more women worked outside the home in 1950 than in 1944, the height of World War II, in the growing cult of motherhood, fulfillment meant meeting the needs of others. Feminism was described in psychology books as a "deep illness," entirely out of place.

America at mid-twentieth century saw an acceleration of postwar trends. As 40 million people moved to the suburbs, the large cities declined in population, political power, and quality of life. Racial lines remained rigid, with census data showing the suburbs to be more affluent than the cities they surrounded—and 98 percent white (see Figure 26.1). Automobile sales skyrocketed, creating whole new industries to service American travelers. Inventions poured forth, from the computer to the polio vaccine. And a new president was elected to guide the country through these anxious, demanding times.

Cold War State of intense geopolitical rivalry, such as existed between the United States and the Soviet Union following World War II, that stopped short of full-scale military conflict.

❖ A New Direction, 1953

Dwight Eisenhower entered the White House on a wave of good feeling. His lack of political experience appeared to be an asset after the turmoil of the Truman years. Americans trusted Eisenhower's judgment and admired his character. They believed that his enormous skills as a military leader would serve him equally well as president of the United States.

Modern Republicanism

Yet few Americans knew where Eisenhower stood on important domestic or international issues. His presidential campaign in 1952 had been intentionally vague. He described himself as a moderate, using the term "modern Republicanism" to define his political approach.

Eisenhower filled his cabinet with prominent business leaders. For secretary of defense, he chose Charles E. ("Engine Charlie") Wilson, former president of General Motors; for secretary of the treasury, Eisenhower selected George Humphrey, a fiscal conservative who believed in smaller government and less

Urban, Suburban, and Rural Americans 1940–1960

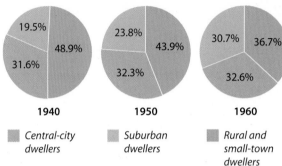

| Central-city dwellers | Suburban dwellers | Rural and small-town dwellers |

FIGURE 26.1

Urban, Suburban, and Rural Americans, 1940–1960
These charts point to a number of important changes. First is the steady loss of population in small-town America. Second is the stagnation of the inner cities, reflecting both a loss of population in the older northern and midwestern cities and a growth in the Sunbelt cities of the South and West. Third is the surge of population in the suburbs, which continues to this day.

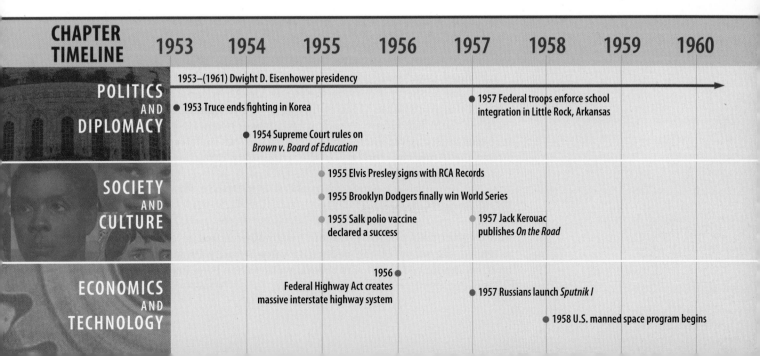

federal spending. Eisenhower had no intention of dismantling popular New Deal programs such as Social Security or unemployment insurance, yet wherever possible, he worked to balance the budget, trim government expenditures, and stimulate private enterprise. "I'm conservative when it comes to money," Eisenhower claimed, but "liberal when it comes to human beings."

In his first year as president, federal spending and federal income taxes were both cut by 10 percent. Eisenhower also opposed expansion of such popular but expensive federal programs as price supports for farmers and cheap public power from government dams and electric plants. In perhaps his most controversial early move, the president strongly supported passage of the Tidelands Oil Act, which transferred coastal oil land worth at least $40 billion from the federal government to the states. Critics, fearing the exploitation of these vital reserves by a few giant corporations, described "Tidelands" as the "most unjustified giveaway program" of the modern era.

A Truce in Korea

One member of Eisenhower's cabinet, Secretary of State John Foster Dulles, stood above the rest. The son of a minister and grandson of a former secretary of state, Dulles trained from his earliest days to serve God and country. Most observers found him arrogant, stubborn, and sour. Yet Eisenhower respected his secretary as a tough, knowledgeable adviser who willingly took the heat for actions the president himself had formulated.

The president's first priority in foreign affairs was to end the Korean conflict. Though willing to accept the same terms that Truman had proposed—two Koreas, North and South, divided at the thirty-eighth parallel—Eisenhower demanded a prompt resolution. To speed this process, Dulles apparently warned the Communist Chinese that the United States would not rule out the use of atomic weapons if the Korean stalemate dragged on. Huge Communist battlefield losses, coupled with the sudden death of Joseph Stalin, helped spur the peace process. In July 1953, a truce was signed that stopped the fighting without formally ending the war. More than 50,000 Americans were killed and 103,000 were wounded in Korea. The Pentagon estimated that 2.4 million civilians died or were seriously injured in the three years of terrible fighting, along with 850,000 troops from South Korea, 520,000 from North Korea, and 950,000 from Communist China.

❖ The Cold War at Home and Abroad, 1953–1954

When Republicans took control of Congress and the White House in 1953, the "Communist issue" gained center stage. On Capitol Hill, 185 of the 221 House Republicans applied for duty on the House Un-American Activities Committee, where Chairman Harold Velde of Illinois vowed to hunt down Communists like "rats." At the White House, President Eisenhower promised both a crackdown on "subversives" in government and a "New Look" in military affairs, designed to streamline American forces for the continuing struggle against "worldwide Communist aggression."

The Hunt for "Subversives"

Shortly after taking office, President Eisenhower issued an executive order that extended the scope of the Federal Loyalty-Security Program. A few months later, he announced that 1,456 federal workers had been fired as "security risks," including "alcoholics," "homosexuals," and "political subversives." The most controversial security case involved J. Robert Oppenheimer, the distinguished physicist who directed the Manhattan Project during World War II. Oppenheimer's prewar association with left-wing radicals was widely known. He had been checked and rechecked by the FBI until 1953, when the Eisenhower administration suspended his top security clearance. Many believed that Oppenheimer's troubles resulted from his public opposition to the building of the hydrogen bomb.

In Congress, the Red-hunting fervor was even more intense. The Senate assault was led by Joseph McCarthy, newly appointed chairman of the Committee on Government Operations and its powerful Subcommittee on Investigations. Filling key staff positions with ex-FBI agents and former prosecutors like Roy M. Cohn, an abrasive young attorney from New York, McCarthy looked for "Communist influence" in the State Department and other government agencies. His hearings did not uncover many Communists. They did, however, ruin numerous careers, undermine worker morale, and make the United States look fearful in the eyes of the world.

Many expected Eisenhower to put the senator in his place. But the new president was slow to respond, telling aides: "I just will not—I refuse to get into the gutter with that guy." Eisenhower changed his mind after McCarthy's subcommittee, spearheaded by Roy Cohn, began to investigate charges that a "Communist spy ring" was operating at Fort Monmouth, New Jersey, home of the Army Signal Corps. Army officials responded that Cohn was harassing the service in order to win preferential treatment for a close friend. Early in 1954, the Senate investigated these conflicting allegations. Furious at the attacks on his beloved army, Eisenhower privately urged Republican Senate leaders to televise the hearings; it proved to be a shrewd move. For thirty-six days, the nation watched the senator's frightening outbursts and crude personal attacks. The highlight of the hearings came on June 9, 1954, when army counsel Joseph Welch sternly rebuked McCarthy for his menacing behavior, asking: "Have you no sense of decency, sir? Have you left no sense of decency?" The spectators burst into applause.

A few months later, the Senate censured McCarthy for bringing that body "into dishonor and disrepute." For McCarthy, things disintegrated quickly: reporters and colleagues ignored him, and his influence disappeared. Unable to get his message across, McCarthy spent his final days drinking in private. He died of liver failure in 1957 at the age of forty-eight.

Senator Joseph McCarthy.
Senator Joseph McCarthy, America's premier Red-hunter, lectured army counsel Joseph Welch (hand on head) about the Communist Party during the celebrated Army–McCarthy hearings in 1954.

Brinksmanship and Covert Action

Like Truman before him, President Eisenhower supported the containment of communism through military, economic, and diplomatic means. But he took a different approach, called the "New Look," reasoning that it was fruitless to match the Communists "man for man, gun for gun," he reasoned. The Korean stalemate showed the folly of that approach. In place of conventional forces, the United States must emphasize "the deterrent of massive retaliatory power." This meant using America's edge in nuclear weapons and long-range bombers to best advantage.

The New Look allowed Eisenhower to cut defense spending by 20 percent between 1953 and 1955. The number of men and women in uniform went down each year, and the production of atomic warheads dramatically increased. Secretary of State Dulles viewed the New Look as a way to intimidate potential enemies with the implied threat of atomic attack. He called this "brinksmanship," claiming that "the ability to get to the verge without getting into the war is the necessary art." Critics, however, saw brinksmanship as a dangerous game. Intimidation meant little, they warned, if the United States did not intend to back up its words.

In 1953, Eisenhower appointed Allen Dulles, younger brother of the secretary of state, to head the Central Intelligence Agency (CIA). Dulles emphasized "covert action" over intelligence gathering—a change the president fully endorsed. Most of the CIA's new work was cloaked in secrecy, and much of it was illegal. Covert action became one of Eisenhower's favorite foreign policy tools.

Iran was a case in point. In 1953, the new government of Mohammed Mossadegh nationalized the British-controlled oil fields and deposed the pro-Western shah of Iran. The United States, believing Mossadegh's government to be pro-Communist, feared for its oil supplies in the Middle East. President Eisenhower thus approved a CIA operation that toppled Mossadegh and returned the young shah to power. A few months later, Iran agreed to split its oil production among three Western nations, with American companies getting 40 percent, British companies 40 percent, and Dutch companies 20 percent. In 1954, the CIA struck again, forcing the overthrow of Guatemala's democratically elected president, Jacobo Arbenz Guzman, on the grounds that he led a pro-Communist regime. He was replaced by a military dictator, General Carlos Castillo Armas, whose government protected American business interests.

Events in Indochina (or Vietnam) did not turn out as well for the United States. Following World War II, nationalist forces in that French colony, led by **Ho Chi Minh,** a popular Marxist leader, began an armed struggle for independence. The United States, viewing Ho (incorrectly) as a puppet of Moscow, supported French attempts to crush the Vietnamese resistance, known as the Vietminh. By 1953, American military aid to France in the Indochina conflict totaled nearly $3 billion. But it failed to turn the tide; instead, the Vietminh grew stronger. On May 7, 1954, after losing a military standoff at Dien Bien Phu—a situation in which Eisenhower refused to intervene—the French surrendered, effectively ending French rule in Vietnam.

At peace talks in Geneva, Switzerland, the two sides agreed to a cease-fire and a temporary partition of Vietnam at the seventeenth parallel, with French troops moving south of that line and Vietminh forces moving north. Free elections were scheduled for 1956, at which time the French were to fully withdraw. However, the United States refused to recognize the Geneva Accords because they knew that Ho Chi Minh would be the certain winner in the proposed election of 1956. Eisenhower and Dulles planned to prevent that election while creating a permanent anti-Communist government in South Vietnam supported by American economic and military aid.

Ho Chi Minh (1890–1969)
Vietnamese leader and first president of North Vietnam. His army was victorious in the French Indochina War, and he later led North Vietnam's struggle to defeat the U.S.-supported government of South Vietnam. He died before the reunification of Vietnam.

To Eisenhower, the survival of South Vietnam became the key to containing communism in Asia. He described the so-called **domino theory** at a press conference about Indochina in 1954. "You have a row of dominoes set up," he began. "You knock over the first one, and what will happen to the last one is a certainty that it will go over quickly. So the possible consequences of the loss [of Vietnam] are just incalculable to the free world."

domino theory A theory that if one nation comes under Communist control, neighboring nations will soon follow.

❖ The Civil Rights Movement, 1954–1955

The 1950s witnessed enormous gains in the struggle for minority rights. In federal courts and in cities throughout the South, African Americans struggled to eradicate the system of racial segregation that denied them dignity, opportunity, and equal protection under the law. Though the Eisenhower administration proved far less sympathetic to the cause of civil rights than the Truman administration had been, the movement for racial justice took on a power and a spirit that would transform the nation in the coming years.

Brown v. Board of Education

In September 1953, Chief Justice Fred Vinson died of a heart attack, requiring President Eisenhower to make his first appointment to the U.S. Supreme Court. Eisenhower offered the position to California Governor Earl Warren, who won prompt Senate approval. Far more liberal than Eisenhower on social issues, Warren would sometimes anger the president in the coming years, but rarely lose his respect.

The major issue facing the Supreme Court in 1953 was civil rights. For more than a decade, a group of talented African American attorneys had been filing legal challenges to segregated public facilities in the South, hoping to erode the "separate but equal" doctrine of *Plessy v. Ferguson.* Led by Thurgood Marshall and William Hastie of the NAACP's Legal Defense Fund, these attorneys targeted specific areas, such as professional education (law, medicine, teaching), to establish precedents for the larger fight.

This strategy worked well. In 1950, the Supreme Court chipped away at the *Plessy* doctrine in two lawsuits addressing graduate school admission brought by the NAACP: *Sweatt v. Painter* and *McLaurin v. Oklahoma.* The new cases touched millions of children, white and black, in twenty-one states and the District of

(© Elliott Erwitt/Magum Photos)

Segregation in the South. Jim Crow was a way of life in the South, where public and private facilities ranging from hospitals to restaurants to cemeteries were racially segregated by law.

Doing History The Long Reach of *Brown*

One of the great spurs to the civil rights movement following World War II was the unanimous U.S. Supreme Court opinion in Brown v. Board of Education, *written by Chief Justice Earl Warren, which overturned the "separate but equal" doctrine set down fifty-eight years before in Plessy v. Ferguson. Racial segregation in the nation's public schools was unconstitutional, the Warren Court ruled, and "any language . . . contrary to this finding is rejected." The opinion stated:*

Today, education is perhaps the most important function of state and local governments. . . . It is required in the performance of our most basic public responsibilities, even service in the armed forces. It is the very foundation of good citizenship. . . . In these days, it is doubtful that any child may reasonably be expected to succeed in life if he is denied the opportunity of an education. . . .

We come then to the question presented: Does segregation of children in public schools, solely on the basis of race . . . deprive the children of the minority group of equal educational opportunities? We believe that it does. . . .

Segregation of white and colored children in public schools has a detrimental effect upon the colored children. The impact is greater when it has the sanction of the law; for the policy of separating the races is usually interpreted as denoting the inferiority of the negro group. A sense of inferiority affects the motivation of a child to learn. Segregation with the sanction of law, therefore, has a tendency to [retard] the educational and mental development of Negro children and to deprive them of some of the benefits they would receive in a racial[ly] integrated school system. . . .

We conclude that in the field of public education the doctrine of "separate but equal" has no place. Separate educational facilities are inherently unequal."

The Brown decision caused a furor in much of the South. Many whites vowed to resist it, including Alabama's governor, George C. Wallace, who promised to "stand in the schoolhouse door" rather than permit two black students to enter the then

Brown v. Board of Education of Topeka (1954) Unanimous Supreme Court decision ruling that segregated facilities in public education were "inherently unequal" and violated the Fourteenth Amendment's guarantee of equal protection under the law. This decision overruled the long-standing "separate but equal" doctrine of *Plessy v. Ferguson.*

Columbia. By 1953, five separate lawsuits had reached the Supreme Court, including **Brown v. Board of Education of Topeka.**

Brown involved a Kansas law that permitted cities to segregate their public schools. With NAACP support, the Reverend Oliver Brown sued the Topeka school board, arguing that his eight-year-old daughter should not be forced to attend a Negro school a mile from her home when there was a white public school only three blocks away. The Supreme Court was badly divided, but Chief Justice Warren insisted that the Supreme Court speak in a powerful, united voice against racial segregation. Anything less, he reasoned, would encourage massive resistance in the South. (See *Doing History: The Long Reach of* Brown.)

On May 17, 1954, the Supreme Court overturned *Plessy v. Ferguson* in a stunning 9–0 decision, written by Warren himself. Relying on the studies of social scientists such as Kenneth Clark, the chief justice claimed that racial segregation had a "detrimental effect" on black children. "In the field of public education the doctrine of 'separate but equal' has no place," he stated. "Separate educational facilities are inherently unequal." The Supreme Court put off its implementation guidelines for a full year, hoping to let passions cool in the South. But there were no timetables, and the wording was intentionally vague. Integration should proceed, it said, "with all deliberate speed."

White southern reaction was intense. "You are not required to obey any court which passes out such a ruling," Senator James O. Eastland of Mississippi told his *all-white University of Alabama. Like other white southern officials, Wallace phrased his objections to Brown in constitutional terms—as a judicial threat to local self-government and the will of the people. He said:*

"The unwelcomed, unwanted, unwarranted and force-induced intrusion upon the campus of the University of Alabama today . . . offers a frightful example of oppression . . . by officers of the Federal Government. . . . Only the Congress makes the law of the United States [and] there has been no legislative action by Congress justifying this intrusion.

When the Constitution of the United States was enacted, a Government was formed upon the premise that people, as individuals, are endowed with the rights of life, liberty, and property, and with the right of local self-government. . . . There can be no submission to the theory that the Central Government is anything but a servant of the people. We are God-fearing people—not Government-fearing people. We practice today the free heritage bequeathed to us by the founding fathers.

I stand here today, as Governor of this sovereign state, and refuse to willingly submit to illegal usurpation of power by the Central Government. I claim today for all the people of the state of Alabama those rights reserved to them under the Constitution of the United States. Among those powers so reserved and claimed is the right of state authority in the operation of public schools, colleges, and universities."

Source: *Brown v. Board of Education,* 349 U.S. 294, 1954; *New York Times,* June 12, 1963.

QUESTIONS for REFLECTION

1. What sort of arguments were used in the *Brown* opinion regarding race and education that went beyond the more traditional interpretations of the Fourteenth Amendment's equal protection clause?

2. Why do you think the Supreme Court waited a full year before issuing guidelines for the implementation of the *Brown* decision?

3. Can you think of other instances in which public officials have accused the federal government, and especially the judicial branch, of exercising too much power while restricting local self-government?

---

constituents. "In fact, you are obligated to defy it." Violence flared across the South. "In one school district after another," wrote an observer, "segregationists staged the same drama: forcing young blacks to enter a school by passing rock-throwing white mobs and white pickets shouting 'Nigger,' 'Nigger,' 'Nigger.'" The Ku Klux Klan came alive in the 1950s, and new groups like the White Citizens' Council were formed to defend segregation and the "Southern way of life."

Many Americans looked to the White House for guidance about civil rights. But Eisenhower had little to say about the issue. When asked about the *Brown* decision, Eisenhower replied: "The Supreme Court has spoken and I am sworn to uphold the constitutional processes in this country; and I will obey."

The Montgomery Bus Boycott

The battle over public school integration was but one of many such struggles in the South during this era. Some were fought by attorneys in federal courtrooms; others involved ordinary men and women determined to challenge the indignities of racial segregation and second-class treatment in their daily lives. "Nothing is quite as humiliating, so murderously angering," said one African American, "as to know that because you are black you may have to walk a half mile farther than whites to urinate; that because you are black you have to receive your food through a window in the back of a restaurant or sit in a garbage-littered yard."

Doing History Online

The Right of Interposition, 1955

Go to the CourseMate website for this chapter and link to Primary Sources. Read the articles online and consider the following questions:

1. If a state were to base its response to the *Brown* decision on the doctrine of interposition, what actions could it potentially take?

2. How could the federal government respond to a state that used interposition as the basis for its opposition to the Supreme Court's decision?

 www.cengagebrain.com

The black people of Montgomery, Alabama, had experienced such treatment for years. Known as "the cradle of the Confederacy," Montgomery enforced segregation and racial etiquette in meticulous detail. Blacks always tipped their hats to whites, always stood in the presence of whites unless told to sit, and always addressed whites with a title of respect. On the local buses, blacks paid their fares in the front, got off the vehicle, and entered the "colored section" through the rear door. They also had to relinquish their seats to white passengers when the front section filled up.

On December 1, 1955, a simple yet revolutionary act of resistance occurred on a crowded Montgomery bus. **Rosa Parks**, a forty-two-year-old black seamstress and member of the local NAACP, refused to give up her seat to a white. The bus driver called the police. "They got on the bus," Parks recalled, "and one of them asked me why I didn't stand up. I asked him, 'Why do you push us around?' He said, '. . . I don't know, but the law is the law and you're under arrest.'"

News of Parks's defiance electrified the black community. Within days a boycott of Montgomery's bus system was begun, organized by local clergymen and the Women's Political Council, the black alternative to the all-white League of Women Voters. Calling themselves the Montgomery Improvement Association (MIA), they chose a young minister named **Martin Luther King**, **Jr.**, to lead the struggle for open seating in public transportation, a small but highly symbolic step.

King, twenty-six years old, was a newcomer to Montgomery. He was selected in part because his youth and vocation made him less vulnerable. The son of a well-known Atlanta pastor, King earned his college degree at Morehouse and his doctorate at Boston University's School of Theology before heading south with his new wife, Coretta Scott King, to serve as pastor of Montgomery's Dexter Avenue Baptist Church in 1954. Dr. King was familiar with the works of Gandhi and Thoreau, and he viewed mass action and nonviolent resistance as essential weapons in the war against racial injustice.

King rallied the Montgomery community with the eloquent passion of his words. "We are here this evening to say to those who have mistreated us so long that we are tired—tired of being segregated and humiliated, tired of being kicked about by the brutal feet of oppression," he exhorted. "We have no alternative but to protest." Blacks formed car pools to get people to their destinations. The churches raised money for fuel, and black-owned garages did repair work free of charge. Many people rode bicycles or simply walked for miles. The **Montgomery bus boycott** nearly bankrupted the city bus system and badly hurt the white merchants downtown. A local participant known as Mother Pollard, bent with age, inspired the movement with her simple remark: "My feets is tired, but my soul is rested."

In November 1956, the federal courts struck down the Alabama law requiring racial segregation in public transportation. A month later, blacks sat in the front of the Montgomery buses without incident. The boycott, lasting 381 days, demonstrated both the power of collective action and the possibility of social change. In 1957, Dr. King joined with other black ministers and civil rights activists to form the Southern Christian Leadership Conference (SCLC), an organization devoted to racial justice through peaceful means. "Noncooperation with evil," King declared, "is as much a moral obligation as is cooperation with good."

Parks, Rosa (1913–2005) Her refusal to give up her seat on a bus to a white man in Montgomery, Alabama, resulted in a citywide boycott of the bus company and stirred the civil rights movement across the nation.

King, Martin Luther, Jr. (1929–1968) African American clergyman whose eloquence and commitment to nonviolence formed the foundation of the civil rights movement of the 1950s and 1960s. He led the 1963 march on Washington at which he delivered his now famous "I Have a Dream" speech. He was awarded the Nobel Peace Prize in 1964 and was assassinated four years later in Memphis, Tennessee.

Montgomery bus boycott Begun in December 1955 as a result of an act of protest by Rosa Parks against the segregated transportation facilities and humiliating treatment facing African Americans in the capital city of Alabama, the boycott soon became an international event.

❖ American Families at Mid-Century

In the 1950s, social commentators analyzed a host of new issues in American life. Some focused on the supposed emptiness of suburban living, the growing cult of domesticity among women, the changing standards of success. Yet what struck virtually all critics and commentators in the 1950s was the impact of television on American life—an impact that altered politics, news gathering, consumer tastes, and popular culture in truly revolutionary ways.

The Golden Age of Television

When World War II ended, there were seventeen TV sets in the United States. The late 1940s saw major changes in television technology, such as the use of coaxial cable and the introduction of color. In 1949, a TV set appeared for the first time in the Sears, Roebuck catalogue—$149.95 "with indoor antenna." A year later, Americans were buying twenty thousand television sets a day.

The two most popular shows of that era were Milton Berle's *Texaco Star Theater* and Ed Sullivan's *Toast of the Town*. Berle, a physical comedian, seemed perfect for a visual medium like TV. His fast-paced humor relied on sight gags instead of verbal banter. What made Sullivan unique was his ability to provide fresh entertainment to Americans of all tastes and ages. Sullivan's Sunday night variety show, mixing opera with acrobats, ran for twenty-three years on CBS. His guests included Elvis Presley, Dean Martin and Jerry Lewis, pianist Van Cliburn, dancer Rudolf Nureyev, singer Lena Horne, and the Beatles. "Ed Sullivan will last," said pianist Oscar Levant, "as long as other people have talent."

Television's potential was impossible to ignore. In 1951, an obscure Tennessee politician named Estes Kefauver became a national figure by holding televised hearings into organized crime. Senator Kefauver grilled prominent mobsters like New York's Frank Costello as 25 million viewers watched in amazement. Nixon's "Checkers speech" and the army–McCarthy hearings further highlighted the impact of television in the political arena. Above all, however, TV possessed the power to sell. Walt Disney struck gold with his three-part series on Davy Crockett, which aired nationally in 1954. Millions of children wore coonskin caps to school. There were Davy Crockett shirts and blankets, toothbrushes, and lunch boxes. One department store chain sold twenty thousand surplus pup tents in less than a week by printing "Davy Crockett" on the flap.

By 1954, three national networks were firmly in place. As the major radio powers, ABC, CBS, and NBC held a decided advantage over potential competitors in technology and talent. Indeed, these networks filled their early airtime by moving popular radio programs like *Jack Benny, Burns & Allen*, and *Amos 'n' Andy* over to TV. The faster television grew, the more its schedule expanded. Important advertisers signed on, sponsoring entire programs such as *Kraft Television Theater* and *Motorola Playhouse*. This, in turn, provided work for hundreds of performers at a time when the motion picture industry was losing ground to television. New York City, the early center of TV production, became a magnet for young actors and writers like Paul Newman, Sidney Poitier, Joanne Woodward, Rod Serling, Neil Simon, and Mel Brooks. Some critics called this era the "golden age" of television.

Many television shows of the 1950s reflected both the yearnings and stereotypes of American society. Popular comedies such as *Father Knows Best, Ozzie and Harriet*, and *Leave It to Beaver* portrayed the charmed lives (and minor problems) of middle-class white families in the suburbs. Mother was a housewife. Dad held a pressure-free white-collar job. The kids were well adjusted and witty. Money was never a problem. No one stayed angry for long. "You know, Mom," said Beaver Cleaver, "when we're in a mess, you kind of make things seem not so messy." "Well," June Cleaver replied, "isn't that sort of what mothers are for?"

(CBS Photo Archive/Hulton Archive/Getty Images)

***Leave It to Beaver* Cast.** No television show captured the idyllic quality of suburban life in post–World War II America better than *Leave It to Beaver*.

Married women in TV sitcoms did not work outside the home. Their husbands would not permit it. This rule even applied to childless couples like Ralph and Alice Kramden of *The Honeymooners*, one of television's rare programs about urban, working-class people. Though racial minorities almost never appeared in these sitcoms, they did play major—if stereotypical—roles in two or three popular shows of the 1950s. The most popular was *Amos 'n' Andy*, an adaptation of the popular radio show created by two white men, Freeman Gosden and Charles Correll, that featured an all-black cast. The NAACP angrily denounced *Amos 'n' Andy* for portraying blacks as "clowns" and "crooks," but others praised the performers for transforming racist stereotypes into "authentic black humor."

By the end of the decade, advertising consumed 20 percent of television airtime, with more money spent making commercials than producing the shows themselves. One study in the 1950s estimated that an American youngster spent eleven thousand hours in the classroom through high school and fifteen thousand hours in front of TV. Another concluded that adults spent more time watching television than working for pay. There were complaints that television tended to isolate people and to shorten their attention spans. As television expanded, other media outlets declined. Newspaper readership went way down, movie attendance dropped, and radio lost listeners. Television was now king. People watched the same programs in Boston and San Diego, in rural hamlets and in cities, in rich areas and in poor. America's popular culture, consumer needs, and general information—all came increasingly from TV.

A New Kind of Music

In the 1950s, a distinctive teenage culture emerged, rooted in the enormous prosperity and population growth that followed World War II. America's young people were far removed from the grim events of the previous two decades. Raised in relative affluence, surrounded by messages that undermined traditional values of thrift and self-denial, these new teenagers rarely worked, yet their pockets were full. By 1956, the nation's teenage market topped $9 billion a year. The typical adolescent spent as much on entertainment as had the average family in 1941.

Nothing defined these 13 million teenagers more clearly than the music they shared. In the 1940s, popular music was dominated by the "big bands" of Glenn Miller and Tommy Dorsey, the Broadway show tunes of Rodgers and Hammerstein, and the mellow voices of Bing Crosby, Frank Sinatra, and the Andrews Sisters. These artists appealed to a broad white audience of all ages. Other forms of popular music—bluegrass, country, rhythm and blues—were limited by region and race.

But not for long. The huge migration of rural blacks and whites to industrial centers during World War II profoundly altered popular culture. The sounds of "race" music, "hillbilly" music, and gospel became readily available to mainstream America for the first time. Record sales tripled during the 1950s, aided by technological advances like the transistor radio and the 45 rpm vinyl disc (or "single"). The main consumers were young people, who acquired new tastes by flipping the radio dial.

In 1951, a Cleveland, Ohio, record dealer noticed that white teenagers at his store were "going crazy" over the songs of black rhythm and blues artists like Ivory Joe Hunter and Lloyd Price. He told a local disc jockey named **Alan Freed**, who decided to play these records on the air. Freed's new program, *The Moondog Party*, took Cleveland by storm. Pounding his fists to the rhythm, chanting "go man, go," Freed became the self-proclaimed father of rock 'n' roll. Freed understood the defiant, sensual nature of rock 'n' roll, the way it separated the young from everyone else. It was their music, played by their heroes, set to their special beat.

Freed, Alan (1921–1965) The self-proclaimed father of rock 'n' roll, he was the first DJ to play black rhythm and blues artists on the radio.

In 1955, a twenty-one-year-old truck driver from Memphis exploded onto the popular music scene. His name was Elvis Presley. Born in rural Mississippi, Presley was surrounded by the sounds of country music, gospel, and blues. As a teenager in Memphis, he listened to WDIA—"the Mother Station of Negroes"— and frequented the legendary blues clubs along Beale Street. Memphis was home to Sun Records, a label with strong southern roots. Signing with Sun Records in 1954, Presley took the region by storm. The press described his unique style as "a cross between be-bop and country" and "a new hillbilly blues beat." It wasn't just the sound. Tall and handsome, with long sideburns and slicked-back hair, Presley was a riveting performer. A fellow artist described young Presley on tour:

> This cat came out in red pants and a green coat and a pink shirt and socks, and he had this sneer on his face. And he stood behind the mike for five minutes, I'll bet, before he made a move. [Meanwhile] these high school girls were screaming and fainting and running up to the stage, and then he started to move his hips real slow like he had a thing for his guitar.

Before long, Elvis was a national sensation. His early hits topped the charts in popular music, country, and rhythm and blues—the first time that had ever occurred. In less than a year, Elvis recorded eight number-one songs and six of RCA's all-time top twenty-five records. When he appeared on *Ed Sullivan*, the cameras carefully shot him from the waist up. The ratings were extraordinary. "I want to say to Elvis and the country," Sullivan told his audience, "that this is a real decent, fine boy." Yet his exaggerated sexuality on stage made him the target of those who believed that rock 'n' roll was a vulgar and dangerous assault on America's youth. "Popular music," wrote one television critic, "has reached its lowest depths in the grunt and groin antics of Mr. Presley."

Such criticism served only to enhance Presley's stature in the teenage world. And his success led the major record companies to experiment more aggressively with black rhythm and blues. At that time, white "cover artists" still were used to record toned-down versions of "race" music for white teenage audiences. In 1956, rock music reached a milestone when **Little Richard's** sensual recordings of "Long Tall Sally" and "Rip It Up" outsold the "sanitized" versions sung by Pat Boone, America's leading white cover artist.

The music that defined this era for most Americans, and for teenagers in particular, was hard-edged rock 'n' roll. It was the car radio blasting Presley's "Hound Dog," Chuck Berry's "Maybellene," and Little Richard's "Tutti Frutti" on a carefree Saturday night. A wop bop a lu bop a lop bam boom!

Little Richard (Richard Wayne Penniman, 1932–) American rock 'n' roll singer noted for his flamboyant style, he influenced many artists including Elvis Presley and the Beatles.

The Beat Generation

Meanwhile, a different sort of youth rebellion emerged in San Francisco and New York. Young writers and poets who called themselves "Beats" attacked mainstream standards and beliefs. The word "beat" described a feeling of emotional and physical exhaustion. The Beats despised politics, consumerism, and technology. They viewed American culture as meaningless, conformist, banal. Their leading poet, Allen Ginsberg, provided a bitter portrait of generational despair in *Howl* (1955).

The Beats linked happiness and creativity with absolute freedom. Their model was Dean Moriarty, the hero of Jack Kerouac's *On the Road* (1957), an autobiographical novel about the cross-country adventures of Kerouac and his friends finding adventure and renewal (not to mention sex and drugs) beyond the confines of middle-class life. *On the Road* became both a national best-seller and a cult book on America's college campuses. In a sense, Kerouac and Presley had something important in common: both appealed to young people who seemed dissatisfied with the apparent blandness of American culture.

❖ Crises and Celebration, 1955–1956

In September 1955, President Eisenhower suffered a heart attack while vacationing in Colorado. The news raised obvious questions about his possible reelection. At age sixty-five, Eisenhower was one of the oldest presidents in American history. How quickly would he recover, if at all? Who would guide the nation in his absence? Fortunately, the fall of 1955 was a time of political tranquility, allowing the president to recuperate. Returning to the White House early in 1956, he announced his plan to seek reelection. The public was vastly relieved. As columnist James Reston noted, Eisenhower was more than a president; he was "a national phenomenon, like baseball."

Conquering Polio

The president's full recovery was not the only positive health news of 1955. On a far larger front, a medical research team led by Dr. Jonas Salk, a virologist at the University of Pittsburgh, announced the successful testing of a vaccine to combat poliomyelitis, the most frightening public health problem of the postwar era. More than fifty thousand polio cases were reported in 1954, mostly of children who took sick during the summer months. The disease produced flulike symptoms in most cases, but a more virulent form, which entered the central nervous system, led to paralysis and sometimes death. Not surprisingly, the epidemic produced a national panic. Cities closed swimming pools and beaches; families cancelled vacations, boiled their dishes, and avoided indoor crowds.

Determined to provide immediate protection against the disease, Dr. Salk tested his polio vaccine on several million schoolchildren in 1954. "It was the largest peacetime mobilization of its kind," wrote one observer, "one in which the mothers of America rose up to save, in many cases, their own children." The testing proved extremely successful. The federal government approved the polio vaccine in 1955, touching off emotional public celebrations. "People observed moments of silence, rang bells, honked horns, blew factory whistles, drank toasts, hugged children, attended church." By 1960, fewer than a thousand new polio cases were reported in the United States.

Interstate Highways

The nation's confidence soared even higher with passage of the Federal Highway Act of 1956, which authorized $25 billion in new taxes on cars, trucks, and gasoline for the construction of forty thousand miles of interstate roads during the next ten years. The huge highway network, linking all cities with more than fifty thousand people, allowed a driver to travel the continent uninterrupted, save stops for food and gas (see Map 26.1). Eisenhower viewed this project as both a convenience to motorists and a boost to the economy. He also invoked Cold War security, warning that cities must be evacuated quickly in the event of nuclear war.

The Highway Act spurred enormous economic growth. Improved roads meant higher oil revenues, soaring car sales, more business for truckers, and greater mobility for travelers. The so-called highway trade took off. Ray Krock opened his first McDonald's in 1955 in Des Plaines, Illinois, a suburb of Chicago. In Memphis, Kemmons Wilson unveiled the first Holiday Inn, featuring a restaurant, a swimming pool, and clean, air-conditioned rooms with free TV. Before long McDonald's golden arches and Holiday Inn's green neon lettering were among the most recognizable logos in America.

(Copyright © Cengage Learning)

MAP 26.1

The National Highway System Proposed in 1957
The ability to drive almost anywhere in the continental United States on a superhighway transformed the nation's economy as well as its culture. Private transportation overwhelmed public transportation. Workers commuted longer distances between their homes and their jobs, and whole new industries arose to service the business traveler and vacationer.

Hungary and Suez

In the fall of 1956, at the height of the presidential campaign, foreign affairs took center stage. From central Europe came a dangerous challenge to the Eisenhower-Dulles rhetoric about liberating nations from Communist oppression. From the Middle East came a crisis that pitted the United States against its most loyal allies: Israel, England, and France.

Following Stalin's death in 1953, Russian leaders called for "peaceful coexistence" between the Communist bloc and "differing political and social systems." In 1956, Soviet Premier **Nikita Khrushchev** stunned the Twentieth Communist Party Congress in Moscow by denouncing Stalin's brutality and hinting at a relaxation of the Soviet grip on central and eastern Europe. The reaction was predictable. Protests flared throughout the Soviet bloc, demanding an end to Russian rule. In Warsaw, angry crowds sacked the Communist Party headquarters, and in Budapest street battles escalated into full-scale civil war.

The Hungarian revolt put Eisenhower on the spot. His administration had vowed to "roll back" the Communist wave, not simply to contain it. Now the time had come to put words into action by supporting the anti-Communist freedom fighters in Hungary. Yet Eisenhower refused to send American troops, or even to airlift supplies to the resisters, for fear of starting an all-out war with the Soviet Union. In October 1956, Russian tanks and troops stormed into Budapest to crush the revolt.

Khrushchev, Nikita (1894–1971)
Soviet politician and Stalin loyalist in the 1930s, he was appointed first secretary of the Communist party in 1953. As Soviet premier, he denounced Stalin, thwarted the Hungarian Revolution of 1956, and improved his country's image abroad. He was deposed in 1964 for failing to establish missiles in Cuba or improve the Soviet economy.

At the very moment of the Hungarian revolt, another crisis erupted in the Middle East, a region of growing interest and concern to the United States. Although American policy supported the new state of Israel, it also recognized the strategic importance and economic power of Israel's Arab neighbors. In 1952, a young Egyptian military officer named Gamal Abdel Nasser had dramatically altered Middle Eastern politics by overthrowing the corrupt regime of King Farouk. As an Arab nationalist, Nasser steered a middle course between the Cold War powers, hoping to play off one side against the other. To the Egyptian people, he promised both the destruction of Israel and an end to British control of the Suez Canal.

The United States tried to woo Nasser with economic aid. It even agreed to finance his pet project, the Aswan Dam, a huge hydroelectric plant on the Nile River. But trouble arose in 1956 when Secretary Dulles withdrew the Aswan offer to protest Egypt's recognition of Communist China. Unable to punish the United States directly, Nasser did the next best thing by seizing the Suez Canal. The move could not be ignored. On October 29, 1956, Israeli armor poured into the Sinai, routing Egyptian forces. Two days later, French and British paratroopers landed near Alexandria and easily retook the Suez Canal.

Eisenhower immediately condemned this invasion. At the very least, he believed, the attack undermined Western interests in the Middle East by forcing Egypt and other Arab states closer to the Soviet bloc. Privately, the White House pressured England, France, and Israel to withdraw. Publicly, the United States supported a UN resolution that denounced the invasion and called for negotiations regarding the canal. On November 6, a cease-fire was signed, ending the crisis but not the ill will.

Events in Hungary and Suez came in the midst of Eisenhower's 1956 reelection campaign. Expecting an easy victory, the president worried most about picking the proper running mate, a critical choice given his advanced age and questionable health. Eisenhower did not believe that Vice President Nixon was the best person to lead the nation in a crisis. "I've watched Dick a long time and he just hasn't grown," Ike told an aide. "So I just haven't honestly been able to believe that he is presidential timber."

In a private meeting, Eisenhower urged Nixon to trade in his vice-presidential hat for a cabinet post. Yet when Nixon resisted, the president backed down, fearing a backlash within Republican ranks. In November 1956, Eisenhower and Nixon trounced the Democratic slate of Adlai Stevenson and Senator Estes Kefauver by almost 10 million votes, a margin of victory even wider than in 1952. Nevertheless, the Democrats easily retained their majorities in both houses of Congress, demonstrating that Eisenhower, who accepted New Deal reforms as a permanent part of American life, remained far more popular than the political party he led.

❖ A Second Term, 1957–1960

Eisenhower returned to office on an optimistic note. Events in Hungary and the Middle East faded momentarily from view. *Time* magazine even praised the president for his moderation "in time of crisis and threat of World War III." The economy was strong; unemployment was low. The nation seemed confident, prosperous, and secure.

Confrontation at Little Rock

These good feelings did not last long. Throughout the South, opposition to the *Brown* decision was spreading, and in 1956, more than one hundred congressmen from the former Confederate states issued a "Southern Manifesto" that vowed to resist court-ordered integration "by all lawful means." A year later, in Little Rock, Arkansas, Governor **Orval Faubus** triggered the inevitable confrontation between national authority and "states' rights" by defying a federal court order to integrate the all-white Central High School. First the Arkansas National Guard, and then a crowd of angry whites, turned away nine black students.

As televised scenes of mob violence in Little Rock flashed around the world, President Eisenhower finally, but firmly, took command. Vowing to use "the full power of the United States . . . to carry out the orders of the federal court," he nationalized the Arkansas Guard and dispatched a thousand fully equipped army paratroopers to surround the high school and escort the black students to their classes. The soldiers remained for months, though peace was quickly restored. Ironically, Dwight Eisenhower became the first president since Reconstruction to protect the civil rights of African Americans through the use of military force.

Faubus, Orval (1910–1994)
Governor of Arkansas in 1957 who triggered a confrontation between national authority and states' rights by defying a federal court order to integrate the all-white Little Rock Central High School.

Sputnik and Its Aftermath

On October 4, 1957, the Soviet Union launched **Sputnik I** (or "traveling companion"), the first artificial satellite, weighing less than two hundred pounds. A month later, the Russians orbited *Sputnik II*, an eleven-hundred-pound capsule with a small dog inside.

The news provoked anger and dismay. Americans had always taken for granted their technological superiority. Even the Soviet atomic bomb was seen as an aberration, most likely built from stolen U.S. blueprints. But *Sputnik* was different; it shook the nation's confidence and wounded its pride. "The time has clearly come," said an alarmed senator, "to be less concerned with the depth of the pile of the new broadloom or the height of the tail fin of the new car and to be more prepared to shed blood, sweat, and tears."

The nation's educational system came under withering fire. Critics emerged from every corner, bemoaning the sorry state of America's schools. In an issue devoted to the "Crisis in Education," *Life* magazine followed a sixteen-year-old Russian student and his American counterpart through a typical high school day. Alexi took difficult courses in science and math. He spoke fluent English, played chess and the piano, exercised vigorously, and studied four hours after class. Stephen, meanwhile, spent his day lounging through basic geometry and learning how to type. The students around him read magazines like *Modern Romance* in

Sputnik I First artificial space satellite, launched by the Soviet Union in October 1957. News of its success provoked both anger and anxiety among the American people who had always taken their country's technological superiority for granted.

(Carl Iwasaki-Time Life Pictures/Getty Images)

Scientists Measuring *Sputnik I* Signals. *Sputnik's* launch in October 1957 raised doubts about America's military and technological superiority in the Cold War era.

their English class. No one seemed to study. The end result, warned the *Life* editors, was a generation of young Americans ill equipped "to cope with the technicalities of the Space Age."

The embarrassments continued. In December 1957, millions watched on television as the U.S. Navy's much-publicized Vanguard rocket caught fire on takeoff and crashed to the ground. (The press dubbed it "Flopnik.") A month later, the army launched a ten-pound satellite named *Explorer I* aboard its new Jupiter rocket. Determined to calm public fears, President Eisenhower insisted that the United States was well ahead of the Soviet Union in nuclear research and delivery systems, but the people thought otherwise, especially after the Russians orbited a third satellite weighing almost three thousand pounds. In fact, however, Eisenhower was correct; the United States was in no real danger of being outgunned.

Eisenhower got this information from the CIA's U-2 spy planes, which crossed the Soviet Union at seventy thousand feet. The U-2 flights were both secret and illegal, a clear violation of Russian air space. But the cameras on board, capable of picking up license plate numbers in the Kremlin's parking lot, provided American intelligence with a detailed picture of the Soviet war machine. Of course, the president could not speak candidly about Russian military power without also admitting the existence of these U-2 flights.

This was an awful dilemma. Critics now demanded expensive programs for weapons research, missile construction, and community fallout shelters to protect against nuclear attack. Eisenhower vigorously opposed these programs, claiming that they undermined economic prosperity and threatened the "very values we are trying to defend." Using his exalted stature as general and war hero, he battled hard—and successfully—to keep military budgets stable during these years. Defense spending increased from $38 billion in 1957 to $41 billion in 1960, a tiny jump after inflation.

Still, the impact of *Sputnik* did not quickly disappear. For the first time, Americans started to view their educational system in terms of national security. This meant greater emphasis on science, mathematics, and foreign language study. In 1958, Congress passed the National Defense Education Act, which funded high school programs in these fields and college scholarships for deserving students. That same year, Eisenhower reluctantly endorsed the creation of the National Aeronautics and Space Administration (NASA), in response to overwhelming public pressure.

End of an Era

In November 1958, the Democrats won a smashing victory in the off-year elections, increasing their majorities in the House (282–153) and the Senate (62–34) to the largest level since 1936. *Sputnik* was partly responsible for this landslide, but so too was an economic recession in 1957 that lingered for the next two years. Determined to avoid the inflationary risks of increased federal spending, Eisenhower did little to counter a steady rise in unemployment and a sharp (if temporary) decline in the annual rate of economic growth.

There were optimistic signs, however. In the summer of 1959, Vice President Nixon visited Moscow at Khrushchev's invitation to open a trade show featuring consumer products from Russia and the United States. Several weeks later, Khrushchev accepted President Eisenhower's invitation to visit the United States. Khrushchev toured an Iowa farm and an IBM plant near San Francisco. At a Hollywood studio, he watched the filming of *Can-Can* and then, offended by the skimpy costumes, launched into a diatribe against capitalist "pornography." The trip ended on a hopeful note with a visit to the presidential retreat at Camp David, where Khrushchev and Eisenhower announced that Eisenhower would visit the Soviet Union in 1960 following a summit meeting of world leaders in Paris. The main issues, they agreed, were nuclear disarmament and the future of Berlin.

The summit meeting was a disaster. As he left for Paris in May 1960, Eisenhower learned that a U-2 spy plane was missing. A few days later, Khrushchev revealed that an American aircraft had been shot down deep inside the Soviet Union. Assuming that the pilot was dead, Eisenhower falsely described the U-2 as a weather research plane that had veered off course during a routine flight over Turkey. But Khrushchev then produced the pilot, **Francis Gary Powers**, frightened but very much alive.

At the summit, Eisenhower took full responsibility for the incident but refused to apologize. Indeed, he justified the U-2 flights by insisting that Soviet espionage inside the United States was rampant and that U-2 photographs were essential to America's defense, given the closed nature of Russian society. In response, Khrushchev turned the summit into a tirade against Western "banditry," adding that Eisenhower was no longer welcome on Soviet soil.

The failure at Paris deeply wounded the president. In his "farewell address" to the people, he warned that years of Cold War tensions were sapping America's strength and concentrating too much power in the hands of "a military-industrial complex." Speaking boldly, at times sadly, he urged the people to be on guard against militarism and greed and to reject a "live for today" mentality. At risk, the president concluded, was "the loss of our political and spiritual heritage."

Powers, Francis Gary (1929–1977) Pilot of a U.S. U-2 high-altitude reconnaissance aircraft shot down over the Soviet Union on May 1, 1960.

The Election of 1960

Who would lead the United States into the next decade? The election of 1960 generated drama from the start. Both major candidates were tough, hard-driving campaigners. Both were born in the twentieth century—a political first—and both entered Congress in 1946 after serving as junior naval officers during World War II. But the similarities ended there.

Richard Nixon, the forty-seven-year-old vice president, grew up in modest circumstances. His Quaker parents ran a small grocery store in Whittier, California, near Los Angeles, where Nixon worked as a boy. After he served in the navy, Nixon's political rise was dramatic. As a new Republican congressman, he played a major role in the Alger Hiss case and then won a U.S. Senate seat in 1950 after accusing his Democratic opponent of being "soft on communism." As vice president from 1953 to 1960, Nixon emerged as the Republican Party's most aggressive defender.

Born to wealth and privilege, John Kennedy grew up in Boston, attended the finest private schools, and graduated from Harvard. His self-made millionaire father, Joseph P. Kennedy, served as ambassador to England under Franklin Roosevelt. Preaching competition and excellence, Joseph Kennedy expected his oldest son, Joe Jr., to become the first Catholic president of the United States. When Joe Jr. died in combat during World War II, the torch was passed to John Kennedy, the next oldest son. In 1943, John barely escaped death himself after his PT boat was rammed by a Japanese warship in the South Pacific.

Elected to Congress in 1946 and to the Senate in 1952, Kennedy did not excel as a legislator. In constant pain from his war wounds, he underwent delicate spinal surgery and then was diagnosed with Addison's disease, an adrenal malfunction that required daily doses of cortisone. While recuperating, Kennedy won the Pulitzer Prize for *Profiles in Courage*, an intriguing book, written almost entirely by his staff, about politicians who took brave but unpopular positions on the great issues of their time.

In 1956, Kennedy ran a close second to Estes Kefauver for the Democratic Party's vice-presidential nomination. Over the next four years, he traveled the country with his glamorous wife, Jacqueline, to line up presidential support. The crowds they drew were so large and adoring that reporters used the word *charisma* to describe the growing Kennedy mystique.

The Republican convention nominated Richard Nixon on the first ballot. As expected, Nixon chose a moderate easterner, Henry Cabot Lodge, Jr., of Massachusetts, to be his vice-presidential running mate. Also winning a first ballot victory, Kennedy surprised almost everyone by selecting Senator Lyndon Johnson, a long-time rival, for the vice-presidential slot. As a Texan with liberal instincts, Johnson was expected to help Kennedy in the South without hurting him in the North.

The two candidates were evenly matched. Nixon campaigned on the eight-year Eisenhower record, reminding Americans that their nation was prosperous and at peace. Kennedy attacked that record without criticizing the popular Eisenhower by name. Portraying the United States as stagnant in a changing world, he promised new leadership "to get the country moving once again."

Kennedy had two main hurdles to overcome: religion and inexperience. No Roman Catholic had ever been elected president, a fact underscored by the crushing defeat of Al Smith in 1928. Religion became an open issue in the 1960 campaign after a group of Protestant ministers issued a statement questioning Kennedy's fitness to govern on the grounds that Roman Catholicism was "both a church and a temporal state." Kennedy confronted this issue in a powerful speech to a Baptist audience in Texas. Vowing to uphold the constitutional separation of church and state, he added: "If this election is decided on the basis that 40,000,000 Americans lost their chance of being president on the day they were baptized, then it is the whole nation that will be the loser in the eyes of history."

Kennedy's other hurdle—inexperience—was removed in a series of televised debates with Nixon that marked the beginning of modern presidential campaigns. The first debate had the greatest impact, as more than 80 million Americans watched on television or listened on radio. Though both candidates spoke well, the handsome, well-groomed Kennedy radiated confidence and charm, while Nixon appeared awkward and ill at ease. Those who heard the debate on radio scored it a draw. Those who saw it on television thought Kennedy the clear victor.

Kennedy won the election with 303 electoral votes to Nixon's 219 (see Map 26.2). Yet the popular vote was the closest since 1888, with Kennedy getting 34,227,000 (49.7 percent) and Nixon 34,109,000 (49.6 percent). A swing

(© David J. & Janice L. Frent Collection/CORBIS)

Kennedy Campaign Button. John F. Kennedy would become the second Catholic and the youngest candidate to run for president on a major party ticket.

MAP 26.2

The Election of 1960

In winning one of the closest presidential contests in American history, John F. Kennedy barely kept the Democratic New Deal coalition together. Several key factors were at work in this election, including the impact of the first televised presidential debates, the Catholic issue, and the suspicion of voter fraud in the key states of Texas and Illinois.

Candidate (Party)	Electoral Vote		Popular Vote	
Kennedy (Democrat)	303	56.5%	34,266,731	49.7%
Nixon (Republican)	219	40.75%	34,108,157	49.5%
Byrd (Independent)	15	2.75%	501,643	0.7%

(Copyright © Cengage Learning)

of several thousand votes in Texas and Illinois, where suspicions of ballot fraud were rampant, would have given the election to Nixon. Kennedy did well among traditional Democrats (minorities, urban dwellers, the working class), and swept the Catholic vote, yet polls showed his religion costing him dearly in rural Protestant areas.

As the 1950s ended, nagging questions remained. Would prosperity and racial justice ever reach into the far corners of the land? Would the civil rights movement retain its momentum and nonviolent stance? Would the nation's expanding Cold War military commitments drain its economic strength—and moral authority? Would the lure of materialism and consumerism undermine precious national values? These questions would dominate the American agenda in the tumultuous years ahead.

CHAPTER REVIEW, 1953–1960

SUMMARY

- The 1953 truce in Korea eased Cold War tensions and ended an increasingly unpopular war.

- The civil rights movement gained dramatic momentum with *Brown v. Board of Education*, the Montgomery bus boycott, and the school integration crisis in Little Rock.

- The condemnation of Senator McCarthy cooled passions surrounding the volatile issue of domestic subversion.

- A distinct youth culture emerged, fueled by the postwar baby boom.

- The launching of *Sputnik* in 1957 raised concerns that the United States was falling behind the Soviet Union in the critical fields of science and technology.

- Senator John F. Kennedy was elected president in 1960 by a razor-thin margin, returning the White House to Democratic control.

IDENTIFICATIONS

Cold War

Ho Chi Minh

domino theory

Brown v. Board of Education of Topeka

Rosa Parks

Martin Luther King, Jr.

Montgomery bus boycott

Alan Freed

Little Richard

Nikita Khrushchev

Orval Faubus

Sputnik I

Francis Gary Powers

MAKING CONNECTIONS: LOOKING AHEAD Ⅲ➡

Chapter 27 considers the turbulent times that followed the relative tranquility of the 1950s, showing the connections between these periods and following the political and cultural events that so badly divided the nation.

1. Did the narrow election victory of John F. Kennedy in the 1960 presidential election send a signal that Americans wanted a change of political course? If so, what sort of change did they have in mind?

2. Would it be possible to build on the major civil rights victories of the 1950s and fulfill the promises of Reconstruction almost a century before—the promises of voting rights, economic opportunity, and equal protection under the law?

3. Would the Cold War with the Soviet Union continue to dominate international relations, and would it expand into other regions of the world?

RECOMMENDED READINGS

Doherty, Tom. *Cold War Cool Medium* (2003). Explores the impact of the Cold War on American popular culture, especially television.

Dudziak, Mary. *Cold War, Civil Rights* (2000). Examines the impact of America's civil rights movement on the international scene.

Guralnick, Peter. *Last Train to Memphis: The Rise of Elvis Presley* (1994). Traces the early years of rock 'n' roll's most popular artist and the reasons for his extraordinary success.

Halberstam, David. *The Fifties* (1993). Offers an encyclopedic account of this decade, from McCarthyism to McDonald's.

Kahn, Roger. *The Boys of Summer* (1971). Recalls the glory days of Major League baseball in a simpler time.

Lewis, Tom. *Divided Highways* (1997). Shows how the building of the interstate highway system transformed American life.

Marling, Karal Ann. *As Seen on TV* (1994). Looks at the rise of visual culture in a new age of leisure.

May, Elaine. *Homeward Bound: American Families in the Cold War Era* (1988). Ties the anxieties associated with anticommunism and the atomic bomb to the national quest for security and stability in the American home.

Oshinsky, David M. *A Conspiracy So Immense: The World of Joe McCarthy* (1983). Explores the life of America's great Red hunter and the era that bears his name.

Ransby, Barbara. *Ella Baker and the Black Freedom Movement* (2003). A biography of a leading civil rights activist and cofounder of the Southern Christian Leadership Conference.

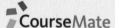 **CourseMate** Go to the CourseMate website at www.cengagebrain.com for additional study tools and review materials for this chapter.

PASSAGES 1960 to 2010

27 The Turbulent Years, 1960–1968

28 Crisis of Confidence, 1969–1980

29 From Reagan to Clinton, 1981–2000

30 A Conservative Nation in a Globalizing World, 2000–2010

Who could have predicted the turmoil and tragedy of the 1960s? The previous decade, after all, gave scant warning that trouble lay ahead. Filled with momentous milestones, such as the National Highway Act and *Brown v. Board of Education*, the 1950s seemed to reflect the optimism and stability of a confident nation—a place of widely shared values and little public complaint.

The tumult of the 1960s began with the jailings and beatings of civil rights workers in the South, which turned many activists against the philosophy of nonviolence. The civil rights movement, in turn, spawned a women's movement, and then a student movement, further challenging the status quo. Meanwhile, the escalating Vietnam War eroded the credibility of American officials and divided the nation in dangerous ways. Against the backdrop of increasing bloodshed in Southeast Asia, the United States endured a horrifying cycle of homegrown violence in the 1960s, including inner-city riots, militant campus upheavals, and the assassination of prominent public figures like President John F. Kennedy, his brother Robert, and the Reverend Martin Luther King, Jr.

The 1970s brought little relief. An American president resigned from office for the first time in the nation's history. The North Vietnamese Communists took over South Vietnam. Americans faced gas shortages, high unemployment, and staggering inflation. They watched with anger and embarrassment as their embassy in Iran was attacked and fifty-two Americans were held hostage for more than a year.

Republican Ronald Reagan won the 1980 presidential election by promising to reverse the nation's apparent decline. Mixing personal charm and optimism with the darker politics of resentment, he attracted mainstream voters by vowing to strengthen family values, reward hard work, and increase respect for America around the world. At the same time, he reinforced the notion among white working-class voters (known as "Reagan Democrats") that the party of Franklin Roosevelt had deserted their interests—that the real enemies of working people were no longer big business and the very rich, but rather big government and the very poor. During the 1980s, the Reagan administration's policies regarding taxes, unions, banking, and antitrust produced one of the most dramatic redistributions of wealth in American history, with the top 1 percent seeing its yearly income rise by 75 percent and the rest of the nation experiencing almost no gain at all. Still, Reagan remained a popular president who articulated the fears and dreams of Americans with extraordinary skill.

Through all the tumult, one certainty remained—the specter of international communism. Although the fear of domestic subversion stirred up by Senator Joseph McCarthy had largely subsided by 1960, the anxieties generated by Soviet power and influence remained solidly in place. During the 1960s, the United States and Russia tangled over Berlin and Cuba, where the placement of offensive missiles led to the most dangerous confrontation of the Cold War. In Vietnam, meanwhile, American officials defended the growing involvement as a test of will against Soviet-inspired aggression. The larger goals, they insisted, were to halt the spread of world communism and maintain American credibility around the globe.

The 1970s brought an apparent thaw in U.S.–Soviet relations. The two sides signed a momentous agreement, known as SALT I, that limited nuclear weapons. President Nixon also visited the Soviet Union as well as Communist China, raising hopes for serious dialogue, or détente. It did not happen. The very idea of negotiating with the Russians over issues such as human rights and arms control offended hard-line anti-Communists who believed that American military power must largely determine the outcome of the Cold War.

The Reagan administration dramatically increased the nation's defense budget. It also funded military

Selma March. Marchers in Selma, Alabama, in 1965 faced constant violence from local police as they demonstrated for the right to vote. Their enormous courage focused world attention on their plight, leading to passage of the Voting Rights Act of 1965.

(Peter Pettus/Library of Congress)

campaigns against leftist rebels and Marxist governments in Africa, Asia, and Latin America. In one instance, it funneled money from a secret arms deal with Iran to illegally finance a right-wing guerrilla army in Nicaragua. President Reagan made no apologies for this activity. The Soviets had created an "Evil Empire," he declared, and it must be confronted.

In fact, that empire was already in trouble. Assuming power in 1985, Soviet Premier Mikhail Gorbachev well understood the problems his nation faced. Believing that communism must become more democratic and market oriented in order to survive, he encouraged the policies known as *glasnost* (openness) and *perestroika* (restructuring). In trying to save communism, however, Gorbachev set in motion the very forces that would bring it down. A wave of protest swept through Eastern Europe, demanding more freedom and closer contacts with the West.

On a trip to West Berlin in 1987, President Reagan encouraged the protesters by demanding: "Mr. Gorbachev, tear down this wall." Two years later, the Communist governments in Eastern Europe began falling like dominoes.

In 1991, the Soviet Union collapsed, and Russians began the painful transition to democratic politics and a free market economy. For the United States, meanwhile, a new set of challenges had emerged. As the world's lone "superpower," it now faced a post–Cold War era marred by ethnic violence in the Balkans, tribal warfare in Africa, military

conflict in the Middle East, and nuclear proliferation around the world. In addition, a booming world birthrate and the specter of global warming raised serious environmental concerns, and the rapid spread of technology and information linked people together in remarkable new ways. During the 1990s, the American economy achieved unprecedented levels of prosperity, but politics took on an especially bitter tone. The Republicans regained control of the House of Representatives in 1994 for the first time in four decades, and a second term for President Bill Clinton seemed doubtful. Yet he won reelection, only to face impeachment arising from a sex scandal in 1998. Despite Clinton's acquittal, his presidency ended under a cloud. In 2000, his vice president, Al Gore, lost a close election to Republican George W. Bush. On September 11, 2001, terrorist attacks on the United States stunned the American people. By mid-decade the nation was involved in wars in Afghanistan and Iraq.

Reelected in 2004, President Bush saw his popularity slide as these conflicts dragged on and the economy slowed down. The first decade of the new millennium was filled with enormous challenges, from domestic terrorism and foreign conflicts to environmental concerns and economic stagnation. All would test the nation's institutions and the resolve of its people. Seeking a new direction, Americans voted for change in the 2008 election when Barack Obama won the presidency with Democratic majorities in both houses of Congress.

POLITICS AND DIPLOMACY

1960: John F. Kennedy elected president
1961: Berlin Wall erected
1962: Cuban missile crisis
1963: President Kennedy assassinated
1964: Lyndon B. Johnson elected president
Civil Rights Act passed
1965: U.S. troop levels in Vietnam exceed 100,000
Malcolm X assassinated
1967: Antiwar protests multiply
1968: Martin Luther King, Jr., assassinated
Robert Kennedy assassinated
Richard Nixon elected president

1970: U.S troops invade Cambodia
1972: President Nixon visits China
Watergate burglary
1973: Vice President Agnew resigns
1974: President Nixon resigns; Gerald Ford becomes president
1976: Jimmy Carter elected president
1977: Panama Canal treaties
1978: Camp David Accords
1979: Hostage crisis in Iran

1980: Ronald Reagan elected president
1981: Reagan survives assassination attempt
Sandra Day O'Connor becomes first female Supreme Court justice
1983: Invasion of Grenada
1984: Geraldine Ferraro becomes first woman nominated for vice president by a major political party
1985: Mikhail Gorbachev becomes leader of the Soviet Union
1986: Iran-Contra scandal begins
1988: George H. W. Bush elected president
1989: Berlin Wall falls

SOCIETY AND CULTURE

1961: Freedom Rides
1962: Students for a Democratic Society formed
1963: Betty Friedan publishes *The Feminine Mystique*
1964: Beatles tour United States
1965: Race riot in Watts
1966: National Organization for Women formed
1967: Haight-Ashbury "summer of love"
1968: Cesar Chavez leads California grape strike
Antiwar protests disrupt Democratic National Convention

1970: Student protesters killed at Kent State and Jackson State
1973: *Roe v. Wade* legalizes abortion
1974: Antibusing protests in Boston
1975: *Saturday Night Live* airs on NBC
1978: Supreme Court upholds affirmative action in *Bakke* case

1981: AIDS epidemic begins in U.S.
1982: Vietnam War Memorial dedicated in Washington
1983: Sally Ride first American woman in space
1984: Summer Olympics in Los Angeles
1985: Rock Hudson dies of AIDS
1986: *Challenger* space shuttle explodes
1988: Antidepressant drug Prozac introduced
1989: Oil tanker *Exxon Valdez* goes aground in Alaska

ECONOMICS AND TECHNOLOGY

1960: Oral contraceptive ("the Pill") marketed
1962: John Glenn orbits the Earth aboard *Friendship 7*
1969: Apollo moon landing

1973: Arab oil embargo triggers energy crisis
1978: National Energy Act passed
1979: Nuclear accident at Three Mile Island

1981: Air traffic controllers strike
1982: Budget deficit exceeds $100 billion for first time
1984: Macintosh computer introduced
1986: Tax Reform Act passed
1988: United States, Canada sign free trade agreement
President Bush approves $300 billion plan to bail out savings and loan industry

1990	2000	2005

1990: Iraq invades Kuwait
1991: Persian Gulf War drives Iraq out of Kuwait
Clarence Thomas–Anita Hill clash before Congress
1992: Bill Clinton elected president
1993: Branch Davidian confrontation in Waco, Texas
1994: Republicans regain control of House of Representatives for first time in 40 years
1995: Bombing of Oklahoma City federal building kills more than 160 people
1996: Clinton reelected
1998: Clinton sex scandal breaks
Clinton impeached
1999: Clinton acquitted by Senate
Kosovo crisis: NATO launches air war against Serbia

2000: Disputed election results in Florida end in Supreme Court ruling that allows George W. Bush to become president
2001: Terrorists attack World Trade Center, Pentagon, on September 11
War in Afghanistan
2002: Republicans regain control of Senate and dominate all branches of government
2003: United States invades Iraq and topples regime of Saddam Hussein
2004: George W. Bush reelected

2005: Chief Justice William Rehnquist dies
John Roberts confirmed as Chief Justice
2006: Democrats regain control of both houses of Congress
2007: Nancy Pelosi becomes first female Speaker of House of Representatives
2008: Barack Obama elected president
Troubled Asset Relief Program (TARP) bill passes to stabilize stock market and banking system
2009: American Recovery and Reinvestment Act passes
Sonia Sotamoyor confirmed as Supreme Court Justice
President Obama receives Nobel Peace Prize
2010: Patient Protection and Affordable Care Act passes
Dodd-Frank Wall Street Reform and Consumer Protection Act passes
Elena Kagan confirmed as Supreme Court Justice

1990: Hubble space telescope launched
1991: Basketball star Magic Johnson reveals he is HIV positive
1993: Toni Morrison wins Nobel Prize for literature
1995: O.J. Simpson acquitted of murder charges in Los Angeles
1996: Virginia Military Institute admits women
1997: Movie *Titanic* sets box office records
1998: Mark McGuire hits record 70 home runs

2000: *Star Wars, Episode 1, The Phantom Menace* opens to long lines and poor reviews
2001: Michael Jordan returns to basketball
2002: Former President Jimmy Carter wins Nobel Peace Prize
2003: *Columbia* space shuttle explodes, killing all seven astronauts

2005: *Hurricane Katrina* devastates New Orleans and Gulf Coast
2007: Former Vice President Al Gore shares Nobel Peace Prize
2008: California Supreme Court legalizes gay marriage in state
2010: Arizona passes controversial immigration bill

1991: Economy enters recession
1993: North American Free Trade Agreement (NAFTA) passed
1995: Budget battle in Congress leads to federal government shutdown in December
1996: Congress passes sweeping welfare reform bill
1997: Federal budget surplus reported

2001: Congress passes Bush's tax cuts
2001: Enron scandal breaks
2002: Hybrid cars, mixing gas with electric power, gain in popularity

2007: Subprime mortgage crisis weakens economy
2008: Economy nears recession
2008: Stock markets plummet worldwide when investment firm Lehman Brothers fails
2009: Congress passes bailout bill to rescue Big Three automobile companies from bankruptcy
Bernard Madoff convicted for operating multi-billion dollar Ponzi scheme
Unemployment rate rises to 10%
2010: Apple's iPad introduced
BP Deepwater Horizon rig explodes, causing catastrophic oil spill in the Gulf of Mexico

27 The Turbulent Years

1960–1968

Early Tests, 1961

Idealism and Caution
The Bay of Pigs
The Berlin Wall
The Freedom Riders
The New Economics

Social and Political Challenges, 1962–1963

The Battle for Ole Miss
The Missiles of October
Trouble in Vietnam
From Birmingham to Washington
Feminist Stirrings

Tragedy and Transition

Kennedy's Assassination
LBJ's Strong Start
Landslide in 1964
The Great Society, 1964–1965
Health Care and Immigration Reform

The Expanding War, 1965–1966

Point of No Return
Early Protests

Doing History: Visions of the
"Multiversity"

The Rights Revolution: Center Stage

Voting Rights
The Watts Explosion
Black Power
"Sisterhood Is Powerful"
The Counterculture

A Divided Nation, 1968

The Tet Offensive
The President Steps Aside
A Violent Spring
The Chicago Convention
Nixon's the One

MAKING CONNECTIONS

◀─▮▮ LOOKING BACK

Chapter 26 examined the promise and prosperity of the United States in the 1950s—a time of great medical and technological advances, the growth of commercial television, an exploding youth culture, and great legal advances and burgeoning movements in the struggle for equal rights. Before starting Chapter 27, you should be able to answer the following questions:

1. What ideological principles and personal qualities defined the Eisenhower presidency? Why did this presidency seem to fit the national mood so well?

2. How did the spread of commercial television both define and reflect the cultural values of post–World War II America?

3. Why did the Soviet launching of *Sputnik* have such a profound effect on U.S. society? Why did it cause so much national soul searching and self-reflection?

4. How did the combination of legal victories and local protests combine to fuel the civil rights movement of the 1950s?

The 1960s opened on an ambivalent note. The gross national product reached $500 billion for the first time, yet talk of economic recession was in the air. The darkest days of McCarthyism were over, yet the fear of communism remained. The development of new products and technologies bred optimism, yet the spread of new weapons caused alarm.

Hints of protest and trouble had begun to appear. In Greensboro, North Carolina, four black college students who sat down at a Woolworth lunch counter and were denied service refused to leave. Word of their defiance triggered sit-in protests across the South, with demonstrators bravely confronting Jim Crow. Half a world away, supporters of North Vietnam's Communist ruler, Ho Chi Minh, announced the formation of a National Liberation Front to overthrow the anti-Communist government of President Ngo Dinh Diem in South Vietnam. Diem didn't seem concerned. With U.S. support, he boasted, his forces would quickly subdue these "Vietcong" [Vietnamese Communists] and bring peace to his land.

❖ Early Tests, 1961

The 1960 election was a landmark event in American political history. At age forty-three, John Kennedy became the first Catholic president, the youngest candidate to win a presidential election, and the first president to be born in the twentieth century. His inauguration on January 20, 1961, seemed to herald a new era of idealism and change. Kennedy declared: "Ask not what your country can do for you; ask what you can do for your country."

Idealism and Caution

The new administration appeared to mirror these words. Young people converged on Washington with a fervor reminiscent of the early New Deal years. Public service became a badge of honor. The new secretary of state, Dean Rusk, came from the Rockefeller Foundation; the new defense secretary, Robert McNamara, left the presidency of the Ford Motor Company to help "streamline" the nation's armed forces. Kennedy chose his younger brother Robert to become attorney general. Under Jacqueline Kennedy's direction, the White House became a center for the arts.

Despite the lofty rhetoric and the fanfare, Kennedy took a measured approach to his early presidential duties, in part because his electoral margin had been so narrow. He also had to contend with a Congress in which conservative Republicans and southern Democrats held the balance of power. Kennedy's early initiatives included an increase in Social Security benefits and a raise in the minimum wage, from $1 to $1.25. A $2.3 billion education bill for school construction and higher teachers' salaries, however, died in committee.

In other areas, the new administration achieved success. By executive order, Kennedy launched the Peace Corps in March 1961. Directed by the president's brother-in-law R. Sargent Shriver, the Peace Corps sent thousands of American volunteers to underdeveloped nations to provide educational and technical assistance. With a tiny budget, it became one of Kennedy's great triumphs, showcasing American idealism and know-how throughout the world. Within three years, almost ten thousand volunteers were at work in forty-six countries. Even more popular, though far more expensive, was the space program. Setting the goal of a manned moon landing "before this decade is out," Kennedy convinced a skeptical

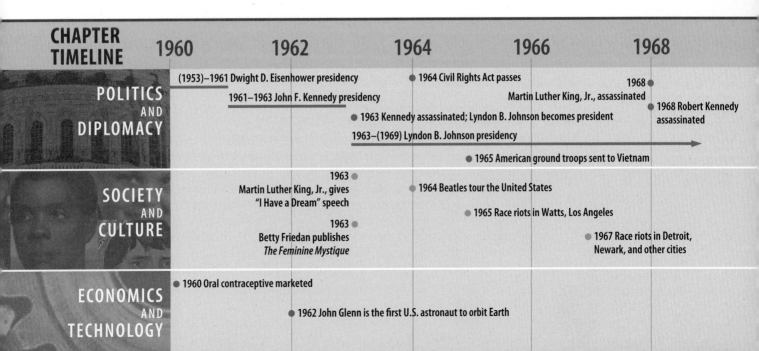

CHAPTER TIMELINE	1960	1962	1964	1966	1968
POLITICS AND DIPLOMACY	(1953)–1961 Dwight D. Eisenhower presidency 1961–1963 John F. Kennedy presidency		● 1964 Civil Rights Act passes ● 1963 Kennedy assassinated; Lyndon B. Johnson becomes president 1963–(1969) Lyndon B. Johnson presidency ● 1965 American ground troops sent to Vietnam	1968 ● Martin Luther King, Jr., assassinated	● 1968 Robert Kennedy assassinated
SOCIETY AND CULTURE		1963 ● Martin Luther King, Jr., gives "I Have a Dream" speech 1963 ● Betty Friedan publishes *The Feminine Mystique*	● 1964 Beatles tour the United States ● 1965 Race riots in Watts, Los Angeles	● 1967 Race riots in Detroit, Newark, and other cities	
ECONOMICS AND TECHNOLOGY	● 1960 Oral contraceptive marketed	● 1962 John Glenn is the first U.S. astronaut to orbit Earth			

Glenn, John (1921–) Astronaut, U.S. Senator (1974–1998). On February 20, 1962, aboard the *Friendship 7*, he was the first American to orbit the earth; in 1998 he was the oldest person to participate in a space flight mission as a member of the space shuttle *Discovery*.

Castro, Fidel (1926–) Cuban revolutionary leader who overthrew dictator Fulgencio Batista in 1959 and soon after established a Communist state. Prime minister of Cuba from 1959 to1976, he served as president of the government and First Secretary of the Communist Party from 1976 to 2008.

Bay of Pigs (1961) Place where fifteen hundred Cuban exiles, supported by the CIA, landed on April 17, 1961, in an unsuccessful attempt to overthrow the new Communist government of Fidel Castro.

Congress to allocate billions of dollars for space research and rocketry, a training program for astronauts, and a mission control center in Houston.

The space race captivated the world. In April 1961, Soviet cosmonaut Yuri Gagarin orbited the globe in less than two hours. A month later, Commander Alan Shepard rocketed three hundred miles from Cape Canaveral in a suborbital flight, and in February 1962, Lieutenant Colonel **John Glenn** orbited the earth three times aboard *Friendship 7* before touching down in the Caribbean. Glenn became a national hero, with ticker-tape parades and a televised address before a joint session of Congress.

The Bay of Pigs

Kennedy inherited his first crisis from the previous administration. As president-elect, he was told of a secret plan, personally approved by Eisenhower, to overthrow the new Marxist government of **Fidel Castro** in Cuba. The plan called for several hundred anti-Castro exiles, trained and equipped by the CIA, to invade Cuba and trigger an anti-Communist revolution. Kennedy agreed that Castro set a dangerous example by aligning Cuba with the Soviet Union; he had promised to "get tough" with Castro during the 1960 campaign. He could not easily back down now.

On April 17, 1961, a brigade of fifteen hundred waded ashore at the **Bay of Pigs,** on Cuba's southern coast. Nothing went as planned. The landing site had sharp coral reefs and swampy terrain, making it hard to unload supplies and move out from the beaches. Local workers quickly spotted the invaders, and news of their arrival sparked no popular uprising against Castro. Kennedy refused to lend vital air and naval support to the brigade in a futile attempt to hide America's role in this disaster. More than a hundred invaders were killed, and the rest were captured. After reviewing the events with his advisers, Kennedy took a walk on the White House lawn. It was "the first time in my life," a friend recalled, "that I ever saw tears come to his eyes."

The Bay of Pigs fiasco left a troubled legacy. On the one hand, it angered Latin Americans and drove Castro even closer to the Russian embrace. On the other, the incident marked Kennedy as a man of action, willing to take chances in the war against communism. His popularity soared. The incident also fueled Kennedy's interest in covert operations and his desire to control them more directly. After removing long-time CIA director Allen Dulles, the president approved a top-secret program, code-named Operation Mongoose, to topple the Cuban government and assassinate its leaders. Its plans included the destruction of Cuba's vital sugar crop and a box of exploding cigars for Castro.

The Berlin Wall

In June 1961, Kennedy met with Soviet leader Nikita Khrushchev in Vienna. Khrushchev tried to bully the new president, threatening to give East Germany full control over road and rail access to West Berlin, in violation of previous guarantees. Berlin was an embarrassment to Khrushchev. The prosperous western sector stood as a model of democratic capitalism behind the Iron Curtain. Each day, more than a thousand refugees from the Communist side poured into West Berlin. At this rate, East Germany would lose most of its skilled workers to the West.

Kennedy met the challenge, declaring that North Atlantic Treaty Organization (NATO) forces would defend the city at all costs. To emphasize this point, the president tripled draft calls, mobilized reserve units, and requested $3 billion in additional defense appropriations, which Congress quickly granted. The crisis ended in August 1961. As the world watched in amazement, workers in East

Berlin constructed a wall of barbed wire and concrete around the western edge of their city, sealing off East Berlin, and eventually all of East Germany, from the non-Communist world. In a tactical sense, Khrushchev achieved his objective of stopping the East German exodus to the West. In a larger sense, the wall became an admission of failure—a monument to freedom denied.

The Freedom Riders

Kennedy's first domestic crisis occurred in the field of civil rights. An integration-ist at heart, the president wanted change to come slowly, without the mass pro-tests and violent incidents that had made headlines around the world. He worried, too, that White House support for immediate desegregation would cost him the goodwill of powerful southerners in Congress.

In 1961, the Congress of Racial Equality (CORE) announced plans to test a recent Supreme Court decision, *Boynton v. Virginia*, which prohibited racial segre-gation in public facilities engaged in interstate transportation. CORE's objective, said its national director, was "to provoke the southern authorities into arresting us and thereby prod the Justice Department into enforcing the law of the land." In May, thirteen "freedom riders"—seven blacks and six whites—left Washington on a Greyhound bus bound for New Orleans, ignoring "white" and "colored" signs that hung by the toilets, lunch counters, and waiting rooms in defiance of federal law. Trouble erupted in Anniston, Alabama, when their bus was firebombed by a white mob. As the passengers struggled outside, they were beaten with fists and clubs.

When the violence continued in Montgomery and Birmingham, Alabama, Attorney General Robert Kennedy urged CORE to end the **freedom rides,** claim-ing that they embarrassed President Kennedy on the eve of his summit with Premier Khrushchev. "Doesn't the attorney general know," a black Alabaman responded, "that we've been embarrassed all our lives?" Ultimately, the violence compelled Kennedy to send in federal marshals to protect the freedom riders. In September 1961, the federal government banned interstate carriers from using any terminal that segregated the races.

freedom riders Interracial groups who rode buses in the South so that a series of federal court decisions declaring segregation on buses and in waiting rooms unconstitutional would not be ignored by white officials.

The New Economics

Despite his increasing focus on civil rights, President Kennedy considered the economy to be his top domestic concern. Economic growth in the Eisenhower years had been steady but increasingly slow. Real wages for an average family rose a remarkable 20 percent in the 1950s, but a series of recessions toward the end of Eisenhower's second term prompted both a drop in factory production and a rise in unemployment. By the time Kennedy took office, more Americans were out of work than at any other time since the end of World War II.

In 1962, Kennedy unveiled an economic program that differed sharply from the spending model of the New Deal and Fair Deal. He proposed a major tax cut for consumers and businesses, designed to stimulate purchasing power and encourage new investment. To prevent inflation, Kennedy lobbied business and labor leaders to respect the wage and price guidelines his administration recom-mended. The Teamsters, Auto Workers, and Steel Workers all agreed to modest wage hikes in 1962, but two weeks later, U.S. Steel, the nation's third largest cor-poration, announced a whopping price increase of six dollars a ton, leading other steel companies to do the same.

Kennedy used his influence to roll back the price increase, winning a major victory in his battle against inflation, although his rough tactics aroused deep anger in the business community. Nevertheless, the economy prospered in the early 1960s, achieving low unemployment, stable prices, and steady growth.

❖ Social and Political Challenges, 1962–1963

Before long, President Kennedy's successes led him to take more confident stands in certain areas, such as U.S.–Soviet relations and the push for civil rights. As events unfolded in 1962, the president faced challenges in familiar places—the Deep South and the waters off Cuba. This time, the stakes were much higher.

The Battle for Ole Miss

In the fall of 1962, a federal court ordered the admission of James Meredith, a black air force veteran, to the all-white University of Mississippi, known as Ole Miss. Governor Ross Barnett led the opposition. A virulent racist, who claimed that "God made the Negro different to punish him," Barnett had kept a previous black applicant from entering Ole Miss by having him committed to a mental hospital. Now Barnett warned that Mississippi would ignore all federal rulings in order to keep segregation in place.

Kennedy responded to Barnett's challenge by dispatching several hundred federal marshals to Ole Miss. They were met by a well-armed mob, more than two thousand strong. In the riot that followed, two people were killed and hundreds were injured, including twenty-eight marshals hit by gunfire. Kennedy rushed in troops and federalized the state Guard. With twenty-three thousand soldiers on campus—five times the student population—Meredith registered for classes under army bayonets. The battle at Ole Miss was over; the larger struggle for Mississippi lay ahead.

The Missiles of October

In October 1962, the world faced the most dangerous confrontation of the entire Cold War. It began with rumors, confirmed by **U-2** spy plane photos, that the Soviets were deploying intermediate-range ballistic missiles in Cuba. Speed was essential, Kennedy believed, for the missiles would become operational in less than a month. In fact, newly declassified documents have shown that a number of these Soviet missiles, carrying warheads nearly the size of the Hiroshima bomb, were already operational in Cuba—a reality of which Kennedy and his advisers were completely unaware.

Castro's need for security was understandable. In addition to Operation Mongoose, the Kennedy administration had imposed an economic embargo on Cuba and engineered its expulsion from the Organization of American States. At Castro's urging, the Soviet Union sent thousands of military advisers to Cuba, as well as defensive missiles to shoot down invading planes. Yet the deployment of offensive weapons, capable of reaching Chicago or Washington with nuclear warheads, was an alarming escalation designed to tip the balance of terror in Moscow's favor.

Kennedy convened an executive committee (known as ex-Comm) to provide a suitable response. Some ex-Comm members recommended immediate air strikes to take out the missile bases. Others, including **Robert F. Kennedy,** proposed a naval quarantine of Cuba. The president chose the latter. A quarantine shifted the burden of responsibility to Khrushchev while allowing both sides to seek a solution short of war.

On October 22, 1962, Kennedy addressed the nation on television. After describing the quarantine, he demanded that Russia remove the missiles and warned that any missile fired from Cuba would be regarded "as an attack by the Soviet Union on the United States," requiring a "full retaliatory response." American forces went on full alert. A U-2 plane over Cuba was shot down, and

U-2 U.S. spy plane. One piloted by Francis Gary Powers was shot down over the Soviet Union in 1960, which led to the angry breakup of a summit meeting in Paris between President Eisenhower and Soviet Premier Nikita Khrushchev.

Kennedy, Robert F. (1925–1968) Attorney general during the presidency of his brother John F. Kennedy. Elected to the Senate in 1964, he was assassinated in Los Angeles while campaigning for the presidency.

its pilot killed. The entire world watched anxiously as Communist-bloc vessels in the Caribbean inched closer to U.S. warships enforcing the quarantine.

On October 26, Kennedy received an emotional note from Khrushchev suggesting a settlement: Russia would remove its missiles if the United States pledged never to invade Cuba. Before the president could respond, however, a second note arrived from Khrushchev demanding that the United States also remove its Jupiter missiles along the Soviet border in Turkey. Robert Kennedy advised his brother to respond to the first note and ignore the second one. On October 27, the president vowed not to invade Cuba if the missiles were removed. In private, meanwhile, Robert Kennedy assured Soviet ambassador Anatoly Dobrynin that the Jupiter missiles would be removed from Turkey in the near future.

On October 28, Khrushchev accepted the deal. The Soviet premier had badly miscalculated the stern American reaction to the placement of offensive missiles in Cuba, though his restraint in the crisis helped to lead to a peaceful solution. Khrushchev soon left office in disgrace, and Kennedy's reputation soared. For two weeks in October, the world had seemed headed for nuclear war.

That fact alone seemed to sober both sides. In July 1963, a direct telephone link, known as the "hot line," was established between the White House and the Kremlin. In August, the United States and Russia joined with ninety other nations to sign the Treaty Banning Nuclear Weapons Tests in the Atmosphere, in Outer Space, and Under Water. A first step had been taken to cleanse the environment of radioactivity—a symbolic step on the road to a safer world.

Trouble in Vietnam

President Kennedy came away from the missile crisis with greater confidence in his ability to manage foreign problems. His primary goal, in military terms, was to replace the Eisenhower-Dulles doctrine of "massive retaliation" with a "flexible response" policy that would maximize his options in any foreign crisis. The plan called for a buildup in nuclear missiles, conventional ground troops, and Special Forces such as the "Green Berets." Not surprisingly, the defense budget rose rapidly in the Kennedy years, giving the United States a sizable advantage over Russia in nuclear weapons.

When Kennedy entered the White House, fewer than a thousand American military advisers were stationed in South Vietnam. Like Eisenhower, Kennedy hoped to formalize Vietnam's temporary partition at the seventeenth parallel by turning the South Vietnamese regime of Ngo Dinh Diem into a military power capable of defending itself against attacks from Ho Chi Minh's Communist

(Malcolm Browne-AP Photo)

Buddhist Protests. Quang Duc, a Buddhist monk in Saigon, burned himself to death in June 1963 to protest the crackdown on Buddhists by South Vietnamese President Ngo Dinh Diem. The Buddhist protests helped bring down the Diem government later that year.

government in the North. U.S. Special Forces were dispatched to train South Vietnam's army, along with CIA personnel to direct covert operations and economic experts to supervise the aid programs intended to stabilize Diem's regime. But Diem was not a promising leader. Educated in the United States, a Catholic in a largely Buddhist land, Diem had little in common with the people he ruled, and he seemed disinterested in popular policies such as land reform and religious toleration necessary to keep him in power.

In 1963, protests erupted in Saigon and other South Vietnamese cities over Diem's autocratic rule. The Buddhists held mass demonstrations against religious oppression, with several monks setting fire to themselves. As the protests escalated, army units attacked Buddhist temples and arrested their priests, sparking even greater protests from the Buddhist majority. That fall, Diem was overthrown in a military coup engineered by South Vietnam's top generals. American officials knew about the coup but did nothing to stop it. To their surprise, the generals murdered Diem and his brother, Ngo Dinh Nhu.

By that time, sixteen thousand American "advisers" were stationed in South Vietnam. For Kennedy, the struggle had become a test of will against "Communist aggression." Yet the president also worried that the use of American troops created a dangerous momentum of its own. "It's like taking a drink," he said. "The effect wears off and you have to take another."

From Birmingham to Washington

In the early 1960s, the fires of social and political protest slowly came alive. Racial injustice was a central issue. Birmingham, Alabama, became the new battleground, as a coalition of civil rights groups, led by Martin Luther King's Southern Christian Leadership Conference, protested discrimination in a city where African Americans had few economic opportunities or political rights. Dr. King hoped to integrate Birmingham with a series of nonviolent protests code-named "Project C," for confrontation. There were sit-ins at lunch counters, kneel-ins at white churches, and voter registration marches to city hall. Birmingham authorities cracked down hard. Led by Commissioner Eugene ("Bull") Connor, city police dispersed the protesters—many of them schoolchildren—with attack dogs and high-pressure fire hoses.

Birmingham Police Dogs.
Led by Eugene ("Bull") Connor, Birmingham police used attack dogs and high-pressure fire hoses to disperse civil rights demonstrators.

(AP Photo-Bill Hudson)

Dr. King was among the hundreds arrested for violating local court orders against marching and picketing. From his jail cell, he defended the morality of civil disobedience, noting that "segregation statutes are unjust because segregation distorts the soul." President Kennedy offered firm support, but Governor George C. Wallace—proclaiming "Segregation Now! Segregation Tomorrow! Segregation Forever"—personally blocked the admission of two black students to the University of Alabama by "standing in the schoolhouse door." When federal marshals arrived, Wallace dramatically stepped aside.

Viewing civil rights for the first time as a moral issue, Kennedy delivered a moving appeal for justice on national television. "One hundred years have passed since President Lincoln freed the slaves," he said, "yet their heirs, their grandsons, are not fully free. . . . And this nation, for all its hope and all its boasts, will not be fully free until all its citizens are free." Later that evening, civil rights activist Medgar Evers was assassinated outside his Jackson, Mississippi, home by a member of the Ku Klux Klan.

In June 1963, Kennedy sent Congress one of the most sweeping civil rights bills of the twentieth century. The bill, which prohibited discrimination in employment, federally assisted programs, and public accommodations such as restaurants and hotels, caused a furor on Capitol Hill. As the bill's momentum stalled, a number of civil rights groups led by A. Philip Randolph, long-time president of the Brotherhood of Sleeping Car Porters, announced a "March on Washington for Jobs and Freedom."

On August 28, 1963, more than two hundred thousand people gathered at the Lincoln Memorial in the largest civil rights demonstration ever held on American soil. They listened to the spirituals of Mahalia Jackson, locked arms in solidarity as Joan Baez sang "We Shall Overcome," the anthem of the civil rights struggle, and rose in thunderous applause to the final words of Martin Luther King's now legendary address, "I Have a Dream."

Martin Luther King, Jr. From the steps of the Lincoln Memorial, Martin Luther King, Jr., delivered his eloquent "I Have a Dream" address to the gathering of two hundred thousand people who had come to Washington to push for passage of a landmark civil rights bill in August 1963.

Feminist Stirrings

In the early 1960s, nonfiction books on a range of subjects helped to spur social movements. The year 1962 had witnessed the publication of two pathbreaking books about the underside of modern society: Michael Harrington's *The Other America*, which examined poverty, and Rachel Carson's *Silent Spring*. Carson, a marine biologist, exposed the contamination of wildlife, water supplies, and farmland by pesticides such as DDT. In 1963, two more seminal works appeared: **Betty Friedan's** *The Feminine Mystique*, which spurred the struggle for women's rights, and James Baldwin's *The Fire Next Time*, which warned of the growing racial divide. "To be a Negro in this country and to be relatively conscious," wrote Baldwin, "is to be in a rage all the time." Such publications helped to fuel movements that would transform modern American society.

The revival of feminism in the 1960s seemed long overdue. More than four decades after winning the vote, American women still played a minor role in government affairs. In 1963, there were no women governors, cabinet officers, or Supreme Court justices. The U.S. Senate contained one female member, Margaret Chase Smith of Maine. Discrimination also pervaded the workplace. Women were increasingly concentrated in low-paying service and clerical jobs despite their rising level of education. Full-time working women earned about 60 percent of the income of men.

Friedan, Betty (1921–2006) Feminist who wrote *The Feminist Mystique* (1963) and founded the National Organization for Women in 1966.

These inequities were highlighted in 1963 by the final report of the Presidential Commission on the Status of Women. Led by Eleanor Roosevelt (who had died in 1962) and Esther Peterson, an assistant secretary of labor, the commission detailed a wide range of problems, including job discrimination, unequal wages, lack of child care, and legal restrictions that prevented women in some states from sitting on juries or making wills. In direct response, President Kennedy issued an executive order banning sex discrimination in federal employment. A few months later, Congress passed the Equal Pay Act of 1963, requiring employers to provide equal wages to men and women who did the same work.

Even more important in terms of the emerging women's movement was the publication of *The Feminine Mystique*. In the opening chapters, Betty Friedan described "the problem that has no name": the emptiness felt by middle-class women who sacrificed their dreams and careers to become the "happy homemakers" of suburban America. Blaming educators, advertisers, and government officials for creating a climate in which femininity and domesticity went hand in hand. *The Feminine Mystique* became an instant best-seller because it voiced the unspoken, desperate feelings of so many women.

❖ Tragedy and Transition

By the fall of 1963, the fast pace and rapid changes of the new decade were leaving their mark. A growing economy, an emerging rights revolution, an expanding war in Southeast Asia, a frantic race to the moon—each would serve to reshape the fabric of American life in the years ahead. First, however, tragedy intervened.

Kennedy's Assassination

In late November 1963, John and Jacqueline Kennedy traveled to Texas on a political tour. The 1964 presidential race was approaching, and Texas, which had narrowly supported the Kennedy-Johnson ticket three years before, could not be taken for granted. The Kennedys took a motorcade through Dallas, with the bubble-top of their limousine removed on a warm and cloudless day. Along the route, people waved from office buildings and cheered from the sidewalks. As the procession reached Dealy Plaza, shots rang out from the window of a nearby book depository. President Kennedy grabbed his throat and slumped to the seat. Texas Governor John Connally was wounded in the back, wrist, and leg. The motorcade raced to Parkland Hospital, where the president was pronounced dead.

Within hours, the Dallas police arrested a twenty-four-year-old suspect named **Lee Harvey Oswald.** Two days later, Oswald was shot and killed in the basement of Dallas police headquarters by Jack Ruby, a local nightclub owner with a shady past. Dozens of theories surfaced about the Kennedy assassination, blaming leftists and rightists, Fidel Castro and the Mafia, the Ku Klux Klan and the CIA. The most logical theory, that a deranged man had committed a senseless act of violence, did not seem compelling enough to explain the death of a president so young and full of life.

Few other events in the nation's history produced so much bewilderment and grief. Charming and handsome, a war hero with a glamorous wife, Kennedy seemed the ideal president for the electronic political age. The media likened his administration to Camelot, a magical place that symbolized courage, chivalry, and hope. The reality was rather different, of course. Kennedy's 1,037 days in office were marked by failures as well as successes, and since his death, evidence of extramarital affairs and other personal shortcomings have raised questions about his character. Still, the president's final months were his most productive by far.

Oswald, Lee Harvey (1939–1963)
Alleged assassin of President John F. Kennedy, he was shot two days later while under arrest.

The Test Ban Treaty offered hope for a safer world, and a new civil rights bill had been sent to Capitol Hill. There is also the suggestion—disputed by some—that Kennedy was rethinking his position on Vietnam. The trip to Dallas shattered those plans.

LBJ's Strong Start

Within hours of the assassination, **Lyndon Baines Johnson** took the presidential oath of office aboard *Air Force One*, with his wife, Lady Bird, and Jacqueline Kennedy standing at his side. As the nation mourned its fallen leader, President Johnson vowed to continue the programs and policies of the Kennedy administration. "All I have," he told a special session of Congress, "I would gladly have given not to be standing here today."

Lyndon Baines Johnson—known as LBJ—bore little resemblance to the president he replaced. Born in the Texas hill country in 1908, Johnson came from a different region, a lower social class, and an older political generation. He seemed crude compared with Kennedy, with his heavy drawl, cowboy boots, and earthy language. Yet few people in Washington knew more about the political process—how things really got done. After running a New Deal program in Texas, Johnson won a seat in Congress, served as a naval officer during World War II, and became a U.S. senator in 1949. Elected Senate majority leader by his Democratic colleagues in the 1950s, Johnson worked efficiently with the Eisenhower White House to craft important legislation on defense spending, highway construction, and civil rights. He entered the White House with three decades of political experience under his belt.

The new president moved quickly to restore public confidence through a smooth transition of power. To calm mounting suspicion of conspiracy, he appointed a seven-member commission, headed by Chief Justice Earl Warren, to investigate the Kennedy assassination and issue a report. To provide stability in the executive branch, he convinced Secretary of State Dean Rusk, Secretary of Defense Robert McNamara, and other key officials to remain at their jobs. One of his first acts as president was to work for the tax cut that Kennedy had supported. He believed that lower taxes would spur economic growth and lower unemployment, thereby increasing federal revenues down the road. In February 1964, Johnson signed a measure that cut taxes by $10 billion over the next two years.

The economy responded. With more money available for investment and consumption, the gross national product shot up 7 percent in 1964 and 8 percent the following year, and unemployment fell below 5 percent for the first time since World War II. Furthermore, the economic boom generated even greater federal revenues, just as Johnson had predicted.

Within weeks after taking office, the president met with Martin Luther King, Jr., and other black leaders to assure them of his commitment to civil rights. "He felt about the race question much as I did," a Texas friend recalled, "namely that it obsessed the South and diverted it from attending to its economic and educational problems." In February, the House of Representatives easily approved the civil rights bill by a vote of 290 to 130, but the bill hit a wall in the Senate, where southern opponents used the filibuster to prevent its passage. Working together, Senators Hubert Humphrey (D., Minnesota) and Everett Dirksen (R., Illinois) gathered bipartisan support. The Senate passed the bill on June 11, 1964. It withheld federal funds from segregated public programs, created the Equal Employment Opportunity Commission, and outlawed discrimination in public accommodations, such as theaters, restaurants, and hotels. Furthermore, a last-minute lobbying effort by Senator Margaret Chase Smith and other women's rights supporters added another category—sex—to the clause in Title VII that

Johnson, Lyndon Baines (1908–1973) Thirty-sixth president of the United States (1963–1968), he succeeded after the assassination of President Kennedy and was elected in a landslide the following year. He piloted a number of important initiatives through Congress, including the Civil Rights Act of 1964 and the Voting Rights Act of 1965.

prohibited employment discrimination based on race, creed, or national origin. President Johnson signed the bill into law on July 2, 1964. Though compliance came slowly, the Civil Rights Act marked a vital turning point in the struggle for equal rights. Quoting Victor Hugo, Senator Dirksen declared that "no army can withstand the strength of an idea whose time has come."

Landslide in 1964

LBJ entered the 1964 presidential campaign on a tidal wave of popularity and goodwill. His early months in office were blunder free. The nation prospered, Vietnam appeared as a distant blip on the screen, and the only war on Johnson's public agenda was the one against poverty, which he promised to wage—and win—after his expected victory at the polls.

The summer of 1964, however, offered signs of trouble to come. In Mississippi, an attempt to register black voters by local activists and northern college students met violent resistance from white mobs. On June 21, three volunteers—James Chaney, Andrew Goodman, and Michael Schwerner—disappeared after inspecting the ruins of a firebombed black church. The incident made the front pages of newspapers across the country. Five weeks later, FBI agents found three bodies buried in an earthen dam. The civil rights workers had been murdered by local Klansmen and police, seven of whom were eventually convicted and sent to jail.

Racial tensions that summer were not confined to the South. In July, a confrontation between residents and police officers in Harlem led to several nights of arson and looting. The trouble was followed by disturbances in the black neighborhoods of Philadelphia, Pennsylvania; Paterson, New Jersey; and Rochester, New York.

At the Democratic National Convention in Atlantic City, moreover, the race issue took center stage. Although the nomination of President Johnson and Senator Humphrey, his running mate, went smoothly, a floor fight erupted over the seating of two rival Mississippi delegations—one composed of state party segregationists, the other representing the biracial Mississippi Freedom Democratic Party (MFDP). Led by **Fannie Lou Hamer**, the twentieth child of illiterate sharecroppers, the MFDP spoke for the disenfranchised black majority in Mississippi. "I was beaten till I was exhausted," Hamer told the national convention. "All of this on account we wanted to register, to become first class citizens. If the Freedom Democratic party is not seated now, I question America." Acting through Senator Humphrey, Johnson offered the Freedom Party two voting delegates and the promise of a fully integrated Mississippi delegation at future national conventions. The compromise pleased no one.

At the Republican National Convention in San Francisco, the simmering feud between moderates and conservatives boiled over, with delegates shouting down opponents with catcalls and boos. After bitter debate, the convention chose Senator Barry Goldwater of Arizona for the presidential nomination and Representative William Miller of New York for the vice-presidential spot. In a defiant acceptance speech, Goldwater promised a "spiritual awakening" for America, adding: "Extremism in the defense of liberty is no vice. Moderation in the pursuit of justice is no virtue." Goldwater's Senate record included votes against Social Security increases, the Nuclear Test Ban Treaty of 1963, and the Civil Rights Act of 1964.

Even in foreign affairs, his least favorite subject, Johnson appeared confident and controlled. In August 1964, two U.S. Navy destroyers, the *Maddox* and *C. Turner Joy*, engaged several North Vietnamese torpedo boats in the Gulf of Tonkin. The truth about why this incident occurred was overshadowed by

Hamer, Fannie Lou (1917–1977) Daughter of illiterate Mississippi sharecroppers, she helped lead the civil rights struggle in Mississippi, focusing on voting rights for African Americans and representation in the national Democratic party.

Johnson's dramatic response. First he ordered U.S. planes to bomb military targets deep inside North Vietnam. Then he requested—and received—a congressional resolution authorizing the president to "take all necessary measures" to repel "further aggression." The **Gulf of Tonkin Resolution** gave Johnson the authority he would need to escalate the Vietnam War. During the 1964 campaign, however, he assured voters that nothing could be further from his mind. "We don't want to get tied down in a land war in Asia," he declared.

The election was never in doubt. Johnson won 61 percent of the popular vote (43 million to 27 million) and forty-four of the fifty states (486 electoral votes to Goldwater's 52). His lopsided margin of victory allowed the Democrats to increase their substantial majorities in both houses of Congress. For Republicans, however, the election returns showed that a new coalition was forming in their ranks, with the party gaining strength among middle-class white voters in the South and Southwest. Furthermore, Goldwater attracted thousands of young recruits who were determined to reshape the Republican Party along more conservative lines. For these legions, 1964 was a beginning rather than an end.

Gulf of Tonkin Resolution (1964) Following reports of a confrontation with North Vietnamese in the Tonkin Gulf in 1964, President Johnson requested, and received, congressional authority to "take all necessary measures" to repel "further aggression" in Vietnam, giving the president formal authority to escalate the war.

The Great Society, 1964–1965

President Johnson viewed his landslide victory as a mandate for change. Anxious to leave his mark on history, he spoke of creating "a great society" for Americans in which the "quality of our goals" exceeded the "quantity of our goods," a society in which poverty, ignorance, and discrimination no longer existed, and the spirit of "true community" prevailed.

The centerpiece of Johnson's expansive vision was his War on Poverty, a concept that President Kennedy and his aides had explored shortly before his death. To maintain continuity, Johnson named R. Sargent Shriver, one of Kennedy's brothers-in-law, to coordinate the numerous programs created by the Economic Opportunity Act of 1964, including the Job Corps, the Neighborhood Youth Corps, and Volunteers in Service to America (VISTA), a domestic service program modeled on the Peace Corps. One aspect of the War on Poverty was its emphasis on community action, which led to the increase of minority participation in local affairs.

Poverty did decline dramatically in this era—the result of an expanding economy as well as federal programs aimed directly at the poor. In 1960, more than 40 million Americans (20 percent of the population) lived beneath the poverty line; by 1970, that figure had dropped to 24 million (12 percent). For all of its problems, the much maligned and seriously underfunded War on Poverty achieved a fair measure of success.

Health Care and Immigration Reform

As Johnson promoted his Great Society programs, a kind of infectious optimism gripped Washington. Nothing seemed politically impossible with Lyndon Johnson in charge, including national health care. When Johnson took office in 1963, a majority of older Americans were without health insurance, one-fifth of the nation's poor had never visited a doctor, and the infant mortality rate showed no signs of declining, despite the introduction of lifesaving vaccines. Johnson believed that medical care for the poor and the elderly was an essential part of the Great Society. Yet the American Medical Association (AMA) and private insurers strongly opposed such intervention, calling it "socialized medicine."

After months of intense lobbying, Congress passed the landmark legislation, known as Medicare and Medicaid, that Johnson requested. Medicare provided federal assistance to the elderly, and Medicaid extended medical coverage to welfare recipients. Both programs grew rapidly, reaching 40 million Americans by 1970. Though supporters pointed with pride to statistics showing both an increase in life expectancy and a drop in infant mortality, critics noted the exploding federal costs, the gaps in coverage, and the inferior quality of health care to the poor.

The Great Society also included a new immigration law, passed in 1965. Though vitally important to the nation's future, it went largely unnoticed at the time. In one bold sweep, the Immigration Act removed the national origins quotas, as well as the ban on Asians, which dated back to 1924. Although it set a ceiling of about three hundred thousand immigrants per year, the law permitted the family members of American citizens (both naturalized and native born) to enter the United States without limit. The impact was dramatic. By the mid-1970s, a majority of legal immigrants came from seven Asian and Latin American countries: Korea, Taiwan, India, the Philippines, Cuba, the Dominican Republic, and Mexico.

❖ The Expanding War, 1965–1966

Despite these domestic achievements, nothing proved as important, or damaging, to LBJ's presidency as the conflict in Vietnam. When Johnson assumed office, there were fewer than twenty thousand American "advisers" in that divided country. Within three years, that number had risen to almost five hundred thousand, with no end in sight. Vietnam quickly became Johnson's war—and ultimately his nightmare.

(National Archives)

Young Marine. Although U.S. troops inflicted heavy casualties on the Vietcong and the North Vietnamese during the Tet offensive of 1968, the intensity of the fighting shocked the American public and increased public criticism of the war.

Point of No Return

Vietnam was part of a larger containment effort that had guided American foreign affairs since the end of World War II. Like Presidents Truman, Eisenhower, and Kennedy, LBJ based his commitment to Vietnam on a series of powerful assumptions, such as saving "democracy" in Asia, halting the spread of communism, and maintaining America's credibility around the globe. "I am not going to lose Vietnam," Johnson declared. His plan was to pressure the Communist enemy in a way that would not divert resources from his cherished domestic programs. The Gulf of Tonkin Resolution gave him the authority to move forward.

A Vietcong attack at Pleiku provided the motive. Pleiku, a market town in the central highlands of South Vietnam, was home to a military airstrip guarded by American Special Forces. In February 1965, a Vietcong mortar barrage killed eight Americans and wounded more than a hundred. Several days later, U.S. warplanes began the massive bombing of North Vietnam. Known first as Operation Rolling Thunder, the air strikes hit targets checked personally by President Johnson. The bombings killed thousands, flattened factories and power plants, and ravaged the economy, yet the flow of Communist troops and supplies into South Vietnam never stopped.

In March 1965, two marine battalions arrived at the huge new U.S. Air Force base in Da Nang, raising the American troop total in South Vietnam above 100,000. By December, troop levels reached 184,000, and they rose each month thereafter. Draft calls zoomed from 100,000 in 1964 to 340,000 by 1966, leading millions of young men to seek student deferments or to join the National Guard in the hope of avoiding combat in Vietnam.

By 1965, at least half of South Vietnam was controlled by Vietcong or North Vietnamese troops. The new South Vietnamese government of General Nguyen Van Thieu appeared more stable than previous ones, but its army was no match for the well-disciplined Communist soldiers. As Johnson saw it, American forces would defend South Vietnam until its people were ready to defend themselves. "We will not be defeated," the president vowed.

American strategy in Vietnam had both a military and political objective: to wear down the enemy with superior firepower and to "win the hearts and minds" of the South Vietnamese people. Neither proved successful. North Vietnam, a nation of 19 million, continued to field a large army despite enormous casualties, while the Vietcong provided able support. Fighting on native soil, these soldiers waged relentless, often brutal war against a "foreign aggressor" and its "puppets" inside South Vietnam. Between 1965 and 1966, U.S. combat deaths rose tenfold, from 636 to 6,664.

Americans fought bravely, and morale at this point remained high. Yet the very nature of the war alienated these soldiers from the people they had come to defend. It would have been trying, under the best of circumstances, to distinguish between innocent civilians and Vietcong. Unfamiliar with the language and culture of Vietnam, Americans increasingly viewed everyone as the enemy.

American planners moved Vietnamese peasants from their ancestral lands to "strategic hamlets" or to cities unprepared for the arrival of thousands of homeless refugees. Between 1960 and 1970, the percentage of South Vietnamese living in urban areas jumped from 20 to 43 percent. Those who remained in the countryside faced terror from all sides. U.S. planes and helicopters defoliated the fields and forests with chemical sprays and pounded suspected enemy strongholds with bombs and napalm (jellied gasoline). In one of the most telling remarks of the war, an American officer explained his mission bluntly: "We had to destroy this town in order to save it."

Early Protests

Even as President Johnson escalated the war in 1965, he expected the Great Society to move freely ahead. A "rich nation" like the United States, he declared, "can afford to make progress at home while meeting its obligations abroad." Fueled by the immense economic prosperity of 1965 and 1966, the Great Society added the Education Act, which extended federal aid to public and private schools, and the Model Cities Act, which provided funds to upgrade urban facilities and services. In addition, LBJ appointed the first African American Supreme Court justice, Thurgood Marshall, and the first African American cabinet member, Robert Weaver, to head the new Department of Housing and Urban Development (HUD).

The momentum did not last. The first rumblings of antiwar protest came from college campuses, where a new group, calling itself **Students for a Democratic Society (SDS)**, was gaining ground. Formed in 1962, SDS issued a "Declaration of Principles" that denounced "racism" and "militarism," among other evils, and promised a new politics based on socialist ideals. Limited at first to elite colleges and major state universities, the organization expanded in direct proportion to the war itself.

The early student leaders called their movement the "New Left." Impatient and idealistic, they identified with the "revolutionary" movements of the emerging Third World. To their eyes, Fidel Castro and Ho Chi Minh represented a fundamental shift in power from the privileged elites to the struggling masses. Vietnam became the New Left's defining issue—a symbol of popular resistance to America's "imperialist" designs. Early in 1965, antiwar students and faculty at the University of Michigan held the nation's first "teach-in" to discuss the consequences of escalation in Vietnam. The idea spread rapidly from campus to campus. On Easter Sunday, a crowd of thirty thousand attended the first major antiwar rally in Washington, sponsored by SDS. (See *Doing History: Visions of the "Multiversity."*)

Students for a Democratic Society (SDS) Formed in Port Huron, Michigan, in 1962, this group became one of the leading New Left antiwar organizations of the 1960s, exemplifying both the idealism and the excesses of radical student groups in the Vietnam era.

Doing History Visions of the "Multiversity"

The student movements of the 1960s had many sources. At the University of California at Berkeley, for example, what began as a protest against campus restrictions on certain types of political activity soon expanded to a full-blown attack on the growing power exerted by corporations and government agencies over American higher education. In 1963, University of California President Clark Kerr coined the term "multiversity" to describe the massive, impersonal institutions that had replaced the smaller, student-friendly colleges of the past. Kerr saw this as progress. Above all, he believed, universities must provide the basic research needed to drive modern societies forward. He wrote:

The basic reality, for the university, is the widespread recognition that new knowledge is the most important factor in economic and social growth. We are just now perceiving that the university's invisible product, knowledge, may be the most powerful single element in our culture, affecting the rise and fall of professions and even of social classes, of regions and even of nations. . . .

This reality is reshaping the very nature and quality of the university. Old concepts of faculty-student relations, of research, of faculty-administration roles are being changed at a rate without parallel. . . . Thus the university has come to have a new centrality for all of us, as much as for those who never see the ivied halls as for those who pass through them or reside there.

Kerr's view offended many students of this era, who found their college experience to be increasingly regimented and dull. Among these students was Mario Savio, a philosophy major who led the growing protests at Berkeley. Addressing eight hundred students during a campus sit-in in 1964, he said:

"We have an autocracy which runs this university. It's managed. . . . It's difficult to get through to anyone in authority. . . . If President Kerr in fact is the manager, then I tell you something—the faculty are a bunch of employees and we're the raw material!

There's a time when the operation of the machine becomes so odious, makes you so sick at heart, that you can't take part! You can't even passively take part! And you've got to put your bodies upon the gears and upon the wheels,

upon the levers, upon all the apparatus—and you've got to make it stop! And you've got to indicate to the people who run it—that unless you're free the machine will be prevented from working at all!!"

Source: Clark Kerr, Foreword to *The Uses of the University* (Cambridge, MA: Harvard University Press, 1963); Mario Savio, "Sproul Hall Sit-In Address," December 2, 1964, in "American Rhetoric, Top 100 Speeches," http:www.americanrhetoric.com/speeches.

QUESTIONS for REFLECTION

1. How much of a generational struggle is evident in Mario Savio's comments?

2. Does Savio's description ring true to young people today?

3. Did Clark Kerr correctly predict the future of higher education in the United States?

❖ The Rights Revolution: Center Stage

The national mood of unity and reconciliation that followed President Kennedy's assassination in November 1963 did not last much beyond the landslide election of 1964. The war in Vietnam created divisions that grew wider by the year. Americans became more skeptical of their leaders and less likely to believe official explanations of events.

Voting Rights

Following passage of the landmark Civil Rights Act of 1964, the struggle for racial justice moved to the next battleground: voting rights in the Deep South. The campaign was already under way in places like Selma, Alabama, where local activists, facing intense white resistance, asked Martin Luther King, Jr., and his Southern Christian Leadership Conference for support.

Voting rights demonstrations in Selma, Alabama, began early in 1965. Local blacks marched daily to the courthouse, where Sheriff Jim Clark—wearing a huge button with the single word NEVER—used force to turn them away. Thousands were arrested, beaten with clubs, and shocked with cattle prods for attempting to register with the local election board. In March, Dr. King decided to lead a protest march from Selma to Montgomery, the state capital, fifty miles away. On March 9—known as Bloody Sunday—a contingent of Sheriff Clark's deputies and Alabama state police attacked the marchers, sending seventeen to the hospital. Violence against protesters continued. James Reeb, a Unitarian minister from Boston, was beaten to death by a gang of whites, and Viola Liuzzo, a civil rights activist from Michigan, was shot and killed by the Klan.

On March 15, President Johnson made a special trip to Capitol Hill to urge passage of a new voting rights bill (see Map 27.1 and Table 27.1). In the most eloquent speech of his career, Johnson said:

> What happened in Selma is part of a larger movement which reaches into every section and state of America. It is the effort of Negroes to secure for themselves the full blessing of American life. Their cause must be our cause, too. Because it is not just Negroes, but really it is all of us who must overcome the crippling legacy of bigotry and injustice. And we shall overcome.

The Watts Explosion

Five days later, on August 11, 1965, a riot erupted in Watts, a black section of Los Angeles, triggering the worst urban violence since World War II. The **Watts riot** began with the arrest of a black motorist by a white highway patrolman. As word of the incident spread, several thousand people—mostly young men—rampaged down Crenshaw Boulevard, looting stores, burning buildings, and overturning cars. The violence flared each evening for a week. At least thirty-four people were killed, a thousand injured, and four thousand arrested, with property damage estimated at $200 million.

News of the Watts riot shocked President Johnson and the rest of the country. "We simply hadn't seen the warnings," recalled Attorney General Ramsey Clark. "We had looked at [civil rights] as basically a southern problem, but . . . in fact the problems of the urban ghettos [were much worse]." Times had changed. By 1965, almost half of America's black population lived outside the South, mostly in large cities, and Watts epitomized the conditions of day-to-day urban life. Inferior schools hampered upward mobility; crime was rampant; public services were poor.

Watts riot (1965) Among the most violent urban disturbances in U.S. history, it erupted in an African American neighborhood in Los Angeles following the arrest of a black motorist. By the time it ended, five days later, thirty-four people were dead, a thousand were injured, property damage topped $200 million, and National Guardsmen had to be called in to restore order.

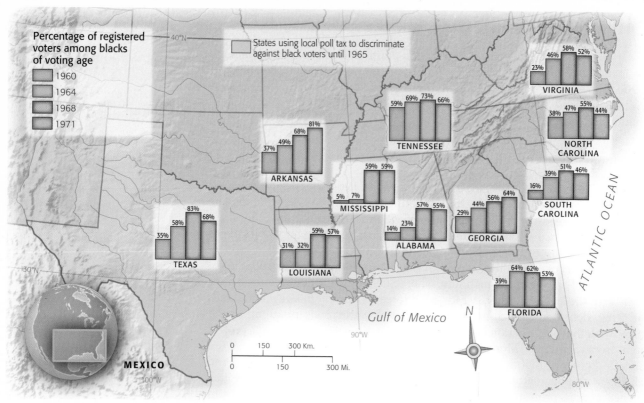

(Copyright © Cengage Learning)

MAP 27.1

Black Voter Registration in the South, 1960–1971

Black voter registration increased dramatically throughout the South following passage of the Voting Rights Act in 1965.

TABLE 27.1
Black Voter Registration

State	1960	1966	Percentage Increase
Alabama	66,000	250,000	278.8
Arkansas	73,000	115,000	57.5
Florida	183,000	303,000	65.6
Georgia	180,000	300,000	66.7
Louisiana	159,000	243,000	52.8
Mississippi	22,000	175,000	695.4
North Carolina	210,000	282,000	34.3
South Carolina	58,000	191,000	229.3
Tennessee	185,000	225,000	21.6
Texas	227,000	400,000	76.2
Virginia	100,000	205,000	105.0

Source: U.S. Bureau of the Census, *Statistical Abstract of the United States: 1982–83* (103d ed.), Washington, D.C., 1982.

Black Power

By the mid-1960s, Dr. King's leadership in the civil rights movement was increasingly criticized. At a 1966 rally in Mississippi, a recent Howard University graduate named Stokely Carmichael, just released from jail following a peaceful protest, shouted, "and I ain't going to jail no more. The only way we gonna stop them white men from whuppin' us is to take over. What we gonna start saying now is **'Black Power.'**" The crowd took up the chant: "Black Power! Black Power! Black Power!" A clearly uncomfortable Dr. King sat behind Carmichael on stage.

Black Power became a symbol of African American unity in the mid-1960s, stressing group strength, independent action, and racial pride. In local communities, black activists lobbied school boards to add African American history and culture to the curriculum. On college campuses, black students pressed administrators to speed up minority recruitment, establish black studies programs, and provide separate living quarters—a demand that alarmed integrationists, black and white. Across the nation, black men and women donned African clothing, took on African names, and wore their hair unstraightened in an "Afro" style. "Black Is Beautiful" became a powerful slogan in this era.

To militants like Stokely Carmichael, Black Power meant a political separation of the races. His position reflected a generational split between "old" civil rights groups such as the NAACP, which viewed racial integration as the key to black advancement, and "new" movement groups like Carmichael's Student Nonviolent Coordinating Committee (SNCC). The separatist impulse had deep roots in the African American community. Its renewed strength in the 1960s was due in large part to a black nationalist movement that appealed to young people in the bleakest neighborhoods of urban America.

Malcolm X was the most popular and controversial Black Muslim leader of the 1960s. Born Malcolm Little, he joined the Nation of Islam while serving a prison term for robbery and adopted the "X" to replace "the white slave-master name which had been imposed upon my paternal forebears by some blue-eyed devil." The Nation of Islam was a black nationalist group, organized in Detroit in 1931, which preached a doctrine of self-help, moral discipline, and complete separation of the races. Black Muslims were forbidden to smoke, drink alcohol, or have sex outside marriage. "Wake up, clean up, and stand up," their motto declared.

Created by Elijah Poole, who renamed himself Elijah Muhammad, the Black Muslims were strongest in the urban ghettos, where their membership reached upward of one hundred thousand with a far larger mass of sympathizers. Assigned by Elijah Muhammad to a temple in Harlem, Malcolm X became a charismatic figure, with his bold statements about the impact of white injustice on black self-esteem. "The worst crime the white man has committed," he said, "is to teach us to hate ourselves." Malcolm X also preached self-defense, saying that blacks must protect themselves "by any means necessary" and that "killing is a two-way street." Such rhetoric made it easy to construe the Black Muslim movement's message as one of violence and hate.

Malcolm X created a public furor by describing the assassination of President Kennedy as an instance of "the chickens come home to roost." Expelled from the Nation of Islam by Elijah Muhammad, he traveled to Mecca on a spiritual pilgrimage and discovered, to his surprise, the insignificance of color in Islamic thought. Assassinated in 1965 by followers of Elijah Muhammad, Malcolm X became a martyr to millions of African Americans, some praising his militant call for self-defense, others stressing his message of self-discipline and self-respect.

One group, the Black Panthers, provided a violent alternative to other black movements of this era. Founded in 1966 by an Oakland, California, ex-convict named Huey Newton, the Black Panthers portrayed themselves as opponents of

Black Power A movement for black racial pride in the 1960s that advocated all-black institutions, not racially integrated ones, as the best vehicles for advancing African American objectives.

Malcolm X (Malcolm Little, 1925–1965) Black Muslim leader who advocated nationalism, self-defense, and racial separation. He split with the Black Muslim movement and formed the Organization of Afro-American Unity, which attracted thousands of young, urban blacks with its message of pride and self-help. He was assassinated by a Black Muslim at a New York rally in 1965.

a "racist-capitalist police state." The Panthers demanded the release of all blacks from prison and the payment of "slave reparations" by whites. The Panthers won modest support through their community work but at the same time, Newton and his aides routinely engaged in extortion, drug dealing, and other criminal acts. Heavily armed, the Panthers became a feared enemy—and primary target—of law enforcement, including the FBI. At least twenty-eight members and eleven policemen were killed in shoot-outs and ambushes between these forces.

"Sisterhood Is Powerful"

The rights revolution of the 1960s included demands for sexual, as well as racial, equality. Both the Equal Pay Act of 1963 and the Civil Rights Act of 1964 were important steps in the battle against gender discrimination, yet progress had been slow. In the fall of 1966, a band of activists formed the National Organization for Women (NOW) to speed the pace of change. At NOW's first convention, the three hundred delegates elected Betty Friedan president. Never radical, NOW pursued its major goals—passage of an equal rights amendment and sexual equality in the workplace—through political means.

NOW grew slowly. Its membership in 1970 totaled fifteen thousand—mostly white, middle-aged, and middle class. Yet NOW's impact on the emerging women's movement was enormous. Some of its members were veterans of the civil rights movement and antiwar protests. Although deeply committed to these causes, they discovered that sexism—the assumption of male superiority—also existed in organizations devoted to justice and equal rights. When asked what positions women filled in his organization, Stokely Carmichael brought roars of male laughter by noting: "The position of women in SNCC is prone."

Determined to confront sexism on all fronts, these "new feminists" developed strategies and communities of their own, in the face of vehement resistance. The most radical feminists viewed men as the enemy, denouncing marriage as "legal whoredom." Such extremism turned off many women from the cause. Surveys of American women in the 1960s showed both a growing sensitivity to issues of sex discrimination and a strong distaste for "women's lib." Most housewives expressed pride in their values and experiences and resented the "elitism" of the feminist movement. As the country artist Tammy Wynette sang: "Don't liberate me, love me." A long and difficult struggle lay ahead.

The Counterculture

The emerging radicalism of America's youth in the 1960s had both a cultural and political base. Bound together with civil rights, women's rights, and the antiwar protests was a diffuse new movement, known as the counterculture, which challenged traditional values.

In 1965, a San Francisco journalist used the term "hippie" to describe a new breed of rebel—passionate, spontaneous, and free. Like the Bohemians of the early 1900s and the Beats of the 1950s, they defined themselves as opponents of the dominant culture, with its emphasis on competition, consumerism, and conformity, an alienation so brilliantly portrayed in Mike Nichols's film *The Graduate* and Paul Simon and Art Garfunkel's "Sounds of Silence." Some young people joined communes, explored ancient religions, or turned to the occult. But far more pervasive were the sexual freedom, the vital new music, and the illegal drug use that marked these turbulent times.

The counterculture spread inward through America from the East and West coasts. In Cambridge, Massachusetts, a Harvard researcher named Timothy Leary became the nation's first psychedelic guru by promoting LSD as the pathway to heightened consciousness and sexual pleasure. In San Francisco, author Ken Kesey (*One Flew over the Cuckoo's Nest*) and his Merry Pranksters staged a series of public LSD parties that drew thousands of participants in 1966. Wearing wild costumes, the revelers danced to the sounds of the Grateful Dead.

To much of the public, San Francisco became synonymous with the counterculture. Acid rock flourished in local clubs like the Fillmore West, where Jimi Hendrix ("Purple Haze"), Steppenwolf ("Magic Carpet Ride"), and the Jefferson Airplane ("White Rabbit") celebrated drug tripping in their songs. In 1967, more than seventy-five thousand young people migrated to San Francisco's Haight-Ashbury district to be part of the much publicized "summer of love." By summer's end, Haight-Ashbury was awash in drug overdoses, venereal disease, panhandling, and prostitution.

At first the national media embraced the counterculture as a "hip" challenge to the blandness of middle-class suburban life. Magazines as diverse as *Time* and *Playboy* doted on every aspect of the hippie existence. Hollywood celebrated the counterculture with films such as *Easy Rider*, about two footloose drug dealers on a motorcycle tour of self-discovery. The smash hit of the 1968 Broadway season was the rock musical *Hair*, depicting a draft evader's journey through the pleasure-filled Age of Aquarius. Yet most young people of the 1960s remained on the margins of the counterculture, admiring its styles and sounds while rejecting its revolutionary mantra. Indeed, most accepted, or even aspired to, America's middle-class promise.

❖ A Divided Nation, 1968

As 1968 began, General **William Westmoreland**, commander of U.S. forces in Southeast Asia, offered an optimistic assessment of the Vietnam War. In his view, American and South Vietnamese (ARVN) troops were gaining strength and confidence as the fighting progressed.

Westmoreland, William (1914–2005) U.S. general; senior commander of U.S. troops in Vietnam from 1964 to 1968.

The Tet Offensive

Four days later, seventy thousand Communist troops assaulted American and ARVN positions throughout South Vietnam. Their lightning offensive, begun on the lunar New Year holiday of Tet (see Map 27.2), took Westmoreland by surprise. In Saigon, Vietcong units reached the American embassy before being driven back. After capturing Hue, one of South Vietnam's oldest cities, Communist soldiers murdered thousands of civilians and dumped their bodies into a mass grave.

As a military operation, the **Tet offensive** failed: using their overwhelming firepower, American and ARVN forces inflicted frightful casualties on the enemy. In psychological terms, however, the Tet offensive marked a turning point. The sheer size of the Communist attacks and their ability to strike so many targets in force made a mockery of Westmoreland's optimistic claims. Reporting from Saigon after the Tet offensive, Walter Cronkite, America's most popular television journalist, claimed that a military victory was nowhere in sight. At best, Cronkite predicted, "the bloody experience of Vietnam is to end in a stalemate."

A stalemate was exactly what Americans feared most. The Tet offensive accelerated Johnson's political decline. His approval rating dropped from 48 to 36 percent, with most Americans expressing skepticism about official claims of military progress in Vietnam.

Tet offensive (1968) Major military operation in South Vietnam launched by the North Vietnamese and Vietcong. Though beaten back, there were tremendous casualties, and coordinated attacks undermined President Johnson's claim that steady progress was being made in Vietnam.

Ho Chi Minh Trail
Enemy supply routes
Major battle of the Tet offensive, January 1968
Major U.S. base during the war
Boat-people refugees after 1975

CHINA

Dienbienphu

MYANMAR (BURMA)

Red R.

Black R.

Hanoi
Haiphong

Harbor mined, 1972

U.S. bombing begins, 1964
Communist-Pathet Lao victory, 1975

NORTH VIETNAM

20°N

Gulf of Tonkin

PLAIN OF JARS

Ca R.

Vinh

Maddox incident, 1964

L A O S

Keo Nua Pass

Vientiane

Mu Gia Pass

U.S. Seventh Fleet operations during the war

Udon Thani   Nakhon Phanom

Demilitarized Zone

17°N

Sépone   Quang Tri
Khe Sanh   Hue

Demarcation Line, 1954

Khon Kaen

Lang Vei

A Shau Valley

South China Sea

T H A I L A N D

Da Nang

Ta Khli

Ubon Ratchathani

Kham Duc

Chu Lai

My Lai

Ratchasima

Quang Ngai

15°N

Dak To

Don Muang

Kontum

Bangkok

Pleiku   An Khe

CAMBODIA (KAMPUCHEA)

Mekong R.

Duc Co

Qui Nhon

U.S. bombing begins, 1969

CENTRAL HIGHLANDS

Tuy Hoa

Ban Me Thuot

Sattahip

Nha Trang

U.S. invasion, 1970

Dalat

Cam Ranh Bay

Communist-Khmer Rouge victory, 1975

Phnom Penh

Bu Dop

SOUTH VIETNAM

110°E

Vietnamese invasion, 1978

Gulf of Thailand

N

Chau Duc

Tan Son Nhut   Saigon   Bien Hoa
Cholon   Long Binh
My Tho   Vung Tau

Mayaguez incident, 1975

Vinh Long
Can Tho   Ben Tre

10°N

CA MAU PENINSULA

Mekong Delta

Vietcong-North Vietnamese victory and U.S. withdrawal, 1975

Ca Mau

100°E   105°E

(Copyright © Cengage Learning)

MAP 27.2

The Vietnam War

The map charts the evolution of American military involvement from the Gulf of Tonkin incident in August 1964 to the surrender of South Vietnam in April 1975. In 1970 and 1971, U.S. and South Vietnamese troops briefly expanded the land war into Cambodia and Laos, stirring further antiwar sentiment inside the United States.

The President Steps Aside

As Lyndon Johnson pondered his political future, the memory of Harry S Truman was fresh in his mind. In 1952, Truman had decided not to seek reelection due to the stalemate in Korea. In 1968, LBJ faced a spirited challenge in New Hampshire from Senator Eugene McCarthy of Minnesota. The main issue now was the stalemate in Vietnam. McCarthy's presidential campaign reflected the deep divisions within Democratic Party ranks. The "peace faction," led by younger activists, hoped to "dump Johnson" by mobilizing antiwar sentiment against him in key primary states. Hundreds of college students arrived in New Hampshire to work for the McCarthy campaign. Long hair and beards were taboo; well-scrubbed volunteers in sports coats and dresses ("be clean for Gene") canvassed house to house. McCarthy came within a whisker of defeating President Johnson in the Democratic primary.

Robert Kennedy. Robert Kennedy's presidential campaign in 1968 both energized and split the Democratic Party, leading, in part, to Lyndon Johnson's decision to announce his political retirement. Kennedy was assassinated after winning the vital California primary in June 1968.

(ILC-DIG-ppmsc-03685]/Library of Congress)

Four days later, Robert Kennedy entered the presidential race. As the former attorney general and a current U.S. senator from New York, he was both a critic of the Vietnam War and a champion of minority causes, especially in the field of civil rights. Millions saw "Bobby" as the keeper of Camelot, the heir to his fallen brother's legacy.

On March 31, 1968, President Johnson announced his political retirement in a stunning televised address: "I shall not seek, and I will not accept, the nomination of my party for another term as your President." A few weeks later, Vice President Hubert Humphrey entered the presidential race as the "regular" Democratic candidate, endorsed by Johnson himself. Humphrey's strategy was to line up delegates without contesting Kennedy or McCarthy in the volatile state primaries, where his chances of winning were slim.

A Violent Spring

Early in April, Martin Luther King, Jr., traveled to Memphis to support a strike of city garbage workers for better wages and conditions. His social vision was ever expanding, as he challenged Americans to confront the "interrelated" evils of racism, militarism, and poverty. On the evening of April 3, King delivered a passionate sermon at a Memphis church. Demanding justice for the poor and the powerless, he seemed to sense the danger he was in. "I've been to the mountaintop," he cried. "I may not get there with you, but I want you to know that we as a people will get to the promised land." The following night, King was shot by James Earl Ray, a white racist, as he stood on the balcony of a hotel. He died instantly, at the age of thirty-nine.

News of Dr. King's death touched off riots in African American communities from Boston to San Francisco. At the White House, President Johnson proclaimed a day of national mourning. Forty-five people died in these national riots, including twenty-four in Washington, D.C.

Among the presidential candidates, Robert Kennedy seemed closest to the message of Dr. King. Centering his campaign on the connection between domestic unrest and the Vietnam War, Kennedy visited migrant labor camps, Indian reservations, and inner-city neighborhoods to highlight the problems of disadvantaged Americans and the work to be done. He also supported the labor strike of

Doing History Online

Martin Luther King and Economic Justice, 1966

Go to the CourseMate website for this chapter and link to Primary Sources. Read the document online. Why did Martin Luther King, Jr., turn his attention to issues other than civil rights in the late 1960s?

 www.cengagebrain.com

Chavez, Cesar (1927–1993) Labor organizer who founded the National Farm Workers Association in 1962.

Cesar Chavez and his National Farm Workers Association against the grape growers in central California.

Chavez, a military veteran, had grown up on an Arizona farm before moving to California in the 1940s. Married, with children, he devoted his life to social causes, first in the barrios of San Jose and then in the fields and orchards where migrant laborers toiled in desperate conditions. Chavez and Robert Kennedy became friends: both men were close to forty years old, both were devout Catholics, and both admired the nonviolence of King and Gandhi in the struggle for justice and social change. As Kennedy campaigned in California, the grape strike was entering its third year. To protest the stalemate, Chavez began a fast that continued for twenty-one days. Despite enormous media coverage, and a national boycott of table grapes, the strike dragged on.

In June 1968, Kennedy took a major step toward the Democratic presidential nomination by defeating Eugene McCarthy in the delegate-rich California primary. That night, after greeting supporters at a Los Angeles hotel, Kennedy was shot and killed by a deranged Arab nationalist named Sirhan Sirhan. The nation went numb. Who could have imagined the horror of four national leaders—John F. Kennedy, Malcolm X, Martin Luther King, Jr., and Robert F. Kennedy—all dead at the hands of assassins?

The Chicago Convention

Throughout the spring of 1968, a coalition of antiwar groups prepared for a massive peace demonstration at the Democratic National Convention in Chicago. Originally expecting five hundred thousand people, the organizers dramatically lowered their estimates following the withdrawal of President Johnson in March and the murder of Senator Kennedy in June. Furthermore, Mayor Richard Daley made it clear that protesters were not welcome in his city. Fearing serious bloodshed at the Democratic convention, Senator McCarthy urged young demonstrators to stay away.

There was reason for concern. The continued military buildup in Vietnam had created a violent cycle of protest and response at home. That spring, thousands of young men burned their draft cards in public; some were beaten by angry crowds. Demonstrators tried to block troop trains and army induction centers, leading to bloody clashes with police. At Columbia University, students from SDS took over several buildings and trashed them to protest "war-related" research on campus. Hundreds were arrested and the university closed down for the semester.

Chicago resembled a war zone in August 1968, with six thousand army troops, five thousand National Guardsmen, and hundreds of Chicago riot police patrolling the streets. Denied permits to rally in public places, the protesters—perhaps four thousand strong—gathered in a park opposite the Hilton Hotel, where many Democratic Party leaders were staying. Conflict was inevitable. Radical speakers from SDS and the Black Panthers harangued the crowd. Abbie Hoffman and Jerry Rubin, founders of the Youth International ("Yippie") Party, held workshops on LSD production and then chose a pig as their candidate.

On the evening of August 28, the demonstrators tried to march to the convention arena. As millions watched on television, the police moved in with clubs and mace, while National Guardsmen fired tear gas at the crowd. Hundreds were badly beaten, including reporters and bystanders, in what investigators later described as a "police riot." Even so, the blame did not rest entirely with one side. "We were not just innocent people who were victimized," Abbie Hoffman admitted. "We came to plan a confrontation." News of the street violence shocked the Democratic convention.

The shaken delegates chose Hubert Humphrey and Senator Edmund Muskie of Maine to be their presidential and vice-presidential nominees. A staunch liberal, Humphrey exemplified the New Deal Democratic tradition of Roosevelt, Truman, Kennedy, and LBJ. His great weakness in 1968 was his loyal (if reluctant) support for Johnson's handling of the war. To many Americans, Humphrey endorsed the very policies that had divided the nation and left the Democratic Party in disarray.

Nixon's the One

Meeting in Miami, the Republicans faced a much simpler task. The Goldwater defeat of 1964 opened the door for candidates with broader political appeal, such as **Richard M. Nixon.** Having lost a bruising election for president in 1960 and another for governor of California in 1962, Nixon kept his fortunes alive by marketing himself as an experienced public figure. After choosing him on the first ballot in 1968, the delegates selected Governor Spiro T. Agnew of Maryland to be his vice-presidential running mate.

Nixon campaigned as the spokesman for America's "silent majority"—the people who worked hard, paid their taxes, went to church, obeyed the law, and respected the flag. In a nation grown weary of urban riots and campus demonstrations, he vowed to make "law and order" his number one domestic priority and to bring "peace with honor" to Vietnam.

For the first time since 1948, the presidential campaign attracted a serious third-party candidate, Governor George Wallace of Alabama. An ardent segregationist, Wallace showed surprising strength in white working-class areas of the North and West, where issues such as rising crime rates and draft deferments for college students were vital concerns. In blunt, sometimes explosive language, Wallace lashed out at "liberal judges," "welfare cheats," and "pot-smoking freaks in their beards and sandals."

On election day (see Map 27.3), Nixon won 43.4 percent of the votes and 301 electoral votes, to 42.7 percent and 191 for Humphrey, and 13.5 percent and

Nixon, Richard M. (1913–1994) Thirty-seventh president of the United States (1969–1974). Known early in his career as a hard-line anti-Communist, he was the first U.S. president to visit Communist China. He also worked skillfully to ease tensions with the Soviet Union. He became the first president to resign from office, due to his involvement in the Watergate scandal.

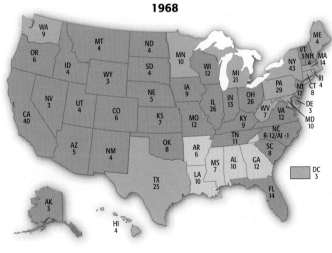

1968

Candidate (Party)	Electoral Vote		Popular Vote	
Nixon (Republican)	301	56.1%	31,785,480	43.4%
Humphrey (Democrat)	191	35.5%	31,275,166	42.7%
Wallace (American Independent)	46	8.4%	9,906,473	13.5%

(Copyright © Cengage Learning)

MAP 27.3

The Election of 1968

In a bitterly fought three-way contest for the presidency, held against the backdrop of a nation badly split by the Vietnam War, Richard Nixon won a razor-thin victory with 43 percent of the popular vote.

46 for Wallace. To a large degree, Richard Nixon rode the political whirlwind that swept America in 1968. His margin of victory against Hubert Humphrey was nearly as narrow as his margin of defeat against John Kennedy in 1960. Yet the combined total for Nixon and Wallace in 1968—almost 57 percent—signaled a major swing to the right. The radical protests of the 1960s had fueled an inevitable backlash against the liberal party in power. The Great Society lay in ruins. The Nixon years had begun.

CHAPTER REVIEW, 1960–1968

SUMMARY

- The Cuban missile crisis was settled peacefully in 1962, ending the most serious nuclear confrontation of the Cold War.

- The war in Vietnam entered public consciousness in 1963, as the number of American military advisers increased and the government of South Vietnam was overthrown in a military coup.

- President Kennedy's assassination in Dallas threw the nation into mourning and brought Lyndon Johnson to the Oval Office.

- Following a landslide victory in 1964, Johnson unveiled plans to create a "great society" modeled after the social programs begun during the New Deal.

- The expanding war in Vietnam pushed Johnson's ambitious domestic agenda to the side.

- Johnson decided not to seek reelection amid growing antiwar protests and racial violence in America's cities.

- The assassinations of Dr. King and Senator Robert Kennedy combined with violent events during the National Democratic Convention to stun the nation in 1968.

- Richard Nixon was elected president, vowing to end the war in Vietnam while restoring "law and order" at home.

IDENTIFICATIONS

John Glenn

Fidel Castro

Bay of Pigs

freedom rides

U-2

Robert Kennedy

Betty Friedan

Lee Harvey Oswald

Lyndon Baines Johnson

Fannie Lou Hamer

Gulf of Tonkin Resolution

Students for a Democratic Society (SDS)

Watts riot

Black Power

Malcolm X

William Westmoreland

Tet offensive

Cesar Chavez

Richard M. Nixon

MAKING CONNECTIONS: LOOKING AHEAD ⅠⅠⅠ➡

Chapter 28 considers the consequences of the tumultuous events of the 1960s. The nation would wrestle with President Nixon's strategy to withdraw U.S. troops from Vietnam and, in an amazing turn of events, watch the president become embroiled in the greatest political scandal in U.S. history.

1. Would a nation as bitterly divided as the United States begin to heal its wounds with a new president at the helm, a president who vowed "to bring the American people together"?

2. Would the "rights revolution" of the 1960s continue to gain momentum in the coming years, and how would its impact be felt in the courts and in the political arena?

3. Was it possible to rekindle interest in the core programs of the Great Society, or would Americans move away from the ideas and proposals that had defined domestic liberalism since the New Deal Era?

RECOMMENDED READINGS

Arsenault, Raymond. *Freedom Riders* (2006). A stirring account of the young civil rights workers who led the struggle for racial justice.

Brennan, Mary. *Turning Right in the Sixties* (1995). Analyzes the impact of Goldwater conservatism on a changing Republican Party.

Farber, David. *Age of Great Dreams* (1994). Provides an excellent synthesis of the political and cultural changes of the 1960s.

Frankel, Max. *High Noon in the Cold War* (2004). A solid history of the Cuban missile crisis seen through the eyes of Khrushchev and Kennedy.

Friedan, Betty. *The Feminine Mystique* (1963). A pathbreaking account of the domestic restrictions placed on women following World War II by those who shape American culture.

Harrington, Michael. *The Other America* (1962). Riveted national attention on the issue of poverty, leading to major government programs and reforms.

Horne, Gerald. *Fire This Time* (1995). Offers an interesting analysis of the Watts riot and the rise of black nationalism.

Karnow, Stanley. *Vietnam* (1983). Remains the best one-volume survey of American involvement in our nation's longest war.

Munoz, Carlos, Jr. *Youth, Identity, Power* (rev. ed. 2000). Carefully examines the origins of the Chicano movement.

McDougall, Walter. "*. . . The Heavens and the Earth*": *A Political History of the Space Age* (1985). Captures both the policy making and the drama behind the race to the moon.

CourseMate Go to the CourseMate website at www.cengagebrain.com for additional study tools and review materials for this chapter.

28 Crisis of Confidence

1969–1980

MAKING CONNECTIONS

◀▮▮▮ **LOOKING BACK**

Chapter 27 examined the impact of the rights revolution, the Vietnam War, and the cultural struggles in the United States during the 1960s, one of the most challenging and bitterly divisive periods in recent history. Before starting Chapter 28, you should be able to answer the following questions:

1. What accounts for the enduring popularity of President John F. Kennedy? Was it his policies, his vision, or were other factors at work as well?

2. In what ways did the assumptions of U.S. leaders regarding Communist expansion remain fixed in the 1960s, and in what ways did they change? Was Lyndon Johnson a prisoner to assumptions that went back to the early days of the Cold War?

3. What impact did the movement for racial equality have on other so-called rights movements in the 1960s? In what ways did the civil rights struggle itself change during this decade?

America United and Divided

The Miracles of 1969
Vietnamization
Confrontation at Home
My Lai and the Pentagon Papers

Activism, Rights, and Reform

Expanding Women's Rights
Minority Power

Doing History: Women Debate
the Equal Rights Amendment

Black Capitalism and Civil Rights
The Burger Court

New Directions at Home and Abroad

Rethinking Welfare
Protecting the Environment
A New World Order
Détente

Four More Years?

The Landslide of 1972
Exit from Vietnam
Watergate and the Abuse of Power
OPEC and the Oil Embargo

Gerald Ford in the White House

The Watergate Legacy
The Fall of South Vietnam
Stumbling Toward Defeat
The Election of 1976

The Carter Years

Civil Rights in a New Era
Human Rights and Global Realities
Economic Blues
The Persian Gulf
Death in the Desert

Richard Nixon had been in politics for most of his adult life. As a congressman, a senator, and a vice president, he thrived on controversy. Bitter defeats in the presidential election of 1960 and the California gubernatorial race of 1962 did not diminish his ambition or ruin his dreams. On the morning after his presidential victory in 1968, Nixon addressed a nation battered by racial turmoil, urban violence, generational conflict, political assassinations, and continuing war. Vowing to unite the country and restore confidence, he recalled a campaign stop he had made in the little town of Deshler, Ohio, where a teenager held up a sign reading, "Bring Us Together." That message, he assured his listeners, "will be the great objective of this administration . . . to bring the American people together." The tragic presidency of Richard Nixon was under way.

❖ America United and Divided

The new era began with optimistic signals and improbable events. For a time, the dark days of 1968 were pushed aside by the miracles of 1969. In January, the New York Jets, led by "Broadway" Joe Namath, won the Super

Bowl by crushing the heavily favored Baltimore Colts. In October, the New York Mets, once regarded as the worst team in Major League baseball history, defeated the Baltimore Orioles in the World Series. Sandwiched between these events were two enormous spectacles, each affecting the nation in a very different way.

The Miracles of 1969

In the summer of 1969, NASA fulfilled John F. Kennedy's bold promise to land a man on the moon "before this decade is out." The lunar mission culminated eight years of extraordinary progress and awful failure, including the 1967 *Apollo 1* disaster in which three astronauts died on the launch pad when their capsule exploded in flames. On July 16, astronauts Neil Armstrong, Edwin "Buzz" Aldrin, and Michael Collins began their 286,000-mile lunar mission—*Apollo 11*—from Cape Kennedy aboard the command vessel *Columbia*. As they neared their destination, Armstrong and Aldrin entered the *Eagle*, a fragile moon module, for the final descent. On July 20, before a television audience of 500 million people, Neil Armstrong put his foot on the lunar surface and said: "That's one small step for man, one giant leap for mankind."

Armstrong and Aldrin spent twenty-one hours on the moon. A television camera beamed back pictures of the men gathering samples, measuring temperature (234 degrees Fahrenheit in sunlight, 279 below zero in darkness), and planting a small American flag. As they rocketed back to Earth, the astronauts provided breathtaking pictures of the world from 175,000 miles away. Other moon missions followed, including the dramatic rescue of *Apollo 13* in 1970.

By studying lunar rocks and photographs, geologists learned that the earth and the moon were formed at the same time—about 4.6 billion years ago—and that both had been pounded for millions of years by a hail of comets, asteroids, and meteorites that helped reshape their outer crust. The moon missions spurred the growth of computer technology and led to numerous product advancements, from fireproof clothing to better navigation systems for jetliners.

(© Elliott Landy/Magnum Photos)

Joe Cocker Performing at Woodstock. Billed as a celebration of the new counterculture, the Woodstock music festival north of New York City attracted 400,000 fans in the summer of 1969.

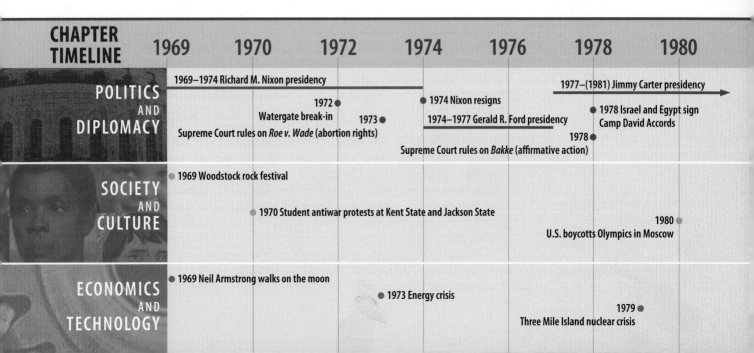

CHAPTER TIMELINE	1969	1970	1972	1974	1976	1978	1980

POLITICS AND DIPLOMACY

1969–1974 Richard M. Nixon presidency

1977–(1981) Jimmy Carter presidency

1972 ● Watergate break-in

1974 Nixon resigns

1973 ● Supreme Court rules on *Roe v. Wade* (abortion rights)

1974–1977 Gerald R. Ford presidency

1978 Israel and Egypt sign Camp David Accords

1978 ● Supreme Court rules on *Bakke* (affirmative action)

SOCIETY AND CULTURE

● 1969 Woodstock rock festival

● 1970 Student antiwar protests at Kent State and Jackson State

1980 ● U.S. boycotts Olympics in Moscow

ECONOMICS AND TECHNOLOGY

● 1969 Neil Armstrong walks on the moon

● 1973 Energy crisis

1979 ● Three Mile Island nuclear crisis

Woodstock A musical festival that was a fusion of rock music, hard drugs, free love, and an antiwar protest. It drew four hundred thousand people to a farm in upstate New York in the summer of 1969.

A month after the moon landing, national attention shifted to an earthly extravaganza, the **Woodstock** Music and Art Fair, on a six-hundred-acre dairy farm in the Catskill Mountains northwest of New York City. Billed as an "Aquarian Exposition," Woodstock fused rock music, hard drugs, free love, and antiwar protest into three days of mud-splattered revelry. Expecting a crowd of perhaps one hundred thousand, the organizers were overwhelmed by the response. More than four hundred thousand people showed up to see Janis Joplin, Jimi Hendrix, Joe Cocker, Joan Baez, the Grateful Dead, and many other bands. Some news reports breathlessly portrayed the event as a cultural watershed; a magazine called Woodstock "the model of how good we will all feel after the revolution." But the mellow portrait of Woodstock soon gave way to the ugly spectacle of Altamont, near San Francisco, where a rock concert featuring the Rolling Stones turned into a bloodbath, with one man beaten to death. In 1970, drug and alcohol addiction claimed the lives of Janis Joplin and Jimi Hendrix. For many young people, the age of innocence was over.

Vietnamization

To bring America together, Richard Nixon would have to end its military involvement in Vietnam. During his inaugural parade on January 20, 1969, Nixon heard the chants of antiwar protesters as his limousine made its way from the Capitol to the White House. The next morning he was handed the weekly American casualty figures from Vietnam: 85 killed, 1,237 wounded—a chilling reminder, he wrote, of the war's "tragic cost."

Vietnamization President Nixon's policy whereby the South Vietnamese were to assume more of the military burdens of the war. This transfer of responsibility was expected to eventually allow the United States to withdraw.

Within weeks, Nixon unveiled a plan, known as **Vietnamization**, to end America's participation in the war. It called for the gradual replacement of U.S. troops by well-trained and supplied South Vietnamese soldiers—a process that included the deployment of American air power and the intensification of peace efforts aimed at getting American and North Vietnamese troops out of South Vietnam. From Nixon's perspective, Vietnamization represented the best solution to a dreadful dilemma. He could not continue a conflict that cost 14,600 American lives and $30 billion in 1968 alone.

Vietnamization did not work well on the battlefield, as time would show. But it did have the advantage of substituting Asian casualties for American ones, which made it popular in the United States. In June 1969, President Nixon announced that twenty-five thousand American combat troops were being withdrawn from Vietnam—the first stage of a pullout to be completed by late 1972 (see Figure 28.1).

Confrontation at Home

Despite Vietnamization and troop withdrawals, the antiwar movement retained considerable force. On November 15, 1969—"Mobilization Day"—hundreds of thousands of people attended rallies in New York, Boston, San Francisco, Washington, and other cities to demand the immediate removal of all American troops from Vietnam. To show his contempt for the protests, President Nixon made a point of listing his schedule that afternoon, which included several hours of watching the Washington Redskins on television.

Kent State University National Guardsmen were sent to this Ohio campus to restore order following a series of antiwar protests in May 1970. They fired into a crowd of students, killing four and wounding nine others.

In March 1970, the White House announced the withdrawal of 150,000 more combat troops over the coming year. The nation's leading antiwar group, the Vietnam Moratorium Committee, responded positively by closing its national office. But a month later, in a startling development, the president told the nation that American troops had just invaded Cambodia to disrupt enemy supply lines that ran through that country along the so-called Ho Chi Minh Trail. "We are a strong people," he said, "and we shall not be defeated in Vietnam."

Nixon misjudged the public reaction. The idea of expanding the war under any circumstances brought protesters back into the streets. At **Kent State University** in Ohio, several thousand students rampaged through the business

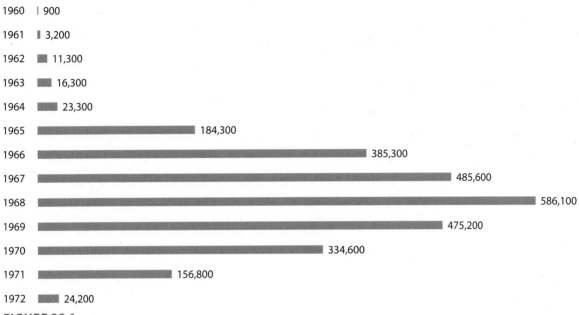

FIGURE 28.1

U.S. Troop Levels in Vietnam, 1960–1972
American troop levels increased dramatically in 1965, following the Gulf of Tonkin incident and the Vietcong attack on U.S. Marines at Pleiku. As the chart shows, troop levels began to decrease significantly in 1969, as newly elected President Nixon started his policy of Vietnamization.
Source: U.S. Department of Defense.

district and clashed with local police. That evening, Kent State's Reserve Officers Training Corps (ROTC) building went up in flames, leading the governor to send in the National Guard. On May 4, the guardsmen confronted five hundred students at a rally, where rocks and bottles were thrown from a distance and tear gas was lobbed in return. Suddenly, without warning, a group of guardsmen fired their rifles at the crowd, killing four and wounding nine others.

Word of the shootings touched off campus protests nationwide. ROTC buildings were attacked, and governors in sixteen more states called out the National Guard. Many colleges shut down for the semester, canceling final exams and mailing diplomas to graduates.

Surveys showed a clear majority of Americans approving of the National Guard's response at Kent State. Many blue-collar workers fumed at the sight of draft-deferred, middle-class students protesting the war from the safety of a college campus while their own sons and brothers were slogging through the jungles of Vietnam. That rage turned to violence in New York City, when several hundred construction workers charged into an antiwar rally and severely beat the demonstrators and onlookers with hammers, pipes, and fists. A week later, President Nixon invited the leader of New York's construction workers' union to the White House, where the two men exchanged gifts and compliments. Meanwhile, the violence continued in fits and spurts.

My Lai and the Pentagon Papers

The news from Vietnam was equally grim. Reports surfaced about a massacre of civilians by U.S. troops at the village of My Lai, a suspected Vietcong stronghold, in 1968. Encountering no resistance, an infantry unit led by Lieutenant William

Calley methodically executed the villagers and dumped their bodies into a mass grave. A number of the women were raped; at least two hundred people, many of them children, were murdered. Evidence of these atrocities was ignored by field commanders until a soldier not connected with the incident sent letters to the Pentagon and the press.

The public reaction to Lieutenant Calley's court-martial verdict (guilty) and sentence (life imprisonment) in 1971 raised the very issues that had divided Americans since the war began. Some believed that Calley acted out of frustration after seeing so many of his fellow soldiers killed. Others blamed a society—as one GI put it—that "forced these kids to die in a foreign land for a cause it refused to defend at home." "Free Calley" signs appeared on car bumpers, in store windows, even in churches. Following numerous appeals and a case review by President Nixon, Calley was paroled in 1974.

Within weeks of Calley's court-martial, another crisis erupted with publication of the Pentagon Papers, a secret report of the decision-making process that led to American involvement in Vietnam. Commissioned in 1967 and containing numerous classified documents within its seven thousand pages, the report was made public by Daniel Ellsberg, a former intelligence officer who had turned against the war. Ellsberg gave a copy to the *New York Times*, which printed the first installment on June 13, 1971.

The report focused mainly on the Kennedy-Johnson years. Yet Nixon viewed Ellsberg's behavior as a threat to his own presidency as well. He feared that continued leaks of classified material might reveal damaging information about current policies, such as the secret bombing of Cambodia. As a result, the White House sought a court injunction to halt further publication of the Pentagon Papers on the grounds that national security was at stake. The Supreme Court rejected this argument, however, ruling 6 to 3 that suppression violated First Amendment guarantees.

Obsessed by the Ellsberg incident, Nixon authorized the creation of a special White House unit, known as the "Plumbers," to "stop security leaks and investigate other sensitive matters." In a tape-recorded conversation on September 18, 1971, Nixon demanded that "the roughest, toughest people [get] to work on this." A few weeks later, the Plumbers carried out their first assignment: burglarizing the office of Ellsberg's psychiatrist in an attempt to gather embarrassing information. Nixon's top domestic adviser, John Ehrlichman, casually informed the president that other "little operations" were planned. "We've got some dirty tricks under way," he said. "It may pay off."

❖ Activism, Rights, and Reform

Political and social activism did not end with the 1960s, as the environmental movement and the antiwar protests clearly showed. While the angry, media-centered radicalism of groups like SDS and the Black Panthers largely disappeared, the movements for women's rights and minority rights remained very much alive, bringing progress and backlash in their wake.

Expanding Women's Rights

On August 26, 1970, feminist leaders organized a nationwide rally to mark the fiftieth anniversary of the Nineteenth Amendment, which had given women the right to vote. Thousands showed up with signs ranging from "Sisterhood Is Powerful" to "Don't Cook Dinner—Starve a Rat Today." The speeches focused on equality for women in education and employment, the need for reproductive freedom, and passage of the **Equal Rights Amendment (ERA)**, an idea first proposed in 1923. (See *Doing History: Women Debate the Equal Rights Amendment.*)

The revived women's movement was already making strides. In 1969, feminist protests forced a number of the nation's best colleges, including Yale and Princeton, to admit women, and the military academies soon followed suit. During the 1970s, female graduates from the nation's law schools rose from 5 to 30 percent of each class and at medical schools from 8 to 23 percent. Yet the number of women elected to public office or promoted to high management positions lagged far behind, and the wages of full-time working women remained well below those of men.

The women's movement had many voices and a wide range of ideas. Handbooks like *Our Bodies, Ourselves* (1971) and *The New Woman's Survival Catalogue* (1972) sold millions of copies by combining a new feminist ideology, based on professional achievement and personal freedom, with medical and psychological strategies for good health. In 1972, *Ms.* magazine was launched, the first feminist magazine to attract a mass circulation. A sampling of its articles showed how dramatically times had changed: "Raising Kids Without Sex Roles," "Women Tell the Truth About Their Abortions," and "Do Feminists Do It Better?"

Minority Power

The political and cultural upheavals of the 1960s had produced a "rights consciousness" that spread dramatically as the decade progressed. For many groups, 1969 was a pivotal year, marking their emergence on the national scene. That summer, for example, a routine police assault against homosexuals at the Stonewall Inn in Manhattan's Greenwich Village turned into days of riots as the patrons fought back, protesting against the harassment of homosexuals. The "Stonewall riot" led to the formation of the Gay Liberation Front, which began the movement to encourage group solidarity within the homosexual community and confront openly the prejudice that gay men and women had suffered, in fearful silence, for so many years.

Equal Rights Amendment (ERA) Congress overwhelmingly passed the Equal Rights Amendment in 1972, but by the mid-1970s conservative groups had managed to stall its confirmation by the states.

(AP Images)

La Raza Unida. Mexican American activists formed La Raza Unida in 1969 to further "Chicano" causes. Jose Gutierrez, left, and Rodolfo "Corky" Gonzalez give the clenched fist sign as they appeared before the national convention of La Raza Unida meeting in El Paso Sept. 2, 1972.

Doing History Women Debate the Equal Rights Amendment

As the women's rights movement gained momentum in the 1970s, new emphasis was placed on passage of the Equal Rights Amendment (ERA) to the U.S. Constitution, which required both congressional approval and ratification by three-quarters of the states. Written by feminist Alice Paul (see Chapter 21) a half-century earlier, the ERA declared that "equality of rights under the law shall not be denied or abridged . . . on account of sex."

The debate over the ERA often focused on the role of married women, especially regarding their family responsibilities. In 1970, feminist leader Gloria Steinem addressed the "sex-based myths" that pervaded American society, such as "women are biologically inferior to men" and "women are already treated equally in this society." She then turned to the issue of child rearing.

Another myth [is] that children must have full-time mothers. American mothers spend more time with their homes and children than those of any other society we know about. . . . The truth is that most American children seem to be suffering from too much mother and too little father. Part of the program of Women's Liberation is a return of

fathers to their children. If laws permit women equal work and pay opportunities, men will then be relieved of their role as sole breadwinner. Fewer ulcers, fewer hours of meaningless work, equal responsibility for his own children: these are a few of the reasons that Women's Liberation is Men's Liberation too.

Among the ERA's staunchest critics was Phyllis Schlafly, an attorney and a mother, who based her opposition to the amendment on the innate differences that separated men from women. To ignore these differences, she warned, would turn the traditional male–female relationship of cooperation into one of endless conflict:

La Raza Unida Formed in 1969 by Mexican American activists, this group reflected the growing demand for political and cultural recognition of "Chicano" causes, especially in the Southwest.

In 1969, Mexican American activists in Texas formed **La Raza Unida**, a political party devoted to furthering Chicano causes and candidates through the ballot. This new party reflected the growing demand for political power and cultural self-determination within the Hispanic community, which had grown from 3 million in 1960 to more than 9 million a decade later. The increase, consisting mainly of Cuban Americans and Puerto Ricans on the nation's East Coast and Mexican Americans throughout the West, provided unique opportunities for change. Political leverage by Hispanic groups spurred Congress to improve conditions for migrant farm workers, many of whom were Mexican American, and to provide federal funding for bilingual education.

In the fall of 1969, several dozen Native Americans took over Alcatraz Island, an unoccupied former federal penitentiary in San Francisco Bay, to publicize the claims and grievances of a younger, more militant generation. "It has no running water; it has inadequate sanitation facilities; there is no industry; there are no health care facilities," said one protest leader, comparing the rocky island to a typical Indian reservation. The group spent nineteen months on Alcatraz, symbolically offering to buy it for "$24 in glass beads and red cloth."

The protest signaled a change in the American Indian community. In the late 1960s, a new group known as American Indian Movement (AIM), inspired

The woman's liberationist . . . is imprisoned by her own negative view of herself and of her place in the world around her. . . . The Positive Woman looks upon her femaleness and her fertility as part of her purpose, her potential, and her power. She rejoices that she has a capability for creativity that men can never have. . . .

The Positive Woman recognizes the fact that, when it comes to sex, women are simply not the equal of men. The sexual drive of men is much stronger than that of women. This is how the human race is designed in order that it might perpetuate itself. The other side of the coin is that it is easier for women to control their sexual appetites. A Positive Woman cannot defeat a man in a wrestling or boxing match, but she can motivate him, inspire him, encourage him, teach him, restrain him, reward him, and have power over him that he can never achieve over her with all his muscle. . . .

The differences between men and women are also emotional and psychological. Without woman's innate maternal instinct, the human race would have died out centuries ago. . . . This is not to say that every woman must have a baby in order to be fulfilled. But it is to say that fulfilment for most women involves expressing their natural maternal urge by loving and caring for someone.

Source: Testimony before Senate Judiciary Committee, May 6, 1970; Schlafly, *The Positive Woman* (New York: Jove Publications, 1977), 10–18.

Map 28.1 clearly shows the regional and cultural divisions over the ERA, with much of the opposition coming from rural and southern states. Only thirty of the needed thirty-eight states voted in the end for ratification, and the amendment died.

QUESTIONS for REFLECTION

1. How do Gloria Steinem and Phyllis Schlafly differ in their views of the biological destiny of the sexes?

2. Why do you think the ERA failed to become part of the Constitution?

3. Have the issues raised by the ERA faded into history, or are they still relevant today?

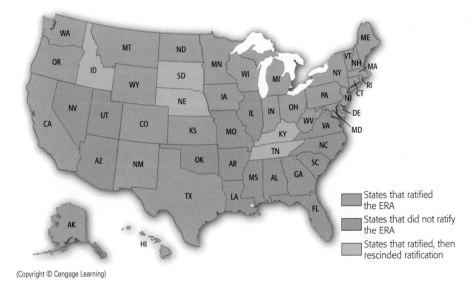

(Copyright © Cengage Learning)

MAP 28.1

The Struggle for the Equal Rights Amendment

When Congress endorsed the ERA, its ratification by three-quarters of the states seemed certain. But opposition mounted quickly, and supporters were never able to reach the magic number of thirty-eight. From a high of thirty-five states, the number fell to thirty, as five states rescinded ratification. A look at the map shows that much of the opposition to the ERA was centered in the South and in rural states.

States that ratified the ERA

States that did not ratify the ERA

States that ratified, then rescinded ratification

by the black freedom struggles, began to preach a philosophy of "Red Power" that rejected the "assimilationist" policies of their elders. In 1972, AIM supported a march on Washington—named the Trail of Broken Treaties—and seized the South Dakota village of Wounded Knee on the Pine Ridge Sioux Reservation in 1973, site of an infamous massacre by federal troops in 1890. They drew attention to both the squalid conditions there and the "broken promises" that stripped Native Americans of their independence and their land. Two Indians were killed in the seventy-one-day standoff with federal agents.

Progress did occur, however. In 1970, the federal government returned forty-eight thousand acres of sacred land to the Taos Pueblo of New Mexico, beginning a process that grew significantly in the coming years. In addition, the Nixon administration targeted minority aid programs for Native Americans living in urban areas, and Congress added funding through the Indian Education Act of 1972. Nevertheless, the alarming rates of suicide, alcoholism, and illiteracy among Native American children continued throughout the 1970s and beyond—a clear warning of how much remained to be done.

Black Capitalism and Civil Rights

Richard Nixon took office at a crucial juncture in the campaign for civil rights. The epic struggles of the 1950s and early 1960s had formally abolished de jure (legal) segregation in public schools and public accommodations—a remarkable achievement—yet serious problems remained. The vast majority of southern children still attended all-white or all-black schools in defiance of *Brown v. Board of Education*, and the situation was little better in the North and West, where de facto segregation in housing and employment kept most neighborhood schools rigidly segregated by race. Furthermore, although the percentage of middle-class African Americans increased substantially in the 1960s, the rate of black unemployment remained twice the national average. This meant a deepening economic split within the African American community.

Civil rights did not rank high on Nixon's domestic agenda. Because most blacks voted Democratic—Hubert Humphrey got 95 percent of their votes in 1968—the president owed them no political debt. On the contrary, he hoped to create a "new Republican majority" by winning over white working-class Democrats, North and South, who feared that minorities were getting too much attention from the federal government.

Nixon's boldest civil rights initiatives related to business and employment. In 1969, he created the Office of Minority Business Enterprise, noting that "people who own their own homes and property do not burn their neighborhoods." More controversial was the administration's proposal, known as the Philadelphia Plan, that required the construction unions—carpenters, electricians, and the like—to set up goals and timetables for hiring black apprentices on government-sponsored projects.

On the emotional issue of public school integration, the president took a more cautious approach. Hoping to win white political converts in the South, he supported the efforts of Mississippi officials in 1969 to postpone court-ordered school integration, while firmly opposing efforts to deny federal funding to segregated schools. When told that Justice Department officials were planning to speed up school integration, the president warned them to "knock off this crap," adding: "Do what the law allows you and not one bit more." As a result, the battle shifted back to the courts, especially the U.S. Supreme Court, where major changes were now under way.

The Burger Court

In 1969, Chief Justice Earl Warren stepped down from the bench. The seventy-seven-year-old Warren had submitted his resignation in 1968, expecting President Johnson to choose a suitably liberal replacement. But problems arose when Johnson nominated his close friend Abe Fortas, an associate justice on the Supreme Court, who was ultimately forced to resign. This gave incoming President Nixon the luxury of appointing two Supreme Court justices at once.

The first choice went smoothly. The Senate quickly confirmed Judge Warren E. Burger, a moderate northern Republican, to replace Warren as chief justice. But due to problems with his first two choices, Nixon had to submit three nominees before the Senate unanimously confirmed his third choice, Judge Harry Blackmun of Minnesota. And the president got to make two more Supreme Court nominations the following year. His selections—William Rehnquist, a prominent Arizona conservative, and Lewis Powell, a distinguished Virginia attorney—were easily confirmed.

The Burger Court proved more independent than most people, including Nixon, had expected. Among other decisions, it upheld publication of the Pentagon Papers and struck down "capricious" state laws imposing the death penalty, thereby halting capital punishment for almost two decades (*Furman v. Georgia*, 1972). In addition, the Burger Court held that state laws prohibiting abortion were unconstitutional because they violated a woman's "right to privacy" under the Fourteenth Amendment (**Roe v. Wade, 1973**). Justice Blackmun's majority opinion permitted a state to outlaw abortion in the final three months of pregnancy, noting, however, that the life and health of the mother must be considered at all times. The following year, almost 1 million legal abortions were performed in the United States.

The Burger Court also confronted segregation in the public schools. Its unanimous ruling in *Swann v. Charlotte-Mecklenburg Board of Education* (1971) served notice that controversial methods like "forced" busing could be used as legal remedies to achieve racial balance. But the idea of transporting children to different neighborhoods in the name of racial integration fueled parental anger and fear. In Boston, a court-ordered plan in 1974 to bus white schoolchildren to Roxbury, a poor black neighborhood, and black children to South Boston, a poor white neighborhood, led to mob action reminiscent of Little Rock, Arkansas, in 1957. Buses were stoned, black students were beaten, and federal marshals rushed in to protect them. Ironically, the schools in both neighborhoods were in awful condition, unlike the wealthy suburban Boston schools, which were not included in the desegregation plan. All too often, forced busing became a class issue, involving poorer people of all races.

Roe v. Wade (1973) Supreme Court decision that, along with *Doe v. Bolton*, legalized abortion in the first trimester.

❖ New Directions at Home and Abroad

Like John F. Kennedy, President Nixon cared more about foreign policy than about domestic affairs. As a moderate Republican in the Eisenhower mold, Nixon endorsed the basic outlines of the modern welfare state, which included Social Security, unemployment insurance, a minimum wage, the right to unionize, and health care for the elderly. Yet Nixon also was convinced that Americans were fed up with wasteful government programs and demonstrations. He tried to find, in his words, a domestic "middle ground."

Rethinking Welfare

President Nixon's immediate domestic goals were to implement a revenue-sharing plan that sent more tax dollars back to the states and localities and to simplify the welfare system. Revenue sharing, designed to limit the power of the national government, was a modest success. Congress passed legislation transferring $30 billion in federal revenue over five years—less than Nixon wanted but more than state and local governments had received in the past.

Welfare reform proved a much harder sell. Here the president looked to domestic adviser Daniel P. Moynihan, a social scientist whose controversial writings on poverty and the African American family reflected a shifting emphasis from equal rights to equal opportunity. Everyone agreed that the current welfare system—Aid to Families with Dependent Children (AFDC)—was seriously flawed. At Moynihan's urging, President Nixon offered an alternative to AFDC, known as the Family Assistance Plan (FAP). The new plan proposed a complete overhaul of the welfare system, guaranteeing a minimum annual income to the poor, beginning at sixteen hundred dollars for a family of four, with additional funding for food stamps. Faced with withering criticism from both liberals, who complained that sixteen hundred dollars was unreasonably low, and conservatives, who opposed the very concept of a guaranteed annual income, the FAP went down to defeat.

To his credit, Nixon did not trim needed programs. He supported Democratic-sponsored measures in Congress to increase food stamp expenditures and provide automatic cost-of-living adjustments (COLAs) for Social Security recipients to help them keep up with inflation. Although Nixon did not care to publicize this achievement, he became the first president since Franklin Roosevelt to propose a federal budget with more spending for social services than for national defense.

Protecting the Environment

On April 22, 1970, millions of Americans gathered in schools, churches, and parks to celebrate Earth Day, an event sponsored by environmental groups like the Sierra Club to educate people about the ecological problems afflicting the modern world. Begun a few years earlier, following the appearance of Rachel Carson's book *Silent Spring*, the environmental movement gained strength after a series of well-publicized disasters, such as the chemical fire that ignited Cleveland's Cuyahoga River. Dire predictions of scientists about population growth, poisoned food and water, endangered species, and air pollution added fuel to the cause. As biologist Barry Commoner noted in his best-selling 1971 book, *The Closing Circle*, "our present course, if continued, will destroy the capability of the environment to support a reasonably civilized human society."

At first, President Nixon showed little interest in environmental problems. Yet Nixon soon considered environmentalism to be a powerful force—one that cut across class, racial, and political lines. Moving quickly, his administration banned the use of DDT in the United States and stopped production of chemical and biological weapons, though not the plant defoliants or napalm used in Vietnam. More significant, the White House supported a bipartisan effort to establish the Environmental Protection Agency (EPA) and pass the Clean Air Act of 1970 and the Endangered Species Act of 1973.

These were notable achievements. The Clean Air Act set strict national guidelines for the reduction of automobile and factory emissions, with fines and jail sentences for polluters. The Endangered Species Act protected rare plants and animals from extinction. Congress also passed the Water Pollution Control Act over Nixon's veto in 1972. The law, mandating $25 billion for the cleanup of America's neglected lakes and rivers, was too costly for the president, though it proved effective in bringing polluted waters back to life. The EPA, meanwhile, monitored the progress of these laws and required environmental "impact studies" for all future federal projects.

A New World Order

Richard Nixon loved the challenge of foreign affairs. Determined to control foreign policy even more rigidly than previous presidents had, Nixon bypassed the State Department in favor of the National Security Council (NSC), based in the White House itself. To direct the NSC, he chose **Henry Kissinger,** a German refugee and Harvard political scientist. Both men agreed that America's bipolar approach, based on the containment of Soviet communism, no longer made sense. They wanted a more flexible policy that recognized the growing strength of Western Europe, Communist China, and Japan. The Nixon-Kissinger approach meant talking with old enemies, finding common ground through negotiation, and encouraging a more widespread balance of world power.

Kissinger, Henry (1912–)
German-born American political scientist, national security advisor (1969–1974), and secretary of state (1973–1977). He shared the 1973 Nobel Peace Prize for helping to negotiate the Vietnam cease-fire.

This innovative thinking, however, did not extend to all parts of the globe. The president still viewed Fidel Castro as a mortal enemy and openly encouraged the CIA to undermine the democratically elected, left-wing government of Chilean president Salvadore Allende, who was overthrown and apparently murdered by right-wing military forces in 1973. "I don't see why we have to allow a country to go Marxist just because its people are irresponsible," Henry Kissinger argued. In Latin America, at least, the New World Order appeared strikingly similar to the old one.

Nixon's skill in foreign affairs lay in his ability to seize opportunities in a rapidly changing world. One of his first moves was to take advantage of the widening rift between Communist China and the Soviet Union. The United States at this time did not even recognize Communist China. Since 1949, American policy had considered the anti-Communist regime on Taiwan the legitimate government of mainland China.

Nixon wanted a new relationship with China for several reasons. The trade possibilities were enormous. Better relations also increased the chances of a peace settlement in Vietnam, while strengthening America's bargaining position with the Soviet Union, which feared any alliance between Washington and Beijing. Most of all, Nixon realized that China must now be recognized as a legitimate world power. The first public breakthrough came in 1971, when an American table tennis team was invited to China for an exhibition tour. Meanwhile, Henry Kissinger secretly visited Beijing to plan a summit meeting between Chinese and American leaders. President Nixon hinted at his future plans in a remarkable magazine interview. "If there is anything I want to do before I die," he said, "it is to go to China."

Nixon arrived there on February 22, 1972—the first American president ever to set foot on Chinese soil. For the next eight days, the world watched in amazement as he walked along the Great Wall and strolled through the Forbidden City. "The Chinese Army band played 'America the Beautiful' and 'Home on the Range,'" wrote the *New York Times*. "President Nixon quoted Chairman Mao Zedong approvingly, used his chopsticks skillfully, and clinked glasses with every Chinese official in sight."

The trip ended with a joint statement, known as the Shanghai Communiqué, that promised closer relations between the two countries in trade, travel, and cultural exchange. Each nation agreed to open a legation (a small staff office that ranks below an embassy) in the other's capital city, beginning the process of diplomatic recognition that would take seven more years to complete. The most important issues, such as human rights and nuclear proliferation, were tactfully ignored. And the most controversial issue—the future of Taiwan—was not resolved, demonstrating the deep rift that still existed. Still, the historic significance of Nixon's visit overshadowed the problems that lay ahead.

Détente

Three months later, the president traveled to Moscow for a summit meeting with Soviet leader Leonid Brezhnev. A master of timing in foreign affairs, Nixon believed that his successful trip to China, coupled with a faltering Russian economy, would make the Soviets more likely to strike a serious deal with the United States. The key issues were arms control and increased trade. Both sides possessed huge atomic arsenals that cost billions of dollars and increased the chances of catastrophic war. The Russians desperately needed grain, heavy equipment, and technical assistance; American farmers and manufacturers saw new markets for their goods.

The Moscow Summit further enhanced the Nixon-Kissinger record in foreign affairs. On May 22, 1972, the United States and the Soviet Union signed the Strategic Arms Limitation Treaty (SALT), which limited the number of long-range offensive missiles (ICBMs), and an antiballistic missile (ABM) agreement, which froze the production of these missiles for the next five years. These initial treaties, committing the superpowers to the principle of arms reduction, represented a stunning breakthrough in Soviet–American relations. Though the economic agreements were less successful, the Moscow Summit provided a solid foundation for **détente**, with both sides pledging to reduce world tensions and coexist peacefully.

détente An easing of tensions among countries, which usually leads to increased economic, diplomatic, and other types of contacts between former rivals.

❖ Four More Years?

After a full term in office, Richard Nixon could look back on a record of notable achievement. Relations with Cold War opponents like the Soviet Union and Communist China had dramatically improved as détente replaced confrontation. Although the Vietnam War continued, the steady withdrawal of American troops meant fewer casualties and an end to the draft. Even the economy looked better, with unemployment and inflation under control.

The Landslide of 1972

Nixon's Democratic challengers faced an uphill battle. From the political right, Governor **George Wallace** of Alabama continued the presidential odyssey he began in 1968, when he had captured five southern states as a third-party candidate. Campaigning this time as a Democrat, Wallace won wide support among white working-class voters for his opposition to forced busing and his attacks on "welfare cheats." After winning the Democratic presidential primary in Florida and running a close second in Wisconsin, Wallace was shot and paralyzed by a would-be assassin, ending his presidential quest.

A few weeks later, on June 17, 1972, five men were arrested while burglarizing the Democratic National Headquarters at the **Watergate** complex in Washington, D.C. Four of them were Cubans who had worked previously for the CIA; they were led by James W. McCord, the security director for Richard Nixon's Committee to Re-Elect the President, known as CREEP. Supervising from a nearby hotel, and later arrested, were two presidential aides—Gordon Liddy and E. Howard Hunt—who belonged to the newly created "Plumbers" unit. Responding to the break-in, Nixon assured the public that no one "presently employed" in his administration was involved "in this very bizarre incident."

At the Republican National Convention in Miami, the delegates enthusiastically renominated the Nixon-Agnew team. The Democratic race, however, proved far more contentious. The candidates included Hubert Humphrey, the 1968

Wallace, George (1919–1998) Governor of Alabama (1963–1967, 1971–1979, 1983–1987), he first came to national attention as an outspoken segregationist. Wallace ran unsuccessfully for the presidency in 1968 and 1972.

Watergate Nixon administration scandal touched off when the Democratic National Headquarters at the Watergate complex in Washington, D.C., was burglarized in 1972. Several top government officials were convicted of crimes and President Nixon was forced to resign in 1974.

presidential nominee; Senator **George McGovern** of South Dakota, the favorite of younger, more liberal Democrats; and Representative Shirley Chisholm of New York, the first African American to seek the presidential nomination of a major political party.

The Democratic National Convention, meeting in Miami Beach, reflected the party reforms that followed the bloody "siege of Chicago" in 1968. The changes were dramatic, with the percentage of female delegates increasing from 13 to 38 percent, blacks from 5 to 15 percent, and those under thirty years old from 3 to 23 percent. Deeply committed to the "rights revolution" of the 1960s, these new delegates proposed a major redistribution of political power and cultural authority in the United States.

The delegates chose George McGovern for president and Senator Thomas Eagleton of Missouri for vice president. The campaign faced trouble from the start. Reporters learned that Senator Eagleton had been hospitalized in the past for mental depression and fatigue, twice undergoing electroshock therapy. As criticism mounted, McGovern replaced Eagleton with former Peace Corps director Sargent Shriver. Appearing weak and opportunistic, McGovern dropped further in the polls. Even more damaging for his campaign was the lack of unity within Democratic ranks. On election day, Nixon overwhelmed McGovern, carrying every state but Massachusetts and winning 61 percent of the popular vote.

Yet Nixon's landslide victory was more limited than it appeared. Ticket splitting flourished in 1972, with the Democratic Party easily retaining control of Congress. Furthermore, the percentage of eligible voters who cast ballots in presidential elections continued to fall, from 62 percent in 1964, to 61 percent in 1968, to 56 percent in 1972. This suggested a growing alienation from the political process—and a hint of the protest to come.

Exit from Vietnam

Richard Nixon's impressive reelection victory seemed a sure sign that passions were cooling and better times lay ahead. The president's first task was to end the Vietnam conflict on honorable terms and secure the release of American prisoners of war. But the key to any settlement, Nixon understood, was the future security of South Vietnam. What would happen after U.S. troops left that country? Would the American sacrifice be in vain?

In the spring of 1972, North Vietnam mounted a major offensive in the South that failed miserably when Nixon ordered massive bombing raids against North Vietnam. Following his reelection that fall, the president increased these air assaults in order to force a peace settlement with the North. "These bastards," said Nixon, "have never been bombed like they're going to be bombed this time." In late December 1972, American B-52s filled the skies over Hanoi and Haiphong, dropping more tonnage than all American planes had dropped in the previous two years. The damage done to North Vietnam was staggering: harbors, factories, railway lines, storage facilities, and sometimes adjoining neighborhoods were destroyed.

On January 27, 1973, an agreement was signed in which the United States agreed to withdraw its remaining troops from Vietnam in return for a North Vietnamese promise to release all American prisoners of war. Nixon also vowed to "respond in full force" if North Vietnam attacked South Vietnam in the future. The United States, he proclaimed, had achieved "peace with honor" at last. But the American exit from Vietnam left the vulnerable South Vietnamese government at the mercy of its Communist opponents. The agreement ended American involvement without guaranteeing South Vietnam's long-term survival.

McGovern, George (1922–)
U.S. senator from South Dakota (1963–1981), he opposed the Vietnam War and was defeated as the 1972 Democratic candidate for president.

The war had divided the country, raised suspicions about government to dangerous levels, and drained billions of dollars from vital domestic programs. More than fifty thousand U.S. soldiers were killed in Vietnam and three hundred thousand were wounded. At least 1 million Asians died, and more would perish in the coming years. As the *New York Times* noted, "There is no dancing in the streets, no honking of horns, no champagne."

Watergate and the Abuse of Power

As 1973 began, Richard Nixon's public approval rating stood at a remarkable 68 percent. With Vietnam behind him, the president appeared ready to launch a successful second term. Yet all that ended in April when the Watergate burglars pleaded guilty to minor charges of theft and wiretapping in order to avoid a public trial. Suspecting a cover-up, federal judge John Sirica convinced the lead burglar, James McCord, to admit that high-ranking White House officials were involved in planning the break-in. This startling confession, combined with the investigative stories of *Washington Post* reporters Bob Woodward and Carl Bernstein, turned the Watergate affair into front-page news.

During the spring of 1973, President Nixon reluctantly appointed Harvard Law School professor Archibald Cox as an independent prosecutor in the Watergate case. The Senate formed a special investigating committee chaired by seventy-three-year-old Sam Ervin of North Carolina. Under Ervin's careful direction, the committee heard sworn testimony from present and former Nixon aides about a "seamless web" of criminal activity designed to undermine the president's critics and political opponents. In meticulous detail, John Dean, the former White House counsel, implicated Nixon himself in a plan to ensure the silence of the imprisoned burglars by paying them "hush money."

Nixon denied any involvement in Watergate, claiming that he had been too busy running the nation to bother with the day-to-day workings of his reelection campaign. Many Americans—and most Republican leaders—took Nixon at his word. As House minority leader **Gerald R. Ford** of Michigan declared, "I have the greatest confidence in the president and am absolutely positive he had nothing to do with this mess."

In July, White House aide Alexander Butterfield stunned the Ervin committee by revealing that Nixon had secretly recorded his Oval Office conversations since 1971. Seeking the truth, Judge Sirica, special prosecutor Cox, and chairman Ervin all demanded to hear the relevant tapes. But Nixon refused to release them, citing executive privilege. When Cox persisted, Nixon ordered Attorney General Elliot Richardson to fire him. Richardson and his top deputy refused, leading to their swift removal. These dramatic developments, known as the "Saturday Night Massacre," produced angry calls for Nixon's impeachment.

There was trouble for the vice president as well. In 1973, a Baltimore grand jury looked into allegations that Spiro Agnew, while governor of Maryland, had accepted illegal payoffs from building contractors. After first denying these charges, the vice president resigned his office and pleaded nolo contendere (no contest) to one count of income tax evasion. He received three years' probation plus a ten-thousand-dollar fine.

Under the Twenty-fifth Amendment, adopted in 1967, the president is obligated to nominate a vice president "who shall take the office upon confirmation by a majority vote of both houses of Congress." To bolster his declining fortunes, Nixon chose the well-respected Gerald Ford, who was quickly confirmed. But the president ran into more trouble when the Internal Revenue Service (IRS) disclosed that he owed $500,000 in back taxes from 1970 and 1971; Nixon had paid less than $1,000 in each of these years.

Ford, Gerald R. (1913–) Thirty-eighth president of the United States (1974–1977), he was appointed vice president when Spiro Agnew resigned and became president when Richard Nixon resigned over the Watergate scandal. As president, Ford granted a full pardon to Nixon in 1974.

"I Am Not a Crook."   As shown in this Herblock cartoon, the release of the Watergate tapes brought down President Nixon by proving his knowledge of illegal activities in the White House.

By this point, public confidence in Nixon had disappeared. The testimony of John Dean, the Saturday Night Massacre, the resignation of Spiro Agnew, the embarrassing IRS disclosures—all cast doubt on the president's fitness to lead. A Gallup poll taken in November 1973 showed Nixon's public approval had dropped to 27 percent. In desperation, the president released transcripts of several Watergate-related conversations (but not the tapes themselves), claiming that they cleared him of wrongdoing. Many thought otherwise. The transcripts contained ethnic and racial slurs, vulgar language (with "expletives deleted"), and strong hints of presidential involvement in a cover-up.

In July 1974, the House Judiciary Committee debated charges of presidential impeachment before a national television audience. Led by chairman Peter Rodino of New Jersey and the eloquent Barbara Jordan of Texas, the committee approved three charges—obstruction of justice, abuse of power, and contempt of Congress—at the very moment that a unanimous Supreme Court ordered Nixon to comply with Judge Sirica's subpoena for the Watergate tapes. On August 5, the president released tapes that showed him playing an active role in the attempt to cover up White House involvement in the crime.

Faced with certain impeachment and removal, Richard Nixon became the first president to resign from office. In a tearful farewell to his staff on August 9, he preached the very advice that he himself was incapable of following. "Always remember," he said, "those who hate you don't win unless you hate them. And then you destroy yourself."

What were the lessons of Watergate? For one thing, Americans learned again that the system of checks and balances put in place by the founding fathers had done its job well. Lawbreaking at the highest level was exposed. A president had resigned his office in disgrace, and the government had moved forward without a hitch. Still, had not it been for the tenacity of reporters Woodward and Bernstein, the intuition of Judge Sirica, and the disclosure of the secret White House tapes, the scandal known as Watergate may never have been exposed.

Someone else had helped as well. For more than thirty years, Woodward and Bernstein had shielded the identity of their most crucial source in the Watergate story, promising to reveal his name only after his death. But in 2005, a ninety-one-year-old former FBI official named W. Mark Felt stepped forward to claim credit for his role. "I'm the guy they used to call 'Deep Throat,'" he declared. Woodward and Bernstein admitted it was true. The biggest remaining mystery of Watergate had finally been put to rest.

OPEC and the Oil Embargo

In the midst of the Watergate scandal, a serious crisis erupted over the nation's energy needs. On October 6, 1973—the Jewish high holiday of Yom Kippur—Egypt and Syria attacked Israel from two sides. After some hesitation, the United States backed Israel, a long-time ally, by airlifting vital military supplies. American aid proved essential in helping Israel repel the attack, and the Organization of Petroleum Exporting Countries (OPEC), led by Saudi Arabia and other Arab nations, responded by halting oil shipments to the United States, Western Europe, and Japan.

The oil embargo created an immediate panic, though the problem had been building for years. As the U.S. economy flourished after World War II, its energy consumption soared. Americans, barely 6 percent of the world's population in 1974, used more than 30 percent of the world's energy. Between 1968 and 1973, America's consumption of imported oil tripled from 12 to 36 percent. This reliance on foreign sources left the United States extremely vulnerable to the OPEC embargo.

As the cold weather set in, President Nixon warned that "we are heading toward the most acute shortage of energy since World War II." In response, the government reduced highway speed limits to 55 miles per hour, lowered thermostats in office buildings to 68 degrees, approved daylight savings time in winter, eased environmental restrictions on coal mining, and pushed the development of nuclear power. Long lines formed at the gas stations, which were closed on Sundays to conserve precious fuel.

The oil embargo ended in April 1974, but its impact lingered. Energy costs rose dramatically, even as supplies returned to normal, because OPEC tripled its price. A gallon of gas in the United States rose from 30 cents (before the embargo) to 75 cents and more. Consumers faced soaring inflation, and manufacturers confronted higher production costs. Some regions, such as the automobile- and steel-producing Midwest, were particularly hard hit; other areas, like the energy-producing Sunbelt, gained in population and political influence.

Above all, the energy crisis shook the foundations of the American dream. For three decades, a booming economy had produced a standard of living unparalleled in terms of material comfort, home ownership, and access to higher education. But after 1973, prosperity could no longer be taken for granted. Following the oil embargo, average weekly earnings in the United States (adjusted for inflation) stopped growing for the first time in thirty years. So too did worker productivity. The increased cost of energy, combined with spiraling federal deficits and aggressive foreign competition in manufacturing and technology, made the American economy vulnerable.

❖ Gerald Ford in the White House

Vice President Gerald Ford, a former football star at the University of Michigan who had served honorably for two decades in the U.S. House of Representatives, seemed the ideal figure to restore public confidence in the presidency. As a Republican Party loyalist, he had opposed most of Lyndon Johnson's Great Society legislation while strongly supporting the war in Vietnam. Yet even Ford's political opponents praised his decency, his integrity, his humble, straightforward ways. As the new president joked, "I'm a Ford, not a Lincoln."

The Watergate Legacy

Gerald Ford inherited a situation in which the legislative branch of government, emboldened by the disasters of Watergate and Vietnam, appeared anxious to restore its former authority by cutting the executive branch down to size. In 1973, for example, Congress passed the War Powers Act that required the president to notify Congress within forty-eight hours about the foreign deployment of American combat troops. If Congress did not formally endorse that action within sixty days, the troops would be withdrawn. In addition, Congress passed the Freedom of Information Act, which gave the American people unprecedented access to classified government material.

The Senate also held a series of spectacular hearings into the abuses and criminal activity of executive intelligence agencies such as the FBI and the CIA. The public learned that FBI agents had routinely harassed, blackmailed, and wiretapped prominent Americans such as Martin Luther King, Jr., and CIA operatives had engaged in illegal drug experiments, money laundering, and bungled assassinations of world leaders like Fidel Castro. These revelations led President Ford to create a monitoring device known as the Intelligence Oversight Board. But Congress, with fresh memories of the Watergate cover-up, formed a permanent watchdog committee to investigate such behavior on its own.

Ford too fell victim to the Watergate morass. During his vice-presidential confirmation hearing in 1973, he had gone on record against a possible presidential pardon for Richard Nixon. Yet in September 1974, President Ford reversed his earlier position by granting Nixon a "full, free, and absolute pardon" for all crimes he "may have committed" during his term in office. Ford hoped that a presidential pardon would finally put the "national nightmare" of Watergate to rest.

In fact, the opposite occurred. By appearing to place one man above the law, Ford saw his own public approval rating plummet from 72 to 49 percent. Richard Nixon barely apologized for Watergate. He never admitted his crimes. Many Americans wanted justice.

The Fall of South Vietnam

In October 1974, at a secret conclave outside Hanoi, the leaders of Communist North Vietnam prepared their final plans for the conquest of South Vietnam. Their main concern was the United States. Would it respond "in full force" to

(© Jacques Pavlovsky/Sygma/CORBIS)

Fall of South Vietnam.
The fall of South Vietnam to the Communists in April 1975 brought America's longest military conflict to an end.

Communist violations of the 1973 peace accords? The North Vietnamese did not think so—and they were right.

The North Vietnamese launched a massive assault in March 1975, overwhelming South Vietnamese forces near the demilitarized zone (DMZ). As North Vietnamese troops advanced, a mixture of chaos and panic gripped South Vietnam, with thousands of soldiers deserting their units and masses of civilians clogging the highways in desperate flight. Ignoring a plea from President Ford, Congress refused to extend emergency aid to South Vietnam. On April 23, Ford ruefully commented that the Vietnam War was "finished as far as America is concerned." Saigon fell to the Communists on April 29.

The humiliating collapse of South Vietnam raised serious questions about the limits of American military power. For those most deeply affected—the veterans of Vietnam—the collapse raised personal questions about the meaning of their sacrifice to the nation and to themselves. With the exception of the POWs, these veterans received no public tributes, no outpouring of thanks. Congress passed no special "GI Bill" to pay for their college tuition, to help them find employment, or to finance their new homes. Some Americans condemned the veterans for serving in an "immoral war"; others blamed them for participating in the nation's first military defeat. "The left hated us for killing," said one dejected veteran, "and the right hated us for not killing enough." A sizable minority of veterans (one out of six, according to the Veterans Administration) suffered from post-traumatic stress disorder, substance abuse, and sometimes both. In addition, some veterans claimed that their exposure to Agent Orange, a toxic herbicide used to defoliate the jungles of Vietnam, had produced high rates of cancer, lung disease, and even birth defects in their children.

Public sentiment softened over time. Opinion polls by the late 1970s showed that most Americans considered the Vietnam veteran to be both a dutiful soldier and the victim of a tragic war. In 1982, the Vietnam Veterans Memorial, a dramatic wall of black granite with the names of fifty-eight thousand Americans who died or went missing in that war, was unveiled on the Mall in Washington, D.C. Attracting large, respectful crowds, the memorial affords recognition for the sacrifices of all who served in Vietnam.

Stumbling Toward Defeat

As his presidency continued, Ford faced a bleak economic picture, darkened by spiraling energy costs, in which unemployment and inflation reached their highest levels in years. "The state of the union," Ford admitted in 1975, "is not good." But there was little consensus on how to fix it. The Republican Ford, believing that a balanced federal budget was the key to cutting inflation, proposed sizable cuts in government programs and a voluntary citizens' campaign to curb rising prices, which he called "Whip Inflation Now" (WIN). The Democratic Congress called for increased federal spending to spur the economy and lower unemployment. Although Ford vetoed more than sixty bills during his brief tenure in office, Congress overrode the president to increase Social Security benefits, fund public works projects, and raise the minimum wage.

In foreign affairs, Ford tried to maintain the policy of détente begun by Nixon and Kissinger, who remained as secretary of state. But unlike Nixon, the new president worried conservatives with his alleged weaknesses as a negotiator. Of particular concern was the Helsinki Accord of 1975, which pledged the United States and the Soviet Union, among other nations, to recognize the Cold War boundaries dividing Eastern and Western Europe and to respect human rights within their borders. Many Americans were dismayed by the formal acceptance of Soviet domination over nations such as Poland and East Germany; many more were skeptical about any Russian promise regarding human rights.

The Election of 1976

Gerald Ford dreamed of winning the White House in his own right. Yet unlike previous incumbents, who normally breezed through the presidential nominating process, Ford faced a serious challenge in 1976 from Ronald Reagan and the Republican Right. With great fanfare, Reagan portrayed Ford as a weak president, unable to tame a Democratic Congress or to confront the Russians at Helsinki. In his sharpest attack, Reagan blasted Ford for opening negotiations aimed at reducing American control of the Panama Canal. "We built it, we paid for it, it's ours," Reagan thundered, "and we should tell [Panama] that we are going to keep it." The president won a narrow victory at the Republican National Convention in Kansas City by agreeing to support a party platform sympathetic to the Reagan forces. For vice president, the Republican delegates selected Senator Bob Dole of Kansas, a tough campaigner with conservative views.

Because Ford appeared so vulnerable in 1976, the Democratic race for president attracted a very large field. Among the candidates was a little-known former governor of Georgia named **James Earl (Jimmy) Carter, Jr.** Few observers took him seriously at the start, and the voters asked, "Jimmy who?" But Carter struck the right pose for the post-Watergate era. A deeply religious man who promised voters, "I will never lie to you," he combined the virtues of small town America with the skills of the modern corporate world. Born in Plains, Georgia, in 1924, Carter attended local schools, graduated with distinction from the U.S. Naval Academy, and spent seven years as a naval officer. He returned to Plains to run the family's farm supply and peanut business, and as the company prospered, he turned to politics, winning the Georgia governorship in 1970. Known as a "new South" politician, Carter supported progressive causes and reached out to black constituents through his concern for civil rights.

Meeting in New York City, the Democratic National Convention chose Carter for president and Senator Walter Mondale of Minnesota for vice president. Carter ran a safe campaign that fall, avoiding controversial issues while claiming that America was no longer "strong" or "respected" in the world. The media, meanwhile, caught Ford in a series of bumbling accidents that made him look

Carter, James Earl (Jimmy) (1924–) Thirty-ninth president of the United States (1977–1981), his successes in office, including the Camp David Accords, were overshadowed by domestic worries and the seizure of American hostages at the U.S. Embassy in Iran. He was defeated by Ronald Reagan in 1980.

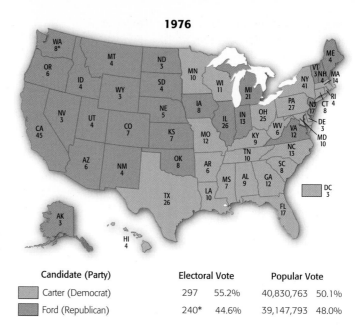

1976

Candidate (Party)	Electoral Vote		Popular Vote	
Carter (Democrat)	297	55.2%	40,830,763	50.1%
Ford (Republican)	240*	44.6%	39,147,793	48.0%

*One Ford elector in Washington voted for Republican Ronald Reagan of California.

(Copyright © Cengage Learning)

MAP 28.2

The Election of 1976

In the first presidential election since Watergate, Democratic challenger Jimmy Carter won a narrow victory over Republican incumbent Gerald Ford by portraying himself as a Washington outsider. Ford hurt himself politically by pardoning Richard Nixon. As the map shows, Carter, a former Georgia governor, swept the South, while Ford, a long-time midwestern congressman, swept the midwest and the west.

clownish and inept. Before long, the comedian Chevy Chase was beginning almost every episode of *Saturday Night Live* by taking a terrible tumble in the role of Gerald Ford. And the president only made things worse for himself with a series of embarrassing verbal blunders, such as his insistence during the televised debate with Carter that "there [was] no Soviet domination of Eastern Europe."

Still, the race was very close. Carter won 40.8 million votes, Ford 39.1 million (see Map 28.2). The electoral count was 297 to 240. Carter swept the entire South (except for Virginia) and the key industrial states of Ohio, Pennsylvania, and New York. Ford did well in the West, carrying every state but Texas. Polls showed Carter with large majorities among both minority voters and working-class whites who had rejected McGovern in 1972.

Jimmy Carter became the first president from the Deep South in more than a century, signifying that region's increased strength—and acceptance—in the national arena. Furthermore, his election witnessed the growing importance of state primaries in the nominating process as well as the influence of the new Fair Campaign Practices Act of 1974. The law provided federal funds to the major candidates and established limits on personal contributions. The result in 1976 was a longer, more expensive presidential campaign season, with television advertising playing an ever larger role.

The Ford–Carter election continued the downward trend in voter turnout, from 55.7 percent in 1972 to 54.4 percent in 1976. Polls showed a growing sense of apathy and disillusionment among the American people. As one bumper sticker put it, "Don't Vote. It Only Encourages Them!"

❖ The Carter Years

The new Democratic administration began with promise and hope. President-elect Carter took the oath of office as Jimmy (not James Earl) Carter and surrounded himself with populist symbolism—giving fireside chats in a sweater and blue jeans, attending town meetings from New Hampshire to New Mexico, and staying overnight in the homes of ordinary Americans. "We must have a new spirit," he declared. "We must once again have full faith in our country—and in one another."

Civil Rights in a New Era

As governor of Georgia, Jimmy Carter had opened the doors of government to minorities. As president, he did much the same thing. Women, African Americans, and Hispanics were appointed to federal positions in record numbers as judges, ambassadors, and White House aides. Women, for example, filled three of Carter's cabinet-level positions and numerous other policy-making roles. In addition, Carter's wife, Rosalyn, greatly expanded the role of first lady by serving as a key adviser to the president and representing him on diplomatic missions.

Although Carter strongly supported civil rights and gave special attention to the plight of minorities in the inner cities, the momentum for racial change in the 1970s had shifted back to the federal courts. During Carter's term, the issue of affirmative action took center stage in *University of California Regents v. Bakke* (1978). Allan Bakke, a thirty-eight-year-old white man, was denied admission to the University of California medical school at Davis. He sued on the grounds that his test scores exceeded those of several black applicants who were admitted under a policy that reserved sixteen of one hundred spots for minorities in each entering class. The policy amounted to "reverse discrimination," Bakke charged, and thus violated his right to equal protection under the law. In a 5-to-4 ruling, the Supreme Court struck down the medical school's quota policy as a violation of Bakke's constitutional rights. But it held that universities might consider race as a factor in admission "to remedy disadvantages cast on minorities by past racial prejudice."

The *Bakke* decision began a passionate debate over affirmative action that continues to this day. Opponents considered it to be a racially divisive policy as well as a dangerous step away from the American tradition of individual rights. Why penalize innocent whites, they argued, for the sins of their ancestors? But supporters of affirmative action viewed it as the surest way to remedy discrimination, past and present. "In order to get beyond racism, we must take race into account," wrote Justice Thurgood Marshall. "There is no other way."

Human Rights and Global Realities

President Carter knew little about foreign affairs, yet he viewed his inexperience as an asset, freeing him from worn-out thinking and stale ideas. He believed that a fresh approach to foreign affairs would move America beyond the "big power" rivalries of the Cold War era. What America needed, he thought, was a foreign policy that stressed democracy and human rights—in short, the idealism of the United States.

Carter scored some impressive successes. Emphasizing human rights in Latin America, he withdrew American support for the military dictatorship in Chile, cut off aid to the repressive Somoza regime in Nicaragua, and encouraged the governments of Brazil and Argentina in their halting steps toward democracy. Carter also presented the Senate with a treaty that relinquished American control over the Panama Canal by the year 2000 and a second one that detailed American rights in the Canal Zone thereafter. Both treaties provoked fierce national debate; both passed the Senate by a single vote.

Carter's greatest triumph occurred in the Middle East. In 1977, Egyptian President Anwar Sadat stunned the Arab world by visiting Israel to explore peace negotiations with Prime Minister Menachem Begin. Their discussions were

Anwar Sadat and Menachem Begin. Anwar Sadat and Menachem Begin shake hands at Camp David, Maryland, as Jimmy Carter, who brought the men together, smiles in the background.

Camp David Accords (1978)
Treaty between Egypt and Israel, brokered by President Carter at Camp David, that returned the Sinai Peninsula to Egypt in return for Egypt's recognition of the state of Israel.

cordial but fruitless, for neither man seemed willing to take the risks that peace demanded. When the talks broke down, Carter invited Sadat and Begin to his presidential retreat at Camp David in Maryland in September of 1978. The **Camp David Accords** led to a historic treaty the following year. Egypt agreed to recognize the state of Israel, which previously had been unthinkable for an Arab nation, and Israel pledged to return the captured Sinai Peninsula to Egypt. The treaty did not consider other vital issues, such as the fate of displaced Palestinians and the future of Israeli-held Arab territory in Gaza and the West Bank, but it was a historic achievement for Carter.

Economic Blues

Early success in foreign affairs, however, could not mask Carter's problems with the troubled economy. During the 1976 presidential campaign, candidate Carter had focused on the high inflation (6 percent) and unemployment (8 percent) that gripped the United States. Combining these figures into a "misery index" of 14, he had promised the American people immediate relief.

Carter's program to stimulate the economy depended on a mixture of tax cuts, public works, and employment programs—a kind of "pump priming" reminiscent of Franklin Roosevelt's New Deal. The Democratic-controlled Congress responded sympathetically by funding large public works projects, reducing taxes by $30 billion, and raising the minimum wage from $2.30 to $3.35 over a five-year span. The good news was that unemployment dropped to 6 percent by 1978; the bad news was that inflation rose to 10 percent—and kept climbing.

Carter changed his approach and attempted to attack inflation by tightening the money supply (through higher interest rates) and controlling the federal deficit. This meant reduced government spending, a turnabout that alienated the Democratic Congress. Moreover, Carter's new policies appeared to increase unemployment without curbing inflation—the worst of both worlds. Before long, the "misery index" stood at 21.

This was not all Carter's fault, of course. The decline of American productivity, the growth of foreign competition, and the surging cost of imported oil had plagued the nation for some time. In 1977, Carter offered a substantive plan for the energy crisis, which he described as "the moral equivalent of war." The plan arrived on the heels of the worst, coldest winter in modern American history.

(© Bettmann/CORBIS)

Three Mile Island Crisis. In March 1979, a mechanical failure at the nuclear power plant at Three Mile Island in Pennsylvania was averted, but the ensuing panic raised awareness of the tremendous risks associated with nuclear power.

Based mainly on reduced energy use, Carter's plan ran into immediate opposition from oil companies, the auto industry, and others who advocated the increased production of fossil fuels and the deregulation of prices. "This country didn't conserve its way to greatness," a Texas oil man complained. "It produced its way to greatness."

The National Energy Act, passed in November 1978, did little to reduce America's energy consumption or its reliance on foreign oil. Carter's original plans to stimulate conservation efforts were overshadowed by incentives to increase domestic energy production through tax breaks for exploration, an emphasis on alternative sources (solar, nuclear, coal), and the deregulation of natural gas. The law did not address, much less solve, the nation's fundamental energy problems—as Americans would soon discover.

The Persian Gulf

In January 1979, a chain of events unfolded that shook the nation's confidence and shattered Jimmy Carter's presidency. The year began with the overthrow of America's dependable ally, Shah Reza Pahlavi of Iran; it ended with the United States appearing helpless and dispirited in the face of mounting challenges at home and abroad.

On a visit to Iran in 1977, President Carter had described it as "an island of stability in one of the most troubled areas in the world." Iran was vital to American interests, as both an oil supplier and a bastion against Soviet influence in the Middle East. Thousands of American workers and their families lived in Iran, and thousands of Iranian students attended college in the United States. Ironically, President Carter's concern for human rights did not extend to Iran, where the army and secret police used widespread torture and repression to keep the shah and his ruling elite in power.

The Iranian Revolution was led by Ayatollah Ruhollah Khomeini, an exiled cleric, and his devoted followers. Their aim was to form a fundamentalist Islamic state. When demonstrations paralyzed Iran, the shah fled his country, leaving the religious fundamentalists in control. One of Khomeini's first moves was to end oil shipments to "the Great Satan" America, thus allowing other OPEC countries to raise their prices even more. In the United States, long gas lines reappeared, and the price reached a dollar per gallon.

With Americans reeling from months of bad news, President Carter went on national television to speak partly about the energy crisis. His address was remarkably candid. Rather than assuring anxious Americans that they had nothing to fear or trying to rally them with ringing phrases about honor and duty, the president spoke of a nation in trouble, struggling with the values of its cherished past. In place of "hard work, strong families, and close-knit communities," he said, too many Americans "now worship self-indulgence and consumption. Human identity is no longer defined by what one does but by what one owns."

Having passionately diagnosed the illness, Carter provided no cure. The "crisis of confidence" deepened. In October, the deposed shah of Iran, suffering from cancer, was allowed to enter the United States for medical treatment. This decision, which Carter viewed as a simple humanitarian gesture, produced an explosive backlash in Iran. On November 4, militant students stormed the American embassy in Tehran, taking dozens of American hostages and parading them in blindfolds for the entire world to see. The militants demanded that the United States turn over the shah for trial in Iran. Otherwise the Americans would remain as captives—and perhaps be tried, and executed, as spies.

Carter had almost no leverage with these militants, who were supported by Khomeini himself. His attempts to settle the crisis through the United Nations were ignored by Iran. His orders to embargo Iranian oil and suspend arms sales were empty gestures because other nations refused to do the same. Freezing Iran's assets in American banks and threatening to deport Iranian students from the United States likewise did nothing to change the fate of the hostages in Tehran. For a time, the American people rallied behind their president: Carter's approval rating jumped from 30 to 61 percent in the first month of the crisis. Yet Carter grasped what many others did not: there was no easy solution to the hostage standoff.

The year ended with yet another nasty surprise. In December, Russian soldiers invaded neighboring Afghanistan to quell a revolt led by Muslim fundamentalists against the faltering pro-Soviet regime. The invasion ultimately backfired; fanatical resistance from Afghan fighters turned the country into a graveyard for Russian troops. Determined to act boldly in the light of the continuing Iran hostage crisis, Carter cut off grain shipments to the Soviet Union and cancelled America's participation at the upcoming Summer Olympic Games in Moscow—a boycott that many nations chose to ignore. More significant, he announced a "Carter Doctrine" for the Persian Gulf, warning that "outside aggression" would "be repelled by any means necessary, including military force." By 1980, the Cold War was heating up again. Afghanistan and its aftermath had dealt a serious blow to détente.

Doing History Online

American Hostages in Iran, 1979

Go to the CourseMate website for this chaper and link to Primary Sources. Read the accounts online. John Limbert and Bill Belk tell different stories about being taken hostage at the American embassy in Iran. Why do their accounts differ so much?

www.cengagebrain.com

Death in the Desert

As President Carter and the American people staggered through the repeated shocks of 1979, one issue dominated the national agenda: the fate of the hostages in Iran. The crisis took on symbolic importance as an example of America's declining power in the world. The television networks flashed nightly pictures of the hostages on humiliating public display in Tehran while frenzied crowds shouted "Death to Carter" and "Down with the United States." In Washington, meanwhile, the president met regularly with the families of the hostages and worked tirelessly to find a diplomatic solution, to no avail. Reluctantly, Carter ordered a secret mission to free the hostages by force.

The result was disastrous. In April 1980, American commandos reached the Iranian desert, where two of their helicopters were disabled by mechanical problems. Another hit a U.S. cargo plane, killing eight members of the rescue mission. The commandos departed without ever getting close to the hostages in Tehran. To make matters worse, the Iranians proudly displayed the burned corpses for television crews. Most Americans blamed the president for the debacle. What little remained of Jimmy Carter's credibility disappeared that fateful day in the Iranian desert.

CHAPTER REVIEW, 1969–1980

SUMMARY

- The spectacular moon landing in 1969 gave a weary and divided nation a welcome reason to celebrate.

- The rights revolution took on even greater momentum as movements for women's rights and minority rights expanded dramatically in universities, the workplace, and the courts.

- Following a string of remarkable successes, including a pathbreaking visit to Communist China and a lopsided reelection victory, President Nixon became the first president to resign his office following revelations of his involvement in the Watergate scandal.

- The collapse of South Vietnam in 1975 ended one of the longest, most divisive chapters in American military history and raised troubling questions about the soundness of U.S. foreign policy in the Cold War era.

- Following decades of unprecedented growth, the American economy entered a period of uncertainty and decline, marked by lower productivity, soaring energy prices, higher interest rates, and runaway inflation.

- The Iran hostage crisis marked a new direction in U.S. relations with the Islamic world.

IDENTIFICATIONS

Woodstock
Vietnamization
Kent State University
Equal Rights Amendment (ERA)
La Raza Unida
Roe v. Wade
Henry Kissinger
détente
George Wallace
Watergate
George McGovern
Gerald R. Ford
James Earl (Jimmy) Carter, Jr.
Camp David Accords

MAKING CONNECTIONS: LOOKING AHEAD Ⅲ➡

Chapter 29 looks at the so-called Reagan Revolution: the attempt by a new president, with a different political philosophy, to restore national confidence and redirect the nation along more conservative lines.

1. How would President Reagan deal with the economic problems facing Americans in this era?

2. How would he differ from previous presidents in his dealings with the Soviet Union and in his personal view of international communism and the Cold War?

3. Was it possible to narrow the social and cultural divisions that had plagued the United States in the 1960s and 1970s, or would they continue to widen over time?

RECOMMENDED READINGS

Carroll, Peter. *It Seemed Like Nothing Happened: America in the 1970s* (1982). A critical overview of American life in the new age of limits.

Chavez, Lydia. *The Color Bind* (1998). Analyzes the political battle surrounding affirmative action in California.

Hull, N. E. H., and Peter Hoffer. *Roe v. Wade* (2001). An excellent analysis of the abortion rights controversy in American history.

Isaacson, Walter. *Kissinger* (1992). A comprehensive biography of the man who helped shape America's foreign policy in the 1970s and beyond.

Kutler, Stanley. *Abuse of Power: The New Nixon Tapes* (1997). The story of a president's demise told through the secret tapes that brought him down.

Lukas, J. Anthony. *Common Ground: A Turbulent Decade in the Lives of Three American Families* (1986). Examines the busing crisis in Boston from several perspectives.

Rudenstine, David. *The Day the Presses Stopped: A History of the Pentagon Papers Case* (1996). Looks at the legal and political issues surrounding the decade's most heralded First Amendment crisis.

Schoenwald, Jonathan. *A Time for Choosing* (2001). Describes the rise of modern conservatism leading to Ronald Reagan's election.

Shilts, Randy. *And the Band Played On* (1987). A superb account of the spreading AIDS epidemic in the homosexual community.

Wandersee, Winifred. *On the Move: American Women in the 1970s* (1988). Highlights the political struggle of women in this decade and the changes that occurred.

CourseMate Go to the CourseMate website at www.cengagebrain.com for additional study tools and review materials for this chapter.

29

From Reagan to Clinton

1981–2000

MAKING CONNECTIONS

◄⁞⁞ LOOKING BACK

Chapter 28 examined the political, economic, and psychological impact of the Watergate scandal, the OPEC oil embargo, the fall of South Vietnam, and other crises on the American people and their vision of the future. Before starting Chapter 29, you should be able to answer the following questions:

1. What impact did the "rights revolution" of the 1960s have on political events in the 1970s? What role did the federal courts play in this process?

2. What were the defining features of the Watergate affair? Why is it considered to be the most significant, and potentially dangerous, political scandal in U.S. history?

3. Though Americans most remember the Iran hostage crisis, the United States achieved some notable successes in foreign policy during the 1970s. What were these successes, and how were they achieved?

The Reagan Revolution

The Election of 1980
Carrying Out the Reagan Agenda
Deregulation
Rivalry with the Soviet Union
Strategic Defense Initiative

Social Tensions of the 1980s

The Challenge of AIDS
New Technologies
The American Family in the 1980s
The Religious Right
The 1984 Presidential Election

Reagan's Second Term

Toward Better Relations with the
Soviet Union
Political Controversies
Reagan and Gorbachev: The Road
to Understanding
The 1988 Presidential Election

The Bush Succession

Bush's Domestic and Economic Policies

Doing History: Debating Ronald
Reagan's Legacy

The Continuing AIDS Crisis
Foreign Policy Successes, 1989–1990
War in the Persian Gulf
The Battle over the Clarence Thomas
Nomination

An Angry Nation

The 1992 Election Campaign
Clinton's Domestic Agenda
Clinton and the World
The Republican Revolution: 1994
Race, Ethnicity, and the Culture Wars

The Republicans in Power

Domestic Terrorism in Oklahoma City
Clinton Resurgent: Bosnia and the
Government Shutdowns
Clinton and the Republican Congress

Clinton: Triumphs and Missteps

The 1996 Election
An Ambitious Foreign Policy
An Economic Boom
The Rise of the Internet
Clinton Impeached and Acquitted

The presidency of **Ronald Reagan** defined the 1980s. Reagan's efforts to redirect the nation toward a smaller and less activist government aroused bitter controversy even while his leadership fostered a mood of renewed optimism. The ensuing administration of George H. W. Bush and the first years of William Jefferson "Bill" Clinton's presidency dealt with the legacy of Reagan and his impact on the nation.

During this period the Soviet Union collapsed, and the Cold War ended. This peaceful transition was an important contribution of the Reagan and Bush administrations. The end of that challenge to American interests revealed other tensions in the world arising from the Middle East, where terrorism became a weapon of choice.

While the economy boomed during the 1980s, the federal government's budget deficits and the national debt increased, and the gulf between the affluent and the poor widened. Under the pressures of global economic change, American businesses became more efficient and less unwieldy. The price, however, was a loss of jobs in many key industries as American workers faced the trauma of "downsizing." The administration of George H. W. Bush faltered as a result. The next president, Bill Clinton, navigated an increasingly hostile political climate while new technology led to rapid growth for some sectors of the American economy.

❖ The Reagan Revolution

When Ronald Wilson Reagan became president of the United States, he was the oldest man ever to assume the nation's highest office. Born in Illinois in 1911, he had been an actor and television personality. Disillusioned with the political liberalism of his youth, he switched to the Republican Party and was elected governor of California in 1966. Reagan's blend of conservative rhetoric and a sunny disposition led to his rise in the 1970s. He lost a race for the Republican presidential nomination to Gerald Ford in 1976 but became the party's nominee four years later with George H. W. Bush as his running mate.

The Election of 1980

The 1980 presidential campaign took place in the shadow of an ongoing crisis involving fifty-two American hostages who had been seized in Iran during the revolution against the shah. A failed military attempt to rescue the hostages in April 1980 undercut Carter's standing with the voters and made his nomination a hollow prize. During the campaign, Reagan assailed Carter's record on the economy and national defense. The president fired back that Reagan was

Reagan, Ronald (1911–2004) Fortieth president of the United States (1981–1989), he represented the ascendancy of conservatism during the 1980s.

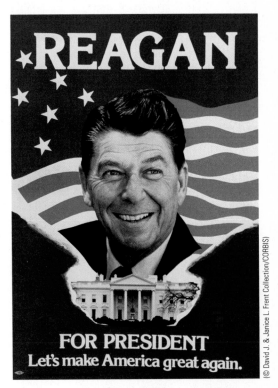

(© David J. & Janice L. Frent Collection/CORBIS)

Reagan in Office. Ronald Reagan conveyed a sense of strong presidential leadership through images like this one that depicted him as an American icon.

CHAPTER TIMELINE	1981	1984	1987	1990	1993	1996	2000
POLITICS AND DIPLOMACY	● 1981 Sandra Day O'Connor is first woman Supreme Court justice				1993–2001 Bill Clinton presidency		
	1981–1989 Ronald Reagan presidency						● 1998 Clinton sex scandals break
				1989–1993 George H. W. Bush presidency			
		1986 ● Iran-contra scandal begins	1989 ● Berlin Wall comes down	● 1991 U.S. defeats Iraq in Gulf War	● 1995 Oklahoma City bombing ● 1994 Republicans retake House of Representatives		
SOCIETY AND CULTURE	● 1981 AIDS epidemic begins in the United States			1993 ● Toni Morrison wins Nobel Prize for Literature			
		● 1983 Sally Ride is first U.S. woman in space	● 1988 Antidepressant Prozac introduced		● 1995 O. J. Simpson murder trial ends in acquittal		
ECONOMICS AND TECHNOLOGY	● 1982 Recession ends	● 1986 Income tax reform passes	● 1988 U.S.–Canada free trade agreement is signed 1993 ● North American Free Trade Agreement signed			● 1996 Welfare reform bill passes	

1980

Candidate (Party)	Electoral Vote		Popular Vote	
Reagan (Republican)	489	90.9%	43,899,248	50.8%
Carter (Democrat)	49	9.1%	35,481,435	41.0%
Anderson (Independent)			5,719,437	6.6%

(Copyright © Cengage Learning)

MAP 29.1

The Election of 1980

The election map reveals the repudiation of Jimmy Carter and his administration in 1980 and the swing to the right that put Ronald Reagan in the White House. Carter's economic record and the foreign policy problems of the late 1970s left him without an effective national political base.

a dangerous and unreliable political extremist. In a televised debate between the two men in late October 1980, Reagan asked viewers: "Are you better off" than in 1976?

Reagan and the Republicans won the election with 44 million ballots for Reagan to 35 million for Carter and 5.7 million for third-party candidate John Anderson. In the electoral college, Reagan garnered 489 votes and Carter 49. The Republicans regained control of the Senate, picking up twelve seats from the Democrats. (See Map 29.1.)

Carrying Out the Reagan Agenda

Reagan said: "We must balance the budget, reduce tax rates, and restore our defenses." His long career in Hollywood had given him a skill in conveying his views that won him the title of the "Great Communicator." He exuded a degree of optimism about his country, sincerity about his positions, and confidence that made him a masterful politician. At the same time, Reagan knew very little about the actual operation of the federal government and displayed scant curiosity about such matters. As a friend put it, "He lived life on the surface where the small waves are, not deep down where the heavy currents tug."

As Reagan started his administration, the Republicans controlled the White House and the Senate, where they commanded a 53 to 46 majority. Democrats remained the majority in the House of Representatives, 242 to 190. In 1980, the inflation rate was over 12 percent, the unemployment rate was above 7 percent, and the prime interest rate had soared to almost 20 percent. The national debt had reached $908 billion.

The administration embraced traditional Republican suspicion of government spending and added to it an aggressive reduction in federal income taxes. The term "supply-side economics" became shorthand for what this program promised to do: the government should lower income and corporate tax rates to give private business and individual taxpayers more money to spend. The predicted surge in productive economic activity would result in an increase in tax revenues, which would prevent large budget deficits.

Reagan's first year in office bolstered his popularity. The release of U.S. hostages in Iran on January 20, 1981, removed that troublesome issue. When Reagan was shot on March 30, 1981, the would-be assassin's bullet came closer to ending his life than the public knew. The president's courage and good humor in this moment of crisis added to the reservoir of goodwill that he commanded. Another event that helped Reagan was his handling of a strike by the Professional Air Traffic Controllers Organization (PATCO). As government employees, the controllers could not legally strike, and the president fired them when they refused to heed a back-to-work order. Clearly, this White House would be tough on organized labor.

During the first half of 1981, a coalition of Republicans and conservative Democrats pushed through legislation that trimmed tax rates by 25 percent over three years. The administration sought budget cuts for a number of discretionary social programs to advance the president's goal of a balanced budget by 1984. Although the budget act, passed in the House on June 25, 1981, promised future reductions in spending, during its first year it provided only $16 billion in immediate cuts. That was $200 billion less than would have been required to achieve a real step toward a balanced budget. The president declined to make cuts in what he termed "the social safety net": Social Security, Medicare, veterans' benefits, Head Start, and school lunch programs. At the same time, his administration increased defense spending.

During the Ford–Carter years, defense budgets had been less than $200 billion annually. Under Reagan, the Pentagon budget rose to nearly $300 billion per year by 1985. The outcome of modest cuts in social programs, sharp hikes in defense spending, and a reduction in tax rates was a growth in the government deficit to $128 billion by 1982. The ballooning federal deficits continued throughout the Reagan era, producing a surge in the national debt. The huge deficits drove economic policy in the years ahead, and future generations were left with a massive debt to fund and pay off.

Deregulation

In his inaugural address, President Reagan proclaimed: "In this present crisis, government is not the solution to our problem; government is the problem." As he attacked large, intrusive government, Reagan advocated an extensive program of deregulation to lessen the government presence in the private sector. Among other areas, this philosophy affected progress on environmental reform. Secretary of the Interior James G. Watt, a conservative who disliked all restrictions on public lands in the West, sought to open new areas for oil drilling, cut back on the acquisition of land for national parks, and put in place other bureaucrats eager to reduce environmental regulations.

The most spectacular and disastrous example of deregulation occurred in 1982, when Congress and the White House lifted restrictions from the savings and loan industry. The Reagan administration also cut back on the number of banking and regulatory examiners. With federal deposit insurance guaranteeing that they would be bailed out, savings and loan operators plunged into ventures that were risky and often illegal. In 1983 and 1984 banks and savings and loan businesses made bad loans, created poorly financed companies, and hired corrupt operators who looted their firms.

By the early 1980s, Social Security, the most popular New Deal program, had reached a funding crisis. During the 1970s, Congress and the Nixon administration had established a system of cost-of-living adjustments (COLAs) that raised benefits for Social Security recipients as the rate of inflation rose. But this caused the cost of Social Security to soar as the population aged. In December 1981, the president appointed a bipartisan panel to address long-range funding of the retirement program. The plan, announced after the 1982 elections, raised payroll taxes to pay for Social Security, taxed some of the benefits of people over age sixty-five who had high incomes, and put off providing for the long-term viability of the system.

Rivalry with the Soviet Union

In 1983, Reagan called the Soviet Union "an evil empire" and said that the Cold War was a struggle between "right and wrong and good and evil." In dealing with the Soviets, the president insisted arms agreements be based on the principle of "trust but verify." But this stern language did not rule out flexibility. Although the new White House team did not like the SALT II Treaty to limit the number of nuclear missiles that Carter had negotiated, it largely observed the pact's provisions.

But the rivalry between the two superpowers flared in Central America. The Reagan administration believed that the victory of the Sandinistas, a pro-Communist faction in Nicaragua, in 1979 represented a serious threat to U.S. interests in the region, especially in neighboring El Salvador. By late 1981, the United States was underwriting a rebellion against the Sandinista regime led by a faction called the **Contras.** Although President Reagan likened the anti-Sandinistas to the patriots of the American Revolution, Democrats in the House objected. In 1982 they blocked funds from being used to oust the Sandinistas.

Contras Nicaraguan military force trained and financed by the United States that opposed the socialist Nicaraguan government led by the Sandinista party.

Reagan and his administration paid a political price for the policies of the first two years. A severe recession continued until almost the end of 1982, causing the Republicans a setback at the polls in the congressional elections. The Democrats gained twenty-seven seats in the House but the Republicans maintained their dominance in the Senate. Nevertheless, President Reagan again urged his fellow Republicans to "stay the course." Shortly thereafter, the economy picked up steam, stimulated by the Reagan tax cuts. The inflation rate declined and unemployment receded. As the recovery gained strength, so did Reagan and his party.

Adding to the president's popularity was the U.S. invasion of the Caribbean island of Grenada in October 1983. Fearing that radicals close to Fidel Castro and Cuba were about to turn Grenada into a Soviet base (an unlikely outcome), the administration launched a powerful invasion force that secured control of the island after a brief struggle. Meanwhile, the war in Nicaragua was not going well for the Contras, and El Salvador was experiencing atrocities from right-wing death squads that murdered their opponents. In 1984, Congress adopted a second, more restrictive, amendment to prevent the government from aiding the Contras.

Contras in Central America.
The Reagan administration sponsored a group in Nicaragua against the Sandinista regime that became known as the "Contras."

(© Susan Meiselas/Magnum Photos)

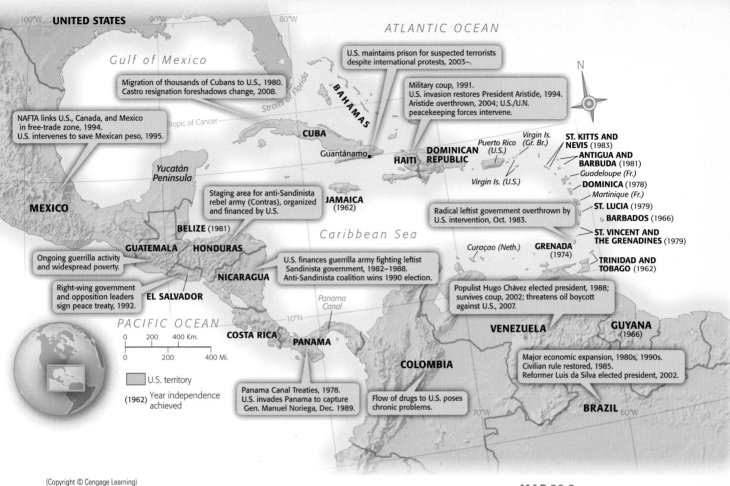

Gulf of Mexico

UNITED STATES

ATLANTIC OCEAN

Migration of thousands of Cubans to U.S., 1980.
Castro resignation foreshadows change, 2008.

U.S. maintains prison for suspected terrorists
despite international protests, 2003–.

Military coup, 1991.
U.S. invasion restores President Aristide, 1994.
Aristide overthrown, 2004; U.S./U.N.
peacekeeping forces intervene.

NAFTA links U.S., Canada, and Mexico
in free-trade zone, 1994.
U.S. intervenes to save Mexican peso, 1995.

BAHAMAS

Straits of Florida

Tropic of Cancer

CUBA

Guantánamo

HAITI

DOMINICAN
REPUBLIC

Puerto Rico
(U.S.)

Virgin Is.
(Gr. Br.)

ST. KITTS AND
NEVIS (1983)

ANTIGUA AND
BARBUDA (1981)

Guadeloupe (Fr.)

DOMINICA (1978)

Martinique (Fr.)

ST. LUCIA (1979)

BARBADOS (1966)

ST. VINCENT AND
THE GRENADINES (1979)

TRINIDAD AND
TOBAGO (1962)

Virgin Is. (U.S.)

Yucatán
Peninsula

MEXICO

Staging area for anti-Sandinista
rebel army (Contras), organized
and financed by U.S.

JAMAICA
(1962)

Radical leftist government overthrown by
U.S. intervention, Oct. 1983.

Caribbean Sea

Curaçao (Neth.)

GRENADA
(1974)

BELIZE (1981)

GUATEMALA

HONDURAS

Ongoing guerrilla activity
and widespread poverty.

NICARAGUA

U.S. finances guerrilla army fighting leftist
Sandinista government, 1982–1988.
Anti-Sandinista coalition wins 1990 election.

Populist Hugo Chávez elected president, 1988;
survives coup, 2002; threatens oil boycott
against U.S., 2007.

Right-wing government
and opposition leaders
sign peace treaty, 1992.

EL SALVADOR

Panama
Canal

VENEZUELA

GUYANA
(1966)

PACIFIC OCEAN

0   200   400 Km.

0   200   400 Mi.

COSTA RICA

PANAMA

COLOMBIA

Major economic expansion, 1980s, 1990s.
Civilian rule restored, 1985.
Reformer Luis da Silva elected president, 2002.

U.S. territory

(1962) Year independence
achieved

Panama Canal Treaties, 1978.
U.S. invades Panama to capture
Gen. Manuel Noriega, Dec. 1989.

Flow of drugs to U.S. poses
chronic problems.

BRAZIL

(Copyright © Cengage Learning)

MAP 29.2

The United States in the Caribbean and Central America, 1981–2008
During the three decades after 1981, the United States took an active role in the Caribbean and Central America with an involvement in Nicaragua during the 1980s, an incursion into Panama in 1989, and continuing issues with Cuba throughout the period. This map shows the extent of the American commitment in the region.

Strategic Defense Initiative (SDI)
Proposed by President Reagan in 1983, a Defense Department program to develop a space-based system to defend against strategic ballistic missiles.

In the Middle East, Reagan's hopes of producing a lasting peace between Israel and its neighbors were also frustrated. The administration did not stop Israel from invading Lebanon in June 1982, and U.S. Marines were sent into the region as part of a multinational peacekeeping force. Two hundred and thirty-nine marines perished when a terrorist bomb blew up a barracks in 1983. The United States subsequently withdrew its remaining soldiers.

Strategic Defense Initiative

In March 1983, the most significant defense policy initiative of the first Reagan term came when the president announced the **Strategic Defense Initiative (SDI).** Reagan envisioned a system of weapons, based in space, that would intercept and shoot down Soviet missiles before they could reach the United States. An appealing vision on the drawing board, critics promptly dubbed SDI "Star Wars" after the hit movie and questioned its technical rationale. But Reagan pressed forward with SDI over the objections of his political opponents and the displeasure of the Soviet Union.

❖ Social Tensions of the 1980s

Besides continued cold war tensions, the 1980s were a time of social change and challenge for Americans. Computers and the Internet began to reshape communications. The rise of the religious Right revealed tensions about fundamental beliefs that would ripple through American history for decades. And the disease known as AIDS caused an ongoing medical tragedy of global proportions.

The Challenge of AIDS

In the early Reagan years Americans learned of a new and deadly disease that scientists called AIDS (for acquired immune deficiency syndrome). The virus originated in Africa and first appeared in the United States in 1981. It ravaged victims' immune systems, and most of those infected were doomed to a painful death. By 1989, the number of confirmed AIDS deaths reached thirty-seven hundred in the United States.

The virus spread within the population through the exchange of body fluids. Mothers who were infected passed the condition on to their children; infected blood was transferred during transfusions. The most vulnerable groups were drug addicts, bisexuals, and homosexuals. Many called for the distribution of condoms to those at high risk for AIDS, but the Reagan administration resisted such actions.

New Technologies

In the 1980s, the nation also experienced the initial stages of a revolution in communications that altered American society. In 1981, International Business Machines (IBM) announced that it would market a computer for home use. Recognizing the potential impact of such a product, two young computer software writers, Bill Gates and Paul Allen of Microsoft, adapted an existing software program and transformed it into DOS (disk operating system), which ran the hardware created by IBM. Important changes followed throughout the decade, including the Lotus 1-2-3 spreadsheet program in 1982, Microsoft Windows in 1983, and the Apple Macintosh computer in 1984.

After January 1983, sales of personal computers rose to more than half a million per year. People found that they could publish books from their desktops, trace financial accounts, make travel reservations, and play a wide assortment of computer games. Growing out of the Advanced Research Projects Agency of the Pentagon was a network of computers founded in 1969. As computer users and researchers exchanged messages over this and other networks in the late 1970s and early 1980s, the National Science Foundation promoted what became known as the Internet as an overall network bulletin board.

Personal Computers. The personal computer appeared in the 1980s and spread into every corner of American life in the decades that followed.

The American Family in the 1980s

The American people responded to troubling changes in the family and its place in society during Reagan's presidency. In 1981, the number of divorces stood at nearly 1.2 million annually, the highest rate ever. At the same time, the number of births to unmarried women rose dramatically during the 1970s. With these developments came a marked increase in the number of single-parent families, which rose from 3.8 million in 1970 to 10.5 million by 1992. The impact of this trend was especially evident among African Americans: by the end of the 1980s, more than 60 percent of all African American families were single-parent families.

One major area of concern for families was the state of the public schools. A series of high-profile national studies suggested that American education was "a disaster area." One national survey, *A Nation at Risk*, asserted that the country faced dire consequences if public education did not undergo sweeping reform.

As families felt the effects of economic and social changes, Americans responded with contradictory approaches. On the one hand, sexual mores became more tolerant. On the other, efforts to recapture "traditional family values" animated many groups on the conservative end of the political spectrum. The boundaries that had governed the depiction of sexual behavior in the media relaxed in significant ways during the 1980s. On prime-time television, viewers could hear language and see sexual intimacy depicted in a fashion that would have been unthinkable a few years earlier.

The Religious Right

A major force in pressing for conservative cultural values was the political power of evangelical Christians. The **Moral Majority,** an organization founded by the Reverend Jerry Falwell of Virginia in 1979, tapped into the evangelical denominations such as the Southern Baptist Convention and assailed abortion, homosexuality, rock music, and drugs. Throughout the 1980s, evangelical Christianity permeated American politics. On cable television, viewers tuned in to Pat Robertson's *700 Club* on the Christian Broadcasting Network that Robertson had founded.

The volatile issue of abortion spurred the rise of the Christian Right. Following the Supreme Court decision in *Roe v. Wade* (1973), the number of abortions in the United States stood at 1.5 million per year. Foes of abortion, most notably in the Roman Catholic Church and among evangelical Protestants, asserted that the unborn baby was a human being from the moment of conception and entitled to all the rights of a living person. The "right-to-life" forces, as they called themselves, pressured lawmakers to cut back on the right of abortion and to enact restrictive laws. They conducted picketing and boycotts of abortion clinics in the 1980s and arranged for massive public demonstrations. The Republican Party became largely antiabortion in its policies and programs. The Democrats were equally committed to what was called "a woman's right to choose" or a "prochoice" position.

Moral Majority Political action group founded in 1979 and composed of conservative, fundamentalist Christians. Led by evangelist Rev. Jerry Falwell, the group played a significant role in the 1980 elections through its strong support of conservative candidates.

The 1984 Presidential Election

At the beginning of 1984, Reagan's popularity rating stood at 55 percent. The Democratic base in the South eroded as the president made substantial gains among what were known as "Reagan Democrats": people who shared the president's social conservatism and disliked the pro–civil rights stances of the Democrats. Even the patriotic pageantry of the Summer Olympics in Los Angeles boosted the president's standing. Reagan's only apparent vulnerability was his age.

Democrats struggled to find a plausible presidential candidate. In the end former vice president **Walter Mondale** of Minnesota turned back the challenges of **Jesse Jackson,** the first credible African American candidate to seek the nomination of a major party, and Senator Gary Hart of Colorado, to lock up the nomination. Mondale came under intense pressure to select a woman as his running mate, and he agreed to the selection of Representative Geraldine Ferraro of New York.

After a stumble in the first of two televised debates, Reagan rebounded in the second appearance with Mondale. When a questioner asked him about his age, the president replied that he would not allow age to be an issue. "I am not going to exploit, for political purposes, my opponent's youth and inexperience," he said. Reagan won by a landslide, carrying forty-nine of the fifty states. The Republicans retained control of the Senate; the Democrats lost seats in the House but maintained their dominance of that chamber.

Mondale, Walter (1928–) Vice president of the United States under Jimmy Carter (1977–1981), he earlier served as a U.S. senator from Minnesota (1965–1977) and was the unsuccessful 1984 Democratic nominee for president.

Jackson, Jesse (1941–) Baptist minister and civil rights leader, he directed national antidiscrimination efforts in the mid-1960s and 1970s.

❖ Reagan's Second Term

The economic boom of the mid-1980s that bolstered Reagan's reelection fostered an atmosphere of moneymaking and social acquisitiveness. Top executives received staggering annual salaries. Wall Street experienced a "merger mania" in which corporations acquired competitors through hostile takeovers.

A sobering moment in the frenetic decade came on January 28, 1986, when the space shuttle *Challenger* exploded, and all seven crew members perished in the disaster. The event happened live before a shocked audience that watched the spacecraft lift off normally and then explode a few seconds later into a mass of wreckage. An official investigation revealed that slipshod technology had contributed to the tragedy.

Toward Better Relations with the Soviet Union

Gorbachev, Mikhail (1931–)
General secretary of the Soviet Communist party (1985–1990) and president of the USSR (1990–1991), he ushered in an era of glasnost (openness) and perestroika (restructuring), and won the Nobel Peace Prize in 1990.

Soviet–American relations entered a new phase when **Mikhail Gorbachev** came to power. Aware of the weaknesses his nation confronted, Gorbachev pursued a more conciliatory policy toward the West while trying to implement a restructuring of Soviet society that came to be known as *perestroika*. He announced reductions in the deployment of Soviet missiles and sought friendlier relations with European nations. Gorbachev and Reagan agreed to hold a summit conference in Geneva in November 1985. Hitting it off, they met again at Reykjavik, Iceland, in October 1986. Again there were no substantive results, but the experience indicated that a genuine arms agreement might be possible.

Political Controversies

In November 1986 the American public learned that the Administration had facilitated the selling of arms to the Islamic regime in Iran that had sponsored terrorist activities for most of the 1980s. Within a month the revelation came that money obtained from the arms sales had been used to support the Nicaraguan Contras in violation of congressional amendments barring the practice. The story emerged that in 1985, members of the National Security Council (NSC) had become convinced that the release of American hostages held in Lebanon could be secured if the United States sold arms to Iran. The evidence that such moderation existed in Iran was largely fanciful. Since disclosure of this new policy would have outraged Americans and provoked congressional investigations, the president's approval of arm sales was kept secret.

North, Oliver (1943–) Member of President Reagan's National Security Council staff and a Marine colonel, he was a central figure in the Iran-Contra scandal.

The actual shipment of weapons to Iran was carried out by Israel, with the United States replacing the transferred munitions. Unfortunately, the Iranians accepted the munitions but released only three hostages. The arms deals generated profits, however, and a member of the NSC staff, Marine Colonel **Oliver North,** had what he later called a "neat idea": those profits from the sale of weapons to Iran should be used to support the Contras in Nicaragua. North's actions violated congressional directives specifically barring the provision of aid to the Contras. Moreover, the use of any funds without legislative approval was illegal. Furthermore, a privately financed, unaccountable, and clandestine foreign policy operation was well outside constitutional limits.

News of the scandal leaked out in October 1986 when the Sandinistas shot down one of the planes taking weapons to the Contras and a captured crew member revealed the Central Intelligence Agency's links to the operation. Early in November, news of the arms-for-hostages deal surfaced in the Middle East. On November 13, 1986, the president told the American people: "We did not—repeat, did not—trade weapons or anything else for hostages, nor will we."

Attorney General Edwin Meese conducted a slow, ineffective probe, but by late November, conclusive proof of the diversion of money to the Contras came out. The president fired Oliver North and accepted the resignation of John Poindexter, the national security adviser. Reagan appointed the Tower Commission, named after its chair, former Senator John Tower of Texas, to look into the White House's role in the scheme, and lawmakers granted immunity to many of the involved individuals in exchange for their testimony. Although everyone concerned professed a desire to get to the bottom of what became known as the **Iran-Contra scandal,** there was little inclination, even among Democrats, to see Ronald Reagan impeached for his role in it. The Tower Commission chastised the president for an inept "management style" that allowed his subordinates to lead him into the scandal. On March 4, 1987, Reagan said that he accepted the commission's findings and reiterated that he had not intended to trade arms for hostages. His poll ratings rose, and once again the public responded to his leadership.

More controversy arose as Reagan pursued his goal of making the federal judiciary more conservative. In the lower courts, Reagan nominated more than half the members of the federal judiciary over his eight years in office. In July 1981, Reagan named the first woman to be appointed to the Court, **Sandra Day O'Connor** of Arizona. The president did not have another opportunity to appoint a justice until Chief Justice Warren Burger resigned in 1986. Reagan elevated Justice William Rehnquist to replace Burger and named Antonin Scalia, a federal appeals court judge, to take the seat that Rehnquist vacated.

In June 1987, after the Democrats had regained control of the Senate, Justice Lewis Powell resigned, and President Reagan named Robert Bork, another federal appeals court jurist, to replace him. During a long career as a legal writer before becoming a judge, Bork had taken many controversial stands on divisive issues. He had opposed the decision in *Roe v. Wade* (1973) that established a woman's right to have an abortion, and he had questioned other decisions in the areas of privacy and civil rights. Senate Democrats, civil rights leaders, and women's groups opposed Bork, calling him a conservative ideologue outside the mainstream of American judicial thinking. His nomination was defeated, but the contentious process had a lasting impact on future Supreme Court nominations. Anthony Kennedy was nominated and confirmed to the Court early in 1988.

Reagan and Gorbachev: The Road to Understanding

The Iran-Contra affair produced changes in Reagan's administration that prepared the way for genuine foreign policy achievements. Former Senator Howard Baker became Reagan's chief of staff, Frank Carlucci was named secretary of defense, and Lieutenant General **Colin Powell** served as the national security adviser. These more pragmatic operators encouraged Reagan to seek further negotiations with the Soviets. By late 1987, negotiators for the two sides had agreed to remove from Europe intermediate-range missiles with nuclear warheads. Tensions between the two countries eased further when the Soviets pulled out of Afghanistan. The improvement in the superpower rivalry helped Reagan regain some of his popularity with the American people as his administration neared its end.

The 1988 Presidential Election

With Ronald Reagan ineligible to seek a third term, Vice President George Bush soon emerged as his Republican successor. **George H. W. Bush** came from an aristocratic New England background but had moved to Texas after combat service in the navy during World War II. Elected to the House of Representatives in 1966, he stayed for two terms and made a losing bid for the Senate in 1970. Service in

Iran-Contra scandal A major scandal of the second Reagan term that involved shipping arms to Iran and diverting money from the sale of these weapons to the Contra rebels in Nicaragua.

O'Connor, Sandra Day (1930–) Appointed by President Ronald Reagan, she was the first woman justice on the Supreme Court.

Powell, Colin (1937–) U.S. general, national security adviser (1987–1989), chairman of the Joint Chiefs of Staff (1989–1993), and secretary of state (2001–2005). He was influential in planning U.S. strategy during the Persian Gulf War.

Bush, George H. W. (1924–) Forty-first president of the United States (1989–1993), he was in office when the Soviet Union collapsed.

the Ford administration as envoy to China and director of the Central Intelligence Agency added to his impressive roster of government posts. He ran against Reagan for the Republican nomination in 1980 and became the vice-presidential choice instead. At the Republican convention in New Orleans, Bush emphasized deficits and taxes. He predicted that Democrats in Congress would pressure him to raise taxes and promised to reject all such proposals. "Read my lips," he declared. "No new taxes!"

With Reagan stepping down, Democrats were hopeful. Massachusetts Governor Michael Dukakis emerged as the leading contender for the nomination. Dukakis emphasized his family's Greek immigrant background and stressed his success in stimulating the Massachusetts economy during the 1980s. As the convention ended, Dukakis had a strong lead in the polls, but his tepid personality—combined with aggressive attacks from Republicans—doomed his candidacy. The most penetrating attack addressed prison furloughs that Massachusetts law granted to jailed criminals. In one case, a black convict named William Horton had been released on furlough, then fled Massachusetts and committed a rape in another state. The Republicans and their surrogates used the "Willie" Horton case in powerful television commercials to portray Dukakis as soft on crime, but the racial dimensions of the incident were also evident. Bush won the election with a solid margin in the electoral vote, though the Democrats retained control of Congress. (See *Doing History: Debating Ronald Reagan's Legacy*.)

❖ The Bush Succession

George H. W. Bush pledged to carry on Reagan's policies, but promised to do so in a more humane and judicious manner. He spoke of a "kinder, gentler" nation and was confident in foreign policy. Bush's secretary of state, James A. Baker, was a close friend and an adroit power broker; the national security adviser, Brent Scowcroft, and the chair of the Joint Chiefs of Staff, General Colin Powell, executed the president's policies with skill and efficiency. The collapse of communism in 1989–1990, the challenge of Iraqi expansionism in the Middle East, and the shaping of a new role for the United States gave Bush and his foreign policy team much to do.

Bush's Domestic and Economic Policies

The first half of the Bush administration went very well. The president relished the art of governing and approached his job by engaging in a frenzy of activity. His press conferences demonstrated his command of information in a way that Reagan had never displayed. As time passed, however, questions arose about Bush's larger goals for his presidency. He called it, in the abrupt shorthand that he often employed, "the vision thing."

The president and his chief of staff, John Sununu, had few domestic goals other than their commitment to uphold the campaign pledge of "no new taxes." Much to the dismay of Republican conservatives, Bush went along with Democratic legislation such as the Clean Air Act and the Americans with Disabilities Act, which involved a growth in the federal bureaucracy and expanded regulations. Any legislation that he did not like, such as an increase in the minimum wage, Bush vetoed. During the first three years of his presidency, Congress failed to override any of Bush's twenty-eight vetoes.

By 1989, however, the Bush administration had to deal with another major domestic issue. The deregulated savings and loan industry had a major collapse that left the taxpayers with a $500 billion cost to bail out depositors for the failed

Doing History Debating Ronald Reagan's Legacy

When Ronald Reagan died in June 2004, one of the authors of this text, Lewis L. Gould, discussed how history might judge the former president. He examined how the reputations of other presidents, from Warren G. Harding to John F. Kennedy, had changed over time and suggested that Reagan would be subjected to the same process of reevaluation and reappraisal. The article, which appeared in the Washington Post, *carried the author's e-mail address for readers' responses. An excerpt from the article and what some e-mail correspondents, pro and con, said about the article illustrate how contentious Ronald Reagan's legacy remains.*

The stakes are high for Reagan's reputation because enough time has passed for a generation of younger Americans to have grown up with only a vague sense of what made him so controversial in his day. For those approaching 30 who were in their mid-teens or younger when Reagan gave way to George H. W. Bush in January 1989, the "Great Communicator" is a historical figure speedily receding into the past. Those who will be entering college this year were born in 1986, as Reagan's second term was winding down. Making the episode of the Reagan years come alive for that new cadre of undergraduates will not be easy. Nothing is quite so dead for young people as the stale disputes of a vanished era, even one that was, in human terms, not so long ago. What was PATCO anyway, or Gramm-Latta, or Iran-Contra?

Responses

Ronald Reagan's legacy has already been imprinted in world history. Perhaps you should listen again to Margaret Thatcher's parting words. Or recall his landslide 49 out of 50 state reelection victory. Or listen to President Reagan's acceptance of blame for sending the Marines to Beirut and for the Iran-Contra mistake.

Why has so little been mentioned of Reagan's domestic legacy, which left not only the poor poorer, but many middle-class families like my own, worse

off. To say nothing of the failed "trickle-down" policy. Why has he repetitively been described as much more popular than he was?

I guess when it comes to you Liberals/Progressives/Commies, no matter what President Reagan did it will never be enough or good or meet your approval. So "we the people" have decided that President Reagan will go down in history as the second best president of the 20th century. There, I have said it. "We the People" do not care what you elitists or commie journalists have to say. All that had to be said and done was said [and] done by President Reagan. It is all in the history books now and no matter how you idiots try to rewrite the history of Reagan, will be of no avail. Eat your hearts out.

Reagan's ability to convince the public that "government is the problem," playing on the public's anger and fatigue after assassinations, civil rights struggles, Vietnam and Watergate, led to the dismantling of hard-won government protections and social programs—not least our public education—that we will never recover. He and his spiritual heirs have led this Cadillac of a country right into a swamp.

Source: Lewis L. Gould, "History in the Remaking," *Washington Post*, June 13, 2004.

QUESTIONS for REFLECTION

1. What accounts for the polarized view of Reagan's accomplishments and his potential historical legacy?

2. What elements in Reagan's political style attracted such devoted followers and repelled others?

3. Where do you think, based on your reading of this chapter and documents that appear in this essay, that Ronald Reagan's historical reputation now stands? How is it likely to change in the future?

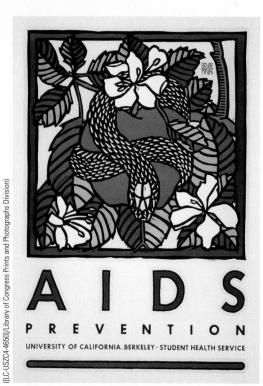

AIDS PREVENTION

UNIVERSITY OF CALIFORNIA, BERKELEY · STUDENT HEALTH SERVICE

AIDS Poster. The AIDS epidemic was frightening to many Americans during the 1980s as warnings about the deadly nature of the disease proliferated.

Tiananmen Square Adjacent to the Forbidden City in Beijing, China, this large public square was the site of many festivals, rallies, and demonstrations. During a student demonstration in 1989, Chinese troops fired on the demonstrators, killing an estimated two thousand or more.

institutions. Congress established the Resolution Trust Corporation to sell off the assets of the failed banks and savings and loans and to obtain as much money as possible from their sale.

The Continuing AIDS Crisis

Both funding for AIDS research and public awareness of the disease increased during the Bush years. Congress created the National Commission on AIDS in 1989, and federal government funds for treatment and research had risen to over $2 billion by 1992. Still, the number of new cases continued to increase, reaching 45,603 in 1992 and 83,814 a year later. AIDS activists wanted more money for research and greater cultural tolerance for those afflicted with the disease, while conservatives like Senator Jesse Helms of North Carolina contended that most AIDS victims were homosexuals who had brought their condition on themselves.

Foreign Policy Successes, 1989–1990

At the end of 1988, Gorbachev had told the United Nations that the nations of Eastern Europe were free to determine their own destiny without Soviet interference. During 1989, the old order in Eastern Europe crumbled. Poland held free elections, Hungary allowed its borders to open, and East Germany eased barriers to travel to West Germany. By the end of 1989, the Cold War seemed to be over, with the United States the victor. The Bush administration handled these developments carefully. Mindful of the nuclear weapons in the hands of the Soviet military, the president avoided gloating over the success of the West. In 1990, Gorbachev renounced the Communist Party's monopoly over political power. Rivals to Gorbachev emerged that year, particularly the new president of the Russian Republic, Boris Yeltsin.

One country where the administration's foreign policy encountered difficulty was China. Student protests during the spring of 1989 led to a brutal crackdown on demonstrators in Beijing's **Tiananmen Square.** The spectacle of students being killed and wounded, as well as the repressive policies of the Chinese government, produced an outcry in the United States. However, Bush believed that it was important to maintain good relations with the Chinese leaders, so the administration's response to the events of June 1989 was muted and cautious.

Closer to home, the Bush administration took more decisive action toward Panama's strongman ruler, Manuel Noriega. Corrupt and deeply involved in the international narcotics trade, Noriega had been on the U.S. payroll for many years as an informant on drug matters. In 1989, his dictatorial regime refused to adhere to the results of national elections. The White House sent additional troops and called for an uprising against Noriega. Noriega declared a state of war on American military personnel and ordered that their families be captured and tortured. In late December, the United States launched an invasion that quickly overcame the Panamanian army. In early 1990, Noriega surrendered, and in 1992 was tried and convicted of drug trafficking in a federal court in Florida. (See Map 29.2.)

By the spring of 1990, President Bush's pledge of "no new taxes" reverberated in the minds of the American people, but Democratic majorities in Congress were forced to consider raising taxes to deal with the budget deficit. In 1989, the president worked out a strategy with Congress that provided for budget savings. With the budget deficit growing, however, the Democrats did not see how spending cuts alone could reduce it, but they were unwilling to propose tax increases unless President Bush agreed to them.

During early 1990, there were signs that the economy had begun to slow down. The gross domestic product had grown slowly in 1989, there had been a slight loss in manufacturing jobs, and producer prices had risen. With a weakening economy, neither side wanted to face the implications of serious budget cuts. Finally on June 26, 1990, Bush announced that dealing with the deficit problem might have to include "tax revenue increases." Republicans reacted with fury. To many, the president had squandered much of the trust that the American people had placed in him in 1988.

War in the Persian Gulf

Foreign policy events soon overshadowed the political fallout from the broken tax pledge. In August 1990, the Iraqi army of Saddam Hussein invaded and seized the oil-rich kingdom of Kuwait. Suddenly the oil supplies of the United States and the industrialized world faced a new threat from the Iraqi dictator.

During the 1980s, Iran and Iraq had fought a brutal and costly war that had drained the resources of both countries. The United States had not taken sides in the conflict, hoping that the two countries, both of which were hostile toward the United States, would exhaust each other. Once the war ended, however, the Bush administration had pursued a conciliatory policy, allowing Iraq to purchase heavy machinery and paying little attention to its efforts to build a nuclear bomb and acquire weapons of mass destruction. But when Iraqi military units rolled into Kuwait in the summer of 1990, Bush decided that the takeover must be resisted, and heavy economic sanctions were put into effect. The United States also deployed American troops in Saudi Arabia to deter Hussein from attacking that country. For the remainder of 1990, the Bush administration moved military forces into Saudi Arabia. The end of the Cold War meant that the United States had the support of the Soviet Union in isolating Iraq from the rest of the world and therefore had much greater freedom of action than would have been the case even two years earlier.

On the domestic side, the budget issue remained unsettled until the president and the Democratic leadership worked out a deficit reduction plan in September 1990, but Republicans thwarted it a few days later. Intense negotiations between the White House and Capitol Hill produced a deficit reduction agreement at the end of October that involved both tax increases and spending cuts. Angry Republicans charged that Bush had capitulated to the opposition; they went into the fall elections in a divided and unhappy mood.

After the elections, Bush stepped up the pressure on Saddam Hussein to leave Kuwait. The United Nations Security Council agreed to the use of armed force against Iraq if Kuwait had not been freed by January 15, 1991. As diplomatic options faded, Congress insisted on a vote over whether American troops should go into combat in the Middle East. The result, on January 12, 1991, was a victory for the president. Five days later, Operation Desert Storm began. In a devastating series of strikes, the allied coalition bombed the Iraqi army into submission. The most that Hussein could do in retaliation was to send missiles against Israel; he also set Kuwaiti oil wells on fire and dumped oil into the Persian Gulf.

The second phase of Desert Storm began on February 24, 1991, with a huge assault of American and allied troops against the weakened Iraqi defenders. A series of encircling maneuvers ousted the Iraqis from Kuwait with huge losses in troops and equipment. Estimates of the number of Iraqi soldiers killed ranged as high as 100,000. American deaths totaled 148, including 11 women. Within one hundred hours, the ground phase of the war ended in a complete victory on the battlefield for the anti-Iraq forces. President Bush decided not to press for Hussein's removal from power, a decision that was later criticized, and key units of the Iraqi army were left intact to fight again against their own people.

CHAPTER 29 • From Reagan to Clinton **1981–2000**

Victory in the Gulf War sent Bush's popularity soaring to record levels; he received approval ratings of nearly 90 percent in some polls. Yet the political dividends from Bush's military triumph did not last long. Hussein bounced back from his defeat to reassert his power in Iraq and, despite United Nations inspections, rebuilt his nation's economy. Other international problems troubled the White House during 1991. In Russia, Gorbachev faced a coup designed to bring hardliners back into power. A rival of Gorbachev, Boris Yeltsin, led demonstrations against the coup, which then failed. The Soviet Union collapsed, and its component nations broke apart. Yeltsin consolidated his power with promises of economic reform and put himself in a position to succeed Gorbachev. With the demise of the Soviet Union, the major threat of the Cold War had ended, but instability in Eastern Europe posed new threats.

One area of turmoil was Yugoslavia, where the Communist government had long suppressed historic rivalries among Serbs, Croats, Bosnians, and other nationalities. Tensions between Christians and Muslims added to the dangerous potential of the situation. Civil war broke out in 1991 as Serbs battled Croats, Slovenes, and Bosnians. The Bush administration recognized Bosnia as an independent nation and thus became involved in a Balkan struggle whose problems spilled over into the next presidency.

The Battle over the Clarence Thomas Nomination

Like Ronald Reagan, George H. W. Bush wanted to continue the conservative trend that the Supreme Court had been following since the 1970s. That goal seemed even more important in the light of the Court's ruling in *Webster v. Reproductive Health Services* (1989), whereby the justices decided in a 5–4 ruling that states could set limits on the ability to obtain an abortion. Any change in the Court could affect the controversy over abortion. When the liberal justice William Brennan retired in 1990, the president named David Souter of New Hampshire to succeed him. The next nomination, in 1991, led to one of the most sensational confirmation struggles in the nation's history. When Justice Thurgood Marshall retired, the president selected African American federal judge **Clarence Thomas,** who had long opposed such programs as affirmative action.

Thomas's qualifications for the Supreme Court were modest, but he seemed to be on the way to easy confirmation until it was revealed that a black law professor at the University of Oklahoma, **Anita Hill,** had accused Thomas of sexual harassment when she had worked for him at the Equal Employment Opportunity Commission during the early 1980s. Her charges led to dramatic hearings in which Hill laid out her allegations and Thomas denied them. A national television audience watched the hearings in fascination. In the end, the Senate voted 52 to 48 to confirm Thomas, who proved to be an intense advocate of conservative positions.

❖ An Angry Nation

Meanwhile, no strong Democratic candidates had emerged to challenge Bush, who had the support of most Republicans. After twelve years of Bush and Reagan, the Republican coalition seemed in solid control of the nation's policy agenda. But Republicans failed to notice that the American people were anxious and fearful as the 1990s began. Major corporations had cut their payrolls to reduce costs in what became known as "downsizing." Large firms like IBM, Procter & Gamble, and Chrysler Corporation trimmed their payrolls dramatically; IBM

Doing History Online

The New World Order

Go to the CourseMate website for this chapter and link to Primary Sources. Based on the documents online, write a thesis paragraph that articulates the principles that guided American foreign policy during the George H. W. Bush presidency.

www.cengagebrain.com

Thomas, Clarence (1948–) Supreme Court justice appointed by George H. W. Bush in 1991, whose confirmation became controversial due to allegations of sexual misconduct made against him.

Hill, Anita (1956–) Government lawyer and law professor who brought charges of sexual misconduct against Clarence Thomas during his confirmation hearings as Supreme Court justice in 1991.

alone reduced its workforce by one hundred thousand. Other businesses moved production facilities overseas in search of lower labor costs. Multinational corporations became a focus of voter anger.

The 1992 Election Campaign

Although the Gulf War had lifted President Bush's popularity, his poll ratings receded from those lofty levels during 1991 and then dropped further. The president seemed out of touch to many Americans. His Democratic opponent was the governor of Arkansas, **William Jefferson ("Bill") Clinton.** Clinton aroused conflicting passions. He was a young southern governor who campaigned as a "New Democrat" with a strong record in education, civil rights, and economic growth in Arkansas. Critics charged that he was a womanizer who had evaded the draft during the Vietnam War. Clinton's business dealings also raised questions.

Racial rioting in Los Angeles during the spring of 1992 underscored the tense nature of national attitudes. Sparked by the acquittal of Los Angeles police officers on trial for beating Rodney King, a black suspect in their custody, the violence showed that passions over race smoldered while political leaders ignored these problems.

Many citizens, especially Republicans, looked for an alternative to a Bush-Clinton matchup. A Texas computer billionaire named Ross Perot emerged as an alternative. Plainspoken and tough talking, the feisty Perot argued that professional politicians lacked the will to engage the nation's problems. Soon a grass-roots movement had Perot on the ballot in every state. He did not say how he would fix the budget deficit and clean up Washington; he would just do so. As the media investigated his previous record in business and politics, evidence of erratic and silly behavior surfaced. Just before the Democratic National Convention, Perot withdrew from the race, giving the Clinton campaign a boost.

The Arkansas governor selected Senator Albert Gore of Tennessee as his running mate. The presence of two southerners on the national ticket defied political wisdom, but the voters liked the youthful and energetic Democratic

Clinton, William Jefferson ("Bill") (1946–) Forty-second president of the United States (1993–2001). He secured passage of the North American Free Trade Agreement (NAFTA) in 1993 and welfare reform in 1996. Impeached for perjury and obstruction of justice in 1998, he was acquitted by the Senate in 1999.

(© Peter Turnley/CORBIS)

Bill Clinton. During his first race for the White House, Bill Clinton sought to convey an image of youthful energy and vigor. At an airport in 1992, he makes a long pass to his running mate, Al Gore, out of camera range.

1992

Candidate (Party)	Electoral Vote		Popular Vote	
Clinton (Democrat)	370	68.8%	44,908,233	43.0%
Bush (Republican)	168	31.2%	39,102,282	37.4%
Perot (Independent)	0	0.0%	19,741,048	18.9%

(Copyright © Cengage Learning)

MAP 29.3

The Election of 1992

This map shows the ability of Bill Clinton to capitalize on the discontent with George H. W. Bush and the Republicans to achieve a landslide electoral victory. Because Clinton received only 43 percent of the vote, however, Republicans soon questioned his legitimacy as president.

team. Clinton's lead in the polls widened before the Republicans held their convention in August, renominating Bush amid an atmosphere in which the conservative social agenda dominated. In a fiery speech, Patrick Buchanan, a conservative commentator, declared a cultural war to reclaim America from liberals, immigrants, and homosexuals. He assailed Hillary Clinton as well. The spectacle added to Bill Clinton's support, especially with women voters in the nation's suburbs.

Perot came back into the race in October 1992 and participated in the debates with Clinton and Bush. Voter interest in the election was high. Bush closed the gap somewhat during the final weeks of the campaign, but the Perot candidacy split the Republican base in many states. The result was a Clinton-Gore victory. Perot made the best popular showing of any third-party candidate but won no electoral votes. The Democrats continued their control of Congress, but the Republicans gained one Senate seat and picked up fourteen members of the House. A notable feature of the 1992 election was the addition of three female members to the U.S. Senate. (See Map 29.3.)

Clinton's Domestic Agenda

Clinton's presidency faltered even before he took office. As one of his first announced priorities, the president-elect indicated that he intended to lift the long-standing ban against declared homosexuals serving in the armed forces. After much debate within the military, the Clinton administration adopted a "Don't Ask, Don't Tell" approach in which gay personnel would not be asked about their orientation and should not be openly homosexual. Meanwhile, the right wing of the Republicans began an assault on the president and his wife that would continue for the next eight years.

After Clinton was inaugurated, an armed confrontation between agents of the Bureau of Alcohol, Tobacco, and Firearms and members of the Branch Davidian religious sect outside Waco, Texas, in April 1993 led to the fiery deaths of many of the Davidians. Opponents of gun control and the federal government contended that the Clinton administration envisioned dictatorial rule. That fear on the far right further sparked discontent with the new president.

During his first two years, Bill Clinton achieved several domestic objectives at a high political cost. With the barest of voting margins in the House and Senate, he secured adoption of an economic package that combined tax increases and spending cuts to lower the deficit for 1993 to $255 billion and for 1994 to $203 billion. Republicans depicted Clinton as returning to a traditional Democratic strategy of raising taxes, and they predicted economic calamity ahead. Clinton responded that the burden of higher levies fell only on the wealthiest Americans. The economy remained strong and the nation was prosperous throughout 1993 and 1994.

Clinton pursued the cause of freer world trade when he advocated passage of the North American Free Trade Agreement (NAFTA), which cleared Congress in late 1993. The trade agreement split the Democrats, and approval came with the help of Republican votes. In late 1994, the White House also secured congressional endorsement of the General Agreement on Tariffs and Trade among nations engaged in international trade (GATT) in a lame-duck session of the Democratic Congress. Again, Republican votes were central to this administration victory.

The major domestic goal of the new administration was reform of the nation's system of health care. Nearly 40 million citizens did not have health insurance, and the costs of medical care were rising at an alarming rate. In a dramatic expansion of the responsibilities for first ladies, the president asked Hillary Clinton to head the task force to prepare a health care plan within one hundred days. Working throughout 1993, Hillary Clinton's planners produced a health care blueprint in September. The plan, which emphasized expanded coverage, managed care, and higher costs for private physicians, soon became the target of attacks from Republicans and the insurance companies as too bureaucratic, complex, and costly. Despite intense lobbying efforts, the "Clinton Health Plan," as it was known, failed to gain support in Congress. By 1994 the health care issue had become a major liability for the Clinton White House.

Despite his domestic accomplishments, President Clinton's popular approval ratings remained low, often below 50 percent of the electorate. From the political right, the president and his wife stirred dislike that bordered on outright hatred. Republicans charged that the Clintons were socialists bent on entrenching homosexuals, bureaucrats, and atheists in power. The Clintons were also dogged by charges of financial improprieties and ethical lapses from their years in Arkansas. Investments that they had made in an Arkansas real estate venture on the Whitewater River became entangled with the failed savings and loan firm run by business associates of the Clintons. The all-purpose label for these and other related scandals was "Whitewater." As subsequent investigations revealed, the allegations had little basis in fact, but an impression of corruption provided a useful weapon to their enemies. The charges against the Clintons led to the appointment of an independent counsel, or special prosecutor, in 1994. When the first counsel, Robert Fiske, failed to find evidence of wrongdoing, angry conservatives had him replaced with another counsel, Kenneth Starr, a former federal judge and Bush administration lawyer.

Also damaging to President Clinton were allegations that he had sexually harassed an Arkansas state employee, Paula Corbin Jones, in 1991. Jones filed a civil law suit in the spring of 1994 in which she claimed that then Governor Clinton had made unwanted sexual advances. The president's lawyers attempted to have the suit delayed until after the end of his administration on the grounds that it disrupted his ability to carry out his official duties.

Clinton and the World

Clinton's first year produced a number of foreign policy problems that created an image of a president out of his depth on the world stage. He inherited heavy U.S. involvement around the globe—Haiti, Bosnia, and Somalia—but the Bush administration had not linked these to any kind of coherent structure other than George H. W. Bush's vague references to a "New World Order." An early disaster came in October 1993, when eighteen American servicemen died in a raid in Somalia that included television footage of crowds dragging the body of an American pilot through the streets. The White House also suffered a setback in Haiti after a peacekeeping force was repulsed by angry inhabits of the islands.

The main foreign policy dilemma of these initial months was Bosnia. With United Nations peace-keeping troops, predominantly British and French, on the ground, the military options for Clinton were limited because the first targets of retaliation would be the allied troops. Throughout 1993, a proper course of action in the Balkans eluded the United States, its allies, and the United Nations.

The administration's foreign relations team did have some success. It obtained the withdrawal of Russian troops from the Baltic Republic of Estonia in 1994. Clinton also brokered peace negotiations among Ireland, Great Britain, and the Irish Republican Army's political arm Sinn Fein. In the Middle East, State Department negotiators facilitated talks between Yasir Arafat of the Palestine Liberation Organization and Prime Minister Yitzhak Rabin of Israel that led to a celebrated handshake on the White House lawn. The United States intervened in Haiti in 1994 and produced the ouster of the military rulers as a prelude to a more democratic government. But the perception that Clinton was ineffective in foreign policy exacerbated his political troubles at home. There was speculation that he would be another one-term president. On the Right, the opposition gathered momentum.

The Republican Revolution: 1994

The political scene was transformed as the congressional elections approached. In the House of Representatives, the Republicans chose as their next leader their ideological champion, Newton ("Newt") Gingrich of Georgia. An adroit political tactician, the burly, rumpled Gingrich used the television coverage of Congress that began in the late 1970s (called C-SPAN) to broadcast his ideas to a national constituency. To dramatize their appeal, Gingrich and the Republicans offered a "Contract with America" as their election platform. Composed of proposals tested in focus groups for their popularity with the voters, the contract promised action on a balanced budget amendment, term limits for Congress members, and making legislators obey the regulations they applied to society.

On election night, the Republicans swept to victory. They had 235 seats in the House to 197 for the Democrats, and they controlled the Senate by a margin of 53 to 47. Newt Gingrich became Speaker of the House and Robert Dole the majority leader. The elections immediately prompted predictions that President Clinton's prospects for regaining the White House in 1996 were bleak. To some observers, it seemed that the election of Clinton had been only a fluke in the movement for conservative ascendancy that began with the election of Ronald Reagan in 1980.

Race, Ethnicity, and Culture Wars

As the drama of the 1994 elections unfolded, Americans spent more time that autumn transfixed by a sensational murder trial. On June 12, 1994, Nicole Brown Simpson, the estranged ex-wife of professional football star Orenthal James "O. J." Simpson, was brutally murdered at her home, along with acquaintance Ronald Goldman. Police suspicions soon focused on Simpson.

Hispanics enter Politics. This photograph, taken in California in the 1990s, shows that Hispanic Americans made their presence felt at the polls, as candidates, and as voters.

The nation was polarized about Simpson's guilt or innocence. Most white Americans believed that strong material evidence pointed to Simpson as the killer, while many black Americans associated his prosecution with earlier examples of racial injustice. These opinions solidified during the protracted trial that began on January 29, 1995, and ended with Simpson's acquittal on October 3. Televised daily on the Cable News Network and Court TV and covered in excruciating detail, the trial played out as a racially charged drama that became a national obsession.

The Simpson trial took place in the context of an ongoing national debate on racial injustice. Since the 1960s, a major weapon in promoting the equality of blacks and other minorities has been the policy of affirmative action in employment, higher education, and government contracts. Affirmative action sought to remedy past discrimination and provide minorities with greater opportunities for advancement. The Supreme Court ruled in the late 1970s that race could be employed in university admissions when the goal was to achieve diversity in the student body.

Unhappiness with affirmative action as a policy led some states, such as California with Proposition 209, to pass a referendum that abolished programs for affirmative action. In the *Hopwood v. Texas* case (1996), a federal circuit court overturned the affirmative action plan of the University of Texas Law School, noting that any effort by the university to promote affirmative action was unconstitutional. Texas adopted a plan to admit the top 10 percent of graduating high school students, irrespective of their race or ethnicity, to its state universities. That allowed students from predominantly minority schools in the state to gain access to the university system. Even though the Supreme Court overruled the *Hopwood* decision in 2003 in the case of *Grutter v. Bollinger*, the larger problem of affirmative action and its consequences remained unsolved during the first decade of the twenty-first century.

A new front in the culture wars opened. These tensions affected the academic world in the debate about the concept of **multiculturalism.** In the 1980s, American academic institutions sought to open up the study of history and literature to a wider range of gender, class, and racial experiences among groups not previously included. (See Map 29.4.) Issues such as the role of black soldiers in the Civil War, Japanese Americans in World War II internment camps, and women in the American Revolution received new emphasis, and Western civilization courses on many campuses gave way to world history.

By the early 1990s, however, multiculturalism had come under attack from enemies on the Right. Conservatives such as Lynne Cheney and David Horowitz accused its proponents of enforcing what was called "political correctness," an insistence on conforming to liberal or radical views on race and gender. Critics of multiculturalism argued that the academic Left used the movement to balkanize society into warring ethnic groups, limited free speech on campus, and repudiated the whole tradition of Western culture.

multiculturalism The effort, particularly in academic life, to embrace the diversity of minority cultures. The movement was especially strong during the 1980s and 1990s.

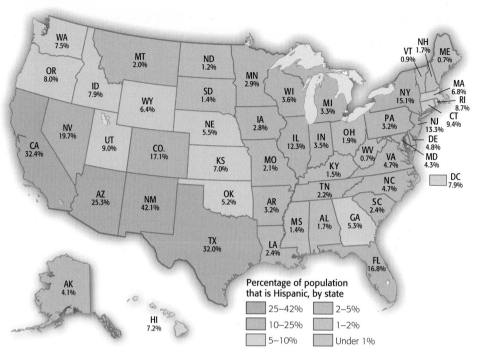

MAP 29.4

The Changing Latino Population of the United States, 2000

Concentrated in the Southwest and California, Hispanics make up a growing and important minority in Illinois, Florida, New York, and elsewhere in the nation. Nearly 60 percent are of Mexican origin, while 10 percent come from Puerto Rico, where they were U.S. citizens. The remaining 30 percent have their origins in the Caribbean, Central America, and South America.

(Copyright © Cengage Learning)

One battlefront in the culture wars was the issue of political and social equality for homosexuals. In the 1990s, homosexuals contended that they should have the right to marry (that is, same-sex marriage) just as heterosexuals did. Identifying their campaign with the civil rights movement of the 1960s, gay groups wanted attacks on those who were openly homosexual to be classified as hate crimes. Meanwhile, conservative groups assailed homosexuality as a sin or a disease. From their enhanced political power after the elections of 1994, Republicans found such "wedge" issues as homosexuality an important contribution to their rise to greater dominance in American politics.

❖ The Republicans in Power

The new Republican majorities in Congress went to work in January 1995 with great energy to implement their "Contract with America." One major initiative was a balanced budget amendment to the Constitution, which failed by a single vote in the Senate. Congress did pass a law to restrict itself from making the states enforce regulations without supplying the necessary funds to do so. Clinton approved the "unfunded mandates" measure on March 22, 1995. The Republicans failed, however, to pass a constitutional amendment imposing term limits on members of Congress. By April, Republicans proclaimed that they had enacted most of the contract within the one hundred days they had set for themselves. Meanwhile, President Clinton accepted some of the Republican ideas in his State of the Union message and praised his own record on the economy.

Domestic Terrorism in Oklahoma City

Then an act of political terrorism shifted the political landscape. On April 19, 1995, an explosion ripped through the Alfred P. Murrah Federal Building in Oklahoma City, killing 168 people. Two suspects, Timothy McVeigh and Terry

Nichols, were quickly arrested and identified as sympathetic to an extremist "militia" movement that sought the violent overthrow of the government of the United States. The glare of publicity revealed that the militia movement, though violent and dangerous, commanded only a small cadre of followers. Yet the backlash against such extremist views after the **Oklahoma City bombing** enabled President Clinton to regain a position of trust and confidence with the American people. The two suspects, McVeigh and Nichols, were both tried and convicted for their roles in the bombing. McVeigh was executed in 2001.

Oklahoma City bombing (1995) Militant right-wing U.S. terrorists bombed the Alfred P. Murrah Federal Building in Oklahoma City in April 1995, causing the deaths of 168 people.

Clinton Resurgent: Bosnia and the Government Shutdowns

Republican overreaching also contributed to the president's rebound in the polls during the remainder of 1995. As congressional Republicans sought to roll back environmental legislation and reduce government regulations on business, Clinton fought back. He cast his first veto as president in June 1995 when he turned down a Republican spending measure that would have trimmed more than a billion dollars from education funding. But the long-running Whitewater saga continued to dog Clinton. Despite the best efforts of Republican lawmakers, congressional inquiries failed to turn up evidence that would incriminate the president or his wife in wrongdoing. Nevertheless, the special prosecutor, Kenneth Starr, continued his investigations.

In Bosnia and Herzegovina, the president succeeded in producing a cease-fire in the conflict and an independent Bosnia. In July 1995, a Bosnian Serb offensive had imperiled several cities that were regarded as "safe havens" for refugees from the fighting. Helped by arms that had come in from Muslim countries, Croatian and Bosnian forces launched a counterattack against the Serbs. At the end of August, Clinton authorized air strikes against the Bosnian Serbs. Within a week, a tentative peace agreement was declared, and a month later a cease-fire was reached. The United States then brokered peace negotiations in Dayton, Ohio, and American and NATO troops were dispatched to help enforce the peace agreement.

Despite successful intervention in the Balkans, the main focus of American politics remained on the running battle between President Clinton and the Republicans in Congress. As budget negotiations over spending produced no result toward the end of 1995, Newt Gingrich and other members of the GOP majority in the House shut down the government as a way of pressuring the White House to agree to their position.

The Republican strategy backfired. Two government shutdowns occurred, a brief one in November and a second that lasted for twenty-one days from mid-December 1995 into early January 1996. Rather than blaming the president for the deadlock, the public put the responsibility on the Republicans. By January 6, 1996, the government had resumed normal operations.

Clinton and the Republican Congress

While President Clinton had the upper hand in the national political arena, the long-running Whitewater saga took an ugly turn for Hillary Rodham Clinton in the early days of January 1996. Kenneth Starr subpoenaed Mrs. Clinton to testify before his Washington grand jury over billing records from her law firm in Arkansas, marking the first time that a first lady had testified in a criminal proceeding while her husband was in office. She spent four hours before the grand jury panel, but like all of the probes into the Clinton's financial affairs, her testimony resulted in no actions against the couple.

As the 1996 election approached, Senator Robert Dole of Kansas became the Republicans' presumed front-runner. A decorated World War II veteran and a gifted lawmaker, Dole had to overcome the age problem (he was seventy-two) and his reputation as a strident partisan. His candidacy was confirmed at the Republican National Convention in late summer. An indifferent speaker at best, Dole campaigned in a frenetic but often unfocused manner.

With the election approaching and polls showing their standing with the public in jeopardy, the Republican majority on Capitol Hill focused on reforming the welfare system. After the GOP passed such a bill, Clinton vetoed the measure, but a compromise proposal came out of Congress at the end of July. The bill produced sweeping changes in caring for the poor. In place of the long-standing Aid for Dependent Children (AFDC) program, lawmakers established a system of block grants to the individual states that emphasized personal accountability over hand-outs. The legislation fulfilled Clinton's 1992 campaign promise to "end welfare as we know it," but it left many Democrats unhappy with the direction of their party.

The waning days of the Congress saw other accomplishments. In August, lawmakers enacted the first raise in the minimum wage since 1991, to $5.15 per hour. Responding to the continuing public unhappiness with immigration problems, Congress included in its spending legislation funds for new personnel for the Immigration and Naturalization Service, the hiring of additional Border Patrol agents, and more severe penalties for bringing in illegal aliens. These achievements undercut Dole's argument that Clinton was not an effective leader.

❖ Clinton: Triumphs and Missteps

Mindful of their public relations disaster in Houston in 1992 when commentator Pat Buchanan emphasized moralism and values issues, the Republicans sought to reassure voters that they were an acceptable and inclusive alternative to the Democrats. Their problem remained, however, of making Senator Dole an exciting figure who could compete with Clinton, an adroit and skilled campaigner.

The 1996 Election

Dole launched his campaign with the promise of a 15 percent tax cut over a three-year period. Reflecting the sentiment within the party for what was known as a "flat tax," an income tax at a low rate for all citizens, he advocated a "fairer, flatter tax" along with prudent spending cuts to find the $548 billion needed to offset his tax reductions. For Dole, long a champion of a balanced budget, the tax cut proposal represented an eleventh-hour conversion to the supply-side ideology of the Reagan wing of his party. He asked former Congressman Jack Kemp of New York to be his running mate. A favorite of conservatives, Kemp's selection lifted the spirits of delegates who saw Dole trailing badly in the polls.

Midway between the conventions of the major parties came the meeting of the Reform Party that Ross Perot had established as the vehicle for his second presidential candidacy. Perot won the nomination easily but did not capture the public's imagination as he had in 1992.

With a commanding lead in the public opinion polls, President Clinton enjoyed a harmonious convention when the Democrats met in Chicago in late August. The platform stressed centrist themes and spoke of a "New Democratic Party." Clinton and Vice President Gore were renominated, and the president promised four more years of prosperity and moderate reform. During

September 1996, the campaign unfolded as though Clinton and the Democrats were certain winners, as Dole failed to crack Clinton's armor with attacks on his character.

Then newspaper reports appeared about improprieties and possible crimes in the fund-raising for the Democratic Party and the Clinton campaign. Money that had flowed into the president's campaign war chest had possible links to the People's Republic of China and Indonesian businesses. Rather than a triumphal march, the waning days of the 1996 election saw Clinton and his party staggering toward the finish line under a severe cloud of scandal. The Democratic ticket won 379 electoral votes and 49 percent of the popular vote to 41 percent (159 electoral votes) for Dole and Kemp. Ross Perot and the Reform Party took 8 percent of the popular vote and no electoral votes. The president carried two staunchly Republican states—Florida and Arizona. However, he fell short of a popular majority.

Although Dole had lost badly, the Republicans retained control of both houses of Congress and even picked up two Senate seats for a 55-to-45 margin over the Democrats. Because they needed sixty votes to block a Democratic filibuster, the Republicans would have to compromise with their opponents to get any legislation passed. The stage was set for another scenario of divided government.

An Ambitious Foreign Policy

For a president who had come into office promoting domestic issues, Clinton seemed to relish the international stage during his fifth year in office. He pushed hard for the North Atlantic Treaty Organization to add members from former Communist states in Eastern Europe; Poland, Hungary, and the Czech Republic were added to the alliance in March 1999. Russian opposition to expansion of NATO was mitigated by the promise that neither nuclear weapons nor large numbers of combat forces would be placed on the soil of the new member states.

In other areas of foreign policy, the world's trouble spots remained volatile. The situation in Bosnia, though improved since the Dayton Agreement, still pitted Serbs, Croats, and Bosnians against each other despite the uneasy peace that American troops in NATO helped maintain. As for the Middle East, tensions between Palestinians and Israelis worsened amid sporadic terrorist violence. The Clinton administration pressed both sides for more movement to implement peace, but progress was elusive.

An Economic Boom

Throughout 1997, the American economy roared into high gear. Unemployment fell to 4.8 percent, and inflation no longer seemed a problem. With jobs plentiful and prices stable, a sense of economic optimism pervaded the nation and kept Clinton's job approval ratings around the 60 percent mark.

Adding to the euphoria was the apparent end of the budget deficit problem that had shaped politics for so many years. Surging tax revenues meant that red ink started to disappear. The 1997 budget deficit was only $25 billion, the lowest since 1974, and 1998 promised the unheard of: a budget surplus. As a result of these trends, Congress and the president worked out a balanced budget agreement in May that was signed into law on August 5. Politicians believed they could look forward to budget surpluses for years to come. This success relied on using the money in the Social Security Trust Fund to offset other spending, but elected officials played down this budgetary sleight-of-hand in their public comments.

The Rise of the Internet

A major force in driving the economic expansion of the 1990s was the rise of the Internet and the World Wide Web, which reshaped the way Americans got their news and communicated with each other. In 1996, 18 million people, or about 9 percent of the population, were accessing the Internet on a regular basis. By 1998, 20 percent of all American households had Internet access. Within three years that figure had risen to almost 51 percent.

Dominating the new field were such corporations as America Online, which provided connections for 30 percent of all Internet users in the country in 1996. Some new online retail firms, such as the bookseller Amazon.com, saw their common stock value soar in 1998 because of the potential growth of their markets. A dot-com boom ensued in which investors poured money into what was seen as the latest hot Internet-related stock. The economic boom of the 1990s depended to a large extent on this expectation of ever-rising Internet profits. The effects of this economic expansion, including rising government revenues, a diffusion of new jobs, and a sense of well-being, helped President Clinton offset the political troubles that threatened to overtake him during the last two years of his administration.

Clinton Impeached and Acquitted

An auspicious start for Clinton in 1997 was dashed when the Supreme Court ruled 9–0 on May 27, 1997, in *Clinton v. Jones* that the sexual harassment lawsuit against the president could go forward while he was in office. Meanwhile, congressional probes on the 1996 campaign scandal indicated that the president and Vice President Al Gore had played a larger role in raising money for their campaigns from wealthy donors than they had earlier admitted, and Kenneth Starr's Whitewater investigation still posed a potential threat to the White House.

Then in mid-January 1998, the public learned that a former White House intern named Monica Lewinsky had been involved in a sexual relationship with President Clinton during her employment. Once the news broke, Clinton asserted that he had not had sex with Lewinsky. Meanwhile, Kenneth Starr investigated whether Clinton had lied under oath in the Paula Jones case when he said he had not had sex with Lewinsky, whether he had obstructed justice, and whether he had asked others to lie on his behalf. This sordid spectacle absorbed vast amounts of television news coverage throughout 1998.

Ultimately, abundant evidence emerged that Clinton and Lewinsky had had sexual contact, a fact that Clinton at last acknowledged on August 17, 1998, when he testified before Starr's Washington grand jury from the White House. That night he told the nation the same thing in a four-and-a-half-minute speech that was widely regarded as a low point of his presidency. A few weeks later, Starr sent a report to the House of Representatives alleging that there were grounds for impeaching Clinton for lying under oath, obstruction of justice, abuse of power, and other offenses. The House Judiciary Committee recommended that an **impeachment** inquiry commence, and the House voted to authorize a probe after the 1998 elections.

The Monica Lewinsky scandal and its fallout left Clinton a wounded president. He retained the ability to achieve foreign policy successes such as a deal he brokered between Israelis and Palestinians in October 1998. But congressional Republicans overplayed their hand. Their moves to impeach Clinton awakened the Democrats and produced a backlash among voters in the 1998 elections. On November 3, the Democrats in the House actually gained five seats; Republican control of the House narrowed to 223–211, a thin majority. In the Senate, the two

impeachment The act of charging a public official with misconduct in office, impeachment is the constitutional procedure for removing presidents who are found guilty of "treason, bribery, or other high crimes and misdemeanors" as interpreted by Congress. Presidents Andrew Johnson, Richard Nixon, and Bill Clinton have been the subject of impeachment proceedings.

parties battled to a draw, with the Republicans holding the same 55–45 edge. Two significant Republican victories came in Florida and Texas, where the two sons of George H. W. Bush, Jeb Bush in Florida and **George W. Bush** in Texas, were elected governor.

Despite the results of the congressional elections, Republican leaders in Congress pressed ahead with the impeachment of President Clinton. In December the House Judiciary Committee, on a nearly party-line vote, sent four articles of impeachment to the full House. That body adopted two articles of impeachment charging President Clinton with perjury in his grand jury testimony in August 1998 and with obstruction of justice in trying to hide his relationship with Monica Lewinsky from members of his staff and the Starr probe. But when the Senate opened its trial in mid-January, it soon became evident that the forty-five Democrats would not vote for conviction and a two-thirds majority to convict and remove the president did not exist.

President Clinton's popularity with the public remained high, and his State of the Union address on January 19, 1999, drove his poll ratings still higher. He was acquitted on both counts when the Senate voted on February 12, 1999. On the perjury count, the total was forty-five Republican senators voting to convict the president and all forty-five Democrats as well as ten Republicans voting for acquittal. On the second article involving obstruction of justice, the Senate split evenly, with fifty Republican votes for conviction and forty-five Democrats and five Republicans voting for acquittal. William Jefferson Clinton remained in office, a wounded chief executive with two years left on his second term.

The impeachment episode reflected the intense emotions that Clinton had provoked during his time in the White House. To the Republicans and other Americans on the right, he was an illegitimate president who had committed crimes in office that warranted his removal. To the remainder of the country, some 65 percent according to most polls, he was a president who was performing well in office and should not be removed. The economy remained prosperous and the Dow Jones Industrial Average hovered around 10,000.

In late March 1999, NATO began air strikes against the Serbian government to stop "ethnic cleansing" of the Albanians near Kosovo. Despite the warning of Clinton's critics, the air campaign ended in success for the NATO forces. The nation turned to the impending presidential contest. In the economy there were signs of a slowdown as the excesses of the dot-com revolution, including speculation and falsified corporate profits, ended the bubble of the late 1990s.

Bush, George W. (1946–)
Forty-third president of the United States (2001–2009).

CHAPTER REVIEW, 1981–2000

SUMMARY

- The United States incurred large budget deficits.

- The nation embarked on a program to build up national defense.

- Computers became an integral part of the economy and communication system.

- There was increasing political polarization over issues such as abortion.

- The Cold War drew to a close with a total victory for the United States and its allies.

- The Middle East emerged as an even more crucial foreign policy challenge during the first Iraq war.

- The United States moved to the right during the presidencies of Ronald Reagan and George H. W. Bush.

- The election of Bill Clinton produced further social tension.

- The Republicans regained control of Congress.

- Political turmoil and partisanship characterized public life in the 1990s, as racial, ethnic, and cultural tensions continued unabated.

- The rise of the Internet and a growing reliance on computers changed the way people did business and communicate.

- Bill Clinton was impeached and acquitted.

IDENTIFICATIONS

Ronald Reagan
Contras
Strategic Defense Initiative (SDI)
Moral Majority
Walter Mondale
Jesse Jackson
Mikhail Gorbachev
Oliver North
Iran-Contra scandal
Sandra Day O'Connor
Colin Powell
George H. W. Bush
Tiananmen Square
Clarence Thomas
Anita Hill
William Jefferson ("Bill") Clinton
multiculturalism
Oklahoma City bombing
impeachment
George W. Bush

MAKING CONNECTIONS: LOOKING AHEAD ⏵

The concluding chapter of the book considers the administration of George W. Bush and the first year of Barack Obama's presidency. During the 2000s, the problem of terrorism arose as a central concern of domestic and foreign policy.

1. Why were policy makers, the media, and the people generally slow to grasp the dangers of terrorism?

2. Has the second Iraq war made the United States more or less safe?

3. Why did so many Americans vote for change in 2008? Do you think Barack Obama is fulfilling those expectations? Why or why not?

RECOMMENDED READINGS

Busch, Andrew E. *Reagan's Victory: The Presidential Election of 1980 and the Rise of the Right* (2005). Argues that the 1980 election marked the end of New Deal liberalism.

Clinton, Bill. *My Life* (2004). The former president's own account of his political rise.

Conason, Joe, and Gene Lyons. *The Hunting of the President* (2000). Looks at the anti-Clinton campaign and its development.

Fitzgerald, Frances. *Way Out There in the Blue: Reagan, Star Wars, and the End of the Cold War* (2000). A critical look at the Strategic Defense Initiative.

Greene, John Robert. *The Presidency of George Bush* (2000). Covers the George H. W. Bush presidency thoroughly.

Johnson, Haynes. *Divided We Fall: Gambling with History in the Nineties* (1994). Covers the Reagan–Bush transition and carries the story down to the start of the Clinton presidency.

Johnson, Haynes. *Sleepwalking Through History: America in the Reagan Years* (1991). Supplies the perspective of a Washington reporter on the 1980s.

Parmet, Herbert. *George Bush: The Life of a Lone Star Yankee* (1997). The best biography of the forty-first president.

Pemberton, William E. *Exit with Honor: The Life and Presidency of Ronald Reagan* (1997). A sound one-volume study of the man and his impact on the nation.

Wilentz, Sean. *The Age of Reagan, 1974–2008* (2008). A thoughtful survey of American politics during these turbulent years.

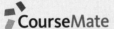 **CourseMate** Go to the CourseMate website at www.cengagebrain.com for additional study tools and review materials for this chapter.

30 A Conservative Nation in a Globalizing World

2000–2010

MAKING CONNECTIONS

◀▦▦ LOOKING BACK

Chapter 29 examined the impact of the Ronald Reagan, George H. W. Bush, and Bill Clinton administrations in the context of the 1980s and 1990s. A key point in the chapter was the nation's rightward shift in political terms and the consequences of that change for foreign policy and domestic priorities. Before starting Chapter 30, you should be able to answer the following questions:

1. What problems confronted the new Reagan administration in 1981 as a result of the events of the Carter administration?

2. What was the international position in economic, political, and military terms relative to the Soviet Union in the early 1980s?

3. In what ways did Ronald Reagan change the role of the president? Which of his achievements have proved the most enduring and which the most controversial?

4. What were the most significant cultural and economic changes Americans experienced during the 1980s and early 1990s?

5. Was the first Iraq war as much of a victory as it was portrayed at the time?

6. How did Bill Clinton benefit from a mood for change and then suffer political reverses because of that same mood?

The Disputed Presidential Election of 2000: Bush Versus Gore

The Presidency of George W. Bush

September 11, 2001, and After
The Dilemma of Iraq
The Erosion of the Bush Presidency

A Society in Crisis

Hurricane Katrina
The Immigration Debate

Doing History: The Torture Debate

Social Activism, Left and Right
Globalization and Economic Troubles
The Climate Change Crisis
The 2006 Midterm Elections

A Change of Course: President Obama

2008: An Historic Election
The "Great Recession"
The Obama Presidency

The presidential administration of George W. Bush, elected as the embodiment of compassionate conservatism and the tradition of Ronald Reagan and his father, prosecuted the wars against terrorism with initial success abroad and political gains at home. By the eve of the 2008 election, however, the president was weakened, and his administration was in disarray. In the process, the institutions of democratic government had been strained and in some areas broken. As candidates in both parties prepared to face the voters in November 2008, a deteriorating economy compounded the challenges before the American people. The electorate confronted the question of whether the conservative policies of George W. Bush and his presidency had protected the nation from harm or created greater threats abroad and economic instability at home.

❖ The Disputed Presidential Election of 2000: Bush Versus Gore

The Republican front-runner in the 2000 presidential election was Governor George W. Bush of Texas, the son of the former president. Elected governor in 1994 and reelected in 1998, the Texan announced his bid for the presidency in mid-1999 and soon amassed a campaign treasury that ultimately reached more than $100 million. Bush promised that he would be "a compassionate conservative" who would "change the tone" in Washington after the partisan discord of the Clinton era. He advocated a $1.6 trillion tax cut and promised to reform the educational system. Bush lost the New Hampshire primary to Senator John McCain of Arizona, but then won a number of primaries to lock up the delegates needed to control the national convention in Philadelphia.

For his running mate, Bush chose Richard "Dick" Cheney, a former House member and secretary of defense in the administration of Bush's father. Cheney headed the vice-presidential selection committee for Bush and ended up recommending himself. Long convinced that the presidency had lost too much power because of Watergate and congressional assertiveness, Cheney intended to increase executive power. He also shared the views of Republican intellectuals who called themselves "neoconservatives." These writers, including William Kristol and Paul Wolfowitz, contended that the United States should exercise military might in the Middle East to oust Saddam Hussein from power. This end could be achieved, they argued, at little cost to the United States, and the resulting victory would persuade the rest of the region to become both democratic and more accepting of the existence of Israel. Neoconservatives saw Clinton as timid and weak in foreign policy, and they longed to reestablish American supremacy.

Albert Gore easily won his party's nomination but had problems separating himself from the scandals of the Clinton years. He also faced a hostile press corps that focused on every lapse to paint Gore as indecisive and opportunistic. Gore emerged from the Democratic convention behind Bush but closed the gap during September 2000. The election hinged on the three presidential debates.

Televised Presidential Debates. The three televised debates between George W. Bush and Albert Gore proved unusually important in deciding the outcome of the 2000 presidential election.

Although neither candidate did well in the debates, Bush exceeded the low expectations that media pundits set for him. Gore was better on substance but was labeled arrogant and condescending. As a result, the race remained tight down to the election. As the votes were counted, the Republicans retained control of the House of Representatives, and the Senate split evenly with fifty Democrats and fifty Republicans. Gore led in the presidential popular vote, but no candidate had an electoral majority. It became clear that the

CHAPTER TIMELINE	2000	2002	2004	2006	2008	2010	2012

POLITICS AND DIPLOMACY

2001–2009 George W. Bush presidency
● 2001 Terrorist attack, September 11
● 2003 Invasion of Iraq
● 2000 Disputed election results in Florida
● 2006 Democrats retake Congress
● 2008 Barack Obama elected president
● 2009 Sonia Sotomayor appointed to Supreme Court
● 2010 Congress passes health care legislation

SOCIETY AND CULTURE

● 2002 Former President Jimmy Carter receives Nobel Peace Prize
● 2005 Hurricane Katrina devastates New Orleans
● 2007 Steroids scandal rocks baseball

ECONOMICS AND TECHNOLOGY

2007 ● Subprime mortgage crisis begins
2008 ● Worldwide markets plunge TARP legislation passed to stabilize banking system
● 2009 Unemployment grows TARP funds extended to Big Three auto companies

2000

Candidate (Party)	Electoral Vote		Popular Vote	
Bush (Republican)	271	50.4%	50,456,169	47.88%
Gore (Democrat)	267	49.6%	50,996,116	48.39%
Nader (Green)	0	0.0%	2,783,728	2.72%

(Copyright © Cengage Learning)

MAP 30.1
The Presidential Election of 2000

The map of the 2000 election reflects the closeness of the electoral vote. Note the extent to which voters were distributed into a pro-Gore coalition on the coasts and a pro-Bush coalition in the interior of the nation, with some key exceptions in the Midwest and the Far West. A comparison with the presidential election of 1896 (see Map 18.1) gives an interesting sense of how partisan alignments changed during the twentieth century.

state of Florida would determine the result because its 25 electoral votes would push either of the two candidates past the 271 electoral votes needed. (See Map 30.1.) State officials put Florida in the Bush column by fewer than six hundred ballots. Gore's forces noted irregularities and flawed ballots in several Democratic counties and sought a recount in those areas.

The Bush camp insisted that the result favoring its man should be final, and charges of fraud, manipulation, and political pressure flashed back and forth throughout November. Finally, the case of *Bush v. Gore* reached the U.S. Supreme Court in mid-December. On the key issue of whether the decision of the Florida Supreme Court ordering a statewide recount should be upheld, the Court ruled 5–4 in favor of Bush in a decision that many commentators dubbed both hasty and partisan. Gore accepted the outcome as final and conceded the election.

❖ The Presidency of George W. Bush

In office, Bush continued to act as permanent campaigner who used the devices of the modern media age to present an image of a strong chief executive. He pushed through Congress a series of tax cuts that, the White House said, were designed to assist the struggling economy. The budget surplus of the 1990s soon disappeared as a brief recession followed the end of the dot-com bubble. Record debt became one continuing legacy of the Bush era.

Like Richard Cheney, Bush believed that the presidency had become weakened, and his administration acted to reassert executive authority. They did so largely by ignoring traditional restraints on presidential power and in many cases flouting the Constitution. The president disregarded congressional laws of which he disapproved and claimed unfettered right to govern as he deemed best. Secrecy and deceit became hallmarks of the Bush era. Unfortunately, the search for absolute power did not include comparable competence on the part of the president. Bush was not a hard worker. He governed more through intuition than through substance, and he longed to be out of Washington. In foreign and domestic policy, the Bush White House mixed arrogance with ineptitude.

Meanwhile, Vice President Cheney functioned as a coexecutive who sought additional presidential power to conduct surveillance of Americans, pursue a foreign policy in which allies counted for little, and make policy in secret. The vice president soon overshadowed the secretary of state, Colin Powell, and the national security adviser, Condoleezza Rice. He proved to be an inept policy maker who believed his own propaganda regarding how easy an invasion of Iraq would be.

September 11, 2001, and After

One issue, international terrorism, had not been of central concern to most Americans during the 1990s. A bombing of the World Trade Center in New York City in 1993 had not shaken the nation out of its indifference to the threat. Other attacks on American embassies in Africa in 1998 and a similar assault on the USS *Cole* destroyer in Yemen in October 2000 had not brought the issue home. The name of the leader of one terrorist group—**Osama bin Laden**—was largely unknown to the average citizen, even though bin Laden, a fundamentalist Muslim of Saudi Arabian origin, sought the violent end of American influence in the Middle East from his base in Afghanistan. Even a frightening report from a prestigious commission in February 2001 warning of a likely terrorist attack on American soil did little to disturb the lack of alertness that pervaded the government and the mass media. President Bush received a briefing on August 6, 2001, that bin Laden was planning an attack somewhere inside the United States, but no sense of imminent danger showed in White House actions.

On the morning of September 11, 2001, two hijacked jetliners slammed into the twin towers of the World Trade Center in New York City. Both buildings collapsed into flames and rubble, and almost three thousand people died. A third airliner crashed into the Pentagon, leaving another two hundred people dead. A fourth plane fell to the ground in rural Pennsylvania after the passengers attacked the hijackers. All air traffic was grounded for several days, consumer spending slumped, and the weakened economy slipped into recession.

This devastating attack on American soil, for which Osama bin Laden and his terrorist network, Al Qaeda, took credit, rattled the nation's morale as it became clear that the terrorists sought nothing less than the destruction of the United States itself. President Bush promised a "war on terrorism" and launched air strikes

bin Laden, Osama (1957–) Saudi-born Islamic radical who masterminded the September 11, 2001, terrorist attacks on the United States.

(© Pool/Don EMMERT/AFP/Getty Images)

Ground Zero. The pictures of Ground Zero where the World Trade Center collapsed became a powerful symbol of the damage the attacks of September 11 had inflicted on the United States and its standing in the world.

and ground troops into Afghanistan to fight its Taliban regime that harbored bin Laden. He rejected any thought of seeking national unity in his government and instead saw the terrorism crisis as a chance to confirm Republican dominance with the voters. Soon the Taliban government had been toppled and Al Qaeda disrupted, but American forces remained in Afghanistan into 2008 as the Taliban resisted the presence of outside troops.

The Dilemma of Iraq

The Bush administration targeted Saddam Hussein and his government in Iraq as the main focus of the antiterrorist effort. The White House argued that Iraq was linked to Al Qaeda, but the evidence for such a connection was thin. Convinced that the invasion of Iraq was necessary both to topple a tyrant and spread democracy in the Middle East, the Bush administration issued warnings that weapons of mass destruction could be used against the United States. This policy led Washington, in the words of a British official, to see that intelligence was "fixed" (or manipulated) around the policy of invading Iraq.

Preparations for war accelerated during 2002 while the White House sought diplomatic support for efforts to curb Hussein and the alleged weapons of mass destruction he possessed. By the autumn of 2002, a United Nations resolution calling on Hussein to admit inspectors had been passed. Hussein said that his government would agree to the resolution, but his previous flouting of the inspections process made the United States suspicious. The administration moved toward war as 2002 ended. The director of the Central Intelligence Agency, George Tenet, responded to a question from President Bush about where weapons of mass destruction existed in Iraq by saying it was "a slam dunk" that they were present.

The terrorist threat validated George W. Bush as a national leader, and his popularity rose to unprecedented high levels. The administration pushed through Congress the Patriot Act of October 26, 2001, which gave broad powers to the federal government to combat terrorism, even at the price of some constitutional guarantees on civil liberties. A year later Congress established the Homeland Security Department on November 25, 2002. The new agency included the Federal Emergency Management Agency (FEMA) despite warnings of the bureaucratic danger of making FEMA part of this unwieldy department. In the congressional elections of 2002, the Republicans, using a strong organization and ample campaign contributions, rode Bush's campaigning and the public confidence in his leadership to victory. Security issues affected the voters more than did the faltering economy and the Democratic emphasis on domestic problems. The GOP regained control of the Senate and widened its majority in the House. As 2003 began, the president and his party seemed poised to enact their conservative agenda.

Meanwhile, preparations for war with Iraq intensified. Secretary of State Colin Powell argued the case for war in a speech to the United Nations in February 2003. Powell's calm, direct presentation convinced many skeptics that Iraq and Saddam Hussein did indeed possess destructive weapons. Although there were doubters at the time, only after the war began did it become apparent that Powell's speech rested on faulty, misleading, and fabricated evidence.

Car Bombing. Exploding cars in attacks designed to kill civilians became a preferred weapon of the insurgency in Iraq during the years after the American invasion.

Dissatisfied with the work of the United Nations weapons inspectors, which found no weapons of mass destruction, the United States had failed to obtain a second United Nations resolution authorizing force. The strong opposition of the international community to an American invasion of Iraq, combined with diplomatic setbacks by the Bush White House, left Washington frustrated. The Bush administration, along with its only major ally, Great Britain, decided that an attack on Saddam Hussein's brutal regime could not be delayed. The Bush administration, from Vice President Cheney to Secretary of Defense Donald Rumsfeld, expected a swift victory on the order of what had occurred during the ground war in the Gulf in 1991. An invasion force of around 145,000 men seemed enough to White House planners even though some generals recommended two or three times that number. Vice President Cheney said that "significant elements" of Hussein's military force were "likely to step aside" once war began. In this mood of confidence about victory, President Bush told the military "Let's go" on March 19, 2003, and the war commenced.

Once launched, the powerful offensive of the American-led coalition swept through Iraq in a dramatic three-week campaign that left the United States in military control of the nation. (See Map 30.2.) Saddam Hussein was either dead or in hiding, the major officials of Iraq were captured, and the symbols of Hussein's rule had been destroyed. On May 1, 2003, President Bush declared the major combat phase of the war at an end.

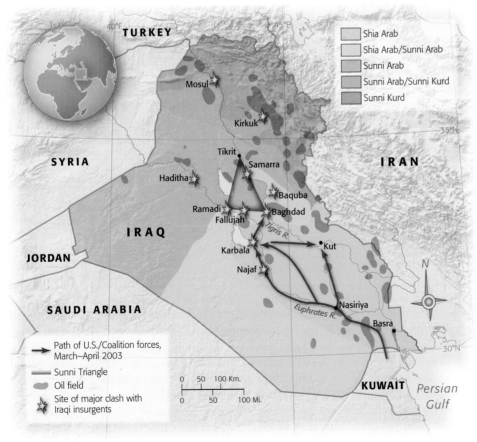

(Copyright © Cengage Learning)

MAP 30.2

The War in Iraq and Its Effects

With Saddam Hussein's overthrow by U.S.-led coalition forces in 2003, violence broke out against American occupiers and within the various ethnic and religious groups in Iraq. The majority Shia Muslims concentrated in the Southeast and the minority Sunni Muslims, who had ruled the country under Saddam earlier, vied for control. By the early months of 2008, reconciliation among these opposing factions was still an elusive goal.

Convinced that they would win an easy victory, the Bush administration had not made plans for the occupation of Iraq. Soon they faced an insurgent movement that resisted the American presence through car bombs, improvised explosive devices that blew up under the lightly armored U.S. vehicles, and guerrilla attacks. By early 2008, almost four thousand American troops had been killed and thousands more wounded. Estimates of Iraqi deaths mounted into the hundreds of thousands. No weapons of mass destruction were found, and inspectors concluded that Hussein had abandoned these efforts after his 1991 defeat.

The Erosion of the Bush Presidency

Angry Democrats looked for a winning presidential candidate in 2004 without success. The election pitted Senator John F. Kerry of Massachusetts against President Bush in a bitterly contested race. Kerry had a war record in Vietnam that was supposed to insulate him from attacks on his patriotism. Instead the Republicans argued that his achievements were bogus, reports that the credulous news media repeated without careful checking. As a result, Bush still seemed the stronger leader in the public mind. Bush won a majority of the popular vote and secured 286 electoral votes to 252 for Kerry. The Republicans picked up seats in both the House and the Senate, and they spoke of a mandate for their conservative philosophy during the four years to come.

Bush's second term, however, got off to a rocky start. The president misjudged the meaning of the election. He mounted an intense effort to change Social Security from an entitlement program to one where individuals would manage private accounts with investments in stocks and bonds. Bush claimed that this shift would produce greater returns for individuals. Critics responded that the Social Security system was not in crisis, private accounts were risky investments, and the president was trying to implement long-term conservative plans to destroy this popular New Deal program.

The war in Iraq, with no end in sight and persistent American casualties each month, became a political liability for the president. Revelations about torture of Iraqi captives in the Abu Ghraib prison near Baghdad undermined the nation's moral standing. An intense debate began about the value of torture as a means of extracting information from prisoners. (See *Doing History: The Torture Debate.*) Bush's poll ratings slipped in the summer of 2005 into the 40 percent range, their lowest levels for his time in office up until then.

❖ A Society in Crisis

Five years into the new century, Americans argued over social and cultural divisions with ever greater intensity. Conservatives pushed forward against what they deemed a secular, irreligious liberal establishment. Liberals felt beleaguered and under siege from religious fundamentalists. Issues of immigration, science, marriage, and economics posed severe challenges to the nation's institutions. Individuals living in the United States, citizens and noncitizens alike, complained that the news and entertainment media were reluctant to address these matters lest they interfere with the pursuit of ratings and profits.

By 2006, the networks and cable television, owned by large corporations and entertainment conglomerates, shaped the way Americans obtained information about everything from sports to politics. These giant corporations emphasized trivial and transient events in their programming and made their political views known even in ostensibly "straight" news reporting. Fox News, which started operations in 1997, behaved as an arm of the Republican Party. Cable News Network (CNN) imitated Fox, with indifferent success. Commentators on the air acted as partisans rather than reporters.

As a counterweight to these forces, individuals on the Internet created websites (known as weblogs) on which they could express their opinions about current events and a host of other subjects. These **bloggers** gained influence as their sites proliferated. In 2003–2004, for example, they propelled Vermont Governor Howard Dean into a brief lead for the Democratic nomination before he gave way to John Kerry. On the Left, such sites as Eschaton, Daily Kos, Talking Points Memo, and Firedog Lake became popular. On the Right, Instapundit and National Review Online (NRO) gained popularity.

bloggers Commentators who post their views on the Internet; derived from the word *weblog*. They became influential in the political process because of the speed with which they could respond to breaking events in politics and international affairs.

Hurricane Katrina

In August 2005, Hurricane Katrina hit the Gulf Coast, devastating large portions of Alabama, Mississippi, and Louisiana. When the levees in New Orleans broke, low-lying areas of the Crescent City became flooded, with hundreds of people dead and large parts of the city uninhabitable. Television viewers across the country saw citizens of New Orleans crowded into the Superdome in horrible conditions, while others clung to rooftops until Coast Guard rescue helicopters could reach them. The social order of the city seemed to have broken down during those desperate days.

Despite ample warnings of the dangers to the city of a Category 4 hurricane and forecasts of where Katrina would hit as landfall approached, city, state, and federal governments performed badly in the crisis. The actions of the federal government represented the greatest shortfall in actual results. President Bush had named inept cronies to head the **Department of Homeland Security** and FEMA, and those two arms of the national government were late, slow, and inefficient in meeting the challenges of the crisis. A terrible disaster worsened because of the shoddy reaction of Washington and the Bush administration. The president's apparent insensitivity to the disaster compounded the damage to his reputation. Once the image of a decisive leader was shattered, he proved incapable of regaining the trust of the American people.

Department of Homeland Security U.S. cabinet department established in 2002 to coordinate defense of the American nation.

Throughout 2006, Republicans were on the defensive in Congress. Polls suggested that voters wanted a change of leadership. The Republican leaders in the House did not cut federal spending as conservatives had promised, and they increased expenditures to record levels. There was no legislative oversight of the executive branch, especially about the increasingly unpopular war in Iraq as casualties among American soldiers and Iraqi civilians mounted. Revelations of corruption among Republican lawmakers further eroded support for the majority. By the fall of 2006, it was evident that the Democrats were poised to make gains in the House of Representatives. Few pundits believed, however, that the Democrats could regain control of the Senate.

The Immigration Debate

Throughout the 1990s and the first decade of the new century, the question of the role of immigrants, both legal and illegal, roiled American politics and culture. Legal immigrants, most of whom were Hispanics and Asians, totaled almost six hundred thousand per year during the early 1990s. Estimates of the number of

Doing History The Torture Debate

In the aftermath of the terrorist attacks of September 11, 2001, the U.S. government argued that it needed to use whatever means necessary to thwart future attacks on the nation. When it captured suspected terrorists, it would be necessary to employ severe interrogation techniques to extract needed information in time to save American lives. Critics alleged, however, that such practices amounted to the torture of prisoners that was banned under U.S. law and the Geneva Convention dealing with combatants held in custody. The Bush administration contended that the Constitution gave the president the power to wage war in the manner the executive deemed best. As a result, courts should not bar the presidency from what were soon called "enhanced interrogation techniques."

The debate focused on the practice of "waterboarding," which simulated drowning by pouring water into a prisoner's mouth to create the perception of imminent death. Defenders of the practice, including many conservatives such as Missouri senator Christopher "Kit" Bond, said that waterboarding was like swimming and involved no torture. Many military officers, however, pointed out that the practice went back to the Spanish Inquisition, had been treated as a crime in American military law and Vietnam, and had achieved dubious results when implemented. These offices recommended that the government cease use of waterboarding. In 2007 the House of Representatives voted to ban waterboarding and similar practices, but the Bush administration said that while it did not use torture, it would continue to interrogate prisoners in ways that brought results from its point of view. Two contrasting views of the issue can be found in the remarks of a Republican presidential candidate, Rudolph Giuliani, in a debate in Iowa in October 2007, and a commentary from Philip Carter, a former military officer, and Dahlia Lithwick, a constitutional writer.

illegal immigrants each year ranged from three hundred thousand to half a million. In the 1990s, the Immigration and Naturalization Service forecast that there might be as many as 13 million immigrants coming to the United States during the next decade.

Debate about the value and cost of this wave of immigrants escalated during the mid-1990s. Studies demonstrated that immigrants, both legal and illegal, contributed more to society in taxes and productivity than they consumed from government services, but the mere increased presence of Hispanics and Asians, the so-called browning of America, produced political conflict, especially in California. In 1994, California voters adopted in an election landslide Proposition 187, a ballot initiative that barred illegal immigrants from receiving state benefits in education and health. After its adoption, court challenges delayed its implementation, but by 1996, the governor ordered many of its provisions into effect. On the national scene, Congress debated immigration restrictions as it decided what to do about reform of the welfare system. The crosscurrents over immigration persisted during the next ten years, with politicians pressed to take action. So volatile was the issue that little constructive work could be done either to stem the flow of illegal immigrants or to assimilate the people who came to the United States legally, seeking a better life.

By 2005, the immigration issue had once again claimed national attention. The estimates of 11 to 12 million people in the country illegally had proven

Giuliani

When Giuliani was asked whether he approved of waterboarding, he said, "It depends on how it is done. It depends on the circumstances. It depends on who does it." Of torture and enhanced interrogation, he then added: "Now on the question of torture. We should not torture. America should not stand for torture. America should not allow torture. But Americans should engage in aggressive questioning of Islamic terrorists who are arrested and apprehended. Because if we don't we leave ourselves open to significant attack. And the line between the two is very delicate and very difficult. But we can't abandon aggressive questioning of people who are intent on coming here to kill us. Or killing us overseas."

Carter and Lithwick

It is the oldest trick in the Bush administration's psychological playbook to claim that we must be one serious badass nation if we are willing to do sick, unspeakable things to our enemies even in the face of international condemnation and in violation of our own laws and ethical rules. But when those sick, unspeakable practices endanger our own soldiers, horrify our allies, and embolden our enemies, we don't look like badasses any more. We just look like sadists. And when those practices don't even work, we look like stupid sadists to boot. There's an easy fix here. Renounce torture. It was once an unremarkable proposition that the United States doesn't stand for senseless sadism. What a tragedy that defending it has suddenly become a point of principle.

QUESTIONS for REFLECTION

1. What in Rudolph Giuliani's mind is the difference between torture and aggressive questioning?

2. How frequent would the use of torture be under Giuliani's program?

3. How do Lithwick and Carter respond to Giuliani's arguments?

4. What does this debate say about the way terrorism and the response to it has affected American values?

to be accurate. In states along the border with Mexico, especially Arizona, groups opposed to immigration proposed the building of fences to stop the flow of entrants into the United States. By 2008 a fence was actually in the process of construction. Corporations that relied on less expensive labor from undocumented immigrants resisted legislation that imposed penalties for employing illegal immigrants. Both sides asked Congress to take action in 2006 and 2007, but the partisan division on the immigration question prevented passage of any bill.

Cable news channels, especially CNN with a commentator named Lou Dobbs, ran repeated stories about the misdeeds, real and less credible, of illegal immigrants. Within the Republican Party, contenders for the party's 2008 presidential nomination filled their speeches with calls for tougher penalties against illegal immigration, which they believed would resonate with the base of the party. In fact, candidates who were the most strident fared less well in the early primaries. Nonetheless, the Republicans risked losses among Hispanic voters, who generally supported a path to citizenship for undocumented workers. As the 2008 election developed, surveys confirmed that the immigration issue might not be as salient politically as the media coverage suggested. However, as the economy slipped into a recession in January 2008, the immigration question retained the potential to regain its power to polarize opinion.

Social Activism, Left and Right

Out of the headlines that dominated the national media during the first decade of the twenty-first century, the descendants of the original inhabitants of North America maintained a tradition of resistance that had existed since the end of the Indian wars during the 1880s and 1890s through the confrontations of the 1970s. Native Americans, faced with such challenges as a suicide rate among young people ten times higher than the national average, have sought to use both legal means and high-profile publicity to alert the nation and the rest of the world to their legitimate grievances. The National Congress of American Indians sued in federal court alleging that the Indian Trust Fund, created under the Dawes act of 1887 (see Chapter 17), had been depriving Indians of their payments for decades. Claims could reach, they said, more than $137 billion.

While some Native Americans saw large revenues from casino gambling, others struggled with poverty, disease, and neglect. A symbolic act in 2007 underscored the depth of Native American anger. Representatives of the Lakota Sioux officially repudiated the treaties the tribe had signed with the United States in 1851 and 1868. The next step was to secure international recognition for the Lakota Nation within the borders of the United States. While such a result was improbable, the protest attracted international attention and reminded the country about the issues that Native Americans had raised, but their conditions were far from resolved.

A cultural issue that aroused strong feelings along the political spectrum was the prospect of gays and lesbians being granted the right to marry their partners and achieve the legal and civil privileges that heterosexual couples enjoyed. In Canada and several European countries, such rights already existed. Religious conservatives regarded this change as a violation of divine law and opposed legislation or court decisions to include homosexuals in marriage law. Gays lobbied through such organizations as the Human Rights Campaign in states such as Massachusetts, whose Supreme Court ruled in 2005 that same sex-marriages could occur, and elsewhere for an equal status under the law for their unions.

While the opponents of same-sex marriages were vocal and intense, the long-term trend seemed to be in the direction of this shift in attitudes toward marriage. Younger Americans, familiar with gays because of people they knew and the television programs that portrayed homosexual characters, tended to be more tolerant and less upset by same-sex unions. In the years after 2001, this issue ebbed and flowed as a matter of public concern. During the early part of the decade, Republicans used referenda on gay marriage as a way to increase the turnout of conservatives during the 2002 and 2004 elections. Polling indicated by 2008 that gay marriage had less salience in this regard.

Conservatives criticized the teaching of evolution with as much intensity as they attacked gay marriage. The cultural battles that had been raging over evolution since the 1920s intensified after 2001. On the right, such lobbying groups as the Discover Institute pushed creationism as an alternative explanation for human origins. The doctrine taught that a divine power had made the universe through what was called "intelligent design." Proponents of this creed contended that the design of the universe could be explained only by a purposeful creator. Creationists lobbied to have their position given equal status with evolution and succeeded in Kansas and Texas. When a school board in Dover, Pennsylvania, adopted an intelligent design curriculum, however, opponents took the board to court. A judge ruled against intelligent design in a setback to the larger movement. As the debate revealed, Americans remain polarized about science and its implications.

Globalization and Economic Troubles

During the opening years of the Bush presidency, after the economic expansion of the late 1990s, the country experienced a mild recession that ended in November 2001. To counter the effects of the downturn, the Federal Reserve System had made credit easier through low interest rates and a growth in the money supply. The tax cuts of the first Bush term added to the stimulus that the economy received. These policies facilitated a boom in housing as new construction and home resales leaped ahead. Homeowners became convinced that the value of their dwellings would always rise. In such circumstances, many borrowers took out large loans without the corresponding income to make payments. They bet instead on the appreciation they would receive when the value of their home rose. Lenders at the same time extended credit on generous initial rates ("teaser loans") to many individuals. Mortgage lenders packaged these loans with other loans and sold them to banks and financial institutions. State and federal regulators paid little attention to these practices. Since these loans did not have the worth of those made by "prime lenders," they were dubbed "subprime" loans in the financial industry.

As long as housing prices rose across the country, few problems seemed evident. In 2007, however, when the housing market softened and foreclosures accelerated, the dubious quality of these subprime loans became evident as banks and lenders incurred staggering losses. Early in 2008, the financial giant Citibank reported losses of $10 billion. Bank of America sought to acquire Countrywide, a major lender, after that firm went into virtual bankruptcy. Other major financial institutions from Merrill Lynch to J. P. Morgan banks wrote down billions of dollars in bad loans.

By early 2008, the housing crisis had spilled over into the larger economy. With billions of dollars in bad loans unlikely ever to be paid, the financial system revealed fundamental weaknesses. Fears of a recession mounted, and the Federal Reserve System in a surprise action cut interest rates by three-quarters of a percent in mid-January 2008. Forecasters warned that the impending recession could be long and deep. Congress responded with legislation to put money into the hands of consumers with tax rebates, but critics questioned whether that move would stave off the looming economic trouble. Because of the place of the American economy in a world in which **globalization** was an increasingly important fact of life, markets in other countries also seemed shaky as 2008 began. After eight years of conservative economic policies under George W. Bush, the United States was now confronted with a huge national debt, a shrunken manufacturing base, and an economy without the resources needed for a quick rebound to prosperity.

globalization The process by which the world's economies are becoming more integrated and interdependent. Those affected by such changes have often protested against the political and economic dislocation that accompanies this trend.

The Climate Change Crisis

For more than a century, scientists had predicted that the accumulation of carbon dioxide that human civilization produced would likely result in the warming of the globe. As a U.S. senator in 1992, Albert Gore, Jr., had written *Earth in the Balance* pointing out this phenomenon and its dangerous consequences. During the next decade and a half, more evidence of global warming accumulated as glaciers melted, ice sheets shrank in the Arctic and Antarctic, and sea levels rose. A scientific consensus emerged that **climate change** was occurring and that humanity was primarily responsible for what was taking place. Dire forecasts told of more catastrophic events if prompt steps were not taken to reduce the extent of carbon emissions in the atmosphere.

climate change Term used by scientists to describe the result of the global warming caused by human activity, especially the burning of fossil fuels.

(© Torsten Blackwood/Pool/epa/CORBIS)

Ice Floe Warning. The evidence of global warming accumulated as melting ice floes appeared in the Arctic and the rate at which the ice disappeared accelerated.

The United States, a major source of carbon emissions from cars, industry, and agriculture, proved reluctant to take any significant steps in the crisis. The Kyoto Treaty of 1999, which sought some steps against climate change, encountered overwhelming opposition in the Senate and then outright rejection from the Bush administration. The White House aligned itself with those who denied that any crisis existed or that the activities of humanity could alleviate the phenomenon.

A 2006 documentary firm produced and narrated by former Vice President Gore, *An Inconvenient Truth*, presented the case for action against climate change and received an Academy Award in 2007. By that year, panels of scientists said that action had to be taken within a decade to stave off the most damaging effects of global warming on agriculture, sea levels, and weather. Other scientists indicated that these projections were too optimistic and that the very existence of human civilization was in jeopardy. The truth about the impact of climate change was likely to determine the future of society in the United States and for civilization itself.

The 2006 Midterm Elections

The congressional elections of 2006 did produce a Democratic majority in the House of Representatives. That in turn led to the election of the first woman Speaker of the House of Representatives, Nancy Pelosi. In the Senate, the Democrats won all of the contested seats possible to achieve a narrow two-vote majority. Harry Reid of Nevada became the new majority leader. Polls indicated that the Democratic intention to scale down or end the war in Iraq had much to do with the Democratic victory.

President Bush drew an opposite conclusion. He accepted the recommendation of conservative advisers that an increase, or "surge," of American forces in Iraq would reduce the violence in that country and promote political reconciliation among the warring factions. Throughout 2007, the American military did achieve a lowering of the resistance to the occupation and eventually a falloff in American monthly troop deaths to around twenty-five per month at the end of the year.

Doing History Online

Barack Obama

Go to the CourseMate website for this chapter and link to Primary Sources. Read online about Barack Obama's remarks at the 2004 Democratic convention.

1. What themes from this 2004 speech on behalf of John Kerry recurred in Obama's presidential campaign in 2008?
2. What part does a sense of hope and possibility play in Obama's evocation of the America he sees in the future?
3. To what extent is the speech partisan in nature? How often does he mention the Democratic Party as an organization?

 www.cengagebrain.com

However, the Iraqis did not take the political steps the surge was designed to promote. By the spring of 2008, troop reductions began to occur, but the prospect of an end to the Iraq war seemed more distant than ever. Some Republicans, such as 2008 presidential candidate John McCain, forecast that American soldiers might still be in Iraq for fifty to one hundred years.

❖ A Change of Course: President Obama

The 2008 presidential election was an important one for the people of the United States for whom great challenges now remained. The nation had come far since its colonial beginnings, with significant accomplishments and sobering defeats. Yet the issues now transcended those of the past. Could its people find a way to survive amid the dangers of terrorism, economic decline, military overreach, and, most of all, the mounting threat of global climate change? The capacity of the society to engage and solve these issues would determine the direction of the American passage in the twenty-first century.

2008: An Historic Election

The 2008 presidential election proved to be a turning point in the nation's history with the election of the first African American chief executive in Barack Obama. The process of choosing the two major party candidates had already identified two clear front-runners by the early months of the year. On the Republican side, Senator John McCain came out of a large field of aspirants to gain the lead by March. His age (he would be seventy-two in 2009), identification with the Iraq War, and lack of fresh economic programs were his minuses; his reputation as a "maverick" lawmaker gave him an appeal with moderates.

Among the Democrats, Senator Hillary Clinton of New York had a strong appeal to the party's base though large elements among the Democrats resisted another Clinton at the head of the ticket. The early leader was Senator Barack Obama of Illinois. He had resisted the Iraq War from the outset. In the quest for delegates, his managers out-dueled the Clinton forces. By mid-June, though their popular vote totals were close, Obama had what proved to be an insurmountable advantage among committed delegates. He sustained that margin and was the presumptive nominee as the Democrats assembled in Denver at their national convention in August. For his running mate, Obama selected Senator Joseph Biden of Delaware. Obama came out of the convention with a united and confident party behind him.

For the Republicans, who met in Saint Paul, Minnesota, in early September, the prospects were less encouraging. Trailing in polls, John McCain had the selection of a prospective running mate as his best chance to shake up the race. He wanted to name Senator Joseph Lieberman of Connecticut, a Democrat who had defected from his party to support the GOP, but party regulars vetoed that suggestion. Instead, the senator made a risky pick of the first-term governor of Alaska, Sarah Palin. Forty-five years old and a novice in national affairs, Palin commended herself to many conservatives as a fresh voice with the ability to articulate traditional family values. Her speech to the Republican National Convention was well received, and the Republican ticket took to the campaign trail with some enthusiasm.

Economic crisis soon transformed the election. Ten days after the end of the Republican convention, the banking firm of Lehmann Brothers failed, and fears of a general financial panic mounted. The stability of other major banks seemed under strain. The Bush administration mounted a major effort to enact

MAP 30.3
The Election of 2008
Barack Obama's success in the 2008 election showed the widespread desire for change among Americans, particularly younger voters.

Candidate (Party)	Electoral Vote		Popular Vote	
Obama (Democrat)	365	68%	69,498,459	52.9%
McCain (Republican)	173	32%	59,948,283	45.6%

(Copyright © Cengage Learning)

financial bailout legislation to preserve the banking system. Federal action to stem the panic that was commencing did work at the end of 2008, but the economic effects of the crisis included a sharp rise in unemployment, further declines in the already weakened housing market, and bleak prospects for additional job creation in the months ahead. The United States found itself in the worst economic situation the nation had confronted since the Great Depression of the 1930s.

Both McCain and Obama endorsed the economic bailout strategy of the Bush administration. By late September and early October, it was clear that the Republican ticket was behind. McCain's pick of Sarah Palin had backfired. In interviews with major television networks, she did less well than in her convention speech. As a result, even though she energized the Republican base, she alienated moderates. Meanwhile, Obama trumped McCain in their televised debates.

On Election Day, Obama achieved a decisive victory. He garnered 69,456,000 popular votes to 59,934,000 for McCain. The electoral vote totals stood at 365 for the Democrat and 173 for the Republicans. (See Map 30.3.) In the House, Democrats added twenty seats to establish a 257–178 ascendancy over the Republicans. As for the Senate, the Democrats had fifty-eight seats to forty-one for the Republicans with one undecided seat in Minnesota. After a long recount process that stretched into 2009, that seat too fell to the Democrats. The switch of a Republican senator, Arlen Specter of Pennsylvania, to the Democratic column in April 2009 put the majority party with sixty votes (including two independents), enough to cut off Republican attempts to filibuster, assuming the often disunited Democrats could agree on a common position. Since they usually could not find such cohesion, their super-majority status did not prove as decisive an advantage as they had anticipated.

The "Great Recession"

Barack Obama was sworn in on January 20, 2009, before one of the largest inaugural crowds Washington had ever seen. He confronted daunting challenges. The most pressing in an immediate sense was the economic crisis, which was becoming the most serious downturn since the Depression of the 1930s.

Foreclosure in Richmond, California, 2009. Lax lending practices and subprime mortgages contributed to the financial crisis as many homeowners found themselves unable to meet their loan obligations. Neighborhoods in California, Arizona, and Florida were hit particularly hard by the housing crash.

(Justin Sullivan/Getty Images)

Acknowledging this, the new president declared in his inaugural address, "Today I say to you that the challenges we face are real, they are serious, and they are many. They will not be met easily or in a short span of time. But know this, America: They will be met."

Many trends came together to produce the gloomy economic situation for the American people. During the years after 2000, budget deficits, tax cuts, and rising housing prices had fueled a speculative bubble in which everyone assumed that home values would rise into the foreseeable future. Lax lending practices included risky "subprime" loans so called because the borrowers lacked the credit for ordinary mortgages. In the process, many homeowners often took on more debt than they could handle. Banks created new financial instruments to market shaky real estate properties. When the inflated home values came under pressure because owners could not pay, the speculative bubble weakened and then collapsed, putting the whole financial system at risk.

The deflationary cycle, once it started, proved difficult to reverse. Jobs disappeared as unemployment rose to more than 10 percent of the workforce. Individuals lost their homes, their savings, and in time all of their assets. More and more Americans, for example, found themselves living on unemployment checks and, in some cases, by late 2009 food stamps as their sole source of income. As government revenues shrank, cities and states cut their budgets further, adding to the numbers of people without jobs. A vicious cycle of cuts and layoffs brought some states to the brink of bankruptcy.

Government struggled to find an adequate response. Conventional thinking argued that society must retrench and live within its means. But to follow that course would accelerate the spiral of unemployment and despair. With huge deficits left over from the 2001–2009 period, government spending to stimulate the economy risked further adding to the red ink for the government. Yet the federal government seemed the only force in society that could alleviate economic strain through job-creation programs and tax cuts. The scale of the crisis meant that the government would have to construct huge programs to accomplish these goals, an idea that troubled many politicians both Democratic and Republican. Could the new Obama administration act in time to stave off disaster?

The Obama Presidency

During 2009, two views of Barack Obama as president emerged. For conservatives the chief executive was an advocate of big government and socialism. Angry voices on the right were heard at "tea parties," which emulated the protests of the American Revolution, claiming that the president was bent on dictatorship. They charged that he had not been born in Hawaii as he claimed and was therefore not eligible to serve as president. That these charges had been disproved many times over meant little to the "birthers," as they became known. Many of these same critics objected to Obama's race and the presence of a black man as president.

The other, more plausible interpretation saw the new administration as cautious and in some cases too timid in its approach to the economic crisis. Although the economic stimulus package came to almost $800 billion, it was modest in terms of the economic crisis that many Americans faced. The combination of tax cuts, payments to states and localities, and increased infrastructure projects was designed to bring the unemployment rate down to 8 percent. However, although the stimulus helped ease the negative impact of the recession on the economy and kept the unemployment rate at around 10 percent, Americans believed by early 2010 that much of the money had been wasted.

One obstacle to Obama's political success was the determined opposition of the Republicans, especially in the Senate, to the administration's initiatives. Although the president called for bipartisan cooperation, the GOP preferred to block even those programs for deficit reduction or health care reform that they had earlier proposed.

President Obama did enjoy some legislative victories. When Justice David Souter retired from the Supreme Court in 2009, the president nominated Sonia Sotomayor, a federal appeals court judge of Hispanic ancestry. Despite strident attacks on her from right-wing critics, she was confirmed and joined Justice Ruth Bader Ginsburg as the two women on the Court. In 2010 they were joined by Obama's second nominee to the court, Elena Kagan. Meanwhile, the Democrats enjoyed a sixty-vote dominance in the Senate, which would enable them, if they could agree, to cut off Republican filibusters. To some degree, this majority was illusory since several Democratic senators, such as Joseph Lieberman of Connecticut (who had switched back to the Democratic

President Barack Obama Meets with Secretary of State Hillary Rodham Clinton. President Obama appointed his opponent for the 2008 Democratic nomination, Hillary Rodham Clinton, as his secretary of state after he won the presidency. In foreign affairs, the new administration sought to renew international friendships that had become strained during the Bush presidency.

(UPPA/Photoshot)

party after the 2008 election) and Ben Nelson of Nebraska, often sided with the Republicans.

In other respects, Obama disappointed the base within the Democratic Party that had supported his candidacy. The administration did not support the repeal of the "Don't Ask, Don't Tell" policy toward gays in the military until January 2010. Many of the Bush policies toward terror suspects were extended and confirmed by the Obama White House. The president's campaign promise to close the facility housing terrorists at Guantanamo Bay, Cuba, remained unfulfilled by the summer of 2010. Most of all, Obama escalated the conflict against the Taliban and Al Qaeda in Afghanistan with a thirty thousand increase in the number of American troops.

The key initiative in Congress was the president's commitment to reform the health care system. Hoping to build a bipartisan consensus, the White House left the fate of the proposal in the hands of Congress. In the Senate, the Democrats involved Republicans in the process of writing the legislation. The GOP members stretched out the deliberations of key committees with promises of eventual support that they never intended to fulfill. The debate dragged on into the winter of 2009–2010 until finally the House and Senate had each enacted its own version of health care measures.

At that point, a special senatorial election in Massachusetts in January 2010 to fill the vacancy created upon the death of Senator Edward Kennedy led to the victory of a conservative Republican, Scott Brown. With that outcome, the Democrats lost their sixtieth vote in the Senate and the ability to shut off a Republican filibuster. At the same time, the majority party lost its political nerve. A retreat from a commitment to health care followed and the prospects for the president's initiative seemed bleak as the winter of 2010 progressed.

That gloomy prediction proved premature. The determination of Speaker of the House Nancy Pelosi and the persistence of President Obama produced a turnaround in Democratic fortunes that achieved passage of a health care package in March 2010. The House adopted the bill that had earlier passed the Senate and the two houses of Congress also enacted a measure to fix some of the more contentious issues in the Senate legislation. By April 1 the health care reform fight had ended in victory for the Democrats, and early polls indicated public approval for the change in health policy.

The effect of President Obama's success on health care remained to be decided as the mid-term elections of 2010 approached. Republicans promised more opposition to Democrats on every issue, including repeal of the health care law, and the Grand Old Party still expected big gains in the congressional elections. American politics remained polarized with the more fervent members of the Republican coalition threatening civil disobedience in the wake of the passage of the health care law.

A disturbing reminder of what the world's dependence on fossil fuels might also entail came in April 2010. An oil well owned by the petroleum giant BP exploded in the Gulf of Mexico, spewing crude oil into the sea at the rate of thousands of barrels per day. Efforts to stop the spill and to clean up the mess dragged on for months, and the ecological and economic damage to coastal states such as Louisiana, Alabama, and Mississippi was catastrophic.

Meanwhile, the climate crisis intensified, thousands of American troops remained in Afghanistan and Iraq, and diplomatic and economic challenges continued to confront Americans and their leaders. The capacity of society to engage and solve these issues would determine the direction of the American passage in the twenty-first century.

CHAPTER REVIEW, 2000–2010

SUMMARY

- George W. Bush was elected president in 2000 in a disputed election that required the Supreme Court's intervention.

- The attacks of September 11, 2001, brought the threat of domestic and foreign terrorism to the forefront of Americans' consciousness.

- Responding to the threat of Al Qaeda, the Bush administration led a group of allies to defeat the Taliban regime in Afghanistan.

- In 2003, the Bush administration targeted Iraq as part of an "axis of evil" and led the country into war. It became a controversial, prolonged conflict with no apparent endgame.

- Global climate change threatened the existence of civilization.

- In 2006, Americans gave Democrats a majority in Congress. In 2008, they elected President Barack Obama, a Democrat who became the first African American to hold that office.

- In December 2007, the United States began to suffer from the most severe recession since the Great Depression; in the fall of 2008, the banking system itself seemed near collapse until the federal government intervened.

- Political divisiveness threatened progress on the difficult issues confronting Americans in the new decade, but Democrats managed to pass health care reform legislation in March 2010.

IDENTIFICATIONS

Osama bin Laden

bloggers

Department of Homeland Security

globalization

climate change

MAKING CONNECTIONS: LOOKING AHEAD ⅠⅠⅠ➡

This is the last chapter of the book, and so these questions are not for further reading. Think about these issues as you ponder the sweep of American history and what could occur during your lifetime as the national passage moves on.

1. In what ways has terrorism altered the nature of the American government?

2. What should the United States do to preserve order while at the same time preserving its democratic heritage?

3. How different will American society be in twenty-five years because of the developments between 2000 and 2010?

4. Should optimism or pessimism be the dominant theme in evaluating the future of the United States in the light of the history you have just finished reading?

RECOMMENDED READINGS

Benjamin, Daniel, and Steven Simon. *The Age of Sacred Terror* (2002). An excellent look at the roots of terrorism and the American response during the 1990s.

Gordon, Michael R., and Bernard E. Trainor. *Cobra II: The Inside Story of the Invasion and Occupation of Iraq* (2006). Analyzes the events that grew out of the invasion of Iraq and the subsequent occupation.

Ricks, Thomas. *Fiasco: The American Military Adventure in Iraq* (2006). A critical examination of the performance of the military in Iraq.

Rivoli, Pietra. *The Travels of a T-Shirt in the Global Economy: An Economist Examines the Markets, Power, and Politics of World Trade* (2005). An incisive look at how globalization has shaped the world economy by focusing on a single product known to all.

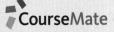 **CourseMate** Go to the CourseMate website at www.cengagebrain.com for additional study tools and review materials for this chapter.

APPENDIX

The Declaration of Independence

The Unanimous Declaration of the Thirteen United States of America

When in the Course of human events it becomes necessary for one people to dissolve the political bands which have connected them with another, and to assume among the Powers of the earth, the separate and equal station to which the Laws of Nature and of Nature's God entitle them, a decent respect to the opinions of mankind requires that they should declare the causes which impel them to the separation.

We hold these truths to be self-evident, that all men are created equal, that they are endowed by their Creator with certain unalienable Rights, that among these are Life, Liberty and the pursuit of Happiness. That to secure these rights, Governments are instituted among Men, deriving their just Powers from the consent of the governed. That whenever any Form of Government becomes destructive of these ends, it is the Right of the People to alter or to abolish it, and to institute new Government, laying its foundation on such principles and organizing its Powers in such form, as to them shall seem most likely to effect their Safety and Happiness. Prudence, indeed, will dictate that Governments long established should not be changed for light and transient causes; and accordingly all experience hath shewn, that mankind are more disposed to suffer, while evils are sufferable, than to right themselves by abolishing the forms to which they are accustomed. But when a long train of abuses and usurpations, pursuing invariably the same Object evinces a design to reduce them under absolute Despotism, it is their right, it is their duty, to throw off such Government, and to provide new Guards for their future security. Such has been the patient sufferance of these Colonies; and such is now the necessity which constrains them to alter their former Systems of Government. The history of the present King of Great Britain is a history of repeated injuries and usurpations, all having in direct object the establishment of an absolute Tyranny over these States. To prove this, let Facts be submitted to a candid world.

He has refused his Assent to Laws, the most wholesome and necessary for the public good.

He has forbidden his Governors to pass Laws of immediate and pressing importance, unless suspended in their operation till his Assent should be obtained; and when so suspended, he has utterly neglected to attend to them.

He has refused to pass other Laws for the accommodation of large districts of people, unless those people would relinquish the right of Representation in the Legislature, a right inestimable to them and formidable to tyrants only.

He has called together legislative bodies at places unusual, uncomfortable, and distant from the depository of their Public Records, for the sole Purpose of fatiguing them into compliance with his measures.

He has dissolved Representative Houses repeatedly, for opposing with manly firmness his invasions on the rights of the People.

He has refused for a long time, after such dissolutions, to cause others to be elected; whereby the Legislative Powers, incapable of Annihilation, have returned to the People at large for their exercise; the State remaining in the mean time exposed to all the dangers of invasion from without, and convulsions within.

He has endeavoured to prevent the Population of these States; for that purpose obstructing the Laws for Naturalization of Foreigners; refusing to pass others to encourage their migrations hither, and raising the conditions of new Appropriations of Lands.

He has obstructed the Administration of Justice, by refusing his Assent to Laws for establishing Judiciary Powers.

He has made Judges dependent on his Will alone, for the tenure of their offices, and the amount and payment of their salaries.

He has erected a multitude of New Offices, and sent hither swarms of Officers to harass our People, and eat out their substance.

He has kept among us, in times of peace, Standing Armies without the Consent of our legislatures.

He has affected to render the Military independent of and superior to the Civil Power.

He has combined with others to subject us to a jurisdiction foreign to our constitution, and unacknowledged by our laws; giving his Assent to their Acts of pretended Legislation:

For Quartering large bodies of armed troops among us:

For protecting them, by a mock Trial, from Punishment for any Murders which they should commit on the Inhabitants of these States:

For cutting off our Trade with all parts of the world:

For imposing Taxes on us without our Consent:

For depriving us in many cases, of the benefits of Trial by Jury:

For transporting us beyond Seas to be tried for pretended offences:

For abolishing the free System of English Laws in a neighbouring Province, establishing therein an Arbitrary government, and enlarging its Boundaries so as to render it at once an example and fit instrument for introducing the same absolute rule into these Colonies:

Text is reprinted from the facsimile of the engrossed copy in the National Archives. The original spelling, capitalization, and punctuation have been retained. Paragraphing has been added.

For taking away our Charters, abolishing our most valuable Laws, and altering fundamentally the Forms of our Governments:

For suspending our own Legislatures, and declaring themselves invested with Power to legislate for us in all cases whatsoever.

He has abdicated Government here, by declaring us out of his Protection, and waging War against us.

He has plundered our seas, ravaged our Coasts, burnt our towns, and destroyed the lives of our people.

He is at this time transporting large Armies of foreign Mercenaries to compleat the works of death, desolation and tyranny, already begun with circumstances of Cruelty and perfidy scarcely paralleled in the most barbarous ages, and totally unworthy the Head of a civilized nation.

He has constrained our fellow Citizens taken Captive on the high Seas to bear Arms against their Country, to become the executioners of their friends and Brethren, or to fall themselves by their Hands.

He has excited domestic insurrections amongst us, and has endeavoured to bring on the inhabitants of our frontiers, the merciless Indian Savages, whose known rule of warfare, is an undistinguished destruction of all ages, sexes and conditions.

In every stage of these Oppressions We have Petitioned for Redress in the most humble terms: Our repeated Petitions have been answered only by repeated injury. A Prince, whose character is thus marked by every act which may define a Tyrant, is unfit to be the ruler of a free People.

Nor have We been wanting in attentions to our British brethren. We have warned them from time to time of attempts by their legislature to extend an unwarrantable jurisdiction over us. We have reminded them of the circumstances of our emigration and settlement here. We have appealed to their native justice and magnanimity, and we have conjured them by the ties of our common kindred to disavow the usurpations, which, would inevitably interrupt our connections and correspondence. They too have been deaf to the voice of justice and of consanguinity. We must, therefore, acquiesce in the necessity, which denounces our Separation, and hold them, as we hold the rest of mankind, Enemies in War, in Peace Friends.

We, therefore, the Representatives of the United States of America, in General Congress, Assembled, appealing to the Supreme Judge of the world for the rectitude of our intentions, do, in the Name, and by Authority of the good People of these Colonies, solemnly publish and declare, That these United Colonies are, and of Right ought to be Free and Independent States; that they are Absolved from all Allegiance to the British Crown, and that all political connection between them and the State of Great Britain, is and ought to be totally dissolved; and that, as Free and Independent States, they have full Power to levy War, conclude Peace, contract Alliances, establish Commerce, and to do all other Acts and Things which Independent States may of right do. And for the support of this Declaration, with a firm reliance on the protection of divine Providence, we mutually pledge to each other our Lives, our Fortunes and our sacred Honor.

The Constitution of the United States of America

We the People of the United States, in Order to form a more perfect Union, establish Justice, insure domestic Tranquility, provide for the common defence, promote the general Welfare, and secure the Blessings of Liberty to ourselves and our Posterity, do ordain and establish this Constitution for the United States of America.

ARTICLE I

SECTION 1 All legislative Powers herein granted shall be vested in a Congress of the United States, which shall consist of a Senate and House of Representatives.

SECTION 2 The House of Representatives shall be composed of Members chosen every second Year by the People of the several States, and the Electors in each State shall have the Qualifications requisite for Electors of the most numerous Branch of the State Legislature.

No Person shall be a Representative who shall not have attained to the Age of twenty five Years, and been seven Years a Citizen of the United States, and who shall not, when elected, be an Inhabitant of that State in which he shall be chosen.

Representatives and direct Taxes[1] shall be apportioned among the several States which may be included within this Union, according to their respective Numbers, which shall be determined by adding to the whole Number of free Persons, including those bound to Service for a Term of Years, and excluding Indians not taxed, three fifths of all other Persons.[2] The actual Enumeration shall be made within three Years after the first Meeting of the Congress of the United States, and within every subsequent Term of ten Years, in such Manner as they shall by Law direct. The Number of Representatives shall not exceed one for every thirty Thousand, but each State shall have at Least one Representative; and until such enumeration shall be made, the State of New Hampshire shall be entitled to chuse three; Massachusetts eight; Rhode Island and Providence Plantations one; Connecticut five; New York six; New Jersey four; Pennsylvania eight; Delaware one; Maryland six; Virginia ten; North Carolina five; South Carolina five; and Georgia three.

When vacancies happen in the Representation from any State, the Executive Authority thereof shall issue Writs of Election to fill such Vacancies.

The House of Representatives shall chuse their Speaker and other Officers; and shall have the sole Power of Impeachment.

SECTION 3 The Senate of the United States shall be composed of two Senators from each State, chosen by the Legislature thereof, for six Years; and each Senator shall have one Vote.[3]

Immediately after they shall be assembled in Consequence of the first Election, they shall be divided as equally as may be into three Classes. The Seats of the Senators of the first Class shall be vacated at the Expiration of the second Year, of the second Class at the Expiration of the fourth Year, and of the third Class at the Expiration of the sixth Year, so that one third may be chosen every second Year; and if Vacancies happen by Resignation, or otherwise, during the Recess of the Legislature of any State, the Executive thereof may make temporary Appointments until the next Meeting of the Legislature, which shall then fill such Vacancies.[4]

No Person shall be a Senator who shall not have attained to the Age of thirty Years, and been nine Years a Citizen of the United States, and who shall not, when elected, be an Inhabitant of that State for which he shall be chosen.

The Vice President of the United States shall be President of the Senate, but shall have no Vote, unless they be equally divided.

The Senate shall chuse their other Officers, and also a President pro tempore, in the Absence of the Vice President, or when he shall exercise the Office of President of the United States.

The Senate shall have the sole Power to try all Impeachments. When sitting for that Purpose, they shall be on Oath or Affirmation. When the President of the United States is tried, the Chief Justice shall preside: And no Person shall be convicted without the Concurrence of two thirds of the Members present.

Judgment in Cases of Impeachment shall not extend further than to removal from Office, and disqualification to hold and enjoy any Office of honor, Trust or Profit under the United States: but the Party convicted shall nevertheless be liable and subject to Indictment, Trial, Judgment and Punishment, according to Law.

SECTION 4 The Times, Places and Manner of holding Elections for Senators and Representatives, shall be prescribed in each State by the Legislature thereof, but the Congress may at any time by Law make or alter such Regulation, except as to the Places of chusing Senators.

The Congress shall assemble at least once in every Year, and such Meeting shall be on the first Monday in December, unless they shall by Law appoint a different Day.[5]

SECTION 5 Each House shall be the Judge of the Elections, Returns and Qualifications of its own Members, and a Majority of each shall constitute a Quorum to do Business; but a smaller Number may adjourn from day to day, and

---

Text is from the engrossed copy in the National Archives. Original spelling, capitalization, and punctuation have been retained.
[1]Modified by the Sixteenth Amendment.
[2]Replaced by the Fourteenth Amendment.

---

[3]Superseded by the Seventeenth Amendment.
[4]Modified by the Seventeenth Amendment.
[5]Superseded by the Twentieth Amendment.

may be authorized to compel the Attendance of absent Members, in such Manner, and under such Penalties as each House may provide.

Each House may determine the Rules of its Proceedings, punish its Members for disorderly Behaviour, and, with the Concurrence of two thirds, expel a Member.

Each House shall keep a Journal of its Proceedings, and from time to time publish the same, excepting such Parts as may in their Judgment require Secrecy; and the Yeas and Nays of the Members of either House on any question shall, at the Desire of one fifth of those Present, be entered on the Journal.

Neither House, during the Session of Congress, shall, without the Consent of the other, adjourn for more than three days, nor to any other Place than that in which the two Houses shall be sitting.

SECTION 6 The Senators and Representatives shall receive a Compensation for their Services, to be ascertained by Law, and paid out of the Treasury of the United States. They shall in all Cases, except Treason, Felony and Breach of the Peace, be privileged from Arrest during their Attendance at the Session of their respective Houses, and in going to and returning from the same; and for any Speech or Debate in either House, they shall not be questioned in any other Place.

No Senator or Representative shall, during the Time for which he was elected, be appointed to any civil Office under the Authority of the United States, which shall have been created, or the Emoluments whereof shall have been encreased during such time; and no Person holding any Office under the United States, shall be a Member of either House during his Continuance in Office.

SECTION 7 All Bills for raising Revenue shall originate in the House of Representatives; but the Senate may propose or concur with Amendments as on other Bills.

Every Bill which shall have passed the House of Representatives and the Senate shall, before it become a Law, be presented to the President of the United States; If he approve he shall sign it, but if not he shall return it, with his Objections to that House in which it shall have originated, who shall enter the Objections at large on their Journal, and proceed to reconsider it. If after such Reconsideration two thirds of that House shall agree to pass the Bill, it shall be sent, together with the Objections, to the other House, by which it shall likewise be reconsidered, and if approved by two thirds of that House, it shall become a Law. But in all such Cases the Votes of both Houses shall be determined by yeas and Nays, and the Names of the Persons voting for and against the Bill shall be entered on the Journal of each House respectively. If any Bill shall not be returned by the President within ten Days (Sundays excepted) after it shall have been presented to him, the Same shall be a Law, in like Manner as if he had signed it, unless the Congress by their Adjournment prevent its Return, in which Case it shall not be a Law.

Every Order, Resolution, or Vote to which the Concurrence of the Senate and House of Representatives may be necessary (except on a question of Adjournment) shall be presented to the President of the United States; and

before the Same shall take Effect, shall be approved by him, or being disapproved by him shall be repassed by two thirds of the Senate and House of Representatives, according to the Rules and Limitations prescribed in the Case of a Bill.

SECTION 8 The Congress shall have power To lay and collect Taxes, Duties, Imposts and Excises, to pay the Debts and provide for the common Defence and general Welfare of the United States; but all Duties, Imposts and Excises shall be uniform throughout the United States;

To borrow Money on the credit of the United States;

To regulate Commerce with foreign Nations, and among the several States, and with the Indian Tribes;

To establish an uniform Rule of Naturalization, and uniform Laws on the subject of Bankruptcies throughout the United States;

To coin Money, regulate the Value thereof, and of foreign Coin, and fix the Standard of Weights and Measures;

To provide for the Punishment of counterfeiting the Securities and current Coin of the United States;

To establish Post Offices and post Roads;

To promote the Progress of Science and useful Arts, by securing for limited Times to Authors and Inventors the exclusive Right to their respective Writings and Discoveries;

To constitute Tribunals inferior to the supreme Court;

To define and punish Piracies and Felonies committed on the high Seas, and Offences against the Law of Nations;

To declare War, grant Letters of Marque and Reprisal, and make Rules concerning Captures on Land and Water;

To raise and support Armies, but no Appropriation of Money to that Use shall be for a longer Term than two Years;

To provide and maintain a Navy;

To make Rules for the Government and Regulation of the land and naval Forces;

To provide for calling forth the Militia to execute the Laws of the Union, suppress Insurrections and repel Invasions;

To provide for organizing, arming, and disciplining, the Militia, and for governing such Part of them as may be employed in the Service of the United States, reserving to the States respectively, the Appointment of the Officers, and the Authority of training the Militia according to the discipline prescribed by Congress;

To exercise exclusive Legislation in all Cases whatsoever, over such District (not exceeding ten Miles square) as may, by Cession of particular States, and the Acceptance of Congress, become the Seat of the Government of the United States, and to exercise like Authority over all Places purchased by the Consent of the Legislature of the State in which the Same shall be, for the Erection of Forts, Magazines, Arsenals, dock-Yards, and other needful Buildings;—And

To make all Laws which shall be necessary and proper for carrying into Execution the foregoing Powers, and all other Powers vested by this Constitution in the Government of the United States, or in any Department or Officer thereof.

SECTION 9 The Migration or Importation of such Persons as any of the States now existing shall think proper to admit, shall not be prohibited by the Congress prior to the Year one thousand eight hundred and eight, but a Tax or duty may be imposed on such Importation, not exceeding ten dollars for each Person.

The Privilege of the Writ of Habeas Corpus shall not be suspended, unless when in Cases of Rebellion or Invasion the public Safety may require it.

No Bill of Attainder or ex post facto Law shall be passed.

No Capitation, or other direct, Tax shall be laid, unless in Proportion to the Census or Enumeration herein before directed to be taken.

No Tax or Duty shall be laid on Articles exported from any State.

No Preference shall be given by any Regulation of Commerce or Revenue to the Ports of one State over those of another: nor shall Vessels bound to, or from, one State, be obliged to enter, clear, or pay Duties in another.

No Money shall be drawn from the Treasury, but in Consequence of Appropriations made by Law, and a regular Statement and Account of the Receipts and Expenditures of all public Money shall be published from time to time.

No Title of Nobility shall be granted by the United States: And no Person holding any Office of Profit or Trust under them, shall, without the Consent of the Congress, accept of any present, Emolument, Office, or Title, of any kind whatever, from any King, Prince, or foreign State.

SECTION 10 No State shall enter into any Treaty, Alliance, or Confederation; grant Letters of Marque and Reprisal; coin Money; emit Bills of Credit; make any Thing but gold and silver Coin a Tender in Payment of Debts; pass any Bill of Attainder, ex post facto Law, or Law impairing the Obligation of Contracts, or grant any Title of Nobility.

No State shall, without the Consent of the Congress, lay any Imposts or Duties on Imports or Exports, except what may be absolutely necessary for executing its inspection Laws: and the net Produce of all Duties and Imposts, laid by any State on Imports or Exports, shall be for the Use of the Treasury of the United States; and all such Laws shall be subject to the Revision and Controul of the Congress.

No State shall, without the Consent of Congress, lay any Duty of Tonnage, keep Troops, or Ships of War in time of Peace, enter into any Agreement or Compact with another State, or with a foreign Power, or engage in War, unless actually invaded, or in such imminent Danger as will not admit of delay.

ARTICLE II

SECTION 1 The executive Power shall be vested in a President of the United States of America. He shall hold his Office during the Term of four Years, and, together with the Vice President, chosen for the same Term, be elected, as follows:

Each State shall appoint, in such Manner as the Legislature thereof may direct, a Number of Electors, equal to the whole Number of Senators and Representatives to which the State may be entitled in the Congress: but no Senator or Representative, or Person holding an Office of Trust or Profit under the United States, shall be appointed an Elector.

The Electors shall meet in their respective States, and vote by Ballot for two Persons, of whom one at least shall not be an Inhabitant of the same State with themselves. And they shall make a List of all the Persons voted for, and of the Number of Votes for each; which List they shall sign and certify, and transmit sealed to the Seat of the Government of the United States, directed to the President of the Senate. The President of the Senate shall, in the Presence of the Senate and House of Representatives, open all the Certificates, and the Votes shall then be counted. The Person having the greatest Number of Votes shall be the President, if such Number be a Majority of the whole Number of Electors appointed; and if there be more than one who have such Majority, and have an equal Number of Votes, then the House of Representatives shall immediately chuse by Ballot one of them for President; and if no Person have a Majority, then from the five highest on the List the said House shall in like Manner chuse the President. But in chusing the President, the Votes shall be taken by States, the Representation from each State having one Vote; A quorum for this Purpose shall consist of a Member or Members from two thirds of the States, and a Majority of all the States shall be necessary to a Choice. In every Case, after the Choice of the President, the Person having the greatest Number of Votes of the Electors shall be the Vice President. But if there should remain two or more who have equal Votes, the Senate shall chuse from them by Ballot the Vice President.[6]

The Congress may determine the Time of chusing the Electors, and the Day on which they shall give their Votes; which Day shall be the same throughout the United States.

No Person except a natural born Citizen, or a Citizen of the United States, at the time of the Adoption of this Constitution, shall be eligible to the Office of President, neither shall any Person be eligible to that Office who shall not have attained to the Age of thirty five Years, and been fourteen Years a Resident within the United States.

In Case of the Removal of the President from Office, or of his Death, Resignation, or Inability to discharge the Powers and Duties of the said Office, the Same shall devolve on the Vice President, and the Congress may by Law provide for the Case of Removal, Death, Resignation or Inability, both of the President and Vice President, declaring what Officer shall then act as President, and such Officer shall act accordingly, until the Disability be removed, or a President shall be elected.[7]

The President shall, at stated Times, receive for his Services, a Compensation, which shall neither be encreased nor diminished during the Period for which he shall have been elected, and he shall not receive within that Period any other Emolument from the United States, or any of them.

Before he enter on the Execution of his Office, he shall take the following Oath or Affirmation:—"I do solemnly swear (or affirm) that I will faithfully execute the Office of President of the United States, and will to the best of my Ability, preserve, protect and defend the Constitution of the United States."

---

[6]Superseded by the Twelfth Amendment.
[7]Modified by the Twenty-fifth Amendment.

SECTION 2 The President shall be Commander in Chief of the Army and Navy of the United States, and of the Militia of the several States, when called into the actual Service of the United States; he may require the Opinion, in writing, of the principal Officer in each of the executive Departments, upon any Subject relating to the Duties of their respective Offices, and he shall have Power to grant Reprieves and Pardons for Offences against the United States, except in Cases of Impeachment.

He shall have Power, by and with the Advice and Consent of the Senate, to make Treaties, provided two thirds of the Senators present concur; and he shall nominate, and by and with the Advice and Consent of the Senate, shall appoint Ambassadors, other public Ministers and Consuls, Judges of the supreme Court, and all other Officers of the United States, whose Appointments are not herein otherwise provided for, and which shall be established by Law; but the Congress may by Law vest the Appointment of such inferior Officers, as they think proper, in the President alone, in the Courts of Law, or in the Heads of Departments.

The President shall have Power to fill up all Vacancies that may happen during the Recess of the Senate, by granting Commissions which shall expire at the End of their next Session.

SECTION 3 He shall from time to time give the Congress Information of the State of the Union, and recommend to their Consideration such Measures as he shall judge necessary and expedient; he may, on extraordinary Occasions, convene both Houses, or either of them, and in Case of Disagreement between them, with Respect to the Time of Adjournment, he may adjourn them to such Time as he shall think proper; he shall receive Ambassadors and other public Ministers; he shall take Care that the Laws be faithfully executed, and shall Commission all the Officers of the United States.

SECTION 4 The President, Vice President and all civil Officers of the United States, shall be removed from Office on Impeachment for, and Conviction of, Treason, Bribery, or other high Crimes and Misdemeanors.

ARTICLE III

SECTION 1 The judicial Power of the United States, shall be vested in one supreme Court, and in such inferior Courts as the Congress may from time to time ordain and establish. The Judges, both of the supreme and inferior Courts, shall hold their Offices during good Behaviour, and shall, at stated Times, receive for their Services, a Compensation, which shall not be diminished during their Continuance in Office.

SECTION 2 The judicial Power shall extend to all Cases, in Law and Equity, arising under this Constitution, the Laws of the United States, and Treaties made, or which shall be made, under their Authority;—to all Cases affecting Ambassadors, other public Ministers and Consuls;—to all Cases of admiralty and maritime Jurisdiction;—to Controversies to which the United States shall be a

Party;—to Controversies between two or more States;—between a State and Citizens of another State;[8]—between Citizens of different States,—between Citizens of the same State claiming Lands under Grants of different States, and between a State, or the Citizens thereof, and foreign States, Citizens or Subjects.

In all Cases affecting Ambassadors, other public Ministers and Consuls, and those in which a State shall be Party, the supreme Court shall have original Jurisdiction. In all the other Cases before mentioned, the supreme Court shall have appellate Jurisdiction, both as to Law and Fact, with such Exceptions, and under such Regulations as the Congress shall make.

The Trial of all Crimes, except in Cases of Impeachment, shall be by Jury; and such Trial shall be held in the State where the said Crimes shall have been committed; but when not committed within any State, the Trial shall be at such Place or Places as the Congress may by Law have directed.

SECTION 3 Treason against the United States, shall consist only in levying War against them, or in adhering to their Enemies, giving them Aid and Comfort. No Person shall be convicted of Treason unless on the Testimony of two Witnesses to the same overt Act, or on Confession in open Court.

The Congress shall have Power to declare the Punishment of Treason, but no Attainder of Treason shall work Corruption of Blood, or Forfeiture except during the Life of the Person attainted.

ARTICLE IV

SECTION 1 Full Faith and Credit shall be given in each State to the public Acts, Records, and judicial Proceedings of every other State. And the Congress may by general Laws prescribe the Manner in which such Acts, Records and Proceedings shall be proved, and the Effect thereof.

SECTION 2 The Citizens of each State shall be entitled to all Privileges and Immunities of Citizens in the several States.

A Person charged in any State with Treason, Felony, or other Crime, who shall flee from Justice, and be found in another State, shall on Demand of the executive Authority of the State from which he fled, be delivered up, to be removed to the State having Jurisdiction of the Crime.

No Person held to Service or Labour in one State, under the Laws thereof, escaping into another, shall, in Consequence of any Law or Regulation therein, be discharged from such Service or Labour, but shall be delivered up on Claim of the Party to whom such Service or Labour may be due.

SECTION 3 New States may be admitted by the Congress into this Union; but no new State shall be formed or erected within the Jurisdiction of any other State, nor any State be formed by the Junction of two or more States, or Parts of

---

[8]Modified by the Eleventh Amendment.

States, without the Consent of the Legislatures of the States concerned as well as of the Congress.

The Congress shall have Power to dispose of and make all needful Rules and Regulations respecting the Territory or other Property belonging to the United States; and nothing in this Constitution shall be so construed as to Prejudice any Claims of the United States, or of any particular State.

SECTION 4 The United States shall guarantee to every State in this Union a Republican Form of Government, and shall protect each of them against Invasion; and on Application of the Legislature, or of the Executive (when the Legislature cannot be convened) against domestic Violence.

ARTICLE V

The Congress, whenever two thirds of both Houses shall deem it necessary, shall propose Amendments to this Constitution, or, on the Application of the Legislatures of two thirds of the several States, shall call a Convention for proposing Amendments, which, in either Case, shall be valid to all Intents and Purposes, as Part of this Constitution, when ratified by the Legislatures of three fourths of the several States, or by Conventions in three fourths thereof, as the one or the other Mode of Ratification may be proposed by the Congress; Provided that no Amendment which may be made prior to the Year One thousand eight hundred and eight shall in any Manner affect the first and fourth Clauses in the Ninth Section of the first Article; and that no State, without its Consent, shall be deprived of its equal Suffrage in the Senate.

ARTICLE VI

All Debts contracted and Engagements entered into, before the Adoption of this Constitution, shall be as valid against the United States under this Constitution, as under the Confederation.

This Constitution, and the Laws of the United States which shall be made in Pursuance thereof; and all Treaties made, or which shall be made, under the Authority of the United States, shall be the supreme Law of the Land; and the Judges in every State shall be bound thereby, any Thing in the Constitution or Laws of any State to the Contrary notwithstanding.

The Senators and Representatives before mentioned, and the Members of the several State Legislatures, and all executive and judicial Officers, both of the United States and of the several States, shall be bound by Oath or Affirmation, to support this Constitution; but no religious Test shall ever be required as a Qualification to any Office or public Trust under the United States.

ARTICLE VII

The Ratification of the Conventions of nine States, shall be sufficient for the Establishment of this Constitution between the States so ratifying the Same.

Done in Convention by the Unanimous Consent of the States present the Seventeenth Day of September in the Year of our Lord one thousand seven hundred and Eighty

seven and of the Independence of the United States of America the Twelfth. In witness whereof We have hereunto subscribed our Names,

Articles in Addition to, and Amendment of, the Constitution of the United States of America, Proposed by Congress, and Ratified by the Legislatures of the Several States, Pursuant to the Fifth Article of the Original Constitution.

AMENDMENT I[9]

Congress shall make no law respecting an establishment of religion, or prohibiting the free exercise there-of; or abridging the freedom of speech, or of the press; or the right of the people peaceably to assemble, and to petition the Government for a redress of grievances.

AMENDMENT II

A well regulated Militia, being necessary to the security of a free State, the right of the people to keep and bear Arms shall not be infringed.

AMENDMENT III

No Soldier shall, in time of peace, be quartered in any house, without the consent of the Owner, nor in time of war, but in a manner to be prescribed by law.

AMENDMENT IV

The right of the people to be secure in their persons, houses, papers, and effects, against unreasonable searches and seizures, shall not be violated, and no Warrants shall issue, but upon probable cause, supported by Oath or affirmation, and particularly describing the place to be searched, and the persons or things to be seized.

AMENDMENT V

No person shall be held to answer for a capital or otherwise infamous crime, unless on a presentment or indictment of a Grand Jury, except in cases arising in the land or naval forces, or in the Militia, when in actual service in time of War or public danger; nor shall any person be subject for the same offence to be twice put in jeopardy of life or limb; nor shall be compelled in any criminal case to be a witness against himself, nor be deprived of life, liberty, or property, without due process of law; nor shall private property be taken for public use, without just compensation.

AMENDMENT VI

In all criminal prosecutions, the accused shall enjoy the right to a speedy and public trial, by an impartial jury of the State and district wherein the crime shall have been committed, which district shall have been previously ascertained by law, and to be informed of the nature and cause of the accusation; to be confronted with the witnesses against

---

[9]The first ten amendments were passed by Congress September 25, 1789. They were ratified by three-fourths of the states December 15, 1791.

him; to have compulsory process for obtaining witnesses in his favor, and to have the Assistance of Counsel for his defence.

AMENDMENT VII

In suits at common law, where the value in controversy shall exceed twenty dollars, the right of trial by jury shall be preserved, and no fact tried by a jury, shall be otherwise reexamined in any Court of the United States, than according to the rules of the common law.

AMENDMENT VIII

Excessive bail shall not be required, nor excessive fines imposed, nor cruel and unusual punishments inflicted.

AMENDMENT IX

The enumeration in the Constitution, of certain rights, shall not be construed to deny or disparage others retained by the people.

AMENDMENT X

The powers not delegated to the United States by the Constitution; nor prohibited by it to the States, are reserved to the States respectively, or to the people.

AMENDMENT XI[10]

The Judicial power of the United States shall not be construed to extend to any suit in law or equity, commenced or prosecuted against one of the United States by Citizens of another State, or by Citizens or Subjects of any Foreign State.

AMENDMENT XII[11]

The Electors shall meet in their respective States and vote by ballot for President and Vice-President, one of whom, at least, shall not be an inhabitant of the same State with themselves; they shall name in their ballots the person voted for as President, and in distinct ballots the person voted for as Vice-President, and they shall make distinct lists of all persons voted for as President, and of all persons voted for as Vice-President, and of the number of votes for each, which lists they shall sign and certify, and transmit sealed to the seat of the government of the United States, directed to the President of the Senate;—The President of the Senate shall, in the presence of the Senate and House of Representatives, open all the certificates and the votes shall then be counted;—The person having the greatest number of votes for President, shall be the President, if such number be a majority of the whole number of Electors appointed; and if no person have such majority, then from the persons having the highest numbers not exceeding three on the list of those voted for as President, the House of Representatives shall choose immediately, by ballot, the President. But in

choosing the President, the votes shall be taken by states, the representation from each state having one vote; a quorum for this purpose shall consist of a member or members from two-thirds of the states, and a majority of all the states shall be necessary to a choice. And if the House of Representatives shall not choose a President whenever the right of choice shall devolve upon them, before the fourth day of March next following, then the Vice-President shall act as President, as in the case of the death or other constitutional disability of the President.—The person having the greatest number of votes as Vice-President, shall be the Vice-President, if such number be a majority of the whole number of Electors appointed, and if no person have a majority, then from the two highest numbers on the list, the Senate shall choose the Vice-President; a quorum for the purpose shall consist of two-thirds of the whole number of Senators, and a majority of the whole number shall be necessary to a choice. But no person constitutionally ineligible to the office of President shall be eligible to that of Vice-President of the United States.

AMENDMENT XIII[12]

SECTION 1 Neither slavery nor involuntary servitude, except as a punishment for crime whereof the party shall have been duly convicted, shall exist within the United States, or any place subject to their jurisdiction.

SECTION 2 Congress shall have power to enforce this article by appropriate legislation.

AMENDMENT XIV[13]

SECTION 1 All persons born or naturalized in the United States, and subject to the jurisdiction thereof, are citizens of the United States and of the State wherein they reside. No State shall make or enforce any law which shall abridge the privileges or immunities of citizens of the United States; nor shall any State deprive any person of life, liberty, or property, without due process of law; nor deny to any person within its jurisdiction the equal protection of the laws.

SECTION 2 Representatives shall be apportioned among the several States according to their respective numbers, counting the whole number of persons in each State, excluding Indians not taxed. But when the right to vote at any election for the choice of electors for President and Vice-President of the United States, Representatives in Congress, the Executive and Judicial officers of a State, or the members of the Legislature thereof, is denied to any of the male inhabitants of such State, being twenty-one years of age, and citizens of the United States, or in any way abridged, except for participation in rebellion, or other crime, the basis of representation therein shall be reduced in the proportion which the number of such male citizens shall bear to the whole number of male citizens twenty-one years of age in such State.

[10]Passed March 4, 1794. Ratified January 23, 1795.
[11]Passed December 9, 1803. Ratified June 15, 1804.

[12]Passed January 31, 1865. Ratified December 6, 1865.
[13]Passed June 13, 1866. Ratified July 9, 1868.

SECTION 3 No person shall be a Senator or Representative in Congress, or elector of President and Vice-President, or hold any office, civil or military, under the United States, or under any State, who, having previously taken an oath, as a member of Congress, or as an officer of the United States, or as a member of any State legislature, or as an executive or judicial officer of any State, to support the Constitution of the United States, shall have engaged in insurrection or rebellion against the same, or given aid or comfort to the enemies thereof. But Congress may by a vote of two-thirds of each House, remove such disability.

SECTION 4 The validity of the public debt of the United States, authorized by law, including debts incurred for payment of pensions and bounties for services in suppressing insurrection or rebellion, shall not be questioned. But neither the United States nor any State shall assume or pay any debt or obligation incurred in aid of insurrection or rebellion against the United States, or any claim for the loss or emancipation of any slave; but all such debts, obligations, and claims shall be held illegal and void.

SECTION 5 The Congress shall have the power to enforce, by appropriate legislation, the provisions of this article.

Amendment XV[14]

SECTION 1 The right of citizens of the United States to vote shall not be denied or abridged by the United States or by any State on account of race, color, or previous conditions of servitude—

SECTION 2 The Congress shall have power to enforce this article by appropriate legislation.

Amendment XVI[15]

The Congress shall have power to lay and collect taxes on incomes, from whatever source derived, without apportionment among the several States, and without regard to any census or enumeration.

Amendment XVII[16]

The Senate of the United States shall be composed of two Senators from each State, elected by the people thereof, for six years; and each Senator shall have one vote. The electors in each State shall have the qualifications requisite for electors of the most numerous branch of the State legislatures.

When vacancies happen in the representation of any State in the Senate, the executive authority of such State shall issue writs of election to fill such vacancies: *Provided,* That the legislature of any State may empower the executive thereof to make temporary appointments until the people fill the vacancies by election as the legislature may direct.

This amendment shall not be so construed as to affect the election or term of any Senator chosen before it becomes valid as part of the Constitution.

Amendment XVIII[17]

SECTION 1 After one year from the ratification of this article the manufacture, sale, or transportation of intoxicating liquors within, the importation thereof into, or the exportation thereof from the United States and all territory subject to the jurisdiction thereof for beverage purposes is hereby prohibited.

SECTION 2 The Congress and the several States shall have concurrent power to enforce this article by appropriate legislation.

SECTION 3 This article shall be inoperative unless it shall have been ratified as an amendment to the Constitution by the legislatures of the several States, as provided in the Constitution, within seven years from the date of the submission hereof to the States by the Congress.

Amendment XIX[18]

SECTION 1 The right of citizens of the United States to vote shall not be denied or abridged by the United States or by any State on account of sex.

Congress shall have power to enforce this article by appropriate legislation.

Amendment XX[19]

SECTION 1 The terms of the President and Vice-President shall end at noon on the 20th day of January, and the terms of Senators and Representatives at noon on the 3rd day of January, of the years in which such terms would have ended if this article had not been ratified; and the terms of their successors shall then begin.

SECTION 2 The Congress shall assemble at least once in every year, and such meeting shall begin at noon on the 3rd day of January, unless they shall by law appoint a different day.

SECTION 3 If, at the time fixed for the beginning of the term of the President, the President elect shall have died, the Vice-President elect shall become President. If a President shall not have been chosen before the time fixed for the beginning of his term, or if the President elect shall have failed to qualify, then the Vice-President elect shall act as President until a President shall have qualified; and the Congress may by law provide for the case wherein neither a President elect nor a Vice-President elect shall have qualified, declaring who shall then act as President, or the manner in which one who is to act shall be selected,

[14]Passed February 26, 1869. Ratified February 2, 1870.
[15]Passed July 12, 1909. Ratified February 3, 1913.
[16]Passed May 13, 1912. Ratified April 8, 1913.

[17]Passed December 18, 1917. Ratified January 16, 1919.
[18]Passed June 4, 1919. Ratified August 18, 1920.
[19]Passed March 2, 1932. Ratified January 23, 1933.

and such person shall act accordingly until a President or Vice-President shall have qualified.

SECTION 4 The Congress may by law provide for the case of the death of any of the persons from whom the House of Representatives may choose a President whenever the right of choice shall have devolved upon them, and for the case of the death of any of the persons from whom the Senate may choose a Vice-President whenever the right of choice shall have devolved upon them.

SECTION 5 Sections 1 and 2 shall take effect on the 15th day of October following the ratification of this article.

SECTION 6 This article shall be inoperative unless it shall have been ratified as an amendment to the Constitution by the legislatures of three-fourths of the several States within seven years from the date of its submission.

AMENDMENT XXI[20]

SECTION 1 The eighteenth article of amendment to the Constitution of the United States is hereby repealed.

SECTION 2 The transportation or importation into any State, Territory, or possession of the United States for delivery or use therein of intoxicating liquors, in violation of the laws thereof, is hereby prohibited.

SECTION 3 This article shall be inoperative unless it shall have been ratified as an amendment to the Constitution by conventions in the several States, as provided in the Constitution, within seven years from the date of the submission hereof to the States by the Congress.

AMENDMENT XXII[21]

No person shall be elected to the office of the President more than twice, and no person who has held the office of President, or acted as President, for more than two years of a term to which some other person was elected President shall be elected to the office of the President more than once.

But this Article shall not apply to any person holding the office of President when this Article was proposed by the Congress, and shall not prevent any person who may be holding the office of President, or acting as President, during the term within which this Article becomes operative from holding the office of President or acting as President during the remainder of such term.

AMENDMENT XXIII[22]

SECTION 1 The District constituting the seat of Government of the United States shall appoint in such manner as the Congress may direct:

A number of electors of President and Vice President equal to the whole number of Senators and Representatives

in Congress to which the District would be entitled if it were a State, but in no event more than the least populous State; they shall be in addition to those appointed by the States, but they shall be considered, for the purposes of the election of President and Vice President, to be electors appointed by the State; and they shall meet in the District and perform such duties as provided by the twelfth article of amendment.

SECTION 2 The Congress shall have power to enforce this article by appropriate legislation.

AMENDMENT XXIV[23]

SECTION 1 The right of citizens of the United States to vote in any primary or other election for President or Vice President, or for Senator or Representative in Congress, shall not be denied or abridged by the United States or any State by reason of failure to pay any poll tax or other tax.

SECTION 2 The Congress shall have power to enforce this article by appropriate legislation.

AMENDMENT XXV[24]

SECTION 1 In case of the removal of the President from office or of his death or resignation, the Vice President shall become President.

SECTION 2 Whenever there is a vacancy in the office of the Vice President, the President shall nominate a Vice President who shall take office upon confirmation by a majority vote of both Houses of Congress.

SECTION 3 Whenever the President transmits to the President pro tempore of the Senate and the Speaker of the House of Representatives his written declaration that he is unable to discharge the powers and duties of his office, and until he transmits them a written declaration to the contrary, such powers and duties shall be discharged by the Vice President as Acting President.

SECTION 4 Whenever the Vice President and a majority of either the principal officers of the executive department or of such other body as Congress may by law provide, transmit to the President pro tempore of the Senate and the Speaker of the House of Representatives their written declaration that the President is unable to discharge the powers and duties of his office, the Vice President shall immediately assume the powers and duties of the office of Acting President.

Thereafter, when the President transmits to the President pro tempore of the Senate and the Speaker of the House of Representatives his written declaration that no inability exists, he shall resume the powers and duties of his office unless the Vice President and a majority of either the principal officers of the executive department or of

---

[20]Passed February 20, 1933. Ratified Decembet 5, 1933.
[21]Passed March 12, 1947. Ratified March 1, 1951.
[22]Passed June 16, 1960. Ratified April 3, 1961.

[23]Passed August 27, 1962. Ratified January 23, 1964.
[24]Passed July 6, 1965. Ratified February 11, 1967.

such other body as Congress may by law provide, transmit within four days to the President pro tempore of the Senate and the Speaker of the House of Representatives their written declaration that the President is unable to discharge the powers and duties of his office. Thereupon Congress shall decide the issue, assembling within forty-eight hours for that purpose if not in session. If the Congress, within twenty-one days after receipt of the latter written declaration, or, if Congress is not in session, within twenty-one days after Congress is required to assemble, determines by two-thirds vote of both Houses that the President is unable to discharge the powers and duties of his office, the Vice-President shall continue to discharge the same as Acting President; otherwise, the President shall resume the powers and duties of his office.

Amendment XXVI[25]

SECTION 1 The right of citizens of the United States, who are eighteen years of age or older, to vote shall not be denied or abridged by the United States or by any State on account of age.

SECTION 2 The Congress shall have power to enforce this article by appropriate legislation.

Amendment XXVII[26]

No law, varying the compensation for the service of the Senators and Representatives, shall take effect, until an election of Representatives shall have intervened.

---

[25]Passed March 23, 1971. Ratified July 5, 1971.
[26]Passed September 25, 1789. Ratified May 7, 1992.

GLOSSARY

Ácoma Town located in New Mexico on a mesa west of the Rio Grande. When the Pueblos defended Ácoma in 1598, the Spanish killed many people, took the survivors prisoner, and destroyed the town.

Adams, John (1735–1826) First vice president (1789–1797) and second president (1797–1801) of the United States. He was a major figure during the American Revolution: he helped draft the Declaration of Independence and served on the commission to negotiate the Treaty of Paris (1783).

Adams-Onis Treaty (1819) Negotiated by John Quincy Adams, this treaty gave the United States control of Spanish Florida and the Oregon Territory, and recognized Spanish authority over southwestern territories from Texas to California.

African American soldiers Finally allowed to enlist in May 1863, African American soldiers accounted for more than one hundred eighty thousand troops and played a major role in the Union victory.

Agricultural Adjustment Act (AAA) (1933) Created under Roosevelt's New Deal program to help farmers, its purpose was to reduce production of staple crops, thereby raising farm prices and encouraging more diversified farming.

Albany Plan of Union (1754) Plan proposed to the Albany Congress of 1754 by Benjamin Franklin to unite the colonies for common defense. The Congress approved the design for an intercolonial government empowered to tax, pass laws, and supervise military defense, but the colonies and British government rejected it.

Allen, Richard (1760–1831) Reverend Allen was a former slave who founded the African Methodist Episcopal church and was a leader of the Philadelphia black community.

American Colonization Society Founded in 1816 to colonize freed slaves on land purchased in Africa and called "Liberia." Members included white slaveholders and opponents of slavery, as well as free African Americans.

American System Political program developed by Henry Clay and John C. Calhoun to strengthen the federal government and promote commerce and industry through a national bank, a strong navy, federally sponsored internal improvement projects, and protective tariffs.

Amistad Cuban slave ship on which forty-nine Africans rebelled in 1839 off the Cuban coast. The ship sailed to Long Island Sound where Spanish authorities demanded they be turned over for punishment. A group of American abolitionists, led by former President John Quincy Adams, won their freedom in 1841. The thirty-five who survived returned to Africa.

Amos 'n' Andy The most popular radio program of the Depression years, it portrayed the lives of two African American men in Harlem as interpreted by two white entertainers, Freeman Gosden and Charles Correll.

Anaconda Plan Term given to the strategy employed by the North during the Civil War in which the Confederacy would be slowly strangled by a blockade.

Anderson, Marian (1897–1993) Opera singer and human rights advocate, she performed on the steps of the Lincoln Memorial before a crowd of seventy-five thousand after being denied the use of Constitution Hall by the Daughters of the American Revolution. She helped focus national attention on the racial prejudice faced by African Americans in all facets of national life.

Andros, Sir Edmund (1637–1714) English colonial administrator in America whose attempt to unify the New England colonies under his governorship (1686–1689) was met by revolt.

annexation of Texas (1845) Incorporation of Texas into the United States as the twenty-eighth state. The Republic of Texas invited U.S. annexation following the Texas Revolution but annexation was delayed by disputes with Mexico. Annexation was hotly debated among supporters and opponents of slavery's expansion.

Anthony, Susan B. (1820–1906) Advocate of woman's suffrage and leader in the woman's rights movement along with Elizabeth Cady Stanton.

Antietam, battle of (1862) Civil War battle near Sharpsburg, Maryland, in September 1862 in which the Union Army stopped the Confederacy's drive into the North. With twenty-five thousand casualties, it was the bloodiest single-day battle of the Civil War.

Appomattox Small Virginia town where Confederate forces under Robert E. Lee surrendered to Ulysses S. Grant on April 9, 1865, generally recognized as bringing the Civil War to an end.

Armstrong, Louis (1901–1971) A trumpeter and a major innovator of jazz.

Articles of Confederation (1781) First Constitution of the United States. Adopted by the original thirteen states in 1781, it remained the supreme law until 1789.

Atlanta Compromise (1895) Speech by Booker T. Washington outlining a program for African American self-help, industrial education, and acceptance of white supremacy.

Atlantic Charter (1941) Composed during a meeting between President Franklin Roosevelt and British Prime Minister Winston Churchill, it listed eight principles for a better world, such as freedom from fear and want, self-determination for all people, and the disarming of aggressor nations. Many see the Atlantic Charter as a guiding force behind the establishment of the United Nations following World War II.

Atlantic slave trade In the 1440s Portugal initiated the trans-Atlantic trade that lasted four centuries. During that time, other European nations participated in a commerce that took more than 10 million people from Africa.

Austin, Stephen F. (1793–1836) Virginian who led efforts to settle U.S. citizens in Texas, negotiated with the Mexican and U.S. governments, commanded Texas forces in the early period of the Texas Revolution, and served as secretary of state for the Republic of Texas.

Aztecs Inhabitants of the Valley of Mexico who founded their capital, Tenochtitlán, in the early fourteenth century. Prior to the arrival of the Spanish, the Aztecs built a large empire in which they dominated many neighboring peoples. Their civilization included engineering, mathematics, art, and music.

baby boom (1946–1964) Increased numbers of births in the years after World War II.

Bacon's Rebellion (1676) Colonial revolt led by Nathaniel Bacon, in which landless freemen attacked neighboring Indians and burned Jamestown in an attempt to gain land and greater participation in the Virginia government.

Bank of North America (1781) The first bank in the United States, modeled on the Bank of England, helped to solve the wartime fiscal crisis. Instead of issuing paper currency through a land office, as farmers wanted, the bank issued money in the form of short-term loans backed by gold and silver plate.

Bank of the United States (1791–1811) National bank established as part of the system proposed by Alexander Hamilton to hold the federal government's funds and regulate state banks. Its chief purpose was to expand the money supply, thus encouraging commercial growth.

Bank War (1832–1834) Attacks by President Andrew Jackson on the Second Bank of the United States. By vetoing the renewal of the bank's charter and removing federal funds to state banks, he effectively destroyed the central bank.

Bataan Peninsula U.S. and Filipino World War II troops surrendered this peninsula in western Luzon, Philippines, to the Japanese in April 1942 after an extended siege; U.S. forces recaptured the peninsula in February 1945.

Bay of Pigs (1961) Place where fifteen hundred Cuban exiles, supported by the CIA, landed on April 17, 1961, in an unsuccessful attempt to overthrow the new Communist government of Fidel Castro.

Bell, Alexander Graham (1847–1922) His invention of the telephone in 1876 changed the nature of life in the United States.

Bell, John (1797–1869) Tennessee-born slaveholder who became the presidential candidate of the Constitutional Union Party, which was founded as a compromise party in 1860.

Bellamy, Edward (1850–1898) Reporter and novelist, the author of the popular utopian novel *Looking Backward* (1888).

Bethune, Mary McLeod (1875–1955) An educator who sought improved racial relations and educational opportunities for black Americans, she was part of the U.S. delegation to the first United Nations meeting (1945).

Bill of Rights (1791) The first ten amendments to the Constitution. These contain basic protection of the rights of individuals from abuses by the federal government, including freedom of speech, press, religion, and assembly.

bin Laden, Osama (1957–) Saudi-born Islamic radical who masterminded the September 11, 2001, terrorist attacks on the United States.

Birth of a Nation, The (1915) Racist movie portrayal of the Reconstruction period in the South that depicted African Americans as ignorant and that glamorized the Ku Klux Klan.

black codes (colonial) Laws passed by colonial assemblies to define slavery and control the black population.

Black Power A movement for black racial pride in the 1960s that advocated all-black institutions, not racially integrated ones, as the best vehicles for advancing African American objectives.

Black Thursday October 29, 1929; the day the spectacular New York stock market crash began.

Bleeding Kansas Nickname given to the Kansas Territory in the wake of a number of clashes between proslavery and antislavery supporters in 1856.

blockade runners During the Civil War, ships that smuggled war supplies and imported goods into the Confederacy during the Union blockade of its coastline.

bloggers Commentators who post their views on the Internet; derived from the word *weblog*. They became influential in the political process because of the speed with which they could respond to breaking events in politics and international affairs.

Blount, William (1749–1800) Governor of the Tennessee Territory and a land speculator the Indians called "dirt king" who, after the Treaty of 1791, ignored President George Washington's guarantee to the Cherokees that they could retain their remaining lands.

Board of Trade and Plantations English government body established in 1696 to gather information and give advice about the colonies.

Bonus Army Thousands of veterans, determined to collect promised cash bonuses early, came to Washington during the summer of 1932 to listen to Congress debate the bonus proposal.

Booth, John Wilkes (1838–1865) An actor and Southern sympathizer who assassinated Abraham Lincoln on April 14, 1865.

bootleggers Enterprising individuals who moved alcohol across the border into the United States from Canada and the Caribbean during Prohibition. Their wares were sold at illegal saloons or "speakeasies" where city dwellers congregated in the evenings.

border ruffians Missouri settlers who crossed into Kansas to lend support for proslavery issues (1855).

Boss Politics Urban "political machines" that relied for their existence on the votes of the large inner-city population. The flow of money through the machine was often based on corruption.

Boston Massacre (1770) Pre-Revolutionary incident growing out of the resentment against the British troops sent to Boston to maintain order and to enforce the Townshend Act.

brain trust Group of prominent academics recruited as a source of ideas for the Franklin Roosevelt presidential campaign.

bread riots (1863) Riots in Richmond and other Southern cities, that occurred when poor women attacked the shops of merchants accused of hoarding food in order to profit from wartime inflation.

Breckinridge, John C. (1821–1875) Born in Kentucky, vice president under James Buchanan (1857–1861), and presidential candidate of the Southern wing of the Democratic Party in 1860.

Brown v. Board of Education of Topeka (1954) Unanimous Supreme Court decision ruling that segregated facilities in public education were "inherently unequal" and violated the Fourteenth Amendment's guarantee of equal protection under the law. This decision overruled the long-standing "separate but equal" doctrine of *Plessy v. Ferguson*.

Brown, John (1800–1859) American abolitionist who, in 1859 with twenty-one followers, captured the U.S. arsenal at Harpers Ferry as part of an effort to liberate Southern slaves. His group was defeated, and Brown was hanged after a trial in which he won sympathy as an abolitionist martyr.

Bryan, William Jennings (1860–1925) Democratic presidential candidate in 1896, 1900, and 1908. Named secretary of state by President Wilson, he pursued world peace through arbitration treaties.

Buchanan, James (1791–1868) Fifteenth president of the United States (1857–1861). He tried to maintain a balance between proslavery and antislavery factions, but his views angered radicals in both the North and South.

Bush, George H. W. (1924–) Forty-first president of the United States (1989–1993), he was in office when the Soviet Union collapsed.

Bush, George W. (1946–) Forty-third president of the United States (2001–2009).

Calhoun, John C. (1782–1850) Vice president of the United States (1825–1832) under John Quincy Adams and Andrew Jackson. In his political philosophy he maintained that the states had the right to nullify federal legislation that they deemed unconstitutional.

Calvin, John (1509–1564) French-born Swiss Protestant theologian who broke with the Roman Catholic Church (1533) and set forth the tenets of his theology, the Reformed tradition including Puritans, Huguenots, Presbyterians, and Dutch Reformed, in *Institutes of the Christian Religion* (1536).

Camp David Accords (1978) Treaty between Egypt and Israel, brokered by President Carter at Camp David, that returned the Sinai Peninsula to Egypt in return for Egypt's recognition of the state of Israel.

Capone, Alphonse "Al" (1899–1947) Chicago gangster; devoted to gaining control of gambling, prostitution, and bootlegging.

Carnegie, Andrew (1835–1919) Scottish-born industrialist and philanthropist, he played a major role in the evolution of the U.S. steel industry.

Carter, James Earl (Jimmy) (1924–) Thirty-ninth president of the United States (1977–1981), his successes in office, including the Camp David Accords, were overshadowed by domestic worries and the seizure of American hostages at the U.S. Embassy in Iran. He was defeated by Ronald Reagan in 1980.

Castro, Fidel (1927–) Cuban revolutionary leader who overthrew dictator Fulgencio Batista in 1959 and soon after established a Communist state. Prime minister of Cuba from 1959 to 1976, he served as president of the

government and First Secretary of the Communist Party from 1976 to 2008.

Catt, Carrie Chapman (1859–1947) Woman suffrage leader; president of the National American Woman Suffrage Association (1900–1906).

Census of 1790, U.S. To fulfill the constitutional requirement for a decennial census, Congress ordered a population count to provide an accurate enumeration for apportioning delegates to the House of Representatives and electoral college.

Champlain, Samuel de (1567–1635) Founder of New France (now Canada), with a temporary base at Port Royal on the Bay of Fundy in 1605 and the main settlement at Quebec on the St. Lawrence River in 1608.

***Charles River Bridge* case (1837)** Supreme Court decision that state charters for internal improvements such as bridges did not imply monopolies; marked a shift toward the definition of economic development as a public good.

Chavez, Cesar (1927–1993) Labor organizer who founded the National Farm Workers Association in 1962.

Chickamaugas Militant Cherokees who allied with Creeks and Shawnees against settlers along the frontier from Kentucky to Georgia during the 1780s and early 1790s.

Churchill, Sir Winston (1874–1965) British politician and writer. As prime minister (1940–1945 and 1951–1955) he led Great Britain through World War II. He published several books, including *The Second World War* (1948–1953), and won the 1953 Nobel Prize for literature.

Civil Works Administration (CWA) The agency tasked with creating jobs and restoring self-respect by handing out pay envelopes instead of relief checks. In reality, workers sometimes performed worthless tasks, known as "boondoggles," but much of the $1 billion budget was spent on projects of lasting value including airports and roads.

Civilian Conservation Corps (CCC) One of the New Deal's most popular programs, it took unemployed young men from the cities and put them to work on conservation projects in the country.

Clay, Henry (1777–1852) American statesman and a founder of the Whig party. He pushed the Missouri Compromise through the U.S. House of Representatives (1820) in an effort to reconcile free and slave states and served

as secretary of state under John Quincy Adams (1825–1829).

Cleveland, Grover (1837–1908) Twenty-second and twenty-fourth president of the United States (1885–1889 and 1893–1897), he was the first Democrat elected to the presidency after the Civil War.

climate change Term used by scientists to describe the result of the global warming caused by human activity, especially the burning of fossil fuels.

Clinton, William Jefferson ("Bill") (1946–) Forty-second president of the United States (1993–2001). He secured passage of the North American Free Trade Agreement (NAFTA) in 1993 and welfare reform in 1996. Impeached for perjury and obstruction of justice in 1998, he was acquitted by the Senate in 1999.

Coercive Acts (1774) Passed by the British Parliament in 1774 in response to the Boston Tea Party, the acts closed the port of Boston, limited the power of town meetings, expanded the governor's control over the courts, and permitted quartering of British troops in private buildings.

Cold War State of intense geopolitical rivalry, such as existed between the United States and the Soviet Union following World War II, that stopped short of full-scale military conflict.

Columbus, Christopher (1451–1506) Italian mariner who sailed for Spain in 1492 in search of a western route to Asia. He located San Salvador in the West Indies, opening the Americas to European exploration and colonization.

***Common Sense* (1776)** Published by Thomas Paine in January 1776, *Common Sense* convinced the American public of the need for independence.

Compromise of 1850 Congressional compromise intended to balance demands among slave and free states. It admitted California as a free state but left the question of slavery open in other new territories; abolished the slave trade in Washington, D.C., but kept slavery legal there; declared that Congress had no power to regulate the interstate slave trade; and created a stronger fugitive slave law.

Conscription Act (1863) Union act instituting military draft; service could be avoided by hiring a substitute or paying a fee.

Constitutional Convention (1787) Fifty-five delegates met in

Philadelphia in May 1787 to reform the U.S. government. They chose to draft a new constitution rather than revise the Articles of Confederation.

containment U.S. national security doctrine during the Cold War. Attributed to State Department officer George Kennan, containment came to define America's political-military strategy for confronting Soviet expansion.

contrabands During the Civil War, term for slaves who made their way to Union lines. By defining the refugees as "contrabands of war," a term used to describe property that could be used in a war effort and was thus subject to confiscation, Union leaders justified the decision not to return escaped slaves to their masters.

Contras Nicaraguan military force trained and financed by the United States that opposed the socialist Nicaraguan government led by the Sandinista party.

Convention of 1800 Negotiated with France by a three-man commission appointed by President John Adams, the convention echoed provisions of the 1778 commercial treaty but voided the defensive alliance, thus eliminating the French claim to U.S. support against Great Britain.

Copperheads Derogatory term used by some Republicans to refer to Peace Democrats, implying that they were traitors to the Union. Peace Democrats thought that the war was a failure and should be abandoned.

Cortés, Hernán (1485–1547) Spanish explorer who conquered the Aztecs initially in 1519, retreated when they rebelled, then defeated them again, aided by a smallpox epidemic, in 1521.

Cotton South Southeastern United States; became a major cotton-producing region following the invention of the cotton gin in 1793 and the eviction of Native Americans from their lands in the decades after 1815. The spread of cotton cultivation led to the development of a vast interstate slave trade.

Crane, Stephen (1871–1900) American naturalist writer, author of *Maggie: A Girl of the Streets* (1893) and *The Red Badge of Courage* (1895).

Crazy Horse (1842?–1877) Native American Sioux leader who defeated George Custer in battle.

Creole Slaving ship sailing from Virginia to New Orleans in 1841 when it was seized by captives and sailed to the Bahamas, a British colony. Britain, which had recently emancipated its own slaves, gave sanctuary to the slaves.

Custer, George Armstrong (1839–1876) Lieutenant colonel famous for his defeat at Little Big Horn by the Sioux Indians.

Dale's Laws (1611) Governor Thomas Dale of Jamestown in 1611 established his "Laws Divine, Morall and Martiall" to bring the colony under control. The harsh punishments became a scandal in England and discouraged emigration.

Davis, Jefferson (1808–1889) United States senator, secretary of war, and then president of the Confederacy (1861–1865). He was captured by Union soldiers in 1865 and imprisoned for two years. Although he was indicted for treason (1866), he was never prosecuted.

Dawes Severalty Act (1887) Congressional legislation that distributed land to the Indians so that it could eventually be sold to whites.

Declaration of Independence (1776) The document, drafted primarily by Thomas Jefferson, that declared the independence of the thirteen mainland colonies from Great Britain and enumerated their reasons for separating.

détente An easing of tensions among countries, which usually leads to increased economic, diplomatic, and other types of contacts between former rivals.

Dix, Dorothea (1802–1887) American philanthropist, reformer, and educator who took charge of nurses for the United States during the Civil War.

dollar diplomacy Term for Secretary of State Philander C. Knox's foreign policy under President Taft, which focused on expanding American investments abroad, especially in Latin America and China.

Dominion of New England In an effort to centralize the colonies and create consistent laws and political structures, James II combined Massachusetts, New Hampshire, Maine, Plymouth, Rhode Island, Connecticut, New York, and New Jersey into the Dominion of New England.

domino theory A theory that if one nation comes under Communist control, neighboring nations will soon follow.

Douglas, Stephen A. (1813–1861) American politician who served as U.S. representative (1843–1847) and senator (1847–1861) from Illinois. He proposed legislation that allowed individual territories to determine whether they would allow slavery (1854), and in the senatorial campaign of 1858 he engaged Abraham Lincoln in a famous series of debates.

Douglass, Frederick (1817–1895) American abolitionist and journalist who escaped from slavery (1838) and became an influential lecturer in the North and abroad. He wrote *Narrative of the Life of Frederick Douglass* (1845) and cofounded and edited the *North Star* (1847–1860), an abolitionist newspaper.

Drake, Sir Francis (1540–1596) English naval hero and explorer who was the first Englishman to circumnavigate the world (1577–1580) and was vice admiral of the fleet that destroyed the Spanish Armada (1588).

Dred Scott **case (1857)** An enslaved man sued for his freedom in 1847, leading to a crucial Supreme Court decision in 1857 in which the Court ruled that African Americans held no rights as citizens and that the Missouri Compromise of 1820 was unconstitutional. The decision was widely denounced in the North and strengthened the new Republican party.

Du Bois, W. E. B. (1868–1963) Initially a supporter of Booker T. Washington's education policy, he later criticized Washington's methods as having "practically accepted the alleged inferiority of the Negro."

Dust Bowl The name given to areas of the prairie states that suffered ecological devastation in the 1930s and then again to a lesser extent in the mid-1950s.

Dutch West India Company Chartered in 1621 by the Dutch government to establish commerce and colonies in America. It received broad powers, including the rights to make war and sign treaties.

Eaton, Peggy (1799–1879) Wife of John Eaton and the central figure in a controversy that divided President Jackson's cabinet into pro- and anti-Eaton factions.

Edison, Thomas Alva (1847–1931) The inventor of the phonograph, electric lights, and countless other products.

Eighteenth Amendment (1919) Constitutional amendment that barred the production and sale of alcoholic beverages. Its adoption represented the national high point of the prohibition movement.

Eisenhower, Dwight D. (1890–1969) U.S. general and thirty-fourth president of the United States (1953–1961). As supreme commander of the Allied Expeditionary Force in World War II, he launched the invasion of Normandy (June 6, 1944) and oversaw the defeat of Germany in 1945.

election of 1840 Whig innovations in campaign slogans, large rallies, and efforts to involve women supporters in this election marked a new style of political campaigning. The election, between Democrat Martin Van Buren and the Whig party's William Henry Harrison, was won by Harrison.

electoral college The group that elects the president. Each state received as many electors as it had congressmen and senators combined.

Elizabeth I (1533–1603) Queen of England (1558–1603), she succeeded the Catholic Mary I and reestablished Protestantism in England. Her reign was marked by several plots to overthrow her, the execution of Mary, Queen of Scots (1587), the defeat of the Spanish Armada (1588), and domestic prosperity and literary achievement.

Ellis Island Immigration station in New York Harbor, opened in 1892, where new arrivals were given a medical examination and questioned about their economic prospects.

emancipation The ending of slavery, initiated in the Emancipation Proclamation of 1863 but not accomplished in many places until the Confederate surrender in 1865.

Embargo Act (1807) Passed by Congress in response to British restrictions on U.S. trade and impressment of American sailors, the act prohibited exportation to all other countries. The policy had serious economic repercussions and was widely violated.

Emerson, Ralph Waldo (1803–1882) American writer, philosopher, and central figure of American transcendentalism. His poems, orations, and especially his essays, such as *Nature* (1836), are regarded as landmarks in the development of American thought and literary expression.

enclosure movement Economic process in which English landlords ended leases for tenant farmers living on their lands, confiscating common fields that peasant communities had shared for grazing their livestock and raising crops.

Enlightenment Philosophical movement of the eighteenth century that emphasized the use of reason to scrutinize previously accepted doctrines and traditions and that brought about many humanitarian reforms.

Enola Gay The B-29 bomber, named after the mother of pilot Colonel Paul W. Tibbets, that dropped the first atomic bomb on the Japanese city of Hiroshima on August 6, 1945, killing more than one hundred thousand people.

Equal Rights Amendment (ERA) Congress overwhelmingly passed the Equal Rights Amendment in 1972, but by the mid-1970s conservative groups had managed to stall its confirmation by the states.

Era of Good Feelings Period in U.S. history (1817–1823) when, the Federalist party having declined, there was little open party feeling.

Erie Canal First major American canal, stretching two hundred fifty miles from Lake Erie across the state of New York to Albany, where boats then traveled down the Hudson River to New York City. Begun in 1818, it was completed in 1825.

Evans, Oliver (1755–1819) American inventor who developed the first application of steam power in an industrial setting. He also developed a method of automating flour mills that had become standard in U.S. mills a generation later.

Farmers' Alliance First started as local groups of angry farmers in Texas during the 1880s, these alliances spread across the South and West and eventually formed into the Farmers' Alliance and Industrial Union in 1889. The Alliance was a forerunner of Populism.

Faubus, Orval (1910–1994) Governor of Arkansas in 1957 who triggered a confrontation between national authority and states' rights by defying a federal court order to integrate the all-white Little Rock Central High School.

Federalist, The Alexander Hamilton, James Madison, and John Jay wrote a series of eighty-five essays in support of the Constitution. First published in newspapers, they appeared in book form as *The Federalist* in the spring of 1788.

Federalists Name assumed by the supporters of the U.S. Constitution of 1787 during the contest for ratification. Also the group supporting policies of Alexander Hamilton that evolved into a political party during the 1790s.

Fillmore, Millard (1800–1874) Thirteenth president of the United States (1850–1853), who succeeded to office after the death of Zachary Taylor. He struggled to keep the nation unified but lost the support of his Whig party.

Finney, Charles Grandison (1792–1875) American evangelist, theologian, and educator. Licensed to the Presbyterian ministry in 1824, he had phenomenal success as a revivalist in the Northeast, converting many who later became noted abolitionists.

fire-eaters Before the Civil War, Southerners who enthusiastically supported Southern rights and, later, secession.

Fitzgerald, F. Scott (1896–1940) Jazz Age novelist; author of *The Great Gatsby* (1925). He and his wife Zelda embodied the free spirit of the Jazz Age.

Ford, Gerald R. (1913–) Thirty-eighth president of the United States (1974–1977), he was appointed vice president when Spiro Agnew resigned and became president when Richard Nixon resigned over the Watergate scandal. As president, Ford granted a full pardon to Nixon in 1974.

Fort Sumter Fort in the harbor of Charleston, South Carolina, that was fired on by the Confederacy on April 12, 1861, triggering the Civil War.

Fort Wagner Fort guarding the approach to Charleston Harbor, South Carolina. In the Union assault on July 18, 1863, nearly half of the 54th Massachusetts Volunteers leading the attack were killed, but their courage helped convince the North to continue recruiting African American soldiers.

forty-niners Prospectors and others, mostly men, lured to California by the gold rush of 1849.

forty-ninth parallel Line of latitude established as the border between the United States and Canada by the Treaty of 1818; extended to the Pacific by President Polk's secret negotiation of the Oregon Treaty in 1846.

Franciscan priests Members of the Roman Catholic order of Saint Francis of Assisi; they served as missionaries in colonial Spanish America.

Franklin, Benjamin (1706–1790) American public official, writer, scientist, and printer. He proposed a plan for union at the Albany Congress (1754) and played a major part in the American

Revolution. Franklin helped secure French support for the colonists, negotiated the Treaty of Paris (1783), and helped draft the Constitution (1787). His numerous scientific and practical innovations include the lightning rod, bifocal spectacles, and a stove.

Franz Ferdinand (1863–1914) Austrian archduke murdered along with his wife in Sarajevo, Bosnia. Austria's ultimatum to Serbia led to the outbreak of World War I.

Freed, Alan (1921–1965) The self-proclaimed father of rock 'n' roll, he was the first DJ to play black rhythm and blues artists on the radio.

Freedmen's Bureau Federal agency created in 1865 to supervise newly freed people. It oversaw relations between whites and blacks in the South, issued food rations, and supervised labor contracts.

freedom riders Interracial groups who rode buses in the South so that a series of federal court decisions declaring segregation on buses and in waiting rooms unconstitutional would not be ignored by white officials.

Free-Soil Party U.S. political party formed in 1848 to oppose the extension of slavery into the territories; merged with the Liberty Party in 1848.

Frémont, John C. (1813–1890) Republican presidential candidate in 1856; western explorer who had supported the Bear Flag Revolt in California during the Mexican-American War.

Friedan, Betty (1921–) Feminist who wrote *The Feminist Mystique* (1963) and founded the National Organization for Women in 1966.

Fugitive Slave Act (1850) Part of the Compromise of 1850, the federal law that provided for the return of escaped black slaves to their owners in the South.

fugitive slave clause (1787) Provision of the U.S. Constitution that prevented free states from emancipating slaves who had escaped from masters in other states.

Gadsden Purchase (1854) A piece of land, 29,670 square miles, purchased from Mexico in 1853 to provide a southern route for a transcontinental railroad; final extension of the southern U.S. border.

gag rule Congressional practice, starting in 1836, to ban consideration of antislavery petitions.

Garner, John Nance "Cactus Jack" (1868–1967) Speaker of the House in 1931 whose answer to the growing budget deficit was to offer a national sales tax. He ran against Roosevelt for the Democratic nomination for president but released his delegates and was in turn rewarded with the vice presidential nomination.

Garrison, William Lloyd (1805–1879) American abolitionist leader who founded the antislavery journal *The Liberator* (1831–1865).

Garvey, Marcus (1887–1940) Jamaican immigrant who promised to "organize the 400 million Negroes of the World into a vast organization to plant the banner of freedom in the great continent of Africa."

Genêt, Edmond (1763–1834) French ambassador who enlisted American mercenaries to assist the French against the British. Genêt's move threatened relations between the United States and Britain.

Geronimo (1829–1909) Apache leader who resisted white incursions until his capture in 1886.

Gettysburg Address (1863) Brief speech given by President Lincoln at the dedication of the Gettysburg Cemetery in November 1863 that declared that the Civil War was dedicated to freedom.

Gibbons v. Ogden **(1824)** Supreme Court case that overturned a steamboat monopoly granted to Robert Fulton and Robert Livingston by New York State. The decision established federal authority over interstate navigation, as an extension of the federal power to regulate interstate commerce.

Gilman, Charlotte Perkins (1860–1935) Feminist who advocated that women should seek economic independence; author of *Women and Economics* (1898).

Glenn, John (1921–) Astronaut, U.S. Senator (1974–1998). On February 20, 1962, aboard the *Friendship 7*, he was the first American to orbit the earth; in 1998 he was the oldest person to participate in a space flight mission as a member of the space shuttle *Discovery*.

globalization The process by which the world's economies are becoming more integrated and interdependent. Those affected by such changes have often protested against the political and economic dislocation that accompanies this trend.

Glorious Revolution (1688) English Revolution against the authoritarian policies and Catholicism of James II. The revolution secured the dominance of Parliament over royal power.

good neighbor policy A new Latin American policy wherein Hoover withdrew the Marines from Nicaragua and Haiti, and in 1930 the State Department renounced the Roosevelt Corollary of 1904.

Gorbachev, Mikhail (1931–) General secretary of the Soviet Communist party (1985–1990) and president of the USSR (1990–1991), he ushered in an era of glasnost (openness) and perestroika (restructuring), and won the Nobel Peace Prize in 1990.

Grant, Ulysses S. (1822–1885) U.S. general and eighteenth president of the United States (1869–1877). He commanded the Union Army during the Civil War.

Grapes of Wrath, The **(1939)** Novel by John Steinbeck depicting the struggle of ordinary Americans in the Great Depression, following the plight of the Joad family as it migrated west from Oklahoma to California.

Great Awakening Immense religious revival during the 1720s to the 1760s that swept across the Protestant world.

Great Compromise (1787) At the Constitutional Convention, plan proposed by the Connecticut delegation for a bicameral Congress with a House of Representatives, with representations based on a state's population, and the Senate, in which each state would be represented equally. Also known as the Connecticut Compromise.

Great Migration A massive movement of blacks leaving the South for cities in the North that began slowly in 1910 and accelerated between 1914 and 1920. During this time, more than six hundred thousand African Americans left the South.

Greeley, Horace (1811–1872) Grant's opponent in the 1872 election. Seen as a political oddball in the eyes of many Americans, the sixty-one-year-old editor favored the protective tariff and was indifferent to civil service reform. He was also passionate about vegetarianism and the use of human manure in farming.

greenbacks Paper currency issued by the Union under the Legal Tender Act of 1862, replacing the notes of individual banks with a unified national currency.

Grimké, Angelina (1805–1879) and Sarah (1792–1873) The first female abolitionist speakers; they were prominent figures in the antislavery movement of the late 1830s.

Gulf of Tonkin Resolution (1964) Following reports of a confrontation with North Vietnamese in the Tonkin Gulf in 1964, President Johnson requested, and received, congressional authority to "take all necessary measures" to repel "further aggression" in Vietnam, giving the president formal authority to escalate the war.

Gullah Creole tongue that evolved in the Lower South from English and various languages from southern Nigeria, the Gold Coast, Angola, and Senegambia.

Halfway Covenant The Puritan practice whereby parents who had been baptized but had not yet experienced conversion could bring their children before the church and have them baptized.

Hamer, Fannie Lou (1917–1977) Daughter of illiterate Mississippi sharecroppers, she helped lead the civil rights struggle in Mississippi, focusing on voting rights for African Americans and representation in the national Democratic party.

Hamilton, Alexander (1755–1804) First U.S. secretary of the treasury (1789–1795), he established the national bank and public credit system. In 1804 he was mortally wounded in a duel with his political rival Aaron Burr.

Handsome Lake (1735–1815) Seneca spiritual and political leader. He advocated peace, the U.S. acculturation policy, abstinence from drinking alcohol and practicing witchcraft, and return to ancestral rituals.

Harpers Ferry Virginia town that was the site of John Brown's raid in 1859, a failed attempt to lead a slave insurrection. It ignited public opinion in both the North and the South.

Harrison, Benjamin (1833–1901) Twenty-third president of the United States (1889–1893), he lost the popular vote but won a majority of the electoral college.

Harrison, William Henry (1773–1841) While governor of the Indiana Territory, he attacked and burned the nativist village of Prophetstown in 1811. The ninth president of the United States (1841), he died of pneumonia after one month in office.

Hartford Convention (1814) Gathering of Federalists in 1814 that called for

significant amendments to the Constitution and attempted to damage the Republican party. The Treaty of Ghent and Andrew Jackson's victory at New Orleans annulled any recommendation of the convention.

Hawthorne, Nathaniel (1804–1864) Massachusetts writer whose novels were mostly set in colonial New England, including *The Scarlet Letter* (1850) and *The House of Seven Gables* (1851).

Hayes, Rutherford B. (1822–1893) Nineteenth president of the United States (1877–1881), he won the most fiercely disputed election in American history.

Haymarket Riot On May 4, 1886, workmen in Chicago gathered to protest police conduct during a strike at a factory of the McCormick Company.

Hearst, William Randolph (1863–1951) The most celebrated publisher of yellow journalism.

Henry, Patrick (1736–1799) Elected to the Virginia House of Burgesses at age twenty-nine, Henry introduced fourteen resolves against the Stamp Act. He was a brilliant speaker and served as governor of Virginia during the Revolution.

Hill, Anita (1956–) Government lawyer and law professor who brought charges of sexual misconduct against Clarence Thomas during his confirmation hearings as Supreme Court justice in 1991.

Hiss, Alger (1904–1996) State Department official accused of espionage at the height of the Cold War, he was convicted of perjury in 1950 in a controversial case.

Ho Chi Minh (1890–1969) Vietnamese leader and first president of North Vietnam. His army was victorious in the French Indochina War, and he later led North Vietnam's struggle to defeat the U.S.-supported government of South Vietnam. He died before the reunification of Vietnam.

Homeland Security U.S. cabinet department established in 2002 to coordinate defense of the American nation.

Homestead strike (1892) Labor uprising of workers at a steel plant in Homestead, Pennsylvania, that was put down by military force.

Hoovervilles Makeshift "villages" usually at the edge of a city with "homes" made of cardboard, scrap metal, or whatever was cheap and available and named for President Hoover who was despised by the poor for his apparent refusal to help them.

Hopkins, Harry (1890–1946) Roosevelt's choice to run the Federal Emergency Relief Administration. He eventually became Roosevelt's closest adviser.

horizontal integration A procedure wherein a company takes over competitors to achieve control within an industry.

House Un-American Activities Committee (HUAC) Formed in the 1930s as a watchdog against Nazi propaganda, HUAC was revived after World War II as a watchdog against Communist propaganda.

Hudson River School Group of mid-nineteenth-century landscape painters, including Thomas Cole, Asher Durand, and Frederic Edwin Church, whose work was influenced by Romanticism and known for its stirring depictions of American landscapes.

Huerta, Victoriano (1854–1916) Mexican general and president (1913–1914). The United States did not recognize Huerta's government, and President Wilson ordered U.S. military intervention in support of his rival, Venustiano Carranza.

Hughes, Charles Evans (1862–1948) Governor of New York (1907–1910), Supreme Court justice (1910–1916), and Republican candidate for president in 1916, when he was defeated by Woodrow Wilson. He served as secretary of state under Presidents Harding and Coolidge (1921–1925) and returned to the Supreme Court as Chief Justice in 1930.

Hull House Settlement house founded in Chicago in 1889 by Jane Addams and Ellen Gates Starr to help solve the troubling problems of city life.

Hurston, Zora Neale (1901–1960) African American novelist who embodied the creative and artistic aspirations of the Harlem Renaissance in the 1920s.

Hutchinson, Anne (1591–1643) English-born American colonist and religious leader who was banished from Boston (1637) for her religious beliefs, which included an emphasis on an individual's direct communication with God.

impeachment The act of charging a public official with misconduct in office, impeachment is the constitutional procedure for removing presidents who are found guilty of "treason, bribery, or other high crimes and misdemeanors" as interpreted by Congress. Presidents Andrew Johnson, Richard Nixon, and Bill Clinton have been the subject of impeachment proceedings.

Impressment Act (1863) Confederate legislation that authorized the seizure of produce and slaves for military purposes, and provided the means for Confederate farmers to appeal unfair prices paid for property seized.

Indian Removal Act (1830) Congressional legislation that set aside land in the Oklahoma Territory for American Indians who were to be removed from the eastern United States. During the next eight years, tens of thousands of Choctaw, Chickasaw, and Cherokee people were transported from their homes on what the Cherokees called the "Trail of Tears."

inoculation Medical procedure tested in 1721 by a Boston doctor, Zabdiel Boylston, to prevent smallpox epidemics. The procedure involved introducing the smallpox virus into an individual's body, thereby giving the person what was usually (but not always) a mild case of the disease.

Interstate Commerce Act (1887) Congressional legislation that set up the Interstate Commerce Commission (ICC) to supervise and regulate the nation's railroads.

Interstate Commerce Commission First federal regulatory agency, established by the Interstate Commerce Act (1887). It had the power to investigate complaints of railroad misconduct and file suit against the companies. The Hepburn Act (1906) gave the commission the authority to establish maximum rates and to review the accounts and records of the railroads.

Iran-Contra scandal A major scandal of the second Reagan term that involved shipping arms to Iran and diverting money from the sale of these weapons to the Contra rebels in Nicaragua.

Iron Curtain Military, political, and ideological barrier established between the Soviet bloc and Western Europe from 1945 to 1989.

Jackson, Andrew (1767–1845) U.S. general and seventh president of the United States (1829–1837). In the War of 1812, he defeated the Red Sticks at Horseshoe Bend (1814) and the British at New Orleans (1815). As president he denied the right of individual states to

nullify federal laws and increased presidential powers.

Jackson, Jesse (1941–) Baptist minister and civil rights leader, he directed national antidiscrimination efforts in the mid-1960s and 1970s.

Jackson, Thomas J. "Stonewall" (1824–1863) Confederate general who commanded troops at both battles of Bull Run (1861 and 1862) and directed the Shenandoah Valley campaign (1862). He was accidentally killed by his own troops at Chancellorsville (1863).

Jamestown First permanent English settlement in America (1607), it was located on the James River in Virginia.

Jay, John (1745–1829) American diplomat and jurist who served in the Continental Congress and helped negotiate the Treaty of Paris (1783). He was the first chief justice of the U.S. Supreme Court (1789–1795) and negotiated the agreement with Great Britain that became known as the Jay Treaty.

Jay Treaty (1794) Treaty between the United States and Great Britain negotiated by John Jay. It settled difficulties arising from violations of the Treaty of Paris of 1783 and regulated commerce and navigation.

Jazz Singer, The **(1927)** One of the first motion pictures with sound, it starred Al Jolson who specialized in rendering popular tunes in blackface.

Jefferson, Thomas (1743–1826) Third president of the United States (1801–1809). As a member of the second Continental Congress, he drafted the Declaration of Independence (1776). His presidency was marked by the purchase of the Louisiana Territory (1803) and the Embargo of 1807.

Johnson, "Jack" (1878–1946) First African American heavyweight boxing champion, taking the title in 1908.

Johnson, Andrew (1808–1875) Seventeenth president of the United States (1865–1869); he succeeded the assassinated Abraham Lincoln.

Johnson, Lyndon Baines (1908–1973) Thirty-sixth president of the United States (1963–1968), he succeeded after the assassination of President Kennedy and was elected in a landslide the following year. He piloted a number of important initiatives through Congress, including the Civil Rights Act of 1964 and the Voting Rights Act of 1965.

joint-stock companies Formed to explore trade routes and establish new

markets, the companies obtained capital by selling shares of stock.

Judiciary Act of 1789 Congressional legislation that established the U.S. Supreme Court of six justices and a system of federal inferior courts, which were restricted primarily to consideration of federal crimes. State courts retained original jurisdiction in most civil and criminal cases, with the U.S. Supreme Court taking appeals from the highest state courts.

Kansas-Nebraska Bill (1854) Congressional legislation drafted by Stephen A. Douglas that provided that people of new territories could decide for themselves whether or not their states would permit slavery.

Kennedy, Robert F. (1925–1968) Attorney general during the presidency of his brother John F. Kennedy. Elected to the Senate in 1964, he was assassinated in Los Angeles while campaigning for the presidency.

Kent State University National Guardsmen were sent to this Ohio campus to restore order following a series of antiwar protests in May 1970. They fired into a crowd of students, killing four and wounding nine others.

Khrushchev, Nikita (1894–1971) Soviet politician and Stalin loyalist in the 1930s, he was appointed first secretary of the Communist party in 1953. As Soviet premier, he denounced Stalin, thwarted the Hungarian Revolution of 1956, and improved his country's image abroad. He was deposed in 1964 for failing to establish missiles in Cuba or improve the Soviet economy.

King, Martin Luther, Jr. (1929–1968) African American clergyman whose eloquence and commitment to nonviolence formed the foundation of the civil rights movement of the 1950s and 1960s. He led the 1963 march on Washington at which he delivered his now famous "I Have a Dream" speech. He was awarded the Nobel Peace Prize in 1964 and was assassinated four years later in Memphis, Tennessee.

Kissinger, Henry (1912–) German-born American political scientist, national security advisor (1969–1974), and secretary of state (1973–1977). He shared the 1973 Nobel Peace Prize for helping to negotiate the Vietnam cease-fire.

Knights of Labor Nineteenth-century labor organization that combined fraternal ritual, the language of Christianity, and a belief in the social equality of all citizens.

Know-Nothings Popular name for the American party, an anti-immigration party of the mid-1850s, derived from members' response to any question about their activities: "I know nothing."

Ku Klux Klan Founded in 1866 as an organization to terrorize blacks in the South during Reconstruction. It was revived in 1915 as a means of enforcing, often through violence and intimidation, the cultural values of rural, prohibitionist America against minority groups including African Americans, Jews, and Catholics.

L'Enfant, Pierre Charles (1754–1825) French-born American architect, who designed Washington, D.C., and its major buildings. His grandiose street plan and Greek and Roman architecture expressed an exalted vision of the republic.

La Follette, Robert M. (1855–1925) Progressive governor (1900–1906) and senator (1906–1925) from Wisconsin; Progressive Party candidate for president in 1924.

La Raza Unida Formed in 1969 by Mexican American activists, this group reflected the growing demand for political and cultural recognition of "Chicano" causes, especially in the Southwest.

La Salle, Sieur de (1643–1687) French explorer in North America who claimed Louisiana for France (1682).

Las Casas, Bartolomé de (1474–1566) Spanish missionary who condemned Spanish colonial policies toward Native Americans. He described atrocities in his book, *A Short Account of the Destruction of the Indies* (1542).

Lee, Ann (1736–1784) Founder of the Shakers in the United States. The sect believed in salvation by confession of sin, equality regardless of sex or race, opposition to slavery and war, sexual abstinence, and assistance to the poor.

Lee, Robert E. (1807–1870) U.S. and Confederate general. He led the Army of Northern Virginia in the American Civil War.

Leisler, Jacob (1640?–1691) German-born merchant and militia captain in New York who in 1689 led a rebellion of merchants and artisans who had been denied economic privileges to trade and mill flour under James II's government.

Leisler was executed for treason when the new governor appointed by William and Mary arrived in 1691.

Lend-Lease (1941) Passed in 1941, this act forged the way for the United States to transfer military supplies to the Allies, primarily Great Britain and the Soviet Union.

Levittown An unincorporated community of 53,286 people in southeast New York on western Long Island, which was founded in 1947 as a low-cost housing development for World War II veterans.

Lewis and Clark Expedition From 1804 to 1806 Meriwether Lewis and William Clark led the Corps of Discovery from St. Louis to the Pacific coast and back. They informed Native Americans that the United States had acquired the territory from France and recorded geographic and scientific data.

Lewis, John L. (1880–1969) U.S. labor leader; president of the United Mine Workers of America (1920–1960) and the Congress of Industrial Organizations (1935–1940).

Liberal Republicans Organization formed in 1872 by Republicans who were not content with the political corruption and the policies of President Grant's first administration.

Liberty Bonds Thirty-year government bonds sold to individuals with an annual interest rate of 3.5 percent. They were offered in five issues between 1917 and 1920, and their purchase was equated with patriotic duty.

Liberty Party U.S. political party formed in 1839 to oppose the practice of slavery; it merged with the Free-Soil party in 1848.

Lincoln, Abraham (1809–1865) Sixteenth president (1861–1865), his election triggered Southern secession. He led the United States throughout the Civil War, strengthened the power of the presidency, and signed into law the Emancipation Proclamation. He was assassinated two days after Lee's surrender.

Lincoln, Benjamin (1733–1810) Revolutionary War general who in 1786–1787 successfully led the army funded by Boston merchants against the Shaysites in western Massachusetts.

Lindbergh, Charles A. (1902–1974) His solo flight across the Atlantic Ocean in 1927 made him an international hero.

Little Richard (Richard Wayne Penniman, 1932–) American rock 'n'

roll singer noted for his flamboyant style, he influenced many artists including Elvis Presley and the Beatles.

Locke, Alain (1885–1954) African American poet and an important member of the Harlem Renaissance.

Locke, John (1632–1704) English philosopher and author of *An Essay Concerning Human Understanding* (1690), which challenged the notion of innate knowledge, and *Two Treatises on Civil Government* (1690), which discussed the social contract.

Long, Huey P. (1893–1935) Populist but dictatorial governor of Louisiana (1928–1932), he instituted major public works legislation; as a U.S. senator (1932–1935), he proposed a national "Share the Wealth" program.

Louisiana Purchase (1803) The acquisition of the Louisiana Territory west of the Mississippi River and New Orleans by the United States from France for $15 million.

Lovejoy, Elijah P. (1802–1837) Abolitionist editor, killed by proslavery advocates in an attack on his printing press in Alton, Illinois.

loyalists Residents of the British colonies who remained loyal to Great Britain during the American Revolution. Also called Tories after the pro-monarchy faction in England.

Lusitania British liner sunk by a German torpedo in May 1915. Among the nearly 1,200 passengers who died were 128 Americans.

Luther, Martin (1483–1546) German theologian and leader of the Reformation. His opposition to the wealth and corruption of the papacy and his belief that salvation would be granted on the basis of faith alone rather than by works caused his excommunication from the Catholic Church (1521). Luther confirmed the Augsburg Confession in 1530, effectively establishing the Lutheran Church.

MacArthur, Douglas (1880–1964) U.S. general. He served as chief of staff (1930–1935) and commanded the Allied forces in the South Pacific during World War II. Initially losing the Philippines to the Japanese in 1942, he regained the islands and accepted the surrender of Japan in 1945. He commanded the UN forces in Korea (1950–1951) until a conflict in strategies led to his dismissal by President Truman.

Madison, James (1751–1836) Fourth president of the United States (1809–1817). Member of the Continental Congress (1780–1783) and the Constitutional Convention (1787), he strongly supported ratification of the Constitution and was a contributor to *The Federalist*.

Malcolm X (Malcolm Little, 1925–1965) Black Muslim leader who advocated nationalism, self-defense, and racial separation. He split with the Black Muslim movement and formed the Organization of Afro-American Unity, which attracted thousands of young, urban blacks with its message of pride and self-help. He was assassinated by a Black Muslim at a New York rally in 1965.

manifest destiny Idea proposed by newspaper editor John L. O'Sullivan in 1845 that the United States was destined to grow from the Atlantic to the Pacific and from the Arctic to the tropics. Providence supposedly intended for Americans to have this area for a great experiment in liberty.

Mann, Horace (1796–1859) Educational reformer and promoter of public school education; first secretary of the Massachusetts Board of Education.

Marbury v. Madison (1803) The first decision by the Supreme Court to declare unconstitutional and void an act passed by Congress that the Court considered in violation of the Constitution. The decision established the doctrine of judicial review, the authority of courts to declare statutes unconstitutional.

Marshall, George C. (1880–1959) U.S. general and statesman. As secretary of state (1947–1949), he organized the European Recovery Plan, often called the Marshall Plan, for which he received the 1953 Nobel Peace Prize.

Marshall, John (1755–1835) American politician and jurist. As chief justice of the United States (1801–1835), he helped establish the doctrine of judicial review.

Marshall Plan Post–World War II U.S. economic aid program, also known as the European Recovery Plan. The plan, costing about $13 billion, helped restore economic confidence throughout Western Europe, raise living standards, curb the influence of local Communist parties, and increase U.S. trade and investment on the European continent.

Maya Inhabitants of the Yucatan Peninsula whose civilization was at its height from 300 to 900 A.D. Their civilization included a unique system of writing, mathematics, architecture, sculpture, and astronomy.

Mayflower Compact (1620) When the *Mayflower* reached Cape Cod and the colonists decided to settle there, they lacked the legal basis to establish a government. Thus, the adult males of the colony signed a mutual agreement for ordering their society, later referred to as the Mayflower Compact.

McCarthy, Joseph R. (1908–1957) U.S. senator from Wisconsin (1947–1957), he presided over the permanent subcommittee on investigations and held public hearings in which he accused army officials, members of the media, and public figures of being Communists. These charges were never proved, and he was censured by the Senate in 1954.

McClellan, George B. (1826–1885) Major general of the United States Army who led forces in Virginia in 1861 and 1862. He was widely blamed for not taking advantage of his numerical superiority to defeat the Confederates around Richmond. McClellan ran against Abraham Lincoln for president in 1864 on the Democratic ticket.

McCulloch v. Maryland (1819) Supreme Court case striking down Maryland's efforts to tax notes issued by the Bank of the United States. The decision established the constitutionality of the bank, the supremacy of federal over state laws, and the principle that the federal government possessed powers implied by but not enumerated in the Constitution.

McGillivray, Alexander (1759?–1793) Son of a Scottish trader and a French-Creek woman, McGillivray served as a Creek leader and allied with Spain to prevent white settlement on Creek lands during the 1780s.

McGovern, George (1922–) U.S. senator from South Dakota (1963–1981), he opposed the Vietnam War and was defeated as the 1972 Democratic candidate for president.

McKinley, William (1843–1901) Twenty-fifth president of the United States (1897–1901), he won by the largest majority of popular votes since 1872.

Melville, Herman (1819–1891) Author of *Moby-Dick* (1851), often considered the greatest American novel of the nineteenth century.

mercantilism Economic policy of the sixteenth to eighteenth centuries. European nations claimed the monopoly to trade with their colonies, which were to serve as markets for goods from the home country and provide raw materials, gold, and silver to increase its wealth.

Metacom (c. 1639–1676) Wampanoag leader who waged King Philip's War (1675–1676) with New England colonists who had encroached on Native American territory.

middle passage Transport of slaves across the Atlantic from Africa to the Americas.

midnight appointments Federal judicial officials appointed to office in the closing period of a presidential administration. The Republicans accused Adams of staying awake until midnight in order to sign the commissions for Federalist officeholders.

Midway Island Location of 1942 decisive World War II naval battle, in which land and carrier-based U.S. planes defeated a Japanese fleet.

midwives Women who traditionally attended at childbirth, treated the ill, and prescribed herbal remedies. They learned their skills through informal apprenticeships and from witnessing the childbirths of neighbors and relatives, and received payment for their services.

Milliken's Bend, battle of (1863) Battle on June 7, 1863, that turned to hand-to-hand combat between African American Union troops and Confederate soldiers during Grant's Vicksburg Campaign. The battle won Union recognition of African American soldiers' fighting abilities.

Missouri Compromise (1820–1821) Congressional legislation that ended the first of a series of crises concerning the extension of slavery.

Mondale, Walter (1928–) Vice president of the United States under Jimmy Carter (1977–1981), he earlier served as a U.S. senator from Minnesota (1965–1977) and was the unsuccessful 1984 Democratic nominee for president.

Monroe Doctrine (1823) U.S. foreign policy statement presented to Congress by James Monroe, declaring U.S. opposition to European interference in the Americas.

Monroe, James (1758–1831) Fifth president of the United States (1817–1825), whose administration was marked by the acquisition of Florida

(1819), the Missouri Compromise (1820), and the Monroe Doctrine (1823).

Montgomery bus boycott Begun in December 1955 as a result of an act of protest by Rosa Parks against the segregated transportation facilities and humiliating treatment facing African Americans in the capital city of Alabama, the boycott soon became an international event.

Moral Majority Political action group founded in 1979 and composed of conservative, fundamentalist Christians. Led by evangelist Rev. Jerry Falwell, the group played a significant role in the 1980 elections through its strong support of conservative candidates.

Morgan, J. P. (Pierpont) (1837–1913) U.S. financier. He purchased Carnegie Steel Company in 1901 for $480 million from Andrew Carnegie, creating United States Steel, which controlled 60 percent of the steel industry's productive capacity.

Morris, "Bill" (d. 1901) Black man burned at the stake in Balltown, Louisiana, for allegedly robbing and raping a white woman; no trial was held.

Morris, Robert (1734–1806) American Revolutionary politician and financier. A signer of the Declaration of Independence, he raised money for the Continental Army, attended the Constitutional Convention (1787), and was financially ruined by land speculation.

Morse, Samuel F. B. (1791–1872) American painter and inventor. He refined and patented the telegraph and developed the telegraphic code that bears his name.

muckrakers The name given to investigative reporters in the early 1900s.

Muller v. Oregon (1908) Case in which the Supreme Court upheld limits on working hours for women.

multiculturalism The effort, particularly in academic life, to embrace the diversity of minority cultures. The movement was especially strong during the 1980s and 1990s.

National American Woman Suffrage Association (NAWSA) This association was formed in 1890 through the efforts of Lucy Stone Blackwell, and its first president was Elizabeth Cady Stanton.

National Association for the Advancement of Colored People (NAACP) Civil rights organization founded in 1909 to fight racial injustice.

National Industrial Recovery Act (NIRA) Enacted on June 16, 1933, this emergency measure was designed to encourage industrial recovery and help combat widespread unemployment.

National Road Federally sponsored road running from the Potomac River at Cumberland, Maryland, to the Ohio River at Wheeling, [West] Virginia, by 1818; extended to Vandalia, Illinois, by 1839.

National Woman's Party Created by Alice Paul, this organization pushed for the Equal Rights Amendment during the 1920s.

National Women's Trade Union League (1903–1950) Labor organization founded by women. It campaigned for better working conditions, protective labor laws, minimum wage regulation, and a ban on child labor.

natural philosophy The study of astronomy, physics, and chemistry, which was introduced into American college curricula under the influence of the Scottish Enlightenment.

Neolin Delaware prophet who preached in the 1760s that Indians must reject Christianity and European goods, particularly rum, and revitalize their ancient culture.

New Deal Term for the domestic programs and reforms instituted by President Franklin D. Roosevelt and his administration in response to the Great Depression of the 1930s.

New Jersey Plan Proposal for the U.S. Constitution drafted by William Paterson, it provided for a one-house (unicameral) Congress in which states had equal representation.

New Nationalism Theodore Roosevelt's far-reaching program that called for a strong federal government to stabilize the economy, protect the weak, and restore social harmony.

"New Negro" A term associated with the Harlem Renaissance of the 1920s that involved a proud assertion of the value of African American culture.

New York City draft riots (1863) Riots, July 13–16, 1863, among working people of New York, many of them recent immigrants, following news of heavy losses at Gettysburg and efforts to replace troop losses through the draft lottery.

Newton, Sir Isaac (1642–1727) English scientist who discovered universal laws that predictably govern the motion of planets, moons, and comets; the motion of falling bodies on earth (gravity); and the ebb and flow of tides.

Nisei A person born in the United States of parents who emigrated from Japan.

Nixon, Richard M. (1913–1994) Thirty-seventh president of the United States (1969–1974). Known early in his career as a hard-line anti-Communist, he was the first U.S. president to visit Communist China. He also worked skillfully to ease tensions with the Soviet Union. He became the first president to resign from office, due to his involvement in the Watergate scandal.

North Atlantic Treaty Organization (NATO) Military alliance, founded in 1949, between the United States and eleven other nations to protect Western Europe from invasion. It was a leading force in the Cold War struggle to contain Soviet aggression, expanding to include new nations over the years.

North, Oliver (1943–) Member of President Reagan's National Security Council staff and a Marine colonel, he was a central figure in the Iran-Contra scandal.

Northwest Ordinance (1787) Adopted by the Congress to establish stricter control over the government of the Northwest Territory ceded to the United States by the states. The ordinance was the most significant achievement of Congress under the Articles of Confederation.

nullification (1828–1833) Argument between leaders in South Carolina and in Washington, D.C., especially President Andrew Jackson, over the relationship between federal and state power. Theorists of nullification, especially John C. Calhoun, argued that a state had the authority to "nullify" a federal law within its own boundaries. The precipitating issue was a tariff, but the debate—eventually settled by compromise over the tariff and a threat of force by the federal government over the issue of authority—was seen as a trial case regarding slavery.

O'Connor, Sandra Day (1930–) Appointed by President Ronald Reagan, she was the first woman justice on the Supreme Court.

Oglethorpe, James (1696–1785) Along with John Viscount Percival, Oglethorpe sought a charter to colonize Georgia, the last of the British mainland colonies. Upon royal approval, he founded the colony with the intention of establishing a society of small farmers, without slavery or hard liquor.

Oklahoma City bombing (1995) Militant right-wing U.S. terrorists bombed the Alfred P. Murrah Federal Building in Oklahoma City in April 1995, causing the deaths of 168 people.

Oñate, Juan de (1549?–1624?) Spanish explorer and conquistador who claimed New Mexico for Spain in 1598 and served as its governor until he was removed on charges of cruelty in 1607.

Oneida Association Utopian community established in 1848 in upstate New York by John Humphrey Noyes (1811–1886) and his followers; practiced "complex marriage," economic cooperation, and gender equality of labor; also known for the community's steel manufacturing.

Opechancanough (1545?–1644?) Brother of Powhatan. In the 1620s Opechancanough organized a military offensive against English settlers.

Operation OVERLORD (1944) Code name for the Allied invasion of Normandy launched on D-Day, June 6, 1944.

Osceola (1800?–1838) Seminole chief who led opposition to Indian removal in the Second Seminole War.

Oswald, Lee Harvey (1939–1963) Alleged assassin of President John F. Kennedy, he was shot two days later while under arrest.

Panic of 1837 Financial crisis that began a major depression that lasted six years.

Panic of 1857 Financial crisis resulting from decreased European demand for American produce and decreased European investment following the Crimean War. The panic led to a wave of bank suspensions, individual bankruptcies, and a two-year depression.

paper currency After the Revolution, Americans hotly debated the issue of paper currency because it had resulted in inflation during the war, when the government used it to pay for goods and services. Many farmers favored issuing paper currency through a land office, which would provide capital based on the value of their land.

Parks, Rosa (1913–2005) Her refusal to give up her seat on a bus to a white man in Montgomery, Alabama, resulted in a citywide boycott of the bus company and stirred the civil rights movement across the nation.

Paul, Alice (1885–1977) A main figure in the radical wing of the woman suffrage movement in the early twentieth century.

Pearl Harbor Site of a U.S. naval base on the southern coast of Oahu, Hawaii, which the Japanese attacked on Sunday, December 7, 1941; the United States entered World War II the following day.

Pemberton, John (1831–1888) Atlanta druggist who in 1886 developed a syrup from an extract of the cola nut that he mixed with carbonated water and called "Coca Cola."

Penn, William (1644–1718) English Quaker leader who obtained a charter for Pennsylvania from Charles II in exchange for a debt owed to Penn's father. Penn intended to establish a model society based on religious freedom and peaceful relations with Native Americans, in addition to benefiting financially from the sale of the land.

Pennsylvania Abolition Society Organization founded in Philadelphia during the revolutionary period that advocated expansion of the state's 1780 act for gradual abolition and provided legal counsel to African Americans to defend their liberty.

Philadelphia Capital of colonial Pennsylvania and Delaware River port founded by William Penn.

piecework Early manufacturing system in which clothing, hats, and portions of shoes were sewn by women, generally working in their own homes, then sent to merchants in nearby cities for assembly and sale.

Pitt, Sir William (1708–1778) British political leader and orator who directed his country's military effort during the Seven Years' War.

Plessy v. Ferguson (1896) Supreme Court decision that approved racial segregation.

Plessy, Homer A. (1863–1925) In a test of an 1890 law specifying that blacks must ride in separate railroad cars, this one-eighth-black man boarded a train and sat in the car reserved for whites. When the conductor instructed him to move, he refused and was arrested.

Plymouth Colony established by the English Pilgrims, or Separatists, in 1620. The Separatists were Puritans who abandoned hope that the Anglican church could be reformed. Plymouth became part of Massachusetts in 1691.

Pope Leader of the successful 1680 Pueblo rebellion against Spanish colonists and priests in New Mexico.

popular sovereignty The concept that settlers of each territory would decide for themselves whether to allow slavery.

Populist Party Also known as the People's Party, the Populists held their first national convention on July 4, 1892. The party platform took a stern view of the state of the nation, with planks endorsing the subtreasury, free coinage of silver, and other reforms.

Port Royal South Carolina port; abandoned by Confederate slaveholders early in the war, this became the site of a well-publicized experiment in the shift from slave to free labor.

Powell, Colin (1937–) U.S. general, national security adviser (1987–1989), chairman of the Joint Chiefs of Staff (1989–1993), and secretary of state (2001–2005). He was influential in planning U.S. strategy during the Persian Gulf War.

Powers, Francis Gary (1929–1977) Pilot of a U.S. U-2 high-altitude reconnaissance aircraft shot down over the Soviet Union on May 1, 1960.

Powhatan (1550–1618) Algonquian leader who founded the Powhatan confederacy and maintained peaceful relations with English colonists after the marriage of his daughter Pocahontas to John Rolfe (1614).

praying towns Established by John Eliot, praying towns were villages in which the Indians were supposed to adopt English customs and learn the fundamentals of Puritan religion.

predestination A theory that states that God has decreed who will be saved and who will be damned.

presidios Forts in colonial Spanish America built in an effort to defend the colonists and missions from Native American opponents.

Prince Henry of Portugal (1394–1460) Henry "the Navigator" established a school for navigators and geographers. He sought to increase the power of Portugal by promoting exploration of trade routes to the East by way of Africa.

Proclamation of 1763 In an attempt to keep white settlers out of the Ohio Valley, the Proclamation of 1763 drew a line along the crest of the Appalachian Mountains from Maine to Georgia and required all colonists to move east of the line.

progressivism Reform movement from 1890 to 1920 that sought to make state and national politics more democratic and government more efficient. The administrations of Theodore Roosevelt and Woodrow Wilson carried out many progressive reforms.

Protestant Reformation Religious rebellion against the Roman Catholic Church that began in 1517 when Martin Luther posted his ninety-five theses on a church door in Wittenberg, Germany.

Pullman, George (1831–1897) Developer of the railroad sleeping car and creator of a model town outside Chicago for his employees.

Pullman strike (1894) Strike by railway workers that led to nationwide unrest.

Puritanism Radical strain of English Protestantism that demanded purification of the Anglican church, including elimination of rituals, vestments, statues, and bishops.

Quakers (Society of Friends) Protestant sect originating in the English Civil War that challenged the authority of the Church of England and New England Puritans.

ratification Process by which the Constitution of 1787 and subsequent amendments must be approved. The original document required ratification by nine state conventions; states that refused to ratify could remain independent or unite under another frame of government.

Reagan, Ronald (1911–2004) Fortieth president of the United States (1981–1989), he represented the ascendancy of conservatism during the 1980s.

Regulators Name used in the late 1760s by the North Carolina Regulator movement and the South Carolina Regulators. Both groups demanded fair representation in the state legislatures but otherwise had distinct goals and membership.

Report on Public Credit (1790) Alexander Hamilton's plan for funding all Revolutionary War debts, including those of the states, by paying the interest with an import duty and excise tax on whiskey.

Republican Party (1790s) Led by Thomas Jefferson and James Madison, the party favored a strict interpretation of the Constitution and opposed Alexander Hamilton's vision of a strong central government and federal privileges for manufacturing and commerce.

Roanoke Island England's first attempt to establish a colony in North America was at Roanoke Island in 1585.

robber barons Railroad industry leaders such as Cornelius Vanderbilt and Jay Gould who became renowned for their ruthless methods against competitors.

Robinson, Jackie (1919–1972) First African American player in the Major Leagues in the twentieth century, he was a second baseman for the Brooklyn Dodgers, had a lifetime batting average of .311, and was inducted into the Baseball Hall of Fame in 1962.

Rockefeller, John D. (1839–1937) Key figure in the development of the oil industry and the growth of large corporations.

Roe v. Wade (1973) Supreme Court decision that, along with *Doe v. Bolton*, legalized abortion in the first trimester.

Roosevelt Corollary (1904) Theodore Roosevelt's extension of the Monroe Doctrine to Latin American states and the right to supervise their behavior.

Roosevelt, Eleanor (1884–1962) Diplomat, writer, and First Lady of the United States (1933–1945) as the wife of President Franklin D. Roosevelt. A delegate to the United Nations (1945–1953 and 1961–1962), she was an outspoken advocate for human rights. Her written works include *This I Remember* (1949).

Roosevelt, Franklin D. (1882–1945) Thirty-second president of the United States (1933–1945), he assumed the presidency at the depth of the Great Depression and helped the American people regain faith in themselves. He brought hope with his inaugural address in which he promised prompt, vigorous action and asserted that "the only thing we have to fear is fear itself."

Rosie the Riveter Symbol of the new breed of working women during World War II.

Ross, John (1790–1866) Cherokee chief who challenged Indian removals in *Cherokee Nation v. Georgia* (1831).

Royal African Company English trading company granted the monopoly from 1672 to 1698 to supply enslaved people from Africa to labor in the English colonies.

royal fifth A tax on silver and gold of which one-fifth of its value went to the king of Spain.

Ruth, George Herman ("Babe") (1895–1948) Boston Red Sox pitcher who was sold to the New York Yankees in 1918 for $400,000. He belted out fifty-four home runs during the 1920 season, and fans flocked to see him play.

Sacagawea (1787?–1812?) Shoshone guide and interpreter who accompanied the Lewis and Clark expedition (1805–1806).

Sacco, Ferdinando Nicola (1891–1927), and Vanzetti, Bartolomeo (1888–1927) Italian immigrants tried for murder in Massachusetts in 1921. The trial attracted worldwide attention because of allegations of bias due to their anarchist beliefs. After exhausting their appeals, they were executed in 1927.

Sanger, Margaret (1883–1966) Social reformer and birth control pioneer. As a public health nurse in New York, she saw women suffering from disease and poverty because of the large number of children they bore. In 1914 she coined the term *birth control* and in 1915 she opened a clinic in Brooklyn. In 1921 she founded the American Birth Control League, which became Planned Parenthood in 1942.

Santa Anna, Antonio López de (1794–1876) Mexican general and politician. Leader of Mexico at the time of the battle at the Alamo. Taken prisoner at San Jacinto, he signed the Treaties of Velasco, which granted Texas its independence and recognized the Rio Grande as the boundary.

Scopes trial (1925) Trial of biology teacher John Thomas Scopes in Dayton, Tennessee, for teaching evolution. The jury found him guilty and assessed a small fine.

Scots-Irish Ulster Scot Presbyterians who settled in New York, Pennsylvania, Delaware, western Maryland, and the southern backcountry.

Scottsboro boys Nine black youths convicted by an all-white jury in 1931 on charges of raping two white women in Alabama. The case became a source of controversy and the focus of civil rights activism in the early 1930s.

Second Bank of the United States (1816–1836) New national bank created to stabilize the economy and distribute scarce money across the country. President Jackson believed the bank had too much power, and he vetoed the rechartering of the bank in 1836.

Second Great Awakening Protestant religious revivals that began in 1797 and lasted into the 1830s.

Seguín, Juan (1806–1890) Tejano cavalry commander who played a key role in defeating Mexican troops at the Battle of San Jacinto, which secured the independence of Texas.

Seminoles Native American people made up of various primarily Creek groups who moved into northern Florida during the eighteenth and nineteenth centuries, later inhabiting the Everglades region as well.

Seneca Falls Convention (1848) First major gathering of women's rights advocates, held in Seneca Falls, New York.

Serra, Junípero (1713–1784) Franciscan missionary who in 1769 established Spanish missions along the Pacific coast from San Diego to San Francisco.

sharecropping Labor system in the South after the Civil War. Tenants worked the land in return for a share of the crops produced, instead of paying cash rent. A shortage of currency in the South made this a common form of land tenure, and African Americans endured it because it eliminated the labor gangs of the slavery period.

Sherman Antitrust Act (1890) Federal legislation designed to curb the growth of large monopolistic corporations.

Sherman, William T. (1820–1891) Union general under Ulysses S. Grant who took Atlanta and led the "March to the Sea."

Shippen, Dr. William, Jr. (1712–1801) Trained in medicine in England and Scotland, Shippen initiated his practice of obstetrics in 1762, giving lectures in anatomy to Philadelphia midwives and doctors. Soon he accepted only male students.

Simms, William Gilmore (1806–1870) Prominent southern essayist, novelist, poet, and proslavery advocate.

Sinclair, Upton (1878–1968) Progressive era writer whose novel *The Jungle* exposed abuses in the meat-packing industry.

Sitting Bull (c. 1831–1890) Lakota Sioux Chief, he defeated George Custer in the Battle of Little Big Horn (1876).

Sixteenth Amendment (1913) Constitutional amendment that made a federal income tax constitutional.

Slater, Samuel (1768–1835) British-born textile pioneer in America. He oversaw construction of the nation's first successful water-powered cotton mill (1790–1793).

Slave Power Before the Civil War, term referring to the disproportionate power that Northerners believed wealthy slaveholding politicians wielded over their constituents and, as a result, over national political decisions.

Smith, John (1580–1631) English colonist, explorer, and writer. His maps and accounts of his explorations in Virginia and New England were invaluable to later explorers and colonists.

Smith, Joseph (1805–1844) American religious leader who founded the Church of Jesus Christ of Latter-Day Saints (1830). He led his congregation from New York State to western Illinois, where he was murdered by an anti-Mormon mob.

Social Darwinism Nineteenth-century philosophy that argued that the social history of humans closely resembled Darwin's principle of "survival of the fittest." According to this theory, human social history could be understood as a struggle among races, with the strongest and the fittest invariably triumphing.

Songhai Dominant West African state in the fifteenth and sixteenth centuries. Askia Mohammed (ruled 1493–1528) expanded the empire; reformed government, banking, and education; and adopted Islamic law.

Sons of Liberty Groups of small merchants, shopkeepers, and craftsmen who successfully opposed the Stamp Act in 1765–1766 by establishing networks to organize boycotts of British goods.

sovereignty Supreme political power. In Spanish and English colonial America, sovereignty rested in the monarch. Under the U.S. Constitution, sovereignty rests in the people (voters).

Special Field Order 15 Issued by William T. Sherman in January 1865, this order reserved land in coastal South Carolina, Georgia, and Florida for former slaves. Those who settled on the land would receive forty-acre plots.

spoils system Initiated by President Andrew Jackson, civil service system by which the victorious political party rewarded its supporters with government jobs.

Sputnik I First artificial space satellite, launched by the Soviet Union in October 1957. News of its success provoked both anger and anxiety among the American people who had always taken their country's technological superiority for granted.

Squanto (d. 1622) Patuxet Indian who helped the Plymouth colonists develop agricultural techniques and served as an interpreter between the colonists and the Wampanoags.

Square Deal Theodore Roosevelt's policy of treating capital and labor on an equal basis.

St. Domingue French West Indies colony in which blacks led by Toussaint L'Ouverture, a former slave, defeated local whites and invading European armies. Napoleon failed to regain control of the island and, in 1804, the victorious rebels established Haiti as an independent nation.

Stamp Act (1765) British law requiring colonists to purchase a stamp for official documents and published papers, including wills, newspapers, and pamphlets.

standing army After the American Revolution, the issue of a standing, or peacetime, army pitted revolutionary ideology against the need for defense.

Stanton, Elizabeth Cady (1815–1902) American feminist and social reformer who helped organize the first woman's rights convention, held in Seneca Falls, New York (1848), for which she wrote a Declaration of Rights and Sentiments calling for the reform of discriminatory practices that perpetuated the subordination of women.

statute for religious freedom (1786) Virginia legislation written by Thomas Jefferson and passed in 1786 that disestablished the Episcopal (Anglican) Church in Virginia.

stock market crash of 1929 The collapse of stock prices that ended the speculative boom of the 1920s and is associated with the onset of the Great Depression.

Stono uprising (1739) Revolt of enslaved Africans against their owners near the Stono River in South Carolina.

Stowe, Harriet Beecher (1811–1896) Author of *Uncle Tom's Cabin* (1852), the most important abolitionist novel.

Strategic Defense Initiative (SDI) Proposed by President Reagan in 1983, a Defense Department program to develop a space-based system to defend against strategic ballistic missiles.

Students for a Democratic Society (SDS) Formed in Port Huron, Michigan, in 1962, this group became one of the leading New Left antiwar organizations of the 1960s, exemplifying both the idealism and the excesses of radical student groups in the Vietnam era.

suffrage The right to vote, extended to African American men by the Fifteenth Amendment (1870). See also woman suffrage.

Sugar Act (1764) British law that initiated the policy of charging duties primarily for revenue rather than for regulating trade. The act reduced the duty on foreign molasses; added timber, iron, and hides to the list of enumerated goods; and increased the powers of vice-admiralty courts.

Sullivan, John L. (1858–1918) Irish American boxing champion of the late nineteenth century.

Sumner, Charles (1811–1874) U.S. senator from Massachusetts (1851–1874), he was a noted orator with an uncompromising opposition to slavery.

Taft, William Howard (1857–1930) Twenty-seventh president of the United States (1909–1913), who split with Theodore Roosevelt once in office. He served as Chief Justice of the United States Supreme Court (1921–1930).

Taney, Roger B. (1777–1864) Chief Justice of the United States (1836–1864). In the *Dred Scott* decision (1857) he ruled that slaves and their descendants could not become citizens of the United States.

Tarbell, Ida (1857–1944) Preeminent crusading journalist, she exposed the abuses of the oil trust in *A History of the Standard Oil Company* (1904).

Taylor, Zachary (1784–1850) U.S. general and twelfth president (1849–1850), he defeated Mexico in the Mexican-American War. As Whig president, he tried to avoid entanglements of both party and region.

Tecumseh (1768?–1813) Shawnee leader who attempted to establish a confederacy to unify Native Americans against white encroachment. He sided with the British in the War of 1812 and was killed in the Battle of the Thames.

Tejanos Mexicans in Texas who supported the revolt for independence from Mexico.

temperance movement Nineteenth century reform movement that encouraged the reduction or elimination of alcoholic beverage consumption.

Tennessee Valley Authority (TVA) Created in 1933 during the New Deal's first hundred days, it was a massive experiment in regional planning that focused on providing electricity, flood control, and soil conservation to one of the nation's poorest regions, covering seven states in the Tennessee Valley.

Tenskwatawa (1768–1834) Called the Shawnee Prophet, he became prominent among the people of the Great Lakes and Ohio Valley. With his brother, Tecumseh, he inspired a nativist movement to resist the U.S. government's acculturation policy and land seizure.

Tet offensive (1968) Major military operation in South Vietnam launched by the North Vietnamese and Vietcong. Though beaten back, there were tremendous casualties, and coordinated attacks undermined President Johnson's claim that steady progress was being made in Vietnam.

Thirteenth Amendment (1865) Constitutional amendment abolishing slavery.

Thomas, Clarence (1948–) Supreme Court justice appointed by George H. W. Bush in 1991, whose confirmation became controversial due to allegations of sexual misconduct made against him.

Tiananmen Square Adjacent to the Forbidden City in Beijing, China, this large public square was the site of many festivals, rallies, and demonstrations. During a student demonstration in 1989, Chinese troops fired on the demonstrators, killing an estimated two thousand or more.

Tilden, Samuel J. (1814–1886) Governor of New York and Democratic candidate for president in 1876. He narrowly lost what has been considered the most controversial election in American history.

Townshend Revenue Act (1767) Conceived by Charles Townshend, the British chancellor of the exchequer, the act placed duties on tea, glass, paper, lead, and paint to help pay British colonial administrative and military costs in North America.

Trail of Tears Forced migration of Indians from southeastern states to what is now Oklahoma, in accordance with the Indian Removal Act (1830). Thousands died on the march known as the Trail of Tears.

transcendentalists Members of an intellectual and social movement of the 1830s and 1840s that emphasized the active role the mind plays in constructing what we think of as reality. A loose grouping of intellectuals in Massachusetts sought to "transcend" the limits of thought in conventional America, whether religious or philosophical.

Treaty of Paris (1783) Signed on September 3, 1783, the Treaty of Paris established the independence of the United States from Great Britain. It set specific land boundaries and called for the evacuation of British troops.

Treaty of Tordesillas (1494) Treaty between Spain and Portugal that located the Line of Demarcation 370 leagues (about 1,000 miles) west of the Azores. It expanded the principle of "spheres of influence."

Treaty of Utrecht (1713) Ending Queen Anne's War between Great Britain and France, the Treaty of Utrecht ceded control of Nova Scotia, Newfoundland, and the Hudson Bay territory to the British.

***Trent* affair (1861)** Diplomatic incident growing out of the Union seizure of two Confederate envoys aboard a British ship, which highlighted the question of whether European countries would recognize Confederate nationhood.

Triangle Shirtwaist Fire (1911) Fire at the Triangle Shirtwaist Company in New York that killed 146 female workers and spurred reform legislation regulating factories and protecting workers.

Triple Alliance Pre–World War I alliance between Germany, Austria-Hungary, and Italy, established in 1882.

Truman Doctrine (1947) Reflecting a tougher approach to the Soviet Union following World War II, President Truman went before Congress in 1947 to request $400 million in military aid for Greece and Turkey, claiming the appropriation was vital to the containment of communism and to the future of freedom everywhere.

Truman, Harry S (1884–1972) Thirty-third president of the United States (1945–1953), he took office following the death of Franklin D. Roosevelt. Reelected in 1948 in a stunning political upset, Truman's controversial and historic decisions included the use of atomic weapons against Japan, desegregation of the U.S. military, and dismissal of General MacArthur as commander of U.S. forces during the Korean War.

trustbuster Term applied to Theodore Roosevelt's efforts to enforce the Sherman Act.

Truth, Sojourner (1797–1883) Former slave who became an advocate for abolitionism and for woman's rights.

Tubman, Harriet (c. 1820–1913) Escaped slave who returned to the South and led hundreds of enslaved people to freedom in the North. Active throughout the 1850s, Tubman became famous as the most active member of the Underground Railroad.

Turner, Nat (1800–1831) American slave leader who organized about seventy followers and led a rebellion in Virginia, during which approximately fifty whites were killed (1831). He was then captured and executed.

Twelfth Amendment (1804) Constitutional amendment requiring electors to draw up distinct lists for president and vice president, thus avoiding the deadlock of 1800 in which Thomas Jefferson and Aaron Burr tied for the presidency.

Twentieth Amendment (1933) Constitutional amendment that moved the presidential inauguration date from four months after the election to January 20.

"twenty negro law" Confederate law exempting from military service one white man for every twenty slaves he supervised.

U-2 U.S. spy plane. One piloted by Francis Gary Powers was shot down over the Soviet Union in 1960, which led to the angry breakup of a summit meeting in Paris between President Eisenhower and Soviet Premier Nikita Khrushchev.

Ulloa, Antonio de (1716–1795) First Spanish governor of Louisiana, who arrived in 1766 and tried to govern jointly with the last French governor.

Universalists Protestant denomination established in 1779 by an Englishman, John Murray. Its message of universal salvation had wide influence, though the Universalist church itself remained small.

vacuum domicilium English legal doctrine meaning that lands not occupied could be taken. It served as a basis for taking Native American territory.

Van Buren, Martin (1782–1862) Eighth president of the United States (1837–1841). A powerful Democrat from New York, he served in the U.S. Senate (1821–1828), as secretary of state (1829–1831), and as vice president (1833–1837) under Andrew Jackson before being elected president in 1836. He unsuccessfully sought reelection in 1840 and 1848.

vertical integration A procedure wherein a company gains control of all phases of production related to its product.

Vesey, Denmark (1767?–1822) American insurrectionist. A freed slave in South Carolina, he was implicated in the planning of a large uprising of slaves and was hanged. The event led to more stringent slave codes in many southern states.

viceroy Governor of a country, province, or colony who rules as the representative of the sovereign.

Vicksburg, battle of (1863) Mississippi battle site under siege by Grant's army for six weeks. Before falling it became the symbol of Confederate doggedness and Union frustration.

Vietnamization President Nixon's policy whereby the South Vietnamese were to assume more of the military burdens of the war. This transfer of responsibility was expected to eventually allow the United States to withdraw.

Virginia and Monitor Two ironclad vessels that fought in the harbor at Hampton Roads on March 9, 1862, in the first American battle between ironclads. Though neither won, the encounter established the importance of ironclads for the remainder of the war.

Virginia Company In 1606 King James I chartered the Virginia Company; one group was centered in London and founded Jamestown, a second group from Plymouth in western England founded the Plymouth colony.

Virginia Plan Constitutional proposal written by James Madison, the Virginia Plan proposed a powerful central government dominated by a National Legislature of two houses (bicameral). It also favored a system of greater representation based on a state's population.

Virginia slave debates (1831–1832) Debates in the Virginia state legislature following Nat Turner's Revolt over proposals to end slavery in Virginia. Although the legislature decided against abolition, the debates revealed white fears and divisions.

Wade-Davis Bill (1864) Congressional legislation for reconstructing the South. The Radical Republicans proposed stringent conditions for states that had seceded to reenter the Union. The bill provided that a majority of citizens in the states sign oaths swearing that they had never supported secession. The bill passed in the Senate and House but was pocket-vetoed by President Lincoln, who favored a more lenient approach.

Walker, David (1785–1830) African American abolitionist and author of *Walker's Appeal … To the Coloured Citizens of the World* (1829), an early and powerful call for black self-awareness and opposition to slavery.

Wallace, George (1919–1998) Governor of Alabama (1963–1967, 1971–1979, 1983–1987), he first came to national attention as an outspoken segregationist. Wallace ran unsuccessfully for the presidency in 1968 and 1972.

Washington, Booker T. (1856–1914) Educator, founder of Tuskegee Institute. He argued that African Americans should emphasize hard work and personal development rather than agitating for social reform.

Washingtonian temperance movement Nineteenth century reform movement that encouraged the reduction or elimination of alcoholic beverage consumption.

Watergate Nixon administration scandal touched off when the Democratic National Headquarters at the Watergate complex in Washington, D.C., was burglarized in 1972. Several top government officials were convicted of crimes and President Nixon was forced to resign in 1974.

Watts riot (1965) Among the most violent urban disturbances in U.S. history, it erupted in an African American neighborhood in Los Angeles following the arrest of a black motorist. By the time it ended, five days later, thirty-four people were dead, a thousand were injured, property damage topped $200 million, and National Guardsmen had to be called in to restore order.

Wells-Barnett, Ida B. (1862–1931) African American journalist and leader of an anti-lynching campaign.

Westmoreland, William (1914–2005) U.S. general; senior commander of U.S. troops in Vietnam from 1964 to 1968.

Whigs (Revolutionary era) Residents of the British colonies who opposed Great

Britain during the American Revolution. Also called patriots, they took the name Whigs from the English party that had opposed the Crown.

Whiskey Rebellion In the early 1790s western Pennsylvania farmers resisted the whiskey tax: they held protest meetings, tarred and feathered collaborators, and destroyed property. In 1794 the Washington administration sent thirteen thousand troops to restore order, but the revolt was over by the time they arrived.

Whitefield, George (1714–1770) Anglican minister who arrived from England in 1739. Called the Grand Itinerant, he promoted the Great Awakening by touring and encouraging New Lights throughout the colonies.

Whitman, Walt (1819–1892) Visionary poet who wrote *Leaves of Grass* (1855), inventing a new American idiom.

Whitney, Eli (1765–1825) American inventor and manufacturer whose invention of the cotton gin (1793) revolutionized the cotton industry. He also established the first factory to assemble muskets with interchangeable parts.

Williams, Roger (1603–1683) English cleric in America who was expelled from Massachusetts for his criticism of Puritan policies. He founded Providence Plantation (1636), a community based on religious freedom, and obtained a charter for Rhode Island in 1644.

Willkie, Wendell (1892–1944) Wall Street lawyer who ran against Franklin D. Roosevelt in his bid for a third consecutive term, which Roosevelt won.

Wilson, Woodrow (1856–1924) Twenty-eighth president of the United States (1913–1921), he was an advocate for the New Freedom and the League of Nations.

Witchcraft hysteria (1691–1692) The prosecution of almost two hundred people in Salem, Massachusetts, and its environs on charges of practicing witchcraft.

Wolfe, James (1727–1759) British general during the Seven Years' War. He defeated the French at Quebec (1759) but was mortally wounded in the battle.

woman suffrage The right of women to vote, which they achieved in 1919–1920 after an intense struggle in congress.

Women of the Army Name given by General George Washington to the approximately twenty thousand women who served in the Continental Army as nurses, cooks, laundresses, and water carriers. They drew rations and were subject to military discipline.

Woodstock A musical festival that was a fusion of rock music, hard drugs, free love, and an antiwar protest. It drew four hundred thousand people to a farm in upstate New York in the summer of 1969.

Wounded Knee, Battle of (1890) The last major chapter in the Indian wars, it was fought on the Pine Ridge Reservation in South Dakota.

writ of habeas corpus Constitutional provision allowing prisoners to petition against unlawful detention. The writ was suspended by Lincoln as a wartime measure to prevent the release of prisoners accused of aiding the Confederacy.

writs of assistance General search warrants; a writ of assistance authorized customs officials to search for smuggled goods.

XYZ Affair (1797–1798) Diplomatic incident in which the French government demanded, through three agents known to the American public as X, Y, and Z, that the U.S. government pay a bribe and apologize for criticizing France.

Yalta Conference (1945) World War II conference where Franklin Roosevelt, Winston Churchill, and Joseph Stalin attempted to establish the political future of a liberated Europe. Though Stalin agreed that Soviet forces would enter the war against Japan within three months of Germany's surrender, his determination to dominate Eastern Europe effectively ended the so-called Grand Alliance.

Yamassees Native Americans who traded with South Carolina merchants but, after enduring fraud and other unfair practices, in 1715 with help from the Creeks waged an unsuccessful war against the colony.

yellow journalism A type of journalism that stressed lurid and sensational news to boost circulation.

Young, Brigham (1801–1877) Mormon leader after the death of Joseph Smith; he led his followers to the Great Salt Lake.

Zimmermann telegram (1917) Secret German diplomatic telegram to the German ambassador in Mexico that was intercepted and decoded by the British. It dangled the return to Mexico of Arizona, New Mexico, and Texas as bait to entice the Mexicans to enter the war on the side of Germany.

INDEX

ABC network, 621

Abortion, 353, 673; religious Right and, 699; rise in, after *Roe v. Wade*, 699; during World War I era, 478

Abraham Lincoln Brigade, 562

Abu Ghraib prison, 726

Acheson, Dean, 598, 603, 607

Acid rock, 657

Acquired immune deficiency syndrome (AIDS), 697, 698, 704

"Active defense" policy (World War II), 569

Activism: by conservatives, 730; gays and lesbians, 699; by Mexican Americans, 670; by Native Americans, 730; women's movement of 1960s, 656, 668–669; in World War II, 575. *See also* Civil rights movement; Protests

Adams, Charles Francis, 354

Adamson Act (1916), 478

Adams, Samuel Hopkins, 443

Addams, Jane, 393, 397, 443, 458

Advanced Research Project Agency, 698

Adventures of Huckleberry Finn, The (Twain), 386

Advertising and advertisements: for the "dream kitchen," 596; electrical items (1920s), 505; emphasizing traditional gender roles, 595; money spent on, 505–506; in the 1920s, 505–506; during Progressive era, 437; on television, 622; for vacuum cleaner, 461

AFDC (Aid to Families with Dependent Children), 674

Affirmative action, 711

Afghanistan: air strikes on, after September 11th attacks, 723–724; Soviet invasion of, 688; Soviet pullout from, 701

AFL. *See* American Federation of Labor (AFL)

African Americans: accomplishments of, in the 1890s, 420; affirmative action and, 711; after emancipation, 340; after Reconstruction, 364; *Amos 'n' Andy* and, 528; in baseball, 511; in *Birth of a Nation*, 475; black codes (colonial) for, 341; Black Muslims, 655; Black Panthers, 655–656; Black Power, 655–656; Booker T. Washington and, 419–420; car ownership by, 504; Centennial International Exhibition and, 358; Clarence Thomas and, 706; Colored Farmers' Alliance, 405; Communist Party and, 559; cowboys, 380; in the defense industry, 574; Eleanor Roosevelt and, 559; excluded from national convention of 1912, 458; failure of Freedman's Savings and Trust Company, 356; Farmers Alliance and, 405; farming and, 384; Fifteenth Amendment and, 345; first to seek presidential nomination of major party, 677; Harlem Renaissance and, 508; higher education institutions for, 510–511; Jackie Robinson, 600–601; "Jack" Johnson, 463; Jesse Jackson, 699; Ku Klux Klan and, 347–348; labor by, 558–559, 574; in the marines, 575; migration from the South, 34, 476–477, 477 (table); militancy, 501–502; New Deal and, 558–559; Niagara Conference (1905), 440; in the 1910s, 440; in the1960s, 672; Pan-Africanism and, 502; political participation by, 343–344, 357, 677; race riots and, 440, 485, 494, 653, 707; racist propaganda and, 356; Reconstruction and, 342, 346, 360; in reform campaigns during the 1890s, 417; Scottsboro boys, 535; Simpson trial and, 711; single parent families among, 698; in Spanish-American War, 427, 428; in Theodore Roosevelt's era, 439–440; unemployment of, 558, 672; as urban residents, 499; in U.S. Supreme Court, 651, 706; violence against, 420, 440, 494, 501, 574; voter registration by, in the South, 654 (map), 654 (table); voting and, 352, 398–399, 440; Watts riot (1965) and, 653; white workers during Great Depression and, 527; women, 353; World War I and, 475–477, 484–485. *See also* Civil rights movement; Lynchings; Segregation

Afrika Korps, 570

Agencies. *See* specific agencies

Agent Orange, 682

Agnew, Spiro T., 661, 678

Agricultural Adjustment Act (AAA), 546, 548, 561

Agricultural Appropriation Act (1906), 447

Agricultural Marketing Act (1929), 527

Agriculture: Agriculture Adjustment Act, 546, 548; Dust Bowl disaster, 546–547; Great Depression and, 524; Mexican farm workers, 548; New Deal programs, 545–546; problems of southern, 383–384; sharecropping, 383–384; tenant and sharecropper organization, 548; World War I "war gardens," 483. *See also* Farms and farming

Aguinaldo, Emilio, 426, 429, 431

Aid for Dependent Children (AFDC), 714

AIDS (acquired immune deficiency syndrome), 697, 698, 704

Aid to Families with Dependent Children (AFDC), 674

Air Force: Luftwaffe, 566, 567; Nazi, 566, 567; Tuskegee Airmen and, 575; Vietnam War and, 650; during World War II, 567

Alabama (ship), 346

Alamogordo, New Mexico, 587

Alaska, 344

Albania, 566, 717

Alcatraz Island, 670

Alcohol consumption: between 1920 and 1930, 502, 502 (table); during Prohibition, 514; temperance movement, 353. *See also* Prohibition

Alcohol, Tobacco, and Firearms, Bureau of, 708

Aldrich, Nelson W., 445, 451
Aldrin, Edwin "Buzz," 665
Alfred P. Murrah Federal Building, Oklahoma City, 712–713
Alger, Horatio, 378, 378 (fig)
Algeria, 578
Allende, Salvadore, 675
Allen, Paul, 698
Allies (World War I), 481–482, 483, 486
Allies (World War II), 578, 579–580
Allison, William Boyd, 446
Al Qaeda, 737
Altamont, California, 666
Altgeld, John P., 415
Amazon.com, 716
Amendments: Equal Rights Amendment, 669, 670, 671, 671 (map); Fifteenth, 345, 351; Fourteenth, 399, 418, 420; Nineteenth, 493, 668; Platt, 430, 550; Seventeenth, 445; Sixteenth, 460; Twentieth, 535
America First Committee, 556
American and South Vietnamese (ARVN) troops, 657
American Aristocracy (film), 477
American Birth Control League, 514
American Civil Liberties Union (ACLU), 512
American Expeditionary Force (AEF), 482, 486
American Federation of Labor (AFL), 378, 448; divisions with, 553; growth of, 455; immigration restriction and, 500; during World War I, 484
The American Indian Gets into the War Game (film), 485
American Indian Movement (AIM), 670, 672
American Liberty League, 550–551
American Medical Association (AMA), 649
American Mercury, 509
American Protective League, 486
American Railway Union (ARU), 414
American Special Forces, 650
Americans with Disabilities Act (1990), 702
American Woman Suffrage Association, 351, 401
America Online, 716
Amoskeag Company textile mills, 454

Amos 'n' Andy (radio program), 528, 551
Amos 'n' Andy (television program), 621, 622
Anarchists, 377
Anderson, John, 694, 694 (map)
Anderson, Marian, 559
Anderson, Sherwood, 463, 509
Andrews Sisters, 622
Anglo-American-Venezuelan commission, 422
Anglo-Saxon supremacy, 402
Animated cartoon, 560
Annexation: Dominican Republic, 346; of Hawaii, 403–404, 426
Anthony, Susan B., 351, 358, 401
Antiballistic missile (ABM) agreement, 676
Anti-Evolution League, 512
Anti-Imperialist League, 429–430
Anti-imperialists, 428–429, 429–430
Anti-Saloon League, 417, 453, 478
Anti-Semitism, 396, 581
Antiwar sentiment, 666–667
Apache Indians, 350–351
Apartments, 394
Apollo 1 disaster (1967), 665
Apollo 11 (1969), 665
Apollo 13 (1970), 665
Apple Macintosh computer, 698
Arabic (torpedo), 475, 479
Arafat, Yasir, 710
Architecture, 510
Ardeness Forest, 567
Argentina, 685
Arizona (battleship), 570
Arkansas Guard, 627
Armas, Carlos Castillo, 616
Armed forces: discrimination and segregation in, 427, 574–575; homecoming for, after World War II, 593; homosexuals serving in, 708, 737; Mexican Americans in, 575; National Security Act (1947) and, 598–599; in Panama, 704; in Persian Gulf War, 705; racism in, 574, 575; in Vietnam, 650, 651. *See also* Army (U.S.); Draft (military); Marines (U.S.); Navy (U.S.)
Armory Show, the (1913), 462
Armour meat company, 385
Arms control: SALT (Strategic Arms Limitation Treaty) and, 676; SALT II Treaty, 696; Soviet Union's

perestroika and, 700; Strategic Defense Initiative, 697
Arms sale, to Iran, 700–701
Armstrong, Louis, 509
Armstrong, Neil, 665
Army (U.S.): Army-McCarthy hearings, 615; Civilian Conservation Corps (CCC) and, 544; in 1889, 401; Mexican Americans serving in, 575; Panama Canal construction and, 441; in the Philippines, 429; reforms in, after Spanish-American War, 428; for Spanish-American War, 427; for World War I, 482, 483
Army Medical Corps, 571
Army Signal Corps, 615
Arthur, Chester, 388, 402
Arts, the: Armory Show (1913), 462; Beat generation, 623; Harlem Renaissance, 508
Assassinations: attempt on George Wallace, 676; attempt on Reagan, 695; of Garfield, 388; of Kennedy, John F., 646; of Kennedy, Robert, 660; of King, 659; of McKinley, 431
Assembly line concept, 461
Assimilation, Native American, 379
Association for the Advancement of Women, 353
Associations, rise of voluntary, 352–353
Astaire, Fred, 560
Aswan Dam, 626
Atlanta Compromise (1895), 419
Atomic bomb: Hiroshima, Japan, 587, 588; increase in production of, 616; Korean War and, 606, 614; Manhattan Project, 587; Nagasaki, Japan, 588; testing, 587–588
Audubon Society, 443
Auschwitz, Poland, 581, 582
Austria-Hungary, Triple Alliance and, 472–473
Automobiles and automobile industry: assembly line concept for, 461; employment at Ford plants, 461–462; first president to travel to inauguration in, 461; General Motors *vs.* Ford Motor Company, 504–505; mass-produced, 436–437; in the mid-twentieth century, 613; Model T, 436–437, 504; number of registered

cars, 1921–1929, 504, 504 (table); during World War I, 484
Aviation, 516–517

B-29 bombs, 587, 588
Babbitt (Lewis), 509
Baby boom, 594, 595
Baden-Powell, Robert, 453
Baez, Joan, 666
Baker, Howard, 701
Baker, James A., 702
Bakke, Allan, 685
Balanced budget, 695
Baldwin, James, 645
Balkans: civil war in (1990s), 706; Clinton's foreign policy in, 710, 715; Dayton Peace Agreement and, 713; World War I and, 473
Ballinger, Richard A., 451, 457
Baltimore, Maryland, African American migration to, 477 (table)
Bank holiday, 544
Bank of America, 731
Banks and banking: banks suspension, 1927–1933, 525 (table); economic bailout, in 2008, 733–734; failure of Freedman's Savings and Trust Company, 356; Federal Reserve system, 460; Great Depression and, 524–525, 526, 534–535, 536; housing crisis (early 2000s) and, 735; Panic of 1893 and, 413
Barker, Ma, 50
Barkley, Alben, 601
Barnett, Ross, 642
Barnum, P.T., 385
Barrow, Clyde, 560
Bartholdi, Frèdèric-Auguste, 386
Barton, Bruce, 506
Baruch, Bernard, 484
Baseball: Babe Ruth and, 511; during early 20th century, 463; in the 1880s, 385–386; Jackie Robinson and, 600–601; World Series (1969), 665; during World War II, 572
Bataan Death March, 571
Bataan Peninsula, 571
Batista, Fulgenico, 550
Battle for Ole Miss, 642
Bay of Pigs, 640
Beat generation, 623
Beatles, the, 621
Bedloe's Island, 386

Begin, Menachem, 685–686
Behavioral psychology, 510
Belgium, 567
Belize, 697 (map)
Belknap, W.W., 355
Bell, Alexander Graham, 358
Bell, Alexander Graham, 375
Bellamy, Edward, 400
Bellamy, Edward, 400
Bellows, George, 462
Berle, Milton, 620
Berlin, Germany, 602
Berlin Olympics (1936), 560
Berlin Wall, 640–641
Bernstein, Carl, 678, 680
Bethlehem Steel, 506
Bethune-Cookman College, 559
Bethune, Mary McLeod, 559
Beveridge, Albert J., 451, 452
Bicycling, 400
Biden, Joseph, 733
Big business: Andrew Carnegie, 374; emergence of, 372–373; John D. Rockefeller and Standard Oil Company, 373–374; merger of railroads, 438; merger of steel companies, 439; railroads and, 371–372; Roosevelt's control over, 447
Billboards, 506
Bin Laden, Osama, 724
Bin Laden, Osama, 723
Biological weapons, 674
Birmingham, Alabama, 644–645
Birth control: coining of term, 478; in the 1870s, 353; laws governing, 477–478; Margaret Sanger and, 478, 514
Birth Control League, 478
"Birthers," 736
Birth of a Nation, The (film), 475
Birthrates, 595
Black codes (colonial), 341
Black, Hugo, 561
Blackmun, Harry, 673
Black Muslims, 655
Black Panthers, 655–656, 660
Black Power, 655–656
Black Thursday, 523
Blackwell, Alice Stone, 351
Blackwell, Lucy Stone, 401
Blaine, James G., 359, 388, 388 (map), 402–403, 404, 407–408
Blair, Frank, 345
Blatch, Harriot Stanton, 452

Bloggers, 727
Bloody Sunday, 653
Board of Indian Commissioners, 349
Bock's Car (B-29 bomb), 588
Bohemian-American National Council, 396
Boll weevil, 476
Bolshevism, 489
Bond, Christopher, 728
Bonds, World War I, 483
Bonus Army, 534–535
Bootleggers, 502
Borah, William E., 489, 491
Bork, Robert, 701
Bosnia, 706, 710, 713, 715
Boss politics, 396–397
"Boston marriages," 477
Boston Red Sox, 511
Boston School Committee, 353
Boston schools, busing in, 673
Boulder Dam, Colorado, 549
Boxer Rebellion, 430
Boxing, 400, 463, 511
Boycotts, grape, 660
Boynton v. Virginia (1961), 641
Boy Scouts of America, 453
Bracero program, 575
Bradwell, Myra, 351
Brain trust, 532
Branch Davidian religious sect, 708–709
Brandeis, Louis D., 418, 449, 479
Brave and Bold (Alger), 378
Brazil, 685, 697 (map)
Breadlines, 523
Brennan, William, 706
Brezhnev, Leonid, 676
British Foreign Office, 480
British Royal Air Force, 567
Broadway musicals, 510
Brooks, Mel, 621
Brotherhood of Locomotive Engineers, 376
Brotherhood of Locomotive Firemen, 376
Brotherhood of Sleeping Car Porters, 574, 645
Brown, Henry Billings, 420
Brown, Oliver, 618
Brown, Scott, 737
Brown v. Board of Education of Topeka (1954), 617–619, 634
Bryan, William Jennings: election of 1896 and, 423–424, 424 (map); election of 1900 and, 431; election

Bryan, William Jennings (*cont.*)
of 1908 and, 450; free silver
policy, 423, 431; fundamentalist
movement and, 511; on reserve
banks, 460; Scopes Trial and,
512–513; as secretary of state, 459,
471; on Treaty of Paris, 429; World
War I and, 475
Bryn Mawr, 351
Buchanan, Patrick, 708, 714
Buddhist protests, 643, 644
Budget and Accounting Act
(1921), 503
Budget deficit. *See* National debt
Buffalo herds, 350
Bulge, Battle of the, 580
Bull Durham, 383
"Bull Moose" Party, 458
Bunau-Varilla, Philippe, 441
Bunyan, John, 443
Bureau of Alcohol, Tobacco, and
Firearms, 708
Bureau of Corporations, 439
Bureau of Indian Affairs (BIA), 527
Bureau of Refugees, Freedmen, and
Abandoned Lands, 340
Bureau of the Budget, 503
Burger Court, 673
Burger, Warren C., 673, 701
Burleson, Albert S., 486, 487
Burma, 570
Burnham, Daniel, 409
Burns & Allen (television
program), 621
Burns, Lucy, 452, 453
Bush, George H.W.: administration
of, 692, 693; approval ratings of,
706, 707; biographical information,
701–702; domestic policies, 702,
704; election of 1988 and, 702;
election of 1992 and, 708, 708
(map); foreign policy successes
under, 704–705; Iran-Iraq war and,
705; Persian Gulf War and, 705–
706; Reagan and, 692; Supreme
Court appointment by, 706
Bush, George W., 635, 720; election
of 2000 and, 720–722, 722
(map); election of 2004 and, 726;
executive authority and, 722–723;
as governor, 717; Hurricane
Katrina and, 727; Iraq and,
724–726; national debt and,
722, 731; poll ratings for, 726;
presidency of, 722–726

Bush, Jeb, 717
Bush v. Gore (2000), 722
Business and businesses: between
1877 and 1914, 364; in the
1980s, 693; antitrust suits
against, 457; civil rights and,
672; during depression of the
1890s, 416; downsizing and,
706–707; employee relations
with, 454; housing crisis and, 731;
immigrant labor and, 472, 729;
media conglomerates, 726–727;
military production (World War
II) by, 571; National Recovery Act
and, 549; overseas investments,
516; railroads and, 370–371;
reasons for U.S. involvement in
World War I and, 557; welfare
capitalism and, 506–507. *See also*
Big business
Butterfield, Alexander, 678
Byrd, Harry F., 630 (map)

Cabinets: of Eisenhower, 613–614;
of Kennedy, John F., 639
Cable cars, 394
Cable News Network (CNN),
711, 727
Cagney, James, 528
California: migration from Dust
Bowl to, 547; Proposition 187 in,
728; Proposition 209 in, 711; racial
violence in, 574–575
Calley, William, 667–668
Cambodia, 666
Camera, invention of Kodak, 375
Camp David Accords (1978),
685–686
Camp David summit meeting
(1960), 628–629
Campfire Girls, 453
Canada: immigration from, 500;
same-sex marriage in, 730; trade
with, 456
Can-Can (film), 628
Candler, Asa, 385, 437
Cannon, Jimmy, 601
Canton, Ohio, 424
Cape Canaveral, 640
Capitalism and capitalists, 378
Capone, Alphonse "Al," 502
Capra, Frank, 560
Carbon filament incandescent
lamp, 375
Cárdenas, Lázaro, 550

Caribbean, U.S. in, 1981–2008, 697
(map)
Carlucci, Frank, 701
Carmichael, Stokely, 655, 656
Carnegie, Andrew, 374, 386, 430
Carnegie Steel Company, 439
Carpetbaggers, 343
Carranz, Venustiano, 472, 480
Cars. *See* Automobiles and
automobile industry
Carson, Rachel, 645, 674
Carter, James Earl (Jimmy):
biographical information, 683; civil
rights and, 685; economic plan of,
686; election of 1976 and, 683,
684, 684 (map); election of 1980
and, 693–694, 694 (map); energy
crisis and, 688; foreign policy
of, 685–686; Iran and, 687–688;
Iranian hostage crisis and, 688–
689; presidential style of, 684–685;
public approval rating, 688
Carter, Philip, 728, 729
Cash register, invention of, 375
Casinos, 730
Castro, Fidel, 640, 646, 651, 675, 681
Casualties: Iraq war, 727; Vietnam
War, 651, 666, 678; World War I,
482; World War II, 583, 584, 585,
588 (table)
Cather, Willa, 509
Catholics and Catholicism: abortion
and, 699; anti-Catholocism, 396;
immigrants, 453; Kennedy, John F.
and, 630
Catt, Carrie Chapman, 443, 478,
485, 493, 514
Cattle raising, 380–381
CBS (Columbia Broadcasting
System), 560, 621
Census: of 1920, 499; on number of
farms (1870), 350; on rural, urban,
and suburban dwellers, 613
Centennial International Exhibition
(1876), 357–358
Central America: funding of Contras
in, 696; U.S. in, 1981–2008, 697
(map). *See also* individual countries
Central Intelligence Agency (CIA):
Chilean government and, 675;
during the Cold War, 616; covert
action and, 616; creation of, 599;
hearings on abuses of, 681; Iran-
Contra affair and, 700; U-2 spy
planes, 628

Central Pacific Railroad, 348, 370
Central Powers, 473
Century of Dishonor, A (Jackson), 379–380
Challenger (space shuttle), 700
Chamberlain, D.H., 387
Chamberlain, Neville, 562, 566
Chaney, James, 648
Chaplin, Charlie, 477, 505
Charitable organizations, 413
Charity Organization Society, 401
Chase, Chevy, 684
Chavez, Cesar, 659–660
Chavez, Hugo, 697 (map)
"Checkers Speech" (Nixon), 621
Chemical weapons, 674
Cheney, Lynne, 711
Cheney, Richard "Dick," 721, 723
Chiang Kai-shek, 516, 538, 603
Chicago, Burlington, and Quincy Company, 438
Chicago Civic Federation, 417–418
Chicago, Illinois, 393–394;
African American migration to, 476, 477 (table); Democratic National Convention, 1932, 532; Democratic National Convention, 1968, 660–661; Haymarket riot in, 377; Hull House in, 393; population growth in, 393–394; race riot in, 494; reform of the 1890s and, 417–418; World's Columbian Exposition in, 409
Chicago Tribune, 355
Chicago Tribune (newspaper), 602
Chicano activism, 669, 670
Child labor, 376; during depression of the 1890s, 416; National Recovery Act and, 549; in 1900, 436; reform in, 454
Child labor laws, 416
Child rearing: Dr. Spock and, 595; in the Progressive era, 436
Children: Boy Scouts for, 453; Girl Scouts for, 453; in Victorian society, 399. *See also* Families
Children's Bureau, 443, 454
Chile, 675, 685
China: Boxer Rebellion (1900) in, 430; dollar diplomacy and, 456; fall to communism, 603; foreign policy with, in the 1920s, 516; Korean War and, 604; Nixon's visit to, 675; Open Door Notes and, 430; Open Door policy, 447, 503;

rape of Nanking, 569; Stimson Doctrine and, 530; Tiananmen Square, 704; U.S. relationship with, under Nixon, 675; Wilson's foreign policy with, 471; World War II casualties, 588 (table)
Chinese Exclusion Act (1882), 398, 453
Chinese immigrants: efforts to restrict, 453; labor by, 377, 380; restrictions on, 398; union opposing labor by, 378
Chisholm, Shirley, 677
Christian Broadcasting Network, 699
Christianity, evangelical, 699. *See also* specific denominations
Chrysler Corporation, 561, 706
Churchill, Winston, 567; Atlantic Charter and, 569; Italian campaign during World War II and, 578–579; Potsdam Conference and, 586; requesting warships from U.S., 568; Yalta Conference and, 585
CIA. *See* Central Intelligence Agency (CIA)
Cigarette-making machine, 383
Cigar Makers International Union, 378
Cincinnati, Ohio, 476
CIO (Congress of Industrial Organizations), 554, 561
Circus, 385
Citibank, 731
Cities: boss politics in, 396–397; Chicago, 393–394; commission government in, 444; in mid-twentieth century, 613; population growth in, 499; progressive reform in, 444; settlement houses in, 393, 397; structure of, 394
Citizenship: for African Americans, 342, 344; for Native Americans, 380
Civilian Conservation Corps (CCC), 544, 545
Civil liberties: internment of Japanese Americans and, 575–576; Patriot Act and, 724; Red Scare and, 494; World War I and, 485
Civil rights: under Carter, 685; Eleanor Roosevelt and, 559; election of 1948 and, 601; Johnson on, 647–648; Mexican Americans

and, 670; Native Americans and, 670–671; Truman's agenda on, 600
Civil Rights Act (1875), 384
Civil Rights Act (1964), 647–648, 656
Civil rights movement: battle at Ole Miss, 642; in Birmingham, Alabama, 644–645; Black Power, 655–656; Bloody Sunday, 653; *Brown v. Board of Education of Topeka* (1954), 617–619; Freedom Riders, 641; Little Rock, Arkansas and, 626–627; March on Washington for Jobs and Freedom, 645; Montgomery bus boycott, 619–620; murder of civil rights activists, 648; Nixon and, 672; sit-in protests, 638; voting rights and, 653; World War II activism and, 575
Civil service, 346, 388
Civil wars: in the Balkans, 706; in China, 603; Russia, 489; Spain, 566; in Spain, 566
Civil Works Administration (CWA), 545
Clansman, The (Dixon), 475
Clark Field, 571
Clark, James Beauchamp "Champ," 457
Clark, Jim, 653
Clark, Kenneth, 618
Clark, Ramsey, 653
Clayton-Bulwer Treaty (1850), 430
Clean Air Act (1970), 674
Clean Air Act (1990), 702
Clemenceau, Georges, 489
Clemens, Samuel L. (Mark Twain), 386
Cleveland, Grover: Cuban Crisis and, 422; election of 1884 and, 388, 388 (map); election of 1888 and, 392–393; election of 1892 and, 408; foreign policy of, 402; Hawaii and, 403, 422; presidency of, 389; protective tariff and, 389; Pullman strike and, 415; Sherman Silver Purchase Act and, 413, 414
Cleveland, Ohio, 622, 674
Climate change, 731–732
"Clinton Health Plan," 709
Clinton, Hillary Rodham, 708; election of 2008 and, 733, 736; health care reform and, 709; Whitewater scandal and, 713

Clinton v. Jones (1997), 716

Clinton, William Jefferson "Bill," 635, 692; allegations against, by political right, 709; approval ratings of, 709, 717; Balkans conflict and, 710, 715; domestic agenda of, 708–709; economy under, 715; election of 1992 and, 707–708, 708 (map); election of 1996 and, 714–715; foreign policy of, 710; health care reform and, 709; impeachment and acquittal of, 716–717; Lewinsky scandal and, 716; national debt and, 709, 715; Oklahoma City bombing and, 713; Republican Congress and, 712, 713; veto by, 713

Closing Circle, The (Commoner), 674

Clothing, women's, 436

Coal miners and coal mining, 356, 439, 594

Coca-Cola, 385, 437

Cocker, Joe, 665, 666

Cocoanuts (film), 528

Cody, William "Buffalo Bill," 385

Cohn, Roy M., 615

Cold War, 612; atomic bomb explosion in Soviet Union and, 603; beginning of, 597; brinkmanship strategy, 616; during Carter years, 688; China's fall to communism and, 603; collapse of Soviet Union and, 706; containment and, 597, 603; defined, 613; détente and, 676, 683; domino theory, 617; end of, 692, 704; in Europe, 1945–1989, 605 (map); House Un-American Activities Committee (HUAC), 599–600; hunt for subversives and, 614–615; "Iron Curtain," 597; Korean War and, 604, 606; McCarthyism, 606–607; in the 1960s, 634; North Atlantic Treaty Organization (NATO) and, 603; Strategic Defense Initiative and, 697; Vietnam and, 616–617

Cole (destroyer), 723

College. *See* Higher education

College football, 511

Collins, Michael, 665

Colombia, 441, 471, 697 (map)

Colorado, 380, 401

Colorado Fuel and Iron Company, 455

Colored Farmers' National Alliance and Cooperative Union, 405

Columbia (space vessel), 665

Columbia Broadcasting System (CBS), 560, 621

Columbian Exposition (1893), 409, 417

Columbia University, 510, 660

COMECON, European members of, 605 (map)

Commercial radio, 505

Commission form of city government ("Galveston Idea"), 444

Committee on Government Operations, 615

Committee on Public Information (CPI), 485

Committee to Re-Elect the President (CREEP), 676

Commoner, Barry, 674

Common Law, The (Holmes), 418

Common Sense Book of Baby and Child Care (Spock), 595

Communism: Berlin Wall and, 640–641; Bolshevism, 489; China's fall to, 603; containment of, 597; domino theory and, 617; fall of South Vietnam and, 681–682; Hungarian revolt (1956), 625; Red Scare and, 494. *See also* Cold War

Communist Party: Abraham Lincoln Brigade, 562; African American writers in, 559; after World War II, 599; election of 1932 and, 535; election of 1936 and, 557, 558; Scottsboro boys and, 55

Compromise of 1877, 360

Computers, personal, 698

Comstock, Anthony, 353

Comstock Law (1873), 477–478

Concentration camps, Nazi, 580–581, 582, 583

Confederacy, amnesty given to, 341

Congress (U.S.): at beginning of Reagan administration, 694; Clinton and Republican, 712, 713; Grant and, 345, 346–347; immigration restriction, 500; term limits on, 712; World War I and, 482. *See also* Elections

Congressional Medal of Honor, 427

Congressional Union, the, 453, 478

Congress of Industrial Organization (CIO), 554, 561

Congress of Racial Equality (CORE), 641

Connally, John, 646

Connor, Eugene "Bull," 644

Conservation: under Taft, 450–451; under Theodore Roosevelt, 449–450

Conservatives/conservatism: allegations against Clinton, 709; blogs, 727; of Coolidge, 507; on homosexuality, 712; in judiciary, 448–449; multiculturalism and, 711; neoconservatives, 721; on same-sex marriage, 730; Taft's presidency, 450–451; on teaching evolution, 730; Theodore Roosevelt's policies and, 448–449

Consumerism: in the 1920s, 510; at beginning of 20th century, 436–437; post-World War II, 596; urban growth and, 394; during World War II, 572

Containment, 597, 603, 616

"Contract with America," 710

Contras, 696, 700–701

Convict-lease system, 398

Coolidge, Calvin, 495; conservative principles of, 507; election of 1920 and, 495; election of 1924 and, 507–508; election of 1928 and, 517; foreign policy of, 515–516; policy goals of, 515

Cooper, Gary, 560

Coral Sea, Battle of the, 582

Corbett, James J. "Gentleman Jim," 400

Corliss steam engine, 358

Cornell University, 351

Corporations. *See* Business and businesses

Correll, Charles, 528

Costello, Frank, 621

Cost-of-living adjustment (COLA), 594, 605

Cost of living index, after World War I, 493

Cotton and cotton industry: decrease in prices of, 506

Coughlin, Charles Edward, 58, 551–552

Counterculture, 656–657

Countrywide (lender), 731

Courts: right of black citizens to sue in federal, 357. *See also* U.S. Supreme Court

Court TV, 711
Cowboys, 380–381
Cox, Archibald, 678
Coxey, Jacob S., 414
Coxey's Army, 414
Cox, James M., 495
Crane, Stephen, 419
Crater Lake, 449
Crazy Horse, 350
Creationists, 730
Credit: autos purchased on, 505; mortgage loans and, 731, 732
Credit card, America's first, 596
Crédit Mobilier Company, 354
Creel, George, 485
CREEP (Committee to Re-Elect the President), 676
Crime and criminals: African Americans and, 398; by Black Panthers, 656; gangsters, 502; organized, in the 1920s, 502, 513; Sacco and Vanzetti case, 500
"Crime of 1873," 356
The Crisis (journal), 508
Croats, 713, 715
Crockett, Davy, 621
Croker, Richard, 397
Cronkite, Walter, 657
Crosby, Bing, 622
"Cross of Gold" speech (Bryan), 423
C-SPAN, 710
C. Turner Joy (ship), 648
Cuba: after Spanish-American War, 430; Batista government in, 550; Bay of Pigs, 640; crisis with Spain (1890s), 422, 425; missile crisis, 642–643; 1980–2008, 697 (map); Operation Mongoose, 640; Platt Amendment and, 430; Spain and, 346; troops to, under Wilson, 472; U.S. acquisition of, 364
Cuban missile crisis, 642–643
Cullen, Countee, 508
Culture: counterculture of the 1960s, 656–657; during the Great Depression, 528–529; Harlem Renaissance, 508; Woodstock music festival, 666. *See also* Literature; Music; Popular culture; Youth culture
Culture wars, 711–712
Currency: battle of gold *vs.* silver standard, 423–424; farmers' grievances on, 404, 407; gold standard, 423, 424; Panic of 1873

and, 356; raising money by coining silver into, 386; Republican discord under Grant on, 346
Custer, George Armstrong, 350
"Custer's Last Stand," 350
Cuyahoga River, fire on, 674
Czech immigrants, 395
Czechoslovakia, 562; Germans marching into, 566; Soviet influence in, 598
Czech Republic, NATO and, 715
Czolgosz, Leon, 431

Dakota Territory, 349
Daladier, Edouard, 562
Daley, Richard, 660
Da Nang, South Vietnam, 650
Danbury Hatters' case *(Loewe v. Lawlor)*, 449
Darrow, Clarence, 513–514
Darwin, Charles, 378
Darwinism, 399–400
Daugherty, Harry, 507
Daughters of the American Revolution, 559
Davis, C. Wood, 406
Davis, John W., 508
Dawes, Henry L., 380
Dawes Severalty Act (1887), 380, 393, 730
Dayton Peace Agreement, 713, 715
D-Day invasion (1944), 579
DDT, banning use of, 674
Dean, Howard, 727
Dean, John, 678
Death penalty, 673
Death rate, in early 20th century, 436
Debates: Nixon-Kennedy, 630; presidential election of 2000, 721
Debs, Eugene Victor: in election of 1912, 458, 459 (map); prison sentence of, 486; Pullman strike and, 414; Red Scare and, 494
Debt. *See* National debt
"Deep Throat," 680
Defense industry: job discrimination in, 574; women in, during World War II, 573
Defense spending: under Eisenhower, 616, 628; during Ford-Carter years, 695; during Kennedy administration, 644; under Reagan, 695. *See also* Military aid

Deflation, 373, 376
De Lôme, Enrique Dupuy, 425
DeMaggio, Joe, 572
Democracy, 442
Democratic National Convention: Atlantic City (1964), 648; Chicago (1932), 532; Chicago (1968), 660–661; for election of 1940, 568; Philadelphia, 1948, 601
Democratic National Headquarters, break-in at, 676
Democratic Party: on abortion, 699; acquittal of Clinton and, 717; African Americans and, 558; boss politics and, 396, 397; congressional election of 1910 and, 452; congressional election of 1930 and, 531; congressional election of 1982 and, 696; congressional election of 1998 and, 716–717; discord in (1920s), 507–508; election of 1868 and, 345; election of 1876 and, 358–359, 358–360; election of 1884 and, 388; election of 1892 and, 407–408, 407–409; election of 1894 and, 415; election of 1904 and, 442; election of 1912 and, 457, 458–459; election of 1920 and, 495; election of 1922 and, 504; election of 1928 and, 466–467, 521, 521 (map); election of 1932 and, 535; election of 1940 and, 568; election of 1948 and, 601, 602; election of 1952 and, 607; election of 1956 and, 626; election of 1960 and, 630 (map); election of 1972 and, 676–677; election of 1996 and, 714–715; election of 2008 and, 733, 734; Farmers Alliance and, 407; gold standard and, 423; during the Great Depression, 531; Ku Klux Klan and, 342, 501; labor unions and, 448; in late 19th century, 286; during Obama presidency, 736–737; Pullman strike and, 415; resurgence of (1870s), 357; in the South, 382
Demonstrations. *See* Marches; Protests
Denmark, 567
Department of Agriculture, 406
Department of Commerce, creation of, 439

Department of Defense, creation of, 598–599

Department of Homeland Security, 727

Department of Housing and Urban Development (HUD), 651

Department of Justice, 445. *See also* Justice Department

Depression (economic): of the 1890s, 415–416; impact of World War I and, 466; mid 1870s, 344; Panic of 1893, 412, 413–415. *See also* Great Depression, the

Deregulation, under Reagan, 695–696

Desert Storm. *See* Operation Desert Storm

Des Moines, Iowa, 444

Détente policy, 676, 683

Detroit, Michigan, 417; African Americans migrating to, 476, 477 (table); auto industry in, 504; racial violence in, 574

Dewey, George, 426

Dewey, John, 419

Dewey, Thomas, 584, 602, 602 (map), 607

DeWitt, John, 576

Dexter Avenue Baptist Church, Montgomery, 620

Diaz, Porfirio, 456, 472

Diem, Ngo Dien, 638, 643–644

Dien Bien Phu, 616

Dillinger, John, 560

Dingley-Tariff Act (1897), 425, 451

Diplomacy. *See* Foreign policy and affairs

Dirksen, Everett, 647

Disabled persons, 702

Discover Institute, 730

Discrimination and prejudice: against Mexican Americans, 472; in the North, after Great Migration, 476–477; "reverse," 685; Truman speaking out against, 600; wage, 573; of women in the workplace, 645. *See also* Race and racism

Disease: AIDS, 697, 698, 704; influenza pandemic, 493; polio, 624; during Spanish-American War, 428

Disney, Walt, 560, 621

Distinguished Unit Citations, 575

Divorce: after World War II, 593; in 1900, 399, 436; in 1916, 477; in the 1920s, 510; rate, in 1981, 698

Dixiecrat Party, 601–602

Dixon, Thomas, 475

Dobbs, Lou, 729

Dobrynin, Anatoly, 643

Dodd, S.T.C., 373–374

Dodge, J.R., 406

Dole, Robert, 710; election of 1976 and, 683; election of 1996 and, 714, 715; tax cut proposal by, 714

Dollar diplomacy, 456

Dolliver, Jonathan P., 451, 452

Domestic policy: of Bush, George H.W., 702, 704; of Clinton, 708–709; of Harding, 503; of McKinley, 425, 431; of Roosevelt, Theodore, 448–450; of Truman, 600. *See also* specific presidents

Dominican Republic (Santo Domingo), 346, 472

Domino theory, 617

Donnelly, Ignatius, 406

"Don't Ask, Don't Tell" policy, 708, 737

Dorsey, Tommy, 622

DOS (disk operating system), 698

Dos Passos, John, 509

"Double V" campaign, 574–575

Douglass, Frederick: on black suffrage, 352; woman's suffrage and, 351

Douglas, William O., 561

Dover, Pennsylvania, 730

Dowd, Mamie, 607

Dow Jones Industrial Average, 717

Downsizing, 706–707

Draft (military): for Vietnam War, 650; for World War I, 482; for World War II, 567–568, 571

Draft cards, burning of, 660

Dreiser, Theodore, 419, 463

Drought, during the Great Depression, 526

Drug use, 656, 657

Dry farming, 382

Du Bois, W.E.B., 440–441, 484, 508

Dukakis, Michael, 702

Duke, James Buchanan, 383

Dulles, Allen, 616, 626, 640

Dulles, John Foster, 614

Dust Bowl, the, 546–547, 547 (map)

Dutch East Indies, 570

Dwellings, in cities of the 1880s, 394

Eagle (moon module), 665

Eagleton, Thomas, 677

Earth in Balance (Gore), 731

Eastern Europe: end of Cold War and, 499, 704 (*See also* specific countries); immigrants from, 364, 394, 395, 500; restricting immigration from, 453

East Germany, 704

Eastland, James O., 617–618

Eastman, Max, 462

East St. Louis, Illinois, 485

Easy Rider (film), 657

E.C. Knight (1895) decision, 418

Economic Opportunity Act (1964), 649

Economy: after World War I, 493; big business and, 373; under Bush Sr., 705; under Clinton, 715; decline and recovery of, 1925–1945, 554 (fig); in 1893, 409; during election of 2008, 733–734; at end of 1920s, 517; during Ford administration, 683; housing crisis and (early 2000s), 731, 735; under Kennedy, 641; in the late 1950s, 628; in the 1920s, 504; in the 1980s, 693; Obama presidency and, 736; oil embargo and, 680–681; Panic of 1873 and, 355–356; Panic of 1893, 413–415; post-World War II, 593–594; railroads and, 370; world, and Great Depression, 524; during World War I, 483–484. *See also* Depression (economic)

Edison, Thomas Alva, 375

Ed Sullivan Show (television program), 623

Education: aftermath of *Sputnik* and, 627–628; in the 1880s, 385; forced busing and, 673; multiculturalism and, 711; National Defense Education Act (1958), 628; national security and, 628; reform in (1890s), 419; at risk, in the 1980s, 698; teaching of evolution and, 511–513. *See also* Higher education; School segregation

Education Act (1965), 651

Egypt: attack on Israel, 680; Camp David Accords and, 685–686; Israel and, 626; World War II and, 570

Ehrlichman, John, 668

Eighteenth Amendment, 483, 493, 545

Einstein, Albert, 563, 587

Eisenhower, Dwight D.: biographical information, 607; brinkmanship strategy of, 616; cabinet of, 613–614; choosing to seek reelection, 624; domino theory and, 617; election of 1948 and, 601; election of 1952 and, 607–608, 610, 613; fiscal policy, 614; foreign policy of, 625–626; hunt for subversives and, 614–615; Korean War and, 614; on Little Rock, Arkansas event, 627; meeting with Khrushchev, 628–629; on Nixon, 626; Normandy invasion and, 579; Supreme Court appointment by, 617; U-2 flights and, 628; Vietnam policy, 616–617; World War II and, 578

Elections: of 1868, 344–345; of 1869, 346; of 1870, 347; of 1872, 354; of 1876, 358–360, 359 (map), 382; of 1884, 388, 388 (map); of 1888, 392–393; of 1890, 404; of 1892, 407–408, 407–409; of 1894, 415; of 1896, 412, 423–424; of 1898 (North Carolina), 420; of 1900, 430–431; of 1904, 442; of 1908, 450; of 1910, 452; of 1912, 457–459, 459 (map); of 1916, 480; of 1918, 488; of 1920, 495; on 1922, 504; of 1924, 507–508; of 1928, 466–467, 521, 521 (map); of 1930, 531; of 1932, 531–532, 533, 535; of 1934, 550–551; of 1936, 557–558; of 1944, 584–585; of 1946, 594; of 1948, 601–602; of 1952, 607–610, 613; of 1956, 626; of 1958, 628; of 1960, 629–631, 639; of 1964, 648–649; of 1968, 659, 661–662, 661 (map); of 1972, 676–677; of 1976, 683–684, 684 (map); of 1980, 693–694; of 1982, 696; of 1984, 699; of 1988, 701–702; of 1992, 707–708, 708 (map); of 1994, 710; of 1996, 714; of 2000, 720–722, 722 (map); of 2006, 732–733; of 2008, 726, 733–734, 734 (map). *See also* Voting and voting rights

Electricity: in the 1920s, 505; invention of electric power, 375; progress and reliance on, 462; radio and, 505

Electric-power cable cars, 394

Eliot, T.S., 509

Elkins Act (1903), 439, 445

Ellington, Duke, 509

Ellis Island, 395

Ellison, Ralph, 559

Ellsberg, Daniel, 668

El Salvador, 696, 697 (map)

Embargo, on Cuba, 642

Emergency quota law (immigration), 500

Emergency Relief and Construction Act (1932), 534

Employers Liabilities Act (1906), 449

Employers, organized labor in the 1930s and, 561

Employment: affirmative action and, 711; firing of federal workers during the Cold War, 614–615; at Ford factories, 461–462. *See also* Labor; Labor unions; Unemployment; Women, in the labor force

Endangered Species Act (1973), 674

Endo v. United States (1944), 577

Energy crisis, 686–688

Enola Gay (airplane), 588

Entertainment: in the 1880s, 385–386; circus, 385; during the Great Depression, 528–529; vaudeville, 385, 463. *See also* Movies; Popular culture; Radio; Sports

Environmental Protection Agency (EPA), 674

Environment, the: climate change and, 731–732; deregulation and, 695; Nixon on, 674; oil spill (2010), 737; *Silent Spring* and, 645, 674

EPIC (End Poverty in California), 551

Equal Employment Opportunity Commission, 647, 706

Equal Pay Act (1963), 646, 656

Equal Rights Amendment (ERA), 514, 668–669, 670, 671, 671 (map)

Equal Rights Association meeting (1869), 351

E. Remington and Sons, 353

Ervin, Sam, 678

Espionage: German, during World War I, 486; House Un-American Activities Committee and, 599–600; U-2 spy planes, 642–643; during World War I, 474

Espionage Act (1917), 486

Estonia, 710

Ethnic cleansing, 717

Ethnic communities, Hispanic, 472

Ethnic neighborhoods, 396

Eugenics, 514

Europe: Cold War in, 1945–1989, 605 (map); same-sex marriage in, 730. *See also* specific country names

European Common Market, members of, 605 (map)

Evangelical Christianity, 699

Evers, Medgar, 645

Evolution, 399–400, 511–513, 730

Ex-Comm, 642

Executive Order 9066, 576

Executive Order 9102, 576

Exodusters, 384

Expansion and expansionism: between 1867 and 1899, 420 (map); annexation of Hawaii, 403–404, 426; critics of, 429–430; under Harrison administration, 402, 404; Hawaii and, 403–404; interest in overseas markets and, 401–402; NATO, 715; Panama Canal and, 441. *See also* Imperialism

Explorer I (satellite), 628

Exports, 402

Factories: Ford assembly plant, 461–462; labor in southern, 383; World War II war production, 571, 572

Fairbanks, Douglas, 477, 506

Fair Campaign Practices Act (1974), 684

"Fair Deal," 599

Fair Employment Practices Committee (FEPC), 574

Fair Labor Standards Act (1938), 563

Falangist government, 562

Fall, Albert B., 507

Falwell, Jerry, 699

Families: average number of children, in 1900, 436; in the 1880s, 385; in the 1980s, 698–699;

Families (*cont.*) in the 1920s, 510; number of children in, World War I era, 477; portrayed on television of the 1950s, 621; post-Civil War, 353; post-World War II, 594–596; in the Progressive era, 436

Family Assistance Plan (FAP), 674

Farewell to Arms, A (Hemingway), 510

Farmers' Alliance, 404–405

Farmers' Alliance and Industrial Union, 405

Farms and farming: African Americans and, 384; after World War I, 466; causes of discontent from, 406; Farmers Alliance, 404–405, 407; during the Great Depression, 527; on the Great Plains, 381–382; grievances of, 1887–1893, 404–405; industrialism and, 382; legislation impacting, late 19th century, 404; in the 1920s, 506; Panic of 1873 and, 356; railroads and, 348. *See also* Agriculture

Farnham, Marynia, 595

Farouk, King, 626

Fascism: in Germany, 555, 562; of Mussolini, 555; in Spain, 562

Father Knows Best (television program), 621

Faubus, Orval, 627

Faulkner, William, 509

FDIC (Federal Deposit Insurance Corporation), 545

Federal Bureau of Investigation (FBI), 494, 681

Federal Deposit Insurance Corporation (FDIC), 545

Federal Emergency Management Agency (FEMA), 724, 727

Federal Emergency Relief Administration (FERA), 545

Federal employment, Cold War and, 614–615

Federal Farm Board, 527

Federal Highway Act (1921), 504

Federal Highway Act (1956), 624

Federal Loyalty-Security Program, 599, 614

Federal Reserve Act (1913), 460

Federal Reserve system, 460, 525

Federal Trade Commission, 442, 460

Felt, W. Mark, 680

FEMA (Federal Emergency Management Agency), 724, 727

Feminine Mystique, The (Friedan), 645, 646

Feminism: in the 1920s, 514–515; in the 1960s, 645–646, 656, 669; Heterodoxy club (1910s) and, 463; portrayed in the 1950s, 612

FERA (Federal Emergency Relief Administration), 545

Ferdinand, Franz, 473

Ferguson, Miriam Amanda, 514

Ferraro, Geraldine, 699

Fifteenth Amendment, 345, 351, 399, 401

Films. *See* Movies

Financier, The (Dreiser), 463

Fire Next Time, The (Baldwin), 645

First ladies: Jackie Kennedy, 629, 646; Rosalyn Carter, 685

First World War. *See* World War I

Fiske, John, 402

Fiske, Robert, 709

Fisk, Jim, 346

Fitzgerald, F. Scott, 510

Fitzgerald, Zelda, 510

Fiume, Italy, 489

Five Civilized Tribes of Native Americans, 393

Five-Power Treaty, 503

Flat tax, 714

Florida: election of 2000 and, 721–722; Ocala Demands and, 407

Flynn, Elizabeth Gurley, 455

Food Administration, 483

Food products: meat inspection and, 447; standardized, 437; toxic chemicals in, 447

Food stamp expenditures, 674

Football, 400, 511, 665

Ford, Gerald R.: chosen as vice-president, 678; the economy and, 683; election of 1976 and, 683–684, 693; fall of South Vietnam and, 682; foreign policy of, 683; Watergate and, 681; Watergate scandal and, 678

Ford, Henry, 435, 436–437, 461, 504–505, 561

Ford Motor Company, 504–505, 561, 562, 571

Fordney-McCumber Tariff law (1922), 503

Foreclosures, 731

Foreign aid: to France, 616; Iran-Contra and, 700–701; Marshall Plan, 598; under Reagan, 634–635; to Soviet Union, 516

Foreign policy and affairs: in the 1920s, 498–499; after Spanish-American War, 430; under Bush, George H.W., 704–706; of Carter, 685–686; of Cleveland, 422–423; of Clinton, 710; of Coolidge, 515–516; covert action, 616; Cuba crisis, 425–426; Cuban Crisis, 1895–1896, 422–423; Cuban missile crisis (1962), 462–463; détente, 676; dollar diplomacy, under Taft, 456; in the early 1890s, 401–404; of Eisenhower, 625–626; of Ford, 683; good neighbor policy, 529, 550; of Harding, 503; interest in overseas markets, 401–402; of Johnson, 648–649; of Kennedy, 640–642; New Deal, 549–550; of Nixon, 675; with the Philippines, 426, 428–429; of Reagan, 696–697, 701; of Roosevelt, Theodore, 441, 447–448; of Wilson, 471–472. *See also* Neutrality

Forrest, Nathan Bedford, 342

Fortas, Abe, 673

Fortune (magazine), 592

Foster, William Z., 494, 535

"Four-Minute Men," 485

Four-Power Treaty, 503

Fourteen Points, the, 487, 489

Fourteenth Amendment, 399, 418, 420, 449

Fox News, 727

France: Four-Power Treaty and, 503; Indochina and, 616; League of Nations and, 490; Nazi invasion of, 567; response to Nazi threat, 562, 567; Suez Canal and, 626; tensions with Germany, 448; war debts of, 529; World War I and, 472, 473, 482, 486; World War II casualties, 588 (table)

Franco, Francisco, 562, 566

Franco-Prussian War of 1871, 473

Frankfurter, Felix, 561

Free blacks, during Civil War, 340

Freed, Alan, 622

Freedmen's Bureau, 340, 342

Freedmen's Savings and Trust Company, 356

Freedom of Information Act, 681

Freedom rides, 641

Free silver policy, 407, 423, 424, 431

Frelinghuysen, Frederick T., 402

Frick, Henry Clay, 408

Friedan, Betty, 595, 645, 646

Friendship 7, 640

Fundamentalism (Christian), 511–512, 513

Furman v. Georgia (1972), 673

Gagarin, Yuri, 640

"Galveston Idea," 444

Galveston, Texas hurricane, 444

Gangster films, 528

Gangsters, prohibition and, 502

Garfield, James A.: assassination of, 388; election of, 388, 388 (map)

Garfunkel, Art, 656

Garland, Judy, 560

Garner, John Nance "Cactus Jack," 531

Garrick Gaieties (musical), 510

Garrison, William Lloyd, 440

Garvey, Marcus, 502, 508

Gates, Bill, 698

GATT (General Agreement on Tariffs and Trade), 709

Gay Liberation Front, 669

Gays and lesbians: in the armed forces, 708, 737; formation of Gay Liberation Front, 669; political and social equality for, 712; same-sex marriage and, 730; Stonewall riot and, 669

Gender roles, traditional, 595

General Accounting Office for Congress, 503

General Agreement on Tariffs and Trade (GATT), 709

General Electric (GE), 462, 506, 523

General Federation of Women's Clubs, 401

General Motors (GM), 504, 561

General Motors Acceptance Corporation, 504

Geneva Accords, 616

Geneva, Switzerland, 616

"Gentlemen's Agreement" (1907), 448

George, David Lloyd, 489

George, Henry, 378

German Americans: antiprohibition sentiment among, 417; election of 1916 and, 480; World War I and, 474, 475, 482, 486

Germany: borrowing money from the U.S., 516; Cuba and, 430; Hitler's message in, 530; immigration restriction from, 500; Munich debacle of 1938, 562; Nazis in, 555; North Africa and, 448; Philippines and, 428; reparation payments and, 524; Sudetenland, 562; tensions with France and Great Britain, 448; Treaty of Versailles and, 489, 492 (map); Tripartite Pact, 570; Triple Alliance and, 472–473; war debts of, 529; World War I and, 472–473, 474, 475, 480–481, 482, 487; World War II and, 580; World War II casualties, 588 (table); Yalta Accords and, 585

Geronimo (Apache leader), 378

Gershwin, George, 510

Gershwin, Ira, 510

GI Bill, 595, 596

Gilbert Islands, 583

Gilded Age, The (Twain), 355

Gillette razors, 437

Gilman, Charlotte Perkins, 401, 417

Gingrich, Newt, 710, 713

Ginsberg, Allen, 623

Ginsburg, Ruth Bader, 736

Girl Scouts, 453

Giuliani, Rudolph, 728, 729

Glasnost, 635

Glenn, John, 640

Glidden, Joseph, 382

Globalization, 731

GNP. *See* Gross national product (GNP)

Gold, discovery of, 350

Golden Gate Bridge, San Francisco, 549

Golden Hour of the Little Flower (radio program), 552

Goldman, Ronald, 710

Gold production, 404

Gold reserves, 413, 423

Gold standard, 346, 356, 404, 408, 423–424

Gold Standard Act (1900), 425

Goldwater, Barry, 648, 649

Gompers, Samuel, 377–378, 448, 455, 484

Gone with the Wind (film), 560

Goodman, Andrew, 648

Good neighbor policy, 529, 550

GOP (Grand Old Party). *See* Republican Party

Gorbachev, Mikhail, 635, 700, 701, 704

Gore, Albert, Jr., 635; *Earth in Balance,* 731; election of 1992 and, 707–708; election of 1996 and, 714–715; election of 2000 and, 721–722, 722 (map); fundraising and, 716

Gosden, Freeman, 528

Gould, Jay, 346, 371, 377

Gould, Lewis L., 703

Government: corruption in, Reconstruction era, 356–357; employment in, 386, 388; Franklin Roosevelt on role of, 533; funding for railroads, 369–370; Hurricane Katrina response by, 727; Nazi, 555; reform in city and state, 444; reform in national, 444–445

Government bonds, 423

Government shutdowns (1995–1996), 713

Governors: female, 514; reform by, 444

Governors Conference on Conservation (1908), 450

The Graduate (film), 656

Grady, Henry, 383

Grand Alliance, 577–581, 592, 597

Grand Coulee Dam, Washington, 549

Grand Old Party (GOP), 404. *See also* Republican Party

Grange, Harold "Red," 511

Grange, the, 348, 356

Grant, Madison, 499–500

Grant, Ulysses S.: administration of, 345–346; election of 1868 and, 344–345; election of 1872 and, 354; on Native Americans, 349; presidency of, 345; scandals during presidency of, 354; tariff policy and, 346

Grape boycott, 660

Grapes of Wrath, The (film), 560

Grateful Dead, 657, 666

Gray, Pete, 572

Greasy Grass (Little Bighorn), 350

Great Britain: *Alabama* and, 346; canal in Central America and, 441; Clayton-Bulwer Treaty, 430; Five-Power Treaty and, 503; Four-Power Treaty and, 503; immigration restriction from, 500; international trade during the Great Depression

Great Britain (*cont.*) and, 529–530; Iraq and, 724–725; League of Nations and, 490; Lend-Lease At and, 568; response to Nazi threat, 567; Suez Canal and, 626; tensions with Germany, 448; Venezuela and, 422; warships sent to (World War II), 568; World War I and, 473, 474, 480–481; World War II and, 567, 578; Yalta Accord and, 585

"Great Communicator," Reagan as, 694

Great Depression, the: banks/banking and, 526, 534–535, 536, 543–544; breadlines, 523; Civilian Conservation Corps and, 544; economic weaknesses leading to, 523–524; election of 1932, 535–536; everyday life during, 527–528; farming during, 527; Hispanic Americans deported during, 527; Hoover's programs to fight, 526–527; Hooverville's and, 528; impact of, 520, 538; international trade and, 529–530; labor during, 527; lack of government programs during, 524–525; lowest point of, 536; mass culture during, 528–529; popular culture in, 559–560; Smoot-Hawley law and, 525; stock market crash of 1929 and, 521–523; unemployment during, 526 (table)

Great Gatsby, The (Fitzgerald), 510

Great Migration, the, 476–477

Great Northern Railroad, 438

Great Plains: Dust Bowl disaster in, 546–547; farming on, 381–382

"Great Recession," 734–735

Great Society, the (1964–1965), 649, 651, 681

"The Great White City," 409

Greece, 597, 598

Greeley, Horace, 354

"Greenbacks," 346

Green Berets, 463

Greenberg, Hank, 572

Green Hornet, The (radio program), 560

Greensboro, North Carolina, 638

Greenwich Village, New York, 462, 463

Grenada, 696, 697 (map)

Griffith, D.W., 475

Gross national product (GNP): in the 1960s, 638; in 1964, 647; during Great Depression, 536; during World War II, 571

Ground Zero, 723

Grutter v. Bollinger (2003), 711

Guadalcanal (island), 583

Guam, 428, 503, 570, 583

Guantanamo Bay, Cuba, 697 (map), 737

Guatemala, 616

Gulf of Tonkin Resolution, 648–649, 650, 667 (fig)

Guzman, Jacobo Arbenz, 616

Hadden, Briton, 509

Haight-Ashbury, San Francisco, 657

Hair (musical), 657

Haiti: Clinton's foreign policy and, 710; troops to, under Wilson, 472; U.S. in, 1998–2008, 697 (map); withdrawing troops from, 503, 529, 550

Hall of Mirrors, Palace of Versailles, 491

Hamer, Fannie Lou, 648

Hammerstein, Oscar, 510

Hanford, Washington, 587

Hanna, Marcus A., 423

Hanson, Ole, 494

Harding, Warren G.: election of 1920, 495; presidency of, 503; reform movement and, 469–470; scandals of, 507

"Hard money," 346

Harlan, John Marshall, 420

Harlem, New York city, 502

Harlem Renaissance, 508

Harriman, Averell, 586

Harriman, E.H., 438

Harrington, Michael, 645

Harrison, Benjamin: in election of 1888, 392–393; election of 1892 and, 407–408; expansionist policy, 404; expansionist policy and, 402, 404; Native American policy, 393

Hart, Gary, 699

Hart, Lorenz, 510

Harvard University, 510

Hastie, William, 617

Hawaii, 403, 422

Hawkins, Coleman, 509

Hayes, Rutherford B.: civil service reform under, 388; election of

1876 and, 359, 360; industry during presidency of, 364; telephone and, 375

Hay, John, 43, 428

Haymarket Riot (1886), 377

Hay-Pauncefote Treaty (1901), 441

Haywood, William D. "Big Bill," 455

Health care: Clinton's reform, 709; under Johnson, 649–650; Medicare and Medicaid, 649–650; Obama's reform, 737

Hearst, William Randolph, 422

Hebrew Immigrant Aid Society, 396

Helms, Jesse, 704

Helsinki Accord (1975), 683

Hemingway, Ernest, 510, 562

Henderson, Fletcher, 509

Hendrix, Jimi, 657, 666

Hepburn Act (1906), 442, 445, 446, 447

Herzegovina, 713

Heterodoxy (club), 463

Higher education: in the 1920s, 510–511; in the late 19th century, 385; "multiversity" and, 652; universities created in the late 19th century, 385; women in, 436, 595, 669. *See also* specific names of universities and colleges

Highland Park, Michigan, 461

Highways, 624, 625 (map)

Hill, Anita, 706

Hill, James J., 438

Hippies, 656

Hirabayashi v. United States (1943), 577

Hiroshima, Japan, 587, 588

Hispanics: cowboys, 380; deported, during the Great Depression, 527; labor by, 472; population of, 2000, 712 (map). *See also* Mexican Americans

Hiss, Alger, 599, 606, 629

Hitler, Adolf: biographical information on, 555; Franco government and, 562; invasion of the Soviet Union, 569; message of, 530; Nazi Germany, 555; nonaggression pact signed by, 566; Stalingrad and, 578; Sudentenland and, 562; suicide of, 580

Hobart, Garret A., 430–431

Ho Chi Minh, 616, 638, 643–644, 651

Ho Chi Minh Trail, 666

Hoffman, Abbie, 660
"Holding company" law, 374
Holiday Inn, 624
Holland. *See* Netherlands
Hollywood, California, 477
"Hollywood Ten," 599
Holmes, Oliver Wendell Jr., 418, 494
Holocaust, the, 580–581
Homeland Security Department, 724
Homestead Act (1862), 381
Homestead strike (1892), 408
Homosexuality: AIDS and, 698; outlawed, 477. *See also* Gays and lesbians
Honduras, 456, 697 (map)
The Honeymooners (television program), 622
Hong Kong, 570
Hoover, Herbert: economic depression and, 520; election of 1928 and, 521, 521 (map); election of 1932 and, 535; election of 1936 and, 557; Food Administration, 483; good neighbor policy of, 529; Great Depression and, 525–527; last days in office, 536; political troubles of, 530–531; Roosevelt *vs.*, 533; stock market crash of 1929 and, 523
Hoover, J. Edgar, 494, 576
Hoovervilles, 528
Hopkins, Harry, 545, 552, 563
Hopwood v. Texas (1996), 711
Horizontal integration, 373
Horne, Lena, 621
Horowitz, David, 711
Horton, William, 702
Hostages, American, 688–689, 693, 695, 700–701
"Hot line," 643
House and Senate Agriculture Committees, 506
House Judiciary Committee, 716, 717
House of Representatives: civil rights bill and, 647; resurgence of Democrats in, 1874, 357; women elected to, 514
House Un-American Activities Committee (HUAC), 599–600, 614
Housing: apartments, 394; tenements, 394
Housing crisis, 731, 735

Howard, Oliver, 342
Howells, William Dean, 394
Howe, Timothy, 344
Howl (Ginsberg), 623
Huerta, Victoriano, 472
Hughes, Charles Evan, 444, 480, 495, 503
Hughes, Langston, 508, 559
Hull House, 393, 394
Human rights: Humphrey on, 601; in Iran, 687; in Latin America, 685–686
Human Rights Campaign, 730
Humphrey, George, 613–614
Humphrey, Hubert: civil rights bill and, 647; election of 1968 and, 569, 661, 661 (map), 662, 672; on human rights, 601
Hungarian immigrants, 395
Hungary, 704; Marshall Plan and, 598; NATO and, 715; revolt by (1956), 625; Soviet influence in, 598
Hunger marchers, 536
Hunt, E. Howard, 676
Hunter, Ivory Joe, 622
Huntington, Collis P., 371
Hurricane Katrina, 727
Hurston, Zora Neale, 508
Hussein, Saddam, 705, 706; invasion of Iraq and, 725; neoconservatives on, 721; war on terror and, 724
Hydroelectric plant, 626
Hydrogen bomb, 615

I Am a Fugitive from a Chain Gang (film), 560
IBM (International Business Machines), 698, 706–707
ICC. *See* Interstate Commerce Commission (ICC)
Ickes, Harold, 558, 559
Idaho, 382, 401
If Christ Came to Chicago (Stead), 417
Illegal immigrants, 727–729
Illinois Railroad Commission, 348
Illinois Women's Alliance, 401
Immigration Act (1965), 650
Immigration and immigrants: between 1901 and 1909, 435, 436 (table); after 1870, 395; communities of, 395–396; debate on, beginning in mid 1990s, 727–729; efforts to restrict, in

early 1900s, 453; employment of, 395–396; impact of Immigration Act on, 650; labor by, 375, 472, 729; in late 19th century, 364; legislation under Clinton, 714; nativist policies and, 448, 453; in the 1950s, 612; number of illegal, 727–728; number of legal, 727; population growth and, 435; post-World War I restriction of, 499–500; quotas, 500, 563; restrictions on, 398, 453, 500; urbanization and, 395 (map); during World War II, 581. *See also* specific groups of immigrants
Immigration and Naturalization Service (INS), 714, 729
Impeachment: of Andrew Johnson, 343; of Clinton, 716; defined, 343, 716
Imperialism: Philippines and, 428; roots of, 402; Spanish-American War, 1898, 426–430
Imports, 402
Inauguration: of Calvin Coolidge, 515; of Franklin D. Roosevelt, 542; moving date of, 535; of Woodrow Wilson, 461
Income. *See* Wages
Income disparities, 524
Income tax, 460
An Inconvenient Truth (documentary), 732
Indian Education Act (1972), 672
Indian Rights Association, 379
Indians. *See* Native Americans
Indian Territory (Oklahoma), 349
Indian Trust Fund, 730
Indochina, 570. *See also* Vietnam
Industrial Workers of the World (IWW), 448, 455, 486, 494
Industry and industrialization: after the Civil War, 368; farming and, 382; impact of, 364; impact on labor, 375–376; inventions and, 374–375; leaving agrarian life for, 409; new workforce and, 375–376; railroad business and network, 369–370; in the South, 383; steel making, 374; textile, 454, 455. *See also* Automobiles and automobile industry; Steel and steel industry
Infant mortality rate, 436
Inflation: in 1980, 694; after World War I, 493; under Carter, 686;

Inflation (*cont.*) Panic of 1873 and, 356; Populist Party and, 407

Influence of Seapower History, The (Mahan), 402

Influenza pandemic, 493

Inner Sanctum (radio program), 560

Inoculation, 70, 71

In re Debs (1895), 414

Insular Cases (1901), 431

Insull, Samuel, 533

Intelligence Oversight Board, 681

Interim Committee, 587

Internal Revenue Service (IRS), 678

International American Conference (1889), 402–403

International Bureau of the American Republics, 403

International Business Machines (IBM), 698, 706–707

International Exhibit of Modern Art (1913), 462

International Garment Workers Union, 454–455

International Harvester, 447, 506

International Ladies Garment Workers Union, 436

International Match Company, 522

Internet, the, 698, 716

Internment camps, for Japanese Americans, 575–577

Interstate Commerce Act (1887), 369, 372

Interstate Commerce Commission (ICC), 372, 416; Hepburn Act and, 445, 446, 447; powers of, 442; railroad rates and, 445

Interstate highways, 624, 625 (map)

Inventions: in the late 19th century, 374–375; typewriter, 353

Ipana Troubadours (radio program), 505

Iran: American hostages in (1979), 688–689; American interest in, 687; Cold War foreign policy with, 616; hostage crisis, 688–689; Shah of, 688; shah of, 687; war with Iraq (1980s), 705

Iran-Contra affair, 700–701

Iranian hostage crisis, 693, 695

Iraq: American invasion of, 724–726; continued occupation of, 732–733; insurgent movement in, 726; invasion of Kuwait, 705; Persian Gulf War and, 705; war with Iran (1980s), 705; weapons of mass destruction and, 724

Iraq War (2003-present), 725–726, 726 (map), 732–733

Irish Americans: antiprohibition sentiment among, 417; boxing, 400; World War I and, 474, 475, 482

Irish immigrants, railroad building and, 348

Iron Curtain, 597

Iron ore industry, 374, 383

Islam, Black Muslims, 655

Islamic terrorism, 723, 729

Isolationism: in the 1920s, 515; after World War I, 498–499; before World War II, 557. *See also* Neutrality

Israel: attacked by Egypt and Syria, 680; Egypt and, 626; invasion of Lebanon, 697; Iran-Contra affair and, 700; neoconservatives on, 721; PLO and, 710; Truman on, 602

Issei, 576

Italian immigrants, 395–396, 500

Italy: League of Nations and, 490; Tripartite Pact, 570; Triple Alliance and, 473; World War II and, 578–579; World War II casualties, 588 (table)

Ithaca, New York, 351

Iwo Jima (island), 584

Jack Benny (television program), 621

Jackson, Helen Hunt, 379–380

Jackson, Jesse, 699

Jackson, Mahalia, 645

James, William, 418–419

Japan: atomic bombing of, 587, 588; bombing campaign of (1945), 587; efforts to restrict immigration from, 453; Five-Power Treaty and, 503; Four-Power Treaty and, 503; "Greater East Asia Co-Prosperity Sphere," 569–570; "Great White Fleet" tour and, 448; League of Nations and, 490; Manchuria and, 447, 529, 530; nativist immigration policies and, 448; naval warfare during World War II, 581–584; Pacific War and, 581–584, 584 (map); Pearl Harbor and, 570; Philippines and, 428; rape of Nanking, 569; Stimson Doctrine and, 530; taking American possessions during World War II, 570–571; tensions with, in 1920s, 503; Theodore Roosevelt's foreign policy with, 447–448; World War II casualties, 588 (table)

Japanese internment, 575–577, 577 (map)

Jay Cooke and Company, 355

Jazz music, 508–509

Jazz Singer, The (film), 505

Jefferson Airplane, 657

Jewish immigration, between 1935–1941, 563

Jews: anti-Semitism, 396, 581; in higher education, 1920s, 510; Hitler's message about, 530; Holocaust and, 580–581; immigrants, 395, 396; immigrating to the U.S., 1935–1941, 563; Kristallnacht and, 562; Nazism and, 555, 562; nominated to U.S. Supreme Court, 479

Jim Crow, 618

Job Corps, 649

Johns Hopkins University, 385

Johnson, Andrew: impeachment of, 343; Radical Republicans and, 341–342; Reconstruction and, 339; reunion with the South under, 341

Johnson, Hugh S., 549

Johnson, "Jack," 463

Johnson, James Weldon, 502, 508

Johnson, Lyndon B.: accomplishments of, 647–648; biographical information, 647; election of 1960 and, 630; election of 1964 and, 649; Ford and, 681; foreign policy of, 648–649; the Great Society and, 649; Gulf of Tonkin and, 648–649; on health care, 649–650; meeting with King, 647; not seeking reelection, 659; Supreme Court nomination by, 673; Vietnam and, 650, 651, 657; voting rights bill and, 653

Johnson, Tom L., 444

Jolson, Al, 505

Jones, Paula Corbin, 709, 716

Jones, Samuel "Golden Rule," 444

Joplin, Janis, 666

Joseph, Chief, 379

Journalism: muckrakers and, 443; "yellow journalism," 422

J.P. Morgan, 731

Judiciary, the. *See also* U.S. Supreme Court
Judiciary, the, under Reagan, 701
The Jungle (Sinclair), 447, 551
Jupiter missiles, in Turkey, 643
Justice Department: Ku Klux Klan and, 347–348; limiting dissent during World War I, 486; Red Scare and, 494. *See also* U.S. Supreme Court

Kagan, Elena, 736
Kalakua, King, 403
Kamikaze planes, 584
Kansas: African Americans moving to, 384; cattlemen in, 380; Farmers' Alliance and, 404, 407
Kansas City Monarchs, 601
Kefauver, Estes, 621, 626, 629
Kelley, Florence, 417, 443, 514
Kellogg's Corn Flakes, 437
Kelly, Florence, 401
Kelly, "Honest John," 397
Kemp, Jack, 714
Kennan, George F., 597
Kennedy, Anthony, 701
Kennedy, Edward, 737
Kennedy, Jacqueline, 629, 646
Kennedy, Joe Jr., 629
Kennedy, John F.: achievements of, during presidency, 639–640; assassination of, 646–647; Bay of Pigs and, 640; Berlin Wall and, 640–641; biographical information, 629; cabinet of, 639; on civil rights, 645; defense spending under, 644; economic program of, 641; economy under, 641; election of 1960 and, 630–631, 630 (map), 639; foreign policy of, 640–642; freedom riders and, 641; moon landing and, 665; Vietnam and, 643–644
Kennedy, Joseph P., 629
Kennedy, Robert F.: assassination of, 660; as attorney general, 639; campaigning in 1968, 659; Chavez and, 660; Cuban missile crisis and, 642–643; election of 1968 and, 659–660; freedom rides and, 641
Kent State University (shootings), 666–667
Kern, Jerome, 510
Kerouac, Jack, 623
Kerr, Clark, 652

Kerry, John F., 726, 727
Kesey, Ken, 657
Keystone company, 477
Khomeini, Ayatollah Ruhollah, 687
Khrushchev, Nikita: Berlin Wall and, 640, 641; Cuban missile crisis and, 642, 643; denouncing Stalin, 625; meeting with Eisenhower, 628–629; visiting the U.S., 628
Kim Il Sung, 604
King, Coretta Scott, 620
King, Martin Luther, Jr.: assassination of, 659; Birmingham, Alabama and, 644–645; criticism of, 655; FBI and, 681; "I Have a Dream" speech, 645; Johnson meeting with, 647; Montgomery bus boycott and, 620; voting rights demonstrations, 653
King, Rodney, 707
Kissinger, Henry, 675
Knights of Labor, 377–378
Knights of the White Camelia, 347
Knox, Frank, 557
Knox, Philander C., 456
Kodak camera, 437
Kodak camera, invention of, 375
Kolster Radio, 522
Korea. *See* North Korea; South Korea
Korean War (1950–1953), 604, 606, 606 (map), 614
Korematsu v. United States (1944), 577
Kosovo, 717
Kraft Television Theater (television program), 621
Kreuger, Ivar, 522
Kristallnacht, 562
Kristol, William, 721
Kroc, Ray, 624
Ku Klux Klan: after World War I, 466; *The Birth of a Nation* and, 475; founding of, 342; Kennedy assassination and, 646; Medgar Evans and, 645; murder of civil rights workers by, 648; practices of, 500–501; resurgence of, 500, 619; threat of violence from, 347–348
Ku Klux Klan Act of 1871, 347, 356
Kuwait, 705
Kyoto Treaty (1999), 732

Labor: of African Americans, 558–559; after World War I, 493–494; employers-worker relations, 454;

during the Great Depression, 527; immigrant workforce, 375, 472, 729; improved, during World War I, 484; industrialism in the South and, 383; industry's impact on, 375–376; in the late 19th century, 376; by Mexican immigrants, 472, 548, 575; by minorities during World War II, 574; in the 1920s, 506–507; steelworker strike, 408; varieties of protest, 454–455; workday, 376, 436, 449, 478. *See also* Child labor; Employment; Labor unions; Wages; Women, in the labor force
Labor strikes. *See* Strikes
Labor unions: competing, 377–378; divisions within, 554; in early 1900s, 448; female workers and, 515; growth of, 455; Knights of Labor, 377; National Recovery Act and, 549; Norris-LaGuardia Act (1932), 534; political parties and, 448; post-World War II, 594; post-World War I strikes, 494; protest b 454–455; rise of, 376–377; sit-dow strikes, 561, 562; Taft-Hartley Act and, 600; women's, 436
Lady, Be Good (musical), 510
La Follette, Robert M., 418, 444, 451, 452, 508
Lake Chautauqua, New York, 353
Lakota Nation, 730
Lakota Sioux tribe, 730
Land grants, railroad, 369–370, 372
Landon, Alfred M., 557, 558
Lansing, Robert, 475
La Raza Unida, 670
Las Gorras Blancas (the White Caps), 398
Lathrop, Julia, 417, 443
Latin America: Carter's foreign policy with, 685; Coolidge's foreign policy with, 516; dollar diplomacy toward, 456; former slaves in, 340; good neighbor policy with, 529, 550; Harding's foreign policy with, 503; Hoover's foreign policy with, 529; International American Conference (1889), 402–403; Panama Canal and, 441; Roosevelt Corollary, 441; Wilson's foreign policy with, 471–472. *See also* specific countries

Latino population, 712 (map)
Lawrence, Massachusetts, 455
Laws: restricting Chinese immigrants, 398; segregation, 398. *See also* Legislation
Lazarus, Emma, 386
League of Nations, 515; debate on, 490, 491; Harding on, 503; Japanese policy and, 530; rejection of, 498; Senate and, 491–492; Wilson's idea on, 481
League of Women Voters, 620
Leary, Timothy, 656–657
Lease, Mary Elizabeth, 407
Leave It to Beaver (television program), 621
Lebanon: American hostages in, 700; Israel's invasion of, 697
Legal reform, 418
Legislation: child labor, 416; limiting dissent during World War I, 486; reform, under Wilson, 478; during World War I, limiting civil liberties, 486. *See also* specific laws
Lehmann Brothers, 733–734
LeMay, Curtis, 587
Lemke, William "Liberty Bell," 558
Lend-Lease (1941), 568–569
Lenin, Vladimir Ilyich, 489
LeRoy, Mervyn, 560
Lesbians. *See* Gays and lesbians
Lever Act (1914), 483
Levittown, 596–597
Levitt, William, 596
Lewinsky, Monica, 716, 717
Lewis, Jerry, 621
Lewis, John L., 553, 554, 612
Lewis, Sinclair, 509
Lexington (ship), 582
Leyte Gulf, Battle of, 584
Liberal blogs, 727
Liberalism, decline of, 600
Liberal Republicans, 346–347, 354, 356
Liberty Bonds, 483, 522
Liberty Island, 386
Libraries, 386
Liddy, Gordon, 676
Lieberman, Joseph, 733, 736–737
Life (magazine), 592
Liliuokalani, Queen, 403, 422
Lincoln Memorial, 559
Lindbergh, Charles A., 556
Lindbergh, Charles A., 516–517
Linotype, invention of, 375

Listerine, 506
Literacy tests, 396, 398, 453
Literature: of the 1920s, 509–510; Beat generation, 623; Edward Bellamy novels, 400; in Greenwich Village, 1910s, 462–463; Mark Twain, 386; naturalism, 419; rags-to-riches novels, 378
Lithwick, Dahlia, 728, 729
Little Bighorn, 350
Little Bighorn, Battle of the, 379
Little Richard, 623
Little Rock, Arkansas, 626–627
Liuzzo, Viola, 653
Lloyd, Henry Demarest, 416
Lochner v. New York (1905), 449
Locke, Alain, 508
Lodge, Henry Cabot, 430, 630; League of Nations and, 491–492; Paris Peace Conference and, 489; Treaty of Versailles and, 490
Lodge, Henry Cabot Jr., 607
Loewe v. Lawlor, 449
Long, Huey P., 551, 558
Long-range offensive missiles (ICBMs), 676
Looking Backward (Bellamy), 400
Los Alamos, New Mexico, 587
Lotus 1-2-3 spreadsheet program, 698
Louisville and Nashville Railroad, 370
Lowell, Josephine Shaw, 401
LSD, 657
Luce, Henry, 509, 592
"Ludlow Massacre" (1914), 455–456
Luftwaffe, 566, 567
Lunar mission, 665
Lundberg, Ferdinand, 595
Lusitania incident, 474–475, 479
Luxembourg, 567
Lynchings: Colored Farmers' Alliance and, 405; contrasting opinions on, 421; in 1890s, 398; by Ku Klux Klan, 501; rate of, 420; during Roosevelt's presidency, 440; women's reform and, 417; during World War I, 485

MacArthur, Douglas: Bonus Army and, 534–535; Korean War and, 604, 606; Pacific War and, 583; in Philippines during World War II, 571
Macune, Charles, 405

Maddox (ship), 648
Madero, Francisco I., 456, 472
Mafia, the, 646
Magazines: in the 1880s, 386; educational system and, 627–628
Maggie: A Girl of the Streets (Crane), 419
MAGIC (Japanese diplomatic code), 570
Maginot Line, 567
Mahan, Alfred T., 402
Main Street (Lewis), 509
Major League baseball, Jackie Robinson and, 600–601
Malaya, 570
Malcolm X, 655
Man and His Mate (movie), 477
Manchu dynasty, 471
Manchuria, 447, 456, 529, 530, 604. *See also* China
Manhattan Project, 615
Manila Bay, Philippine Islands, 426
Man Nobody Knows, The (Barton), 506
Manufacturing, in the South, 383. *See also* Industry and industrialization
Mao Zedong, 538, 603
Marches: by African Americans during World War II, 574; Bonus Army, 534–535; civil rights, 645; hunger, 536; by Native Americans, 672; voting rights (Bloody Sunday), 653
March on Washington for Jobs and Freedom, 645
Marines: withdrawn from Latin America, under Harding, 503
Marines (U.S.): African Americans in, 575; in Haiti, 550; in Israel, 697; in World War II, 583
Marriage: after World War II, 595; changes in, during 1920s, 510; changes in status of women and, 436; in the 1950s, 612; Victorian morality and, 399. *See also* Divorce
Marshall Field's (department store), 454
Marshall, George C., 570, 598, 607
Marshall Islands, 583
Marshall Plan, 598
Marshall, Thurgood, 617, 651, 685
Martin, Dean, 621
Marx Brothers, 528

Mary Noble, Backstage Wife (radio program), 528
Masaryk, Jan, 598
The Masses (magazine), 462, 486
Matisse, Henri, 462
Maxwell House Hour, The (radio program), 505
Mayer, Louis B., 505
McAdoo, William G., 484, 507–508
McCain, John, 721, 733, 734, 734 (map)
McCall's (magazine), 612
McCarthy, Eugene, 659, 660
McCarthyism, 606–607
McCarthy, Joseph R. and McCarthyism, 539, 606–607, 608, 609, 615
McCloy, John J., 582, 583
McClure, Samuel S., 443
McClure's Magazine (magazine), 443
McCord, James, 676, 678
McCormick Company, 377
McDonald's, 624
McGovern, George, 677
McKay, Claude, 501, 508
McKinley Tariff Act (1890), 403, 404, 414
McKinley, William: assassination of, 431, 434; Boxer Rebellion and, 430; congressional election campaigns and, 428; Cuba crisis and, 425–426; domestic policy, 425, 431; election of 1894 and, 415; election of 1896 and, 412, 423, 424, 424 (map); election of 1900 and, 430–431; as the first modern president, 431; foreign policy with Spain, 425–426; on free silver, 424; gold standard and, 425; imperialism and, 429–430; Paris Peace conference with Spain, 428–429; on the Philippines, 426; on the protective tariff, 387, 431
McLaurin v. Oklahoma (1950), 617–618
McNamara, Robert, 639, 647
McNary, Charles, 568
McNary-Haugen Plan, 504, 515
McPherson, Aimee Semple, 511
McVeigh, Timothy, 712–713
Meat-packing industry, 447
Media: on counterculture of the 1960s, 657; sexual behavior depicted in, 699. *See also* specific media

Media conglomerates, 726–727
Medicaid, 649–650
Medical students, female, 595
Medicare, 649–650
Medicine: polio vaccine, 624. *See also* Health care
Meese, Edwin, 701
Mein Kampf (Hitler), 555
Mellon, Andrew, 503, 515
Memphis, Tennessee, 342
Mencken, Henry L., 509
Menlo Park, New Jersey, 375
Mercury Theater, 560
Meredith, James, 642
Mergers, business, 438–439
Merrill Lynch, 731
Merry Pranksters, 657
Mesa Verde, 449
Metro-Goldwyn-Mayer (MGM), 505
Mexican Americans: conflict in New Mexico, 397–398; deportation of, during Great Depression, 527; political activism (1960s) by, 670; prejudice and, 472; serving in World War II, 575; violence against, 574–575
Mexican immigrants: after 1910, 472; farm workers, 548; labor by, 472, 575; prejudice against, 472
Mexico, 697 (map); Franklin D. Roosevelt's foreign policy in, 550; immigration from, 500; overthrow of Madero, 456; Pancho Villa and, 480; Vera Cruz incident and, 472; Wilson's foreign policy with, 472
MGM (Metro-Goldwyn-Mayer), 505
Microsoft, 698
Microsoft Windows, 698
Middle-class: post-World War II, 594; reform by women in the 1890s, 401; in Victorian society, 399
Middle East: Camp David Accords (1978), 685–686; Clinton's foreign policy in, 710; neoconservative view on, 721; Persian Gulf War (1990–1991), 705–706; tensions from, 692. *See also* specific countries
Midway Island, 582
Migration: of African Americans to Kansas, 384; of African Americans to the North, 476–477, 477 (table); Dust Bowl disaster and,

547; during World War II, 572, 574
Military. *See* Armed forces
Military aid: to France, 616; under Reagan, 634–635
Military draft. *See* Draft (military)
Military spending: during the Cold War, 603; for World War II, 571
Militia: railroad strike and, 377
Militia movement, 713
Miller, Glenn, 622
Minimum wage: Clinton and, 714; Kennedy and, 639; for women, 506; World War I and, 484
Mining: western industry, 380
Minnesota, 348, 404
Minorities: college experience for, 510; portrayed on television programs of the 1950s, 622. *See also* specific minority groups
Minor v. Happersett (1875), 351
Minor, Virginia, 351
Mississippi Freedom Democratic Party (MFDP), 648
Missouri (ship), 588
Mitchell, Margaret, 560
Mobilization Day (1969), 66
Mobsters, 502
Model A automobile, 504–505
Model Cities Act (1966), 651
Model T automobile, 436–437, 462, 504
Modern Women: The Lost Sex (Farnham/Lundberg), 595
Molotov, V.M., 578, 586
Mondale, Walter, 683, 699
Monkey Business (film), 528
Monopolies, 373
Monroe Doctrine: Roosevelt Corollary and, 441; Treaty of Versailles and, 490; Venezuela-Great Britain crisis and, 422
Montana, 380, 382
Montgomery bus boycott, 619–620
Montgomery Improvement Association (MIA), 620
Moon landing, 665
Morality, Victorian, 399–400
Moral Majority, 699
Morgan, J.P., 416, 438, 439, 451
Morgenthau, Morgan, 572
Morocco, 578
Morrill Land-Grant Act (1862), 381
Morris, "Bill," 440
Morrow, Dwight, 516

Moscow Summit (1972); 676
Mossadegh, Mohammed, 616
Mothering, concept of, 595
Motion pictures. *See* Movies
Motion picture studios, 505
Motorola Playhouse (television program), 621
Movies: in the 1920s, 505; emerging popularity of (1910s), 463; during the Great Depression, 529; in the Great Depression, 559–560; House Un-American Activities Committee (HUAC), 599; rise of the, 477; silent, 477; sixties counterculture, 656, 657
Moynihan, Daniel P., 674
Mr. Deeds Goes to Town (film), 560
Mr. Smith Goes to Washington (film), 560
Ms. (magazine), 669
Muckrakers, 443, 447
Muhammad, Elijah, 655
Muller v. Oregon (1908), 449
Multiculturalism, 711
Multinational corporations, 706–707
"Multiversity," 652
Munich debacle of 1938, 562
Munn v. Illinois (1877), 348, 371–372
Muscle Shoals, Alabama, 515
Music: of the 1950s, 622–623; the Beatles, 621; Broadway musicals, 510; jazz, 508–509; Presley, Elvis, 623; sixties counterculture, 657; swing, 529; Woodstock festival, 666
Musicals, 528
Muskie, Edmund, 661
Muslims, Black, 655
Mussolini, Benito, 530, 555, 562, 578
My Lai massacre, 667–668

NAACP. *See* **National Association for the Advancement of Colored People (NAACP)**
NAFTA (North American Free Trade Agreement), 709
Nagasaki, Japan, 588
Nagumo, Chuichi, 570
Namath, Joe, 664–665
Napalm, 674
NASA. *See* National Aeronautics and Space Administration (NASA)
Nasser, Gamal Abdel, 626
Nast, Thomas, 396

National Aeronautics and Space Administration (NASA), 628, 669
National American Woman Suffrage Association (NAWSA), 401, 443, 452–453, 478, 485
National Association for the Advancement of Colored People (NAACP): on *Amos 'n' Andy*, 622; formation of, 440–441; Legal Defense Fund, 617; Marcus Garvey and, 502; Truman speaking at convention of, 600
National Association of Colored Women, 417, 420
National Broadcasting Company (NBC), 505, 560
National Commission on AIDS, 704
National Congress of American Indians, 730
National Consumers League, 443
National Credit Corporation, 526
National debt: after Bush, George W.'s presidency, 731; after World War II, 572; under Bush, George W., 722; Bush, H.W. deficit reduction plan, 705; Clinton lowering the, 709; decreased during Clinton's presidency, 715; growth of, under Reagan, 695; in 1980, 694
National Defense Education Act (1958), 628
National Energy Act (1978), 687
National Guard: at Chicago Democratic Convention, 660; Kent State shootings and, 667; "Ludlow Massacre" (1914) and, 455–456; Vietnam War draft and, 650
National health insurance, Truman's proposals for, 600
National Industrial Recovery Act (NIRA), 548
Nationalist Socialist Party, 530
National Labor Relations Act (1935), 553–554, 561
National Labor Relations Board (NLRB), 554, 562
National Labor Union (NLU), 376
National Liberation Front, 638
National Monuments Act (1906), 449–450
National Organization for Women (NOW), 656

National Origins Quota Act (1924), 500, 563
National parks and monuments, 449–450, 449 (map)
National Professional Football League, 511
National Recovery Administration (NRA), 548, 549
National sales tax, 531
National Science Foundation, 698
National Security Act (1947), 598
National Security Council (NSC), 599, 675, 700
National Security Council Paper 68 (NSC 68), 603
National Socialist (Nazi) Party, 555
National Union for Social Justice, 552
National War Labor Board, 484
National Woman's Party, 478, 514
National Woman Suffrage Association, 351, 401
National Women's Trade Union League, 436
National Youth Administration, 552; Office of Negro Affairs, 559
A Nation at Risk (study), 698
Native Americans: Battle of Wounded Knee, 397; buffalo herds and, 350; Centennial International Exhibition and, 358; citizenship for, 380; cowboys, 380; Custer's Last Stand and, 350; Dawes Severalty Act and, 380, 393; in early 2000s, 730; during Great Depression, 527; military force used against, 350–351; national policy on (1800s), 379–380; peace policy toward, 349; post-Civil War policies on, 348–349; reservations, 349, 349 (map); resistance by, 379, 397
Nativism, 396, 448, 453
NATO. *See* North Atlantic Treaty Organization (NATO)
Naturalism, 419
Naturalism, literary, 419
"Natural selection," 378
Naval warfare: *Lusitania* incident, 474–475; World War II, 569–570, 581–584. *See also* Submarines and submarine warfare
Navy (U.S.): Clayton-Bulwer Treaty of 1850 and, 430; in 1889, 401; Five-Power Treaty and, 503; "Great

White Fleet" tour and, 448; in Gulf of Mexico, 472; Gulf of Tonkin, 648–649; imperialism and, 402; race discrimination in, 575; radio usage and, 462; recruiting, or World War I, 481; renewal of Washington Naval Conference pacts, 529; segregation in, 575; Spanish-American War, 426, 427; Vanguard rocket fire, 628; violence against Mexican Americans by, 574–575; World War I and, 474

NAWSA. *See* National American Woman Suffrage Association (NAWSA)

Nazi concentration camps, 580–581, 582, 583

Nazi Germany, 555; blitzkrieg, 567; concentration camps, 580–581, 582, 583; Kristallnacht and, 562; neutrality debate and, 556; Sudentenland and, 562. *See also* Hitler, Adolf

Nazi-Soviet Pact, 569

NBC (National Broadcasting Company), 505, 560, 621

Nebraska, 380, 404

Negro leagues, 511

Neighborhood Youth Corps, 649

Nelson, Baby Face, 560

Nelson, Ben, 737

Nelson, Donald, 571

Neoconservatives, 721

Netherlands: Jewish immigrants and, 563; Nazi invasion of, 567

Neutrality: in the early 1930s, 555, 557; Nazi and fascist aggression and, 556; during World War I, 474, 475, 479; in World War I, 474; World War II and, 569

Neutrality Acts, 556

New Deal, the, 534; African Americans and, 558–559; Agricultural Adjustment Act (AAA), 546; Civilian Conservation Corps (CCC), 544; Civil Works Administration (CWA), 545; criticisms of, 550–552; defined, 544; Eisenhower and, 614; Federal Emergency Relief Administration (FERA), 545; foreign diplomacy of, 549–550; National Industrial Recovery Act (NIRA), 548; the "second," 552–554; Tennessee Valley Authority, 545

New England's Women's Club, 353

New Freedom policy, 471–472

New Freedom programs, 458, 461

New Guinea, 583

"New Look" approach to containment, 616

Newman, Paul, 621

New Nationalism, 452, 458

"New Negro," 485

New Negro, The (Locke), 508

New Orleans, Louisiana: Hurricane Katrina and, 727; riots in, 342; White League and, 357

New Republic (magazine), 607

Newspapers: yellow press, 422

Newton, Huey, 655–656

New Woman's Survival Catalogue, The, 669

New World Order, 675, 710

New York (city): African American intellectual life in, 508; African American migration to, 477 (table); architecture, 510; Harlem, 502, 508; Harlem neighborhood in, 502; immigrant self-help societies in, 396; Italian immigrants in, 365; September 11th terrorist attacks in, 635, 723; Statue of Liberty in, 386; Tweed Ring in, 396; World Trade Center bombing in, 723

New York (state): Levittown in, 596–597

New York City Working Women's Society, 401

New York Post (newspaper), 608

New York Society for the Suppression of Vice, 353

New York Stock Exchange, 521

New York Yankees, 511

Nez Perce Indians, 379

Niagara Conference (1905), 440

Nicaragua, 697 (map); dollar diplomacy and, 456; foreign policy in 1920s with, 516; Iran-Contra affair and, 700; support for Contras in, 696; troops to, under Wilson, 472; withdrawing troops from, during Great Depression, 529

Nicholas II, Tsar, 482

Nichol, Mike, 656

Nichols, Terry, 712–713

Nimitz, Chester, 583, 584

Nine-Power Treaty, 503, 530

Nineteenth Amendment, 493, 668

92 Infantry, Italy, 575

Nisei, 576

Nitze, Paul, 603

Nixon, Richard M.: accomplishments of first term, 676; biographical information, 629; "Checkers speech," 621; civil rights and, 673; election of 1952 and, 607–608; election of 1956 and, 626; election of 1960 and, 629, 630–631, 630 (map); election of 1968 and, 661–662, 661 (map); election of 1972 and, 677; environmentalism and, 674; foreign policy of, 675; Internal Revenue Service (IRS) and, 678; the "Plumbers" and, 668; public approval rating of, 678, 679; resignation of, 680; social service spending under, 674; Supreme Court nomination by, 673; uniting the country and, 664; Vietnam and, 666, 677; Vietnamization and, 666; visit to China, 675; visit to the Soviet Union, 676; Watergate scandal and, 676, 678–680, 681; welfare system and, 673–674

NLRA. *See* National Labor Relations Act (1935)

NLRB (National Labor Relations Board), 554, 562

NLU (National Labor Union), 376

Nobel Peace Prize, 448

Nonrecognition, policy of, 516

Noriega, Manuel, 704

Normandy invasion (1944), 579–580

Norris, Frank, 419

Norris-LaGaurdia Act (1932), 534

North Africa, World War II and, 578

North American Aviation, 574

North American Free Trade Agreement (NAFTA), 709

North Atlantic Treaty Organization (NATO): air strikes against Serbia and, 717; Berlin Wall and, 640; Dayton Peace Agreement and, 713; Eastern European countries added to, 715; European members of, 605 (map); formation of, 603

North Carolina: election of 1898, 420

North Dakota, 382

Northern Pacific Railroad, 355, 370, 438
Northern Securities Company, 438, 439
North Korea, 604
North, Oliver, 700, 701
North, the, African American migration to, 476–477, 477 (table)
North Vietnam, 616, 677, 681–682. *See also* Vietnam; Vietnam War
Norway, Nazi invasion of, 567
NSC. *See* National Security Council (NSC)
Nuclear Test Ban Treaty (1963), 648
Nuclear weapons: Cuban missile crisis and, 643; Russia testing, 538–539; spending on, during Kennedy years, 643; Strategic Defense Initiative (SDI), 697. *See also* Atomic bomb
Nureyev, Rudolf, 621
Nye, Gerald P., 557

Oak Ridge, Tennessee, 587
Obama, Barack, 635; challenges of, 734–735; election of 2008 and, 733, 734, 734 (map); presidency of, 736–737
Oberlin, Ohio, 417
Ocala Demands, 407
O'Connor, Sandra Day, 701
Octopus, The (Norris), 419
Office of Minority Business Enterprise, 672
Office of Price Administration (OPA), 572
Office of the Alien Property Custodian, 507
Oil and oil industry, 687–688, 695, 705
Oil consumption, 680
Oil embargo, 680–681
Oil reserves, leased to private oil companies, 507
Oil spill (2010), 737
Okinawa, 584
Oklahoma: Indian removal and, 349, 379; prohibition in, 453
Oklahoma (ship), 570
Oklahoma City bombing (1995), 712–713
Old Age Revolving Pensions Limited plan, 552
Olney, Richard, 422
Olsen, Floyd, 551

Olympic Games: Berlin, 1936, 560; Summer, 1980, 688; Summer, 1984, 699
Omaha, Nebraska, 407
One Flew Over the Cuckoo's Nest (Kesey), 657
O'Neill, Eugene, 463
One Man's Family (radio program), 528
On the Origin of Species (Darwin), 378
On the Road (Kerouac), 623
OPEC (Organization of Petroleum Exporting Countries), 680, 687–688
Open Door Notes, 430
Open Door policy, 447, 503, 530
Operation Desert Storm, 705
Operation Mongoose, 640, 642
Operation OVERLOAD (Normandy invasion), 579–580
Operation Rolling Thunder, 650
Operation TORCH, 578
Oppenheimer, J. Robert, 615
Oregon, 381
Organization of Petroleum Exporting Countries (OPEC), 680, 687–688
Organized crime, in the 1920s, 502
Orlando, Vittorio, 489
Oswald, Lee Harvey, 646
The Other America (Harrington), 645
Ottoman Turks, 473
Our Bodies, Ourselves (handbook), 669
Our Country: Its Possible Future and Its Present Crisis (Strong), 402
Ovington, Mary White, 440
Owens, Jesse, 560
Ozzie and Harriet (television program), 621

Pacific War, 1942–1945 (World War II), 581–584
Paddle Your Own Canoe (Alger), 378
Pahlavi, Riza (Shah of Iran), 687, 688
Palace of Versailles, 491
Palestine Liberation Organization (PLO), 710
Palin, Sarah, 733, 734
Palmer, A. Mitchell, 494, 495
Pan-Africanism, 502
Panama, 697 (map); Noriega and, 704; treaty on Panama Canal with,

550; Wilson's foreign policy with, 471–472
Panama Canal, 441, 550, 683, 685
Pan-American Conference (1933), 550
Panay (gunboat), 569
Panic of 1873, 355–356, 357, 360
Panic of 1893, 409, 412, 413–415
Paper currency, 346
Paramount Pictures studio, 477, 505
Pardons: under Johnson, 341
Parenting, Victorian morality and, 399
Paris (musical), 510
Paris Peace Conference, 489
Parker, Alton P., 442
Parker, Bonnie, 560
Parker, Ely, 349
Parks: in cities, 394, 397; national, 449–450, 449 (map)
Parks, Rosa, 620
Patriot Act (2001), 724
Patronage (spoils) system, 386, 388
Patrons of Husbandry, 348
Patterson, Ben, 405
Paul, Alice, 452–453, 478, 514, 670
Payne-Aldrich Tariff Act, 451
Payne bill, 451
Payne, Sereno E., 451
PB oil spill (2010), 737
Peace Corps, 649
Peace policy (Native Americans), 349
"Peace without Victory" speech (Wilson), 481
Pearl Harbor, 569–570, 576
Peek, George, 506
Pehle, John H., 582, 583
Pelosi, Nancy, 732, 737
Pemberton, John, 385
Pendleton Act (1883), 388
Penniman, Richard Wayne (Little Richard), 623
Pennsylvania: Homestead strike in, 408; labor strikes and, 356; September 11th terrorist attack and, 723
Pennsylvania Railroad, 374
Pensions, 276
Pentagon Papers, 668, 673
Pentagon, the, 698
People's Party. *See* Populist Party
People's Republic of China. *See* China
Per capita income: in early 1900s, 437; of farmers in the 1920s, 506; during World War II, 572

Perestroika, 635, 700
Perkins, Charles E., 446
Perot, Ross, 707, 708, 714
Pershing, John J., 480, 482
Persian Gulf region, 687–688
Persian Gulf War (1990–1991), 705–706
Personal computers, 698
Peterson, Esther, 646
Philadelphia: African American migration to, 477 (table)
Philadelphia Plan, 672
Philippines: Japan taking over, 570–571; Spanish-American War and, 426; U.S. acquisition of, 428; U.S.-Japanese relations and, 503; Wilson's foreign policy with, 471; World War II and, 583, 584
Philosophy: pragmatism, 418–419
Phonograph, invention of, 374–375
Picasso, Pablo, 462
Pickford, Mary, 477
Pilgrim's Progress (Bunyan), 443
Pinchot, Gifford, 451
Pine Ridge Sioux Reservation, 672
Pingree, Hazen, 417
Pit, The (Norris), 419
Pittsburgh, Pennsylvania, 408, 476
Planned Parenthood, 514
Platt Amendment (1901), 430, 550
Playboy (magazine), 657
Pleiku, 650
Plessy v. Ferguson (1896), 420, 617
PLO (Palestine Liberation Organization), 710
"Plumbers" unit, 676
Poetry, 386
Poets and poetry, 509
Poindexter, John, 701
Poitier, Sidney, 621
Poland: end of Cold War and, 704; German invasion of, 566–567; immigration from, 500; Marshall Plan and, 598; NATO and, 715; World War II casualties, 588 (table)
Polio, 624
Polish immigrants, 395
Polish National Alliance, 396
"Political correctness," 711
Political participation: by African Americans, 343–344, 357, 677; Fifteenth Amendment and, 345; by women, 514, 645, 677; of

women and minorities, under Carter, 685. *See also* Voting and voting rights
Politics: from 1877–1887, 386–387; Ku Klux Klan and, 347–348, 501; in late 19th century, 364; in the 1990s, 635; during Reconstruction, 341, 343, 353–354, 356–357; reform governors, in 1890s, 418; television's impact on, 621; urban political machines, 396–397
Polk, Leonidas, 407
Pollard, "Mother," 620
Pollock v. Farmers' Loan and Trust Co. (1895), 418
Poll taxes, 398
Poole, Elijah, 655
Popular culture: in the Great Depression, 559–560; music of the 1950s, 622–623; rags-to-riches novels, 378; Social Darwinism in, 378. *See also* Entertainment
Population: of Chicago, 393–394; immigrant, 727–728, 727–729; Latino, 2000, 712 (map); of Mexican American community, 670; in 1901, 435; in the 1950s, 612; urban growth, 393–394, 499
Populist Party: on agrarian discontent, 406; on coining silver, 407; defined, 407; election of 1894, 415; election of 1982, 408; Farmers Alliance and, 407; William Jennings Bryan and, 423–424
Populists, 364
Port Chicago, California, 575
Porter, Cole, 510
Portsmouth, Treaty of, 447
Potsdam Conference (1945), 586–587
Pound, Roscoe, 418
POUR (President's Organization of Unemployment Relief), 526
Poverty, 394
Powderly, Terence V., 377
Powell, Colin, 723, 724
Powell, Colin, 701
Powell, Lewis, 673, 701
Powers, Francis Gary, 629
Pragmatism, 418–419
Prejudice. *See* Discrimination and prejudice
Premarital sex, 399, 515
Presidency: limiting power of, 343; Taft on power of, 450

Presidential Commission on the Status of Women, 646
Presidential vetoes, 342
President's Organization of Unemployment Relief (POUR), 526
Presley, Elvis, 621, 623
Price, Lloyd, 622
Prime interest rate, in 1980, 694
Prisoners of war, torturing, 728, 729
Procter and Gamble, 706
Proctor, Redfield, 426
Professional Air Traffic Controllers Organization (PATCO), 695
Profiles in Courage (Kennedy), 629
Progress and Poverty (George), 378
Progressive Citizens of America, 601
Progressive Party, 458; in election of 1912, 458, 459, 459 (map); election of 1916 and, 480
Progressivism: defined, 442; events of the 1890s and, 419; immigration restrictions and, 453; journalism and, 443; labor protest, 455–456; limiting child labor and, 454; local and state reform and, 444; national government reform and, 444–445; prohibition and, 453; reform in cities and states, 444; reforms, 442–443; waning spirit of, 493; Wilson and, 460–461; woman suffrage and, 452–453; women and, 443; workplace reform, 454
Prohibition: Anti-Saloon League and, 453; compliance with, 503; ending of, 545; faltering, in the 1920s, 513–514; impact of, 502; reform campaigns in 1890s and, 417; Volstead Act and, 493; Webb-Kenyon Act, 453; Woman's Christian Temperance Union (WCTU) and, 401; World War I era and, 478, 483; World War I's impact and, 466, 470
Promontory, Utah, 348
Propaganda: racist, 356; watchdog against Communist, 599–600; during World War I, 474
Proposition 187 (California), 728
Proposition 209 (California), 711
Protective tariff, 346, 354, 386, 387
Protestants and Protestantism, 399–400

Protests: Chicago Democratic National Convention (1968), 660–661; labor, 454–455; during Panic of 1873, 355; by Vietnamese Buddhists, 643, 644; against Vietnam War, 651, 666–667; voting rights, 653; for woman suffrage, 478. *See also* Marches; Strikes

Public Enemy, The (film), 528

Public libraries, 386

Public opinion: on Calley's prison sentence, 668; on Carter, 688; on Roosevelt, Franklin D., 585–586; on Roosevelt, Theodore, 450; on Truman, 606, 607; on Vietnam veterans, 682; World War I, 474; during World War II, 577

Public Works Administration (PWA), 548–549, 558–559

Puerto Rico, 427, 428

Pulitzer, Joseph, 422

Pullman, George, 369, 414

Pullman strike (1894), 414–415

"Pumpkin Papers," 599–600

Pure Food and Drugs Act (1906), 443, 447

PWA. *See* Public Works Administration (PWA)

Quarantine Speech (1937), 555

Quotas, immigration, 500, 563

Rabin, Yitzhak, 710

Race and racism: affirmative action and, 711; in the armed forces, 574, 575; eugenics and, 514; immigration restriction and, 500; Jackie Robinson and, 600–601; racial violence and, 574–575; relations after World War I, 494; Simpson trial and, 711; during World War I, 475–477

Race riots: after World War I, 494; in Atlanta, Georgia (1906), 440; in Los Angeles, 1992, 707; Watts riot (1965), 653; during World War I, 485

Radiant Toaster, 462

Radical Reconstruction, 343, 382

Radical Republicans, 341–342

Radio: advertising and, 506; Father Coughlin on, 552–553; "fireside chats" on, 544; first inauguration broadcast over, 515; during the Great Depression, 528; growth of the, 505; *The Moondog Party* on, 622; in the 1930s, 560; "War of the Worlds" episode on, 560

Radio Corporation of America (RCA), 505, 521–522

Radiola radio, 505

Radio stations, 505

Rags-to-riches novels, 378

Railroads and railroad building: Central Pacific, 348; during depression of the 1890s, 416; farmers and, 348; funding, 369–370; Interstate Commerce Act (1887), 369; land grants, 369–370, 372 (map); merger of companies, 438; Panic of 1873 and, 355; Railroad Network, 370, 370 (map); regulation of, 445–447; regulatory commissions and, 371–372; as a social and political issue, 371; in the South, 383; standard time zones and, 369; Union Pacific, 348; during World War I, 484

Railroad strikes, 376–377, 414–415, 594

Rainey, Ma, 509

Randolph, A. Philip, 574, 645

Rankin, Jeanette, 570

Rape of Nanking, 569

Rauschenbusch, Walter, 400–401

Ray, James Earl, 659

RCA (Radio Corporation of America), 505, 521–522

Reagan, Ronald, 692; agenda of, 694–695; attempted assassination of, 695; biographical information, 693; Contras and, 696; deregulation under, 695–696; election of 1980 and, 693–694, 694 (map); election of 1984 and, 699; Ford and, 683; foreign policy of, 696–697; funding military campaigns, 634–635; Gorbachev and, 700, 701; Iran-Contra scandal and, 701; legacy of, 703; presidency of, 634; second term of, 700–702; Strategic Defense Initiative and, 697; strengths and weaknesses of, 694; Supreme Court appointments of, 701

Recession: in the 1920s, 517; after September 11th terrorist attacks, 723; Obama's presidency and, 734–735; during Reagan administration, 696. *See also* Depression (economic)

Reconstruction, 338–360; Andrew Johnson and, 339; black suffrage during, 352; Centennial International Exhibition, 357–358; election of 1868, 344–345; election of 1872 and, 354; election of 1876, 358–360; Fifteenth amendment, 345; Freedmen's Bureau, 340, 342; the "Gilded Age" and, 355; government corruption and, 356–357; political reunion with the South, 341; politics during, 353–354; reasons for failure of, 360; resurgence of Democrats and, 357; wartime, in the South, 340; women's rights and, 352; women's suffrage and, 351, 352

Reconstruction Act (1867), 342, 343–344

Reconstruction Finance Corporation (RFC), 530–531, 534

Red Badge of Courage, The (Crane), 419

Redeemers, the, 382

"Red Power," 672

Red River War, 350

Red Scare, 493, 494–495. *See also* **McCarthy, Joseph R.** and McCarthyism

Reeb, James, 653

Reed, John, 463

Reed, Thomas B., 430

Reform and reform movements: in the army, 428; birth control, 478; in child labor, 454; in the 1890s, 400–401, 416–418; end of, 563; at end of 19th century, 365; legal, 418; pragmatism and, 418–419; progressivism, 442–443; tariff, 450–451, 459–460; women and progressive, 443–444; workplace, 454; during World War I era, 466, 470, 475, 478–479. *See also* New Deal, the

Reform Party, 714

Regulation: contrasting opinions on, 446; expansion of, under Roosevelt, 445–447; on food safety, 447; of railroad rates, 445, 447; of railroads, 371–372

Regulatory commission, for railroads, 371–372

Rehnquist, William, 673, 701
Reid, Harry, 732
Religion: fundamentalist, 466,
   511–512; reform of 1890s and,
   400–401; Religious Right, 697,
   699; in Victorian society, 399–400
Reparation payments, 524;
   by Germany, 516; Japanese
   internment camps, 577; World
   War II, 585
Republican National Convention: in
   1896, 423; in 1964, 648
Republican Party: on abortion,
   699; acquittal of Clinton and,
   717; African American voting
   and, 344; Clinton and, 712, 713;
   congressional election of 1910
   and, 452; congressional election
   of 1982 and, 696; congressional
   elections of 1994 and, 710;
   congressional elections of 1998
   and, 716–717; corruption among
   southern, 356–357; dissatisfaction
   with, in 2006, 727; election of
   1868 and, 344–345; election
   of 1872 and, 354; election of
   1876 and, 359–360; election
   of 1884 and, 388; election of
   1888 and, 392–393; election
   of 1894, 415; election of 1896,
   412; election of 1896 and, 423,
   424; election of 1908 and, 450;
   election of 1912 and, 457, 458,
   459, 459 (map); election of
   1920 and, 495; election of 1928
   and, 521, 521 (map); election
   of 1930 and, 531; election of
   1936 and, 557; election of 1940
   and, 568; election of 1946 and,
   600; election of 1952 and,
   607–609; election of 1956 and,
   626; election of 1960 and, 630
   (map); election of 1964 and, 648;
   election of 1968 and, 661–662,
   661 (map); election of 1996
   and, 714, 715; election of 2008
   and, 733, 734; Fox News and,
   727; Grant and, 346–347; labor
   unions and, 448; in late 19th
   century, 386; McCarthyism
   and, 607; Obama and, 736; on
   protective tariff, 346, 450–451;
   Reconstruction Act and, 342,
   343; on Treaty of Versailles, 491;
   Wilson and, 488

Republic Steel, 561–562
Reservations, Native American, 349,
   349 (map)
Reserve Officers Training Corps
   (ROTC), 667
Resolution Trust Corporation, 704
Reston, James, 624
Reuther, Walter, 612
Revenue Act (1932), 534
Reverse discrimination, 685
Revolts and rebellions: Boxer
   Rebellion (1900), 430; in Hungary
   (1956), 625
Reykjavik, Iceland, 700
RFC (Reconstruction Finance
   Corporation), 530–531, 534
Rhee, Syngman, 604
Rhythm and blues music, 622
Rice, Condoleezza, 723
Richardson, Elliot, 678
Rickey, Branch, 600, 601
Righteous and Harmonious Fists, 430
Right, the. See Conservatives/
   conservatism
"Right-to-life" movement, 699
Riots: after King's assassination, 659;
   against harassment of homosexuals,
   669; Haymarket Riot (1886), 377;
   race, 440; during Reconstruction,
   342; Stonewall riot, 669; "zoot-
   suit," 575. See also Race riots
Robber barons, 371
Robertson, Pat, 699
Robinson, Jackie, 600–601
Rockefeller Center (New York city),
   510
Rockefeller, John D., 455
Rockefeller, John D., 373–374
Rock 'n' roll music, 622–623
Rockwell, Norman, 573
Rodgers and Hammerstein show
   tunes, 622
Rodgers, Richard, 510
Roe v. Wade (1973), 699, 701
Roe v. Wade (1973), 673
Rogers, Ginger, 560
Rolling Stones concert, 666
Roman Catholic Church. See
   Catholics and Catholicism
Rommel, Erwin, 570, 578
Rooney, Mickey, 560
Roosevelt Corollary, 441
Roosevelt, Eleanor, 514, 531;
   feminist movement and, 646;
   minority rights and, 559

Roosevelt, Franklin D., 520;
   Atlantic Charter and, 569; atomic
   bomb and, 587; on the bank
   crisis, 543–544; biographical
   information, 531–532; bombing
   of concentration camps and,
   582; building a strong defense,
   567–568; civil rights legislation
   and, 559; death of, 585–586; at
   Democratic National Convention,
   532; election of 1920 and, 495;
   election of 1932 and, 532, 535;
   election of 1936 and, 557–558;
   election of 1944 and, 584–585;
   on enemy during World War II,
   577; fireside chats of, 544; foreign
   policy of, 549–550; on the Great
   Depression, 543; Holocaust and,
   581; inaugural speech, 542; Italian
   campaign during World War II,
   578–579; Japanese internment
   and, 576; Jewish immigration and,
   563; meeting with Hoover, 536;
   neutrality and, 556, 566; polio of,
   532; progressive views of, 532; on
   role of government, 533; on the
   second front during World War II,
   578; speeches of, 532, 556; third
   term of, 568; U.S. Supreme Court
   and, 561; Yalta Conference and,
   585. See also New Deal, the
Roosevelt, Theodore, 365; African
   Americans and, 439–440;
   assassination of McKinley and,
   431, 434; biographical information,
   437; on business mergers, 439;
   coal strike and, 439; death of, 495;
   election of 1900 and, 431; election
   of 1904 and, 442; election of
   1912 and, 458; election of 1916
   and, 480; expansion of regulation
   under, 445–447; foreign policy of,
   441, 447–448; as governor, 444;
   muckrakers and, 443; national
   parks and monuments established
   under, 449–450, 449 (map); New
   Nationalism and, 452; Nobel Peace
   Prize and, 448; Panama Canal and,
   441; on the presidency, 437–438;
   prior to becoming president, 437;
   progressivism and, 434–435; public
   opinion on, 450; regulation of
   business under, 445–447; Spanish
   American War and, 427; Spanish-
   American War and, 430; Square

Roosevelt, Theodore (*cont.*) Deal and, 439; Taft and, 457; as a trustbuster, 439; William Howard Taft and, 450

Root-Takahira Agreement, 448

Rosie the Riveter, 573

Ross, Nellie Tayloe, 514

Rouge River automobile plant, 504

Rough Riders, 427, 437

Royal Navy, 480

Royal Oak, Michigan, 551

Rubin, Jerry, 660

Ruby, Jack, 646

"Rum runners," 502

Rumsfeld, Donald, 725

Rural America, 613 (fig)

Rusk, Dean, 639, 647

Russell, H.H., 417

Russia: Bolshevism and, 489; NATO expansion and, 715; nuclear bomb testing by, 538–539; purchase of Alaska from, 344; revolution in (1917), 486; World War I and, 473, 481–482, 487; World War II and, 578. *See also* Soviet Union

Russian immigrants, 395, 472

Ruth, George Herman "Babe," 511

Sacco, Ferdinando Nicola, 495, 500

Sadat, Anwar, 685–686

Sailors. *See* Navy (U.S.)

Saipan (island), 583

Sales tax, 531, 534

Salk, Jonas, 624

SALT II Treaty, 696

SALT I Treaty, 676

Same-sex marriages, 730

San Bernadino, California, 472

Sandinistas (Nicaragua), 696, 700

San Francisco, California, 657

Sanger, Margaret, 478, 514

San Juan Hill, Battle of, 427

Santo Domingo (Dominican Republic), 346

Sarajevo, Bosnia, 473

Sarnoff, David, 505

Saturday Night Live (television program), 684

"Saturday Night Massacre," 678

Saudi Arabia, 705

Savings and loan industry, 695, 702, 704

Savio, Mario, 652

"Scabs," 454

Scalawags, 343

Scalia, Antonin, 701

Scandals: Democratic fundraising, 1996, 715; of Harding, 507; Iran-Contra affair, 700–701; Lewinsky, 716, 717; under Ulysses S. Grant, 346, 354–355; Watergate, 676, 678–680, 681; Whitewater, 709, 713

Schechter Poultry Company v. United States (1935), 549

Schlafly, Phyllis, 670, 671

School and Society, The (Dewey), 419

School segregation: *Brown v. Board of Education of Topeka* (1954), 617–619; Little Rock, Arkansas and, 626–627; under Nixon, 672

Schurz, Carl, 43, 354

Schwerner, Michael, 648

Scopes, John T., 512, 513

Scopes Trial (1925), 512–513

Scotland, 381

Scottsboro boys, 535

Scowcroft, Brent, 702

Sears catalog, 437

Sears, Richard Warren, 437

Sears, Roebuck and Company, 437

Sears, Roebuck catalog, 620

SEC (Securities and Exchange Commission), 545

Second World War. *See* World War II

Second World War, The (Churchill), 567

Securities and Exchange Commission (SEC), 545

Sedition Act (1918), 486

Segregation: of African Americans, 419–420; of African American soldiers during Spanish-American War, 427; in the armed forces, 574–575; Booker T. Washington and, 419–420; *Brown v. Board of Education of Topeka* (1954) and, 617–619; of children of Japanese ancestry, 448; freedom rides and, 641; in higher education, 510–511; Little Rock, Arkansas and, 626–627; Montgomery bus boycott and, 619–620; in the 1910s, 440; in the 1960s, 672; under Nixon, 672; *Plessy v. Ferguson* (1896), 420; in professional baseball, 600–601; in the South (1870s and 1880s), 384–385; spread of, in 1890s, 398–399; Theodore Roosevelt and, 440; under Wilson, 475–476

Selassie, Haile, 555

Selective Service Act (1917), 482

Selective Service System, 571

Selma, Alabama, 653

Senate (U.S.): Democrats in, during Obama presidency, 736–737; direct election of senators, 445; League of Nations and, 491–492; Treaty of Versailles and, 491–493; women in, 708

Senate Finance Committee, 451

Senate Foreign Relations Committee, 346

"Separate but equal" doctrine, 617

September 11th terrorist attacks, 635, 723

Serbia and Serbs, 473, 713, 715, 717

Serling, Rod, 621

Servicemen's Readjustment Act (1944), 593

Settlement homes: Hull House, 393; positive impact of, 397; progressivism and, 443

700 Club (television program), 699

Seventeenth Amendment, 445

Sex and sexuality: depicted in the media, 699; in the 1920s, 514–515; in the 1980s, 699; premarital, 399, 477, 515; rock 'n' roll music and, 623; Victorian morality and, 399; World War I era attitudes toward, 477–478

Sexism, 656

Seymour, Horatio, 345

Shafter, William R., 427

Shah of Iran, 687, 688

"The Shame of the Cities" (articles), 443

Shanghai Communiqué, 675

Sharecropping, 339 (map), 340, 383–384

Shaw, Anna Howard, 452

Sheep raising, 381

Shepard, Alan, 640

Sherman Antitrust Act (1890), 48, 404, 416, 418, 431, 438, 439

Sherman Silver Purchase Act, 404, 413–414, 423

Shipbuilding, during World War I, 484

Shopping districts, 394

Showboat (musical), 510

Shriver, R. Sargent, 649, 677

Sicily, 578

Sierra Club, 443, 674

"The Significance of the Frontier in American History" (Turner), 409

Silent movie era, 477

Silent Spring (Carson), 645, 674

Silver: battle of gold standard *vs.*, 423–424; coinage of, 356, 386, 407; Sherman Silver Purchase Act, 413

Simon, Neil, 621

Simon, Paul, 656

Simpson, Nicole Brown, 710

Simpson, Orenthal James "O.J.", 710–711

Sims, William S., 483

Sinatra, Frank, 622

Sinclair, Upton, 551

Sinclair, Upton, 447

Singapore, 570

Single parent families, 698

Sinn Fein, 710

Sioux Indians, 350, 397

Sirhan Sirhan, 660

Sirica, John, 678

Sister Carrie (Dreiser), 419

Sit-down strikes, 561

Sitting Bull, 350

Sixteenth Amendment (1913), 460

Skyscrapers, 510

Sloan, Alfred P., Jr., 504

Smith, Alfred E., 466–467, 507–508, 521, 521 (map), 630

Smith, Bessie, 509

Smith, Margaret Chase, 608, 609, 645, 647–648

"Smoked Yankees," 427

Smoking, 383

Smoot-Hawley Tariff Act (1930), 525, 529

Snow White and the Seven Dwarfs (film), 560

Soap operas, 528

Social Darwinism, 378, 400

Social Gospel, the, 401

Socialist Party, 448; in election of 1912, 458, 459 (map); in election of 1932, 535; in election of 1936, 557, 558

Socialists and socialism, 444

Social Security, 674; deregulation and, 695–696; increase in benefits, under Kennedy, 639; reform of, under Bush, 726; Roosevelt's plan for, 553

Social Security Act (1935), 553, 561

Social Security Trust Fund, 715

Sociological jurisprudence, 418

Solomon Islands, 583

Somalia, 710

Somme River, 482

Somoza regime, Nicaragua, 685

"Sooners," 393

Sorosis clubs, 352–353

Sotomayer, Sonia, 736

Souls of Black Folks, The (Du Bois), 440

"Sounds of Silence" (Simon/Garfunkel), 656

Soup kitchens, 413

Souter, David, 706, 736

South Dakota, 382, 397, 404

Southern Christian Leadership Conference (SCLC), 620, 644, 653

Southern Manifesto, 626–627

Southern Pacific Railroad, 370

Southern Railway, 370

Southern Tenant Farmers' Union (STFU), 548

South Korea, 604

South, the: African Americans migrating from, 476; black voter registration in, 654 (map), 654 (table); industrialism in, 383; in the late 19th century, 382–385; the "new," 382–383; problems of agriculture in, 383–384; racial segregation in, 384–385; during Reconstruction, 345–346; Reconstruction Act and, 343; Reconstruction in, 358 (map); sharecropping in, 339 (map); wartime Reconstruction in, 340

South Vietnam, 617, 643–644, 677, 681–682. *See also* Vietnam

Southwest, the: Mexican farm workers in, 548

Soviet Union: Afghanistan and, 688, 701; arms control and, 676; Berlin Wall and, 640–641; Bolshevism and, 489; collapse of, 635, 706; Cuban missile crisis and, 642, 643; Eisenhower's visit to, 628–629; Franklin D. Roosevelt's foreign policy with, 549–550; Gorbachev and, 700; impact of World War II on, 585; Korea and, 604; Marshall Plan and, 598; Nixon's visit to, 676; Persian Gulf War and, 705; Poland and, 566; post-World War II relations with, 592–593; Reagan

and, 696; receiving U.S. aid during World War II, 569; relations with U.S., in the 1970s, 634–635, 676; relations with U.S., under Reagan, 701; *Sputnik,* 627; Strategic Defense Initiative (SDI) and, 697; threat of, in Greece and Turkey, 597–598; Truman Doctrine and, 598; Truman on blockade of West Berlin, 602; U-2 spy planes and, 628, 629; U.S. aid to, 516; World War II and, 570, 578; World War II casualties, 588 (table); Yalta Accords and, 585, 586. *See also* Cold War

Space exploration: explosion of *Challenger,* 700; impact of *Sputnik,* 627–628; during Kennedy's presidency, 640; manned moon landing, 665; *Sputnik,* 627

Spain: Cuba and, 346, 422, 425–426; fascism in, 562; Spanish-American War (1898), 426–430; Spanish Civil War, 566

Spanish-American War (1898), 426–428, 427 (map)

Sparkman, John, 607

Speakeasies, 502

Speeches: of Franklin D. Roosevelt, 532, 533, 542; of Joseph McCarthy, 608, 609; Nixon's "Checkers speech," 609; Roosevelt's Quarantine speech, 556; Wilson's "Peace Without Victory," 481

Spencer, Herbert, 378

Spies and spying. *See* Espionage

Spirit of St. Louis (airplane), 516

Spock, Benjamin, 595

Spoils system, 386, 388

Sports: boxing, 463; college football, 510; in the 1880s, 385–386; in late 19th century, 400; in the1920s, 511; Super Bowl (1969), 664–665; World Series (1969), 665. *See also* Baseball

Spruance, Raymond A., 583

Sputnik I, 627

Sputnik II, 627

Square Deal, 439

SS *Titanic* (ship), 462

Stalingrad, Soviet Union, 578

Stalin, Joseph, 559; death of, 614; Franco government and, 562; Khrushchev denouncing, 625;

Stalin, Joseph (*cont.*) nonaggression pact signed by, 566; Potsdam Conference and, 586; World War II and, 578–579; Yalta Conference and, 585

Standardized food products, 437

Standard Oil Company, 373–374, 416, 443, 447

Standard time zones, railroads and, 369

Stanford University, 385

Stanton, Edwin, 343

Stanton, Elizabeth Cady, 351, 352, 358, 401, 452

Starr, Ellen Gates, 393

Starr, Kenneth, 709, 713, 716

"Star Wars," 697

State rights, 627

States: progressive reform in, 444; Reconstruction and, 343–344, 358 (map)

States' Rights (Dixiecrat) Party, 601–602

Statute of Liberty (New York city), 386

Stead, William T., 417

Steel and steel industry: Andrew Carnegie and, 374; Carnegie Steel Company, 439; Homestead strike, 408; merger of companies, 439; Republic Steel, 561–562; steel production (in tons), 374 (table); strike by, 408, 494; United States Steel, 439, 447, 457; vertical integration, 374; during World War I, 484

Steffens, Lincoln, 443

Steinbeck, John, 548, 560

Steppenwolf, 657

Stevens, Alexander H., 341

Stevenson, Adlai, 607, 626

Stewart, Jimmy, 560

Stimson Doctrine, 530

Stimson, Henry L., 530, 575, 587

Stock market crash of 1929, 521–524

Stone, Lucy, 351

Stone Mountain, Georgia, 475

Stonewall riot, 669

Strategic Arms Limitation Treaty (SALT). *See* SALT II Treaty; SALT I Treaty

Strategic ballistic missiles, 697

Strategic Defense Initiative (SDI), 697

Streetcars, 394

Strikes: after World War I, 494; coalminer, 439; by farmers, 405; International Ladies Garment Workers Union, 454–455; Knights of Labor and, 377; miner, 594; during Panic of 1873, 355–356; by Professional Air Traffic Controllers Organization, 605; Pullman (1894), 414–415; railroad, 376–377, 414–415, 594; "sit-down," 561, 562; steelworkers, 408, 494; by steelworkers, 408, 494; textile mill, 455; U.S. Supreme Court ruling on, 414; violence during, 561–562

Strong, Josiah, 402

Student Nonviolent Coordinating Committee (SNCC), 655

Students for a Democratic Society (SDS), 651, 660

Submarines and submarine warfare: World War I, 474–475, 479, 481, 482–483; during World War II, 578

Subprime loans, 731, 735

Substantive due process, doctrine of, 418

Subtreasury plan, 407

Suburbia, 596–597, 613

Sudentenland, 562

Suez Canal, 570, 626

Suffrage, 352; African Americans, 341, 342, 352; defined, 351; reform campaigns of the 1890s and, 417. *See also* Woman suffrage

Sugar trade, 422

Sullivan, Ed, 621

Sullivan, John L., 400

"Summer of love" (1967), 657

Sumner, Charles, 342, 346

Sun Also Rises, The (Hemingway), 510

Sunni Muslims, 735 (map)

Sun Records, 623

Sununu, John, 702

Super Bowl (1969), 664–665

"Supply-side economics," 694

Supreme Court. *See* U.S. Supreme Court

"Survival of the fittest" doctrine, 378

Sussex (ship), 479

Sussex Pledge, 479

Swann v. Charlotte-Mecklenburg Board of Education (1971), 673

Sweatt v. Painter (1950), 617

Swift and Company (meatpacking firm), 454

Swing music, 529

Syria, 680

Taft-Hartley Act (1946), 600

Taft, Robert, 607

Taft, William Howard, 365, 484, 607; biography, 450; conservation and, 451; conservative presidency of, 450–451; in election of 1908, 450; in election of 1912, 459 (map); on presidential power, 450; prohibition and, 453; on protective tariff, 450–451; Republican internal warfare and, 450, 452; Roosevelt and, 457; Woodrow Wilson and, 451

Taiwan, 675

Taliban regime, 724, 737

Tammanay Hall, 397

Tampico, intervention in, 472

Taos Pueblo, New Mexico, 672

Tarbell, Ida, 443

Target Committee, 587

Tariffs, 386, 387; Cleveland on, 389, 408; election of 1908 and, 450; Grant and, 346; McKinley on, 431; McKinley Tariff Act (1890), 403, 404; Panic of 1893 and, 414; political debate on, in 1880s, 386, 387; protective, 346, 354, 386, 387; Republican Party divided over, 448; Smoot-Hawley, 525, 529; Taft on, 450–451; Theodore Roosevelt on, 438; Wilson-Gorman Tariff Act (1894), 414; under Woodrow Wilson, 459–460; Woodrow Wilson on, 458

Taxation: under Bush Sr., 704–705; Coolidge's presidency and, 515; during Great Depression, 534; income, 460; for interstate roads, 624; under Johnson, 647; political debate on, in late 19th century, 386–387; raised, under Clinton, 709; World War II financed by, 571

Tax rebates, 731

Taylor, Frederick Winslow, 45, 454

"Teach-in," 651

Tea parties, 736

Teapot Dome Scandal, 507

Technology: developments in, in early 1900s, 461–462; personal